I0831443

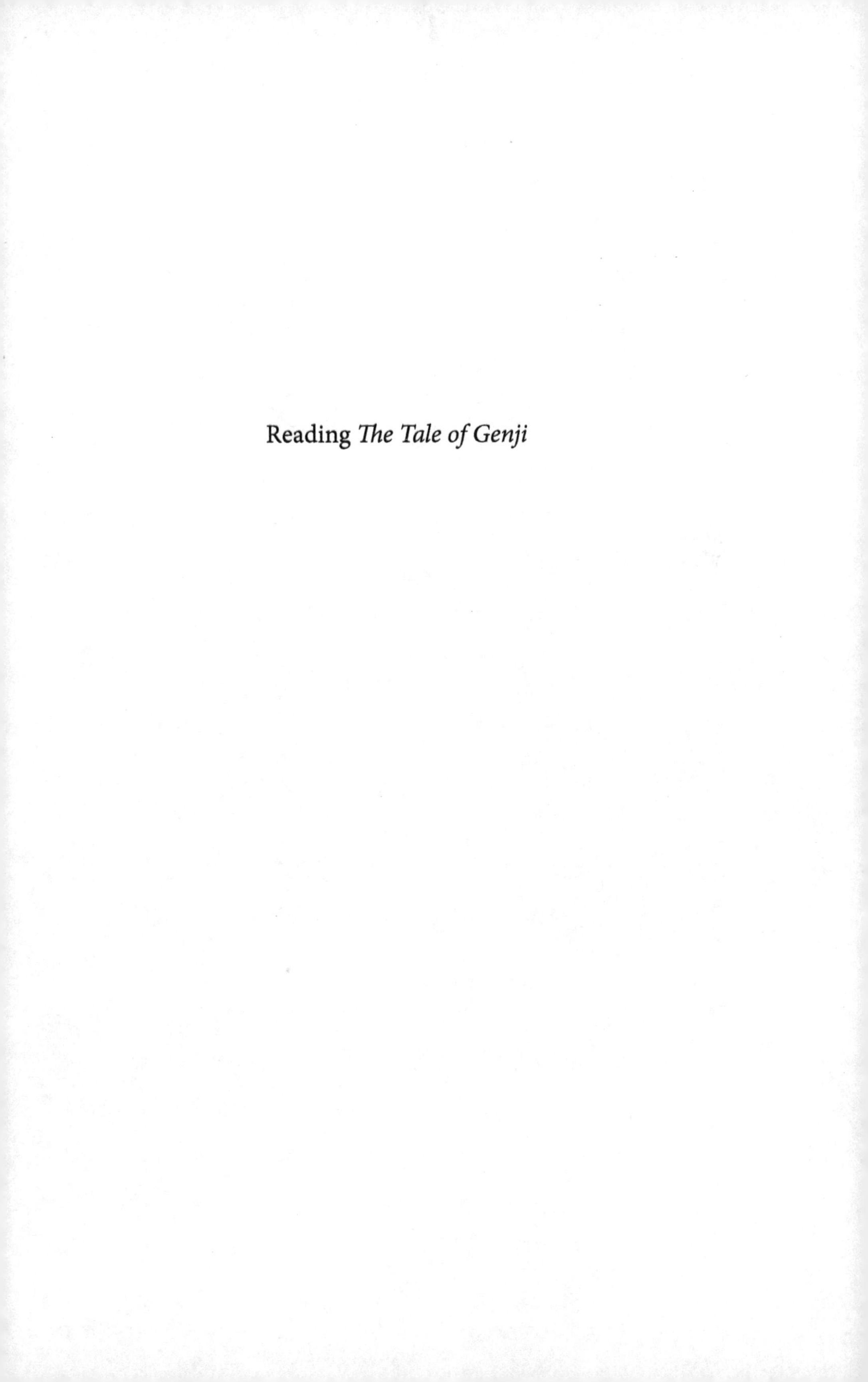

Reading *The Tale of Genji*

Reading *The Tale of Genji*

SOURCES FROM THE FIRST MILLENNIUM

Edited by
Thomas Harper and Haruo Shirane

TRANSLATIONS AND INTRODUCTIONS BY
Patrick Caddeau, Lewis Cook, Wiebke Denecke,
Michael Emmerich, Thomas Harper, Michael Jamentz,
Christina Laffin, James McMullen, Gaye Rowley,
Satoko Naito, Haruo Shirane, Tomi Suzuki,
and Hitomi Yoshio

COLUMBIA UNIVERSITY PRESS
New York

Columbia University Press wishes to express its appreciation for assistance given by the Japanese Literary Studies Fund of Columbia University toward the cost of publishing this book.

Columbia University Press
Publishers Since 1893
New York Chichester, West Sussex
cup.columbia.edu

Copyright © 2015 Columbia University Press
All rights reserved

Library of Congress Cataloging-in-Publication Data

Reading the Tale of Genji : sources from the first millennium / edited by Thomas Harper and Haruo Shirane ; translations and introdutions by Patrick Caddeau, Lewis Cook, Wiebke Denecke, Michael Emmerich, Thomas Harper, Michael Jamentz, Christina Laffin, James McMullen, Gaye Rowley, Satoko Naito, Haruo Shirane, Tomi Suzuki, and Hitomi Yoshio.
pages cm
Includes bibliographical references and index.
ISBN 978-0-231-16658-4 (cloth)
ISBN 978-0-231-53720-9 (e-book)
1. Murasaki Shikibu, 978?– Genji monogatari. I. Harper, Thomas J., editor. II. Shirane, Haruo, 1951– editor.

PL788.4.G43R37 2015
895.63'14—dc23

COVER IMAGE:

Tosa Mitsunobu, *The Picture Contest* (*E-awase*), Illustration to Chapter 17 of *The Tale of Genji* (*Genji monogatari*), Muromachi period, dateable to 1509–1510. (Harvard Art Museums/Arthur M. Sackler Museum, Bequest of the Hofer Collection of the Arts of Asia, 1985.352.17.A. Photo: Imaging Department © President and Fellows of Harvard College)

COVER DESIGN:

Milenda Nan Ok Lee

For Professor Ii Haruki

to whose scholarship, guidance, and encouragement

every contributor to this volume

is deeply indebted.

Contents

Illustrations

Abbreviations and Periods of Japanese History

The following abbreviations for multivolume series are used in the notes.

GMKS	Genji monogatari kochū shūsei. 30 vols. Tokyo: Ōfūsha, 1978–.
GR	Gunsho ruijū. 29 vols. Reprint. Tokyo: Zoku Gunsho Ruijū Kanseikai, 1959–1960.
KT	Shinpen kokka taikan. 20 vols. Tokyo: Kadokawa Shoten, 1983–1992.
MNZ	Ōkubo Tadashi and Ōno Susumu, eds., Motoori Norinaga zenshū. 23 vols. Tokyo: Chikuma Shobō, 1968–1993.
NKBT	Nihon koten bungaku taikei. 102 vols. Tokyo: Iwanami Shoten, 1957–1968.
NKBZ	Nihon koten bungaku zenshū. 51 vols. Tokyo: Shōgakukan, 1970–1976.
SNKBT	Shin Nihon koten bungaku taikei. 105 vols. Tokyo: Iwanami Shoten, 1989–2005.
SNKBZ	Shinpen Nihon koten bungaku zenshū. 88 vols. Tokyo: Shōgakukan, 1994–2002.
SNKS	Shinchō Nihon koten shūsei. 82 unnumbered vols. Tokyo: Shinchōsha, 1976–1989.
T	Takakusu Junjirō et al., eds., Taishō shinshū daizōkyō. 100 vols. Tokyo: Taishō Issaikyō Kankōkai, 1924–1932.
ZGR	Zoku gunsho ruijū. 37 vols. and 3 supplementary vols. Tokyo: Zoku Gunsho Ruijū Kanseikai, 1959–1960.

Unless otherwise stated, the text of *The Tale of Genji* cited is the six-volume *Genji monogatari*, edited by Abe Akio, Akiyama Ken, and Imai Gen'e, NKBZ 12–17. Each quotation is identified by volume and page number in the following form: 12:345.

For a bibliography on the reception of *The Tale of Genji*, see Haruo Shirane, ed., *Envisioning The Tale of Genji: Media, Gender, and Cultural Production* (New York: Columbia University Press, 2008). A regularly updated bibliography of English-language scholarship on *The Tale of Genji* may be found at http://www.gayerowley.com/teaching/genji-bibliography/.

The periods of Japanese history are as follows.

Nara	710–784
Heian	794–1185
Kamakura	1192–1333
Muromachi	1336–1573
Country at war (Sengoku)	1467–1615
Edo	1603–1868
Meiji	1868–1912
Taishō	1912–1926
Shōwa	1926–1989
Heisei	1989–

Chapter Titles of *The Tale of Genji*

In the many references to the chapters *of The Tale of Genji* in this volume, the original Japanese titles are cited. They are not translated because there is no unanimity among the three modern English translations, and no one set of titles is clearly superior to the other two. In lieu of providing translations, therefore, we have compiled the following list of chapter titles from the translations by Arthur Waley, Edward Seidensticker, and Royall Tyler.

	Murasaki Shikibu	Arthur Waley	Edward Seidensticker	Royall Tyler
1	Kiritsubo	Kiritsubo	The Paulownia Court	The Paulownia Pavilion
2	Hahakigi	The Broom-Tree	The Broom Tree	The Broom Tree
3	Utsusemi	Utsusemi	The Shell of the Locust	The Cicada Shell
4	Yūgao	Yugao	Evening Faces	The Twilight Beauty
5	Wakamurasaki	Murasaki	Lavender	Young Murasaki
6	Suetsumuhana	The Saffron-Flower	The Safflower	The Safflower
7	Momiji no ga	The Festival of Red Leaves	An Autumn Excursion	Beneath the Autumn Leaves
8	Hana no en	The Flower Feast	The Festival of the Cherry Blossoms	Under the Cherry Blossoms
9	Aoi	Aoi	Heartvine	Heart-to-Heart
10	Sakaki	The Sacred Tree	The Sacred Tree	The Green Branch

	Murasaki Shikibu	Arthur Waley	Edward Seidensticker	Royall Tyler
11	Hanachirusato	The Village of Falling Flowers	The Orange Blossoms	Falling Flowers
12	Suma	Exile at Suma	Suma	Suma
13	Akashi	Akashi	Akashi	Akashi
14	Miotsukushi	The Flood Gauge	Channel Buoys	The Pilgrimage to Sumiyoshi
15	Yomogiu	The Palace in the Tangled Woods	The Wormwood Patch	A Waste of Weeds
16	Sekiya	A Meeting at the Frontier	The Gatehouse	At the Pass
17	Eawase	The Picture Competition	The Picture Contest	The Picture Contest
18	Matsukaze	The Wind in the Pine-Trees	The Wind in the Pines	Wind in the Pines
19	Usugumo	A Wreath of Cloud	A Rack of Cloud	Wisps of Cloud
20	Asagao	Asagao	The Morning Glory	The Bluebell
21	Otome	The Maiden	The Maiden	The Maidens
22	Tamakazura	Tamakatsura	The Jeweled Chaplet	The Tendril Wreath
23	Hatsune	The First Song of the Year	The First Warbler	The Warbler's First Song
24	Kochō	The Butterflies	Butterflies	Butterflies
25	Hotaru	The Glow-Worm	Fireflies	The Fireflies
26	Tokonatsu	A Bed of Carnations	Wild Carnations	The Pink
27	Kagaribi	The Flares	Flares	The Cressets
28	Nowaki	The Typhoon	The Typhoon	The Typhoon
29	Miyuki	The Royal Visit	The Royal Outing	The Imperial Progress
30	Fujibakama	Blue Trousers	Purple Trousers	Thoroughwort Flowers

	Murasaki Shikibu	Arthur Waley	Edward Seidensticker	Royall Tyler
31	Makibashira	Makibashira	The Cypress Pillar	The Handsome Pillar
32	Umegae	The Spray of Plum-Blossom	A Branch of Plum	The Plum Tree Branch
33	Fuji no uraba	Fuji no Uraba	Wisteria Leaves	New Wisteria Leaves
34	Wakana, jō	Wakana, Part I	New Herbs, Part One	Spring Shoots I
35	Wakana, ge	Wakana, Part II	New Herbs, Part Two	Spring Shoots II
36	Kashiwagi	Kashiwagi	The Oak Tree	The Oak Tree
37	Yokobue	The Flute	The Flute	The Flute
38	Suzumushi	(Not translated)	The Bell Cricket	The Bell Cricket
39	Yūgiri	Yugiri	Evening Mist	Evening Mist
40	Minori	The Law	The Rites	The Law
41	Maboroshi	The Mirage	The Wizard	The Seer
42	Niou Miya	Niou	His Perfumed Highness	The Perfumed Prince
43	Kōbai	Kobai	The Rose Plum	Red Plum Blossoms
44	Takekawa	"Bamboo River"	Bamboo River	Bamboo River
45	Hashihime	The Bridge Maiden	The Lady at the Bridge	The Maiden of the Bridge
46	Shii ga moto	At the Foot of the Oak-Tree	Beneath the Oak	Beneath the Oak
47	Agemaki	Agemaki	Trefoil Knots	Trefoil Knots
48	Sawarabi	Fern-Shoots	Early Ferns	Bracken Shoots
49	Yadorigi	The Mistletoe	The Ivy	The Ivy
50	Azumaya	The Eastern House	The Eastern Cottage	The Eastern Cottage
51	Ukifune	Ukifune	A Boat upon the Waters	A Drifting Boat

	Murasaki Shikibu	Arthur Waley	Edward Seidensticker	Royall Tyler
52	Kagerō	The Gossamer-Fly	The Drake Fly	The Mayfly
53	Tenarai	Writing-Practice	At Writing Practice	Writing Practice
54	Yume no ukihashi	The Bridge of Dreams	The Floating Bridge of Dreams	The Floating Bridge of Dreams

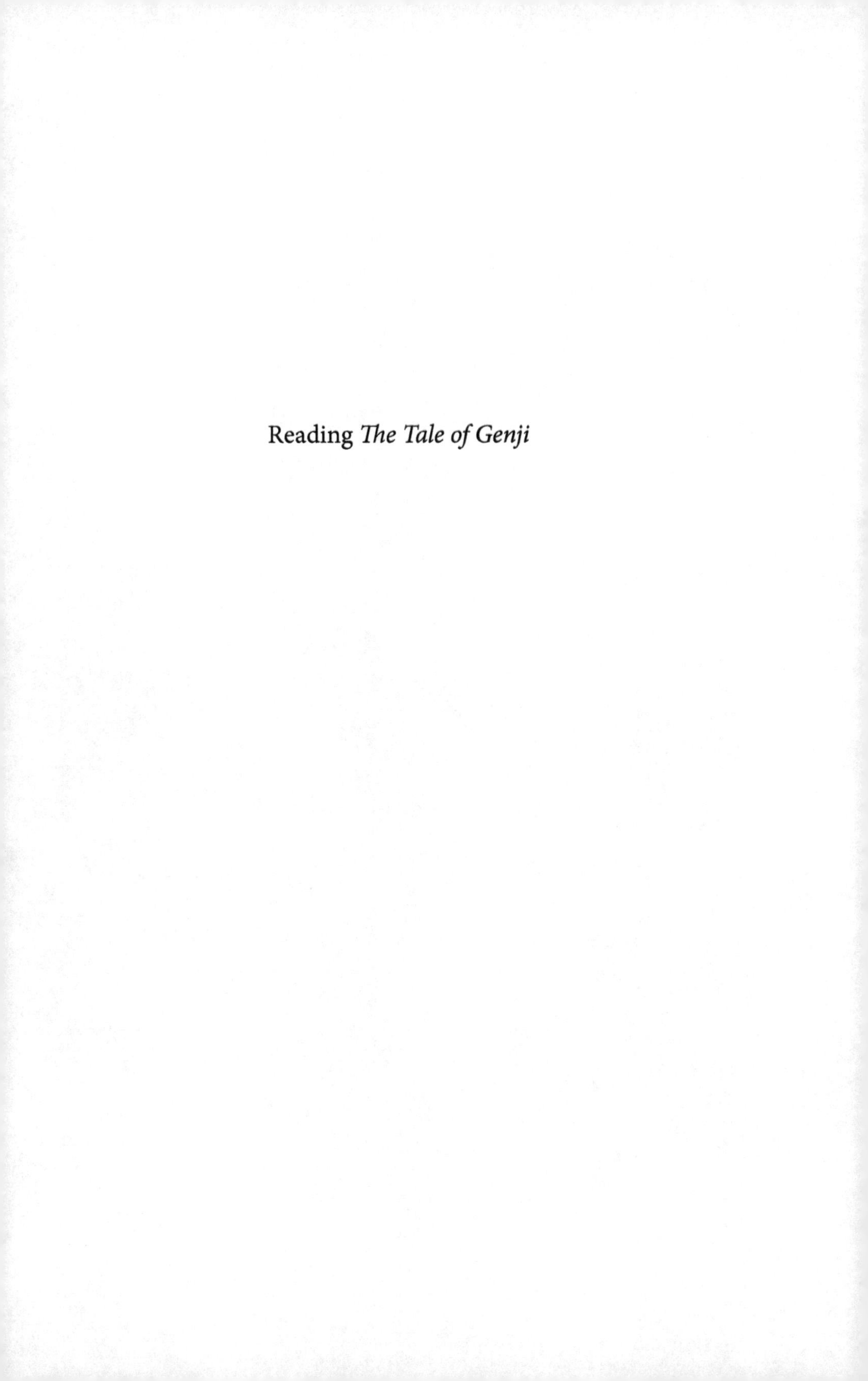

Reading *The Tale of Genji*

Introduction

THE TALE OF GENJI, written in the early eleventh century by a woman known as Murasaki Shikibu, has become a world classic and is still regarded as Japan's finest work of literature. Since the early twentieth century, *The Tale of Genji* has been called the world's first novel, giving us distinctive and memorable characters, realistic settings, and a deep interior view of the life of the nobility, particularly that of women of the middle ranks, in the heyday of Heian court society. The tale, which eventually grew to the fifty-four chapters that we have now, attracted notice from Murasaki Shikibu's male contemporaries. The *Tale of Genji Illustrated Scrolls* (*Genji monogatari emaki*, twelfth century), containing the earliest extant text of *The Tale of Genji*, were probably commissioned by a retired emperor or empress, revealing that within a century and a half of its appearance, *The Tale of Genji* had become a text prestigious enough to be associated with the apex of court culture.

In subsequent centuries, *The Tale of Genji* was read, commented on, illustrated, dramatized, rewritten, and translated in so many ways and by so many different poets, dramatists, and painters that the history of its reception represents no less than a cultural history of Japan. Over the centuries, *The Tale of Genji* passed from the hands of aristocrats to those of Buddhist monks and educated samurai and then to urban commoners; from poets of *waka* (classical poetry) to those of *renga* (classical linked verse) in the late medieval period to poets of *haikai* (popular linked verse) in the Edo period. *Genji* has had a particular fascination owing to its own poetry (795 *waka* "composed" by characters in the story), its narrative of imperial politics, and its focus on the roles of women and the traditional arts. Most major texts enjoy a certain popularity among a particular group of readers, but *The Tale of Genji* has had the capacity to be many things to many different communities over a thousand-year span and continues to underpin what can be called a *Genji* industry, which extends far beyond the borders of Japan. This book brings to an anglophone audience for the first time many of the textual landmarks in the reception of *The Tale of Genji* over the past millennium. These texts, which have been chosen from thousands that exist, tell us not only about how the tale was read and interpreted but also about the ever-changing cultural contexts that altered the significance of *The Tale of Genji* for a wide range of readers. Each translation is preceded by an introduction that provides a historical frame for understanding the selection.

The book begins with a chapter on early discussions of fiction (*monogatari*), providing a broad context for understanding the genre to which *The Tale of Genji* originally belonged and which it would alter irreversibly. The second chapter, "*Genji* Gossip," reveals the early responses, probably in large part by women readers, to *The Tale of Genji* and includes a variety of what could be called *Genji* contests, which compare characters and scenes in *Genji*. The next chapter, on the early canonization of *The Tale of Genji*, demonstrates the ways in which the prose and poetry of this work of fiction were read in relation to classical Japanese poetry and how poetry was involved in the canonization of *The Tale of Genji*. The fourth chapter, "Obsequies for *Genji*," looks at the Buddhist-inflected reception of *The Tale of Genji* as attested by various medieval texts based on the belief that the author had been condemned to hell for writing the tale. These texts are connected primarily with rites meant to offer posthumous salvation to the author and, by implication, redemption of *The Tale of Genji* itself. The fifth chapter is devoted to *Genji* apocrypha, a subgenre of texts that attempted to fill perceived gaps in the tale, including that left by what appeared to some readers to be an unfinished story. The sixth chapter introduces medieval commentaries, which appeared as early as the thirteenth century and became the most influential mode of *Genji*'s reception in the medieval period. Originating in interlinear glosses, these commentaries trace and explicate literary sources, historical references, social customs, poetic allusions, and obscure words. They also address the complex position that *The Tale of Genji* held in relation to its literary predecessors and to contemporary secular and religious discourses, including the larger issue of fictional versus historical discourse. The seventh chapter discusses translations of major Edo-period treatises on *The Tale of Genji* by such prominent Confucian and *kokugaku* (nativist studies) scholars as Kumazawa Banzan (1619–1691), Andō Tameakira (1659–1716), and Motoori Norinaga (1730–1801). Here *The Tale of Genji* becomes a battleground for differing views of the role of literature; debates over aesthetics, morality, and politics; and the controversial role of *The Tale of Genji* in women's education. The final chapter brings us to the modern period, with particular attention to the pre–World War II years, when *The Tale of Genji* was inextricably linked to the emergence of the modern novel and was translated repeatedly into contemporary Japanese.

Poetry and Issues of Fiction

The Tale of Genji was first canonized not merely as a *monogatari*, a genre held in low regard for most of the premodern period, but also as a source of and inspiration for *waka*, which had become the premier literary genre by the mid-Heian period. By the late twelfth century, *Genji* had become an important source for poetic diction and topics. Equally significant, it had become one foundation for allusive variation, a major poetic device from the thirteenth century onward. Poets such as Fujiwara no Teika (1162–1241) were interested not only in the 795 *waka* contained in *Genji* but also in its often lyrical prose and poetically evocative scenes. In the fifteenth and sixteenth centuries, digest versions of *Genji* were compiled by *renga* poets who relied on poetic associations derived from the text. *The Great Mirror of Genji* (*Genji ōkagami*, ca. early fifteenth century), one of the most popular digests, had the alternative title *Poetic Words in the Genji* (*Genji utakotoba*) and enabled its readers to become familiar with the poems in *Genji* without having to read the entire fifty-four chapters.

For many centuries, Japanese literature consisted of a body of selected, authoritative texts and *hon'i*, essential lexical associations, which made up the heart of the literary canon. *Renju gappekishū* (*Gathered Gems*, ca. 1476), a handbook for *renga* poets composed by Ichijō Kanera (1402–1481), lists 886 key poetic words, divided into forty-one categories, that are followed by lists of associated words (*yoriai*) used to link verses in *renga*. An example is "For mountain person (woodcutter): Suma, hedge, pink, and 'to lose favor' (*The Tale of Genji*)."[1] If the previous verse (*maeku*) included the word "mountain person" (*yamagatsu*), one could create a link in the next verse by using the word "Suma," "hedge," "pink," or "to lose favor," each of which was associated in the collective poetic memory with "mountain person." All these associated words derive from specific scenes and poems in *The Tale of Genji*, related to either Genji's exile in Suma and Akashi or the "Yūgao" chapter.

Even *kokugaku* scholars like Motoori Norinaga, who attempted to eliminate Buddhist and Confucian discourse from discussion of *The Tale of Genji* and asserted its value as prose fiction, regarded *waka* and *monogatari* as of identical essence. As Norinaga notes in *Shibun yōryō* (*Essence of Murasaki Shikibu's Writings*, 1763), "Apart from this *monogatari*, there is no Way of Poetry, and apart from the Way of Poetry this *monogatari* would not exist. The Way of Poetry and this *monogatari* are of quite the same essence."[2] A full poetics of prose fiction did not develop until the early nineteenth century, with Takizawa Bakin (1767–1848) and Hagiwara Hiromichi (1815–1863) under the influence of Chinese vernacular fiction theory. Even modern literary scholarship on *The Tale of Genji* can be seen as an extended attempt to escape from this long tradition of defining literature as poetry—from the hegemony of *waka*—and to reread *Genji* purely as a *monogatari* or a psychological novel.

Gender and Reception

In the words of the modern scholar Tamagami Takuya (1915–1996), *The Tale of Genji* was originally written by a woman, for women, and about women. Indeed, the initial readers and consumers of *Genji* were women of the imperial court, and the primary readers of *Genji* during the first century after its appearance were aristocratic women. Nonetheless, few traces of women's reception remain, in contrast to the subsequent flood of male commentary on the text. This book, however, provides a rare example of female reception that survives in the *Mumyōzōshi* (*A Nameless Notebook*), thought to have been written in 1200/1201, which describes a women's literary tradition beginning in the ninth century with Ono no Komachi and argues for the elevation of the literary status of fictional tales over that of diaries and nonfiction. Other glimpses of female reception are visible in the texts in the "*Genji* Gossip" chapter and in the late medieval commentaries by Kaoku Gyokuei (b. 1526).

The practice of *Genji* obsequies (*Genji kuyō*)—rites for the salvation of the author of *The Tale of Genji*—suggests that by the late twelfth century the position of aristocratic women readers vis-à-vis *The Tale of Genji* was much more ambivalent than the relationship of men to *Genji*. There is a stark contrast between the poet Fujiwara no Shunzei (1114–1204), who was responsible (along with his son Teika) for the early canonization of *The Tale of Genji*, and his wife, Bifukumon'in Kaga (d. 1193), who also loved *The Tale of Genji* but feared that it would have a negative impact on her afterlife and thus was involved in *Genji kuyō* rituals. In contrast to the medieval commentaries on *Genji* written by men, which focus on diction or textual sources, both poetic and historical, women's writings on *Genji* such as *Sarashina Diary* (*Sarashina nikki*, ca. 1059) and *A Nameless Notebook* (*Mumyōzōshi*, ca. 1200) focus on the fate of the female characters. For women readers, *Genji* appears to have been a vehicle for exploring and understanding their own lives. Indeed, *The Tale of Genji* may well have been written by Murasaki Shikibu, at least in part, as a guide for women on how to survive at court and in aristocratic society, and later women readers saw *Genji* as representing various models of living and coping. Many versions of *Genji* gossip or games were lists of judgments on the "superlative female character," "superlative nun," and so on in *The Tale of Genji*. Although the dating and authorship of these texts are uncertain, they bear a strong resemblance to *The Pillow Book* (*Makura no sōshi*, 997) and its entertaining lists of superior or inferior things. *A Nameless Notebook* also compares the male and female characters in *Genji* with each other according to varying criteria.

Tale of Genji Variations and Apocrypha

Another major stream of medieval reception is the fictional reincarnations of *The Tale of Genji*. From the late Heian period through the Kamakura era, *The Tale of Genji* became the object of constant reinvention, with prominent borrowings of plots, scenes, and characters from *Genji*. Before *The Tale of Genji*, Heian tales drew on narrative archetypes such as the courtship narrative or the exile of the young noble, but after *The Tale of Genji*, the tale itself became an archetype for subsequent fictions. Late-eleventh-, twelfth-, and thirteenth-century readers took pleasure in finding small differences between similar scenes, much as *waka* poets took pleasure in allusive variation. Even in the Muromachi period, *otogizōshi* (short fictional tales) like *Kachō fūgetsu* (*Flowers and Birds, Wind and Moon*) use characters from *The Tale of Genji* or create new variations on the plot.

Due to space limitations, these narrative reincarnations cannot be included here, but the volume does present a number of apocrypha that attempted to fill in what were perceived to be gaps in the existing *Tale of Genji*.

Linked Verse, Nō Drama, and Painting

The powerful warlords of the late medieval period, faced with constant battle and social and political chaos, were drawn to the world of *The Tale of Genji*, as is manifest in their deep interest in *renga*, which frequently alluded to the Heian court tale, and through their patronage of nō drama, which often depicted characters from *The Tale of Genji*. Nijō Yoshimoto (1320–1388), a *waka* scholar and *renga* poet, was probably the individual most responsible for making a knowledge of *Genji* indispensable to *renga*. As Yoshimoto notes in *Kyūshū mondō* (*Dialogue at Kyushu*), "If the poet uses the *Man'yōshū* all the time, the appearance [*sugata*] of *renga* will become rough," but if *renga* relied solely on "the first three imperial anthologies, beginning with the *Kokinshū*, one would feel that the language was weak."[3] In Yoshimoto's view, *Genji* was perfectly positioned between those two extremes. One consequence was that Yoshimoto brought *Genji* into late medieval *renga* in the same way that Shunzei had brought *Genji* into *waka* in the late twelfth century.

For warrior leaders, who typically had far less education than members of the aristocracy, *The Tale of Genji* represented a connection to a heritage of court culture that they did not possess. One result was that powerful warlords and shoguns repeatedly commissioned *Genji* paintings in a variety of genres (scroll paintings, albums, and large illustrated screens), which became a major form of *Genji* reception in the late medieval and Edo periods. Powerful warriors also took lessons on *The Tale of Genji* from learned nobles such as Sanjōnishi Sanetaka (1455–1537), the author of an influential commentary on *Genji*. In this situation, *renga* masters, who often were Buddhist priests and/or commoners, formed a key link between the new warrior class and the classical tradition. *Renga* masters like Sōgi (1421–1502), the author of *Notes on the Rainy Night's Discussion* (*Amayo danshō*, ca. 1485), became influential teachers of *The Tale of Genji*. The *renga* manuals and *Genji* digests written by *renga* poets in turn provided the foundation for the *Tale of Genji* nō plays, particularly the genre of women's plays, based mainly on female figures (such as Utsusemi, Yūgao,

Rokujō, and Ukifune) from *The Tale of Genji*. Owing to considerations of space, *Genji* nō plays and *Genji* paintings cannot be included here, but anyone interested in the cultural history of *The Tale of Genji* must consider these two major streams of *Genji* reception. In fact, the phenomenon of *Genji* painting expands in the Edo period in the form of *ukiyo-e* (literally, "pictures of the floating world") and new visual genres.[4]

Edo Treatises, Imperial Transgression, and Women's Education

Roughly speaking, *Genji* commentary passed from the hands of *waka* scholars to *renga* masters (Muromachi period) to *haikai* masters (Edo period), exemplified by Kitamura Kigin (1624–1705), to Confucian and *kokugaku* scholars in the eighteenth and nineteenth centuries. The publication of Kigin's *Kogetsushō* (*Moonlit Lake Commentary*, 1673), with its headnotes and interlinear commentary, enabled a new and expanded audience of commoners to gain access to *Genji*. The *Kogetsushō* was printed, thereby permitting mass distribution, as opposed to the manuscript transmission of the preceding period. One result of this new print culture was that *Genji* was adapted into the vernacular, parodied, and reconstructed for popular consumption, in versions ranging from Ihara Saikaku's (1642–1693) *Kōshoku ichidai otoko* (*Life of an Amorous Man*, 1682) to Ryūtei Tanehiko's (1783–1842) *Nise Murasaki inaka Genji* (*Fraudulent Murasaki's Bumpkin Genji*, 1829–1842), both of which presented contemporary versions of the Shining Genji. At the same time, *Genji* scholarship also passed into the hands of *kokugaku* scholars like Motoori Norinaga, who attempted to bring new techniques of philological analysis to *Genji* and criticized Buddhist and Confucian readings that had permeated earlier views of *Genji*.

Throughout the early modern and modern periods, *The Tale of Genji* was attacked as a form of imperial betrayal, owing to the secret liaison between Genji and his stepmother (the Fujitsubo Empress), which results in the ascent of their illegitimate son to the throne. Some commentators, such as Andō Tameakira, found ways to defend this by arguing that *The Tale of Genji* was intended to show the negative consequences of such acts. The most famous defense, however, was that of Motoori Norinaga, who stressed that *The Tale of Genji* was not intended to demonstrate the consequences of good or evil acts, as Buddhist and Confucian commentators had argued. Instead, Murasaki Shikibu described these painful love affairs and transgressions in order to reveal the depths of human emotion, so that readers could "know *mono no aware*" or "sensitivity to emotion."

By looking at the Edo-period commentaries of both Confucian and *kokugaku* scholars and by placing them alongside the proliferation of *Genji*-related prose fiction and the emergence of women's educational texts, which included passages from *Genji* as models of elegant writing, we get a much more complex picture than that of the standard literary histories, which place Norinaga's theory of *mono no aware* at the apex of Edo-period *Genji* reception. As the proliferation of women's educational textbooks indicates, *The Tale of Genji* had attractions that made it useful for women's education and a suitable part of an upper-class daughter's trousseau, but it also had aspects, particularly its eroticism and episodes of adultery, that made it a precarious subject for its advocates.

Modern Reception and the Modern Novel

In the early Meiji period, *The Tale of Genji* was overshadowed by the new literary genres imported from the West. However, with the importation of the nineteenth-century European notion of "literature," which valued prose fiction, *Genji* was soon recanonized as a "novel," which, in the Spencerian evolutionary scheme, was considered the most advanced literary form. In *Shōsetsu shinzui* (*Essence of the Novel*, 1885–1886), an influential statement of the value of the novel as "art," Tsubouchi Shōyō (1859–1935) defined *The Tale of Genji* as a "realistic novel" (*shajitsu shōsetsu*) that depicts contemporary upper-class society.

The fate of *The Tale of Genji* was also closely tied to the rise of nationalism, through the institutional establishment of the new fields of national literature (*kokubungaku*) and national language (*kokugo*), which were thought to embody national character and were set, particularly after the Sino-Japanese War (1894–1895), in opposition to Chinese, which had been an integral part of Japanese literature for more than a thousand years. Fujioka Sakutarō's (1870–1910) *Kokubungaku zenshi: Heianchō-hen* (*Complete History of National Literature: Heian Literature*, 1905), which marks the beginning of modern scholarship on Heian literature, defines *Genji* in the context of both the novel and the nation: "Not only is *The Tale of Genji* the most important Heian novel, it is our nation's number-one novel of all time." Thus by the turn of the century, *The Tale of*

Genji had been recanonized as a predecessor of the modern "realistic novel," placed in government-approved textbooks, and made a central part of the national language and literature curriculum. By the 1920s, *Genji* was being viewed and read in Japan as a part of "world literature."

Starting in the mid-Meiji period, *The Tale of Genji* also became the source of inspiration for novels and short stories by such writers as Ozaki Kōyō (1867–1903), Higuchi Ichiyō (1872–1896), and Izumi Kyōka (1873–1939). A major literary turning point was the modern Japanese translation of *The Tale of Genji* by the noted *tanka* poet Yosano Akiko (1878–1942). Her first modern translation, *Shin'yaku Genji monogatari* (*New Translation of The Tale of Genji*, 1912–1913), which radically abbreviated the original text, transformed *Genji* into a modern novel, thus making it part of modern Japanese literature. Her second translation, *Shinshin'yaku Genji monogatari* (*New New Translation of The Tale of Genji*, 1938–1939), was a translation of the entire text (except for the *waka*, which were left in the original). It was succeeded by a series of twentieth-century translations by major novelists—such as Tanizaki Jun'ichirō (1886–1965), Enchi Fumiko (1905–1986), and Setouchi Jakuchō (b. 1922)—a phenomenon that was followed in the 1980s and 1990s by full *manga* translations, notably *Asaki yume mishi* (*Fleeting Dreams*, 1979–1993) by Yamato Waki (b. 1948).

In the Shōwa period, *The Tale of Genji* continued to inspire such noted novelists as Tanizaki Jun'ichirō, Kawabata Yasunari (1899–1972), and Mishima Yukio (1925–1970). As Tanizaki's postwar novella *Yume no ukihashi* (*The Bridge of Dreams*, 1960) suggests, *The Tale of Genji* contains themes and plot patterns—such as a young man's search for the image of a lost mother (Genji / Fujitsubo), death as a result of forbidden or unattainable love (Kashiwagi / Third Princess), a man and a woman unable to unite as a result of excessive self-consciousness (Kaoru / Ōigimi)—that continue to appeal to the interests of modern Japanese writers, dramatists, and filmmakers.

HARUO SHIRANE

Notes

1. Kidō Saizō and Shigematsu Hiromi, eds., *Renga ronshū*, Chūsei no bungaku (Tokyo: Miyai Shoten, 1972), 1:129.

2. *Shibun yōryō*, in *Motoori Norinaga shū*, ed. Hino Tatsuo, SNKS 60 (Tokyo: Shinchōsha, 1983), 213. In revising *Shibun yōryō* for use as the introductory chapters

to *Genji monogatari Tama no ogushi* (*The Tale of Genji: A Little Jeweled Comb*, 1799), Norinaga eliminated the passage in which this sentence appears.

3. Ijichi Tetsuo, ed., *Renga ronshū* (Tokyo: Iwanami Shoten, 1953), 1:94.

4. For an overview of the dramatic and visual reception of *The Tale of Genji*, see Haruo Shirane, ed., *Envisioning The Tale of Genji: Media, Gender, and Cultural Production* (New York: Columbia University Press, 2008). For translations of *Genji* nō plays, see Janet Goff, *Noh Drama and The Tale of Genji: The Art of Allusion in Fifteen Classical Plays* (Princeton, N.J.: Princeton University Press, 1991).

Chapter 1

Early Discussions of Fiction

THE IMPACT OF *THE TALE OF GENJI* on its first readers, and their responses to it, can be fully appreciated only within the context of the romances or tales (*monogatari*) they were reading before the appearance of *Genji* and what was being said about them, by both their devotees and their detractors. Only three prose fictions of any length survive from the century before *Genji*: *The Tale of the Bamboo Cutter* (*Taketori monogatari*), *The Tale of the Hollow Tree* (*Utsuho monogatari*), and *The Tale of the Lady in the Lower Room* (*Ochikubo monogatari*). That such tales abounded we know from the many titles mentioned here and there, but none of the texts survive.[1] The same is true of readers' reactions. We catch only brief glimpses of women copying tales and gossiping about them. In the end, however, it is Murasaki Shikibu herself who gives us the clearest and most discursive picture of the literary landscape of which *Genji* was to become a part. In chapter 17, "Eawase," she describes a matching of old romances and tales, similar, perhaps, to something she herself may have witnessed. In chapter 25, "Hotaru," she sets forth, in the guise of Genji lecturing his ward Tamakazura, what are generally taken to be her own views of fiction and its possibilities. And in her diary, she describes the making of the first bound volumes of *Genji*, as well as the reactions of Fujiwara no Michinaga (966–1027), the patron who financed the project, and of the Ichijō Emperor (980–1011; r. 986–1011) to whom it was presented. Few though they may be, these documents sketch a court in which tales of the fantastic—of a princess sent to Earth as an exile from the moon, of a young man raised in the hollow of a tree who eventually marries the emperor's first daughter—formed the principal fare of readers. Then suddenly there appeared a tale—*The Tale of Genji*—that depicted a known world, and did so with a compelling sense of reality that readers had never before seen. Their reactions to this startling phenomenon, and the preconceptions in which they are rooted, are described in the documents translated in this chapter.

One problem that arises in discussing, in English at least, the development of prose fiction in Japan is that the terminology used in Japanese is only partially congruent with that used in the West. In both cases, a long and revered tradition of "classical" literature forms the background against which vernacular prose fictions evolve—in Japan, the Chinese classics; and in the West, Greek and Roman. Nor are the new genres greatly dissimilar: both are constituted of tales of the marvelous and the improbable, the absurd and the ideal. In the West, it was language itself that gave this new genre its name. Fictions were first called "romances" because they were written in (or translated into) the vernacular "romance languages" rather than Latin or Greek. In Japan, they were called "tales"—literally, "talk of things"—a word that refers here to the act of oral storytelling but in other contexts may denote "chat" or even the "babbling" of babies. If this were all there was to it, the writer of English could simply translate *monogatari* as either "romance" or "tale," the former emphasizing origins in the vernacular as well as similarity of subject matter and the latter, the orality of the narration. But further developments in the "progress of romance"[2] make the choice more complex. In both Japan and the West, these tales of worlds that might have been if dreams came true gave way to representations of known worlds such as those in which their readers actually lived. In Europe, the realist turn is conventionally dated to the appearance of *Don Quixote*, and in Japan, needless to say, to *Genji*.

The great difference between the two traditions is that in Europe the realist turn marked the rise of a genre of fiction so new, and eventually so voluminous, that it seemed to require a new name: novella, nouvelle, novel.[3] In Japan, *Genji* so overwhelms its predecessors that it has no successors; there is no need for a new word because there is only one work of such towering novelty. The novelty itself was as clearly recognized in Japan as it was in Europe. The "old romances," as they came to be called in English, became *furu-monogatari* or *mukashi monogatari* in Japan. The author of the *Kagerō Diary* (*Kagerō nikki*) complains bitterly of their shortcomings, and Murasaki Shikibu herself distinguishes old from new with complete clarity in the "Hotaru" chapter of *Genji*. Yet *The Tale of Genji* continues to be called a *monogatari* along with its far more fanciful forebears of the same name. Therefore, when discussing *Genji* in English, I am reluctant to call it a "novel" when no comparable term exists in Japanese. Neither is it a "romance." Although acceptable in the title, "tale" is less than ideal as a generic designation, for it fails to suggest any quality that would distinguish *Genji* from its predecessors. Another approach to the problem is not to translate *monogatari* at all but instead to attempt to force the word into the English language, as has been done with haiku and nō and even hiragana. But haiku and nō and hiragana have a far stronger claim to naturalization, for there are no even remotely comparable terms in English that might serve to translate them. *Monogatari* is not untranslatable. To use it as if it were is only to evade the issue, and risks implicating whatever one has to say in a welter of ideological and ahistorical claims for the "non-novelistic" narratological uniqueness of all Japanese works that bear the name.[4] In the end, then, a conservative compromise seems to be the least problematic solution. In this volume, *furu-monogatari* and *mukashi monogatari* are translated as "old romances"; references to *monogatari* other than *Genji* are rendered as either "romance" or "tale," depending on which seems more appropriate to the work in question; and *Genji* itself is always, as its readers termed it, a "tale."

T. HARPER

KAGERŌ DIARY, CA. 974
(*Kagerō nikki*)
THE MOTHER OF MICHITSUNA

This prologue to the *Kagerō Diary* records the first surviving objection to "the old romances" (*furu-monogatari*) on the grounds of their remoteness from the reality of the reader's own life.[5] The same objection is voiced by Tamakazura in *The Tale of Genji* itself, and no doubt other readers harbored similar feelings. But the author of the *Kagerō Diary*—a woman we know only as "the Mother of Michitsuna" (935–995)—not only voiced her objection but then wrote a memoir of her own life in as unidealized a manner as she could. Paradoxically, the prologue begins as if it were itself another "old romance" but soon settles down into an unvarnished account of her experience of marriage to a "man of the highest rank." It is highly likely that Murasaki Shikibu read this memoir, and it may well have served as an example to her of the hitherto unexplored possibilities of prose fiction.

T. HARPER

The times, such as these have been, have passed, and there was one who lived through them, uncertain as they were, with nothing to which she could cling. Even her looks were not the equal of others', nor was she particularly bright. It was only natural, she thought, that she should be as useless as she was. Yet as the days passed with nothing to do but live through them and she looked into some of the old romances, of which there were so many about, all of them laden with all the same old lies, it occurred to her that it might be interesting to describe in a diary even the lot of someone of no consequence. Life with a man of the highest rank, you ask? Here's an example! But those bygone years are now but a blur, so there are many places where, well, that will just have to do.

TRANSLATED BY T. HARPER

EARLIER COLLECTED POEMS OF THE GREAT KAMO PRIESTESS, CA. 983
(*Dai Sai'in saki no gyoshū*)

PRINCESS SENSHI

The following is a brief sampling from a collection of 394 poems compiled by Princess Senshi (964–1035), a daughter of the Murakami Emperor (926–967; r. 946–967).[6] She is known as the Great Kamo Priestess (Dai Sai'in) because she served in that position through five imperial reigns, from 975 until she was finally allowed to retire in 1031, a total of fifty-seven years. Several collections of her poetry survive. This one is particularly notable for its glimpses into the daily lives of the princess and her retinue, as well as their literary activities, such as poetry competitions (*uta-awase*), the copying of tales, and the appointment of the princess's ladies-in-waiting to positions in the fanciful "Bureau of Poetry" (Uta no Tsukasa) and "Bureau of Romances" (Monogatari no Tsukasa).

T. HARPER

On about the twentieth day,[7] when Her Highness promoted the Deputy Director to Director of the Bureau of Poetry, the new Deputy Director said:

mi wa naredo sakidatazarishi hana nareba / kotakaki e ni zo oyobazarikeru
Though it has borne fruit, never has this flower been one to lead the way,
nor, therefore, shall it ever bloom upon a branch so high.

When she said this, Her Highness replied:

shizueda to itaku na wabi so sue no yo wa / kotakaki mi ni zo narimasarubeki
Pray lament not so the lowliness of the branch upon which you bloom,
for in times to come, surely you shall fruit high in the tree.

After these bureaus had been established, when it was suggested that the Deputy Director of the Bureau of Romances might well serve jointly in the Bureau of Poetry, the Director of Romances said to the Deputy Director of Poetry:[8]

uchihaete ware zo kurushiki shiraito no / kakaru tsukasa wa tae mo shinanamu[9]
To go on thus, speaking for myself, would be quite excruciating.
Far rather would I that these bureaus should be abolished.

In reply:

shiraito no onaji tsukasa ni arazu tote / omoiwaku koso kurushikarikere
True though it be, that we are not colleagues of the self-same bureau,
that you should set yourself apart from us is hurtful indeed.

When Her Highness commanded that fresh copies of the romances be made and the old texts were distributed among the members of the bureau, the Director of Romances sent some to Minbu's place, saying:

yomo no umi ni uchiyoserarete . . . neyoreba kakisuteraruru mokuzu narikeri[10]
Of all those washed ashore from across the far seas . . .
these writings are but a heap of abandoned dregs of weed.

Minbu, because she had not been in attendance for long, wrote:

kakisutsuru mokuzu o mitemo nageku kana / toshi heshi ura o hanarenu to omoeba
When I peruse even these abandoned dregs of writings—ah, I sigh,
to think how far away are those shores where I spent so many years.

TRANSLATED BY T. HARPER

PREFACE TO *THE ILLUSTRATED THREE TREASURES*, 984
(*Sanbōe*)

MINAMOTO NO TAMENORI

The Illustrated Three Treasures is a collection of Buddhist homilies compiled for the edification of an unhappy princess who was soon to enter holy orders as a nun. Princess Takako (Sonshi, 966–985) served from her third to her tenth year as the High Priestess of Kamo. In 980, her fifteenth year, she became a Dame of Honor (*nyōgo*) to the Enyū Emperor (959–991; r. 969–984). Barely a month after her arrival, the imperial palace burned down, and many people apparently blamed the disaster on the princess. Two years later (982), after the death of the uncle who was her last living backer at court, she secretly fled the palace and cut her hair short. At this point, someone seems to have commissioned the scholar Minamoto no Tamenori (941?–1011) to compile a collection of homilies that might guide the young lady to a somewhat happier life.[11] A profusely illustrated edition of the *Three Treasures* was completed in 984.[12] In the following year, the princess took vows and shortly thereafter died of unknown causes.[13]

The argument of this particular homily is the seemingly universal one: that fiction seduces and misleads the imagination, encouraging not only immoral behavior but also a waste of time on frivolities that might better be spent in spiritual pursuits.

T. HARPER

To pass the time of day at a game of go may be diverting, yet how fruitless to waste one's thoughts in striving and contention. The koto, too, can be a pleasant companion of an evening, but one is apt to grow overfond of its music.[14] And romances—these are but for the amusement of women. They flourish in greater profusion than weeds on the wooded graves of old; they are as numerous as the grains of sand on the rocky strand. To creatures that lack the gift of speech they give words; to insentient objects they impart feelings—even to trees and grasses, mountains and rivers, birds and beasts, fishes and insects. Their words flow forth unchecked, as flotsam on the sea; unlike reeds at the river's edge, they have no root in truth. *The Old Trickster* [*Iga no taome*], *The Tosa Minister* [*Tosa no otodo*], *The Fashionable Colonel* [*Imameki no chūjō*], [and] *The Lady of the Inner Chamber* [*Nakai no jijū*]—these and all their ilk describe the dallying of men and women as if it possessed all the beauty of flowers and butterflies. They are the very roots of sin. They count for not so much as a drop of dew in the Grove of Letters.

TRANSLATED BY T. HARPER

THE PILLOW BOOK, 997
(*Makura no sōshi*)

SEI SHŌNAGON

This fragment from *The Pillow Book* is from Sei Shōnagon's (b. ca. 965) description of an exchange with a lover, Fujiwara no Tadanobu (967–1035), who seems to be losing interest in her. Shōnagon's sharp reply to one of Tadanobu's messages, scrawled in charcoal at the bottom of the missive, quickly becomes the talk of the court, whereupon Shōnagon sets out to tell the empress of her triumph.[15] When she arrives, however, she finds the empress and her gentlewomen in the midst of a heated discussion of *The Tale of the Hollow Tree* (*Utsuho monogatari*), and before Shōnagon can say a word about herself, she is asked to offer an opinion of the two rivals of the first section of this tale. The scene that Shōnagon alludes to, in the "Fukiage" chapter, describes a musical contest in which Fujiwara no Nakatada and Minamoto no Suzushi play the koto in the presence of the emperor at the Festival of Autumn Leaves. Both men have fine old instruments of illustrious lineage and are privy to esoteric techniques passed down secretly from great masters of the past. As a result, they play so consummately as to disrupt the course of nature itself. A wind arises to set the clouds racing; the moon and stars flicker unnaturally; hail the size of pebbles falls; thunder roars and lightning flashes; a blanket of snow covers the earth, only to melt the instant after it falls; and finally a heavenly maiden descends and dances to their music. As a reward for this stunning performance, the emperor grants the hand of his own daughter, the First Princess, to Nakatada, and that of Princess Atemiya, the most sought-after beauty in the land, to Suzushi.[16] The episode provides a glimpse of the kind of reading material favored by ladies of the court before the appearance of *Genji*.

T. HARPER

On the Twentieth or So of the Second Month of Last Year (996)

When the sun had set, I went to the Empress's chamber, where quite a number of people were gathered. Her Majesty was attended by her own gentlewomen, who were absorbed in an argument over which of the romances were good and which bad, and what it was they didn't like about them. Even Her Majesty had something to say on the merits and demerits of Suzushi and Nakatada. "Come now," someone said to me, "tell us what *you* think, and be quick about it. Her Majesty insists that Nakatada is ill bred."[17] "What?" I said. "Suzushi does play the koto well enough that a maiden came down from heaven to dance, but he's a perfectly horrid person. And did the Emperor give *him* one of his own daughters, as he did Nakatada?"[18] When I said this, the ladies partial to Nakatada took heart. "So there!" one of them said. To which the Empress replied, "Well, all that aside, if you had seen Tadanobu when he attended us today, I expect you'd have been beside yourself admiring *him*." "Oh yes, indeed," her ladies said, "even more the picture of perfection than he usually is!" "Well, it was he," I said, "whom I came to tell you about in the first place, but all this talk of romances has prevented me." Then I told her all that had happened.

TRANSLATED BY T. HARPER

THE TALE OF GENJI
(*Genji monogatari*)

MURASAKI SHIKIBU

Eawase

Beneath a veneer of aesthetic refinement and connoisseurship, "Eawase" is an intensely political chapter of *Genji*.[19] In the aftermath of Genji's triumphal return from exile in Suma and Akashi, the Suzaku Emperor is living in retirement, and the new Reizei Emperor, still a boy in his thirteenth year, has ascended the throne. As in every new reign, new opportunities arise for the exercise of power through the new sovereign. This time, the competitors are Genji and Tō no Chūjō, friends and rivals since boyhood, but with the stakes so much higher now, their rivalry is no longer as friendly as it once was. The new emperor is in fact Genji's son by his father's wife, the Fujitsubo Empress, but since even the emperor himself is unaware of this relationship, it affords Genji no political leverage. Moreover, Tō no Chūjō has already placed one of his daughters in the palace as the new Kokiden Dame of Honor, and the emperor has taken quite a liking to her. Should their union produce a son, Genji's chances at supreme power would be seriously threatened. Accordingly, he and the Fujitsubo Empress Mother decide that Genji should adopt the daughter of another of his former lovers, the late Rokujō Consort, and place her in the palace as the Umetsubo Dame of Honor. The only problem with this stratagem is that the new lady arrives on the scene after a long period of service as the High Priestess of Ise, and she is already in her twenty-second year, nine years older than the emperor. Something will have to be done to make this grown woman more attractive to the boy than a girl of his own age and entice him to spend his time with her. Just as in the real world described by Murasaki Shikibu in her diary, this sort of seduction is accomplished by means of art and literature, lavishly patronized by the backers of both ladies.

T. HARPER

The Empress Mother, too, was in the palace. When His Majesty heard that someone unusually lovely was coming, he took a very charming interest in it all. For his age he was quite knowing and grown up. The Empress Mother had told him, "With so grand a lady as she is, you must be very well behaved when you meet her." Secretly he worried that he might feel uncomfortable with a grown-up. But when she arrived at the palace, far into the night, it turned out that she was very modest seeming and dignified and looked so small and frail that he thought her quite lovely.

By now he was on such familiar terms with the lady in the Kokiden that he felt very close to her and, in a touching way, at ease in her company. But this new lady was so dauntingly serene of manner, and the Minister [Genji] treated her with such respect and deference, that he knew he hardly dared slight her. Accordingly, at night he allowed both to attend him in equal measure, but by day, for more carefree and childlike amusements, it was to the other quarter he was most likely to go. The Acting Middle Counselor [Tō no Chūjō] had plans of his own in begging this favor for his daughter, and the new arrival, challenging her, left him feeling, in countless ways, ill at ease. . . . And so the two vied, each in her own way, for the imperial favor.

His Majesty delighted, above all else, in pictures. Perhaps because he took such particular interest in this art, he was exceptionally skilled at painting. Because the former High Priestess of Ise, now his Dame of Honor, painted beautifully, his affections shifted to her. More and more it was to her that he went, and as they painted together, they drew ever closer. He had been partial, as well, to some of the young Privy Gentlemen who were students of the art. But this was nothing compared to the way he was smitten by the charming sight of this lovely creature, absorbed in her painting, so individual in style, reclining fetchingly there beside him, when now and again in such an attractive way she would pause with her brush poised. He went to her very often now and favored her far more than he had before.

When the Acting Middle Counselor heard of this, fiercely competitive and thoroughly modern man that he was, he raged to himself, "Am I to let them leave me in the lurch?" He summoned the most skilled artists, enjoined them to strict secrecy, and had them paint a collection of magnificent pictures on papers of unparalleled quality. "Pictures based on tales are what will most appeal to him," he told them. Then, carefully selecting all the most interesting texts, he had them illustrate them. There was also to be a set of familiar scenes of the successive seasons, which he arranged in an original way, joining them with passages of text, for presentation to His Majesty. They were so well done that His Majesty wanted to view them with the other lady, too. Yet the Acting Middle Counselor would not willingly let them go but kept them strictly to himself, guarding them jealously from being taken.

When he heard about this, the Minister [Genji] smiled. "It seems the Acting Middle Counselor will never grow up," he said to the Emperor. "He's as childish as ever. It's quite shocking he should cause you such distress, purposely hiding his pictures and not giving you the chance to share them. Well, I have some much older pictures; let me give you those."

Thus are established the terms of the competition between the two ladies for the emperor's affections. The emperor is fond of pictures, and still being a boy, he will find pictures that go with stories the most enjoyable. Both ladies will therefore be lavishly equipped to please him: Tō no Chūjō's daughter with newly painted scenes in the modern style, and Genji's ward with the finest of old paintings. The next level of escalation is carried out by the empress mother herself, who arranges that the rivalry be brought into the open with all the highly ordered formality of a poetry contest.

When he heard that Genji was assembling a collection of paintings, the Acting Middle Counselor went to even greater lengths to equip his own with decorative spindles, covers, and cords. It was a lovely time of year, around the tenth of the Third Month, when skies are clear and hearts free of care; and at court there was a hiatus between ceremonials, with the result that both ladies were spending all their time in pursuits of this sort. "If that's how it's to be," Genji decided, "I shall show His Majesty some pieces that will delight him even more." And he set about collecting with even greater determination. Both sides now had a great many pieces of several sorts. Illustrated tales seemed to be what they found the most deeply touching and enjoyable. On the Umetsubo side they concentrated on the best known and most interesting of the old tales, while in the Kokiden they chose to illustrate those that dazzled and charmed their own day, the modish flair of which, at a glance, was far greater. All the Emperor's own gentlewomen who took an interest in such things likewise busied themselves passing judgment this way and that.

It was a time when the Empress Mother, too, had come to the palace, and, having seen all that was going on, she was loath to miss out; so, to the neglect of her devotions, she turned to viewing paintings. Hearing His Majesty's gentlewomen debating the merits of this one and that, she divided them into two sides, Left and Right. On the side of the Umetsubo, there were Hei no Naishi no Suke, Jijū no Naishi, and Shōshō no Myōbu; and on the Right, Daini no Naishi no Suke, Chūjō no Myōbu, and Hyōe no Myōbu. These were some of the brightest and most knowledgeable women of their time, and Her Majesty listened with fascination to the wit with which each argued her own point of view.

First, that "great progenitor of all tales," *The Old Bamboo Cutter*, was matched against the "Toshikage" chapter of *The Hollow Tree*. "In its very antiquity, as age after age piles up on it, like the joints of the pliant bamboo itself, this work may be somewhat lacking in glamour. But the story of Princess Kaguya, unsullied by this sordid world, destined to rise nobly to the lofty heavens, seems something out of the Age of the Gods, something no frivolous sort of woman is ever likely to comprehend." The Right responded: "The heavens to which Princess Kaguya rose may well be beyond us, indeed incomprehensible to anyone. But her destiny in this world is tied to the bamboo, which suggests low birth. She may have illumined a single household, but never did she stand alongside the brilliance that shines within the august precincts of the palace. Abe no Ōshi throws away thousands and thousands in gold, only to have his hopes for the skin of the fire rat vanish in flames within an instant. How very depressing. And Prince Kuramochi, who knows full well the depth of the princess's feelings, that she is as unattainable as the land of Hōrai itself, nonetheless makes a fake jeweled branch and then ruins it. There's still another defect." The paintings were by Kose no Ōmi [fl. 901–922] and the text was in the hand of Ki no Tsurayuki [881?–945?], both done on official court papers backed with patterned Chinese silk, with a cover of violet tinged in red, on a sandalwood spindle, a perfectly ordinary sort of mounting.

"Now Toshikage," they went on to say, "though nearly drowned by violent wind and waves, then cast away in a strange land, nonetheless accomplishes the goal he has set out to attain. Ultimately, he displayed, both in the foreign court and in our own land, the magnitude of his rare talent, for which he shall always be known. And in keeping with the profound significance of this tale, the pictures, too, combine the styles of both China and Japan, the many points of interest in which are beyond comparison." They were done on a stiff, gleaming white paper, mounted with a cover of blue on a spindle of yellow jade. The paintings were by Tsunenori [fl. 946–967] and the text in the hand of [Ono no] Michikaze [894–966], all so modern and glamorous as to dazzle the eye of the beholder. The Left had no cogent counterargument.

Next *The Tales of Ise* was matched against *Jōsanmi*,[20] and again it was no simple decision. Here, too, the Right's choice was appealing and lively, depicting scenes in the modern world, particularly in and around the palace, which made it all the more worthy of attention. Hei no Naishi:

> *ise no umi no fukaki kokoro o tadorazute / furinishi ato to nami ya ketsubeki*
> "Without our ever even exploring the depths of the sea of Ise,
> must the waves wash away all those traces of the past?

Are we to sully the name of Narihira in favor of some common tale of dalliance set forth in meretricious finery?" On the Right, Daini no Naishi no Suke:

> *kumo no ue ni omoi noboreru kokoro ni wa / chihiro no soko mo haruka ni zo miru*
> "To the heart of one whose aspirations soar to heights above the clouds[21]
> even the vast depths of your sea seem far distant below."

"To be sure," said the Empress Mother, "the lofty aspirations of the Palace Guardsman's elder daughter are not to be slighted, yet neither dare we defame the name of Narihira, the Ariwara Colonel of the Bodyguards.

> *miru me koso urafurinurame toshi henishi / ise o no ama no na o ya shizumemu*
> Worn and shabby it may, at a glance, appear; yet after all these years
> is the fame of the fisher from Ise now to be sunk?"

And so this women's talk raged on inconclusively, in a dispute that elicited poem after poem yet failed to decide on any one scroll. The younger gentlewomen, who knew very little of such things, were simply dying to see them. But no one, whether in the service of the Emperor or the Empress Mother, got even so much as a glimpse, so jealously were they guarded.

The Minister had arrived at the palace and was much amused by the reckless spirit with which these arguments flew to and fro. "If it is all the same to you," he ventured to say, "shall we settle this matter in the presence of His Majesty?" He had anticipated that this was how things might turn out and had purposely held back the choicest pieces in his collection, to which he had added, for reasons of his own, those two scrolls from Suma and Akashi.

This round ends in an uneasy draw, the supporters of the classics saved from near total defeat only by the forceful intervention of the empress mother. But Genji is unruffled; this is all as he has planned it. The final round, and the final decision, must be witnessed by the emperor himself in the presence of all the notables of the court. Ultimately this contest is not about romances or pictures at all but about which of the two young ladies, now ranked equally as dames of honor, will be appointed the new empress. And that will be determined by whichever of the two competing backers can prove himself the more powerful in this contest. When Genji decides to deploy not only the wealth of his collection but also his own overwhelming talents in the cause of the Umetsubo Dame of Honor, by displaying the scrolls he himself painted while in exile, the victory of his candidate is virtually ensured. Two years later, the full implications of the "picture contest" become apparent. The Umetsubo lady, with Genji's backing, is proclaimed the new empress, and Tō no Chūjō, furious at the humiliation of his own daughter, withdraws the Kokiden lady from palace service.[22]

TRANSLATED BY T. HARPER

Hotaru

The following passage from the "Hotaru" chapter of *Genji* is often described as Murasaki Shikibu's "defense" or "discussion of fiction" (*monogatari-ron*).[23] There is a sense in which such a description is entirely just, yet it is important to keep in mind that this is not simply literary criticism couched in the voice of a fictional character. It is first and foremost a piece of dramatic writing, and any ideas that find their way into it are inevitably inflected by their literary function.

Genji has amorous designs on Tamakazura, the long-lost daughter of Yūgao, one of his youthful loves. The girl is living in Genji's Rokujō mansion, having arrived in the capital only a few months earlier after living for many years in Kyushu. As the rainy season wears on and Genji's women while away the tedium with illustrated romances, Tamakazura takes a particular fancy to this new (to her) form of entertainment. Genji's discussion of fiction begins, therefore, when he finds the girl utterly engrossed in these romances and, for reasons of his own, wants to discourage her from taking what she reads too much to heart. His first ploy is to denigrate fiction as deceptive and untrue, but when she reacts defiantly to this charge, Genji quickly concedes that she may well have a point and proceeds to fabricate a defense of fiction that he hopes will be more to her taste and make her more amenable to his advances. In the end he fails, and we see from his demand that his own daughter not be exposed to any love stories that his "defense of fiction" was entirely insincere.

This is not to say, however, that the ideas expressed in this passage must not be associated with Murasaki Shikibu, for in fact she talks about fiction here in ways that it had never been discussed before. In *The Pillow Book*, and even in "Eawase," the worth of romances is determined by entirely extraneous qualities, such as the birth, accomplishments, and likability of the characters. Here, for the first time, fiction is discussed in terms of its intrinsic qualities and its possibilities. Whatever the dramatic function of this discussion, its content is revolutionary.

As we shall see further on in this volume, Motoori Norinaga (1730–1801) was the first commentator to single out this passage and explicate its literary significance. One wonders, of course, why commentators of the medieval era, many of whom were extremely intelligent readers of *Genji*, did not do this earlier. But perhaps this "oversight" is only an indication that their awareness of the dramatic qualities of the passage was more acute than Norinaga's.

T. HARPER

The rains this year had persisted much longer than usual, and the ladies of the household were amusing themselves whole days at a stretch with illustrated tales. The Akashi lady had produced some very nice work of this sort, too, which she would pass on to the young lady, her daughter. But the lady in the Western Wing [Tamakazura] was even more intrigued by such things and would spend night and day copying and reading. She had a number of young gentlewomen who were quite proficient and who had told her all sorts of astonishing tales of people's lives. Yet in none of them, it seemed to her, whether fact or fiction, was there anyone at all like herself. For some reason, the young lady in *Sumiyoshi*,[24] a heroine, of course, at the time of her adventures, seemed still to be highly regarded in the present day, though her narrow escape from the Superintendent of Finance did call to mind the ferocity of the Viceregal First Secretary.[25]

His Lordship [Genji] found her unable to take her eyes off these things, which were scattered everywhere around the room. "What a mess!" he said. "You women seem to have been born only to be deceived by people, and without your even raising a complaint. You know perfectly well that there's very little truth in any of these, and yet here you are, captivated and deceived by all this nonsense, copying away as if you were quite unaware that it is a stifling hot day and your hair is all in a tangle." He smiled and went on. "Yet without these old stories, how indeed would you while away this interminable tedium? For among these fabrications are some that show us people's feelings in so real a manner as to make us feel that this is life as it really is. One thing follows another so plausibly that even though we know it to be sheer nonsense, still, for no good reason, we are deeply moved. And so we may see some lovely little lady stricken with grief and find that we ourselves are quite caught up in her woes. And then, there are those who so dazzle us with their grandiloquence that we are taken in by things we know could never happen. Upon a calmer hearing we would only be annoyed; yet, incredibly, we still appreciate whatever it was that so fascinated us at first. Lately when I have stopped to listen to our young [Akashi] lady's women reading to her, I have been struck by what extraordinary tellers of tales we have these days.

Such stuff could come only from the mouth of someone well accustomed to lying, it seems to me, but perhaps I am wrong."

"Isn't it rather that it takes a person who is quite accustomed to lying even to imagine such things?" she asked, pushing away her inkstone. "For my part, I accept them as completely true."

"That was rude of me to run them down so, wasn't it? As they say, everything that has gone on in the world since the Age of the Gods is recorded in [these tales]. The histories of Japan are really very one-sided. But these must give you all the choice little details," he said with a smile. "It isn't that they describe the events of some person's life exactly as they happened. But rather that some things one sees and hears about people as they go through life, whether good or evil, are so intriguing and overwhelming that one cannot shut them all away in one's heart but wants to pass them on to subsequent generations—and so sets out to tell the story. Should one mean to describe someone favorably, one may select every good quality imaginable. Or instead one may defer to the tastes of others and gather in all manner of evils and marvels. But in neither case will these depart from the realities of this world we live in. In other courts, their scholarship and their styles of writing differ from our own, while even in this land of Yamato, works of old differ from those of the present day. To be sure, there is a distinction to be drawn between deeper language and shallow language, yet to dismiss them all as empty fabrications runs counter to the facts of the matter. Even in the Holy Law that the Buddha in his beneficence has expounded for us, there are what we call the Expedient Truths [*hōben*], which, owing to the contradictions they contain, the unenlightened doubtless view with suspicion. In the Vaipulya sutras [Hōdōkyō], these are quite numerous, but in the final analysis they all share a single aim. And this disparity between enlightenment and delusion, you see, is comparable to the difference between good and evil in these people. Given its fair due, then, nothing whatever is utterly bereft of benefit, is it?" He made quite a case for tales as something of particular value.

"But where in any of these old stories will you find a tale of such an earnest old fool as I? Even the most distant of those young ladies could hardly be as coldhearted and oblivious seeming as you. But come," he said, drawing closer to her, "let us create a story that never before has been known, and let it be told to all the world." She cringed and hid her face. "Even if we do nothing of the sort," she said, "this alone is bizarre enough to set everyone gossiping."

"You think this is bizarre? You really are one of a kind, it seems to me." He slid still closer until he sat right at her side, in a manner that was terribly suggestive.

omoiamari mukashi no ato o tazunuredo / oya ni somukeru ko zo tagui naki
"Overcome with longing, I have searched through the records of the past, yet
nowhere do I find a child so heedless of her father.

Even in the Way of the Buddha there are dire warnings against unfilial behavior." When she refused to look up at him, he stroked the hair away from her face. So bitterly reproachful was he that finally she managed to say,

furuki ato o tazunuredo ge ni nakarikeri / kono yo ni kakaru oya no kokoro wa
"Search the annals of antiquity though you may, indeed there are none:
no parents in all the world who harbor such thoughts as these."

He felt shamed and troubled her no further. But now that this had happened, whatever was to become of her?

Lady Murasaki, too, had quite a penchant for tales, which she procured on the pretext that they were for the young lady [from Akashi]. "My, but these are beautifully painted, aren't they," she said, looking at an illustration of *The Tale of Kumano*.[26] It was a picture of a little girl, innocently napping, that brought to mind memories of her own past. "How precocious they must have been," Genji said, "even little girls like this! You know, I really should be regarded as something of a model; I'm sure few others would have exercised such patience as I did." True enough; not many others had assembled such a collection of amours.

"I do hope, though," he went on, "that you won't read any tales of such loose behavior to our young lady. It's not that she would admire those girls who carry on clandestine affairs, but it could prove disastrous should she come to think it entirely normal that such things go on in this world." Well, isn't that just the limit! The lady in the Western Wing [Tamakazura] would surely have fumed, could she have heard him say this.

TRANSLATED BY T. HARPER

THE DIARY OF MURASAKI SHIKIBU, 1010
(*Murasaki Shikibu nikki*)
MURASAKI SHIKIBU

The Diary of Murasaki Shikibu contains a number of references to *The Tale of Genji*, as well as other unnamed fictions.[27] The first of these is a comment by Fujiwara no Kintō (966–1041). Kintō is nowadays best known as a man of letters. As the compiler of *Chinese and Japanese Poems for Chanting* (*Wakan rōei shū*, 1013), he played an important part in the popularization of the *Hakushi monjū* (*Bo Juyi's Collected Works*) in Japan, and his treatise *The Newly Compiled Essence of Poetry* (*Shinsen zuinō*, date unknown) became one of the most frequently cited authorities by composers of *waka*. He is also the compiler of the third imperially commissioned anthology of Japanese poetry, the *Shūishū* (ca. 1005–1007). Here, however, it is not as a man of letters that he speaks. The occasion of his remark is the fiftieth-day celebration of the birth of a prince (1008) to Empress Shōshi (988–1074), which, according to Murasaki Shikibu, very early on showed signs of becoming a "frightfully drunken evening." Murasaki writes:

> The Commander of the Left Gate Guards, Kintō, peered in. "I beg your pardon," he said, "but is our little Murasaki in attendance hereabouts?" "There's certainly no one in sight that bears any resemblance to Genji," I thought to myself as I sat there, "why then should his lady be here?"

Kintō clearly has read enough of *The Tale of Genji* to address its author jokingly as "little Murasaki" (*waka*-Murasaki). Indeed, it may be that the nickname by which we now know her, "Murasaki Shikibu," originated in references of this sort. It is likely, too, that Kintō was aware of the project that Murasaki describes shortly thereafter in her diary, the production of a luxurious edition of *Genji* that the empress planned to present to the emperor on her return to the palace. As with so many works of art and literature of the time, the aim of this project was not simply aesthetic but political as well. For Fujiwara no Michinaga, the father of the empress, to perpetuate his rule over the land, it was essential that his daughters continue to produce male heirs through whom he, as regent, could wield power. To this end, he spared no expense in equipping his daughters with paintings, furnishings, books, and the like that the emperor might find entertaining and entice him to spend his time with the woman who possessed them and not some rival nobleman's daughter. In this sense, the first edition of *The Tale of Genji* was very much a tool of seduction, and it is highly likely that Murasaki's talent for writing such tales was the reason she was summoned to serve Michinaga's daughter Shōshi in the first place. She herself laments that a reputation for being "fond of her tales, conceited, always with a poem at the ready" had preceded her and that it took some doing to counter this (as she saw it) misapprehension. This passage also makes it clear that at this point in the textual history of *Genji*, at least two versions of the tale were in circulation. Scholars now reckon that the version presented to the Ichijō Emperor was little more than half the length of the present fifty-four-chapter *Genji* and that the purloined version probably contained additional chapters that were not considered suitable for such a felicitous occasion as presentation to the emperor.

T. HARPER

Though the time had drawn near for Her Majesty to return to the palace, her people were rushing frantically about while the Empress busied herself with bookbinding. At daybreak I would wait upon her, and we would first pick out the papers in a variety of shades, put them in proper order, attach the texts of the tale, write to the persons concerned, and distribute them. Then we would spend the day at the task of assembling the pages and stitching them together. "What's this?" His Lordship said. "You with a child, and doing all this out in the cold!" Even so, he would bring us fine thin papers, brushes, ink, and even an inkstone, which Her Majesty gave to me. He made a terrible grudging fuss over this. "You're always in here waiting on her," he scolded me, "and now you make off with this." But then he gave me some excellent papers and brushes.

In my room I had hidden some texts of the tale that I had sent home for, and while I was in the presence, His Lordship slipped in there, rummaged about for them, and gave them all to the Chief Palace Attendant.[28] I lost every one of the texts I had revised so carefully, which made me quite apprehensive about what this would do to my reputation.

The little prince was making gurgling sounds [*on-monogatari*] by now. No wonder His Majesty was so eager to see him.

Once this task is completed, she leaves briefly to visit her own home before returning to the palace. The change of scene brings back depressing memories of listless days between her husband's death and the time she was summoned to serve the empress, which in turn make even her accomplishment in writing Genji *pale in her own eyes.*

As I gazed out at the dreary grove in the garden here at home, I was beset with confusion and melancholy. The tedium of all those years I had spent, day in and day out, amid the color of the blooms and the song of the birds; gazing, spring and autumn, at the changing patterns in the sky, at the moonlight, the frost, and the snow; hardly aware of anything but that one season or another had come; all the while helpless to dispel the forlorn thought of "what, oh what"[29] was to become of me? Still, there were those of like mind with whom I could discuss this frivolous tale of mine, and it was comforting to correspond with them. There were those, as well, whom I could approach only through somewhat distant connections. Yet all the while I was only pottering about with this thing [*The Tale of Genji*], whiling away the tedium with worthless words. I felt I hardly counted for enough to go on living in this world, but for the moment at least, I had avoided doing anything I need be ashamed of or regret. How dismal my lot is now that I've tasted all these things to the fullest. I made an attempt to read the *Tale* again, but it no longer seemed what it once had, and that was depressing. How worthless and shallow I must now appear to those with whom I'd found such comfort in discussing it. The very thought fills me with such shame I'm no longer able to write to them.

On another visit home, some disused books catch her eye.

There are two large cabinets, both piled full to capacity. One is filled with old poems and romances that have become a nest of the most unspeakable insects that go creeping and scampering so repulsively that no one ever opens it anymore. In the other are Chinese books that no one has touched since the person who so carefully stacked them there passed away. When loneliness threatens to overwhelm me, I take out one or two and look through them, at which point my women get together and mutter behind my back, "If Madam's going to go on like this, she'll come to no good. What sort of woman is it who reads books in Chinese? Once upon a time they used to stop us reading even the scriptures." When I hear them, I want to say, "Well, I've never seen one of these women who's supposed to have lived to a ripe old age because she's abstained from everything she's supposed to." But that would be thoughtless. They may even be right.

In the following year (1009) she relates an incident involving the Ichijō Emperor and one of her fellow gentlewomen.

There is a certain Lady Saemon no Naishi who for some strange reason has decided that she dislikes me and, without my knowledge, has been saying the most unpleasant things about me behind my back. Once, while His Majesty was having *The Tale of Genji* read to him, he remarked, "This lady must have been reading *The Chronicles of Japan*.[30] She is very learned indeed." Whereupon this woman, on no more than her own whim, immediately spread it about among the Privy Gentlemen that I had been "putting on the most pretentious airs of learning." Then she began calling me "Lady Chronicles." How perfectly ludicrous. I have always been careful to avoid that sort of thing, even among the women of my own household. Why would I ever presume to make a display of my learning in such a place as this?

In the same year, she also records an exchange of poems with Fujiwara no Michinaga, the father of Empress Shōshi and the patron of the luxurious first edition of Genji. *Michinaga seems to assume, at least for purposes of the mischief he intends, that the author of a tale of the amours of the Shining Genji must herself be strongly inclined that way.*

His Lordship saw *The Tale of Genji* there in front of the Empress, and after making the usual senseless jokes, he wrote upon a piece of paper upon which were placed some plums:

sukimono to na ni shi tatereba miru hito no / orade suguru wa araji to zo omou
Known as she is as a wanton, as is the plum for its bitterness,
there must be none who pass her by without plucking the fruit.

I replied:

hito ni mada orarenu mono o dare ka kono / sukimono zo to wa kuchi narashiken
When no fruit has ever been plucked from this tree, who is there who can say
that I might be quite as wanton as the plum is bitter?[31]

Shocking! At night, when I was asleep in the room on the bridgeway, I heard someone tapping on the door, but frightened, I made not a sound the whole night through. The next morning:

yo mo sugara kuina yori ke ni naku naku zo / maki no toguchi ni tatakiwabitsuru
The whole night through, more even than the water rail did I cry and cry
tapping tapping wearily away at your cedar door.

I replied:

tada naraji to bakari tataku kuina yue / akete wa ika ni kuyashikaramashi
Tapping tapping at my door as persistently as did this water rail,
had I opened it, how much might I have to regret.

TRANSLATED BY T. HARPER

SARASHINA DIARY, CA. 1059
(*Sarashina nikki*)

THE DAUGHTER OF SUGAWARA NO TAKASUE

The Daughter of Sugawara no Takasue (b. 1008), born in the year that the luxurious edition of *The Tale of Genji* was compiled and presented to the Ichijō Emperor, provides the earliest-known description of the experience of reading the tale. Her *Sarashina Diary*,[32] of course, is not a diary at all but a memoir, written when she was fifty-one or fifty-two, shortly after the death of her husband. Hence, all the events she describes are seen in retrospect and, moreover, are colored by her grief at her recent bereavement. To judge from the frequency with which she refers to *Genji*, however, and the amount of space she allots to it in a journal covering almost forty years, her involvement with *Genji* must have been one of the most deeply felt experiences of her life.

T. HARPER

I was born and brought up in a province more remote than the far end of the Eastern Sea Road, so you can well imagine what a countrified creature I was. How I first came by the notion I do not know, but I had heard there were these books called tales, and oh! how I longed to read them. On days and evenings when time hung heavy on our hands, I would listen to my elder sister and my stepmother talking of this tale or that, or of Genji the Shining One. This only made me long to hear more, but I could hardly expect them to recite them from memory. In my impatience I had a life-size statue of the Healing Buddha[33] made, and when no one was around, I would go in secretly to it, kneel down with my head to the floor, and pray fervently: "Grant that I may soon go up to the capital, and there let me read all the tales there may be."

In the same year, both her wishes came true: after an arduous three-month journey, she and her family arrived in the capital.

We were not yet settled and the house was still in turmoil, but I was so impatient that I pestered my mother repeatedly to find some tales for me to read. She wrote to a relative in service at Sanjō Palace, Emon no Myōbu, who, surprised and delighted to hear of our return, sent us some lovely booklets that the Princess had given her, all packed in the lid of a writing box. I was overjoyed and read them night and day. That was the start, and soon I began to wish for more, but we were not yet settled in the capital, and who was there to seek out tales for me?

An epidemic in the spring of the next year, 1021, claimed the life of her nursemaid. This disaster so saddened the author that she "lost all interest in tales."

When I continued in this downcast state, my mother took pity on me and tried to console me by obtaining some tales for me to read, and then I began to recover my spirits. I read about little Murasaki and yearned to read the rest, but there was no one whom I could ask, and since we were still not settled in the capital, we could not find a copy. I was most impatient and curious, and in my heart I would pray, "Let me see the entire *Tale of Genji*, from the very first volume." When I went with my mother on a retreat to Uzumasa,[34] I could pray for nothing else. As soon as we returned home, I felt sure that I would then be able to read it through, but I never got to see it. I was completely downcast, but while still bemoaning my fate, I went to visit my aunt, who had just returned from the country. "What a lovely girl you've grown to be," she said, making a great fuss over me. Then just as I was about to leave, she said, "What shall I give you? Nothing terribly practical, to be sure. Let me give you something you really want." And she gave me the fifty-odd volumes of *Genji*, all in their own box; and *Zai Chūjō*, *Tōgimi*, *Serikawa*, *Shirara*, and

Asauzu[35] as well. She put them all in a bag for me, and I was overjoyed to have them to take home for my own. Before I had been able to read only bits and pieces, and didn't really know how the story went. Now I had the whole *Genji* to read from the very first volume. When I lay down alone behind my screens, drew it to me, and started to read, I would not have changed places even with the Empress. All day and as far into the night as I could keep my eyes open, I read with the lamp close by me. And since I did absolutely nothing else, I soon knew parts of it by heart, a grand accomplishment, I thought. But then I had a dream in which a monk in a yellow surplice came to me and said, "Study the fifth scroll of the Lotus Sutra immediately!"[36] I told no one; neither did I make any attempt to study it. Tales consumed all my attention. I thought myself terribly unattractive at the time, but when I grew up, I thought, I would be beautiful, with very long hair. Surely I would grow up to be like Genji's Yūgao or Kaoru's Ukifune, I thought, silly fool that I was.

Ten years later, she seems not to have changed her ways. Though in hindsight she felt she could have spent her time to better advantage, at twenty-three she remained as addicted to reading tales as she had been at twelve.

And so I went on wasting my time on the most frivolous thoughts. When I did happen to make one of my rare pilgrimages, it was not to pray, as others did, that I might become a better person. In those days most people began to read the sutras and to perform religious devotions at age sixteen or seventeen, but such things did not interest me in the least. All I could manage to think of was how I might live hidden away in the mountains like Ukifune. And there would be some very noble and handsome gentleman, like Genji in the tale, who would call on me perhaps once a year. In my loneliness I would gaze out upon the cherry blossoms, the autumn leaves, the moon, or the snow while I waited for one of his charming letters. I actually thought this would come true someday.

In 1036, her parents, much against their better judgment, were persuaded to let her try a term of service at court. Her first stay was to be for one night.

I was so absorbed in tales that I maintained no social relations with friends or relatives. I spent all my time at home with my old-fashioned parents and never went out other than to view the cherry blossoms or the moon. And so when I went to court, it all seemed more like a dream than reality.

Four years later, after the death of her father and probably after her marriage to Tachibana no Toshimichi (1001–1058), her tone begins to change to one of disillusionment.

Thereafter, other things seemed to keep me occupied. I completely forgot about tales and became more serious and sober. How many years and months I had utterly wasted, all the while neglecting my devotions and making no pilgrimages! And what about all those hopes and dreams I had had—could such things really exist? Is there really anyone like Genji to be found in this world? Certainly it is no place where you will find anyone like the lady whom Kaoru kept hidden away at Uji. What a lunatic I had been, I thought.

In 1046, she makes a pilgrimage to Hatsuse, and when passing through Uji she remarks:

We arrived at the ferry at Uji. . . . It seemed the boat would never come to take us across, and as I looked around, I was very curious to know where the daughters of Prince Hachi no Miya had lived and where Kaoru had ensconced his lady. It was every bit as lovely a place as I had imagined. Then at long last we crossed and went to see the Uji Mansion,[37] where I could not help thinking that the Lady Ukifune must have lived in just such a place.

Her last mention of tales comes in the entry for 1058, shortly after her husband's death.

If in the past I had not spent all my time thinking about worthless tales and poems but had devoted myself night and day to the performance of my devotions, then perhaps I might not have suffered such a fate.

TRANSLATED BY T. HARPER

Notes

1. "Nearly 240 titles" for which no texts survive are mentioned in Heian- and Kamakura-period sources. See Matsuo Satoshi, "San'itsu monogatari," in *Nihon ko-*

ten bungaku daijiten (Tokyo: Iwanami Shoten, 1984), 3:92–95. The *Tales of Ise* (*Ise monogatari*), too, predates *Genji*, but its prose passages are mere fragments by comparison with *Taketori*, *Utsuho*, and *Ochikubo*.

2. Clara Reeve's title of her history of the genre, *The Progress of Romance*, 2 vols. (1785; repr., New York: Facsimile Text Society, 1930).

3. This is by no means the only construction of the history of prose fiction in the West. Another asserts that "Romance and the Novel are one," traces the origins of the genre to Greek and Roman sources, and sees its progress to the present day as "a continuous history of about two thousand years" (Margaret Anne Doody, *The True Story of the Novel* [London: HarperCollins, 1997]). The subject remains under continual and vigorous debate.

4. For example: "In the Heian tale, plot and character, together with syntax, fuse into an all-embracing time-flow which affords the reader an occasion to feel and reflect on his being and non-being in life (which may be at the same time non-life)" (Masao Miyoshi, "Translation as Interpretation," *Journal of Asian Studies* 38, no. 2 [1979]: 98). A similar line is pursued at greater length by Miyoshi's protégé Richard Okada in *Figures of Resistance: Language, Poetry, and Narrating in The Tale of Genji and Other Mid-Heian Texts* (Durham, N.C.: Duke University Press, 1991). Readers of this book should also consult Haruo Shirane, "Review of *Figures of Resistance*," *Journal of Japanese Studies* 20, no. 1 (1994): 221–28.

5. Translated from *Tosa nikki, Kagerō nikki*, ed. Kikuchi Haruhiko, Kimura Masanori, and Imuta Tsunehisa, SNKBZ 13:89.

6. Translated from *Dai Sai'in saki no gyoshū chūshaku*, ed. Ishii Fumio and Sugita Jurō (Tokyo: Nihon Koten Bungakukai Kichōbon Kankōkai, 2002).

7. Probably the twentieth day of the Sixth Month of Eikan 1 (983), according to *Dai Sai'in saki no gyoshū chūshaku*, 123.

8. This preface (*kotobagaki*) is fraught with textual problems. The translation follows the reconstruction of the text proposed in *Dai Sai'in saki no gyoshū chūshaku*, 122.

9. The "pillow word" (*makura kotoba*) *shiraito no* in this and the following poem is used in an unconventional manner, thus rendering it virtually untranslatable. For a detailed explication of its use here, see *Dai Sai'in saki no gyoshū chūshaku*, 122.

10. As the ellipses indicate, either something is missing from the text or it has been incorrectly copied.

11. Translated from Minamoto no Tamenori, *Sanbōe*, ed. Mabuchi Kazuo and Koizumi Hiroshi, SNKBT 31:5–6.

12. Although none of the illustrations survives, some versions of the text note the position of the pictures.

13. This account follows Mabuchi Kazuo's introduction to Minamoto no Tamenori, *Sanbōe*, NKBT 31:2. Other sources reconstruct the chronology of her life differently.

14. An example of how this notion translates into the terms of "everyday life" is seen in *Genji monogatari* ("Tenarai," 17:308), in which the sister of Yokawa no Sōzu complains that her brother no longer allows her to play the koto because it distracts from the *nenbutsu*, and the young Major disingenuously encourages her to do so despite these warnings, because music and dancing are among the delights enjoyed in paradise.

15. Translated from Sei Shōnagon, *Makura no sōshi*, ed. Matsuo Satoshi and Nagai Kazuko, SNKBZ 18:144–45.

16. *Utsuho monogatari* 1, ed. Nakano Kōichi, SNKBZ 14:532–35. Shortly thereafter, however, Suzushi is prevailed on to relinquish Atemiya to the crown prince and accept her younger sister instead.

17. Probably because he grew up in the hollow of a huge tree.

18. Sei Shōnagon's disparagement of Suzushi is the cause of some puzzlement among modern commentators. In extant texts, Nakatada and Suzushi are playing in unison when the heavenly maiden descends; it is not Suzushi's skill alone that entices her. Nor is anything said about Suzushi's character that would seem to justify so harsh a judgment of him. Does this mean that the *Utsuho* text that Shōnagon read differed markedly from those now extant? Or should we read her criticism as referring to Suzushi's playing rather than his person, that although he played well enough to attract the maiden, he was undistinguished in comparison with Nakatada? There is also the possibility, of course, that Sei Shōnagon is just being provocative. See Sei Shōnagon, *Makura no sōshi*, SNKBZ 18:144n.10; and *Makura no sōshi*, ed. Watanabe Minoru, SNKBT 25:96n.16. This translation follows the lead of these commentators.

19. Translated from "Eawase," NKBZ 13:363–73.

20. No longer extant.

21. Probably referring to the heroine of *Jōsanmi*, who seems to be the daughter of a palace guardsman who becomes a favorite of the emperor.

22. We should note what a virtuoso performance the depiction of this contest is. As Tamagami Takuya points out, before *Genji*, although there had been poetry contests, there had never been a picture contest of any sort, much less one in which victory was decided not by the pictures themselves but by the texts they illustrated. The scene depicted here is thus entirely the creation of Murasaki Shikibu's imagination, and the "wit with which each [lady] argued her own point of view" is entirely the author's own (Tamagami Takuya, *Genji monogatari hyōshaku* [Tokyo: Kadokawa Shoten, 1965], 4:41–42). Tamagami also notes that the picture contest held in the household of Princess Shōshi in 1050, in which the basis of judgment was the poems inscribed on them, as well as that in *Rokujō Sai'in-ke utaawase* (1055), in which single poems from each of eighteen newly composed tales were matched in nine rounds, may well have been inspired by the "Eawase" chapter of *Genji*.

23. Translated from "Hotaru," NKBZ 14:202–7.

24. *Sumiyoshi monogatari*. No longer extant. A newer version bearing the same title dates from the Kamakura period.

25. A high-ranking official in the Dazaifu hierarchy from whom Tamakazura herself escaped only narrowly.

26. No longer extant.

27. Translated from *Murasaki Shikibu nikki zenchūshaku*, ed. Hagitani Boku, 2 vols. (Tokyo: Kadokawa Shoten, 1971). Many passages in this text are highly elliptical and ambiguous, and interpretations of them sometimes differ considerably. In most cases, I followed Hagitani, who at least has given a great deal more thought to the text than any other commentator. I also consulted Richard Bowring's excellent translation, *The Diary of Lady Murasaki* (London: Penguin, 1999), likewise based

on Hagitani's text and commentary, and am indebted to him for more than one felicitous rendition of a difficult phrase.

28. His second daughter, Kenshi (994–1027).

29. *Shūishū* 507, circumstances of composition unknown, author unknown.

yo no naka o kaku ii-ii no hate hate wa / ika ni ya ikani naramu to suramu
Having said this of life and then said that, in the end, the very end,
what, oh what, do you suppose is to become of us?

This has proved to be a highly versatile poem. It appears twice in *Shūishū*, first as a "Miscellaneous" poem (507) and later as a "Lament" (1314), while in *Shūishō* it is a "Love" poem, and in *Hōbutsushū*, a religious poem (92). It all depends on whether *yo no naka* is taken to refer to life in general, life's sorrows, life in love, or life in a state of delusion.

30. *Nihongi* is often used as an abbreviated title of the historical work *Nihon shoki* (720), but here it probably is used more generally to refer to all histories of Japan written in Chinese.

31. *Murasaki Shikibu nikki zenchūshaku*, 2:387.

32. Translated from Daughter of Sugawara no Takasue, *Sarashina nikki*, ed. Inukai Kiyoshi, NKBZ 18:283, 298–99, 301–3, 317, 328, 332, 345–46, 359.

33. Yakushi Nyorai.

34. That is, the temple Kōryūji, in the western quarter of Kyoto.

35. *Zai Chūjō* (*The Ariwara Colonel*) is a variant title of *Ise monogatari*. The other works no longer survive.

36. Scroll 5 of the Lotus Sutra describes how a young girl, the Dragon King's daughter, attains enlightenment.

37. Uji-dono, the villa of Fujiwara no Michinaga's son Yorimichi (992–1074). Now known as the Byōdō-in.

Chapter 2

Genji Gossip (Plus a Bit of Good Advice)

"CRITICISM," ONE EMINENT CRITIC WRITES, "is in effect—or should be—what happens when people get excited about works of art and want to share that excitement with others."[1] The texts in this chapter are the earliest known discussions of *The Tale of Genji*. They are also, in the most literal sense, exactly the sort of "criticism as conversation" described here as ideal. They are the record of people (probably women) who are excited about *The Tale of Genji* and are sharing their excitement with one another.

We already have glimpsed the scenes of some of this discourse: the Bureau of Romances at the court of the Great Kamo Priestess; Sei Shōnagon happening upon the empress's gentlewomen "absorbed in an argument over which of the romances were good and which bad"; and the "picture contest" in which "this sort of women's talk" raged back and forth as they disputed the merits and demerits of the *Tales of Ise* and the *Tale of Jōsanmi*. The appearance of *The Tale of Genji* could only have made the conversation livelier.

Yet because it was nothing but "women's talk" (*onna-goto*)—mere "gossip" as we have termed it here—very little of what was said about *Genji* survives. The earliest record of any discussion of *The Tale of Genji* is in a work of fiction entitled *A Nameless Notebook* (*Mumyōzōshi*), which dates from about 1200. Thereafter come a few cryptic enumerations of favorite scenes, chapters, characters, and the like, some in the form of lists and others presented as "matches" (*awase*). Then nothing. The texts collected here are the last gasp of a once lively critical colloquy. With them, the genre died.

For the years that produced this meager record of *Genji* gossip were also the years in which began a great flood of scholarship that was to produce the first (and still) "definitive" texts of *Genji*; a sea of commentary (the favored metaphors are of droplets, brooks, rivers, and seas) whose full extent is still unknown; and myriad other tokens of veneration, from allusive poems and apocryphal supplements to learned treatises and reference works. In all, it constitutes the world's richest record of the reception of a work of fiction. For this we can only be grateful, as we may owe the very survival of *The Tale of Genji* to it. Yet for all its beneficence, this flood also did some damage. It overwhelmed, and probably drowned, another sort of voice that was beginning to be recorded at about the same time. This was the voice of gossip, which must have been the principal form of attention paid to *Genji* in the first two centuries of its existence. The canonization of *Genji* was not achieved without cost.

Genji gossip apparently still has detractors. One modern scholar, whose taste runs to abstraction and theory, denigrates his colleagues who practice "chapter-by-chapter analysis" and "character analysis" of *Genji* as "repeating the same old tricks," as do the women in *A Nameless Notebook* gossiping about "wonderful chapters" and "adorable people."[2] Yet as the critic from whom we borrowed the concept of "criticism as conversation" says, "That is as much a part of what we are as is the making of works of art."[3]

T. HARPER

A NAMELESS NOTEBOOK, CA. 1200
(*Mumyōzōshi*)

The earliest surviving record of any discussion of *The Tale of Genji* is found in *A Nameless Notebook*.[4] Although clearly a work of imaginative literature, its portrayal of the tone and matter of this night of animated gossip and good-natured debate is so true to those described in works that do purport to record reality that there seems no reason to doubt its authenticity. This sort of activity must have gone on all the time, and *Genji* must have been—as it certainly was to this group of women—one of their favorite subjects about which to gossip the night away.

Most of the other works translated in this chapter are irretrievably anonymous and impossible to date, even roughly. In *A Nameless Notebook*, however, mentions of the names and titles of persons, poetic anthologies, and era designations enable us to date the text with reasonable certainty to 1200/1201 and to identify the author as someone closely associated with the Mikohidari house of Fujiwara no Shunzei and his son Teika. Although

Shunzei himself has been suspected to be the author, the most likely candidate is the woman known as the "daughter of Lord Shunzei" (1171–1253?). She actually was Shunzei's granddaughter. But because her real father had been implicated in the infamous "Shishigatani plot" against the Heike and her mother had returned to service in the household of Princess Hachijōin (1137–1211), their child was raised in her grandparents' home and thus came to be known as their "daughter."

The discussion of *Genji* constitutes about a third of *A Nameless Notebook*.[5]

T. HARPER

Some three and eighty years I have passed in vain pursuits, the mere thought of which fills me with grief—that I happened to be born a human in this life and yet have ended up with nothing to show for it in the next.[6] In my grief, I shaved my head and donned these dark-dyed robes. In appearance at least, I have entered upon the Way of the Buddha, though in my heart I remain unchanged from of yore. As the months and years mount up, I find it ever more difficult to forget the past and long even more for loved ones from of old; and so often do I break down, secretly weeping silent tears, that these dark sleeves never dry. In search of solace, I set out every morning, basket on my elbow, brushing away the dew as I wend my way through the tussocks in the fields, picking flowers to proffer to the Buddha. Such has been my sole pursuit for so many years that my hair has grown as white as snow and my face has become a sea of wrinkles. Even I myself care less and less to look at the reflection in my mirror, and if the sight is repellent to me, how much the more am I reluctant to be seen by others. Thus it was that as I ambled through the Eastern Hills, following one path and another, picking flowers as I went, the sun setting lower and lower, I realized that I had wandered too far from home to return; I would have to find some place to spend the night.

She finds a charmingly dilapidated villa with a courtyard overgrown with wormwood, "such as the Shining Genji made his way through, brushing away the dew." She detects the scent of fine incense coming from a chapel and the strains of a koto from inside the main house and then overhears the voices of three or four young ladies who have caught sight of her and are comparing her, quite favorably, with Ono no Komachi and Prince Siddhartha. A moment later, they appear before her and urge her to tell them the story of her life. The old woman begins with a rambling account of her service at court, lapses into a lament about her own current shabbiness and ugliness, recites a bit of the Lotus Sutra, and finally lies down. "Let's stay up all night and you tell us stories," the girls say, but the old woman pretends to go to sleep. By this time a few more mature women have joined the group, and they begin to discuss the things they would find the most difficult to do without. For one it is the moon, for another letters, for yet another dreams, and still others tears, the Buddha Amida, and ultimately the Lotus Sutra.[7]

"Of all things meritorious and efficacious, none of which I could ever describe in indifferent terms, I can think of nothing more magnificent than the Lotus Sutra. After two or three readings, one tires of even the most fascinating and magnificent of illustrated romances. But this [the Lotus] one could listen to in its entirety a thousand times over and every time find it as wondrous as ever, every word as fresh as the first time one heard it—in short, utterly magnificent. For it is not merely that it is, as proclaimed, 'without equal, without parallel,' but that 'the Lotus is first and foremost.' I shouldn't have to remind you of this anew, but it can happen that even something as wondrous as this, handed down from ages past, may not be valued all that highly. And yet, when I think how our encounter with it [the Lotus] should call to mind our good fortune in having chanced to be born as humans, I cannot but wonder why, in so magnificent a work as *Genji*, there appears not a word from a single verse or a single phrase of this scripture. For what else has she failed to write not a single word about? This, it seems to me, is its greatest, and indeed its only, flaw."

When she said this, the voice of a very young lady spoke up from within the group: "Could it be that Murasaki Shikibu never composed any poems on the Lotus Sutra?"

"Oh come now," the woman replied, "it seems a pity anyone should think such a thing. Why, even in my own graceless compositions, I make a point of showing that I've read the Lotus—not merely for the sake of lives to come, but also lest anyone happening to hear them should think me lacking in sensibility. Yet a person of her stature—how could she possibly have failed to do so? For she appears, after all, to have been a deeply devout woman, fearful of her fate in lives to come, diligent in the performance of her devotions, both morning and evening, and not at all attached to the things of this world." And thus she began.

"Even so, just to have written *Genji*! I've thought and thought about this, and I find it so amazing that I just don't see how the karma of a single lifetime could account for it. Indeed, I suspect it is the answer to her prayers to the Buddha. Those tales that came after *Genji*, I should think, must have been quite easy to write. And one day, someone, following her example, may manage to produce something that surpasses *Genji*. But with only the likes of *Utsuho*, *Taketori*, and *Sumiyoshi* as examples of what a tale might be, and then to produce something as great as *Genji*—I just don't see how it could be the work of a mere mortal."

And again, the same young voice: "It's such a pity I haven't read it yet. Do tell us the story. We're ever so eager to listen."

"But how could I tell you such a long story just from memory?" the woman said. "Let me tell it to you when I have a text to consult." Then they all chimed in:

"Oh, but tell us tonight!"

"Yes, it would be just the thing to dispel the tedium of an evening like this."

The Chapters of Genji[8]

"Of all the chapters," one woman asked, "which do you find the most poignant?" Whereupon, one after another, all the others spoke up.

"Could any chapter possibly surpass 'Kiritsubo'? From those opening words, 'In a certain reign (whose can it have been?) . . .' on through to Genji's coming-of-age ceremony—really, what with the beauty of the writing and the matter of the story alone, this chapter is just packed with touchingly poignant moments."

"The rainy night ranking in 'Hahakigi' is fascinating in so many ways."

"'Yūgao' seems to me a totally touching and heartrending chapter."

"'Momiji no ga' and 'Hana no en,' each in its own way, are ineffably alluring and lovely chapters."

"'Aoi' is a most touchingly beautiful chapter."

"'Sakaki,' when she [the Rokujō Consort] is about to leave for Ise, is exquisitely beautiful."

"And after the old Emperor [Kiritsubo no In] passes away and the Fujitsubo Empress becomes a nun—this is particularly moving."

"'Suma' is an exquisitely moving chapter. When he [Genji] is about to leave the capital, and then his life far from home—these are such moving scenes."

"And in 'Akashi,' when he moves from the one shore to the other. Then when he leaves that shore to return to the capital and says:

miyako ideshi haru no nageki ni otorame ya / toshi furu ura o wakarenuru aki
'Do I lament any less than that spring when I left the capital,
this autumn as I part from this shore of so many years?'
["Akashi," 13:259]

When he left the capital, he must have realized that this was not the end of everything, that he would one day return, and in this he must have found much to console himself. But this shore—why would he ever come here again? He must have felt that this was the very last he would ever see of it, so it was only natural that everything should so capture his attention."

"'Yomogiu' is such a charming chapter."

"In 'Asagao,' when Lady Murasaki is in such distress, it is so piteous."

"In the seventeenth series,[9] 'Hatsune,' 'Kochō,' and some of the others are both beauteous and magnificent."

"And that morning after the typhoon there were so many alluringly beautiful moments."

"'Fuji no uraba' is a very satisfying and joyous chapter."

"The 'Wakana' chapters, both of them, are full of troubling incidents but fascinating nonetheless."

"In 'Kashiwagi,' the death of the Commander of the Right Gate Guards is very moving."

"'Minori' and 'Maboroshi' are replete with deeply moving moments."

"The other 'Uji' chapters are rather different from 'Kojima.'[10] There is the language, and indeed everything else about them. . . . But the death of the elder Princess as well as the story of the younger Princess are really quite. . . ."

The Women in Genji

The young lady said, "Who are the most wonderful women?"

"The Kiritsubo Mistress of the Wardrobe and the Fujitsubo Empress."

"Lady Aoi has such self-control."

"And of course, Lady Murasaki."

"Akashi, too, is so exquisitely refined."

"As for impressive women, the Oborozukiyo Chief Palace Attendant. When you stop to think that it was on her account that Genji was banished, that is impressive."

"Impressive, too, when the Emperor says, 'For which of us do these tears of yours fall?'"[11]

"The Asagao Princess seems to be a very strong-willed woman. [Genji] is so very persistent, and yet her will remains firm to the end. That I find most impressive."

"Utsusemi, too! But in her it's just disgusting. And the way she goes on mingling in society after she becomes a nun; that, too, is distasteful."

Then someone said, "Why is it that some people say Utsusemi didn't really give in to Genji, and some say she did?"

"Well, in 'Hahakigi' she herself plainly says, 'Why didn't I give in to him?' But sometimes, it seems, people misread this and say she did."[12]

"The elder Princess in Uji, now *she* is really impressive! And Chūjō, in the service of the Rokujō Consort, is impressive for a lady-in-waiting."

"Now an attractive woman—that would be Hanachirusato. She isn't at all good looking or imposing, but she holds her own among the finest and is held in no lower regard than any of them. It is she who cares for that earnest young man, the Commandant [Yūgiri], as her own son, which is impressively attractive" ["Otome," 14:61].

"So yes, she adopts the earnest young man as her ward. But why must a child born to someone as lovely as Lady Aoi have such an ugly foster mother?" She seemed so angry when she said this that everyone burst out laughing.

Again: "You won't like me for saying this, but I'd call Suetsumuhana attractive. Even when the Deputy Viceroy invited her,[13] she firmly refused and would not move from her old home, even though the hardships she endured there might well have killed her. Then, after waiting and waiting, when she sees him [Genji] making his way [through the weeds], murmuring, 'Does her heart remain as it was before, here in this patch of wormwood?' ["Yomogiu," 13:338], she seems to me more magnificent than anyone else. For a woman who was good looking and in every other way exceptional, this would be nothing special. But for a woman of her sort, isn't this a stroke of fate more miraculous than becoming a buddha?"

"It's frightening the way the Rokujō Consort so often ventures forth as a malign spirit, but as a person, she is wonderfully refined and attractive."

"And her daughter, the Empress [Akikonomu no Chūgū], behaves with such superb self-control that she really must be counted among the most refined of women, yet for some reason I just can't bear her. It's quite off-putting the way the Genji Minister is so excessively solicitous of her."

"The young lady Tamakazura I'd certainly describe as attractive. Her looks, her features, her character, her good nature—everything about her is quite what one would expect of a fine lady. Further, to her great good fortune, her fathers, both natural and adoptive, are Ministers of State, each in his own way held in no mean regard at court. As well connected as she was, even as a mere Chief Palace Attendant, she might have inspired the affection of the Reizei Emperor. Or if that was not to be, she should at least have become the wife of the [Hotaru] Prince Minister of War, who had so deeply adored her for so many years. But instead she becomes the wife of that perfectly horrid Commandant Higekuro, who keeps her under such constant close watch that she goes through life unable ever to see that fine man, her adoptive father [Genji]. How very depressing and distressing."

"Yet it hardly seems she could be kin to so hapless a creature as Yūgao; she is so excessively self-assured and so knowing. It seems to me quite out of place for someone of her sort to tell [Genji] there is 'no parent in the whole world with feelings the likes of yours.'[14] I expect, though, that those years in Kyushu must have been terribly degrading. Even so, for the most part, her demeanor is attractive."

"A pitiable person—that's Lady Murasaki. I feel such sympathy for her; she is so to be pitied, and all the people around her are so terribly ill natured. Everyone, from her father, the Prince, to her great-uncle, the Prelate, they're all so unpleasant. Her stepmother's attitude is only to be expected in such a relationship, but did she really have to be so mean to someone who was to rise so high in the world?"

"Now Yūgao, she's just too terribly pathetic. It really doesn't seem fair that someone like her should have such a shocking daughter, so unlike her mother. Someone of her sort we might remember more fondly had she just passed away, leaving no trace behind her."

"The wife of that earnest fellow the Commandant [Yūgiri], the 'New Wisteria Leaves' lady [Kumoinokari], seems not to have been a woman of any great elegance or beauty, but somehow, from the time he was a boy, he always had a soft spot in his heart for her."

"And the younger Princess in Uji, she's just so pathetic. At first she didn't seem so, but when the Prince Minister of War [Niou] becomes the son-in-law of that earnest young fellow [Yūgiri] and she becomes so despondent, that's really pitiful. And most of all, every time I read that passage in which she says, 'For just this touch of scent, are we to be driven apart?' I feel like my tears will never, ever stop."[15]

"The Third Princess we really must describe as pathetic. But then there is that passage when she recites, '"Soak your sleeves with evening dew," do you tell me, as at day's end . . . ?' and then says, 'But as I recall, she tells him to "Await the moon."'[16] Heartrending though this is, it's somehow offensive when someone so hopelessly ineffectual turns out to have a lascivious side to her. People of her sort are charming only when they are totally childlike and guileless. His Lordship's discovery of that shocking letter, too, was entirely the result of her own wrongheadedness. Had she given any thought to the situation she was in, the slightest hint that he [Genji] might stay over should have impelled her to urge him on his way. But instead, clever girl that she imagines herself, she puts on her heartbroken act and convinces him to stay—thus giving rise to that dreadful disaster."[17]

"The lady at writing practice [Ukifune]—now, she would have to be described as despicable. But being in so many ways extraordinarily troubled, she recites:

> *kane no oto no tayuru hibiki ni ne o soete / waga yo tsukinu to kimi ni tsutaeyo*
> 'To the fading echo of the bell pray add the sound of my weeping,
> to carry the word to her that my life draws to an end.' ["Ukifune," 17:187]

Whereupon she casts herself away, and that is pitiful indeed. When Commandant Kaoru heard of her affair with the Prince Minister of War [Niou], he wrote:

> *nami koyuru koro to mo shirazu sue no matsu / matsuramu to nomi omoikeru kana*
> 'Unaware that a time had come when waves would rise above Mount Sue,
> I thought only that you must pine for me, true to the end.'
> ["Ukifune," 17:168]

So firm was her resolve that she returned [his letter] to him unopened, saying, 'You must have the wrong address.'"

The Men in Genji

Again, it was the same young lady who asked, "Who are there among the men?"

"I'm very reluctant to try all over again to assess the merits and demerits of the Genji Minister, but there are so many things about him that one might wish were otherwise. First of all, the Ōuchiyama Minister [Tō no Chūjō].[18] From the time they were young, they were inseparable, the closest and most intimate of friends. There's the rainy night discussion. And then [the time when] he says:

> *morotomo ni ōuchiyama o idetsuredo / yuku kata misenu isayoi no tsuki*
> 'Though together we left the palace, the moon above Ōuchiyama,
> this sixteenth night, gives no hint where it might now be bound.'
> ["Suetsumuhana," 12:346]

And again when he draws his sword and threatens Genji in the quarters of Gen no Naishi no Suke ["Momiji no ga," 12:414]. I couldn't begin to describe all the episodes of this sort. But above all, when [Genji] was living in exile in Suma, [Tō no Chūjō] went there to visit him, undeterred by the trouble it would cause him in that scheming world of the court. Could one ever forget such deep compassion, no matter how many years might pass? And yet [Genji], heedless of this, takes an adopted daughter [Akikonomu], with whom he has no blood relationship, and sets her up in competition with the Minister's [daughter, the Kokiden] Dame of Honor, a terribly mean-spirited deed ["Eawase," 13:363–64]. At the picture competition, he produces two scrolls of his own pictures from Suma, which bring about the defeat of the Dame of Honor ["Eawase," 13:377–78]. That is just too deplorable. And when [Genji] goes to Suma, he does not take Murasaki, who is utterly heartbroken, with him. Then, when you might expect he'd at least be cleansing his mind in the constant performance of devotions, he becomes the son-in-law of the Akashi Novice and spends whole days with this would-be minstrel, playing the koto to his heart's content as if he hadn't another care in the world. And later in life, when everything had settled down and you might think he had finished with such things, he starts all over again and takes up with the Third Princess, like a man rejuvenated. As if this weren't unseemly enough, when he discovers her affair with the Commander of the Right Gate Guards, even though the [young] man is too frightened even to appear in public, he forcibly summons him, teases and toys with him, and finally kills him with his withering gaze. That was a positively malevolent deed. This side of him, it seems to me, is utterly lacking in serene dignity."

"The [Hotaru] Prince Minister of War strikes me as a man of no outstanding merits or faults. Of all his many brothers, Genji is particularly close to him, and it's rather charming that he is the first person he consults on any matter whatever. But his failure to persuade Tamakazura is perfectly pathetic."

"The Ōuchiyama Minister [Tō no Chūjō] is a very fine man. Above all, when he goes to visit Genji in Suma, he is simply magnificent. To be sure, it was cruel of him to cause that earnest fellow [Yūgiri] such pain and distress, yet he does have his reasons. When he relents, giving them his consent without a trace of enmity, he apparently handles the matter very graciously."

"That earnest fellow the Commandant, though his airs of propriety—so excessive that he hardly seems a youth—are rather chilling, his gravitas surpasses even that of the [Genji] Minister.[19] It's extraordinary the way he is unswayed by the several proposals that come his way and waits patiently until 'the new wisteria leaves yield.'[20] I wonder if even a woman could manage that. But what a shock, years later, when he at last is living with the woman he longed for, he takes up with that unremarkable Princess Ochiba, ruins his reputation for earnestness, and emerges a man transformed."

"At the outset, the Kashiwagi Commander of the Right Gate Guards is a fine young man. From the time he was known as the 'Rocky Spring Colonel'[21] until 'the new wisteria leaves yield,' he is quite quick-witted.[22] But how irritating that he should become so infatuated with the Third Princess that he would give his life for her. Both of them [Kashiwagi and Yūgiri] caught sight of her, but the earnest fellow was upset by it, thinking, 'Oh, no!' How very disappointing that [Kashiwagi] should be so transfixed by her ["Wakana, jō," 15:132–35]. When that earnest gentleman caught a glimpse of Lady Murasaki and seemed lost in reverie that morning after the typhoon, he was just splendid ["Nowaki," 14:268]. When [Kashiwagi] is dying, it is indeed touchingly pitiful, and yet, one wonders, isn't it rather unseemly that he should feel so sorry for himself? Was it really as bad as all that?"

"His younger brother the Kōbai Grand Counselor at the rhyme-guessing contest when he sings 'Takasago' ["Sakaki," 13:133–34], and in 'Fuji no uraba,' when he was called Ben no Shōshō and sang 'Fence of Rushes' ["Sakaki," 14:431], was a wonderfully talented person. In later years, after Genji dies, he behaves quite distastefully, going around grumbling enviously when Commandant Kaoru becomes the son-in-law of the

Emperor, rather like the proverbial bat on an island where there are no birds."[23]

"Even leaving aside his dallying as a young man (as they say we must), Prince Minister of War Niou is lustful and lascivious to a scandalous degree, all of which is quite unbecoming. It's rather touching, though, that, having been a favorite of Lady Murasaki, he lives in the Nijō mansion."

"Commandant Kaoru seems like a totally magnificent man; from beginning to end, there's not a single thing about him that one would wish otherwise. Even if he were actually the son of the Shining Genji, you'd never expect him to be so when you consider what a hopeless creature his mother the Princess was, as surely you would had Lady Murasaki given birth to him. Rare indeed are the likes of him, whether in stories or, even more so, among people in the real world, whether past or present."

Then another woman said, "True enough, but isn't the man somewhat lacking in warmth and passion? It's a pity, really, that Ukifune and the younger Sumori lady find him less attractive than the Prince Minister of War."

"That's not the Commandant's fault!" another said. "That's because those women are so horrid; they're just obsessed with lust. But the Sumori Lady, who is a woman of great refinement, speaks of 'Niou the cherry and Kaoru the plum,' which seems to suggest that she finds *him* [Kaoru] far and away more attractive."[24]

Moving Scenes (aware naru koto)

Again it was the same young lady who said, "Well, that gives me a rough idea of what the people are like. So tell me some of the stories that you found moving or magnificent and that made a deep impression on you."

"Aren't you a greedy little pest," someone said, and they all laughed and laughed.

"One touching passage is that in which the Emperor laments the death of the Kiritsubo Mistress of the Wardrobe:

> The imagination, after all, has its limits, and thus the brush could hardly have done justice even to the lady in the "Song of Everlasting Sorrow." [This lady's] looks, more graceful than plume grass bending

with the wind, more exquisitely appealing than a little pink wet with dew, could never be adequately described in terms of the beauty of flowers or the song of birds.

> *tazuneyuku maboroshi mogana tsute nite mo / tama no arika o soko to shirubeku*
> 'Would there were a wizard to go and seek her out, so that I might know,
> if only by report, the place where her spirit resides' ["Kiritsubo," 12:111],

His Majesty said, and even after the wicks of the lamps had burned down, he remained lost in reverie, unable to sleep.[25]

From which you can imagine what the remaining sixty chapters are like."

"And then there's the scene of Yūgao's death: The sky is clouded, the wind is cold, and, sunk in reverie, he murmurs:

> *mishi hito no keburi o kumo to nagamureba / yūbe no sora mo mutsumashiki kana*
> 'Gazing at these clouds, thinking them to be smoke from the pyre of my love,
> the sky, even on an evening like this, seems dear to me.' ["Yūgao," 12:262]

Then he hums 'Long indeed are these nights.'"[26]

"When Lady Aoi dies, that too is touching. On the night of the funeral, her father the Minister is distraught, which of course is deeply moving. When [Genji] is about to change into gray mourning, he thinks that if he had died first, she would have worn mourning dyed an even deeper shade, and he chants:

> *kagiri areba usuzumigoromo asakeredo / namida zo sode o fuchi to nashikeru*
> 'Bound as I am, these mourning robes are dyed but a shallow shade of gray,
> yet my tears plunge these sleeves into a pool of deep purple.'" ["Aoi," 13:42]

"And then there is the passage: 'A wild wind blew, the autumn rain poured down while his tears, he felt, raced to outdo the storm. To himself, he murmured, "Has she become rain, or has she become cloud? There is no knowing now."'[27] Whereupon, the First Secretary Colonel [her brother Tō no Chūjō] arrived.

> *mishi hito no ame to narinishi kumoi sae / itodo shigure ni kakikurasu kana*
> 'Even the clouded skies above, where she whom I loved has turned to rain,
> now darken only the more in this autumnal downpour.'" ["Aoi," 13:49]

"Another very moving scene is the one in which the little girl, wearing a formal gown dyed a deeper shade of mourning than was usual, is in attendance, looking dreadfully downcast. Quite touched by her, because she is so exceptionally lovely, [Genji] comforts her saying, 'You may think of me now [as you did of her],' and she breaks down weeping right there in his presence."

"And it is poignantly moving when his mourning comes to an end and Genji is to leave. All the ladies, too, who have waited on him these several days, are about to go their separate ways, and each of them laments her parting with him."

"And when the Minister sees the scraps of paper that Genji has been practicing on and he weeps—everything in this chapter is moving."

"When Genji departs for Suma, too! The scene in which he goes to Lady Aoi's old home to take his leave and says,

> *toribeyama moeshi keburi mo magau ya to / ama no shio yaku urami ni zo yuku*
> 'Might one mistake them for the smoke that rose from Toribeyama,
> the salt maker's fires on that shore I'm so loath to go and see?'"
> ["Suma," 13:160]

"And when he looks in the mirror to comb his sidelocks and, in spite of himself, is touched by the beauty of his own face, now grown so thin. 'Am I really as thin as I look in this mirror?' he says [to Murasaki]:

> *mi wa kakute sasuraenutomo kimi ga atari / saranu kagami no kage wa hanareji*
> 'Though my body may wander afar, here by your side, in this mirror
> that never leaves you, the image of me shall not depart.' ["Suma," 13:165]

When he says this, Lady Murasaki's eyes fill with tears as she looks up at him.

wakarutomo kage dani tomaru mono naraba / kagami o mitemo nagusaminamashi
'Were it so that even though we part, your image at least remains,
then might I indeed be consoled just looking into the mirror.'"[28]
["Suma," 13:165]

"And at the Lower Kamo Shrine, when he takes leave of the deity:

uki yo oba ima zo wakaruru todomaramu / na oba tadasu no kami ni makasete
'Now, as I remove myself from this world of sorrows, I commend
to thee, god of Tadasu, the good name I would leave behind.'"
["Suma," 13:173]

"And at dawn on the day he departs, when Lady Murasaki says:

oshikaranu inochi ni kaete me no mae no / wakare o shibashi todometeshikana
'How I wish, in exchange for my life, which I would give with no regrets,
I might delay but a moment this parting we now face'
["Suma," 13:178];

that was just appalling.[29] Even as insignificant a woman as Hanachirusato would seem to have said:

tsukikage no yadoreru sode wa sebakutomo / tometemo mibaya akanu hikari o
'Narrow though they be, these sleeves of mine wherein dwells the light of the moon,
how I wish they might stay its glow, of which I never tire.'"
["Suma," 13:167]

"And when he arrives at that shore, he watches the waves roll in and return to the sea and chants 'how I envy them . . .'[30] and then, 'Might these skies that I now gaze on be the same as for her?'"[31]

"And 'Mournful autumn winds blew, and though the sea was somewhat distant, the waves that it raised as it "blew down from beyond the barrier,"[32] as Viceroy Yukihira had put it, sounded very close indeed.'[33] He recites:

koiwabite naku ne ni magau uranami wa / omou kata yori kaze ya fukuramu
'Waves on this shore, sounding so like my own wailing as I languish here:
does this wind blow from the quarter of those for whom I yearn?'"
["Suma," 13:191]

"Then there is the passage in which 'On the night of the fifteenth of the Eighth Month, he longed to hear the music in the duty room at the palace, and as he recalled times past and thought how they all must be gazing at the moon, he fixed his eyes on the face of the moon and sang, "Two thousand leagues away, the heart of a friend . . ."'" ["Suma," 13:194].[34]

"And the passage, 'Yes,' he recalled, 'the cherry blossoms before the South Hall would be in in full bloom. Only a year ago at the Blossom Festival, how fine the Emperor looked, and the Crown Prince. . . .' He recited:

itsu to naku ōmiyabito no koishiki ni / sakura kazashishi kyō wa kinikeri
'Ever and always do I yearn for those people of the great court,
and the more so this day when once I adorned my cap with blooms.'"
["Suma," 13:204]

"And then the time when Ōuchiyama [Tō no Chūjō] comes and they compose nostalgic poems for each other and exchange poems in Chinese" ["Suma," 13:204–8].

"In Akashi, in a letter to [Murasaki at] the Nijō mansion that was even more detailed than usual, he writes:

shioshio to mazu zo nakaruru karisome ni / miru me wa ama no susami naredomo
'I now break down in a briny flood of tears, for only on a whim
did this fisherman seek his pleasure while gathering seaweed.'
["Akashi," 13:249]

Her reply:

uranaku mo tanomikeru kana chigirishi o / matsu yori nami wa koeji mono zo to
'And to think that in all innocence, I trusted you, for you'd promised:
never would waves wash over the pine-clad hill where I wait.'
["Akashi," 13:249]

This is most moving."

"And all that happens around the time of the death of Kashiwagi, Commander of the Right Gate Guards, is moving. He wants to send a letter to the Third Princess, 'but his hand trembles so that he gives up trying to write all that he feels.

ima wa tote moemu keburi mo musubōre / taenu omoi no nao ya nokosamu
"Even then when the end is come and smoke rises from my burning pyre,
these unquenchable flames of yearning surely shall remain.
["Kashiwagi," 15:281]

Pray tell me at least that you pity me," he says, "that I may have something to light the dark path I choose to wander."' To which she replies:

tachisoite kie ya shinamashi uki koto o / omoikogaruru keburikurabe ni
'How I wish I too might die, that my smoke might rise together with yours;
then could we compare whose flames of sorrow burn the brighter.
["Kashiwagi," 15:286]

Do you suppose I shall be far behind you?' She's nasty, that Princess!"

"And when his [Kashiwagi's] father the Minister is rambling on about one thing and another, 'he looks up at the sky and gazes into the distance. The evening clouds are misted the gray of mourning, and then he notices that the blossoms have fallen from the branches, just today.

ko no shita no shizuku ni nurete sakasama ni / kasumi no koromo kitaru haru kana
"Drenched with tears for the loss of a child, a topsy-turvy spring is this,
that I should be the one to wear the mist-gray of mourning."'
["Kashiwagi," 15:325]

This passage is very moving."

"As is, I need hardly say, all that happens around the time of the death of Lady Murasaki. The earnest gentleman [Yūgiri] catches a brief glimpse of her lying there after all life had left her.

inishie no aki no yūbe no koishiki ni / ima wa to mieshi akegure no yume
'Lost in fond memories of that autumn evening so long ago,
and now I see her, departed, as in a dream at dawn.' ["Minori," 15:498]

He must be recalling the time he saw her in the confusion after the typhoon."

"In 'Maboroshi,' when he [Genji] hears the gentlewoman say, 'What a lot of snow has fallen!' the memory of that excruciating snowy night, as vivid as if it were happening that very moment, fills him with remorse and sadness.[35] He recites:

ukiyo ni wa yukikienamu to omoedomo / omoi no hoka ni ware zo hodo furu
'Though I wish only to vanish, as shall this snow, from the world of pain,
yet as unforeseen as was this flurry, I linger on.'"[36] ["Maboroshi," 15:510]

"And then there's the passage in which even the room and its furnishings make him feel lonely, and just to look around leaves him forlorn.

ima wa tote arashi ya hatemu nakihito no / kokoro todomeshi haru no kakine o
'My time is come, I say, yet can I simply let it run to ruin,
this spring garden that she, now gone, cared for so lovingly?'" ["Maboroshi," 15:516]

"And when he tears up her letters, to have them made into sutra paper:

kakitsumete miru mo kanashiki moshiogusa / onaji kumoi no keburi to mo nare
'Naught to be gained gathering up these, like sea grasses, and reading them;
let your smoke join that from her pyre in that same cloud on high.' ["Maboroshi," 15:534]

Everything about 'Maboroshi' is perfectly poignant."

"And when the elder Princess in Uji dies, this is touchingly sorrowful. Since there were restrictions, Commandant Kaoru himself did not change into clothes of a different color, but seeing that those women who were particularly close to her had changed into the darkest shades, [he wrote]:

kurenai ni otsuru namida no kai naki wa / katami no iro o somenu narikeri
'To no avail do I shed these tears, blood-red like my robe though they be,
for never may I dye it the dark hue of remembrance.' ["Agemaki," 16:321]

The bell of the temple across the way sounds, moving him to turn his headrest on end and think, 'So another day has come to an end.'[37] And then 'he sits down on a rock by the garden brook and for a time remains there.'[38] He says:

taehatenu shimizu ni nado ka naki hito no / omokage o dani todomezarikemu
'How is it that these pure waters, which flow on forever, yet retain
no faint reflection of the face of the departed one?' ["Azumaya," 17:78]

This is so wonderfully touching; I really do envy her. To have had such a man as this, even if she did have to die, must have been just magnificent. That's what I think."

Magnificent Moments (imijiki koto)

"And speaking of things magnificent: At dawn, on one of his secret visits to Rokujō, her gentlewoman Chūjō escorts him out. 'He draws her aside and sits her down for a moment by the base of the rail outside the corner room. . . .

saku hana ni utsuru chō na wa tsutsumedomo / orade sugiuki kesa no asagao
"Though loath to be known as one who flits to whatever flower is in bloom,
what a shame to pass by without plucking this morning face.

So what shall we do?" he says, taking her hand in his . . .' ["Yūgao," 12:222]

asagiri no harema mo matanu keshiki nite / hana ni kokoro o tomenu to zo miru
'So you are not inclined even to wait for the morning mists to clear;
I take it then that our flower has no hold on your heart.'
["Yūgao," 12:222]

The way her answer deflects his advances seems to me just magnificent."

"And when he passes the gate of a place he has been visiting secretly, he has one of his guardsmen, who has a good voice, chant:

asaborake kiri tatsu sora no mayoi ni mo / sugiukarikeru imo ga kado kana
'Lost though I am in the mists that rise in the dim first light of day,
I am loath to pass it by, this gate of my beloved.' ["Wakamurasaki," 12:321]

After he chants the poem twice, a serving woman of some sensibility comes out.

tachitomari kiri no magaki no sugiuku wa / kusa no tozashi ni sawari shimo seji
'If indeed you are loath to pass by this rustic fence, shrouded in mist,
then surely this flimsy gate of grass should not deter you.'"
["Wakamurasaki," 12:321]

"And 'Hana no en' is quite magnificent. Right from the start, when she says, 'Naught can compare with a night lit by a misty moon,' everything that happens is most magnificent. And after [the Suzaku] Retired Emperor secludes himself in the mountains, he [Genji] goes back to her again, but it has been a very long time, and he is ill at ease.

shizumishi mo wasurenu mono o korizuma ni / mi mo nagetsubeki yado no fujinami
'Not that I forget being sunk in Suma, yet neither have I learned:
I'd cast myself again into your wisteria waves.' ["Wakana, jō," 15:77]

This, too, seems to me quite magnificent."

"And all that happens when the High Priestess is about to depart [for Ise] is somehow awe inspiring and impressive.

> *akatsuki no wakare wa itsumo tsuyukeki o / ko wa yo ni shiranu aki no sora kana*
>
> 'Partings at break of day are always dew drenched with tears, and yet this time
> the autumn sky is like nothing I have ever known.' ["Sakaki," 13:81]

Likewise, when 'the pine crickets chirp to one another as if they understand the occasion.'"[39]

"And when she asks, 'Who, when I am far off in Ise?'[40] That, too, is magnificent."

"As I mentioned briefly before, everything at the time he is banished is utterly magnificent."

"And when he passes the palace of the Hitachi Princess, he recalls that 'this is a grove I've seen before' ["Yomogiu," 13:334], whereupon he alights from his carriage and sends Koremitsu ahead to clear the way. When he says, 'This wormwood certainly is dewy,' he [Genji] thinks, sorrowfully,

> *tazunetemo ware koso towame michi mo naku / fukaki yomogiu no moto no kokoro o*
>
> 'Search though I must, I shall find out for myself whether in these trackless
> depths of wormwood, her heart remains as once it was of yore.' ["Yomogiu," 13:338]

So saying, he proceeds further, with Koremitsu leading the way, brushing the dew from the wormwood, guiding him in. Say what I may, no words can describe how splendid this is."

"The morning after the typhoon, when Genji and that earnest young man the Commandant [Yūgiri] go around looking in on his several women, is just splendid. The quarters of the [Akikonomu] Empress are particularly lovely. In the [Akashi] Princess's quarters, it is most impressive when he requests an inkstone and paper and writes a letter. He feels a bit awkward when he takes the inkstone and begins to write, but then he decides that needn't trouble him.[41] His [Yūgiri's] feelings [for Kumoinokari] must have been quite intense.

kaze sawagi murakumo mayou yūbe ni mo / wasururu ma naku wasurarenu kimi

'Even on this evening when the wind rages and thick clouds roam the sky,
not for a moment do I, can I, forget you, my love.' ["Nowaki," 14:275]

Then he ties [the letter] with a piece of autumnal grass, whispers something, and sends it off. Just superb! There are also a great many superb scenes involving the sisters at Uji, but it would tiresome of me to go on like this."

Pitiful Scenes (itōshiki koto)

"Lady Murasaki when he [Genji] departs for Suma."

"In 'Otome' when she [Kumoinokari] is berated as being destined to marry a man of the sixth rank, she murmurs to herself, 'The wild geese high above in the clouds; do they, too, feel as I do?'[42] The earnest young man, standing outside, hears this and says, 'Is Jijū with you? Pray do open up!' ["Otome," 14:42]. This passage is quite pitiful."

"In 'Wakana,' Lady Murasaki is sleeping alone, her sleeves soaked with tears and frozen stiff, lying there in a state of desolation. At daybreak he comes back and knocks; she pretends to be asleep and her people don't open the door" ["Wakana, jō," 15:62–63].

"The morning after the younger of the Uji Princesses [receives] Commandant Kaoru for the first time [since her marriage], he sends to her:

itazura ni waketsuru michi no tsuyu shigemi / mukashi oboyuru aki no sora kana

'So thick is the dew on this path down which I've made my way, all in vain,
that the autumnal sky calls to mind those days long ago.' ["Yadorigi," 16:419]

When [her husband] the Prince Minister of War [Niou] arrives, he takes her to task for the scent [of Kaoru] that permeates her robes. She doesn't even bother to answer him, which irritates him, and he says,

mata hito mo narekeru sode no utsuriga o / waga mi ni shimete uramitsuru kana
'This scent on your sleeve, so intimate has it become with someone else,
pierces my very being, arouses me to anger.' ["Yadorigi," 16:424]

The lady,

minarenuru naka no koromo to tanomeshi o / kabakari nite ya kakehanarenamu
'This robe, this intimacy we share, in which I have placed all my trust:
is it to be cast aside for such a trifle as this?' ["Yadorigi," 16:424]

And so saying, she breaks down crying. This episode is truly pitiful."

Disappointments (kokoroyamashiki koto)[43]

"He does not take Lady Murasaki with him to Suma, and yet he writes, unbidden, to tell her that he has taken up with the Akashi lady ["Akashi," 13:248–49]. 'The boat that rows seaward from the shore . . . ,'[44] she says resentfully, but he shows her only the cover sheet of the letter ["Miotsukushi," 13:286]. The two scrolls of pictures from Suma, which usually he kept hidden away, he takes out for the picture competition. She says:

hitori ite nagameshi yori wa ama no sumu / kata o kakute zo miru bekarikeru[45]
'Rather than stay here, all alone, passing the days in fretful worry,
I should have seen these pictures of the place where fishers dwell.
["Eawase," 13:368]

I might then have found some comfort in my anxiety.' This could just as well have been placed with the 'pitiful things.'"

"He takes up with the Third Princess and causes Lady Murasaki such anguish. On the first day of the New Year he makes the rounds of his various ladies' quarters, thinking diffidently, 'It would be a shame if she [Murasaki] were to be upset so soon,' despite which he spends the night with the Akashi lady ["Hatsune," 14:144]. Even the Ōuchiyama Minister has a falling out with Genji, and their relationship is strained. Tamakazura becomes the wife of Commandant Higekuro. In 'Yūgiri,' when the

Consort [Ochiba no Miya's mother], is about to die, she writes a letter to him [Yūgiri]:

ominaeshi shioruru nobe o izuko tote / hitoyo bakari no yado o karikemu
'Where do you think this is, this moor where the maidenflower withers away,
that you should take but a single night's lodging here with her?'
["Yūgiri," 15:412]

This very earnest gentleman, the Commandant [Yūgiri], takes in the Ochiba Princess, and keeps her along with his first wife."

Shocking Things (asamashiki koto)

"Yūgao is possessed by a tree spirit. Genji, on the night of the downpour, stays late with the Oborozukiyo Palace Attendant and is discovered by her father the Minister. Genji discovers the letter from the Commander of the Right Gate Guards to the Third Princess. The lady at writing practice [Ukifune] disappears. If she had just done away with herself, that would be all very well; but she is possessed by something and then is discovered by people on a pilgrimage to Hatsuse, all of which is terribly spooky," she said. "But you can remember all these splendid things and touching things only when you have the book there in front of you. It's difficult to talk about them from memory. I'll read through it at leisure and tell you about it another time. This is only small part of it; I've hardly done it justice at all."

Following this discussion of Genji *is an even longer section discussing several later tales, starting with* Sagoromo monogatari *and* Yoru no nezame *and moving on to several other lesser works, most of which no longer survive. Toward the end, "this same young lady" raises yet another objection.*

"You know, though, that all these are fictions and falsehoods. Tell us about some that describe things that actually happened. I've heard that *Tales of Ise* and *Tales of Yamato* are about things that really happened, which, I think, is very, very impressive. Tell us a bit about those, too."

"This *Tales of Ise*, as they call it, was written simply to depict the amorous exploits of Narihira. Is there anyone in all the world, whether of high station or low—anyone with a bit of brain, at least—who hasn't read *Ise* and *Yamato* and knows nothing about them? There's no need for us to discuss *them* in any detail. And [Narihira's] wanderings beyond the region of the capital—when he questions the *miyako* [capital] bird by the banks of the Sumida River, when he yearns for his lady love at Yatsuhashi [Eight Bridges][46]—show only that there apparently was nowhere he wouldn't go in the course of his quest. *Tales of Yamato* is just more of the same and needn't detain us. Everyone's read it and knows all about it. If you're curious about the merits of the poems in these books, just look them up in the *Kokinshū*. All the good ones are in there."

That matter disposed of, the talk then turns to anthologies of Japanese poetry, the content of which elicits surprisingly little comment. What does concern them, however, is the fact that no woman has ever been commissioned to compile one. As one woman says at the beginning of this passage, "Ah, how I wish that I might have the chance, like the third-rank novice [Shunzei], to compile an anthology."

"There is no creature more unfortunate than woman. Since ages past, many women of refined sensibility have been well versed in the Way [of Poetry], but never has one of them compiled an anthology of any sort. Now that's a great pity."

"Oh, but compiling an anthology isn't necessarily such a great accomplishment. Murasaki Shikibu wrote *Genji*; Sei Shōnagon composed *The Pillow Book*; and all those tales we've just been talking about—aren't most of them the work of women? Though I say so myself, these are not to be dismissed."

"Then why is it that I can't seem to write anything that will last through the ages? Never mind those pampered daughters and high-ranking wives who seem to live in such seclusion. For someone like me, who serves at court, goes about with her face in full view, and is known to almost everyone, it seems a dreadful shame that no one ever says, 'Now *there's* someone! One of these days *she* will. . . .' I'll probably end up never writing anything that lasts through ages to come."

"But how often does that ever happen? Just to write one worthless cripple of a poem and get it into an anthology, for a woman at least, seems to be very difficult, much less finding words that will keep her name alive through ages to come. We don't hear of many who've done that. They're few and far between, it seems to me."

"But who are the ones who did?" the same young lady asked. "I'd like to be able to call to mind all those women, past or present, [who are] known for their refinement and then imitate the ones who seem even just a little better than the rest."

"Well, you know what they say: imitating people is something you must never do. It can get you in deep trouble," someone said, laughing.

From here the discussion moves on easily to those few women who did achieve fame for their literary talents: Ono no Komachi, Sei Shōnagon, Izumi Shikibu, and, finally, Murasaki Shikibu. The fascination of this subject is sufficient to rouse from slumber the old woman whose unintended visit initiated this long evening's conversation. "There were many things I was just dying to say in response," she says. "But there was no point in that, so I pretended to be still asleep, not even moving my body."

"But such things [as musical talent] last only as long as one lives," someone said. "It's too bad that that it can't be passed on for later generations to hear. There have been any number of men and women who, in their time, were superbly talented musicians, but who among them has left behind a single note for posterity? When someone composes a poem, in Japanese or Chinese, and signs one's name to it, a hundred or even a thousand, years may pass, yet it still feels, here and now, as if one were face to face with the author. This is such a moving experience, which is why I wish I could write even one word to leave behind for later generations. I know I'll sound like I'm repeating myself, but what makes me so envious and seems so wonderful is how the Great Kamo Priestess sent to inquire whether the Jōtōmon'in Empress had any stories with which they might while away the tedium. The Empress summoned Murasaki Shikibu and asked, 'What shall we offer her? What do we have that's at all remarkable?' Murasaki replied. 'We had better make something new for her.' 'Then you write it,' the Empress said. And how magnificent: in response to the command, she wrote *The Tale of Genji*."

"But they also say she hadn't yet entered service at court, that she was still at home when she wrote it. And that's why she was summoned to serve at court and why they called her Murasaki Shikibu. I wonder which is correct? In the book that they call her diary, it does say, 'When I first came to court, everyone thought I must be so grand and refined a lady that they would feel uncomfortable in my company; but then to their surprise, it appeared I was actually rather absentminded and inexperienced and couldn't even write the number "one," so my colleagues came to feel I wasn't at all that sort.'"

"And how splendid that although she thinks His Lordship [Michinaga] so magnificent, she never speaks of him with the least hint of intimacy or familiarity. Yet even though she describes the Empress Mother [Shōshi] as incomparably magnificent, it somehow seems out of character that she should reveal how adoringly and fondly she waited upon her and how wonderfully friendly His Lordship was. I suppose, though, that's just the sort of people they were."

From here, the talk moves on to the subject of empresses, with which the colloquy winds down to an end. The old woman continues to ponder whether she herself might say something when the "same young lady" again speaks up.

"At this rate we'll spend the whole night talking about nothing but women. We haven't even mentioned a single man; that's just scandalous."

"Right you are, and that's a subject well worth attending to, be they men of the past or the present. There must be any number of marvelous stories. So if it's all the same to you, shall we start with Emperors?"

"What you really should do, you know, is read Yotsugi's *The Great Mirror* and the like. What can we say that would top them? And so saying . . ."

TRANSLATED BY T. HARPER

The Lists

The four texts translated under this rubric constitute one small subgenre of *Genji* gossip: lists of superlatives.[47] Almost nothing is known of their provenance, and none survives in its original form. They are customarily assigned to the Kamakura or the early Muromachi period mainly because they seem out of place in the company of later, more tendentious works. There is speculation, based on traces of feminine insight that some scholars claim to detect, that one or more lists may have been written by a woman. Affinities have been noted with Sei Shōnagon's lists and, more interestingly, with digest versions of *Genji*. But in the end, no one has much more to say about them than did the anonymous copyist of *A Key to Genji*, who in 1650 said the most important thing: that they are a delight to read.

The order in which the lists are arranged here is an attempt to represent what may well have been a genetic relationship among them.[48] *A Key to Genji* appears to be a riposte to *Forty-Eight Exemplars from Genji*.[49] They share twenty-nine categories, many of which appear in the same order in both texts; and where *Forty-Eight Exemplars* states the obvious (Man: Genji, Pretty Face: Fujitsubo), *Key* tends to offer less conventional choices (Kaoru, Akikonomu). *Exemplars from Genji* seems to be even more closely related to *Forty-Eight Exemplars*.[50] Thirty-six categories are shared, and more than half appear in identical order. The fourth and last list, which has no title because the only surviving copy of it bears no title, appears to be related to all of the previous three. It shares thirty-seven categories with the list that precedes it, and only two of its total of forty-seven categories are new. In contrast, almost all its responses are original, not only in the "answers" they offer to the questions implied, but also in the extreme allusiveness of those answers. Although we know nothing about when or by whom these lists were written, they at least afford us glimpses of the critical colloquy from which they grew.

A transliteration of each entry's original heading follows its translation. When necessary, brief expository comments and quotations immediately follow the entry rather than in the notes.

T. HARPER

FORTY-EIGHT EXEMPLARS FROM GENJI
(*Genji shijū-hachi monotatoe no koto*)

Man [*otoko*]. It need hardly be said again that the Shining Genji is the very foundation of this tale. And of course, Commandant Kaoru's very genuine thoughtfulness is without parallel.

Woman [*onna*]. Who but Lady Murasaki?

Pretty Face, Good Looks [*mime katachi*]. Fujitsubo.

Character [*kokorobase*]. The elder of the Uji sisters.

Good Karma [*kahō*]. The Akashi lady.

Chapter [*maki*]. "Suma."

Poem [*uta*].

furusato o izure no haru ka yukite mimu / urayamashiki wa kaeru karigane
My old home village: in what spring shall I ever go see it again?
How I envy the wild geese returning whither they came. ["Suma," 13:206–7]

Prose Passage [*kotoba*].

> The drop of dew that will fall if the sprig of *hagi* [bush clover] is plucked, the crystal of frost that will melt away if lifted from the bamboo leaf.[51] ["Hahakigi," 12:156]

Extraordinary Scene [*koto naru tokoro*]. [Tō no Chūjō's dance] "Garden of Willows and Flowers," which was thought rare even for the past four illustrious reigns and which would surely be regarded as a model for ages to come ["Hana no en," 12:432].[52]

Wondrous Event [*medetaki koto*]. The appointment of the Akashi Empress.[53]

Moment of Joy [*ureshiki koto*]. One can well imagine how Kumoinokari felt when [her father] the Minister relented and accepted [Yūgiri] as his son-in-law ["Fuji no uraba," 14:428].

Sight to Be Seen [*miru koto*]. The dance "Waves of the Blue Ocean" at the palace rehearsal ["Momiji no ga," 12:383].

Hopeful Moment [*tanomoshiki koto*]. When the Akashi lady says ". . . today let her hear the first song of the little warbler." ["Hatsune," 14:140:

> *toshitsuki o matsu ni hikarete furu hito ni / kyō uguisu no hatsune kikaseyo*
> For the sake of the one who has pined away these many months and years,
> today let her hear the first song of the little warbler.]

Desolate Place [*wabishiki koto*]. The mansion of the Hitachi Princess [Suetsumuhana].

Heartbreaking Scene [*itōshiki koto*]. When Kashiwagi, on the verge of death, is visited by Yūgiri and tries to talk to him ["Kashiwagi," 15:30].

Disgusting Deed [*nikuki koto*]. When the Right Bodyguards Major learns that Ukifune is not the daughter of the Governor of Hitachi [and] marries her younger sister instead ["Azumaya," 17:16].

Marvelous Moment [*mezurashiki koto*]. When Rokujō-in [Genji] first sees the newborn First Prince, son of the Akashi Empress and the Emperor ["Wakana, jō," 15:102–3].[54]

Perfection [*aramahoshiki koto*]. When Genji, at the firming-of-the-teeth celebration, "shows Murasaki the mirror" ["Hatsune," 14:138–39].[55]

Ineptitude [*kokoro okuretaru koto*]. Taifu no Myōbu produces the garment box ["Suetsumuhana," 12:371].

Magnificent Thing [*imijiki koto*]. Commandant Kaoru supersedes all the Princes to become the Emperor's son-in-law ["Yadorigi," 16:462–63].

Unpleasant Moment [*muzukashiki koto*]. When the ashes from the censer are dumped on Commandant Higekuro ["Makibashira," 14:357].

Grief [*kanashiki koto*]. Nakanokimi's feelings when the elder Uji sister dies and she is left behind ["Agemaki," 16:320–21].

Devastation [*mune tsubururu koto*]. Kojijū's feelings when she realizes that Genji has seen Kashiwagi's letter ["Wakana, ge," 15:240–41].

Longing [*koishiki koto*]. Lady Murasaki's feelings when Genji leaves for Suma and she must remain behind in the capital ["Suma," 13:182].

Heartless Deed [*kokoronaki koto*]. The musicale in the Kokiden, held just after the Kiritsubo Mistress of the Wardrobe has died and the Emperor is sunk in grief ["Kiritsubo," 12:111–12].

Amusing Thing [*okashiki koto*]. The Ōmi lady aspires to become Chief Palace Attendant and composes a petition requesting that she be appointed to the post ["Miyuki," 14:315–16].

Affecting Scene [*aware naru koto*]. When the Emperor dispatches Yugei no Myōbu to call on the mother of the Kiritsubo Mistress of the Wardrobe, who has survived her daughter ["Kiritsubo," 12:102–13].

Moment of Shame [*hazukashiki koto*]. When Genji says to the Third Princess, "What shall he answer . . . growing from the rock?" ["Kashiwagi," 15:314:

ta ga yo ni ka tane wa makishi to hito towaba / ikaga iwane no matsu wa kotaen
Should anyone ever ask him who planted the seed, and in what reign,
what shall he answer, this little pine growing from the rock?]

Thing of Beauty [*omoshiroki koto*]. The music played by the ladies of the Rokujō mansion, each on her individual instrument ["Wakana, ge," 15:177].

Unfortunate Thing [*hoi naki koto*]. That Lady Murasaki never had children.

Irritating Thing [*modokashiki koto*]. That Ukifune, finding it impossible to choose between the love of Commandant Kaoru and the Prince Minister of War [Niou], simply abandons them both and tries to do away with herself.

Wretched Situation [*kokoro uki koto*]. The Oborozukiyo Chief Palace Attendant, with Genji secreted behind her curtains, is discovered by her father the Minister ["Sakaki," 14:135–38].

Deplorable Thing [*urameshiki koto*]. That "earnest young man" [Yūgiri] spends alternate nights with Kumoinokari, who has loved him since long past when he was wearing the green sleeves [of the sixth rank], and with Princess Ochiba—fifteen days each per month ["Niou Miya," 16:14].

Astonishing Event [*asamashiki koto*]. When Yūgao, at that "certain estate," is possessed by a spirit.

Absolutely Perfect Response [*tsukizukishiki koto*]. When Koremitsu asks, "How many Rat-Day sweets am I to provide" ["Aoi," 13:66]?

Surprising Thing [*omowazu naru koto*]. Kogimi fails to accompany Genji to Suma ["Sekiya," 13:351].

Mortification [*kuyashiki koto*]. The Rokujō Consort, fearful lest she become a laughingstock, departs for Ise ["Sakaki," 13:75].

Desperation [*kokorozukushi naru koto*]. Genji's feelings as he laments [to Fujitsubo] "rare will be the nights we can meet again." ["Wakamurasaki," 12:306:

mitemo mata au yo mare naru yume no uchi ni / yagate magiruru waga mi to mogana

Though with you now, yet rare will be the nights we can meet again; would that
I myself might be swirled away with this dream we now live.]

Regrettable Thing [*ushirometaki koto*]. That Kojijū revealed Kashiwagi's feelings ["Wakana, ge," 15:208–24].

Unsettling Event [*kokoromotonaki koto*]. When the Third Princess joins the company at the Rokujō mansion, and Murasaki—who is so unaccustomed to sleeping alone and who now so often must—conceals her sleeves, which are soaked from crying the whole night through ["Wakana, jō," 15:63].

Disgraceful Behavior [*hitowaroki koto*]. When Genji stops to inquire after Suetsumuhana, her ladies complain of their lot ["Yomogiu," 13:336–37].

Timorousness [*kokoro yowaki koto*]. Commander of the Right Gate Guards Kashiwagi calls at the Rokujō mansion, senses that he is not welcome, and immediately falls into a decline ["Wakana, ge," 15:268–71].

Rare Event [*arigataki koto*]. Ukifune, in Ono, watches and listens while robes are prepared to be offered in her memory by those she left behind, all of whom think her dead ["Tenarai," 17:348].

Anguish [*kokorogurushiki koto*]. The feelings of the elder sister in Uji, who, in a state of anguish at the thought of what might become of her younger sister, dies ["Agemaki," 16:317].

Fearsome Thing [*osoroshiki koto*]. The amorous designs of the Kyushu First Secretary on Chief Palace Attendant Tamakazura, as in his poem, "Should my feelings ever change; by the god in Matsura . . ." ["Tamakazura," 14:91:

kimi ni moshi kokoro tagawaba Matsura naru / kagami no kami o kakete chikawamu

If ever my feelings for you, my love, should change—then this I swear before the God of the Mirror Shrine in Matsura . . .][56]

Enviable Thing [*urayamashiki koto*]. The splendor in which the Akashi lady went, in place of Lady Murasaki, to serve [as her daughter's guardian] in the Shigeisha ["Fuji no uraba," 14:440–41].

TRANSLATED BY T. HARPER

A KEY TO GENJI
(*Genji kai*)

I have no idea who compiled this list of high points in *The Tale of Genji*. As I leaf through it, I find any number of passages at which I nod in perfect agreement. If some seem to me to miss the mark, well, not all people think alike. In any case, this work has afforded me so many moments of mirth that for the sheer delight of it, I have made a copy. Should more points strike my fancy, I may see fit to add them.[57]

The Very Best in Genji

Man [*otoko*]. Commandant Kaoru.

Woman [*onna*]. Lady Aoi.

Nun [*ama*]. The Novice [Third] Princess.

Monk [*sō*]. The Prelate of Yokawa.

Good Looks [*sugata*]. The Palace Attendant Oborozukiyo.

Pretty Face [*mime*]. The Akikonomu Empress.

Hair [*kami*]. Suetsumuhana's. It says it was longer than her height and lay in thick waves on the hem of her robes ["Suetsumuhana," 12:367].

Disposition [*kokoro*]. The Akashi lady.

Beautiful Voice [*koe yoki hito*]. The Kōbai Minister of the Right; as a boy, it was he who sang "Takasago" ["Sakaki," 12:133–34].

Good Karma [*kahō*]. The Kiritsubo Mistress of the Wardrobe.

Best Chapter [*suguretaru maki*]. "Wakana."

Extraordinary Scene [*koto naru tokoro*]. The Ōmi lady playing go while [her father] the Minister watches ["Tokonatsu," 14:234–35; in fact, she is playing backgammon].

Poem [*uta*].

> *yogatari ni hito ya tsutaen taguinaki / ukimi o samenu yume ni nashitemo*
> Shan't we become the stuff of gossip even so, even though I make
> of my wretched life a dream from which there is no waking?
> ["Wakamurasaki," 12:306]

Sight to Be Seen [*miru koto*]. The picture contest.

Sounds to Be Heard [*kiku koto*]. The ladies' musicale ["Wakana, ge," 15:177–86].

Joyful Event [*ureshiki koto*]. Suetsumuhana is taken into Genji's household ["Yomogiu," 13:344].

Heartbreaking Thing [*itōshiki koto*]. The Suzaku Emperor, in a letter to the Third Princess, writes, "Though you follow far behind on this Way of escape from the world . . ." ["Yokobue," 15:335:

> *yo o nogareirinamu michi wa okurutomo / onaji tokoro o kimi mo tazuneyo*[58]
> Though you follow far behind upon this Way of escape from the world,
> do seek out your old father at our common journey's end.]

Vulgar Thing [*nikuki koto*]. The Yūgao lady writes her "I would venture" poem on a fan and sends it out to him. ["Yūgao," 12:214:

> *kokoroate ni sore ka to zo miru shiratsuyu no / hikari soetaru yūgao no hana*
> It seems, I would venture, that you might just be he, the glistening dew
> come to shed your light upon the face of the moonflower.]

Forlorn Moment [*kokorobosoki koto*]. When Rokujō-in [Genji] ponders the possibility that this might be the last year he will hear the Invocation of the Holy Names ["Maboroshi," 15:534].

Moment of Astonishment [*mezurashiki koto*]. When the Reizei Emperor hears the secret of his birth revealed to him ["Usugumo," 13:439–42].

Unacceptable Behavior [*ukerarenu koto*]. Utsusemi continues to mix in society after she has become a nun ["Hatsune," 14:149–51].

Perfection [*aramahoshiki koto*]. Lady Murasaki's dwelling.

Ineptitude [*kokoro okuretaru koto*]. Suetsumuhana's behavior, no matter what she does.

Obsessive Behavior [*setsu naru koto*]. Genji's visits to Fujitsubo's gentlewoman [Ōmyōbu] ["Wakamurasaki," 12:305–6].

Splendid Thing [*imijiki koto*]. Hanachirusato becomes Yūgiri's guardian ["Otome," 14:61].

Place of Elegance [*yū naru koto*]. Among those of all the ladies Genji called upon that New Year's Day, the apartments of the Akashi lady ["Hatsune," 14:143–45].

Deplorable Deed [*wabishiki koto*]. Genji forces himself on the [Fujitsubo] Empress while she is visiting her home ["Wakamurasaki," 12:305–6].

Devastating Scene [*mune tsubururu*[59] *koto*]. After Lady Murasaki dies, Yūgiri sees her and recites the poem ". . . now this, as in a dream dreamt in the darkness before dawn." ["Minori," 15:498:

> *inishie no aki no yūbe no koishiki ni / ima wa to mieshi akegure no yume*
> Even while still yearning after that autumn evening so long ago,
> now this, as in a dream dreamt in the darkness before dawn.]

Thing of Beauty [*omoshiroki koto*]. The Festival of Cherry Blossoms.

Matter of Anxiety [*obotsukanaki koto*]. As the time of the birth of the Akashi Princess draws near, Genji worries, "Surely by now . . ." ["Miotsukushi," 13:275].

Time of Anguish [*urewashiki koto*]. When the Kashiwagi Commander of the Right Gate Guards lay helpless in his yearning for the Third Princess ["Wakana, jō/ge," 15:139–41, 208–13].

Grief [*kanashiki koto*]. Ukon's feelings when she realizes that Yūgao is dead ["Yūgao," 12:240–43].

Amusing Thing [*okashiki koto*]. The wording of the Ōmi lady's letter ["Tokonatsu," 14:240–41].

Shame [*hazukashiki koto*]. Ukifune's feelings on reading his "engulfed in waves" poem. ["Ukifune," 17:168; the poem in which Kaoru lets her know that he knows about her affair with Niou:

nami koyuru koro to mo shirazu sue no matsu / matsuramu to nomi omoikeru kana

Never did I imagine that even now they were engulfed in waves
but thought only they must be waiting, the pines of Sue.][60]

Affecting Scene [*aware naru koto*]. Just before he is to leave for Suma, Genji sets out to pay his respects at the grave of the late Emperor and, on the way, visits the [Fujitsubo] Empress, now a nun ["Suma," 13:170–72].

Irritating Incident [*modokashiki koto*]. The battle of the carriages when the [Rokujō] Consort goes to view the procession ["Aoi," 13:16–18].

Wretched Situation [*kokoro uki koto*]. The Retired Minister [Tō no Chūjō] writes to the Ochiba Princess, "I think fondly of you, yet hear such hateful things of you." ["Yūgiri," 15:471:

chigiri are ya kimi o kokoro ni todomeokite / aware to omou urameshi to kiku

Perhaps for some karmic bond between us? You are ever in my thoughts.
I think fondly of you yet hear such hateful things of you.]

Wondrous Occasion [*medetaki koto*]. When Genji makes his pilgrimage to Sumiyoshi to give thanks for prayers answered, he takes the Akashi lady back to the capital ["Miotsukushi," 13:292–98; not until the following chapter, "Matsukaze," does she actually come to the capital].

Deplorable Deed [*urameshiki koto*]. Genji allows Murasaki to see only the outside of the letter from Akashi ["Miotsukushi," 13:286–87].

Shocking Behavior [*asamashiki koto*]. The Minister of the Right walks straight into her chamber when Genji is with the Oborozukiyo Chief Palace Attendant ["Sakaki," 13:136–38].

Absolutely Perfect Response [*tsukizukishiki koto*].[61] When the guardsman says, "That flower is called the 'Evening Face'" ["Yūgao," 12:210].

Embarrassing Thing [*katawaraitaki koto*]. Suetsumuhana composes her "Chinese robe" poem. ["Suetsumuhana," 12:372:

karakoromo kimi ga kokoro no tsurakereba / tamoto wa kaku zo tobochitsutsu nomi

This Chinese robe of mine: because your heart, my love, is so very cold, its sleeves are forever soaked, like this, with my tears.]

Fretful Time [*omoiwazurau koto*]. When Nakanokimi moves from Uji to the Prince Minister of War's [Niou's] mansion ["Sawarabi," 16:342–55].

Fright [*osoroshiki koto*]. The Yūgao lady's feelings at that "certain estate" ["Yūgao," 12:233–44].

Surprising Thing [*omowazu naru koto*]. When Genji goes to Suma, he does not take Murasaki with him.

Satisfying Occasion [*kokoro yuku koto*]. When the Akashi nun moves to the capital ["Matsukaze," 13:391–97. The old woman herself is very sad; the satisfaction must be that of the writer].

Anguish [*kokorogurushiki koto*]. Nakanokimi's feelings when the Prince Minister of War [Niou] becomes Yūgiri's son-in-law ["Yadorigi," 16:373–402].

Deplorable Thing [*urameshiki koto*]. The Akikonomu Empress wins the picture contest ["Eawase," 13:375–78].

(COPIED) KEIAN 3 (1650), ELEVENTH MONTH, SIXTEENTH DAY

TRANSLATED BY T. HARPER

EXEMPLARS FROM GENJI (*Genji monotatoe*)

Man [*otoko*]. "'Only the name itself is so very grand,' they protest, but . . ." Genji ["Hahakigi," 1:129; the quotation is not precise].

Woman [*onna*]. The Akikonomu Empress.

Pretty Face [*mime*]. The Kiritsubo Mistress of the Wardrobe.

Disposition [*kokoro*]. Lady Murasaki.

Good Karma [*hō*]. The Akashi lady.

Chapter [*maki*]. "Kashiwagi."

Poem [*uta*].

ima wa tote moemu keburi ni mo musubōre / taenu omoi no nao ya nokosan[62]

Even then when the end is come and smoke rises from my burning pyre, these unquenchable flames of yearning surely shall remain.

["Kashiwagi," 15:281]

Prose Passage [*kotoba*].

> *Suma ni wa kokorozukushi no akikaze*[63] *ni umi wa sukoshi tōkeredo Yukihira no Chūnagon no seki fukikoyuru to iiken uranami no yoru yoru wa ito chikō kikoete* . . . ["Suma," 13:190: In Suma, though the sea was a bit distant, the waves raised by the mournful autumn winds that "blew in past the barrier," as Middle Counselor Yukihira described them, sounded very close as they rolled in, night after night.]

Extraordinary Event [*koto naru tokoro*]. When construction of the Rokujō mansion, with its gardens of the four seasons, is completed and Genji's household moves in ["Otome," 14:72–77].

Wondrous Event [*medetaki koto*]. When the Akashi Princess goes to court as a Dame of Honor, she is permitted to ride in Lady Murasaki's hand-drawn carriage ["Fuji no uraba," 14:442].

Moment of Joy [*ureshiki koto*]. At Hatsuse, after years of anxiety, Ukon finds Tamakazura ["Tamakazura," 14:98–104].

Sight to Be Seen [*miru koto*]. That evening when [the dance] "Waves of the Blue Ocean" puts to shame even the tints of the autumn leaves ["Momiji no ga," 12:387].

Heartening Feeling [*tanomoshiki koto*]. Genji's feelings when the late Emperor appears to him in a dream and commands him, "Be gone from this shore" ["Akashi," 13:219].

Desolate Feeling [*wabishiki koto*]. Gate Guards Commander Kashiwagi's feelings on the day of the rehearsal for the celebration of the Retired Emperor's birthday, when he is summoned to the Rokujō mansion and "forced to take the cup and drink, time and again" ["Wakana, ge," 15:262–71].

Heartbreaking Scene [*itōshiki koto*]. When the Akashi Princess is about to board the carriage to go to Lady Murasaki, she clutches her mother's sleeve and says, "You too, mother" ["Usugumo," 2:423–24].

Disgusting Thing [*nikuki koto*]. [Kumoinokari's] nursemaid "mutters" about [Yūgiri] being "fated to the sixth rank" ["Otome," 14:51].

Moment of Gloom [*kokorobosoki koto*]. When at dawn Genji sets out to pay his respects at the late Emperor's grave, the moon goes behind a cloud ["Suma," 13:173–74].

Incredible Thing [*mezurashiki koto*]. Ōmyōbu somehow contrives to arrange [Genji's] dreamlike meeting with the Usugumo Empress Mother [Fujitsubo] ["Wakamurasaki," 12:305].

Perfection [*aramahoshiki koto*]. If only Chief Palace Attendant Tamakazura could have been married to the Hotaru Prince Minister of War.

Unacceptable Behavior [*ukerarenu koto*]. Gen no Naishi's "'mother's mother' he used to call me" poem. ["Asagao," 13:474:

toshi furedo kono chigiri koso wasurarene / oya no oya[64] *to ka iishi hitokoto*
Though years pass and I grow old, this bond with the child I cannot forget,
though it was "mother's mother" his father used to call me.

The old woman's poem flirtatiously reminds Genji both of their own previous "affair" ("Momiji no ga," 12:407–18) and that his father the late Emperor used to call her *oba otodo* (Dame Granny).]

Difficult Matter [*muzukashiki koto*]. Commandant Kaoru's advances toward Nakanokimi after she has become the wife of the Prince Minister of War [Niou] ["Yadorigi," 16:412–18].

Ineptitude [*kokoro okuretaru koto*]. Taifu no Myōbu produces the garment box ["Suetsumuhana," 12:371–76].

Magnificent Thing [*imijiki koto*]. Commandant Kaoru, in preference to all the princes, is granted the cup of betrothal as the Emperor's son-in-law ["Yadorigi," 16:462–63].

Grief [*kanashiki koto*]. Genji's feelings at that "certain estate" when Yūgao is possessed by a tree spirit and he waits for Koremitsu to respond to his summons ["Yūgao," 12:242–44].

Longing [*koishiki koto*]. On that moonlit night in Suma, [Genji recalls past evenings of] music at court ["Suma," 12:194].

Shock [*mune tsubururu koto*]. The first time Genji goes to court to see the [future] Renzei [*sic*] Emperor, his father remarks how much the child resembles him ["Momiji no ga," 12:401].

Heartless Words [*kokoronaki koto*]. When [Genji] says, "How touching that [the *yamabuki*] blooms more brilliantly than ever, as if it had no idea that this spring she who planted it is no longer with us,"[65] [the Third Princess] replies, "'Spring is a stranger to this dark valley'" ["Maboroshi," 15:518].[66]

Disheartening Situation [*ajikinaki koto*]. The [Rokujō] Consort's distress at her own "weakness in waiting for the procession of the man who had caused her such unhappiness," even though "he passed her by as if she were not so much as a 'clump of bamboo'" ["Aoi," 13:17].[67]

Deep Emotion [*aware naru koto*]. Genji's feelings as he takes out the heart-rending letters that Murasaki wrote while he was away in Suma, writes in the margin of one of them, ". . . let your smoke join that from her pyre in that same cloud on high" and burns them. ["Maboroshi," 15:533–34:

kakitsumete miru mo kai nashi moshiogusa / onaji kumoi no keburi to mo nare[68]

Naught to be gained gathering up these, like sea grasses, and reading them;
let your smoke join that from her pyre in that same cloud on high.]

Moment of Shame [*hazukashiki koto*]. "'How distressing that my [the Suzaku Emperor's] death might trouble you less than this separation from someone [Genji] still so close by.' . . . Tears were streaming from her [Oborozukiyo's] eyes. 'See there?' he said, now smiling at her. 'For whom are those shed'" ["Suma," 2:189–90; in extant texts, the Emperor does not smile]?

Moment of Terror [*osoroshiki koto*]. At that "certain estate," in the "dim, flickering light of the lamp . . . there comes the creak of footsteps approaching from behind" ["Yūgao," 12:243].

Depressing Thing [*hoi naki koto*]. Whatever it was that possessed the Commandant [Yūgiri]. The [Suzaku] Retired Emperor had dropped pointed hints concerning the Third Princess, yet he coldly passed her by, only to "pick up the fallen leaf" that the Gate Guards Commander [Kashiwagi] never loved. ["Wakana, jō/ge," 4:18–19, 185; the quotation is from Kashiwagi's poem lamenting the fact that he had married the Second Princess (Ochiba) rather than the Third Princess:

morokazura ochiba o nani ni hiroikemu / na wa mutsumashiki kazashi naredomo

From that crown of vines intertwined, why did I pick up the fallen leaf?
Though in name she would seem a harmonious adornment.
("Wakana, ge," 15:224)]

Wretched Situation [*kokoro uki koto*]. [Genji's] note is discovered by the Chief Palace Attendant's [Oborozukiyo's] father the Minister ["Sakaki," 13:137–39].

Deplorable Deed [*urameshiki koto*]. When Murasaki, as if to herself, speaks of him as being "far out at sea," Genji pretends his sighs are but for the scenery [in Akashi] and lets her see only the outer wrapping of his letter [from the Akashi lady]. ["Miotsukushi," 13:286–87; Murasaki quotes a phrase from *Kokin rokujō* 1888:

Mikumano no ura yori ochi ni kogu fune no / ware oba yoso ni hedatetsuru kana

The boat rowing far out to sea from these lovely shores of Kumano travels farther and farther away, leaving me behind.]

Moment of Panic [*asamashiki koto*]. The thoughts that must have passed through Kojijū's mind when she realized that, yes, His Lordship [Genji] sees that pale green letter ["Wakana, ge," 15:240–41].

Absolutely Perfect Response [*tsukizukishiki koto*].[69] When [Genji] stops and speaks of her as a flower that he would be "loath to pass without plucking," Chūjō replies less directly, [as if he were referring to her mistress]. ["Yūgao," 12:222:

Genji: *saku hana ni utsuru chō na wa tsutsumedomo / orade sugiuki kesa no asagao*

Though loath to be known as one who flits to whatever flower is in bloom,
what a shame to pass by without plucking this morning face.

Chūjō: *asagiri no harema mo matanu keshiki nite / hana ni kokoro o tomenu to zo miru*

So you are inclined not to wait even for the morning mists to clear;
I take it then that our flower has no hold upon your heart.]

Surprise [*omowazu naru koto*]. The Palace Attendant Tamakazura rejects the elegant and handsome Prince Hotaru, whose "love for her burned as brightly as that of the insect whose cry cannot be heard" ["Hotaru," 14:193], and becomes the wife of Commandant Higekuro, though she claims to feel no affection for him ["Makibashira," 14:341–44].

Mortification [*kuyashiki koto*]. Commandant [Kaoru's] feelings when, with his heart set on the elder Princess, he relinquishes the younger Princess to Prince Niou, soon after which [the elder sister] dies ["Agemaki"].

Desperation [*kokorozukushi naru koto*]. "All through the day . . . he [Genji] would sit gazing off into space, and once the sun had set, he would go to Ōmyōbu and press her [to intercede on his behalf with Fujitsubo]" ["Wakamurasaki," 12:305].

Lamentable Thing [*ushirometaki koto*]. [Niou's] bitter resentment of that unmistakable "scent on your [Nakanokimi's] sleeve that pierces my body." ["Yadorigi," 16:424:

matahito ni narekeru sode no utsuriga o / waga mi ni shimete uramitsuru ka na

This scent on your sleeve, so intimate has it become with someone else,
pierces my very being, arouses me to anger.]

Time of Anxiety [*kokoromotonaki koto*]. In Suma, when [Genji] awaits replies to letters he has sent by messenger to the capital ["Suma," 13:180].

Rare Persons [*arigataki koto*]. Tō no Chūjō, who went to Suma with no thought for the problems it might create for him at court ["Suma," 13:204–5]. The lady at writing practice [Ukifune], who was actually distressed that she was loved by two men ["Ukifune," esp. 17:176–78].

Thing of Beauty [*omoshiroki koto*]. Tō no Chūjō's dance, "Garden of Willows and Flowers," which he had practiced with more than the usual care ["Hana no en," 12:424].

Humiliation [*kuchioshiki koto*]. The Rokujō Consort's feelings when she is pushed out of the way in the battle of the carriages ["Aoi," 13:16–18].

Curiosity [*yukashiki koto*]. What the Imperial Adviser Colonel [Yūgiri] must have imagined that morning after the typhoon when he went [to Rokujō], found the shutters not yet raised, and heard indistinct voices, first that of a woman and then His Lordship [Genji] laughing in response ["Nowaki," 14:262–64].

Embarrassing Scene [*katawaraitaki koto*]. The Ōmi lady confronts that "very proper young man" [Yūgiri] with her "just tell me which port is yours" poem. ["Makibashira," 14:390:

okitsufune yorube namiji ni tadayowaba / sao sashiyoramu tomari oshieyo

Little boat all at sea; if you're wandering the waves with no place to go,
then I'll pole on out to you; just tell me which port is yours.]

TRANSLATED BY T. HARPER

[UNTITLED]

The one surviving manuscript of this text remained unknown to *Genji* scholars until a transcript of it was published by Morikawa Akira in 1974.[70] It is now in the possession of Mrs. Suzuki Myō of the village of Nijō near the southern tip of the Izu Peninsula, whose ancestors were the custodians of Nakanoin Nakako (1591?–1671) from 1609 to 1623. Nakako was the daughter of the great *Genji* scholar Nakanoin Michikatsu (1556–1610) and was banished from the imperial court for her involvement in the so-called dragon-scale scandal (*gekirin jiken*, 1609). Fortunately, her ship, though bound for the desolate island of Niijima, was wrecked on the tip of the Izu Peninsula, and she was able to spend her years of exile rather comfortably with the Suzuki family. When she was pardoned and returned to Kyoto, she left behind the manuscripts she had brought with her. It is tempting to identify the allusiveness and accuracy of the quotations in this text as marks of the involvement of her father, Michikatsu, but of course nothing can be proved.

Man [*otoko*]. Kaoru.

Woman [*onna*]. The older [Uji] Princess.

Nun [*ama*]. [She (Ukifune), who said,] "Is that not his scent?" ["Tenarai," 17:344:

> *sode fureshi hito koso miene hana no ka no / sore ka to niou haru no akebono*
>
> He who brushed my sleeve is himself nowhere in sight, and yet is that not his scent on the blossoms, so radiant this spring dawn?]

Monk [*hōshi*]. The holy man of Uji.

Looks [*mime*]. "Even compared to the bloom of the cherry, her [Murasaki's] beauty surpassed that of the real thing" ["Wakana, ge," 15:184].

Disposition [*kokoro*]. The Akashi Novice.

Good Karma [*hō*]. The Akashi lady.

Best Chapter [*suguretaru maki*]. "Sakaki."

Extraordinary Scene [*koto naru tokoro*]. "When he raised his head from his pillow and listened to the tempest that raged all around him, he felt as if the waves might overwhelm him even where he lay. Though unaware that he wept, his tears were enough to set his pillow afloat" ["Suma," 13:190].

Poem [*uta*].

ōkata no uki ni tsukete wa nagekutomo / itsu ka kono yo wa somukihatsubeki
Deplore though I may this world, so utterly dismal in every way,
when shall I ever be able to turn my back on it? ["Sakaki," 13:125]

Spectacle [*miru koto*]. The tumult he creates as it culminates in the "Suma" chapter.

Sounds to Be Heard [*kiku koto*]. The music played by the assembled ladies ["Wakana, ge," 15:177–82].

Joyful Moment [*ureshiki koto*]. When Tamakazura encounters Ukon ["Tamakazura," 14:98–104].

Desolation [*wabishiki koto*]. The feelings of the Chief Palace Attendant [Oborozukiyo] when she is discovered by her father the Minister, with a man secreted in her chamber ["Sakaki," 13:135–38].

Pathetic Scene [*itōshiki koto*]. "They told her she must 'make obeisance in the direction of her parents,' but having no idea what direction that might be, she [Ukifune] could not restrain herself [and broke down weeping]" ["Tenarai," 17:326].

Disgusting Thing [*nikuki koto*]. "The wicks in the lamps had been trimmed and the oil exhausted, and still he [the Kiritsubo Emperor] remained awake"—while in the Kokiden there was music ["Kiritsubo," 12:112].

Moment of Melancholy [*kokorobosoki koto*]. When she [Ukifune] wrote, "to the fading toll of the bell . . ." ["Ukifune," 17:187:

kane no oto no tayuru hibiki ni ne o soete / waga yo tsukinu to kimi ni tsutaeyo
To the fading echo of the bell pray add the sound of my sobs,
to carry the word to her that my life has run its course.]

Wondrous Thing [*mezurashiki koto*]. Tō no Chūjō seeks him [Genji] out in Akashi ["Suma," 13:204–8].

Unacceptable Behavior [*ukerarenu koto*]. "Only to find you crowned with the garland of another," [writes Gen no Naishi], still youthfully refusing to grow old. ["Aoi," 13:23:

hakanashi ya hito no kazaseru aoi yue / kami no yurushi no kyō o machikeru
All for naught! I awaited this day, ordained by the gods for our tryst,
only to find you crowned with the garland of another.]

Perfection [*aramahoshiki koto*]. The dwelling at Unrin'in ["Sakaki," 13:108–13].[71]

Negligence [*kokoro okuretaru koto*]. The letter beneath the cushion ["Wakana, ge," 15:240].

Magnificent Thing [*imijiki koto*]. "'I am the son of King Wen, the younger brother of King Wu,' he [Genji] chanted, and splendid it was just to hear him proclaim the names" ["Sakaki," 13:135].

Discomfort [*muzukashiki koto*]. His feelings when the "new leaves of wisteria" yield. ["Fuji no uraba," 14:430; when Tō no Chūjō, quoting this phrase from *Gosenshū* 100, finally yields his daughter Kumoinokari to Yūgiri:

haru hi sasu fuji no uraba no uratokete / kimi shi omowaba ware mo tanomamu
These new leaves of wisteria, bathed in spring sunlight, now yield to you;
if you shall but love me, then will I place my trust in you.]

Shock [*mune tsubururu koto*]. Jijū's feelings when [Genji] spies the pale green wrap of the letter from Yokobue [Kashiwagi] ["Wakana, ge," 15:240–41].[72]

Poignant Longing [*koishiki koto*]. When the [Fujitsubo] Former Empress, now a nun, said, "Do mists rise to part us?" ["Sakaki," 13:118:

kokonoe ni kiri ya hedatsuru kumo no ue ni / tsuki wo haruka ni omoiyaru ka na
Do ninefold mists rise to part me from him in the palace? For now I can but imagine from afar the moon above the clouds.]

Heartless Deed [*kokoronaki koto*]. When the Prince Minister of War [Niou], wishing to see the fish weirs, as well as to view the autumn leaves, journeys to Uji, the Gate Guards Commander and the Chamberlain of the Empress, with a whole train of Privy Gentlemen in tow, arrive on the scene ["Agemaki," 16:282–84].

Sorrow [*kanashiki koto*]. He appends the words "Let your smoke join that from her pyre in that same cloud on high." ["Maboroshi," 15:534:

kakitsumete miru mo kai nashi moshiogusa / onaji kumoi no keburi to mo nare[73]
Naught to be gained gathering up these, like sea grasses, and reading them;
let your smoke join that from her pyre in that same cloud on high.]

Amusing Scene [*okashiki koto*]. The burst seam in the Unmeiden ["Momiji no ga," 12:415].

Deep Emotion [*aware naru koto*]. He dreamed that [his father said to him,] "I plunged into the sea and made my way along this shore . . ." ["Akashi," 13:219].

Moment of Shame [*hazukashiki koto*]. When he [Genji] said, "What shall he answer, the little pine growing from the rock?" ["Kashiwagi," 15:314:

ta ga yo ni ka tane wa makishi to hito towaba / ikaga iwane no matsu wa kotaen
Should anyone ever ask him who planted the seed, and in what reign,
what shall he answer, this little pine growing from the rock?]

Rare Thing [*arigataki koto*]. His [Genji's] kindness in trudging through the deep growth of wormwood ["Yomogiu," 13:337–38].

Heartrending Scene [*setsu naru koto*]. "This 'smoke' shall itself be my keepsake of the world I once lived in," he said, weeping ever more uncontrollably. ["Kashiwagi," 15:286; Kashiwagi refers to the "smoke" in the Third Princess's poem:

tachisoite kie ya shinamashi uki koto o / omoimidaruru keburi kurabe ni
How I wish I too might die, that my smoke might rise together with yours;
then could we compare whose flames of sorrow burn the brighter.]

Beautiful Moment [*omoshiroki koto*]. "The Crown Prince urges him to 'adorn your cap with this' [sprig of blossoms]. Unable to decline, he [Genji dances the passage in which he] gently flips his sleeve over his arm . . ." ["Hana no en," 12:424].

Bitterness [*netaki koto*]. The feelings of the Sanjō lady [Kumoinokari] in saying "rather than resent the lot . . ." ["Yūgiri," 15:461:

naruru mi wo uramuru yori wa matsushima no / ama no koromo ni tachi ya kaemashi
Rather than resent the lot of one grown too close and then cast aside,
might I not better exchange it for the robes of a nun?]

Exasperating Thing [*modokashiki koto*]. She [the Third Princess] detains him [Genji], saying, "'Let your sleeves be moist,' do you tell me?" And then he sees the letter. ["Wakana, ge," 15:239:

yūtsuyu ni sode nurase to ya higurashi no / naku wo kiku kiku okite yukuramu
"Let your sleeves be moist with evening dew," do you tell me?
You hearken to the cry of the evening cicada, yet rise up to leave.]

Awe-Inspiring Scene [*tōtoki koto*]. The dedication of the Paradise Mandala that Lady Murasaki had made before she died ["Maboroshi," 15:526, 529].

Splendid Thing [*medetaki koto*]. That the Akashi Empress bears so many princes.

Miserable Situation [*kokoro uki koto*]. For someone [Ukifune] who must have felt that she had once brushed sleeves with the brilliance of the sun and moon [Kaoru and Niou] to be forced to converse with the Major, the former son-in-law of the Ono nun ["Tenarai," 17:315–16].

Resentment [*urameshiki koto*]. Her [Murasaki's] feelings when finally she can say only, ". . . last for ever and ever." ["Wakana, jō," 15:58:

me ni chikaku utsureba kawaru yo no naka o / yukusue tōku tanomikeru kana
Before my very eyes it shifts and then changes, this bond between us,
and I had trusted it to last for ever and ever.]

Agony [*kokorogurushiki koto*]. The feelings of the Ono Consort[74] when, convinced that it had been only a one-night affair, she died ["Yūgiri," 15:423–24].

Uncertainty [*obotsukanaki koto*]. "Whom might I ask, and why is it so," he [Kaoru] said. ["Niou Miya," 16:18:

obotsukana tare ni towamashi ikani shite / hajime mo hate mo shiranu waga mi zo
This uncertainty: Whom might I ask, and why must it be my fate that
I know nothing of whence I come or whither I shall go?]

Absolutely Perfect Response [*tsukizukishiki koto*]. The guardsman says, "A very human sort of name" ["Yūgao," 12:210].

Shock [*asamashiki koto*]. Their feelings when having taken everyone to the conference on promotions, they [Genji, the Minister of the Left, and so on] hear that Lady Aoi has suddenly expired ["Aoi," 13:39].

Pitiful Thing [*katawaraitaki koto*]. When he [Genji] wrote, "Though it appeared to be a flower of the deepest shade . . ." and straightaway sent it to the lady [Suetsumuhana]. ["Suetsumuhana," 12:373–74; the source of this allusion does not survive in any extant anthology. Most medieval commentators suggest that Genji is quoting from some version of the following poem:

kurenai no iro koki hana to mishikadomo / hito o aku dani utsuroinikeri
Though it appeared to be a flower of the deepest shade of crimson,
your love for me, like a garment washed in lye, has faded.[75]

In fact, Genji never sends the note to the Princess.]

Mortification [*kuyashiki koto*]. After Lady Murasaki dies, he [Genji] recalls how insensitive he had been ["Maboroshi," 15:508–9].

Unexpected Thing [*omowazu naru koto*]. When, in reply to the [Suzaku] Emperor in the mountain temple, Lady Murasaki writes, "Do not force yourself . . ." ["Wakana, jō" 15:69:

somuku yo no ushirometaku wa sarigataki / hodashi wo shiite kake na hanare so
If concerns of the world you have left behind still weigh upon your mind,
then you mustn't force yourself to break the ties that bind you.]

Fearsome Thing [*osoroshiki koto*]. The god of Suma ["Suma," 13:210].

TRANSLATED BY T. HARPER

The Matches

Isn't it a delight to win a matching contest?
Sei Shonagon, *The Pillow Book*

The next four texts constitute another subgenre of *Genji* gossip. Whereas the lists of the previous section resemble concise sets of minutes taken at gossip sessions such as that depicted in *A Nameless Notebook*, the matches in this section cast the same sort of material in the format of a formal poetry contest (*utaawase*). Here the emphasis is almost entirely on characters in *Genji* and their feelings, rather than on scenes, chapters, and such. And rather than simply state (or suggest) which is the superlative exemplar in each category, two alternatives are offered for judgment, and then a case is made for the side deemed the winner. In the first text, *The Feelings of People in Genji: A Match,*[76] both the comparisons and the final judgments are expressed in prose. However, in the next two texts, *Genji: A Contest*[77] and *The Feelings of People in Genji: A Match*,[78] the judgments are rendered in the form of poems. In the last text, by far the most discursive of the four, a selection of women in *Genji* are matched against similarly situated women in the *Tales of Ise*, ostensibly for the entertainment of an emperor. Again, the most that can be said of the provenance of any of these texts is that they probably were written by women connected to the imperial court, sometime after the appearance of *A Nameless Notebook*.[79]

T. HARPER

THE FEELINGS OF PEOPLE IN GENJI: A MATCH
(*Genji hitobito kokoro kurabe* [Awa no Kuni Bunko text])

Item. Which would have been the more painful [*kokorogurushi*]: the Emperor's grief when the Wisteria Court Mistress of the Wardrobe, sensing that the end was near, left the palace ["Kiritsubo," 12:97–98], or Genji's grief when Lady Murasaki, knowing that her time had come, took the Five Vows? ["Wakana, ge," 15:232]

It was upsetting indeed when the Consort,[80] sensing that the end was nigh, left the palace, yet there was still some hope that she might live. How must Genji have felt when Murasaki, with whom he had lived from the time she wore her hair in tails, knowing that her time had come, took the final step and cut short her hair?

Item. Which is the more forward [*hashijika nari*]: the Chief Palace Attendant [Oborozukiyo] gazing out at the misty moon ["Hana no en," 12:426], or the Yūgao lady's "shed your light . . ." poem? ["Yūgao," 12:212]

For someone to come peeping just when she expected it least—when she found the late night moon irresistible and she was gazing out at it thinking that no one would be listening—that was frightening. But for that shadow behind the gate to send out her "shed your light . . ." poem was most forward.

[*kokoroate ni sore ka to zo miru shiratsuyu no / hikari soetaru yūgao no hana*
It seems, I would venture, that you might just be he, the glistening dew
come to shed your light upon the face of the moonflower.]

Item. Whose shame [*hazukashisa*] and fright [*osoroshisa*] would have been greater: the Oborozukiyo Palace Attendant's when her father the Minister, found Genji hiding in her chamber ["Sakaki," 13:137–38], or the Third Princess's when Genji picked up the letter from the Commander of the Gate Guards [Kashiwagi]? ["Wakana, ge," 15:240]

One can well imagine her shame and fright in that chamber; even so, her father the Minister must have lacked any sense of shame [*hazukashiki ke*]. He seems even to have had other people compose his poems for him. But the fright and shame when Genji discovered the letter must simply have devastated her. Surely this was the more wretched.

Item. Whose distress [*migokoro, omoi*] would be the greater: Lady Murasaki's when Genji departed for Suma, leaving her behind in the capital, when she would have "given her life" to detain him ["Suma," 13:178], or the Akashi lady's when Genji was recalled? ["Akashi," 13:253–61]

That [Murasaki] should so grieve that she would "give her life" demonstrates how far from shallow her feelings were. But the Akashi lady was of mean rank, added to which was the loneliness of life amid the "huts of crude mountain folk" ["Suma," 13:199]. And with her parents in such a state of agitation, how much more distressed must she have been?

[Murasaki's poem; "Suma," 13:178:

oshikaranu inochi ni kaete me no mae no / wakare o shibashi todometeshikana
How I wish, in exchange for my life, which I would give with no regrets,
I might delay but a moment this parting we now face.

Genji's poem; "Suma," 13:199:

yamagatsu no iori ni takeru shibashiba mo / koto toikonan kouru satobito
As often as crude mountain folk kindle fires of brushwood in their huts,
would that you should inquire after me, my loved ones at home.]

Item. Who is the more quick-witted [*kokorotoshi*]: Genji when he read the letter he found under the Third Princess's cushion and knew that it was from [Kashiwagi] the Commander of the Gate Guards ["Wakana, ge," 15:240], or Koremitsu, who understood immediately what was meant when Genji told him to "bring the Boar's Day cakes tomorrow evening"? ["Aoi," 13:65–66]

When she leaves the letter under her cushion, allowing it to be seen, anyone would be bound to suspect something of this sort. When "the waters of the mountain spring well forth," he is certain to know it. Koremitsu's "Baby Rat Day" is indeed "quick-witted."

> [The "mountain spring" is perhaps that of a poem in *Shokusenzaishū* (1071) by the Kameyama Retired Emperor on the subject of "secret love" (*shinobu koi o*):
>
> *shirasebaya iwa moru mizu no tayori ni mo / taezu kokoro no shita ni seku to wa*
>
> Would that I might let her know: what the message hidden in my heart
> might tell her were those waters to well forth from the rocks.
>
> Koremitsu's quick-witted phrase *ne no ko* means "baby rat" but also suggests, homophonically, Genji's intention to "sleep with the child," Murasaki.]

Item. Which was the more repellent [*utomashi*]: the Rokujō Consort's several apparitions as a malign spirit, or Higekuro's wife dumping the ashes from the censer on him?

It was not merely that the Consort's resentment manifested itself as a disconsolate shade. That her obsession should be so great that even after death her spirit took flight and censured the most intimate converse between Genji and Murasaki, which no one else could have heard—this surely was the more repellent. The frenzy with which Higekuro's wife dumped the ashes from the censer on him was shocking, but the lady was not in her right mind; surely she can be forgiven.[81]

Item. Which would have been the more deeply touching [*aware fukashi*]: when, just before Ukifune disappeared, the Prince [Niou] himself went to her, but she was under heavy guard and he heard of her pitiful plight [from Jijū; "Ukifune," 17:182–83], or the feelings of the Commander of the Right Gate Guards [Kashiwagi] when he was near death as a consequence of [his affair with] the Third Princess, yet was unable to be with her and could talk about their relationship only with [Ko]jijū? ["Kashiwagi," 15:279–88]

It must have been sorrowful indeed when at about the time [Ukifune] was thinking of ending her life, the Prince Minister of War [Niou] went [to Uji], only to be kept apart from her and learn of her piteous condition from another. Yet it must have been even worse [for the young lady], despairing as she did of choosing between them, only to have the Commandant [Kaoru] learn what was going on, thus deciding her to end it all. Near death on account of the Third Princess and yet unable to be with her, the Commander of the Right Gate Guards could talk only with [Ko]jijū, and merely hearing of her plight made him apprehensive of the future of the "pine that grows from the rock" ["Kashiwagi," 15:314]. What, then, must have been his "darkness of heart" as he perished?

> [*ta ga yo ni ka tane wa makishi to hito towaba / ikaga iwane no matsu wa kotaen*
> Should anyone ever ask him who planted the seed, and in what reign,
> what shall he answer, this little pine growing from the rock?]

Item. Which would have been slightly the more sorrowful [*sukoshi kanashi*]: Genji's feelings when he saw Yūgao perish before his very eyes ["Yūgao," 12:238–44], or the Prince Minister of War's [Niou's] bewilderment when Ukifune vanished without a trace? ["Kagerō," 17:193–98]

When Yūgao passed away, [Genji] could take some solace in the thought that the span of her life may well have been predestined ["Yūgao," 12:253]. One can imagine the commotion when Ukifune was nowhere to be found; yet it was in the Prince's nature that he could divert himself with whatever else chance might offer. But the grief [of seeing] Yūgao's lifeless body, perished like a drop of dew—or even just hearing someone tell the story—surely [Genji's] lamentations were the greater.

Item. Whose joy would have been the greater [*nao ureshi*]: Lady Murasaki's when she first saw Genji on his return from Akashi ["Akashi,"

13:261–62], or Ukon's when she discovered Tamakazura, the Chief Palace Attendant, at Hatsuse? ["Tamakazura," 14:101–12]

When [Genji] departed for Akashi, he did not travel so far away that [Murasaki] need feel as desolate as she might have had they been separated by the seas; there still was hope that they might be together again. But what must have been Ukon's joy when, after all those years of longing for her lost one [Tamakazura], pleading to the gods and buddhas, the two should chance to meet, and she found the girl even lovelier than she had been as a child?

Item. Which is more the painful to contemplate [*katawaraitashi*]: when the Hitachi Princess [Suetsumuhana] presented Genji with the garment box ["Suetsumuhana," 12:372–73], or the Ōmi lady when she met her father the Minister and spoke so presumptuously to him? ["Tokonatsu," 14:234–39]

The Ōmi lady's presumptuous replies were painfully ridiculous, but her father could not help but see how devoted to him she was and forgive her. When the Hitachi Princess produced that old-fashioned garment box, it was distressing even to the feelings of an onlooker.

Item. Which transgression was slightly the more forgivable [*sukoshi tsumi yurusaru*]: Fujitsubo's affair with Genji, or the Third Princess's affair with [Kashiwagi,] the Commander of the Right Gate Guards?

For the Emperor's sake, Fujitsubo did ultimately turn her back on the world with unflinching resolve, yet her replies [to Genji] invariably seem far too peevish. But one does feel sorry for the Commander of the Right Gate Guards when, having had no sympathy from the Third Princess, he sends her his "smoke from my burning pyre" poem ["Kashiwagi," 15:281], thinking the end had come and he might perish without ever receiving a reply.

[*ima wa tote moen keburi mo musubōre / taenu omoi no nao ya nokoramu*
Even then when the end is come and smoke rises from my burning pyre,
these unquenchable flames of yearning surely shall remain.]

Item. Which is the more shocking [*omowazu nari*]: Tamakazura, the Chief Palace Attendant, ignoring the proposals of the Reizei Emperor and the [Hotaru] Prince Minister of War, only to become the wife of Commandant Higekuro [between "Fujibakama" and "Makibashira"], despite saying she cares nothing for him; or Utsusemi, whom we would pity and recall how lovely she had once been, if only she had gone into seclusion in some mountain retreat after turning her back on the world ["Sekiya," 13:354]? But just when the woman should have been devoting herself to tranquil reflection and repentance, she allowed herself to be brought back and live with [Genji's] other women ["Hatsune," 14:149–51].

It is indeed unseemly that Utsusemi went to live among all those other ladies after she had become a nun. Still, once she turns her back on the world, her resolve is firm, and never does she entertain any thoughts that might transgress the Buddha's precepts. It is a pity that after Tamakazura had been so firm with the Reizei Emperor and the Prince Minister of War, Commandant Higekuro should force himself on her. She was always fretting about one thing or another, though, and most likely she found some peace of mind in settling once for all on this rather coarse gentleman. But then—the deed done—she has the gall to take her "little pines" [sons] with her and refer [to Genji] as her "great rock" ["Wakana, jō," 15:51]—now *that* was shocking.

[*wakaba sasu nobe no komatsu o hikitsurete / moto no iwane o inoru kyō kana*
I bring with me today these little pines, plucked from freshly sprouting fields,
as I pray that the great rock whence I sprang may long endure.]

Item. Which would have been slightly more heart-rending [*ima sukoshi kokorozukushi*]: the parting at the shrine in the fields when [Genji] laments that "dawn partings will always be drenched with dew, but . . . " ["Sakaki," 13:81], or that winter's evening, "trudging along icy shores" by the ferry crossing at the Uji River? ["Ukifune," 17:146]

The setting, the touching beauty of the scene before his eyes when they parted at the shrine in the fields, would indeed have left their mark on the man's feelings. But surely one's heart must go out to the spectacle of [Niou's] distress, so "lost to her" that he would "trudge through the snow."

[Genji's poem to the Rokujō Consort; "Sakaki," 13:81:

akatsuki no wakare wa itsumo tsuyukeki o / ko wa yo ni shiranu aki no sora kana
Though partings at dawn will always be dewy and drenched with tears,
never before have I seen such autumnal skies as this.

Niou's poem to Ukifune; "Ukifune," 6:146:

mine no yuki migiwa no kōri fumiwakete / kimi ni zo madou michi wa madowazu
I trudge across snowbound mountain peaks, along ice-lined shores,
never losing my way as I have lost myself to you.]

Item. Who is the more resolute [*kokorozuyoshi*]: the Asagao High Priestess, or the elder Uji sister?

The Asagao High Priestess is past her prime; she is of lesser rank than the most exalted ladies, and she would have been well aware what the [Rokujō] Consort had been through ["Aoi," 13:13]. Although the elder Uji sister realized that his [Kaoru's] devotion to her was of many years standing, she managed to elude him until her death. *That* is incomparable.

TRANSLATED BY T. HARPER

GENJI: A CONTEST
(*Genji monoarasoi*)

Which is the more profound [*fukashi*]: the Emperor's feelings that autumn when the Mistress of the Wardrobe in the Paulownia Court sensed that her time was come, and he found it so maddeningly difficult to give her leave to depart the palace ["Kiritsubo," 12:97–98], or Genji's grief when Lady Murasaki passed away? ["Minori," "Maboroshi"]

tsuki mo senu kokoro no yami no fukaki yo ni / kumogakurenishi aki zo kanashiki
In the limitless depths of that night of ceaseless darkness in his heart,
that autumn when she was hidden in cloud, *that* was sorrow.

Which is slightly the more forward [*ima sukoshi hashijika nari*]: the Yūgao lady when she sent out her "it seems that you might just be he, the glistening dew . . . " poem ["Yūgao," 12:211], or the Third Princess, in pursuit of her cat, being seen by Kashiwagi? ["Wakana, jō," 15:132–33]

te ni naraishi neko no kagoto mo arinubeshi / amari zo kakeshi yūgao no hana
At least she could blame it on her pet kitten, tamed by her own hand,
but the girl with the moonflower face has gone just too far.

[Yūgao's poem; "Yūgao," 12:214:

kokoroate ni sore ka to zo miru shiratsuyu no / hikari soetaru yūgao no hana
It seems, I would venture, that you might just be he, the glistening dew
come to shed your light on the face of the moonflower.]

Who are closer friends: Genji and Tō no Chūjō in earlier days, or the Prince Minister of War [Niou] and Commandant Kaoru during their Uji period?

iro mo ka mo tagui wa onaji tazunekoshi / suma no tabine ni shiku mono zo naki
In both substance and essence, they are of quite the same order,
but naught
can equal that journey to visit his friend in Suma. ["Suma," 13:304-8]

Genji, who gleamed as with a bright light, or Commandant Kaoru, who radiated fragrance? ["Niou Miya," 16:19–22]

minamoto o musubishi mizu wa kiyokeredo / nagare no sue ya sumimasaruran
Though the waters be pure where they rise from the Minamoto wellspring,
can they possibly be clearer yet further down the stream?

Who feels himself to be the greater fool [*nao oroka nari*]: Genji when he discovered the letter from the Kashiwagi Commander of the Gate Guards beneath her cushion ["Wakana, ge," 15:240], or Commandant Kaoru when he first heard of the Prince Minister of War's [Niou's] dalliance with the lady at writing practice [Ukifune]? ["Ukifune," 17:161–63]

> *tamafuda no kayoishi naka wa tsurakeredo / shitone no shita ni shiku mono wa naki*
> Their bond, linked by those lovely letters, was painful to him,
> but naught can equal what lay beneath that cushion of hers.

Which would be the more difficult to conceal [*shinobigatashi*]: Genji's feelings after the Yūgao lady passed away ["Yūgao," 12:247–49], or the Prince Minister of War's [Niou's] feelings after the young lady at writing practice [Ukifune] vanished without a trace? ["Kagerō," 17:206–12]

> *ukifune no ato no namida wa kawakanedo / kiku dani kanashi yūgao no tsuyu*
> The wake of that small boat adrift, those tears of his, never do they dry;
> yet the dew on the moonflower, sad even to hear of it.

The terrible grief felt [*kokoro no monoganashisa*] by the Rokujō Consort when she left the capital, saying, "Whose [thoughts are likely to follow me] as far as Ise?" ["Sakaki," 13:87], or by Hanachirusato when [Genji] left for Suma and she spoke of her "sleeves, narrow though they be," while in those dark-hued sleeves "dwelled the face of the moon, itself wet with tears"? ["Suma," 13:167]

> *tachibana no hana chiru sato no kayoiji ni / yasose no nami ya tachimasaruran*
> More so than upon the path to the village where orange blossoms fall
> shall there be tears as the waves of myriad rapids rise.

[Genji's poem; "Sakaki," 13:86:

> *furisutete kyō wa yukutomo suzukagawa / yasose no nami ni sode wa nureji ya*
> Though today you abandon me and leave, at the Suzukagawa
> will not the waves of its myriad rapids soak your sleeves?

The Rokujō Consort's reply; "Sakaki," 13:87:

suzukagawa yasose no nami ni nurenurezu / ise made tare ka omoiokosemu
Whether wet or not by waves in the myriad rapids of the Suzukagawa,
whose thoughts are likely to follow me as far as Ise?

Hanachirusato's poem; "Suma," 13:167:

tsukikage no yadoreru sode wa sebakutomo / tometemo mibaya akanu hikari o
Narrow though they be, these sleeves of mine wherein dwells the light of the moon,
how I wish they might stay its glow, of which I never tire.

Both the *Genji* narrator and Hanachirusato allude to a poem by Ise; *Kokinshū* 756:

ai ni aite monoomou koro no waga sode ni / yadoreru tsuki sae nururu kao naru
How appropriate that now, in my despair, even the face of the moon
that dwells in my sleeves should itself be wet with tears.]

Which is the more distressing [*kokorogurushi*]: the enormity of her dumping the ashes in the censer on Commandant Higekuro ["Makibashira," 14:357–58], or the spirit of the Rokujō Consort venturing forth to possess Lady Aoi? ["Aoi"]

takimono no hitori no hai ya musebiken / kuyuru omoi wa iro ni izutomo
The ashes in the brazier of the perfume censer must have been stifling,
though they did give vent to the smoke of her smoldering feelings.

Whose profound prudence [*kokoro fukasa*] is rarer [*arigatashi*]: the Asagao Princess, who died stubbornly firm in her determination that she should never be rumored to be frivolous ["Asagao," "Otome"], or the elder Princess in Uji, who strongly urges him [Kaoru] to transfer his affections [to Nakanokimi]? ["Agemaki"]

utsurowade yaminishi hana no tsuyu bakari / fukaki iro aru uji no kawanami
Deep is the hue of the river waves at Uji, but not so much so
as the dew on that blossom, withered yet not faded.

Which, finally, is the more frivolous [*kokoro karoshi*]: the Third Princess allowing herself to be seen by Kashiwagi ["Wakana, jō," 15:132–33], or the lady at writing practice [Ukifune] giving herself up to the Prince Minister of War [Niou]? ["Ukifune," 17:115–17]

iroiro ni utsurou hana wa ada naredo / nao kashiwagi no mori no shita tsuyu
Fickle indeed is the fading flower as it shifts from shade to shade,
yet even more so is the dew beneath the grove of oak.

Genji's devotion [*kokorozashi*] in having advanced the career of the Akikonomu Empress and treated her so wonderfully out of pity for [her mother] the Rokujō Consort, who had died in the depths of despair, or his having cared so solicitously for Tamakazura, the Chief Palace Attendant, as a keepsake of [her mother Yūgao, whose life had been as ephemeral as] the dew on the moonflower?

tamakazura kokoro ni kakete shinobedomo / nao mi ni shimu wa aki no yūgure
Tamakazura he cherishes with a particular fondness;
yet even more poignant is that evening in autumn.

Which would have been the more bewildering [*magiretarikemu*]: Genji's feelings when he could learn nothing about the identity of Yūgao ["Yūgao"], or his anxiety [*obotsukanasa*] when, despite running hither and yon, he could not work out where Oborozukiyo, the Chief Palace Attendant, lived? ["Hana no en"]

[The puzzle of] Yūgao's identity originates in the contemptible circumstances in which she lived; but he is calmed by her manner, so much less pretentious than that of the others, and ultimately he comes to trust her. Oborozukiyo's quarters, at the Third Door, lay in an awesome location. He had no idea of her whereabouts and was utterly at a loss for any means of finding her. In addition, the contrary manner of her "grassy moor" poem weighed so heavily on his mind that this would have seemed to him far the more bewildering.

> *hikari sou tasogaredoki no hana yori mo / oboroge naranu fukaki yo no tsuki*
> More so than that flower upon which he casts his glow in the twilight
> was the full moon, shining clear and unmisted, late that night.

[Oborozukiyo's poem; "Hana no en," 12:427:

> *ukimi yo ni yagate kienaba tazunetemo / kusa no hara oba towaji to ya omou*
> Were I, poor thing, suddenly to vanish from this world, you might inquire,
> do you mean, but not seek out my grave on the grassy moor?

The judgment poem draws its diction from two poems:
Yūgao to Genji; "Yūgao," 12:214:

> *kokoroate ni sore ka to zo miru shiratsuyu no / hikari soetaru yūgao no hana*
> It seems, I would venture, that you might just be he, the glistening dew
> come to shed your light on the face of the moonflower.

Genji to Oborozukiyo; "Hana no en," 12:426:

> *fukaki yo no aware o shiru mo iru tsuki no / oboroge naranu chigiri to zo omou*
> One who appreciates the beauty of this late night as the moon sets
> feels our bond to be every bit as clear and unmisted.]

The Imperial Adviser Colonel [Tō no Chūjō] makes his way to Suma, and as they talk of the capital, their "drunken sorrow" grows deeper and they recall how "tears fill the wine cups of spring" ["Suma," 13:204–8; quoting *Hakushi monjū*, 1107]. This seems a noble and exemplary deed [*arigataki tameshi*]. Neither does the deep devotion of Commandant Kaoru ever diminish, resolved as he is to look after the Prince Novice [the Eighth Prince], even into the next life. He undertakes, too, the guardianship of the Princesses, discreetly yet unceasingly ["Hashihime," 16:150–51; "Shiigamoto," 16:171]. This, too, surely, is noble [*arigataki*].

When the Imperial Adviser Colonel pointedly ignores the troublesome political consequences and goes openly to that wave-beaten shore, that is truly noble [*makoto ni arigataki*]; and yet, given the intimacy of their familial relationship, and even more so their friendship, like birds who fly wing to wing, it is only natural that he should show such affection. Yet the Commandant's noble behavior [*arigatasa*] surely is without precedent. In admiration of the principles that made [the prince] an "ascetic, though yet of this world," he seeks him out deep in the mountains ["Hashihime," 16:124–27], never flags from beginning to end, even making his way through snows that block out the heavens ["Shiigamoto," 16:197], and then rebuilds his "straw-thatched hermitage" as a temple ["Yadorigi," 16:443–45].

nochi no yo mo kono yo mo fukaki kokoro ni wa / tachiokurekeri suma no uranami
Whether in worlds to come or in this present world, to such deep feeling they are inferior—those waves that beat on Suma's shore.

At the festivities beneath the cherry blossoms before the Southern Hall ["Hana no en," 12:423–24], "the poems were so superb and the dances and the music in such perfect harmony" that [the Minister of the Left] thought their magnificence unequaled in "these past four reigns of enlightened sovereigns" and, moreover, that they "must stand as a model for reigns yet to come." Particularly memorable, too, in so many ways, [Genji thought], was [Tō no Chūjō's dance] "Garden of Willows and Flowers" ["Hana no en," 12:432]. In the women's concert at the Rokujō mansion ["Wakana, ge" 15:175–76], of the countless tunes of one sort and another that come to mind, one can imagine how superb the sound of that Azuma koto ["Wakana, ge," 15:192] must have been—which was the instrument, was it not, to which the Commandant [Yūgiri] had listened so intently? ["Wakana, ge," 15:181]

Of the many different beauties at the women's concert, one calls to mind, too, the appearance [*katachi*] of each of the ladies, at which time images of an unseen world form in one's mind. And when [Genji] hears the Third Princess playing her *kin*, looking [as frail and delicate as new strands of willow that might] "tangle even in the breeze from a warbler's wings" ["Wakana, ge," 15:183], and deems her touch superior even to the sound of [Murasaki's] Azuma koto ["Wakana, ge," 15:192–93], *that* is unforgettable [*sutegataki*]. But how memorable must have been the "Spring Warbler" that the Genji Colonel casually danced "just a hint of" and then retired ["Hana no en," 12:424]. The somewhat more conscientiously prepared "'Garden of Willows and Flowers,' which truly must stand as a model for reigns yet to come," is likewise exceptional.

> *momochidori saezuru haru no kai arite / yanagi no hana no itodo yukashiki*
> Following upon the beauties of spring, flights of plovers chirping,
> one longs only the more for the willows and the flowers.

The quick wit [*kokorotosa*] of Koremitsu when he asks, "How many Baby Rat Day sweets?" ["Aoi," 13:65–66], or the quick wit of Commandant Kaoru's guardsman when he detects the letter from Prince [Niou] at Uji? ["Ukifune," 17:161–63]

It was quick-witted of Commandant Kaoru's guardsman to realize that this was a letter from the Prince and to go as far as to send someone to follow [the messenger] and find out where he came from; but then, Tokitaka[82] was of common origins. Anyone seeing someone at the door delivering a letter attached to a branch of cherry could have guessed what was going on. If you really place a higher value on sharpness [*kadokadoshiki*] in such matters, then Koremitsu's hinting at "Baby Rat Day" is the more impressive.

> *tamazusa no kayou yukue o tazunetemo / ne no ko no kazu wa nao zo masareru*
> Though the one identifies the source of this traffic in love letters,
> "How many for Baby Rat Day" is by far the better.

> [Koremitsu's quick wit consists of not only his recognition of Genji's meaning but also the words with which he expresses his perception: *ne no ko* means "baby rat" but also suggests that Genji intends to "sleep with the child."]

Despite Genji's circumspection, on account of the cruel things that are being said about him, just as he is leaving Fujitsubo's quarters, [Tō no Ben] chants, "A white rainbow crosses the sun; the Crown Prince falls to the earth [*sic*]" ["Sakaki," 13:117]. How must Genji have felt to hear such effrontery? And how cruel Genji is when the saké cup comes around to [Kashiwagi,] the Commander of the Gate Guards: although he appears to be in high spirits, he decides to feign drunkenness and persists in forcing him to drink ["Wakana, ge," 15:270–71].

When [Tō no Ben] chants, "A white rainbow crosses the sun," that was something said simply because, as a rule, people of a particular faction are swayed by the way things go in their own world and act accordingly. What can anyone do about that? When [Kashiwagi,] the Commander of the Gate Guards, declines to come because he is so terribly frightened ["Wakana, ge," 15:259–63] and [Genji] decides to summon him forcefully and then torments him, that is quite shocking.

> *shizariki* [*sic*] *tada naozari no koto no ha mo / moemu kemuri ni musebu beshi to wa*[83]
>
> . . . even the words of the simplest careless utterance
> may cause one to choke on the smoke of a smoldering pyre.

> [The writer misquotes the second clause of the passage from *Records of the Historian* chanted by Tō no Ben: *taishi chi ni ochitariken* (the Crown Prince has fallen to the earth). The version in the *Genji* text reads *taishi ojitari* (the Crown Prince trembles). Tō no Ben is the nephew of the Kokiden Consort and the grandson of the Minister of the Right. His effrontery lies in the suggestion that Genji, like the Crown Prince in the *Records*, harbors treasonous designs against the emperor.]

Which was the occasion of greater mental anguish [*kokorogurushisa*]? On a spring morning at the Rokujō mansion, around the time Genji is visiting the Third Princess, he goes to the quarters of Lady Murasaki, humming to himself, "The snows that yet remain." The lady retracts and conceals the sleeve of her robe, which is wet with tears, and greets him warmly ["Wakana, jō," 15:62]. Or the evening when the Prince Minister of War [Niou] is to become Yūgiri's son-in-law, he makes all manner of promises [to Nakanokimi], telling her that "you are not to look at the late night moon alone" and trying in various ways to comfort her? She thinks neither one thing nor another but feels only that her pillow might float away ["Yadorigi," 16:390–91].

Murasaki, who for years had been accustomed to having no rival, now must have felt overcome with grief. Yet she could still count on [Genji] to deem her superior to his many others. They had been together since he had fallen in love with her long ago as a little girl, so she could take heart in the knowledge that he was not likely to lose all interest in her. The Prince Minister of War [Niou] was of an innately amorous disposition, and his affections had shifted. This was the end, she realized: a wretched state. Her inconsequential rank had left her humiliated, forlorn, and so anguished that she could hardly believe she had really left home and made her way down that mountain path. The Princess's feelings as she pondered that "piercing autumn [wind]" were of quite another order.

tsuyu wakuru kusa no yukari wa ada naraji / mi ni shimu aki no kaze zo kanashiki
So her kin, from whom she'd parted brushing aside the dew, had not been wrong;
sorrowfully blows that autumn wind, piercing to the bone.

["Autumn wind" alludes to Nakanokimi's own poem ("Yadorigi," 16:393):

yamazato no matsu no kage ni mo kaku bakari / mi ni shimu aki no kaze wa nakariki
Even there in the shade of the pines in my old home in the mountains,
never did the autumn wind blow so piercingly as this.]

COPIED THIS TWENTIETH YEAR OF ŌEI (1413),
SEVENTH MONTH, FIRST DAY

KAMEWAKAMARU[84]

TRANSLATED BY T. HARPER

THE FEELINGS OF PEOPLE IN GENJI: A MATCH
(*Genji hitobito kokoro kurabe* [Suzuki manuscript])

Which is the more profound [*fukashi*]: the Emperor's feelings when the Mistress of the Wardrobe in the Paulownia Court sensed that her time was come, and he found it so painfully difficult to give her leave to depart the palace ["Kiritsubo," 12:97–98], or Genji's feelings when Lady Murasaki passed away?[85] ["Minori," "Maboroshi"]

tsuki mo senu kokoro no yami no fukaki yo ni / kumogakurenishi ato zo kanashiki
In the limitless depths of that night of ceaseless darkness in his heart,
it was after she was hidden in cloud; *that* was sorrow.

Which is the more forward [*hashijika nari*]: the Yūgao lady when she sent out her "it seems that you might just be he, the glistening dew . . ." poem ["Yūgao," 12:212], or the Third Princess, in pursuit of her cat, being seen for the first time by Kashiwagi? ["Wakana, jō," 15:132–33]

tenarekoshi neko no kagoto mo arinubeshi / amari zo nageshi yūgao no hana
At least she could blame it on her pet kitten, tamed by her own hand;
but the girl with the moonflower face is just too forward.

[Yūgao's poem; " Yūgao," 1:214:

kokoro ate ni sore ka to zo miru shiratsuyu no / hikari soetaru yūgao no hana
It seems, I would venture, that you might just be he, the glistening dew
come to shed your light on the face of the moonflower.]

Who are closer friends: the Prince Minister of War [Niou] and Commandant Kaoru during their Uji period, or Genji and Tō no Chūjō in their earlier days?

iro mo ka mo tagui wa onaji tazunekoshi / suma no tabine ni shiku mono zo naki
In both substance and essence, they are of the same order, but nothing
can equal that journey to visit his friend in Suma. ["Suma," 13:304-8]

Genji, who gleams as with a bright light, and Commandant Kaoru, who radiates a pervasive fragrance? ["Niou Miya," 16:19–22]

minamoto o musubishi mizu wa kiyokeredo / nagare no sue ya sumimasaruran
Though the waters be pure where they rise from the Minamoto wellspring,
can they possibly be clearer yet further down the stream?

Who feels himself to be the greater fool [*nao oroka naru*]: Genji when he discovered the letter from the Kashiwagi Commander of the Gate Guards beneath her cushion ["Wakana, ge," 15:240], or Kaoru when he first heard of the letter that Prince Niou sent to Miyanokimi? ["Ukifune," 17:161–63]

tamazusa no kayoishi naka wa tsurakeredo / shitone no shita ni shiku mono zo naki
Their bond, linked by those lovely letters, was a painful one,
but naught can equal what lay underneath that cushion of hers.

[The writer apparently confuses Ukifune with her cousin Miyanokimi. In extant *Genji* texts, Niou does not send a letter to Miyanokimi.]

Which would be the more hurtful [*urameshi*]: Lady Murasaki's anguish when the Lord of Rokujō [Genji] welcomed the Third Princess as his wife and treated her so solicitously ["Wakana, jō"], or the Sanjō lady's [Kumoinokari's] grief when Commandant Yūgiri took the Ochiba Princess to wife? ["Yūgiri"]

murasaki no yukari mo tsurashi yūgiri no / ochiba iro tsuku enishi aritomo
Painful it was for her of affinities with purple [Murasaki], fated though
the fallen leaves [Ochiba] were to be tinged by the evening mists
[Yūgiri].

Which would be the more difficult to lament openly [*wabigatashi*]: Genji's feelings after the Yūgao lady passed away ["Yūgao," 12:247–49], or the Minister of War's [Niou's] feelings when the lady at writing practice [Ukifune] vanished without a trace? ["Kagerō," 17:206–12]

ukifune no ato no namida mo kawaranedo / kiku dani kanashi yūgao no tsuyu
The wake of that small boat adrift, those tears of his, never will they
change;
yet the dew on the moonflower, sad even to hear of it.

The mental anguish felt [*kokoro no monoomowashisa*] by the Rokujō Consort when she left the capital, saying, "Whose thoughts are likely to follow me to Ise?" ["Sakaki," 13:87], or Hanachirusato, when [Genji] left for Suma and she spoke of her "sleeves, narrow though they be," while in those dark-hued sleeves "dwelled the face of the moon, itself wet with tears"? ["Suma," 13:167]

tachibana no hana chiru sato no kayoiji ni / yasose no nami ya tachimasaruran
More so than upon the path to the village where orange blossoms fall
shall there be tears as the waves of myriad rapids rise.

[Genji's poem; "Sakaki," 13:86:

furisutete kyō wa yukutomo suzukagawa / yasose no nami ni sode wa nureji ya
Though today you abandon me and leave, at the Suzukagawa
shall not the waves of its myriad rapids soak your sleeves?

The Rokujō Consort's reply; "Sakaki," 13:87:

suzukagawa yasose no nami ni nurenurezu / Ise made tare ka omoiokosemu
Wet or not wet by waves in the myriad rapids of Suzukagawa,
whose thoughts are likely to follow me as far as Ise?

Hanachirusato's poem; "Suma," 13:167:

tsukikage no yadoreru sode wa sebakutomo / tometemo mibaya akanu hikari o
Narrow though they be, these sleeves wherein dwells the light of the moon,
how I wish they might stay its glow, of which I never tire.][86]

Which is the more frightful [*osoroshi*]: the enormity of her [Higekuro's wife] dumping the ashes on Commandant Higekuro ["Makibashira," 14:357–58], or the spirit of the Rokujō Consort venturing forth to possess Lady Aoi? ["Aoi"]

takimono no hitori no hai ya musebiken / kuyuru keburi no iro ni izutomo
The ashes in the brazier of the perfume censer must have been stifling,
though they did give vent to the smoke of her smoldering anguish.

Whose profound prudence [*kokoro fukasa*] is the rarer [*arigatashi*]: the Asagao Princess, who died quite stubbornly firm in her determination that she should never hear herself called frivolous ["Asagao," "Otome"], or the elder Princess in Uji, who strongly urges him [Kaoru] to transfer his affections [to Nakanokimi]? ["Agemaki"]

utsurowade yaminishi hana no iro bakari / fukaki iro aru uji no kawanami
Deep is the hue of the river waves at Uji, but not so much so
as the hue of that blossom, withered yet never faded.

Which, finally, is the more frivolous [*kokoro karoshi*]: the Third Princess allowing herself to be seen by Kashiwagi, the Commander of the Gate Guards ["Wakana, jō," 15:132–33], or the lady at writing practice [Ukifune] giving herself up to the Prince Minister of War [Niou]? ["Ukifune," 17:115–17]

> *iroiro ni kokoro no hana wa ada naredo / nao kashiwagi no mori no shita tsuyu*
> Fickle indeed is the flower of the heart, shifting from shade to shade;
> yet even more so is the dew beneath the grove of oak.

Genji's devotion [*kokorozashi*] in having advanced the career of the Akikonomu Empress and treating her so wonderfully out of pity for [her mother] the Rokujō Consort, who had died in the depths of despair for her reputation; or his having cared so solicitously for Tamakazura, the Chief Palace Attendant, as a keepsake of [her mother Yūgao, whose life had been as ephemeral as] the dew on the moonflower?

> *tamakazura kokoro ni kakete omoedomo / nao mi ni shimu wa aki no yūkaze*
> For Tamakazura he feels a most particular affection,
> yet even more poignant is that evening breeze in autumn.

[Genji's] beauty at the autumn leaves festivities when he danced the Blue Waves in the glow of the setting sun ["Momiji no ga," 12:383], or Yūgiri's beauty under the blossoms at the musicale in the "Wakana" chapter? ["Wakana, ge," 15:180]

> *tachimayou hana no nioi wa fukakeredo / yūhi kagayaku aki no momijiba*
> Rich indeed was the fragrance wafting about the radiant blossoms,
> yet those autumn leaves all aglow in the evening sun. . . .

Which is the more touching [*aware*] instance of parental love for a child: the letter the Retired Minister [Tō no Chūjō] sent to the Ochiba Princess in which he vented his resentment, saying, "I hold you ever in my heart . . ." ["Yūgiri," 15:471], or the one that the Prince Minister of War [Niou], in a state of desperation, wrote to Commandant Higekuro, in which he spoke of the "bird that flits about and roosts"? ["Makibashira," 14:376]

izure to mo waki zo kanetaru katagata ni / ko o omou michi no michishiba no tsuyu
Which is the more so? One hesitates to distinguish one from the other; parental love is a path fraught on both sides with perils.

[Tō no Chūjō's poem; "Yūgiri," 15:471:

chigiri are ya kimi o kokoro ni todomeokite / aware to omou urameshi to kiku
Perhaps some karmic bond between us? I hold you ever in my heart; I think fondly of you yet hear such hateful things of you.

The author seems to confuse Hotaru Hyōbukyō no Miya, a former suitor of Tamakazura, with Shikibukyō no Miya, the father of Higekuro's rejected wife. Moreover, Hotaru's note is sent not to Higekuro but to Tamakazura herself. It is thus no expression of parental love at all but the complaint of a rejected lover ("Makibashira," 14:376):

miyamagi ni hane uchikawashi iru tori no / mata naku netaki haru ni mo aru kana
So you mean to flit about and roost in such a gnarled old mountain tree? Well, this new song of yours proclaims a spring of great rancor.]

Which more nearly approaches perfection [*aramahoshi*]: that auspicious scene when [Tamakazura] expresses her [congratulations on Genji's fortieth birthday] in terms of the pines that sprout from the rock, tinted so deeply with the green of spring ["Wakana, jō," 15:51], or that autumn evening when their converse was so intimate that even the slightest glance conveyed affection? ["Kagaribi," 14:246–50]

iro kaenu iwane no matsu no shitaogi ni / tsuyu okimasaru aki no yūgure
On the reeds that grow, shaded beneath the ever unfading green pine, dewdrops form yet more profusely of an autumn evening.

[The author's memory of Tamakazura's poem is slightly skewed, as the pines in this episode spring not from the rocks but from the fields:

wakaba sasu nobe no komatsu o hikitsurete / moto no iwane o inoru kyō kana
I bring with me today these little pines, plucked from freshly sprouting fields,
as I pray that the great rock whence I sprang may long endure.]

When Commandant Yūgiri catches sight of Lady Murasaki from a far corner on the morning after the typhoon ["Nowaki," 14:256–59], or when the Commandant [Yūgiri] glimpses the scene in which the Akashi Empress appears even more imposing than before in her robes? ["Nowaki," 14:274–77]

morotomo ni fukaki ko no ma o yuku tsuki no / honoka ni mieshi kage zo wasurenu
Both are as unforgettable as the light of the moon faintly glimpsed
from deep in a grove as it passes a gap in the trees.

Which is the more touching [*aware*]: when his attendant monk told the Renzei [*sic*] Emperor about that "dream they had lived, in which the nights they [Genji and Fujitsubo] met were so rare" ["Usugumo," 13:439], or [Kaoru's] joy when the nun Ben produced the brocade bag and showed it to him? ["Hashihime," 16:154–55]

mukashi mishi au yo mare naru yumeji ni mo / fukaki namida no tsuyu no tamazusa
Even on that path of dreams, where long ago on nights so rare they met,
the dew of tears lies deep, from those few little letters.

[The quotation is from Genji's poem to Fujitsubo ("Wakamurasaki," 12:306):

mitemo mata au yo mare naru yume no uchi ni / yagate magiruru waga mi to mogana
Though with you now, yet rare will be the nights we can meet again; would that
I myself might be swirled away with this dream we now live.]

After the Princess Second Rank [the Third Princess] moved to the Rokujō mansion, [Murasaki], in an excess of unbearable insecurity, gazed out at "green leaves on the hills" and thought, "so autumn is come" ["Wakana, jō," 15:82], or when the Prince Minister of War [Niou] proceeded to the mansion of the Minister of the Left [Yūgiri, actually the Minister of the Right], [Nakanokimi], bereft of all consolation, gazed out at the moon as it rose bright and clear, as it had above Mount Abandoned Crone, and mused that her life was more miserable now than it had been even in the wretched "shade of the pines"? ["Yadorigi," 16:392–93]

mizutori no aoba no yama o nagametemo / mi ni shimu hodo no aki wa nakariki
Gaze though she may at the hills green with new leaves where waterfowl sport,
her autumn was not so sharp as a lover's indifference.

[The reference to the moon shining on Obasuteyama alludes to *Kokinshū* 878:

waga kokoro nagusamekanetsu sarashina ya / obasute yama ni teru tsuki o mite
O Sarashina! My heart is inconsolable even as I gaze
at the moon that shines down on Mount Abandoned Crone.

The "shade of the pines" is from Nakanokimi's own poem ("Yadorigi," 16:393):

yamazato no matsu no kage ni mo kaku bakari / mi ni shimu aki no kaze wa nakariki
Even there in the shade of the pines in my old home in the mountains
never did the autumn wind blow so piercingly as this.]

TRANSLATED BY T. HARPER

THE WOMEN IN ISE AND GENJI: A MATCH IN TWELVE ROUNDS
(*Ise Genji jūniban onna awase*)

Most attempts to date *The Women in Ise and Genji*, based principally on comparison with *Ise monogatari* texts of known provenance, have proved inconclusive, and thus in most reference works *Onna awase* is described as dating from the Kamakura period.[87] More recently, however, a study based on close comparison of the *Onna awase* text with a number of *Genji* digests has revealed correspondences with fifteenth-century digests that are so numerous and so close that we can now confidently assume that *Onna awase* must have been composed sometime after *Genji monogatari teiyō* was completed in 1432.[88] Even more significantly, these correspondences reveal a great deal about the way the text was composed. As Oda Keiko, the author of this study, points out, by the later Muromachi period, "common readers" (*ippan dokusha*) could no longer read the raw text of *The Tale of Genji*. Whatever knowledge of *Genji* they possessed came more from digest versions than from the original. *Onna awase* is a fascinating illustration of such an understanding. Readers of this translation will no doubt notice many discrepancies between the *Genji* described by the author of *Onna awase* and the *Genji* written by Murasaki Shikibu. Story lines are garbled, characters and chronology confused, and poems misquoted. One at first suspects an understandable imprecision of memory. *The Tale of Genji* is a vast work; no one could memorize it perfectly, and it would not have been easy to check every detail with the resources available at the time. But in fact, many of these discrepancies can be traced to the text of one or another of the *Genji* digests. They are not imprecise versions of the *Genji* text; rather, they are "correctly" cited or quoted from inaccurate digests. Some of the more conspicuous inaccuracies are pointed out in the notes. Unfortunately, however, no evidence has yet been discovered that would support even a guess at the identity of the author of *Onna awase*.[89]

T. HARPER

It was in a recent reign, I believe, toward the middle of the Second Month, when the cherry blossoms before the South Hall were at their peak, on a tranquil day when even the breeze, cognizant perhaps of the occasion, blew but softly. As the Emperor himself was to grace the day, not one of his ladies failed to attend him: the Empress, of course, and every Dame of Honor, every Mistress of the Wardrobe was there. Musicians were summoned, each painstakingly selected for the perfection of his particular art, so that the strains of woodwinds and strings resonated throughout this dwelling in the clouds, while dancers, likewise, performed with consummate brilliance. "Though these sleeves flutter not in the shade of autumn leaves,"[90] said the Emperor, beaming, "who would not be touched by the sights we have seen today?" His gentlewomen, one and all, appeared loath even to venture a reply. As the saké cups made their rounds, all strove to do their best by the topic, "Blossoms Blooming with Smiles of Joy." And thus they passed the entire day absorbed in the pleasures of composition, in both Chinese and Japanese. When it was agreed that [they should meet] again the next day, though blooms of *hagi* [bush clover] these were not, the face of the moon did indeed smile upon them.[91]

The Empress summoned a lady called Dainagon. "Since His Majesty would view [the blossoms] again tomorrow, to complement the fine music already requested, you must put together a few pairs of women who appear in the old romances. Now, if you discuss them only in terms of their office and rank, what sort of contest would that be? So present them to His Majesty, judging them only on the basis of their gentility and character as exhibited in the particular circumstances of one passage and another." So saying, the Empress herself called for her inkstone and was pleased to draw up a list of people, in twelve pairs, just as they happened to occur to her, those from *Tales of Ise* on the Left and those from *The Shining Genji* on the Right. As she accepted [the list], Lady Dainagon said, "There do seem to be numerous instances of matching objects, be they poems, pictures, perfumes, fans, or whatever else might suit the occasion—but those sorts of things one can compare on the basis of particulars and thus judge which are the winners and losers. How, though, is one to judge the feelings of people of the distant past well enough to compare them?" Thus did the deluded darkness of a dim mind find its way into even such an endeavor as this. If only there were some precedent, she thought, that would permit her to escape the august imperial command. For should she state her judgments, item by item, the distress of it, as with an old jewel left too long unpolished, could not help but arouse in her an unsettling sense of trepidation.

Round 1

Left	The Empress Mother of the Fifth Ward	Win
Right	The Kiritsubo Mistress of the Wardrobe	

On the Left is the Empress Mother of the Montoku Emperor.[92] During His Majesty's august reign, she did no little bit to nurture the realm and benefit her subjects, while to His Majesty, too, she was a source of sound counsel. In the Zhou dynasty, the Consort of King Wen, desiring to perpetuate the reign, understood that keeping peace in the realm was a matter of winning the allegiance of people and that to win the allegiance of people, nothing could equal familial relationship. And so she sought out daughters from each of her subjects of good family and presented them to His Royal Highness. Might even the example of this woman be something this lady has taken to heart? In nobility of character and appearance it is hard to say [who else] she might be compared with. In *Yotsugi's Tale*, this lady is likened to the cherry blossoms. Her father, too, merely for expatiating on his own old age, attained unwarranted repute.[93] Having given birth to a child who becomes Emperor, she caused her entire line to achieve rank. Quite magnificent!

On the Right, the Kiritsubo Mistress of the Wardrobe. Her father was a Grand Counselor, or some such, but he seems to have died. Having no means of support, she enters service in the palace and there finds favor with the Emperor, who persists in spending day and night with her. Not one of those around her fails to take umbrage at this. This sort of thing has happened in foreign lands, they say—there could well be trouble here, too—and the realm grows more and more distressed by it. Before long, she gives birth to a Prince. It must have been when the child was in his third year that his mother, the Mistress of the Wardrobe, fell ill. She shows no sign of recovery, and in the summer of that year she is in such agony that she wishes to return to her home. The Emperor is utterly inconsolable. He has long wished at least to raise her to the rank of Empress,[94] but what then of the censure of the court? No, he says, that would be going too far, and so he decrees that she be granted the privilege of a hand carriage. The Mistress of the Wardrobe:

> *kagiri tote wakaruru michi no kanashiki ni / ikamahoshiki wa inochi narikeri*
> In my grief, now that the end has come and I tread this path that parts us,
> far more do I wish that my destination should be life. ["Kiritsubo," 12:99]

And thus in the end she passes away. In the palace, His Highness, sunk in grief, longs for a wizard so that he might know whither her spirit has gone ["Kiritsubo," 12:111]. During the period of mourning, the young Prince's grandmother, now an old nun,[95] takes him in. In her rustic thatched retreat, a desolate place buffeted by stormy winds, it is an even more dew-drenched autumn than usual. In the palace, His Highness, concerned in addition to all else about the Prince, deigned to send Lady Myōbu to the nun.

> *miyagino no tsuyu fukimusubu kaze no oto ni / kohagi ga moto o omoi koso yare*
> At the sound of the winds that bring dew down on the moors of Miyagi,
> my heart goes out to that place where the young *hagi* grows.
> ["Kiritsubo," 12:105]

Her reply:

> *araki kaze fusegishi kage no kareshi yori / kohagi ga ue zo shizugokoro naki*
> Since the withering of the tree in whose shade he sheltered from the rough winds,
> my heart can't but tremble for the fate of the young *hagi*.
> ["Kiritsubo," 12:110]

No sooner has the period of mourning passed than the Prince returns to the palace where he grows up as if he were the ward of the Kokiden Empress.[96] In the spring of his seventh year, he embarks on the study of reading. When a physiognomist from Korea arrives, he is taken to the Kōrōkan to meet him. This man foretells his future triumphs, and, because his appearance is so radiant, dubs him the "Shining Lord." In keeping with the precedent of the sage kings, he dons the court cap of an adult for the first time in his twelfth year and is granted the name Minamoto. In the reign of the Reizei Emperor, he is made Honorary Emperor in Retirement, after which, I believe, he was addressed as Lord of the Rokujō Estate. As the mother of this extraordinary man who so astonished the world, for both his talents and his virtues, this Mistress of the Wardrobe suffers considerable humiliation at court in her own day. Reticent though I am to presume, having been selected to judge this entertainment today, how dare I not at least pay homage to the shade of this wise and noble Prince?

Round 2

Left	The Nijō Empress	Draw
Right	The Usugumo Empress Mother	

On the Right, the Empress Mother. After the death of the Kiritsubo Mistress of the Wardrobe, His Majesty was so utterly despondent that he could hardly even distinguish morning from evening. "Yet with whom else . . . ?" he would sigh, grasping her pillow. As he grew ever more lax in the performance of his duties at court, there arose a flurry of alarm in which some expressed doubts over the very future of the reign. In the hope that something might be done, they sought out this lady, and from time to time he would take comfort in her company. She was aged fourteen or fifteen, and perhaps for her natural radiance, so they say, she was dubbed "Princess Radiant Sun." She was given quarters in the Wisteria Court, and in looks she came more and more to resemble her of the past. To the Shining Lord she looks like his real mother, and he becomes her close companion, waiting upon her morning and night. For her part, in her childish way, she treats him as her playmate, and thus it was that they come to hold frightfully inappropriate feelings for each other. Never would Her Highness be able to reveal this, but then, to her particular distress, she gave birth to a Prince. As the child matures, he comes to resemble Genji most remarkably, so that in the larger world, at least among those of discernment, some feel distinctly uneasy about what they see. Her Highness the mother, caught as she is in this impossible state of affairs, can but bear her anguish in silence, wondering all the while whether it can really be so, which in itself seems, at least slightly, to assuage her sense of guilt. But Genji, lamenting the shock of her total change of heart:

> *yosoetsutsu miru ni kokoro wa nagusamade / tsuyukesa souru nadeshiko no hana*
> Though I liken him to this pink, it brings my heart no satisfaction,
> this little flower upon which the dew of my tears fall. ["Momiji no ga," 12:402]

Before long, this boy succeeded to the throne, and Genji came to determine the course of worldly affairs. From this we realize that, indeed, the rank, even of the children of Emperors, appears to derive from the mother's side.

The Empress of the Left was betrothed to the Crown Prince when she was very young and had been raised with great care. However, a man, who held the rank of Colonel, made reckless advances toward her and persisted in courting her. When his parents and brothers forcefully restrained him, he turned away from the world in disgust and went into hiding outside the capital. Nonetheless, by night he would go to her, and probably because this proved to no avail, he intoned:

itazura ni yukite wa kinuru mono yue ni / mimakuhoshisa ni izanawaretsutsu
Though to no avail I go to you, only to return once again;
even so I go on, drawn by my desire to see you. [*Ise* 65; *Kokinshū* 620]

With nothing else, apparently, that he could do, he even prayed to the buddhas and gods that he might forget her. Exorcisms of various sorts were performed, but he longed for her still more than before.

koi seji to mitarashigawa ni seshi misogi / kami wa ukezu mo narinikeru kana
To those many lustrations performed at the river Mitarashi
that I might love no more, the gods, alas, have paid no heed.
[*Ise* 65; *Kokinshū* 501]

Back in the palace, His Majesty's love for her is anything but shallow, and her cousin the Empress Mother looks after her with the utmost devotion. Thus the light of the world seems to have shone upon her, for toward the end of the Jōgan era [858–876] she gives birth to a Prince, and in the following year, I believe, rises to the rank of Empress.

Both these ladies, though of the most exalted lineage, were also tainted by a tinge of shadow in their lives, and since their personal qualities, too, are much the same, this match is a perfect draw.

Round 3

Left	The daughter of Aritsune	
Right	Lady Murasaki	Win

On the Left: Inasmuch as the Colonel's father, the Prince, lived not far from the home of Ki no Aritsune, the boy and the girl played together throughout their childhood. And with the blooming of the blossoms in spring and the tinting of the leaves in autumn, they vowed passionately to love each other forever. As they grew up, the girl's parents were not inclined to be as permissive as they had been in the past. From time to time, however, her mother may have shown signs of sympathy, for she intoned:

miyoshino no tanomo no kari mo hitaburu ni / kimi ga kata ni zo yoru to naku naru
I seem to hear the goose that alights on the fields of Miyoshino
crying that it is in your direction she would fly. [*Ise* 10]

Delighted, the man replies:

waga kata ni yoru to naku naru miyoshino no / tanomo no kari o itsu ka wasuremu
The goose in the fields of Miyoshino that seems to you to cry
that she would come my way: when could I ever forget her? [*Ise* 10]

On what occasion might it have been? The woman:

amagumo no yoso ni mo hito no nariyuki ka / sasuga ni me ni wa miyuru mono kara
Like the clouds far above, you fade ever further into the distance,
though to the eye you still remain so clearly visible. [*Ise* 19; *Kokinshū* 784]

The man replies:

amagumo no yoso ni nomi shite furu koto wa / waga iru yama no kaze hayami nari
That the clouds above remain so far distant can only be because
the winds around the mountain where they dwell blow so harshly. [*Ise* 19; *Kokinshū* 785]

It is written that he says this because she has another man. According to this account, apparently, he himself found another lover elsewhere, and whenever he visited her, the [first] woman would see him off as if nothing had changed. The man was suspicious of this and, pretending to leave, lingered in the shadows and watched her. She makes herself up immaculately and, until late at night, plays her koto. Then, swallowing her resentment, she retires, saying:

kaze fukeba okitsu shiranami tatsutayama / yowa ni ya kimi ga hitori koyuran
Tatsutayama, higher than the white waves that rise when the winds blow:
in the middle of the night my love must cross all alone. [*Ise* 23]

Even when the man was on his deathbed, this woman wailed, "I've been counting on you to light my way along the path of darkness, and now you're going to abandon me and go on ahead?" The man:

shiru ya sa wa ware ni chigireru yo no hito no / kuraki ni yukanu tayori ari to wa
Know'st thou? That any woman in this world who has pledged her love to me
thereby forms a bond such that she'll never walk in darkness?[97]

Some cheek, that!

On the Right: This lady loses her mother when she is very young, and her nursemaid, a nun, brings her up. Genji, for reasons of his own, pays a visit to the retreat of the Prelate of the Northern Hills. This nursemaid, as it happens, is related to the Prelate and comes regularly to the Northern Hills, where she would stay in order to perform her devotions. Of course, she also brings the little lady with her. With so much idle time on his hands, Genji finds life in this mountain abode, whose sights were so unfamiliar to him, both strange and fascinating. He would look in here and look in there, leaving no corner of the place unexplored in his wanderings. What is this, and what is that? he would ask his retainers. During this time, he catches sight of a hermitage that, though enclosed by a brushwood fence like all the others, has a garden grove of particular elegance and beauty. He summons Koremitsu and sends him to investigate, whereupon he reports that the younger sister of the Prelate seems to have once been the wife of someone called the Inspector Grand Counselor. Although she lives in the capital, from time to time she comes up here for the merit that these visits will bring her in the afterlife. And the young and very pretty little girl there is the daughter of the Prince Minister of War and a granddaughter of the nun. Well then, His Lordship thinks, he will look into this more closely, and peering in on her, he could see that she was indeed no ordinary creature. It was obvious to him what [a beauty] she would grow up to be, and right away, as seems to have been his wont, reckless thoughts ruled his heart. He drops delicate hints to both the Prelate and the nun.

hatsukusa no wakaba no ue o mitsuru yori / tabine no sode mo tsuyu zo kawakanu
From the moment I first caught sight of the new leaves of this young slip,
the dew-drenched sleeves of this weary traveler have yet to dry.
["Wakamurasaki," 12:290]

The nun's reply:

makura yū koyoi bakari no tsuyukesa o / miyama no koke ni kurabezaranan
The dewfall of but a single night on a makeshift pillow:
compare it not with that on the moss deep in these mountains.
["Wakamurasaki," 12:291]

His Lordship pleads most fervently for the little lady, and it is with no little regret that he brings himself to leave the mountain village and return home.

yūmagure honoka ni hana no iro o mite / kesa wa kasumi no tachi zo wazurau
Having glimpsed indistinctly in the dusk the beauty of this flower,
I am loath now to leave with the rising mists of morning.
["Wakamurasaki," 12:296]

What with the First Secretary Colonel, the Controller of the Left,[98] and several other lesser courtiers having come to meet him, as well as [the Emperor's] inquiries from the palace and various other matters demanding his attention, he returns home. From the following morning, he sends a steady stream of messengers, though without revealing the full extent of his apprehension, which is as deep as those mountains. Months went by, during which the old nursemaid passed away, and the nursemaid Shōnagon, with two or three other ladies, had gone back to the mansion in the capital. The girl's father, the Prince, he heard, was about to move her to his home as a keepsake [of her mother], but [Genji] has his contacts, through whom he brings her to the Nijō mansion as a matter of urgency, where he is most solicitous of her. Before long, he becomes as close to her as if she were his own daughter, teaching her the koto and calligraphy.[99]

> *te ni tsumite itsushika mo min murasaki no / ne ni kayoikeru nobe no wakakusa*
> How I long to pluck, and eventually make mine, this wildflower sprung from the root of *murasaki* she so resembles. ["Wakamurasaki," 12:314]

It was from about the time of this poem that he began to feel amorously inclined toward her. Even at the time of his setback in Suma, it is written, it was, above all, concern for this lady that troubled him night and day ["Suma," 13:153–54]. Because she had no children, she was drawn to the Way of the Buddha from a very early age. Of her own volition, she has a thousand magnificent sets of the Lotus Sutra made and dedicates them with great splendor and ceremony ["Minori," 15:481–84].

Of this pair, the lady of the Left likewise enjoys unparalleled renown for her allure, of both appearance and person. Yet [the man] had his reasons, however slight, for mentioning "the mountain where they dwell." This practice of matching things is, after all, just a quest for trifling flaws, as in the raillery of old women.[100] Despite how difficult it is to avoid going astray, has the lady of the Right ever done anything amiss in matters conjugal? Am I not right, then, I wonder, in deeming her the winner?

Round 4

Left	The lady who died of love	
Right	Lady Aoi	Win

The lady of the Right, the only daughter of the Minister [of the Left] and his wife the Princess, was raised with the greatest affection and care. On the day that the Shining Lord was granted the surname Genji, it was arranged, through the good offices of the Emperor himself, that he become her husband. They then take up residence together, and a very fine match it is. Her elder brother, the First Secretary Colonel, having grown up in like manner, was the envy of all the spectators at the autumn leaves festivities when he danced to the music of both Left and Right. Though they were born humans, just like the rest of us, people would say, apparently their sins of the past were lighter and their progress on the path to Buddhahood greater for them to have been blessed with such exceptionally fine looks and character. In such terms were the two of them praised as models of their age. The lady is of a very dignified character and, even after longer acquaintance, is frightfully reticent and shy of people. Even when spoken to, she will not readily respond. She averts her gaze and her face turns bright red. Such is the great charm of her character. Even when Genji came down with malaria, went off to the Northern Hills [to be cured], and then returned home again,[101] she slipped out, as was her wont, and hid, quite unwilling to come out [and receive her husband]. Only after the Minister [her father] spoke firmly to her did she, after an interval, make an appearance. And there she sat, precisely where she was placed, as stiff and proper as a princess in a painting. How satisfying it would be, Genji thinks, if I could chat with her about things that are on my mind or tell her about that place in the mountains, in return for which she would say something interesting in reply. Never, though, does she relent; she regards him as a nuisance, to be kept at a distance. Painful though it is, with the passing years, they grew only further apart. "I do wish that once in a while you could behave normally with me," he says. "Even when I was suffering so unbearably, you never asked how I felt. That isn't unusual, of course, but it does hurt." She slowly turned away and replied, "So you, too, find it painful, not being asked after?" There was a haughty beauty in the sharp glance she shot back at him. Even so, she gave birth to a child, and not long thereafter she suddenly fell ill. The court is thrown into a frenzy, and several rites are performed, but the possessing spirit is tenacious, and finally she passes away. From the Rokujō Consort:

hito no yo o aware to kiku mo tsuyukeki ni / okururu sode o omoi koso yare
Hearing, with grief, of what this life can hold for us brings the dew
of tears,
but above all my heart goes out to the sleeves of him left behind.
["Aoi," 13:44]

In reply, Genji:

tomaru mi mo kieshi mo onaji tsuyu no yo ni / kokoro okuran hodo zo hakanaki
For those of us who stay, as for those who go, it's the same world of dew:
too insubstantial ever to set one's hopes upon it. ["Aoi," 13:46]

Regarding the infant lord as a keepsake of her:

shimogare no magaki ni nokoru nadeshiko o / wakareshi aki no katami to zo miru
This little pink that lingers on at the base of my frost-withered hedge
I look upon as a keepsake of an autumn now past. ["Aoi," 13:50]

And again, his lamentations having calmed him:

naki tama zo itodo kanashiki neshi toko no / akugaregataki kokoro narai ni
Even greater must be the sorrow of the departed one's spirit,
when I find it so hard to forsake this bed where we slept. ["Aoi," 13:58]

On the Left: His Lordship her father is fonder of this lady than any of the others, and he raises her with great affection and care. Suddenly, however, she falls ill. He stays constantly by her side, offering vows and the like, but all to no avail. When she is near death, she tells him that she had fallen in love with this man and that as time passed she has grown only weaker and weaker. When her parents sent word of this, the man, in a frenzy, came to her [but it was too late]. Lamenting the bond that has ended in her death, he went into seclusion for several days. It was in the Sixth Month, and only late at night did it grow at all cool. Watching the fireflies flit back and forth high above him:

tobu hotaru kumo no ue made inubeku wa / akikaze fuku to kari ni tsugekose
Fireflies, if, as you flit to and fro, you can fly above the clouds,
pray go and tell the wild goose the autumn winds now blow. [*Ise* 45]

It is very difficult to decide the winner of this round. When we examine poetry competitions of the past that match "Requited Love" and "Unrequited Love," are there any in which Requited Love is deemed the winner? I find the depth of devotion in the lady of the Left, who died of love, exceptionally touching. But lacking any precedent, I declare the Right the winner. Still, I can hardly hold back my tears when I think how difficult it will be ever to dispel the blind attachment of the lady of the Left.

Round 5

Left	The lady who told of her dream	
Right	The Oborozukiyo Chief Palace Attendant	Win

On the Right: The Chief Palace Attendant [Oborozukiyo] is the younger sister of Kokiden, mother of the Crown Prince. She goes to view today's cherry blossom festivities, which take place around the twentieth of the Second Month. In the dusky beauty of early evening, as Genji lurks near the third portal of the Kokiden, there comes from within a youthful voice of exceptional beauty, chanting, "Naught is there to equal a night lit by a misty moon." Genji goes to her, takes her in his arms, and gently conceals her. The girl murmurs her discomfort, but to no avail. As dawn approaches, still feeling as if she were dreaming:

uki mi yo ni yagate kienaba tazunetemo / kusa no hara oba towaji to ya omou

Were I, poor thing, suddenly to vanish from this world, you might inquire, do you mean, but not seek out, my grave on the grassy moor? ["Hana no en," 12:427]

Thus he begins, in great secrecy, to visit her. This lady had been destined for the Crown Prince. But when this blot upon her reputation is revealed, the Empress Mother bursts into tears of rage. After the old Emperor dies, she tells the Crown Prince, and Genji is sent off to Suma. To him on that shore:

namidagawa minawa mo ukite kienubeshi / nagarete nochi no yo o mo matazu shite

This froth, anguished, floating on a river of tears, soon shall vanish, flowing away without awaiting a world yet to come. ["Suma," 13:170]

And from Suma, ostensibly to her nursemaid Chūjō:

> *korizuma no ura no mirume mo yukashiki ni / shio yaku ama yo ikaga omowan*
> Unrepentant, here on Suma's weed-strewn shore, I yet long for our trysts;
> and you, seaside maid, how bright burns the fire in your salt kiln?
> ["Suma," 13:181]

On the Left: The lady who told the story of her dream [*Ise* 63] may at first have been the wife of some ordinary man. Later a gentleman of rank may have taken a fancy to her, and she had children. Then this, too, in the inevitable vicissitudes of life, came to an end. How about the Colonel? she wonders. But there would have been no way she could say such a thing, so she tells the story of a false dream. We see this same word [*yumegatari*] when Genji broaches the subject of Murasaki to the Prelate ["Wakamurasaki," 12:286]. It was of no consequence to the Colonel whether or not he loved her, so he came and slept with her. But, then, what was the occasion this next time?

> *momotose ni hitotose taranu tsukumogami / ware o kou rashi omokage ni miyu*
> An old grayhead, but one year short of a hundred, seems to fancy me,
> for her visage, an apparition, arises before me. [*Ise* 63]

On the Right, Genji's chance encounter with the Chief Palace Attendant, with whom he trysts for the first time at the Cherry Blossom Festival, is quite exceptional and exciting. On the Left, this lady seems to me just a bit past her prime; I am inclined, therefore, as the old song says, to "scorn the dotard's head, white as frost,"[102] and declare the Right the winner.

Round 6

Left	Ono no Komachi	Win
Right	The Third Princess	

On the Right: Because the cares that weigh on his mind grow heavier with every passing day, the Suzaku Emperor relinquishes his reign to the Crown Prince. He has two Princesses for whom his love knows no bounds and for whom he is deeply concerned what might become of them [after his death].[103] The Kashiwagi Commander of the Right Gate Guards undertakes to care for the Second Princess, as does the Lord of the Rokujō mansion [Genji] for the Third Princess. The Third Princess, in particular, is a girl whose looks were of exceptional allure. One imagines her beauty might be something on the order of all that one hears about the distinguishing marks of the Buddha. For indeed, what sort of flower could ever surpass the sight of a green willow swaying in the wind, its strands strung with drops of early morning dew? Its beauty, one feels, fairly bursts forth before one's very eyes. Though His Lordship was very deeply enamored of her, the Kashiwagi Commander of the Right Gate Guards by chance caught a glimpse of her and thereafter yearned distractedly for her. He must have persuaded her nursemaid Jijū to pass his letters to her from time to time. At the time, Lady Murasaki was ill and His Lordship was spending all his time with her. Once she is feeling a bit better, he goes to the Princess. His arrival appears to have taken her by surprise, and the clutter had not been straightened up. She hastily tucked Kashiwagi's letter under her cushion. But His Lordship found it, and what was written there clearly revealed the affair. He took it and returned home, after which he was unable to feel any genuine affection for her. And when it went so far that she bore a child, [Genji] could do nothing but lament that even he should suffer such mortification. He went several times to the birthing room, just as if it were his own child, and at the fiftieth-day celebration, he took the infant in his arms and drew near the Princess's ear:

ta ga yo ni ka tane o makishi to hito towaba / ikaga iwane no matsu wa kotaen
Should anyone ever ask him who planted the seed, and in what reign,
what should he answer, this little pine growing from the rock?
["Kashiwagi," 15:314]

The Princess collapses in a faint. When he makes similar insinuations to the Commander [Kashiwagi], he falls ill and eventually dies. When near death, he sent to Jijū:

ima wa tote moen keburi mo musubōre / taenu omoi no nao ya nokosan
Even then when the end is come and smoke rises from my burning pyre,
these unquenchable flames of yearning surely shall remain.
["Kashiwagi," 15:281]

The Princess, when she sees it:

tachisoite kie ya shinamashi uki koto o / omoikogaruru keburikurabe ni
How I wish that I too might die, that my smoke might rise together with yours;
then could we compare whose flames of sorrow burn brighter.
["Kashiwagi," 15:286]

The Princess, unable even to take proper leave of her father the Emperor, cut her hair short,[104] after which they called her the Cloistered Princess.

The lady of the Left is a great lover. Even so, none of her liaisons can compare with those of the lady of the Right, whose looks and character are quite superior. In addition, her repute in the Way of Japanese Poetry is anything but commonplace. This is an art that began in the far-off age of the gods; nonetheless, the texts of antiquity mention but one or two persons knowledgeable in both the lore of the past and the essence of poetry—and in this number they include Komachi. In other lands, too, women apparently renowned for superior looks and character are as numerous as grains of sand on a beach. Yet in the arts, though one finds painters and calligraphers, those renowned for their Chinese poetry are few. In antiquity, Izanami no Mikoto composed her "Ah, splendid!"[105] and Shitateru Hime her "Weaver Maid high in the heavens,"[106] while in more recent times Sotoori Hime wrote "movements of the spider,"[107] and Uneme her "Asakayama,"[108] all of them poems by no means shallow in feeling. The names of women who appear in the several imperial anthologies are too numerous to mention. Inclusion in the *Kokinshū*, however, would be utterly impossible without Tsurayuki's approval. As we amble through the *Kokinshū* itself, even the women included there, though their compositions are by no means undistinguished, must all yield pride of place to Komachi.

Round 7

Left	The Dame of Honor and former High Priestess of Ise	
Right	The Asagao High Priestess of Kamo	Win

On the Right: From the time she was serving as the High Priestess of Kamo, Genji persisted in importuning her, even within those sacred precincts, but she coolly pays no heed to his advances. When her father the Prince [Momozono] dies, he [Genji] inquires after her:

hito shirezu kami no yurushi o machishi ma ni / kokora tsune naki yo o sugusu kana
All the while I've been waiting, in secrecy, for sanction from your god,
many are the years of uncertainty I have endured. ["Asagao," 13:464]

Her reply:

nabete yo no aware bakari o tou kara ni / chikaishi koto wa kami ya isamemu
Were I to ask, even in the most ordinary way, how you feel,
surely my god would forbid it as a breach of my vows. ["Asagao," 13:464]

And again, Genji:

mishi ori no tsuyu wasurarenu asagao no / hana no sakari wa sugi ya shinuramu
That bluebell that once I knew and shall never, even slightly, forget:
has its beauty at the peak of bloom perhaps now faded? ["Asagao," 13:466]

Thus even though he does his utmost to persuade her, she seems to treat this gentleman with the utmost coolness. From her late father she inherits the Momozono Palace, and there she spends her days in devotional practices, so it is said.

On the Left: The Colonel goes to Ise as an emissary from the palace. Because word had come down from [her mother] the Empress that he should be received with greater consideration than the usual, she [the priestess] could not, it seems, lodge him at any great distance from her own sleeping chamber. Thus, around the first quarter of the Hour of the Rat, the woman goes to him, and they remained in intimate converse until the third quarter of the Hour of the Ox.[109] Then, at daybreak, from the woman:

kimi ya koshi ware ya yukikemu omohoezu / yume ka utsutsu ka nete ka samete ka
Was it you who came to me or did I go to you; I cannot tell;
was it a dream; was it real; was I sleeping or awake? [*Ise* 69; *Kokinshū* 645]

In reply, the Colonel:

kakikurasu kokoro no yami ni madoiniki / yume utsutsu to wa yohito sadameyo
In the pitch-black darkness of the human heart I wandered bewildered:
whether that was a dream or real, let someone else decide.[110]
[*Ise* 69; *Kokinshū* 646]

It is said that because this was forbidden by the gods as improper, the unwanted [child] was given to the Takahashi house and that even now [his descendants] are not permitted to enter the presence of the deity.[111]

On the Right: Even after relinquishing her position, this lady still retains her reverential respect, saying, "My god forbids it." On the Left: Even so, inasmuch as she is present in the actual precinct of the gods, it is hard to believe that this lady lacked such scruples. What am I to make of this? Quite baffling!

Round 8

Left	Ise	Draw
Right	The Akashi lady	

On the Left: She seems always to have been in the service of the Shichijō Empress Dowager. The Kanpyō [Uda] Emperor often looked upon her with favor, and she bore him a Prince. In the Way of Japanese Poetry, she is said to have gained considerable repute. This Way, being the very quintessence of this ancient land of ours, her accomplishment does her no little credit. Because of the work's title, some say that it was she who wrote and compiled the *Tales of Ise* and presented it to the Uda Emperor, for which reason it was so entitled. This is high praise indeed.

On the Right: Her father, the Governor of Harima, even after his term of office had ended, for whatever reasons was unable to assuage his disappointment and remained behind, devoting himself to observances for the next life; yet he had a daughter. So lovingly and carefully had he raised her that even in the capital many had heard of her and yearned secretly that somehow they might have her for their own. But he had counseled her that even if he himself should end his days there on the seashore, she, rather than accept some ordinary husband, should instead throw herself into the sea. And then he hears of Genji being sent to Suma, which makes him hope that by some means he might entice him to move to his own shore. He could well imagine what would have befallen the traveler's lodging place in the recent tidal wave, so he set out in a small boat to fetch him away. Genji, no doubt seeing in this the fulfillment of the portent of his dream, moves down the coast. The Novice does his utmost to make the dwelling, in keeping with its surroundings, a place of great beauty. In dreary hours, when time hangs heavy on his [Genji's] hands, the strains of his koto would make those moments only the more poignant. On one occasion, the Novice comes and plays beautifully one or two pieces on his lute. Then, pressing Genji to play the koto, he at long last hints at the subject of his daughter, remarking awkwardly that in her hands the music of this instrument has the power to calm his troubled mind. Before long, a letter arrives at the daughter's place:

ochikochi o shiranu kumoi o nagamewabi / kasumuru yado no kozue o zo tou

Gazing, downcast, at the skies, I know not whether it be near or far;
I ask of the misted treetops, where lies that lodging he hinted at?
["Akashi," 13:238]

No doubt because this was so sudden, she seemed loath to reply, so the Novice, in her stead:

nagamuran onaji kumoi o nagamuru wa / omoi mo onaji omoi naruran

To one who is gazing at those same skies that you must be gazing at,
her feelings must be those same feelings that you now feel.
["Akashi," 13:238]

And again, Genji:

ibuseku mo kokoro ni mono o nayamu kana / yayo ya ikani to tou hito mo nami

How I suffer from it, this nagging doubt that I harbor in my heart,
for I've no one to ask of me, "I say, now, how are you?" ["Akashi," 13:239]

Told, "Well this time . . . ," the daughter herself replies:

> *omouran kokoro no hodo yo yayo ikani / mada minu hito o kiki ka nayamamu*
> I say now, then, what sort of feelings might these be that you seem to feel?
> Do you suffer having heard of someone you've never known?
> ["Akashi," 13:239]

Fearing a tidal wave, he [the Novice] seems to have moved his daughter away to a house by the hill. Then Genji comes, and when he plays the koto, his thoughts more likely turn to her than to people in the capital. In the Eighth Month of the following year, he is summoned to return. The lady was in a delicate condition, and seeing him this last time was deeply painful to her. As a keepsake, he asks her to play for him and, leaving behind his own koto:

> *naozari ni tanomeokikeru hitokoto o / tsuki senu oto ni ya kakete shinoban*
> This halfhearted promise, this koto that you leave me; to its music,
> blended with my ceaseless weeping, shall I entrust my hopes.
> ["Akashi," 13:239]

She gives birth in Akashi, and he sends a nursemaid to rear the child. Later she moves to the capital, and Murasaki raises her child, who is betrothed to the Crown Prince and becomes the mother of the nation. Glorious indeed was her lot in life!

Of this pair, I cannot decide who is the lovelier. The Right is described as a lady far from commonplace, who can depend on her child to rise to the heights and prosper throughout her life. The Left, too, is a lady of no mean talent. Attracted as one is to those of such high repute, these two seem to me equals; and thus, perhaps, this round must be deemed a draw.

Round 9

Left	The elder sister of the daughter of Aritsune	Win
Right	The Utsusemi lady	

The lady of the Left: I have tried to trace where she fits into the *Tales* as a whole. In the first section, she appears fleetingly, and farther on it says, "There were two sisters. One of them had a husband of mean station who was poor, and the other a husband of high rank" [*Ise* 41]. Then it seems to say that "the one who had the husband of mean station, at the end of the Twelfth Month, washes his overcloak." This must be an old expression meaning something like when we [now] say, "I wash myself," "I wash my clothes," or whatever. The substance of this section seems to me rather shallow, does it not? It sounds as if they considered a woman's caring for her husband as something noble, so I suppose this is just a case of ideas current at the time being reflected in the words of an old text. The "robe of green" would indicate the sixth rank. This may be why they call him a man of mean station.

murasaki no iro koki toki wa me mo haru ni / no naru kusaki zo wakarezarikeru
When the purple color of affinity is deep, the plants on the moor,
as far as the eye can see, are all as one to me.[112] [*Ise* 41; *Kokinshū* 868]

On the Right: Utsusemi lived near the Nakagawa, and [Genji's visits there, ostensibly to avoid] directional taboos are not without ulterior motives. He seems to claim the coolness of the garden stream as his pretext. When he arrived, guided by Kogimi, he was lodged very close to the women's bedchamber. So he peered in, and there she was playing go with her stepdaughter. When they were finished and the girl crooked her fingers counting the score, "ten, thirty," and so on, her hostess laughed and asked, "Are you counting all the bathtubs in Iyo?" This woman is always very restrained and prone to caution. "Let yourself go, just once," I feel like telling her. And that's the story.

When the girl called Ōmi no Kimi, or something, was playing backgammon, she must have thought she was going to lose, so she picked up the dice, lightly rubbed them together, raised her face and prayed, her tongue flying at frightful rate, "Make it low! Make it low!" This so embarrassed her father the Minister, who was watching from a place of concealment, that he exclaimed, "Horrid!" snapped his fingers in disgust, and fled. That's reasonable enough, isn't it?

Anyhow, that night Utsusemi must have slipped out, and since only the stepdaughter [Nokiba no Ogi] remained behind, he unwittingly slept with her. Genji:

honoka ni mo nokiba no ogi no musubazuba / tsuyu no kagoto o nani ni kakemashi
Had I never, even briefly, tied a knot with that reed 'neath the eaves
what excuse would I have to voice my dewdrop of complaint?
["Yūgao," 12:264]

The daughter:

honomekasu kaze ni tsuketemo shitaogi no / nakaba wa shimo ni musubōretsutsu
Even this faint whisper of wind touches the lowly leaves of this reed
as with frost, leaving it but little less chilled than before.
["Yūgao," 12:265]

He takes the gown [that Utsusemi] slipped off and left behind and, in the morning, when he returns home, sends it back to her:

utsusemi no mi o kaetekeru ko no moto ni / nao hitogara no natsukashiki kana
Here beneath the tree where the cicada has shed its shell for another,
I yet go on longing for her as she was before. ["Utsusemi," 12:203]

In reply:

utsusemi no ha ni oku tsuyu no kogakurete / shinobi shinobi ni nururu sode kana
As when dew forms on the cicada's wings, hidden within the tree,
secretly, ever so secretly, are my sleeves dampened.[113] ["Utsusemi," 12:205]

After [her husband] Iyo no Suke dies, [Genji] takes her in and places her among his many other attendants ["Hatsune," 14:149–51].

She of the Right, although apparently spoken of as fickle, is not the sort of person who deserved to be married to someone like Iyo no Suke. But her parents are gone and she has lost all means of support, so this was the life to which she is doomed. And he [Genji] being no ordinary person, she would have found it difficult to raise her voice and call out when he burst in on her so unexpectedly. On the Left, given as I am to understand that this is a lady of incomparable virtue, I award to her the character "Win."

Round 10

Left	The daughter of the Middle Counselor	
Right	The Yūgao lady	Win

On the Right: In the story the First Secretary Colonel tells on that rainy night ["Hahakigi," 12:157–60], he was seeing a certain woman to the exclusion of all others, and she even bore him a child. They are exceptionally attached to each other, but then he hears that his wife has said some nasty things to her. Of her own accord, she steals away and goes into hiding, and he has no idea where she has gone. The name she gave the child, he tells them, is "the pink." Thinking that perhaps it might find its way to him, she wrote this poem and left it behind:

yamagatsu no kakiho arutomo oriori wa / aware o kakeyo nadeshiko no tsuyu
Ruined the hedge about this mountain hut may be; yet from time to time,
pray let the dew of your kindness touch the pink that grows there. ["Hahakigi," 12:158]

When the Consort of the late Crown Prince was living in the vicinity of Rokujō, Genji visits her in the greatest secrecy. His old nursemaid, Daini no Menoto, is ill. Her home is in Gojō, and, not without ulterior motives, he decides to pay her a visit. As he departs, he summons one of his men and commands him to pick one of the white flowers blooming in profusion by a small house behind a board fence of some sort. "What flower is that?" Koremitsu asks, and from inside [the house] someone says, "It is called an evening face. Its stems are rather pitiful, but present it to him on this." She held out a fan. He takes it and sees written on it:

kokoroate ni sore ka to zo miru shiratsuyu no / ikari soetaru yūgao no hana
It seems, I would venture, that you might just be he, the glistening dew
come to shed your light on the face of the moonflower. ["Yūgao," 12:214]

In reply:

yorite koso sore ka to mo mime tasogare ni / honobono mieshi hana no yūgao
Come a bit closer then, won't you, and see for yourself who it might be,
evening face flower, whom I glimpsed but faintly in the dusk.
["Yūgao," 12:215]

He halts his carriage and has Koremitsu ask the name of the master of the house. It is the home of Yōmei no Suke, he tells him; they said he is away in the country. And so [Genji] stays that evening. This would have been the night of the fifteenth of the Eighth Month. From neighboring houses comes the noise of something called a treadle mortar, and then the sounds of someone performing austerities preparatory to a pilgrimage to Mitake, chanting all the while, "Hail to him who shall lead us in lives to come!" [Genji's] ears are offended in the extreme. This place will be most unpleasant, he thinks, and in a single carriage, he escorts her to a certain estate. When he says that he has never experienced anything like this, she replies:

yama no ha no kokoro mo shirade yuku tsuki wa / uwa no sora nite kage ya kienan
All unknowing how the mountain feels, might the moon that moves toward it,
in its apprehension, disappear from the skies above? ["Yūgao," 12:215]

The place is an utter ruin. Owls shriek in the trees. The rampant chrysanthemums have the look of a lair of foxes. Late at night, a tree spirit or something comes and possesses the girl. Genji is aghast and dazed. He draws his sword and tries to find it, but it is nowhere to be seen. The lamps, too, had burned low, and there was only the sound of footsteps. He called for Koremitsu, but his words were in vain. When the lamps were lit again, there was only her dead body, and naught was there he could do. Later he was chagrined to learn that this was the place where the Uda Emperor [867–931; r. 887–897] is said to have brought one of his consorts, and that this same sort of thing happened while he was disporting himself with her.[114] In a single carriage, he takes her to a place just opposite Higashiyama Rokudō,[115] and when she rose in smoke from the pyre, he feels as if he were dreaming. Returning to his home:

mishi hito no kemuri o kumo to nagamureba / yūbe no sora mo natsukashiki kana
Gazing at these clouds, thinking them to be smoke from the pyre of my love,
the sky, even of an evening like this, seems dear to me. ["Yūgao," 12:262]

Her nursemaid, a woman called Ukon, Genji takes into his service as a reminder of her.

As for the lady on the Left: Long ago, in the [Ariwara] clan, a Prince was born. At the grandfather's, the Colonel:

waga kado ni chihiro aru kage o uetsureba / natsu fuyu tare ka kakurezarubeki
Now that within our gates is planted this tree whose shade shall be so vast,
be it summer or winter, who shall not find shelter here? [*Ise* 79]

For the Ariwara, descended from Princes, yet in so few generations having fallen so low, gloom had become a way of life. Taking his brothers to see the Nunohiki Waterfall, the Commander of Guards [Narihira]:

waga yo oba kyō ka asu ka to matsu kai no / namida no taki to izure takakemu
These tears I shed, hoping my day might come, whether today or tomorrow:
which is higher, the stream they form or this waterfall? [*Ise* 79]

And their host [Yukihira]:

nukimidaru hito koso arurashi shiratama no / ma nakumo chiru ka sode no sebaki ni
Someone would seem to have undone them, for these pearls, these tears of mine,
scatter ceaselessly, though my sleeves be too small to catch them. [*Ise* 79]

To those in straits they find as lamentable as this, the birth of a Prince must open up a truly bright and promising future.

What, then, of Left versus Right? The lady of the Right enjoys an unequaled reputation for the cheerful charm of her disposition. And the Left is famous for the way she seems to have risen to the occasion, for this [child] was Prince Sadakazu,[116] and it is clear that people of the time said he was the son of the Colonel [Narihira]. Yet one is reluctant to set at naught the writings of those of the past, so I cannot but declare the Right to be the winner.

Round 11

Left	The Somedono Palace Attendant	Draw
Right	The Yomogiu lady	

On the Right: Faithful to her father's dying wishes, she lives on in the old palace. Genji becomes fond of her and begins writing to her. Her looks and such, he is told, are not those of an ordinary person, though there does seem to be something a bit backward about her. She seems unable to adjust to anything out of the ordinary, such as his [Genji's] banishment to Harima or the [dwindling] number of her attendants, which may well be why he looks down on her, both her character and her person, and only very rarely comes to call on her. Even after his return, neither is able to make immediate contact with the other. Her palace is rank with wormwood and weeds, the galleries leaking and rotting from exposure, while the Princess continues to inhabit this corner and that of what remains. She seems unwilling to part with any of her father's treasures, a veritable mountain of which he had accumulated, all of them now rotting away. Her servants, too, one by one drift away, and only one or two of those who were closest to her remain. When even Jijū, who was like a nursemaid to her, is offered a place with the man who was to go down to Kyushu as the Assistant Viceroy, the lady:

> *tayumajiki suji to tanomishi tamakatsura / omoi no hoka ni kakehanarenuru*
> Never would they part, I had always trusted, these long glistening strands, when to my surprise they depart, for someplace far away. ["Yomogiu," 13:331]

Jijū replies:

tamakatsura taete wa yamaji yuku michi no / tamuke no kami mo kakete chikawan
Part they may, these long glistening strands, but never shall there be an end;
that I swear by the gods of all the roads I shall travel. ["Yomogiu," 13:332]

In another year, when Genji recalled their relationship and paid her a visit, groping his way through the murky forest of wormwood:

tazunetemo ware koso towame michi mo naku / fukaki yomogi ga moto no kokoro o
Though I search her out, still I must see for myself if her feelings remain
as they were before, in this trackless waste of wormwood. ["Yomogiu," 13:338]

It distresses him to see how she is living, as does also his own failure to visit her of late. He summons people from his estates, makes all the necessary repairs, and restores the place to its past glories before her very eyes. He also summons a number of people, high, middling, and low in rank, and places them in her service. Later he moves her to his Rokujō mansion,[117] where he treates her with particular care, so they say.

On the Left: She was reputed to be a woman of great distinction, and the Colonel's affair with her was by no means a casual one. They had a child together; but life in this world being what it is, they grew apart, and then he hears that another man is seeing her.

aki no yo wa haruhi wasururu mono nare ya / kasumi ni kiri ya chie masaruran
On this autumn evening, are those days of springtime something you forget?
Is autumn mist better by a thousand times than spring haze? [*Ise* 94]

The woman's reply:

chiji no aki hitotsu no haru ni mukawame ya / momiji mo hana mo tomo ni koso chire
How could thousands upon thousands of autumns compare with one spring day?
Even so, both crimson leaves and blossoms flutter and fall. [*Ise* 94]

Of this pair, which am I to decide is the one? On the Right, her devotion, never ceasing to see him while she lived in that house in the wormwood, I find touching and noble. The Left, too, is a woman of exceptional charm, who exhibits no shortcomings, and thus can in no way be faulted. This is a draw.

Round 12

Left	The Hatsukusa lady	Draw
Right	The Tamakazura Palace Attendant	

On the Left: Seeing how beautiful his younger sister is:

urawakami neyoge ni miyuru wakakusa o / hito no musuban koto o shi zo omou
This young sprout, looking so fresh and youthful, so inviting to sleep with,
I fear may be bound in attachment to another man.

The girl's reply:

hatsukusa no nado mezurashiki koto no ha zo / ura naku mono o omoikeru kana
Why ever should you say such strange things to me, to this first sprout of spring,
when in all innocence, my thoughts have been only for you? [*Ise* 49]

I expect there are those who have made love to a woman with words of this sort. In addition, relations between brother and sister seem not to be all that unusual; such a thing may well have happened. It appears, though, that he was deeply enamored of his sister, does it not? In a later section, a man named Fujiwara no Toshiyuki was courting a woman. Because she was still young, she was unskilled at letter writing; and not even knowing how to write prose, she could hardly compose poems. And so, it says, the man of the house wrote out a draft for her. [Her suitor writes]:

tsurezure no nagame ni masaru namidakawa / sode nomi hijite au yoshi mo nashi
In the long rains of my languor, this river of tears goes on rising;
my sleeves are soaked through, for no way is there that we can meet.

The reply, composed by the man [Toshiyuki] on the woman's behalf:

asami koso sode wa hitsurame namidakawa / mi sae nagaru to kikaba tanomamu
So shallow this river of tears that surely only your sleeves are soaked;
when I hear that you are washed away, then shall I trust you. [*Ise* 107]

The Palace Attendant on the Right, when she is very young, travels to a faraway place in the company of her nursemaid and there vanishes from sight. As time passes and she grows to adulthood, many men yearn to have her for their own. Her nursemaid is always saying that she will never let the girl end up sunk in such a shocking situation, that she must somehow get her back to the capital and entrust her to the care of her father the Minister, but then she [the nursemaid] dies. It is her daughter who, in compliance with her [mother's] wish, takes the girl back to the capital. As they passed Thunder Bay:

uki koto no mune nomi sawagu hibiki ni wa / hibiki no nada mo sawarazarikeri
What with the thunderous tumult these miseries arouse in my breast;
Thunder Bay and its pirates hardly trouble me at all. ["Tamakazura," 14:95]

Even in the capital, they know of no particular person to whom they can turn for help, so first of all, they make a pilgrimage to Hatsuse, where they pray that she might be reunited with her father. Whereupon Ukon, who happens to be there on a pilgrimage herself, guides them back, and she is placed in Genji's care. Says Ukon:

futamoto no sugi no tachido o tazunezu wa / furukawa nobe ni kimi o mimashi ya
Had I never come and sought out this place where the twin cedars stand,
would I ever have encountered you here by this Old River? ["Tamakazura," 14:110]

Genji assiduously teaches her the koto and the *biwa* and suchlike. To [Kashiwagi], the girl's elder brother, he hints that he has acquired a lovely daughter. At some point, the brother becomes interested in her. He recites:

omoutomo kimi wa shiraji na wakikaeri / iwa moru mizu no iro shi mieneba
Long though I may, I expect you are unaware of it, for waters
that well from the rocky spring have no color to be seen. ["Kochō," 14:169]

Later he talks to her about this, and she is amused.[118] Genji, too, from time to time hints at his own interest in her, but she ignores him, pretending she does not understand.

omoikane mukashi no ato o tazunuredo / oya ni somukeru ko zo tagui naki
Overcome with longing, I have searched through the records of the past, yet
nowhere do I find a child so heedless of her father. ["Hotaru," 14:206]

The woman's reply:

furuki ato tazunuredo ge ni nakarikeri / kono yo ni kakaru oya no kokoro wa
Search the annals of antiquity though you may, indeed there are none:
no parents in all the world who harbor such thoughts as this. ["Hotaru," 14:206]

This much there was, but I somehow doubt that after such a cold response, he would have gone all the way. But I just don't know![119] She becomes the wife of Commandant Higekuro, bears him several children, and prospers immensely.

In regard to this pair: Coming back to the Left, even though this is phrased in amorous terms, there is no evidence to suggest that she gives in, at least to her real elder brother. Nor is it at all illogical that this should be so. As for the Right, since obviously she is not his real daughter, even if she were to acquiesce, it would by no means be a sin. Thus I deem them evenly matched, indeed a perfect draw.

Contestants of the Left

The Empress Mother of the Fifth Ward, daughter of Chūjinkō Yoshifusa[120]
The Grand Empress Mother of the Second Ward, daughter of the Chancellor (appointed posthumously) Lord Nagara (802–856), her mother the daughter of Fusatsugu
The daughter of Aritsune, her mother the daughter of Yoshikado
The lady who died of love, daughter of the Third Ward Minister of the Left, Lord Yoshimi (813–867)
The lady who told of her dream, daughter of the Commander of the Right Palace Guards, Ki no Natora
Ono no Komachi, daughter of the Dewa District Magistrate, Ono no Tsunetaka
The Dame of Honor and former High Priestess of Ise, honored daughter of the Montoku Emperor
Ise, daughter of the Governor of Ise, Tsugikage
The elder sister of the daughter of Aritsune
The daughter of the Middle Counselor, her mother the daughter of Natora
The Somedono Palace Attendant, daughter of Yoshimi
The Hatsukusa lady, daughter of Prince Abo, honored granddaughter of the Nara Emperor

Contestants of the Right

The Kiritsubo Mistress of the Wardrobe, daughter of a Grand Counselor
The Usugumo Empress Mother, honored daughter of a previous Emperor

Lady Murasaki, daughter of the Prince Minister of Ceremonial
Lady Aoi, daughter of his [Genji's] sponsoring Minister
The Oborozukiyo Chief Palace Attendant, honored younger sister of Kokiden
The Third Princess, honored daughter of the Suzaku Retired Emperor
The Asagao High Priestess of Kamo, daughter of the Prince Minister of Ceremonial
The Akashi lady, daughter of the former Governor of Harima
The Utsusemi lady, daughter of a Middle Counselor
The Yūgao lady, daughter of a Colonel, Third Rank
The Yomogiu lady, daughter of Prince Hitachi
The Tamakazura Palace Attendant, daughter of the Retired Chancellor

THE FOREGOING COPIED FROM THE AUTHORITATIVE TEXT IN THE HAND OF LORD YANAGIWARA SUKESADA (1495–1578)
TRANSLATED BY T. HARPER

THE NURSEMAID'S LETTER, CA. 1264
(*Menoto no fumi*)

ABUTSU

The nun Abutsu (d. 1283) was known for her accomplishments as a *waka* poet and her travel record, *The Diary of the Sixteenth-Night Moon* (*Izayoi nikki*, ca. 1283). During her lifetime, she was renowned as a teacher of poetry and an expert on *The Tale of Genji*. Works from the medieval period to the 1930s hail Abutsu as the founder of the Reizei line of the Mikohidari literary house and praise her as a paragon of motherly virtue. At the opposite end of the spectrum, Abutsu's rival poets in the medieval period, as well as some modern scholars, portray her as a conniving widow who mined the literary fortunes of her husband, Fujiwara Tameie (1198–1275), heir to the Mikohidari lineage of Shunzei (1114–1204) and Teika (1162–1241). Allies and rivals alike, however, recognized Abutsu as one of the leading *Genji* experts of her time, who sparred with the likes of Minamoto no Chikayuki (fl. ca. 1265) and his younger brother Sojaku (fl. ca. 1294), and whose reading of the tale left an indelible impression on the young Asukai Masaari (1241–1301).

Masaari's diary, *Visits to Saga* (*Saga no kayoi*, 1269), describes an encounter with Abutsu during the Ninth Month of Bun'ei 6 (1269), when Tameie was tutoring him in reading *Genji*. He noted: "On the seventeenth day, I went [to see Tameie] in the afternoon. We began *Genji*, and the mistress of the house was called to act as the reader.[121] She read from behind her blinds. It was truly fascinating and differed from others' ways of reading.[122] She appeared to follow a particular tradition."[123] Masaari's comments demonstrate the respect that Abutsu had garnered from her peers as a scholar and teacher of *Genji* and the pride that she placed in the Mikohidari lineage.

The *Genji* commentary *Shimeishō* (ca. 1294) notes an altercation between Abutsu and its author, Sojaku, concerning the interpretation of a section of the "Yūgao" chapter. After hearing that Abutsu had criticized his brother Chikayuki's reading as mistaken, Sojaku went to her residence to debate this. The *Shimeishō* ardently defends Chikayuki's views against Abutsu's and argues that such interpretive discrepancies arose from Abutsu's not possessing an authoritative copy of *Genji* transcribed by the "daughter of Shunzei." While there are few extant sources documenting Abutsu's interpretations of *Genji*, her writings draw heavily from the work, and her recorded advice shows that a successful court lady was expected to have a scholarly understanding of the text.

Abutsu was also known by the appellation Ankamon'in no Shijō, and most of her forty-eight poems in imperial anthologies appear under this name. At fifteen, like her sisters, she entered the court of Ankamon'in, a salon that fostered various other successful female poets. Study of *The Tale of Genji* was an important aspect of Abutsu's education, and her mastery of the work is what brought her to the attention of her future husband, Tameie, who commissioned her to produce a copy of the tale for his daughter. Abutsu's memoir *Fitful Slumbers* (*Utatane*, ca. 1265)[124] weaves numerous references to *Genji* into its depiction of a failed love affair, reclusion, and tonsure, events thought to have taken place soon after she became an attendant to Ankamon'in. One of the reasons she may have closely imitated the tale in her memoir was to prove her capabilities as a *Genji* expert to Tameie as their relationship progressed.

Abutsu's marriage to Tameie provided her with a vast repository of literary sources that had been passed down in the Mikohidari family, from Tameie's grandfather Shunzei and father, Teika. During the ten years leading up to Tameie's death in 1275, Abutsu secured for her children important literary manuscripts and a landed estate, all of which became objects of legal disputes, as described in *The Diary of the Sixteenth-Night Moon*. Tameie moved with Abutsu to the Saga region of Kyoto, where they lived close to Mount Ogura in a villa he had inherited from his father.

Around 1264, Abutsu produced *The Nursemaid's Letter*, a work that became the most widely circulated didactic text among women of the medieval period.[125] It was originally designed as a lengthy response to a letter from her daughter Ki no Naishi (b. ca. 1251), who had entered the court service of Retired Emperor GoFukakusa (1243–1304; r. 1246–1259) at the age of six and who was approximately thirteen years old when the text was sent to her. Abutsu had probably just moved to Saga to reside with Tameie, which made it more difficult to see her daughter, born of a previous marriage while Abutsu lived in Matsuo. Concerned about her daughter's future at court, Abutsu drew from her own experience serving Ankamon'in to produce a letter of advice for success as an attendant. The advice must have proved useful, for it was later abridged and circulated as a didactic manual for women, *Teachings of the Courtyard* (*Niwa no oshie*), a forerunner of the women's educational texts that became popular during the early modern period. The content of *The Nursemaid's Letter* describes the necessary skills, practices, and comportment needed for a woman serving at court, including how to interact well with all levels of courtiers, appropriate musical and literary arts to learn, and the merits of Buddhist practice.

The title of the work, which was likely provided by a later reader, implies that Abutsu was Ki no Naishi's wet nurse (*menoto*) rather than her birth mother. In the letter, Abutsu intentionally distances herself, as both a gesture of humility and a means of supporting her daughter's position at Emperor GoFukakusa's court. With her stepfather Tameie's support, Ki no Naishi had the opportunity to rise within the ranks, and later she indeed gave birth to a child of the retired emperor.

The letter that Abutsu composed for her daughter had greater influence than she likely anticipated. The handbooks for women that followed, such as *The Nursemaid's Book* (*Menoto no sōshi*, late fourteenth century), drew heavily from *The Nursemaid's Letter* in title and content. Even Lady Nijō, author of *The Unrequested Tale* (*Towazugatari*, ca. 1306), appears to have heeded Abutsu's advice.[126]

The following sections show that for a woman to have a successful career at court, she needed a reading knowledge and an ample understanding of *Genji*, which meant not only memorizing the work but also being able to analyze it in a scholarly manner with the aid of various textual guides.[127] The extant sources that refer to Abutsu's expertise, and the advice she provides to Ki no Naishi in *The Nursemaid's Letter*, suggest a network of *Genji* transmission among women serving in imperial salons during the Kamakura period and a tradition of interpretation and debate that was at least somewhat open to women's participation.

CHRISTINA LAFFIN

As in trying to part the reeds at the Bay of Naniwa, until you are able to discern the good from the bad in all things, you will endure various hardships. I have thought to protect you faithfully, but now we must lead lives apart,[128] and I constantly lament this fate.[129] When I read your letter, I was particularly moved to see that you asked about "teachings." It pains me to think that you must, no doubt, be concerned about such things. Recently, others no longer even think of me, and I receive no news from the capital bird, so I envy the waves that are certain to return, and [I] resent the name of Yatsuhashi, with its spider-legged bridges, forever pulled in all directions, like my thoughts.[130] Among the feelings that prevent me from departing, I feel sadder still when I dwell on the despair that you must surely feel.

Most people do not begin to comprehend things properly until after [they reach] thirty. While in their twenties, their views are even less settled. As someone who has not yet reached twenty, even though you may feel troubled, you appear more mature than people several years older than you. Accordingly, I have set down all [my instructions] in detail, with hopes that you will understand everything and have various opportunities to examine them.

Even though it may be difficult to follow in the footsteps of Hitomaro and Akahito, or Murasaki Shikibu—who gazed at the reflection of the moon on the waves at Ishiyama Temple and composed *The Tale of Genji* through to the meeting of Ukifune with the Master of the Law[131]—rather than feeling melancholy and discouraged, concentrate on the hue of the moon and the scent of the flowers, and gather your thoughts and write poems.

Nothing is more unfortunate than failing to memorize *Genji* and other important tales. In particular, consider the texts that I have copied and gathered for you to be a memento of me and read them carefully. In the case of *Genji*, make sure that you can discuss even the guides to difficult passages and the various catalogs. Read [them] thoroughly so that all is clear and nothing is left uncertain. To help you do so, I will leave handbooks on the difficult passages [*nangi*] and catalogs [*mokuroku*] in a wooden chest for you.[132]

You should be able to recite by heart all of the upper and lower hemistichs of poems from the *Kokinshū* and *Shinkokinshū*. It would truly be regrettable to think that you were memorizing the poems and yet, despite my urgent request, were finding it tedious and failed to apply yourself.

What I have written down may be clumsy and my thoughts scattered. Though it may seem unsightly, I have written this in response to your strong wish and the uncertainty of life after I depart. Perhaps you can think of this as the beginning of my farewell. As I set off toward an unknown realm, remember my words, even though I may have let my brush flow foolishly and said I know not what, feeling as though I were drowning in bitter tears. I have left out much and have included many awkward things. Even so, I hope you will feel sympathy for me each time you read this.

Although I believe I have produced only useless words, even among the grains of sands there is sure to be a jewel swaying in the waves. If anything in this letter should catch your attention, then it will surely serve you well.

With great respect for Ki no Naishi from someone dwelling beneath the clouds.

TRANSLATED BY CHRISTINA LAFFIN

Notes

1. Gabriel Josipovici, "The Magician's Doubts: Nabokov and the Risks of Fiction," *Times Literary Supplement*, August 26, 1994.

2. Fujii Sadakazu, "Kodai-chūsei dokusha ron," *Kokubungaku: Kaishaku to kanshō* 45, no. 10 (1980): 49.

3. Josipovici, "Magician's Doubts."

4. Translated from *Mumyōzōshi*, ed. Kuboki Tetsuo, SNKBZ 40; and *Mumyōzōshi*, ed. Kuwabara Hiroshi, SNKS.

5. For a complete translation, see Michele Marra, "*Mumyōzōshi*: Introduction and Translation," *Monumenta Nipponica* 39, no. 2 (1984): 115–46; 39, no. 3 (1984): 281–306; 39, no. 4 (1984): 409–34. Readers are warned, however, that this translation contains many errors and should be used only with great caution.

6. Opinion is divided whether the old woman is saying that she is in her eighty-third year at the present moment in the narrative or that she was eighty-three when she entered religious orders. This translation follows the former interpretation, but the verb inflections are indefinite, and the ambiguity cannot be resolved grammatically.

7. *Mumyōzōshi* has more than its share of the problems that plague so many texts of this vintage, in which the dialogue is unmarked and the speakers are only rarely identified. Although the text consists almost entirely of dialogue, only two of the seven or eight speakers, the old woman and the youngest girl, are ever identified. Since no two editors punctuate the text in the same way, the translator is often forced to decide unilaterally where one speech ends and another begins and is almost never able to say who the speaker might be. This problem becomes worse in the latter part of the discussion of *Genji*, when the narrative becomes less a conversation than a series of lists that seem to foreshadow the lists translated in the next section of this chapter.

8. This and all subsequent section titles for which no Japanese equivalents are given do not appear in the original text but have been added by the editors of the texts consulted. They are retained in the translation as an aid to readers. Those titles for which Japanese equivalents are given are, of course, listed in this text.

9. The so-called ten Tamakazura chapters.

10. An alternative title for "Ukifune."

11. *Ika naru kata ni otsuru namida ni ka*. Extant texts of *Genji* read: *Sari ya. Izure ni otsuru ni ka* ("Suma," 13:190).

12. The quotation from "Hahakigi" is nowhere to be found in extant texts of *Genji*, and ambiguities in the sentence in which it is embedded further complicate the problems of this passage. This translation follows the version suggested by Kuwabara, which reads "'Hahakigi' *ni iu, 'Nani tote uchitokezarikeri'*" (*Mumyōzōshi*, 29), rather than "'Hahakigi' *to iu na nite . . .* ," and takes *miete* to be unvoiced and affirmative, rather than voiced and therefore negative.

13. "Yomogiu," 13:323. Suetsumuhana is invited to join the household of the newly appointed deputy viceroy of Dazaifu and to move with them to his post in Kyushu. It is not the deputy himself who issues the invitation, however, but his wife, an aunt of Suetsumuhana who has married beneath her station.

14. "Hotaru," 14:206. This scene is translated in chapter 1 of this volume. Commentators interpret *Mumyōzōshi*'s criticism of Tamakazura as follows: Genji once loved Tamakazura's mother, Yūgao, and it is Tamakazura's resemblance to her mother that now arouses Genji's untoward amorous urges. For the daughter to rebuff his advances, inspired as they are by her own mother, is rude.

15. "Yadorigi," 16:424. When Niou returns home, he detects Kaoru's scent in the room and berates Nakanokimi for what he assumes to be her infidelity:

mata hito ni narekeru sode no utsurika o / waga mi ni shimete uramitsuru kana

This scent on your sleeve, so intimate has it become with someone else,
pierces my very being, arouses me to anger.

Nakanokimi replies:

minarenuru naka no koromo to tanomishi o / kabakari nite ya kakehanarenan
This robe, this intimacy we share, in which I have placed all my trust:
is it to be cast aside for such a trifle as this?

16. "Wakana, ge," 15:239. The passage in question describes one of Genji's infrequent visits to the Third Princess. After staying for two or three days, he announces his impending departure with the words, "Well, before the way grows hard to find . . . ," an allusion to the poem (*Man'yōshū* 709 and/or *Kokin rokujō* 371):

yūyami wa michi tadotadoshi tsuki machite / kaere waga seko sono ma ni mo mimu
In the dusk the way will be hard to find, so await the moon, my love,
before you return; and in the meantime let us make love.

The Third Princess recognizes the poem he alludes to and reminds him that it ends with the lady urging the man not to leave but to linger. From this, Genji draws his own conclusions as to what she wishes to do "in the meantime." The princess then follows up her allusion with a poem describing her own hurt feelings:

yūtsuyu ni sode nurase to ya higurashi no / naku o kiku kiku okite yukuramu
"Soak your sleeves with evening dew," do you tell me, as at day's end you rise
to leave, listening all the while to the shrilling cicadas?

Genji takes this at face value and decides to stay the night. The next morning, while searching for his fan, he discovers the incriminating letter from Kashiwagi that the princess had slipped carelessly under her cushion.

17. The death of her lover Kashiwagi.

18. So nicknamed for his poem quoted in the text.

19. Tō no Chūjō describes him in similar terms in "Fuji no uraba," 14:428.

20. "Fuji no uraba," 14:430, the scene in which Tō no Chūjō finally offers his daughter Kumoinokari to Yūgiri, chanting the phrase "new wisteria leaves" in an allusion to *Goshūishū* 100:

haru hi sasu fuji no uraba no uratokete / kimi shi omowaba ware mo omowamu
These new leaves of wisteria, bathed in spring sunlight, now yield to you;
if you will but love me, then shall I place my trust in you.

21. After a poem he sends to Tamakazura in "Kochō," 14:169:

omoutomo kimi wa shiraji na wakikaeri / iwa moru mizu ni iro ni mieneba
Long though I may, you are not likely aware of it, for the waters
that well from the rocky spring have no color to be seen.

22. "Fuji no uraba," 14:430. When Tō no Chūjō, feigning drunkenness, finally signals his approval of the union between Yūgiri and his daughter Kumoinokari, it falls to Kashiwagi to handle the logistics of getting the two into the same room, which, given Yūgiri's somewhat dull "earnestness," requires a good bit of "quick wit" on Kashiwagi's part.

23. A bat that has no opportunity to compare itself with birds is apt to think itself a superior creature.

24. Most commentators assume that both Sumori no Nakanokimi (the younger Sumori lady) and Sumori no Kimi (the "Sumori" lady) mentioned here refer to the younger daughter of Hachi no Miya and that she is so called for her poem, written as a child and addressed to her widowed father ("Hashihime," 16:115):

> *naku naku mo hane uchiki suru kimi nakuba / ware zo sumori ni narubekarikeru*
>
> Were it not for you, sheltering us under your wings, weeping all the while,
> I should surely have been left in the nest, the unhatched egg.

The same commentators also note, however, that the opinions of Niou and Kaoru that this lady is reported to hold seem to contradict each other. This translation, therefore, follows an interpretation suggested by Inaga Keiji, in which he takes "Sumori no Nakanokimi" and "Sumori no Kimi" as references not to a single person but to two separate persons, the daughters of Hotaru Hyōbukyō no Miya who are courted by both Niou and Kaoru in the no longer extant chapter "Sumori." We know from the "old *Genji* genealogies" (translated in chapter 5 of this volume) that Sumori no Nakanokimi is having an affair with Niou and that as soon as he drops her, she takes up with his brother, the Second Prince. We know, too, that her elder sister, Sumori no Sanmi, much prefers Kaoru to Niou. Inaga's reading assumes, of course, that the *Genji* text in the possession of the *Mumyōzōshi* author included "Sumori" and that she regarded this chapter as authentic. But his interpretation also resolves all the incongruities and provides good reason for describing Ukifune and Sumori no Nakanokimi as "horrid" and "lustful." The phrase "Niou the cherry and Kaoru the plum" is not found in extant texts of *Genji* but may have been used in "Sumori." See Inaga Keiji, *Genji monogatari no kenkyū: seiritsu to denryū* (Tokyo: Kasama Shoin, 1967), 486–88.

25. This "quotation" from *Genji* agrees only patchily with texts based on the Aobyōshi-bon. It is closer to, but still not identical with, the Kawachi-bon texts. The two lines of texts are compared in Murasaki Shikibu, *Taikō Genji monogatari shinshaku*, ed. Yoshizawa Yoshinori and Kinoshita Masao (Tokyo: Kokusho Kankōkai, 1971), 1:17–18.

26. He is alluding to "Bright the moon, fierce the wind, sad the sound of the fulling block; long indeed are these nights in the Eighth Month, the Ninth Month" (*Hakushi monjū*, 19).

27. From a poem by Liu Mengde (772–842).

28. Extant texts of *Genji* read *wakaretemo* and *nagusametemashi*, rather than *wakarutomo* and *nagusaminamashi*.

29. Presumably because the degree of passion expressed in Murasaki's poem is deemed unseemly? In support of this interpretation, on which all commentators agree, Kuwabara notes that in an earlier passage of *Mumyōzōshi*, the speaker says, "When you're upset with someone, when life in this world seems painful, when something seems just too dreadful or wonderful, at any time whatever, when strong feelings threaten to overcome you, if you just recite 'Namu Amida Butsu,' whatever may be troubling you will vanish and you will feel relief" (*Mumyōzōshi*, 45n.8, 20n.5).

30. "Suma," 13:178, alluding to *Ise monogatari* 7:

itodoshiku sugiyuku kata no koishiki ni / urayamashiku mo kaeru nami kana
Only the more do they make me long for the place whence I have just come;
how I envy them, these waves that return whither they came.

31. "Suma," 13:179:

furusato o mine no kasumi wa hedatsuredo / nagamuru sora wa onaji kumoi ka
Though mountain peaks shrouded in mist now stand between me and our old home,
might these skies that I now gaze upon be the same for her?

32. *Shokukokinshū* 868:

tabibito wa tamoto suzushiku narinikeri / seki fukikoyuru suma no urakaze
The traveler's sleeves, by now soaked through with tears, have grown chill
as the wind that buffets Suma's shore blows down from beyond the barrier.

33. Extant texts of *Genji* describe Yukihira as a Middle Counselor (*chūnagon*) rather than a viceroy (*sochi*) and differ in other minor ways from this quotation.

34. Extant texts of *Genji* differ slightly. The allusion is to *Hakushi monjū*, 724.

35. "Wakana, jō," 15:62–63. While sleeping with the Third Princess, Genji dreams of Murasaki and leaves before dawn to return to her. Her women make him wait, gazing at the snowy garden, for some time before letting him in.

36. Extant texts of *Genji* read *omoitsutsu*.

37. The allusion is to *Shūishū* 1329:

yamadera no iriai no kane no koe goto ni / kyō mo kurenu to kiku zo kanashiki
With every toll of the evening bell from the temple in the mountains,
how sad to think, "Yet another day has come to an end."

38. Extant texts of *Genji* read *itamaite*, rather than *shiri kakete*.

39. "Sakaki," 13:81. Extant texts of *Genji* read *nakikarashitaru koe mo* (chirp in rasping voices), rather than *nakikawashitaru* (chirp to one another).

40. "Sakaki," 13:87:

Suzukagawa yasose no nami ni nurenurezu / Ise made tareka omoiokosemu
Whether I am soaked or not in the ripples of Suzukagawa,
who is likely to care when I am far off in Ise?

41. Yūgiri at first feels "a bit awkward" because the inkstone the waiting lady brings him is not her own but the Akashi Princess's; yet when he considers the low regard in which this lady's mother is held, he "decides that needn't trouble him" ("Nowaki," 14:274–75nn.18–20).

42. Teika, in *Okuiri*, cites:

kiri fukaki kumoi no kari mo waga goto ya / hare sezu mono no kanashikaruramu
The wild geese high above in misty clouds, do they too feel as I do,
full of sorrow, beset by cares that cannot be dispelled?

The poem is otherwise unknown.

43. Here, as noted previously, the narrative becomes more a series of lists than a conversation. In this translation, these lists—each consisting of a subject heading followed by a series of events the description of which ends in *koto*—are treated as the words of the woman who ends the discussion, probably the same woman who at the outset expresses her reluctance to embark on the subject without a text of *Genji* to refer to.

44. From *Ise shū*, 380:

mikumano no ura yori ochi no kogu fune no / ware oba yoso ni hedatetsuru kana
The boat that rows seaward from the shore of beautiful Kumano
leaves me behind as it travels ever further away.

45. Extant texts of *Genji* read *nagekishi*, rather than *nagameshi*.

46. Described in *Ise monogatari* 9.

47. For a comprehensive discussion of the art of the list in Japanese literature, see Jacqueline Pigeot, "La list éclatée: Tradition de la liste hétérogène dans la littérature japonaise ancienne," *Extrême-orient–extrême-occident* 12 (1990): 109–38.

48. The text of *Forty-Eight Exemplars from Genji* is in Shigematsu Nobuhiro, *Shinkō Genji monogatari kenkyū shi* (Tokyo: Kazama Shobō, 1961), 142–45; and Abe Akio, Oka Kazuo, and Yamagishi Tokuhei, eds., *Genji monogatari*, Kokugo kokubungaku kenkyū shi taisei 3 (Tokyo: Sanseidō, 1960), 112–14; only forty-six "exemplars" survive. The text of *A Key to Genji* is in Shigematsu, *Shinkō Genji monogatari kenkyū shi*, 145–47; and Abe, Oka, and Yamagishi, eds., *Genji monogatari*, 115–17. The text and a brief discussion of *Exemplars from Genji*, the third "list" translated here, are in Inaga Keiji, "Meiō ninen okugaki mugedai *Genji* shō shoshū

'*Genji monotatoe* (kadai)' kaisetsu, honkoku," *Kokubungaku kō* 33 (1964): 35–39; the text alone is in Inaga, *Genji monogatari no kenkyū*, 601–13. This printing of the text is collated with twenty-eight fragments of what appears to be another copy of the same text, which are appended to a copy of *Genji kokagami* owned by Professor Katagiri Yōichi. These fragments are extremely useful in resolving some of the textual difficulties in Inaga's text. The entire *Genji shō* is reproduced in Teramoto Naohiko, *Genji monogatari juyō shi ronkō, zoku hen* (Tokyo: Kazama Shobō, 1982), 769–98. As the title of Inaga's article indicates, the list itself has no title. The title attached to the translation is Inaga's provisional title.

49. Shigematsu, *Shinkō Genji monogatari kenkyū shi*, 134–35.

50. Inaga, "'*Genji monotatoe* (kadai),'" 35–37. This article contains a useful list displaying the correlation of categories in the three texts.

51. The dewdrop may allude to *Kokinshū* 223. The source of the frost crystal is uncertain. Here both are metaphors for willing women.

52. In fact, the Minister of the Left praises Genji's arrangement of the festivities as the finest that he has seen in four reigns. Genji returns the compliment by insisting that the contribution of the minister's son, rather than his own, would be the one remembered by history.

53. There is mention here of dissatisfaction in certain quarters that a member of Genji's faction would probably be appointed empress, but the appointment itself is never described. In "Minori," she is referred to as *kisaki* (empress).

54. At this point, "the Emperor" is still the crown prince and does not accede to the throne until the following chapter. Genji's daughter is also not yet the empress.

55. . . . *ue ni wa ware* [*mochiikagami o*] *misetatematsuramu* (let me offer my lady New Year's felicitations).

56. The poem, composed by a country bumpkin, is a non sequitur. What the first secretary intends to swear is never stated.

57. Someone indeed added the two entries entitled *urameshiki koto*.

58. Extant texts of *Genji* read *wakareirinamu*.

59. Abe, Oka, and Yamagishi's text reads *tsuburu*; the *-ru* is emended from Shigematsu.

60. Kaoru here employs the metaphor for absolute fidelity made famous by *Kokinshū* 1093:

kimi o okite adashigokoro o waga motaba / sue no matsuyama nami mo
koenan
Should ever I neglect you, my love, and even think to be faithless,
then shall the pine-clad Sue mountains be engulfed in waves.

61. Abe, Oka, and Yamagishi's text reads *tsukizukishi*; the *-ki* is emended from Shigematsu.

62. Extant texts of *Genji* read *nokoran*, rather than *nokosan*.

63. The allusion is to *Kokinshū* 184.

64. Compare *Shūishū* 545.

65. He is alluding to *Kokinshū* 851.

66. She is quoting *Kokinshū* 967.

67. Compare *Kokinshū* 1080.

68. Extant texts of *Genji* read *o*, rather than *mo*.

69. The text here reads *tsurezure naru*. The emendation follows Inaga's suggestion in *Genji monogatari kenkyū*, 609.

70. Morikawa Akira, "*Genji* hitobito kokoro kurabe," *Seikei kokubun* 7 (1974): 34–41.

71. Urin'in is the currently preferred reading.

72. The text reads *yofuhe*, which I take to be a scribal error for *yokobue*. Kashiwagi is never called Yokobue in *Genji*, but he is admired for his prowess on this instrument, and the letter is indeed from him. The Yokobue no Kimi in "Wakana, ge," 15:193, seems to be Yūgiri's son.

73. This transcription follows the version of the poem given in this text, in which the final syllables read *to mo nare*. Extant texts of *Genji* read *to o nare*.

74. The mother of Ochiba no Miya, although she is never called by this name in *Genji*.

75. Ii Haruki, *Genji monogatari hikiuta sakuin* (Tokyo: Kasama Shoin, 1977), 59.

76. Translated from Abe, Oka, and Yamagishi, eds., *Genji monogatari*, 108–12.

77. Translated from Ichiko Teiji, "Shiryō shōkai: *Genji* monoarasoi," *Chūsei bungaku* 5 (1960): 12–13.

78. Translated from Morikawa, "*Genji* hitobito kokoro kurabe," 37–39. The manuscript is untitled. The title given here is that appended by Morikawa to his transcription of the Suzuki-ke text, probably because of its clear genetic relationship to the Awa no kuni bunko text, which has this title. Actually, however, it has much more in common with *Genji monoarasoi* than with *Kokoro kurabe*. Ten of the first eleven entries are identical (or nearly so) with those of *Genji monoarasoi*.

79. Hirata Sakura, "Kichōsho shōkai: *Genji monoarasoi*," *Toshi no fu: Meiji Daigaku Toshokan kiyō* 3 (1999): 146–61.

80. She is here referred to as Miyasudokoro, although she is never called that in *Genji*.

81. "Intimate converse" (*mutsugoto*) probably refers to Genji's conversation with Murasaki in which he expatiates on the subject of other women he has known, during which he describes the Rokujō Consort in most unflattering terms ("Wakana, ge," 15:200–201). Shortly thereafter, Murasaki is taken ill, and the cause of her affliction turns out to be the wayward spirit of the maligned lady (15:224–28).

82. The author of this text has inadvertently reversed the last two syllables of this name, which should read Tokikata. Tokikata is the son of Niou's nursemaid. He thus grows up with the prince, becomes his closest retainer, and handles all the practical details of such transactions.

83. The lower hemistich of this poem is a speculative reconstruction of a corrupt original that reads *moen [sic] ni kemuri ni musubu [sic] beshi to wa*.

84. The identity of the copyist is unknown, but the same name appears on a manuscript of *Izumi Shikibu zoku shū*.

85. Perhaps a scribal error here? The latter part of the sentence reads, redundantly, *Murasaki no Ue usetamaishi Genji no on-omoi ni kumogakuretamaishi Genji no mi-gokoro. . . .* The translation follows the otherwise identical *Genji monoarasoi* text.

86. Both the *Genji* narrator and Hanachirusato are alluding to a poem by Ise, *Kokinshū* 756:

ai ni aite monoomou koro no waga sode ni / yadoreru tsuki sae nururu kao naru
How appropriate that now, in my despair, even the face of the moon
that dwells in my sleeves should itself be wet with tears.

87. These attempts and the evidence against them are summarized in Ōtsu Yūichi, *Gunsho kaidai*, ed. Zoku Gunsho Ruijū Kanseikai (Tokyo: Zoku Gunsho Ruijū Kanseikai, 1961), 12:80–81.

88. Oda Keiko, "*Ise-Genji jūniban onna awase* no seiritsu kiban," *Kokugo kokubun* 54, no. 11 (1985): 1–21.

89. Surviving manuscripts of *Ise Genji jūniban onna awase* differ very little from one another and usually only in ways that help the reader make better sense of the text. None has been annotated or even edited more than minimally. Readers who wish to consult the original should be warned, however, of one major defect that has found its way into some printed editions of the text. Two of the surviving texts lack a large section of round 12, which seems to have been omitted by a copyist who inadvertently turned two pages instead of one, thus missing the reverse of one fold and the obverse of the following fold. The texts consulted in making this translation are in Abe, Oka, and Yamagishi, eds., *Genji monogatari*, 117–32; Katagiri Yōichi, ed., *Ise monogatari no kenkyū, shiryō hen* (Tokyo: Meiji Shoin, 1969), 73–94; and Nakashima Shōji, "Fukui Shiritsu Toshokan zō *Ise Genji jūniban onna awase* honkoku," *Mita kokubun* 21 (1994): 18–31, and "Honokuni Bunko zō *Ise Genji jūniban onna awase*," in *Yakaku gunpō: kodai chūsei kokubungaku ronshū*, ed. Ikeda Toshio (Tokyo: Kasama Shoin, 2002), 375–400. The first two of these texts contain the defective round 12, but the last two are complete. The textual history of this work has been very little studied to date, but a report on research in progress is given in Nakashima Shōji, "Fukui Shiritsu Toshikan zō *Ise Genji jūniban onna awase* ni tsuite," *Kyūko* 26 (1994): 24–26.

90. As when Genji dances in "Momiji no ga."

91. Moonlight reflected (*yadoru*) in dewdrops on the leaves of *hagi* (bush clover) was traditionally a harbinger of autumn, as in Teika's poem, *Shūi gusō* 226:

aki no iro o shirasesomu to ya mikazuki no / hikari o migaku hagi no shitatsuyu
Might we then call them the first sign that autumn is come—these dewdrops on
the *hagi* that so heighten the glow of the crescent moon?

92. Junshi (809–871). See *Ise monogatari* 4, 5, 65.

93. Junshi's father was Fujiwara no Fuyutsugu (775–826). It is not she, however, but her niece Akirakeiko/Meishi (829–900) who is so described (*Ōkagami*, vol. 2) in a poem composed by her father, Fujiwara no Yoshifusa (804–872), "when he saw a vase of cherry blossoms standing before the Somedono Empress":

toshi fureba yowai wa oinu shika wa aredo / hana o shi mireba monoomoi mo nashi

The years pass and I have grown old; yet even so, when I gaze upon these cherry blossoms I haven't a care in the world.

Perhaps the "unwarranted repute" (*aranu na*) that accrues to Yoshifusa is the honor of having this poem included in *Kokinshū* 52?

94. *Kisaki no kurai*; actually, he wishes only that he had named her a Dame of Honor (*nyōgo*) ("Kiritsubo," 12:101).

95. She is nowhere described as a nun in *Genji*.

96. This may be based on the brief passage in which Kokiden is so charmed by Genji that she allows him inside her blinds immediately after seeing him ("Kiritsubo," 12:114), but there are no further grounds for saying that she raised the boy. She does not, of course, hold the rank of empress in this chapter, nor does the appellation Kokiden no Miya, as she is called here, appear anywhere in *Genji*. Only much later, in "Sakaki," is she referred to as Ōkisai no Miya (Empress Mother).

97. This poem appears neither in *Ise monogatari* nor in any of the prose works or imperial anthologies indexed in *Kokka taikan*. A variant version of it can be found in *Genji ichibu no nukigaki narabi ni Ise monogatari*, as Oda points out in "*Ise-Genji jūniban onna awase* no seiritsu kiban," 16 (manuscript in Hōsa Bunko):

shirurame ya ware ni narenishi yo no hito / kuraki ni yukanu tayori ari to wa

Yet another variant occurs in *Aro monogatari*, SNKBT 52:92:

shirurame ya ware ni au mi no yo no hito no / kuraki ni yukanu tayori ari to wa

98. Brothers of Genji's wife.

99. The text is corrupt here. I am grateful to Professor Miyakawa Yōko for pointing out that *hodokurau* may be a mistake for *hodo nau*, as the kana orthography of both phrases can be very similar in some hands. The translation is based on this possibility.

100. The text is corrupt here; the translation is based in part on speculation.

101. The passage that follows, up to and including the description of her "sharp glance," follows almost verbatim the text of "Wakamurasaki," 12:300–301.

102. *Wakan rōei shū* 279, by Minamoto no Shitagō (911–981): "*Ominaeshi*. The color of this flower resembles that of steamed millet. It is commonly called 'maiden flower' [*jorō hana*]. Hearing that name, I wished I might propose in jest that we be married, but surely she would scorn this dotard's head, white as frost" (*Wakan rōei shū*, ed. Sugano Hiroyuki, SNKBT 19:153–54).

103. Actually he has four daughters, but only the second and third are depicted as characters in *Genji*. The first and fourth are mentioned only once in passing.

104. The chronology of events is reversed here. Only after describing her tonsure does the *Genji* text mention that she is too weak to bid her father farewell.

105. Not a poem at all, but the deity's exclamation of delight on encountering her male counterpart, Izanagi no Mikoto. See *Kojiki*, NKBT 1:55.

106. *Kojiki*, NKBT 1:119. The singer of the song is here designated by her alternative name, Takahime no Mikoto.

107. *Kokinshū* 1110:

waga seko ga kubeki yoi nari sasagani no / kumo no furumai kanete shirushi mo

Tonight is the night that my love shall come to me; for in the crab-like movements of the spider, I saw a sign that told me so.

108. *Man'yōshū* 3807:

asakayama kage sae miyuru yama no i no / asaki kokoro o waga omowanaku ni

Shallow like this mountain spring in which I see reflected Mount Shallow;
that shallow I know they are not, the feelings of my love.

109. Either 11:00–11:30 P.M. to 2:00–2:30 A.M. or midnight to 3:00 A.M., depending on the system of reckoning time that the author of *Ise monogatari* is using.

110. Most texts of *Ise monogatari* read *koyoi*, rather than *yohito*.

111. This judgment draws on a tradition that a child was born of the liaison, described in *Ise monogatari* 69, between Ariwara no Narihira and Princess Yasuko (d. 913), a daughter of the Montoku Emperor who served for eighteen years as the High Priestess of Ise. It was arranged by the then acting governor of Ise, Takashina Mineo, that the unwanted child be adopted by his son Takashina Shigenori and be given the name Takashina Morohisa (b. 866). Later, when Shigenori's own son unexpectedly took vows, Morohisa became the heir to the Takashina line. Because his true parentage was by then an open secret, members of the Takashina house thereafter discreetly refrained from worshipping at the Ise shrine. See *Sonpi bunmyaku*, 4:111. All texts of *Onna awase* give the name of this house as Takahashi, some glossing the characters 高階 as Takahashi. Current opinion seems not to accept this pronunciation.

112. In the *Kokinshū*, this poem is attributed to Narihira, with the headnote, "Composed upon sending an overcloak to the man who was married to his wife's younger sister."

113. Not exactly a reply, but a poem written in the margin of Genji's letter. The poem is not Utsusemi's own; she quotes from the *Ise shū* 442 (Nishi Honganji-bon).

114. The "certain estate" is thought to have been modeled on the Kawara no In, built by Minamoto no Tōru (822–895) and inherited after his death by the Uda Emperor (867–931; r. 887–897). Among many stories of the haunting of this mansion by its former owner, one recorded in *Gōdanshō* (GR 21:309) tells how the emperor takes one of his ladies, the Kyōgoku Consort, there and is attacked by the ghost of Tōru while engaged with Her Ladyship in some "bedroom business" (*bōnai no koto*). The ghost demands the consort for himself; the emperor is enraged by the ghost's insubordination; and the lady ends up "half dead." No mention of this incident is found in any extant text of *Genji*, but medieval commentaries from *Kakaishō* onward regard Genji's recollection that "one hears of such things in the old tales"

("Yūgao," 12:241) as a reference to the *Gōdanshō* story. One wonders, too, whether the upper hemistich of Genji's poem addressed to Yūgao, the reply to which is quoted in *Onna awase*, might have seemed to a knowing reader to be a portent of things to come:

inishie mo kaku ya wa hito no madoiken / waga mada shiranu shinonome no michi

Might others long ago have gone astray in much the same manner?
To me this dawn road we travel is something I've never known.

115. A popular designation of the temple Chinkōji, which stood opposite the entrance to the Toribeno cremation ground.

116. 875–916. Current reference works describe him as the son of the Seiwa Emperor (850–878; r. 858–876) and the daughter of Ariwara no Yukihira.

117. Actually he moves her to the Nijō mansion.

118. "Fujibakama," 14:331–34. Actually it is Tamakazura's intermediary, Saishō, who is amused.

119. The reader whose knowledge of *Genji* derives principally from digest versions has good reason to wonder whether Genji slept with Tamakazura, as Oda points out in "*Ise-Genji jūniban onna awase* no seiritsu kiban," 15–16. Some digests say he did not; others say he did.

120. The genealogical confusion mentioned earlier is apparent here as well. The Fifth Ward Empress was the daughter of Fujiwara no Fuyutsugu, not Yoshifusa.

121. Abutsu is referred to as *onna aruji*. The term translated as "reader" is *kōji*.

122. Masaari may have found Abutsu's reading unusual because he was not used to hearing *Genji* read by a woman, but this could also refer to Abutsu's rhythm, her enunciation, or her following a Mikohidari style of reading. See Tabuchi Kumiko, *Abutsu-ni to sono jidai: Utatane ga kataru chūsei* (Kyoto: Rinsen Shoten, 1999), 160.

123. The implications of this phrase are unclear. The original reads *narai abekameri* and implies that Abutsu's particular style of narration follows a tradition she has learned from her own family or Tameie's. See *Asukai Masaari nikki zenshaku*, ed. Mizukawa Yoshio (Tokyo: Kazama Shobō, 1985), 61.

124. For a recent annotated text, see Abutsu, *Utatane*, ed. Fukuda Hideichi, in SNKBT 51.

125. Until recently, *Menoto no fumi* was thought to have been written right before Abutsu set out for Kamakura to defend a court case in 1279, because it described Abutsu's being far away from her daughter. For a summary of the various theories and a reexamination of the dating of this work, see Iwasa Miyoko, "*Menoto no fumi* kō," *Kokubun tsurumi* 26 (1991): 1–11.

126. Nijō's advice from her father on taking the tonsure should she lose the affections of her patron, GoFukakusa, is from a section of *Menoto no fumi* suggesting a similar course of action.

127. Translated from the Gunsho ruijū-bon version of the unabridged (*kōhon*) *Niwa no oshie*, in *Abutsu-ni zenshū*, ed. Yanase Kazuo, expanded ed. (1958; Tokyo: Kazama Shobō, 1981).

128. The phrase *onoga yoyo ni*, translated here as "lead lives apart," is found in *Ise monogatari* 21, which describes a couple who eventually part. The phrase also appears in *The Tale of Genji* in a poem composed by Genji for Tamakazura, which Abutsu seems to be citing here:

mase no uchi ni ne fukaku ueshi take no ko no / ore ga yoyo ni ya oiwakaru beki
Must that dear bamboo, so young when I planted her deep in my garden,
grow up with the passing years to a life apart from mine?

Murasaki Shikibu, *The Tale of Genji*, trans. Royall Tyler (New York: Viking, 2001), 1:448.

129. "This fate" or, more literally, "was this sort of promise made?" refers to *Shūishū* 992:

Sent to a woman's residence:

au koto wa kokoro ni mo arade hodo fu tomo / saya wa chigirishi wasure hatene to
Time may have passed without any expectation of meeting with you,
yet was a promise made for you to forget about me completely?

130. Abutsu uses three images from *Ise monogatari* to emphasize her and her daughter's sadness at separating. The "capital bird" appears in episode 9, in which one of the travelers composes this poem:

na ni shi owaba iza koto towamu miyakodori / waga omou hito wa ari ya nashi ya to
If you be true to the name you bear, Capital Bird,
then let me ask: does the one I love live, or does she not?

Abutsu's envy of "the waves that are certain to return" refers to episode 7, in which the protagonist looks out to sea and composes this poem:

itodoshiku sugiyuku kata no koishiki ni / urayamashiku mo kaeru nami kana
The direction from which I came seems dearer still as we proceed;
how enviable are the waves that return.

Finally, the "spider-legged" Yatsuhashi Bridge is the famous scene of the Eight Bridges (Yatsuhashi) of Mikawa Province, found in episode 9. Abutsu takes the phrase "spider-legged bridges, forever pulled in all directions, like my thoughts" (*kumode ni omou koto taenu*) from *Gosenshū* 570:

uchiwatashi nagaki kokoro wa yatsuhashi no / kumode ni omou koto wa taeseji
The lengths to which my patient heart extends, my thoughts forever pulled
in all directions, like the spider-legged eight bridges of Yatsuhashi.

131. Abutsu refers to the penultimate chapter of *The Tale of Genji*, in which Ukifune is taken in by the prelate of Yokawa (called here the *nori no shi* [master of the law]). By the medieval period, popular legend held that Murasaki Shikibu composed the "Suma" and "Akashi" chapters while in retreat at Ishiyama Temple, inspired by the moon reflected on the waters of Lake Biwa.

132. The "chest" is a *kokarabitsu*, a wooden box with legs, used to hold clothing and items of daily use. The "catalogs" (*mokuroku*) likely included information like lists of the chapter titles.

Chapter 3
Toward Canonization

THAT SEA CHANGE IN ATTITUDES toward *The Tale of Genji* that we sum up under the convenient rubric of "canonization" is in fact a shifting amalgam of forces, some in concert, some in conflict, never quite coalescing in total consensus, yet yielding ultimately what one scholar aptly describes as the transformation of *Genji* from "a women's romance into a men's classic."[1] Very little documentation of this process, which spanned at least two centuries, survives, but the scattering of sources that we do have allows us at least roughly to chart its progress. We can assume, first of all, that the sense of wonder at the tale's greatness, as expressed by the Ichijō Emperor, was shared by most of Murasaki's readers and was the initial and indispensable impetus of the canonization process. Certainly it was what drove the *Sarashina* diarist when she "lay down behind her screens" and read *Genji* "all day and as far into the night as I could keep my eyes open." In contrast, however, we have seen how the reading of fictions of any sort may have been dismissed—even by Genji himself—as mere "amusement for women" or, more severely, as the "very root of sin," the creation of which could condemn an author to hell. To make a classic out of a work against which such objections could be leveled would prove to be a formidable task, far more difficult than the canonization of, say, a doctrinal or historical or philosophical text.

The documents collected here, describing events toward the end of the twelfth and the beginning of the thirteenth century, reveal not only what a sense of awe still prevailed among those most directly responsible for the canonization of *Genji*, but also a key element in the process of canonization: the association of *The Tale of Genji* with the composition of *waka*, poetry in Japanese. *Waka* was the premier genre of all the literary arts practiced in Japan, rivaled only by the composition of poetry in

Chinese. When it became permissible to draw the diction and conception of poems from *Genji* and to allude in poetry to scenes and events in *Genji*—and when the many poems "composed" by characters in *Genji* were themselves admitted into the canon of *waka*—the way then opened for all the other forms of attention normally reserved for literary classics to be applied to *Genji*: the collation, recension, and verification of texts; the compilation of commentaries; the construction of genealogies; the rendition of pivotal scenes in paintings. This process is sometimes described as dragging *Genji* into the canon as the handmaiden of *waka*, but the documents collected here suggest that what in fact happened was that *Genji* overwhelmed and subsumed the canon. This, as Harold Bloom has noted, is "the strongest test for canonicity. . . . One breaks into the canon only by aesthetic strength."[2] This is not to say, however, that the old objections simply vanished. Some readers still clung to them and periodically had to be refuted. As Inaga Keiji put it, "Though the *Genji*'s status as a classic had become unshakable, there lingered, throughout the medieval era, an unsteadiness in its stance."[3]

T. HARPER

SENZAISHŪ, 1188

COMPILED BY FUJIWARA NO SHUNZEI AND ANNOTATED BY KITAMURA KIGIN

Fujiwara no Shunzei (1114–1204) may not have been the first person to draw on *The Tale of Genji* when composing poetry. He was, however, the first to accord poems based on *Genji* the distinction of being included in an imperially commissioned anthology of Japanese poetry (*chokusenshū*). The seventh imperial anthology, the *Senzaishū*, edited principally by Shunzei, contains two anonymous love poems that take both their conception and their diction from *Genji* and are explicitly labeled as *Genji* poems. The commentary that follows each poem, explaining the use its author made of *The Tale of Genji* and the resultant poetic effects, is by the Genroku-era (1688–1704) scholar Kitamura Kigin (1624–1705), in his edition of the first eight imperial anthologies, *Hachidaishū shō* (1682).[4]

T. HARPER

Two Poems on the Topic of Love, Based upon The Tale of Genji

misebaya na tsuyu no yukari no tamakazura / kokoro ni kakete shinobu keshiki o
Would that I might show the love hidden in my heart, like a diadem bejeweled with tears shed for her who vanished like the dew. [869]

In the "Tamakazura" chapter of *Genji*, Ukon, in telling Genji about Tamakazura, says, "I have discovered someone related to the lady who vanished like the dew on the moonflower" [14:114]. In employing these words in this poem, the author uses *tamakazura* [diadem] to refer to women in general. As there is also an implicit association with the verb "to wear," the poem thus means "I wish to show my hidden love that I wear like a diadem in my heart."

ausaka no na o wasurenishi naka naredo / sekiyararenu wa namida narikeri
Though I've forgotten the very name Ausaka, barrier where lovers meet, no barrier can ever stop these tears of mine. [870]

In the "Sekiya" chapter of *Genji*, when Genji makes his pilgrimage to Ishiyama, the Utsusemi lady, returning from Hitachi, by chance encounters him at Ausaka Mountain. She composes the poem:

yuku to ku to sekitomegataki namida o ya / taenu shimizu to hito wa miruramu
These tears I could not stop, as I both left and return to this barrier: will people think them but the ceaseless spring of Meeting Slope? [13:351]

The poem *ausaka no* . . . thus means "My feelings are like Utsusemi's. She did not requite Genji's love, and after that night when the direction of his own home was inauspicious, she would never meet him again. She had, so to speak, forgotten the name Ausaka, the barrier where lovers meet. But like her, my longing for you has not ceased, and so I find it difficult to stop my tears." A "love poem based on *The Tale of Genji*" can be simply a poem about love that includes the name of a chapter in the tale, or the entire conception [*kokoro*] may be taken from the tale. There are numerous examples of such poems in subsequent anthologies.

TRANSLATED BY T. HARPER

POETRY CONTEST IN SIX HUNDRED ROUNDS, 1193
(*Roppyakuban utaawase*)

FUJIWARA NO SHUNZEI

The *Poetry Contest in Six Hundred Rounds* is the locus classicus of Fujiwara no Shunzei's often quoted and extremely influential pronouncement that "to compose poetry without having read *Genji* is simply inexcusable." The full significance of his judgment emerges with greater clarity, however, when we compare it with an earlier round of the same contest in which Shunzei recognizes an allusion to *Genji* but criticizes the poet for executing it ineptly, considering only the source and ignoring its context.

T. HARPER

Summer II, "Evening Faces," Round 18

Left Draw Ariie Ason (Fujiwara no Ariie, 1155–1216)

mugura hau shizu ga kakine mo iro haete / hikari kotonaru yūgao no hana
The fence around the hovel, too, overgrown with weeds, glows with color;
its gleam a thing apart is the flower of the evening face.

Right Takanobu Ason (Fujiwara no Takanobu, 1142–1205)

tasogare ni magaite sakeru hana no na o / ochikatabito ya towaba kotaemu
The name of that flower blooming there, indistinct in the gathering dusk:
I say, yonder person, should I ask, would you answer me?

The Right comments: I wonder if one can speak of a "fence glowing with color."

The Left comments: The poem that goes "I would ask you, yonder person" [*Kokinshū* 1007] would not seem to be about evening faces.

The Judgment: However colorful the fence, aren't the words "glows with color" rather repetitive? As for the poem of the Right: The poem composed in reply to "yonder person" reads "when spring comes" [*Kokinshū* 1008]. It cannot be about evening faces. In *Genji*, he [Genji] sees a white flower that is in bloom just then, and says ". . . of yonder person," which his guardsman hears, understands, and says, "That is called an 'evening face.'" This poem is not exactly in error, but it is composed with *Genji* alone in mind. This is unacceptable.[5] It does a disservice to *Genji* as well. But one can hardly settle on the Left's "glows with color" as the winner. A draw, shall we say?

The round in which Shunzei's pronouncement appears reads as follows:

Winter I, "Sear Fields," Round 13

Left Win A lady of the court (Fujiwara no Yoshitsune, 1169–1206)

mishi aki o nani ni nokosan kusa no hara / hitotsu ni kawaru nobe no keshiki ni
Is there naught wherewith I might capture this autumnal scene I have known,
this grassy moor transformed to a totally withered plain?

Right Takanobu Ason

shimogare no nobe no aware o minu hito ya / aki no iro ni wa kokoro someken
Can there be one who sees not the touching beauty of frost-withered fields
once his heart has been tinged by the brilliant tints of autumn?

The Right objects: "Grassy moor" [*kusa no hara*] has an unpleasant ring to it.

The Left comments: The poem of the Right is old-fashioned.

The Judgment: The words of the poem of the Left, "Is there naught wherewith I might capture . . . transformed to a totally withered plain," are lovely indeed. The Right's objection to "grassy moor" seems quite inadmissible. Although Murasaki Shikibu is more accomplished as a writer of prose than as a poet, [the poems in] "Hana no en" are particularly lovely. To compose poetry without having read *Genji* is simply inexcusable. The poem of the Right does not appear flawed in either concept or diction, but its style is rather ordinary. The poem of the Left is superior and should be declared the winner.[6]

TRANSLATED BY T. HARPER

What seems to have aroused Shunzei's ire is the objection of the poet of the Right that "'grassy moor' has an unpleasant ring to it." The objection was not groundless. "Grassy moor" was often used as a euphemism for "graveyard," and at the time of this competition, it still lacked the imprimatur of use in an imperially commissioned anthology. Shunzei, however, seems to take it for granted that anyone who has read *Genji* would immediately recognize these words as alluding to a poem in the "Hana no en" chapter. After seducing Oborozukiyo, the somewhat careless daughter of the Minister of the Right, Genji says to her, "Do tell me your name, else how shall I write to you? Surely you cannot think we shall never meet again?" Oborozukiyo replies coquettishly with this poem:

uki mi yo ni yagate kienaba tazunetemo / kusa no hara oba towaji to ya omou
Were I, poor thing, suddenly to vanish from this world, you might inquire,
do you mean, but not seek out my grave on the grassy moor? (12:426–28)

For Shunzei, this precedent from *Genji* was sufficient sanction for the use of "grassy moor" in a poetry contest. Even so, his criticism of the Right is not entirely fair. As we have seen, Takanobu himself alludes to *Genji*, however ineptly, in an earlier round. Shunzei knows very well that he does not "compose poetry without having read *Genji*." But only "reading" it is not enough. One must be sufficiently steeped in the tale to allude to it with a knowledge of its sources as well as its events, and to recognize the faintest allusions to it in the poems of those who are thoroughly versed in it. Shunzei might better have said that to compose poetry without studying *Genji* was simply unforgivable. It is interesting to note, too, that in both rounds, the object of Shunzei's anger was Fujiwara no Takanobu, the son of his own wife by a previous marriage.[7] It is tempting to wonder whether this relationship may have had something to do with Shunzei's uncharacteristic display of emotion. Whatever his motives, however, they in no way diminished the influence of his pronouncement in the eyes of later poets. It is quoted repeatedly in the commentaries on *Genji* of later centuries.

LORD SHUNZEI'S MEMORIAL IN JAPANESE SCRIPT, SUBMITTED IN 1200

(Shōji ninen Shunzei Kyō waji sōjō)

FUJIWARA NO SHUNZEI

When Fujiwara no Shunzei learned that his rivals in the Rokujō school of poets had connived to have his son Teika excluded from participating in a hundred-poem sequence (*hyakushu*) to be sponsored by the GoToba Retired Emperor (1180–1239; r. 1183–1198), he composed a memorial in protest against this injustice.[8] In this document, he argues both for Teika's merits and against the ignorance and incompetence of the leader of the Rokujō school, Fujiwara no Kiyosuke, and his associate Fujiwara no Norinaga. As the following excerpt illustrates, Shunzei was particularly derisive of their lack of knowledge of *Genji*, which he considered indispensable to the composition of poetry. The fact that he writes in Japanese rather than Sino-Japanese (*kanbun*) indicates that he intends the document not as an official memorial but as a communication to be submitted informally through gentlewomen in the service of the retired emperor. His protest was successful, and in the end both Shunzei and Teika were named to take part in the project.

T. HARPER

As a rule, it is strictly by virtue of their vast knowledge of poetry that the "authorities," as they style themselves, judge contests and compile anthologies. If their judgments of what is good and what is bad should be entirely in error, they do damage to the entire Way of Poetry. I happened to hear that this person called Norinaga had compiled an anthology, which he entitled *Shūi kokin* [*Gleanings Old and New*].[9] On that occasion, Kiyosuke assisted him, and they produced the work in close collaboration. It is truly dreadful. In the first place, the poem "Of a spring night, neither shining brightly nor yet completely clouded . . ."[10] they took to be on the subject of "summer nights" and placed it in the summer section. In the "Hana no en" chapter of *The Tale of Genji*, which takes place in the Second Month, it is this poem that the Chief Palace Attendant [Oborozukiyo] is depicted as quoting when she speaks of "the light of a misty moon" [12:426]. But Norinaga and Kiyosuke have not read *Genji*, and certainly have not read [*Hakushi*] *monjū*. In one of his poems Haku

Kyoi writes, "Neither bright nor dark, the misty moon; neither warm nor chill, the gentle breeze." This is the Chinese poem upon which the Japanese poem is based. Knowing neither of them, they describe it as a poem on "summer nights" and place it in the summer section. Both Norinaga and Kiyosuke are a disgrace.

TRANSLATED BY T. HARPER

EXPLICATING MURASAKI, BEFORE 1294
(*Shimeishō*)

SOJAKU

There is no reason whatever to doubt the veracity of the following account by Sojaku (active 1289–1293) of the cooperation between Minamoto no Mitsuyuki and Fujiwara no Shunzei.[11] Several sources attest to their close and continued collaboration in the collation and recension of their family texts of *Genji*. Chronological constraints, however, make it all but impossible to date this particular episode with any precision. Obviously it could not have taken place later than 1204, the year of Shunzei's death. Yet it is known for certain that in that year, Mitsuyuki and his son Chikayuki were living in Kamakura and probably had lived there for the previous six years. Were Shunzei and Mitsuyuki the only persons involved, it could at least be dated confidently sometime before 1198. In that year, however, Mitsuyuki's son Chikayuki, the intermediary between the two older scholars, was, at most, eleven, hardly an age at which he might be entrusted with such a mission. Ikeda Kikan dates their collaboration with Shunzei to around 1201[12] but offers no evidence to support his surmise. It is possible that circumstances, unrecorded in the few sources that survive from those tumultuous times, brought the three protagonists together before Shunzei's death. But with no documentation, we can only speculate how the events described here might have come about.[13] Whatever the timing, however, the story illustrates vividly the seriousness and meticulousness with which the two houses approached the task of establishing an authoritative text of *Genji*.

T. HARPER

Of those many works called *The Tale of Genji*, the one with the title *The Tale of the Shining Genji* is the work of Murasaki Shikibu. The text that had been handed down in this house, however, was fraught with mistaken readings perpetuated from the past. Thus my late father, Superintendent of Accounts [*dai kenmotsu*] Mitsuyuki, in order to assist those who might find it confusing and to set right the errors it contained, punctuated and added ideographic glosses [*reiji o tsuku*] to the text. Even so, these amendments were based only upon personal judgment, and he wished to seek the advice of someone of greater learning. With this in mind, he went to the mansion of His Lordship, Third Rank, of the Fifth Ward [Shunzei], and discussed the matter with him. [Shunzei] said he would be delighted to help, that indeed this was something he himself had been wanting to do for years. And what he accomplished in the end proved to be the major achievement of the final years of his life. Of those who attended my father throughout this process, I, Chikayuki, was the only one who never missed a day.

Now, when we opened Lord Shunzei's copy of the "Kiritsubo" chapter and examined it, we noted that in the passage in which it is written "The figure of Yang Guifei in the paintings lacked the radiance of life. For there are limits to the powers of even the most gifted artist, while the lady herself was said to resemble the lilies of the royal pond, the willows of the Weiyang Palace . . ." [12:111], the phrase "willows of the Weiyang" had been marked for deletion.[14] At this point he sent me, Chikayuki, as a messenger, to inquire why. "Yang Guifei," I [Chikayuki] said, "is always likened to the lily and the willow and Kiritsubo, to the maidenflower [*ominaeshi*] and the pink [*nadeshiko*]. Two phrases for each is what one usually hears. But in Your Lordship's [Shunzei's] text, 'willows of the Wei-yang' is deleted. What might be the reason for this?"

Shunzei replied, "How could you imagine that I have done this of my own accord [*jiyū ni*]? This phrase was marked for deletion in a manuscript written entirely in the hand of Imperial Attendant Grand Counselor [*jijū dainagon*] Yukinari. His being a contemporary of Murasaki Shikibu, I assume that this was done in consultation with her, and so I have marked this text accordingly. Though I did have my doubts, in the course of several readings, I came upon a passage in 'Wakana' that made me realize why the deletion makes the passage more interesting." I returned and reported this [to my father Mitsuyuki], whereupon he asked, "Where in 'Wakana' is the passage His Lordship says he associates with this one?" When I said I had not asked him about that, he said, "Your sole mission as my messenger was to discuss what was needed to dispel these doubts. You've been utterly negligent and bereft of reason. So be quick about it now; you must study that text until you can clear up this question."

He was absolutely right, so I shut myself away and read "Wakana" at least sixty times over until finally I understood. When the Fiftieth-Year Festivities for the Suzaku Cloistered Emperor are being arranged at the command of Rokujō-in [Genji], and a practice session is held for the women's concert, the ladies of the mansion are compared to various things. Here it is written: "When he peered in at the [Third] Princess, she looked lovely, but so much smaller than the others that she gave the impression of being naught but a pile of robes. Her charms were not yet fully developed, yet her bearing was most graceful—like green willow fronds in the middle of the Second Month when they have just begun to sprout, still so delicate that they seem they might be blown into disarray by the breeze of a warbler's wings. While over a long gown of cherry blossom pink, her hair cascaded, both left and right, quite like willow fronds" [15:183]. I realized then that "willows of the Weiyang" at the beginning of the book was superfluous. Immediately, I told my father, and he said, "There are many men of great cultural accomplishment here in the capital, but quite apart from His Lordship's superior learning in all things Japanese, there is no one who can equal the acuity of his grasp of this tale. As a result, he's hit on something extremely interesting." Since he [Shunzei] had marked this phrase for deletion, we too, in our humble text, shall mark it for deletion.

TRANSLATED BY T. HARPER

Two versions of this narrative survive, one in *Genchū saihishō*, compiled principally by Mitsuyuki and Chikayuki, and the other in *Shimeishō*, compiled by Chikayuki's younger brother Sojaku. The latter version is translated here because it is more complete. The former version, however, ends with an interesting passage not included in the latter, in which Chikayuki notes: "As I recall, however, 'willows of the Weiyang' was written into the family manuscript of the lay monk and Kyōgoku Middle Counselor [Teika]. I inquired further about this from the daughter of Lord Shunzei [ca. 1171–1254],[15] who said, 'It is probably a scribal error that has been handed down over the years and thus was copied into this text as well. The phrase must have been deleted because it smacks too much of parallelism.'" Modern scholars, however, tend to think that the retention of "willows of the Weiyang" in the Aobyōshi-bon is the result of a conscious aesthetic choice by Teika rather than an overlooked scribal error.[16]

DIARY OF THE JUNTOKU RETIRED EMPEROR, 1220
(*Juntoku-in gyoki*)
THE JUNTOKU RETIRED EMPEROR

The Juntoku Emperor (1197–1242; r. 1210–1241) was a son of and successor to the GoToba Emperor, and like his father, he was banished to the remote island of Sado for his part in the Jōkyū Rebellion. Only fragments of his diary survive, in the form of quotations like the following comment on *The Tale of Genji*, quoted in the introductory section of *Kachō yosei*, compiled by Ichijō Kanera.[17] The emperor's remarks are somewhat repetitive, with frequent references to the Buddhist concept of "inexplicable" wonder and mystery, usually associated with the scriptures. But there is no mistaking his fondness for *The Tale of Genji*.

T. HARPER

Of tales, there are, all told, a great many, some based on actual events, some fictional. The language of *The Tales of Ise* is nothing extraordinary, though those parts that are well written are splendid. *The Tales of Yamato* is far inferior. These aside, you will find nothing, even should you exhaust the lot of them, for they all are quite worthless. *The Tale of Genji*, however, is something inexplicable. It could hardly be the work of an ordinary person. When Murasaki Shikibu began writing, the Ichijō Emperor read it and remarked that she must be very well versed in the *Annals of Japan*. The imperial pronouncement struck jealousy in the heart of Lady Saemon no Naishi, and she dubbed Murasaki "Lady Annals." Yet truly, all the arts, all the Ways, are epitomized in this one volume. This is inexplicable and unprecedented. There are some, it is rumored, who maintain that the poems of *Genji* are inferior and that the poems of *Sagoromo* are superior. How pitifully ridiculous. The two are hardly to be discussed on the same day. To be sure, there are some poems in *Sagoromo* that are not to be despised, but they do not approach the poems in *Genji*. The two are as different as clouds and mud. In the Way of Poetry, those who know and those who know not are as water is to fire. In the first place, the flow of the phrases [*kotobatsuzuki*] in *Genji* could not be the work of any mortal. This is something inexplicable. Second, the poems are superb. Who could approach them? Third, there is the way it is constructed [*tsukurizama*]. Nothing has ever surpassed the beauties she has created out of her own imagination, nor indeed has their like ever been seen. The poems, too, are inexplicable, indeed the finest in this realm of mine. Neither is the prose at all the work of any mortal. But those who fail to comprehend such fine points can hardly be expected to distinguish good from bad.

TRANSLATED BY T. HARPER

FULL MOON DIARY, 1225
(*Meigetsuki*)
FUJIWARA NO TEIKA

The following entry from *Full Moon Diary*, the diary of Fujiwara no Teika (1162–1241), is thought to describe the completion of his carefully collated "Text in Blue Covers" (Aobyōshi-bon).[18] Taken at face value, this would suggest that for about thirty years, Teika did not have a copy of *Genji*. Yet his collection of poems from *Genji* and the compilation of *Monogatari nihyakuban utaawase* would have required access to a copy of the text, causing scholars to speculate that he may have been able to use another text that he considered less than authoritative. In any case, this entry from his diary is an invaluable record of the high regard in which Teika held *Genji*.

T. HARPER

[1225, Second Month,] Sixteenth Day. Skies again cloudy. In the evening, rainfall. Since the Eleventh Month of last year, I have had the women and girls of the household copying the fifty-four chapters of *Genji monogatari*. Yesterday we finished the covers. Today we write the chapter titles. For several years, I have neglected this, and we have not had a copy of the work in the household. [It was stolen in the Kenkyū era (1190–1198).][19] Having no authoritative text, I inquired about in an attempt to obtain one. Yet though I compared various texts, all were in the worst state of disorder and did nothing to resolve any points of doubt. "Wild words and fancy phrases,"[20] though it may be, this is a work of extraordinary genius. "The more I look up to it, the higher it seems; the more I probe into it, the more solid it seems."[21] How dare anyone discuss it thoughtlessly?

TRANSLATED BY T. HARPER

ORAL TRANSMISSIONS OF THE GOTOBA RETIRED EMPEROR, 1225–1227

(*GoToba no In gokuden*)

THE GOTOBA RETIRED EMPEROR

Shunzei's dictum, once voiced, was accepted, in a general way, without challenge by the poetic community. Some, however, wished to attach certain provisos. One of these is the following by the GoToba Retired Emperor (1180–1239; r. 1183–1198).[22]

T. HARPER

Item. Shakua [Shunzei], Jakuren, and others have said that when composing poems for a poetry contest, one is by no means free to compose just as one pleases. Still, such poems are not fundamentally different in nature. "Consider carefully the sense of the topic, and avoid the poetic ills," they said. "One need not avoid using diction [*kotoba*] from *Genji* and other romances so long as one does not derive poetic conceptions [*kokoro*] from such works." As a rule, it has likewise been unacceptable in hundred-poem sequences to draw the conceptions of poems from tales, but in recent times the practice has not been objected to.

TRANSLATED BY T. HARPER

CONVERSATIONS WITH THE KYŌGOKU MIDDLE COUNSELOR, CA. 1229

(*Kyōgoku Chūnagon sōgo*)

COMPILED BY FUJIWARA NO NAGATSUNA

Conversations with the Kyōgoku Middle Counselor, compiled by Fujiwara no Nagatsuna (dates unknown) sometime after the Eighth Month of 1229, purports to record the sayings of Fujiwara no Teika and Fujiwara no Ietaka (1158–1237), a claim generally accepted as authentic.[23] The following comment by Teika, in addition to noting some forms of attention that we have seen evidence of elsewhere, suggests another, more abstract, benefit of reading *Genji* to the would-be composer of poetry, that of calming the mind, thus putting the poet in a proper mood to compose elegantly.

T. HARPER

The manner in which people read *The Tale of Genji* has changed of late. They will take a poem from it and use it as the source of an allusion in a poem of their own. Or they will pose as experts on precedent, argue over whose child Lady Murasaki was, and construct genealogies, or whatever it is they call them. In times past, there was none of this. Their most deeply felt concern was not disputing Murasaki's ancestry, or searching out poems to which they themselves might allude, it was the inexpressible beauty of the language. When one reads Murasaki Shikibu's writing, one's mind clears, and then one can compose poems of graceful style and diction.

TRANSLATED BY T. HARPER

PREFACE TO *SINO-JAPANESE POEMS ON THE TALE OF THE SHINING GENJI*, 1290–1291
(*Fu Hikaru Genji monogatari shi*)

The *Sino-Japanese Poems* were composed in 1291 by an anonymous author. The text consists of a Sino-Japanese (*kanbun*) preface,[24] followed by fifty-four Sino-Japanese poems (*kanshi*), one on each of the chapters of *The Tale of Genji*, and concludes with a biographical poem on Murasaki Shikibu. The *Sino-Japanese Poems* are both unique and puzzling. As Sino-Japanese texts on a vernacular tale, they transpose the romantic *Tale of Genji* into the academic world of canonical scholarship, replacing the vernacular with the more prestigious *kanbun* and switching from a courtly, elegant, and amorous space to an academic, antiquated, and official male world.

The most fascinating aspect of this text is its elusive form and argument. Formally, it resembles *kanshi* poems introduced by prefaces, like those composed on canonical Chinese works such as the *Analects*, the *Book of Filial Piety*, and the *Three Histories* on special occasions. At times, the preface calls for elevating *The Tale of Genji* to canonical status on a par with the Chinese curriculum: Genji's son Yūgiri is given disproportionate attention because he can be presented as a paragon of Confucian virtue based on his formal training at the Academy. By the same token, the *Sino-Japanese*

Poems present an early formulation of later mainstream interpretive wisdom, which claims for *Genji* the status of history (as seen in the "Hotaru" chapter) and points to the tale's value as moral instruction through the three teachings of Confucianism, Buddhism, and Shinto. At the same time, the *Sino-Japanese Poems* seem to parody the world of the Academy, picking up on Murasaki Shikibu's entertaining invectives against the dull and dusty doctors in the "Otome" chapter. To make things even more complex, the vernacular tradition, too, is sometimes treated with deprecation. Although the indeterminacy of their genre and their agenda has deterred scholars from studying the *Sino-Japanese Poems*, this makes them even more significant in the context of the early reception of *The Tale of Genji*.

WIEBKE DENECKE

The Tale of the Shining Genji is a profound text of our nation. If you skim it and know little about it, you may consider it a playful toy, but if you ponder it and study it well, you will take it as the foundation of devoted learning. It records events since the divine age and describes those of the human age, just as the illustrious volumes [the *Nihon shoki*] by our courtiers and princes do. In assembling hundreds of texts into one book, it is like Sima Qian's [ca. 145–86 B.C.E.] *Records of the Historian*. Who would ever call it "a go-between of flowers and birds"?[25] In short, it sums up all of Japanese and Chinese writing.

This is the gist of *The Tale of Genji*: As four generations of benevolent sovereigns succeed one another, their magnificent abundant virtue spreads everywhere, and their bond with the Three Dukes and the Hundred Officials, who admire [their ruler's] transformative moral power, is like a fish in water.[26] At one time [Genji] enters the flowery curtains of the female palace quarters and ties the knot in secret [with Fujitsubo], just as Colonel Ariwara [no Narihira] abandoned himself to beautiful ladies. At another time, [the Akashi] lady from humble origins becomes his consort, just as [Major] Katano's lady rises to prosperity. Now, the way the Crown Prince brought glory to his Eastern Palace, the way the high officials conducted palace affairs, [and] the ways of the silk-clad beauties of the inner quarters and of the heirs of the aristocracy—the battlement, the bulwark [to their ruler]—all this is in keeping with the laws of the sage governance of sage eras and absolutely *had* to be recorded by the Left and Right Historians.[27]

What is more, when discussing principles of government, [*The Tale of Genji*] reveres the Confucian way of the "Three Relations" and the "Five

Constants."[28] With the procession to Ōharano at Mount Oshio [in the "Miyuki" chapter], it describes hunting outings. In discussing the divinations for the High Priestess of Ise, it pays its respects to the *kami* [gods], and when showing the deep tenets of the manifest and secret teachings, it turns to the Buddha.[29] It is not just about the lifting of brocade curtains to host banquets under moon-drenched blossoms in the courtyards of the Orchid Bureau [Secretariat] and the Emperor's Pear Garden [theater], or about how to make merry by rushing the imperial chariot over the gateways of waters and rocks in detached palaces and estates. No, it reaches moments like these: That Genji sighs [in exile] on the shores of Suma and Akashi, yet later reaches the exalted station of Honorary Retired Emperor or that with Aoi's and Murasaki's descent to the underworld of the Yellow Springs, he alone has to face the law of destiny, showing that worldly fortunes are unstable, that heavenly destiny is in the hands of [Zhuangzi's] dream world of Southern Blossoms, that people's pleasures and sorrows change easily, and that our evanescent life succumbs to the autumn at [Luoyang's cemetery] Beimang Hill!

How great that there is the beloved heir of the Genji clan [Yūgiri], a disciple of the Apricot Terrace[30] in Locust Tree District.[31] Tirelessly he studied at night, the snow substituting for a cantilevered lamp. He reviewed unremittingly while fireflies shed their light on his five-colored bamboo mat.[32] When they finally had him take the exam for the "Literary Scholar" degree, his talent ascended unencumbered like a scaly [dragon] at Dragon Gate.[33] In his position as Adviser, he showed the utmost loyalty, and his reputation spread far as he was "taking wing" in the "Phoenix Palace."[34] To love learning and to serve one's father is the beginning of filial piety. He fastened his purple sash[35] and ascended to the position of the three highest ministers. Meanwhile, because he helped with "affairs" at the morning court, he was called "Yūgiri," meaning "Evening Affairs/Mist." Meeting with enlightened times, he exercised ministerial powers on behalf of the realm. This is the significance of the saying that "he governed the world through *wen*"[36] and is a good part of the [tale's] essential meaning.

Alas, texts that illuminate reality through fiction are [tales of the] marvelous, like that about the prince from the eastern state of Wu and the lord from the western state of Shu,[37] and parables like the one [in the Lotus Sutra] about the old man's destitute house or about the people lost in the Phantom City are wonderful for instructing the people. They are not written in elegant Confucian wording but do rely on the Lotus

Sutra that the World-Honored Buddha pronounced at Eagle Peak. The [tale's] meaning pervades the esoteric and exoteric, and its words adumbrate past and present; isn't that precisely the appeal of this literary work?

In my idleness, I opened a copy [of the tale], and stirred by a thousand feelings, I have composed [poems] about its principal appeal. Not a single one is missing from its fifty-four chapters, and I've not left out a single one of the thirty-two rhyme categories. Moreover, at the end I added a short biographical composition on the author. Although the tale violates the "Six Poetic Principles,"[38] I could not resist singing its high praises.

Unfortunately, my "Lu-ish" dullness[39] is incorrigible; I am worlds apart from Bo Juyi's ancient style; and since it's hard for me to get used to the "Hymns of Zhou" [from the *Classic of Poetry*], I am ashamed to play around with the evanescent words of Murasaki Shikibu. That is what [Zhuangzi] means when he says that the wisdom of a frog in the well knows nothing about the turtle in the ocean and that the happy quail on the fence does not envy the giant *peng* bird in the clouds. Natural principle makes it thus.[40]

In the fourth year of Shōō [1291] of our imperial calendar. Drawn up in the crisp coolness of the Eighth Month.

TRANSLATED BY WIEBKE DENECKE

Notes

1. G. G. Rowley, *Yosano Akiko and The Tale of Genji* (Ann Arbor: Center for Japanese Studies, University of Michigan, 2000), 17–33.

2. Harold Bloom, *The Western Canon: The Books and School of the Ages* (New York: Harcourt Brace, 1994), 28–29.

3. Inaga Keiji, *Genji monogatari no kenkyū: seiritsu to denryū* (Tokyo: Kasama Shoin, 1967), 4.

4. Translated from Kitamura Kigin, *Hachidaishū shō*, ed. Yamagishi Tokuhei (Tokyo: Yūseidō, 1960), 2:434.

5. Probably because it fails to take proper account of the *Kokinshū* poems (1007, 1008) in the background of this episode in "Yūgao," 12:210. See Fujiwara no Shunzei, *Roppyakuban utaawase*, ed. Kubota Jun and Yamaguchi Akiho, SNKBT 38:102–3.

6. Translated from Shunzei, *Roppyakuban utawase*, 186–87

7. Takanobu is perhaps best known as the painter of the two magnificent portraits of Minamoto no Yoritomo and Taira no Shigemori.

8. Translated from Fujiwara no Shunzei, *Shōji ninen Shunzei Kyō waji sōjō*, ed. Inoue Muneo, in *Karon shū*, ed. Hisamatsu Sen'ichi, Chūsei no bungaku (Tokyo: Miyai Shoten, 1971), 1:271–76.

9. No longer extant.

10. By Ōe no Chisato (dates unknown):

teri mo sezu kumori mo hatenu haru no yo no / oborozukiyo ni shiku mono zo naki
Of a spring night, neither shining brightly nor yet completely clouded;
naught is there to compare with the light of a misty moon.

This poem first appears in Chisato's anthology *Kudai waka* (*Japanese Poems on Chinese Themes*, 894).

11. Translated from Sojaku, *Shimeishō, Kakaishō*, ed. Tamagami Takuya (Tokyo: Kadokawa Shoten, 1968), 16.

12. Ikeda Kikan, ed., *Genji monogatari jiten* (Tokyo: Tōkyōdō, 1960), 2:532.

13. For a detailed discussion of this problem, see Ikeda Toshio, *Kawachi-bon Genji monogatari seiritsu nenpu kō: Minamoto Mitsuyuki ittō nenpu o chūshin ni* (Tokyo: Kichōhon Kankōkai, 1977), 50–52.

14. The word translated here is *misekechi* (visible deletion), which means that the word(s) to be deleted are not defaced or obliterated but are left fully legible, with only a light mark at their side—often two dots at the left in the space between lines—to indicate that they should be omitted when the text is read or copied.

15. Actually his granddaughter, but traditionally called his daughter because she was adopted by Shunzei when her father was implicated in the unsuccessful Shishigatani plot to overthrow the Taira in 1177.

16. See, for example, Takeda Munetoshi, *Genji monogatari no kenkyū* (Tokyo: Iwanami Shoten, 1954), 142.

17. Translated from Ichijō Kanera, comp., *(Matsunaga-bon) Kachō yosei*, ed. Ii Haruki, GMKS 1:10.

18. Translated from Fujiwara no Teika, *Meigetsuki*, ed. Nanba Tsuneo et al. (Tokyo: Kokusho Kankōkai, 1970), 2:411.

19. Inaga suggests that the text stolen was Shunzei's own (*Genji monogatari no kenkyū*, 494).

20. *Hakushi monjū*, 70.

21. *Analects*, 9:10.1.

22. Translated from Hisamatsu Sen'ichi and Nishio Minoru, eds., *Karon shū, Nōgakuron shū*, NKBT 65:144.

23. Translated from Fujiwara no Nagatsuna, comp., *Kyōgoku Chūnagon sōgo*, ed. Kubota Jun, in *Karon shū*, ed. Hisamatsu, 1:332–38. The work is known by several different titles, the most common of which is *Sendatsu monogatari*.

24. Translated from the text in GR 9:270–71.

25. A defense against the accusation in the Sino-Japanese preface to the *Kokinshū* that some *waka* poets abuse their art for trivial love exchanges.

26. Like the proverbially close bond between Liu Bei (161–223), the ruler of the kingdom of Shu, and his general Zhuge Liang.

27. According to the Confucian classic *Book of Rites*, the Left and Right Historians recorded, respectively, the ruler's words and actions.

28. "Three Relations" are between ruler and subject, father and son, and husband and wife. Although the lists of "Five Constants" differ, one includes the Confucian virtues of benevolence, righteousness, ritual, wisdom, and trustworthiness.

29. Three examples of how *The Tale of Genji* addresses the "Three Teachings" of Confucianism, Shinto, and Buddhism.

30. Confucius's school near Qufu in present-day Shandong Province.

31. A poetic name for the university.

32. Yūgiri studies in same way as did the famously poor scholars Che Yin and Sun Kang, who compensated for their lack of money for lamp oil with the light of fireflies and moonlight reflected from snow.

33. The gates to the examination facilities, hence a metonymy for success in the official examinations.

34. A metaphor for successful court service is that of becoming a feathered immortal.

35. A sign of high rank.

36. Yūgiri is described in the words that the *Book of Rites* uses for the virtuous King Wen (twelfth century B.C.E.) of the Zhou dynasty. The character *wen* 文 of King Wen's name has a broad spectrum of meanings, ranging from "pattern" and "ornament" to "cultivation," "sophistication," and "literature."

37. In Zuo Si's (ca. 253–307) "Three Capitals Rhapsody," a lord from Shu, a prince from Wu, and a master from Wei compete in a fictional dialogue over the respective advantages of their capitals.

38. The "Six Poetic Principles" are listed in the "Great Preface to the *Book of Poetry*" as narration (*fu*), comparison (*bi*), evocative image (*xing*), Airs (*feng*), Odes (*ya*), and Hymns (*song*). They are a revered staple of Chinese and Japanese poetics.

39. A pun on the word 魯 *lu* (J. *ro*). It both means "dull" and is the name of Confucius's home state of Lu.

40. This phrase echoes one in the Sino-Japanese preface to the *Kokinshū* that describes *waka* poetry as the product of human instinct in response to the world.

Chapter 4
Obsequies for *Genji*

"OBSEQUIES FOR *GENJI*" is a rough translation of *Genji kuyō*, a term for which there is no precise English equivalent. A *kuyō* is a dedicatory service in which the merit acquired in preparing for and performing the rite is assigned to another person, usually deceased, in order to diminish that person's suffering and speed his or her progress toward Buddhahood. The title *Genji kuyō* was applied to various such rites performed on behalf of Murasaki Shikibu, her readers, her hero the Shining Genji, and even *The Tale of Genji* itself.

The reason that such rites were thought necessary lies in the doctrine of Buddhist morality that counts four of the "ten evils" (*jūaku*) as "sins of the word" (*kugō*): falsehood (*mōgo*), equivocation (*ryōzetsu*), slander (*akku*), and frivolous or specious talk (*kigo* or *kigyo*).[1] As these were commonly held to apply to both the written and the spoken word, the writer of almost any sort of secular literature could be considered a sinner, for even the use of ornamented or poetic language could be construed as *kigo*. Writers of fiction stood in the greatest danger, for they were guilty of *mōgo* as well. And the danger was great, for the commission of any of these sins, depending on the seriousness of the deed, could result in a sentence to hell, rebirth as an animal, or a term as a hungry ghost (*gaki*, Sk. *preta*).[2]

In Murasaki Shikibu's day, these strictures seem not to have troubled many readers or writers very deeply. A few devotees of Chinese literature, members of the Society for the Advancement of Learning,[3] had taken to chanting a passage from the *Hakushi monjū* that had found its way into the Japanese anthology *Wakan rōeishū* (NKBT 73:200): "May the worldly writings of my present incarnation, all these wild words and fancy phrases [*kyōgen kigo*], be transformed into hymns of praise of the Buddha's teachings in age on age to come and cause the wheel of the dharma forever to turn." And the *Sarashina* diarist, while reading *Genji* "night and day," seems to have been visited in a dream by "a monk in a yellow surplice" who warned her that she might better be spending her time studying the fifth chapter of the Lotus Sutra.[4]

A century or two later, however, when the peace and tranquillity of Heian had been shattered by the disturbances and uprisings that culminated in outright warfare in the capital region, even *The Tale of Genji* came to seem a threat to its readers' welfare, not only in the present, but also in lives to come. It was at this time, in the later twelfth and early thirteenth centuries, that Murasaki Shikibu began to appear in women's dreams, telling of her suffering in hell for having written *Genji* and begging her readers to destroy their copies of the tale and sponsor the performance of rites to propitiate her sin. These rites, a considerable number of which were indeed performed, are what came to be called *Genji kuyō*.

Very few documentary remains of the rites survive, but from those that do we can reconstruct with reasonable accuracy the form that they took. Like any dedicatory rite, they consisted principally of creating merit that then could be assigned to someone in need of it. Merit might be accumulated in myriad ways, from building grand temple complexes and casting bells to simply reciting scripture. But in all the *Genji kuyō* of which we know, the requisite merit was created by making a complete copy of the Lotus Sutra. The sponsor of the rite would enlist the aid of twenty-eight like-minded readers of *Genji* and ask each of them to make a copy of one chapter of the Lotus. When they had finished, each copyist would then compose a poem based on the content of the chapter that he or she had copied, to be submitted with that chapter. These chapters would then be collected and dedicated to a temple. In preparation, the officiating monk would compose a "proclamation" (*hyōbyaku*) stating the purpose of the rites and designating the beneficiary, which he would read or chant aloud during the dedication. No doubt there were other elements as well—invocations, chants, responsories, benedictions, and the like—but no record of them remains.

As alien as such notions and practices may seem to modern sensibilities, it is important to remember that in medieval Japan, they were not oddities found on the fringes of *Genji*'s readership. *Genji kuyō* were a significant current in the very mainstream of literary activity in that era. Only fragments of documentation survive, but many of them, in one way or another, involve members of the Mikohidari branch of the Fujiwara clan and their clients, the most prestigious of all literary coteries. One occasion about which we have some knowledge appears to have been sponsored by no less a figure than Bifukumon'in Kaga (d. 1193), the wife of Fujiwara no Shunzei (1114–1204) and the mother of Fujiwara no Teika (1162–1241). Another was sponsored by the paramour of Fujiwara (Saionji) no Kintsune (1171–1244), whose sister was married to Teika. Kaga's son by a previous marriage, Takanobu (1141–1205), tells us not only that Murasaki Shikibu had appeared to his mother in a dream, but also that he himself had copied one of the chapters of the Lotus Sutra to be dedicated at the rites held under her auspices. Another chapter—perhaps for the same rites—was copied by Kaga's son-in-law Fujiwara no Muneie (d. 1189), who was married to another of Teika's sisters. *Ima monogatari*, which contains an elaborate description of Murasaki Shikibu's appearance in readers' dreams, is thought to have been written by Takanobu's son Nobuzane (d. 1265?). And recent research has determined with near certainty that Takanobu's father, Tametsune (Jakuchō, b. 1113), was the author of *Ima kagami*, which contains an entire chapter delineating and debating Murasaki Shikibu's "sins."

Entering the realm of speculation—although of a conservative sort—we recall that every *Genji kuyō* had to involve at least twenty-eight participants, the number of persons required to copy one chapter each of the Lotus Sutra. Given that Shunzei's wife was among the prime movers of these occasions, it is tempting to conclude—indeed, all but impossible *not* to conclude—that Shunzei and Teika and the "daughter" of Shunzei,[5] as well as other members of the Mikohidari house and their clients, were directly involved in some of the many obsequies for *Genji*.

Almost all the known documents relating to *Genji kuyō* are translated in this chapter; only those that duplicate, or nearly duplicate, those translated have been omitted. These documents are arranged not in strict chronological order but in a sequence intended to illustrate the steps in the process just described. Accordingly, the "Progress of Fiction" chapter of *Ima kagami*, in which Murasaki's "sins" are described, comes first. Following this are the accounts of Murasaki's appearance in dreams, the poems composed after copying chapters of the Lotus Sutra, the proclamations for the dedicatory services, and finally a Muromachi-period story in which these materials were put to dramatic use.

T. HARPER

THE MIRROR OF THE PRESENT, CA. 1170
(*Ima kagami*)
FUJIWARA NO TAMETSUNE

By the latter part of the twelfth century, *The Tale of Genji* was firmly ensconced in the classical canon of Japan and an object of scholarly attention, required reading for all men and women of letters. Yet for a work of prose fiction, this position of preeminence proved decidedly less comfortable than for the more orthodox forms of literature. The century and a half that had passed since the composition of *The Tale of Genji* had been marked by warfare and a steady decline in the wealth and power of the aristocrats of the world of the Shining Genji. While this unsettled state of affairs unquestionably heightened late-Heian aristocrats' appreciation for Murasaki Shikibu's brilliant depiction of their past glories, it also inspired a new earnestness in religion, one consequence of which was an upsurge in moral misgivings about the ultimate worth of literature—misgivings from which no form of imaginative writing was totally exempt, but which aroused particular objections to fictions in prose. So as admiration for *Genji* grew, its expression took on a melancholic and defensive tone as the devout attempted to justify their attachment to a work that plainly violated the moral precepts of Buddhism. "The Progress of Fiction" (Tsukuri-monogatari no yukue) is one of the earliest such defenses.

The defense constitutes the final chapter of the historical tale *The Mirror of the Present*[6] and is cast in the form common to all works of the "Mirror" genre, in which a preternaturally aged person, encouraged by an audience of inquisitive pilgrims, gives a rambling, firsthand account of times long past. The narrator of *The Mirror of the Present* is a "toothless and doddering" woman more than 150 years old, who as a young girl had served as a lady-in-waiting to Murasaki Shikibu. While gathering fern shoots in the vicinity of her home, she encounters a band of pilgrims returning from the temple at Hatsuse who, upon learning her age and identity, begin to ply her with questions. Toward the end of the day, one of the pilgrims laments the severity of Murasaki's punishment for having written so "insinuating and suggestive" a tale, and the work closes with the old woman's attempt to defend the writings of her former mistress. The ensuing conversation provides an excellent epitome of the arguments for and against fiction that were to be rehearsed again and again throughout the medieval era in Japan.

Strict interpretation of Buddhist moral precepts led to the conclusion that any sort of fiction was a form of "falsehood" (*mōgo*) and that highly literary or poetic writing broke the commandment against "specious, fancy language" (*kigo* or *kigyo*). As a tale of "amorous intrigues," *The Tale of Genji* was further censured for corrupting morals and exciting passions. The cumulative force of these several strictures can be gauged by the widespread credence given the legend mentioned by the first pilgrim, that Murasaki Shikibu had been cast into hell for writing *Genji* and that her readers were in danger of like retribution.

Defenders of *Genji* argued not against the basic validity of these charges, but for a more subtle interpretation of the precepts on which they were based. One line of reasoning held that *Genji*, though not "true" in the literal sense, was a moral fable and therefore a form of "expedient truth" (*hōben*) such as the Buddha had used in preaching to those incapable of grasping more sublime expressions of the dharma. The immoral acts depicted in the novel could thus be seen as serving the same purpose as those related by the Buddha in his parables: to illustrate graphically the true nature and consequences of wrongdoing in order to inculcate in the reader an abhorrence of evil. Buttressing this argument was the popular belief in bodhisattvas who appeared in human form in order to "lead us humans to enlightenment." The narrator of *The Mirror of the Present* is only one of many to suggest that Murasaki was "no ordinary person" but an avatar of the bodhisattva Avalokitésvara (J. Kannon), while the pilgrims suspect that the old woman herself might be a supernatural being.

Another line of argument resorted to in "The Progress of Fiction" was based on the doctrine of the "Middle Way" expounded by the Indian sage Nāgārjuna (ca. 150–250).[7] In its original form, this was a complex metaphysical postulate that held, among other things, that all sensory perceptions are illusory; hence all distinctions between true and false, right and wrong, good and evil, and so forth, are meaningless. Seeming differences are only seeming; all ultimately partake of a single Absolute. In Japan, however, this doctrine was often interpreted in ways more utilitarian than metaphysical. Objections to literature could thus be confuted by citing, as the old woman does, the passage from the Nirvana Sutra that says "even coarse and insinuating language partakes of Absolute Truth,"[8] or the Chinese poet Bo Juyi's (772–846) prayer that the "wild words and fancy phrases" of his poetry might lead the way to enlightenment.

For all their grounding in scripture, however, the old woman's arguments derive their cogency no less from their appeal to a predilection for intuited over reasoned truth. From this cast of mind grew the conception of Japanese poetry as primarily a vehicle for the "meditations of the heart," without which one could not fully apprehend the "essential nature" of things. When the narrator claims that "to stir people's hearts can be a virtue" and that *The Tale of Genji* "reveals the workings of a feeling heart," she is in effect claiming these same functions for fiction and, in so doing, basing her argument on one of the most incontrovertible tenets of Japanese literary theory.

Others, however, like the first pilgrim who speaks, were not content with sophistry and felt that Murasaki's sins required justification as well as propitiation. It was from this attitude that the practice of *Genji kuyō* grew.

T. HARPER

The Progress of Fiction (Tsukurimonogatari no yukue)

Again the pilgrim spoke: "How true it is I do not know, but so often we hear that Murasaki Shikibu, for crafting so insinuating and suggestive a tissue of lies in her *Tale of Genji*, was in the afterlife doomed to be consumed in smoke, like seaweed in the salt fires. This so upsets me that, vain though it may be to hope for her deliverance, I should like to make some offering for the repose of her soul."

"Yes," the old woman replied, "that is indeed what everyone says. And yet in Japan, as in China, the writings of the wise have always brought comfort to people's hearts and have illuminated the way for dimmer minds; this hardly deserves the name of falsehood [*mōgo*]. To describe what never did happen, protesting behind a face of innocence that it is actually true, to lead others to think well of evil—to utter any sort of lie [*soragoto*] is sinful indeed. But is *The Tale of Genji* really such an empty fabrication? Meretricious [*kigo*] or specious [*zōego*] you might call it, but these hardly seem the most monstrous of sins. To take the life of any living creature or to steal even the least of a person's treasures—these are horrible sins for which the offender may be plunged to the very depths of hell. But I find it hard to imagine that such should be the lot of Murasaki Shikibu, though to be sure I have no knowledge of what retribution she might now be suffering. To stir people's hearts can, after all, be productive of virtue. And though to excite the passions may perhaps prevent one's release from the cycle of rebirth, this is hardly so serious a transgression as to condemn one to hell. It is difficult enough to comprehend the affairs of our own time; but in China, the poet Bo Juyi composed works amounting to seventy-some volumes, which greatly stirred people's hearts with their elegant phrases and ingenious conceits—and this man, we are told, was the incarnation of Manjusrī. Indeed, the Buddha himself, when he preached in parables, invented stories of events that never occurred, and these certainly are not to be regarded as falsehoods. For a mere woman to have written such a marvelous book as this, well, it doesn't seem to me she could have been any ordinary person. More than likely, she was Gadgadasvara or Avalokitésvara or some other supernatural being, come to us in the form of a woman to preach the dharma and lead us to enlightenment."

A child in her company then said: "I can see how some women who have led others to enlightenment might indeed have been Avalokitésvara incarnate—such as Queen Vimaladattā, who led the king before the Buddha and persuaded him to reform his wicked ways,[9] or Queen Shrīmālā, whose praise of the Buddha, inspired by her parents' epistles, will transmit the dharma to generations yet unborn.[10] But *The Tale of Genji* is such a farrago of amorous intrigues, all set forth as the very truth, that it corrupts people's minds and excites their passions. How are we to regard this as the sacred and holy dharma?"

"Yes," the old woman said, "there is some truth in what you say. Yet when you consider what an extraordinary and marvelous work *Genji* is; that she has written not just a scroll or two but a book of sixty chapters; that nowhere is it flawed by frivolity; that in the past as in the present it has brought pleasure even to emperors and empresses, who have made magnificent copies of it and have prized it above all their treasures—when you consider all these things, I say, what in fact strikes one as odd is that anyone could consider its author sinful. By showing the deeply sinful, it inspires one to chant the holy name of the Buddha and thus can serve as a first step toward the enlightenment of those for whose deliverance we pray. By revealing to us the workings of a feeling heart, it wins over to the path of righteousness those mired in the miseries of life; in demonstrating the evanescence of this world, it is by no means without effect as an exhortation to the Way of the Buddha. And when you further consider that it depicts one who, though grieved at having to leave behind his loved ones yet keeps the precepts of the Novice,[11] and a woman who guards her chastity until death in obedience to her father's dying injunctions,[12] it is plain to see that this tale was intended as an object lesson. When readers see how Genji, who enjoyed the boundless favor of the Emperor and was blessed with the best of all possible karmas, yet dies as though all this had been but a dream or an illusion, they cannot but realize how ephemeral are the things of this world. And then there is the Emperor, who relinquishes his throne to his younger brother and retires to a hermitage in the western hills:[13] here is another example of one devoted to the Way of the Buddha and learned in the dharma, one indeed that calls to mind that Emperor of old in the "Devadatta" chapter of the Lotus Sutra.[14] Vasubandhu has written at the beginning of his treatise[15] that nothing but the wisdom to distinguish right from wrong can rescue the heart lost in darkness, for so deep are the depths of delusion that the ignorant only drift on as though upon a bottomless sea. And so the Buddha in his benevolence has given us this means to discern the true nature of things and turn us in the way of enlightenment—this seed of the propagation of his dharma—that even coarse and insinuating language can lead the way to the Truth of the Absolute. To be sure, *The Tale of Genji* is not the untainted holy word of the dharma, and many passages describe the amorous intrigues you speak of. Yet under the pure morning light of the dharma, surely anyone with such great compassion as to pray for the deliverance of Murasaki Shikibu—whether because she found comfort in her book or was deeply touched by it—surely such a person must form a very deep bond of good karma."

As she spoke, the pilgrims, in their eagerness to hear more, lost all thought of their destination. Yet loath though they were to part from her, the sun had begun to set, and they went their separate ways.

"Perhaps one day we shall all meet again," she said, "for I hope in some future life to become a buddha and preach the dharma, as I've done here today, under the Tree of Enlightenment."

These words convinced the pilgrims that she could be no ordinary mortal. But later, when they sought her at the place where she said she lived, she was not to be found. Filled with regret that they had not sent one of their number to follow her, they proceeded on their way.

TRANSLATED BY T. HARPER

COLLECTED POEMS OF THE MOTHER OF ACTING MIDDLE COUNSELOR LORD SANEKI
(*Gon Chūnagon Saneki Kyō no haha shū*)

THE MOTHER OF ACTING MIDDLE COUNSELOR LORD SANEKI

The composer of the majority of poems in this collection, a woman known to us only as "the mother of Acting Middle Counselor Lord Saneki," was once a *shirabyōshi*, a female entertainer who danced and sang wearing male court costume. Hers is the only personal poetry collection by a *shirabyōshi* to have survived, and as such it provides evidence of the rich store of cultural knowledge possessed by such women, knowledge that in this case included familiarity with *The Tale of Genji*. Over the course of a long relationship with a low-ranking member of the Taira warrior house, Chikakiyo (d. 1275), "the mother of Acting Middle Counselor Lord Saneki" gave birth to several children, including at least one son as well as Chikakiyo's fourth and fifth daughters. For a time, she also was involved with the much higher-ranking Saionji Kintsune (1171–1244), who had risen to the office of Grand Minister of State before taking vows (administered by Myōe) in 1231. "Lord Saneki" (1239–1267) was her son by Kintsune, and she was pregnant with another of his children, a daughter, when he died in 1244. She also outlived Chikakiyo and several of her children by him. We do not know when she died, but one source suggests sometime between 1293 and 1299. Through her lover Kintsune, whose elder sister was married to Fujiwara no Teika, the mother of Lord Saneki also was distantly connected to the great poet and scholar of *Genji*.[16]

Collected Poems of the Mother of Acting Middle Counselor Lord Saneki consists of 887 poems divided between two volumes. The collection is thought to have been compiled near the end of the thirteenth century by someone other than the author herself. In the words of one twentieth-century scholar, "It bears no sign of deliberate editing."[17] Only one manuscript survives, in the Shoryōbu imperial archives. Although the manuscript is not dated, the titles of the two volumes are in the hand of the Reigen Emperor (1654–1732; r. 1663–1687), indicating that it was copied in the mid-seventeenth century.

In addition to the five "obsequies for *Genji*" (*Genji kuyō*) poems translated here,[18] the collection includes a series of nine poems based on chapter titles of *The Tale of Genji*[19] and ten poems inspired by someone's remark that "in *The Tale of Genji* it is first and foremost the 'ranking of women' [*shinasadame*] that one must comprehend."[20]

G. G. ROWLEY

141. At a time when I was reading *The Tale of Genji* day and night, I saw Murasaki Shikibu in a dream, and for her enlightenment I sponsored obsequies at which the Lotus Sutra was dedicated.[21] When the disquisition was delivered, I wrote the following:

nori naranu koto ya wa aru to murasaki no / fukaki kokoro o tazunete zo tou
So profound a mind has she that I would seek her out and inquire of
Murasaki Shikibu: Be there aught not of the Law?

142. On the occasion of a sudden downpour early one evening, to my younger daughter:

murasaki no kusaba mo ima ya moeiden / koyoi ichimi no ame sosogu nari
How the leaves of the *murasaki* must now be sprouting green and bright,
this evening when the rain pours equally upon us all.[22]

143. Her reply:

ima ya kono minori no ame ni murasaki no / karenishi nobe no kusa mo moyuran
Blessed now at last by the rain of the Law, how must the parched fields and plains
of *murasaki* be sprouting brightly with their new growth.

144. Sent to my elder daughter, with a copy of "Lauds for *Genji*" [*Genji* kōshiki] that I had written:

naniwa-e no ama no susabi mo minori zo to / kakioku ato o aware to wa miyo
Pray look with pity on the traces of these words I write,
for even this trifle by a fishermaid at Naniwa is of the Law.

145. Her reply:

hikari aru nori no tamamo o kakioku ya / satori nagisa no ama no ko no tame
Is it for the sake of that fishermaid's child on the shore of enlightenment
you gather the glistening sea grasses of the Law?

TRANSLATED BY G. G. ROWLEY

COLLECTION OF FUJIWARA NO TAKANOBU
(*Fujiwara no Takanobu Ason shū*)
FUJIWARA NO TAKANOBU

Fujiwara no Takanobu (1141–1205) was the son of Bifukumon'in Kaga, born to her before her marriage to Fujiwara no Shunzei. We therefore know that the excerpt from this particular *Genji kuyō* was sponsored by Shunzei's wife.[23]

T. HARPER

When Mother sponsored a dedication of the complete [Lotus] Sutra for the benefit of Murasaki Shikibu and I undertook to copy the "Dharani" chapter,

yume no uchi mo mamoru chikai no shirushi araba / nagaki nemuri o samase
to omou

Should this vow that Mother keeps, even in her dreams, one day be
fulfilled,
may it awaken her [Murasaki Shikibu] from the long sleep of delusion.

TRANSLATED BY T. HARPER

NEW IMPERIAL COLLECTION OF POETRY, 1235
(*Shinchokusen wakashū*)
FUJIWARA NO MUNEIE

Fujiwara no Muneie (d. 1189) was married to a daughter of Fujiwara no Shunzei, so it is possible that the following poem was composed for the *Genji kuyō* sponsored by Bifukumon'in Kaga,[24] but no documentary proof of such a connection survives. The "rain of the dharma" is a metaphor used in the "The Parable of Medicinal Herbs" chapter of the Lotus Sutra to describe the teaching of the Buddha, which, like the rain, waters all plants equally but does not result in equal growth in all.

Poem 602

Upon sending "The Parable of Medicinal Herbs" to be dedicated at rites of bonding with the Buddha, for the benefit of Murasaki Shikibu.

ACTING GRAND COUNSELOR MUNEIE

nori no ame ni ware mo nuren mutsumashiki / wakamurasaki no kusa no yukari ni

By the rain of the dharma, would that I, too, might be blessed, for my close affinity with the tender young *murasaki* sprouts.

TRANSLATED BY T. HARPER

A DEDICATORY PROCLAMATION FOR *THE TALE OF GENJI*, CA. 1166
(*Genji* ipponkyō)

CHŌKEN

This proclamation (*hyōbyaku*)[25] employs Bo Juyi's double-edged rhetoric that both justifies secular literature as an instrument to propagate Buddhism and apologizes for erroneously creating it in the first place.[26] Bo Juyi's formulation is quoted verbatim in the proclamation and is applied to prose fiction as a genre and to *The Tale of Genji* in particular. The collective project for which this proclamation was composed—the copying of a complete text of the Lotus Sutra[27]—involved the apparently unprecedented painting of scenes from *Genji*, which were attached to the sutra scrolls. The work is anomalous also in that it was composed of intricately crafted couplets, characteristic of Sino-Japanese (*kanbun*) parallel prose, although it was undoubtedly read out, or sung, as Japanese.

The author of this proclamation, the Tendai prelate Chōken (1126–1203), was a son of Fujiwara no Michinori (Shinzei, 1106–1159), a talented and learned scholar who amassed a vast collection of Chinese books and was renowned for producing a superb picture scroll of Bo Juyi's "Song of Everlasting Sorrow." Shinzei is better known, however, as a political figure who acquired sufficient power to punish his enemies in the Hōgen uprising (1156) by reactivating the death penalty after a 346-year hiatus. Three years later, in the Heiji uprising (1159), Shinzei was dragged from the hole in which he was hiding and beheaded. The source of Shinzei's power was the influence of his second wife, Fujiwara Tomoko (Kii no Nii), who served as wet nurse to the GoShirakawa Emperor and whose name has been suggested as one of the painters of the twelfth-century *Genji monogatari emaki* (*The Tale of Genji Illustrated Scrolls*). Fortunately, because Chōken was not one of those whom his father had installed in a position of power, he was not implicated in the Heiji uprising and was banished only briefly to Shimotsuke (present-day Tochigi Prefecture). Afterward, he went on to found the first hereditary line of Buddhist preachers, known as the Agui school. Chōken's eloquence is known to have startled his audiences at times, often moving them to tears and occasionally even to laughter.

The date of the dedicatory service for which this proclamation was composed is unclear, but the author, Chōken, was most active from the 1160s to the 1180s. On another occasion, he employed the same logic of *kyōgen kigo* in a sermon meant to justify the composition of *waka*. The proclamation from that service appears to date from the year 1166 and is therefore thought to indicate roughly the date of the *Genji* proclamation.

On the basis of a pair of *waka* and their headnotes found elsewhere, the sponsor of the service for which this proclamation was composed was long assumed to have been Bifukumon'in Kaga, the mother of Fujiwara no Teika. The attribution in the Sōanshū manuscript, however, makes it clear that the project's principal sponsor was another lady-in-waiting, known as Tosa no Naishi. Unfortunately, her actual name, dates, and family are unknown. We know only that she was a poet of some renown who was associated with Shun'e and his Karin'en circle of poets, who frequently composed *waka* on topics taken from *Genji*, and also with Kamo no Shigeyasu and his circle.[28]

MICHAEL JAMENTZ

Tosa no Naishi, a nun in service to the Retired Emperor, urged various people to copy out the [Lotus] Sutra, each doing one chapter and providing paintings of scenes from *Genji* for the covers.[29]

Considering the pleasures of literature and the appeal of the classics, we see that the purposes of these writings vary and their significance differs. The sutras of the buddhas and the treatises of the bodhisattvas reveal the sources of the precepts and wisdom; they have opened the gate of the nirvana of enlightenment since the distant past. The writings of the Duke of Zhou[30] and the *Analects* of Confucius concentrate on the Way of benevolence, righteousness, propriety, and wisdom.[31] They clarify the principles of the relationships between lord and subject, parent and child. Although these two types differ, one being scriptural and the other secular, together they conform completely to the true principles of this world and the next.[32] Moreover, the Scribe of the Left[33] has recorded in detail times of tranquillity and turbulence in the realms of a hundred kings, and periods of security and peril for all the world within the four seas.[34] The verses of the poets who compose in Chinese take objects of nature as their topics and describe, as suits their fancy, the pleasures of spring scenery and the views of autumn vistas.

In addition to these genres, in our own realm, we have what we call *waka*. Composing them is an established custom of the people of Japan. In this land, there also exist what we call tales. They are the products of both past and present. They include *Ochikubo*, *Iwaya*, *Nezame*, *Shinobine*, *Sagoromo*, *Ōgi nagashi*, *Sumiyoshi*, *Mitsu no Hamamatsu*, *Sueba no tsuyu*, *Ama no hagoromo*, *Kaguyahime*, *Hikaru Genji*,[35] and so forth. Such works as these tales do not recount the good and evil deeds of people of the past, nor do they record the ancient matters of past reigns. Through falsehood, they create events that never happened and people that never existed. They invent ages and reigns, creating something out of nothing. Although the stories they tell are truly beyond counting, all of them merely describe relations between men and women.

Among these, *The Tale of the Shining Genji*, which was the creation of Murasaki Shikibu, is composed of sixty fascicles and organized in forty-nine chapters.[36] Its language is drawn from both secular and Buddhist texts. The elegant discourse between men and women is cleverly crafted throughout. Of all tales, from past to present, it stands alone in its excellence. Its alluring language is exquisite, greatly exciting the passions. For those men and women who favor amorous pursuits and those, whether high or low, who value superficial luster, this tale is the stuff of their idle talk and so nurtures untoward thoughts in the hearts of others.[37] Thus sheltered maidens in the recesses of their homes read it and are furtively driven to springtime longings. Lonely men, reclining on their cold mats, open it and languish vainly in autumnal reverie.

It is thus that the ghost of the one who created it as well as those who have perused it are assuredly bound in sin, trapped in the cycle of birth and death. All of them will be plunged onto the blades of the saber-branched trees of hell. As a consequence, the ghost of Murasaki Shikibu has long since been appearing in people's dreams, warning them of the gravity of this sin.

Therefore, our grand sponsor, the eminent nun, in her piety, has attempted, on the one hand, to save the author's soul and, on the other, to rescue those who have read or listened to the tale. She has urged in particular those who have entered the path of Buddhism as well as those still of this world, both high and low, to copy the true word of the twenty-eight chapters of the Lotus Sutra and to illustrate each chapter with a scene from *Genji* at the beginning of each scroll, thereby truly turning delusion into enlightenment. The chapters of the sutra have thus been matched to the chapters of the tale in order to transform these amorous words into the seeds of wisdom.

In the past, Bo Juyi vowed to "make the error of wild words and fancy phrases into the karmic cause of praise for the one vehicle of the Buddha and to create karmic opportunities to turn the wheel of the dharma."[38] Now in order to save others, the nun seeks to transform the excesses of those alluring words found in its several chapters so as to adhere to the cosmic law of immutable truth and to create a karmic source for unsurpassed, true enlightenment.

That was but a passing moment, and this, too, is but a moment. Let us together depart the sea of suffering and ascend to the shore of enlightenment.

OFFICIANT, AGUI HŌIN CHŌKEN[39]
TRANSLATED BY MICHAEL JAMENTZ

THE STORY OF OBSEQUIES FOR GENJI
(*Genji kuyō sōshi*)

SEIKAKU

Yet another proclamation (*hyōbyaku*) composed for dedicatory rites on behalf of Murasaki Shikibu is attributed to Chōken's son Seikaku (1167–1235),[40] who succeeded his father as head of the Agui line of preaching prelates. This work survives independently in various sources and is even reprinted in Kitamura Kigin's great commentary *Kogetsushō*. The most interesting context in which it is found, however, is a Muromachi-period (1333–1568) story (*otogizōshi*), in which its origins are "explained." The story is probably a fiction but is not implausible. Unlike his father's proclamation, Seikaku's is written in Japanese[41] and incorporates every chapter title from *Genji* in a lyrical, though often syntactically loose, setting of Buddhist doctrine, the whole forming a continuous flow from "Kiritsubo" to "Yume no ukihashi." Even if it was not composed impromptu, as the story claims, it is nonetheless an impressive performance of the principle of non-duality.[42]

T. HARPER

Seikaku Hōin,[43] of the temple Agoin,[44] had two residences, East and West. The Eastern Residence was a tranquil place, undisturbed by visitors, where he could compose his thoughts and prepare his sermons. The only resident was a young acolyte named Zebun. The Western Residence was where his disciples always gathered for study and where he received callers. In the inner quarters, as they were called, the ladies of the household lived and managed his private affairs.

One day around the middle of the Third Month, back when he was still known as Seikaku the Grand Prelate, he was composing a sermon at his Eastern Residence. Dressed in a sleeveless robe of rough silk, with a hempen surplice thrown over his shoulder, and shod in sandals worn down at the heel, he was circumambulating the veranda,[45] when from an easterly direction he heard the sounds of an approaching carriage. To the east, a rushing stream flowed down the valley; carriages did not normally pass that way. What might be the meaning of this? he wondered, listening intently. Whereupon the carriage halted before his own gate, and someone pounded vigorously on the doors. Whoever might this be? he thought with a start. He called to Zebun,

"Come now! Can't you hear that pounding at the gate?"

The boy had been napping, and still half-asleep, never questioning who it might be, he threw open both the left and right panels. The Prelate took refuge behind the wooden door at the carriage landing, peering out from which he spied a fawn-colored carriage adorned with large eight-petal crests and hung with long tinted curtains beneath the blinds. . . .[46] Five or six lackeys, clad in white cloak and trousers, were in attendance. They pushed the gate wide open and swiftly entered the compound. Who could this be? the Prelate wondered; but Zebun had fled, and there was no one else he could command to make inquiries in his stead. He could only gaze wide-eyed at the scene. They unhitched the carriage and turned it to face the wooden door. The Prelate himself handed them the straw mat for the carriage landing, whereupon the lackeys pushed the door shut again and shunted the carriage into position.

As he watched, a gentlewoman of twenty-two or twenty-three alighted, wearing crimson trousers and a diaphanous gown. Then the Prelate saw another woman gently alight, a nun of twenty-four or twenty-five, fine featured with a pale white complexion, wearing a pale persimmon robe next to her skin and over it a black robe with white trousers. The Prelate slid open the panel door and took refuge inside. He was quite perplexed what sort of people these might be, but when he cleared his throat, the gentlewoman spoke.

"Might we have a word with you?" she said.

"Concerning what . . . ?" he replied.

"A person from the Eastern Hills who wishes to speak with you has made her way hither," she said.

"But whose dwelling do you imagine this might be, that you should make your way here?" When he said this, a look of doubt crossed her face.

"I had our attendants drive the carriage in here, thinking this was the residence of the preaching Prelate. But am I perhaps mistaken?"

"From time to time, I do preach a poor sermon of sorts," the Prelate replied, "but I can hardly imagine who from the Eastern Hills might honor me with a visit."

"Were she some grand personage, I should gladly tell you who comes from the Eastern Hills. But she lives deep in a valley you may never even have heard of. Even if I were to tell you, I doubt that you would have heard of her; we are not the sort whose names are well known. She simply wishes to meet you and speak with you."

In the meantime, the Prelate had changed into a somewhat more presentable robe, donned a silken surplice, and come to sit by the sliding panel.

"I am no one toward whom you need feel reticent," the gentlewoman said. "Could you perhaps slide the panel open a bit?"

Since the gentlewoman herself showed no reticence, there seemed no need for the monk to do so, and he slid the panels all the way open. And there sat the nun, facing north, directly opposite him, as in a formal audience. But when she turned her gaze slightly to the west, he could see from her face and bearing that she was no ordinary woman. Even when she was about to speak, the expression that spread from ear to ear across her face bespoke great reluctance to do so.

"I am loath even to speak of this," she said, "but since childhood, my thoughts have been deeply tainted by a storybook called *Genji*, which I found utterly fascinating. But in the spring of this past year, I came to my senses and, as you see, became a nun. I am now determined to give my undivided attention to thoughts of the hereafter. Yet, those things that for long I read still linger, unforgotten, in my mind, and I find myself thinking, 'Now it was in this chapter that such and such happened . . . ,' which distracts me from my devotions when I am chanting the *nenbutsu*. I know full well how grievously sinful this is, and so in atonement, I purposely tore up several chapters of this book,[47] both those I myself had copied and those I had had others copy for me, and had them remade as sutra rolls, onto which I copied, in my own hand, the entire Lotus Sutra.

"Were I a person of any consequence, it would behoove me to extend an invitation to you; but being of such mean station, I would hardly dare ask that you honor me with a visit. Neither would I be able to offer you such recompense as I would wish. Even so, it would be a terrible shame to request this of a rude monk from a rustic mountain temple. And so, hoping at least to forge an initial bond with the Way of the Buddha, I have, despite all, come to you. Might I beg of you, then, if only for form's sake, to sound your chime on my behalf?"

The Prelate replied: "That I, Seikaku, make my way through this life as a preacher of the dharma is well known to all and sundry. But to conduct rites of dedication to the Buddha or in praise of the scriptures would require that I prepare a written proclamation, for which I would need advance notice from your good self. Your command that I do so this very moment, here in your presence, I am hard put to obey."

"It is nothing so very grandiose that I require," Her Ladyship the nun said. "I dare hope that you might in some small way oblige me only because I place such great faith in you. Please, I pray you, simply sound your chime for me."

"It would indeed be too heartlessly cruel of me to send away one whose devotion is so great. Very well, then—here and now, if only for form's sake, let me offer you my humble services."

Overjoyed, her gentlewoman summoned their lackeys and had them bring in the sutra box. The fabric of the pouch in which it was wrapped hinted to him that its contents would bear no resemblance to anything commonplace, and when he saw the sutra box that they produced from it—redolent with the rich scent of a renowned incense, its polished lacquer surface adorned with a scene strewn in gold dust, the scattering cherry petals in mother-of-pearl, with silver edging in the Chinese fashion—it was obvious that this was something quite exceptional. Then the box was opened, revealing sutra scrolls of extraordinary magnificence, with cover papers of deep blue and spindles of crystal. The Prelate summoned Zebun and had the boy bring him his battered old lectern. He assumed that the gentlewoman would first place a protective layer of paper on it, but she took up the scrolls, one after another, and set them out in a row. She could see perfectly well how decrepit a lectern it was, fraught with broad cracks between its slats. "And yet a gentlewoman can bring herself to use such a thing?" he thought, marveling only the more how very gracious she was. He, of course, had an incense burner at hand, but to give the rite a special touch, he had a sprig of star anise brought in, which he used to sound the chime. Then unobtrusively, he made triple obeisance and began, there and then, almost inaudibly, to chant a full catalog of the chapters of *Genji*:

***Kiritsubo** no yūbe no kemuri, sumiyaka ni hosshō no sora ni noboru,*
In the evening, smoke rising from the pyre of the lady of the **Paulownia Court** ascends swiftly to the heavens of the dharma nature,

***Hahakigi** no yoru no kotoba wa, tsui ni kakuju no hana o hirakan.*
While those trifling words spoken that night in the **Broom Tree** ultimately shall cause flowers to bloom on the tree of enlightenment.

***Utsusemi** no munashiki kono yo o itoite,*
Despising this world, as empty as the **Cicada's Shell**,

***Yūgao** no tsuyu no inochi o kanji,*
Contemplating her whose life was as fleeting as dew on a **Moonflower**,

***Waka [Waga?] murasaki** no kumo no mukae o ete,*[48]
And receiving the welcome of those who come for us on **Delicate Purple** clouds,

***Suetsumuhana** no utena ni za seshimen.*
Then shall we be seated on the throne of the **[Saf]flower** of the Lotus.

***Momiji no ga** no aki no yūbe ni wa, ochiba o nozomite, ui o kanashimi,*
On the autumn evening of the **Celebration of Autumn Leaves**, gazing at those leaves as they fall, lamenting the impermanence of all phenomena,

***Hana no en** no haru no ashita ni wa, hika o kanjite mujō o satorite,*[49]
On the spring morning of the **Cherry Blossom Festival**, observing the fluttering petals, awakening to the impermanence of all things,

*Tamatama busshō ni **Afu hi [Aoi]** nari.*[50]
Then perchance shall come that **Day of Encounter** with our own Buddha nature.

***Sakaki**-ba no, sashite jōsetsu wo negaubeshi.*
Proffering a sprig from the **Sacred Tree**, pray then for rebirth in the Pure Land.

***Hana chiru sato** ni kokoro o todomu to iedomo, aibetsu rikū no kotowari manugaraegatashi.*[51]
And though our hearts may long to linger in this **Village of Falling Flowers**, there is no escaping the truth that all must know the pain of parting with loved ones.

*Tada subekaraku wa, shōji ryūrō no **Suma** no ura o idete,*
What must, above all, be done is to depart that desolate shore of **Suma**, where one wanders in the endless cycle of birth and death,

*Shichi enmyō no **Akashi** no ura ni itaran ga tame nari.*[52]
So as to arrive at the shore of total **Understanding** of the Four Modes of Wisdom.

***Miotsukushi, Sekiya** no yukiau michi o nogarete, hannya no kiyoki migiri ni omomuki,*
Avoiding that way where they who come via the **Channel Markers** and the **Barrier Gate** chance to meet and making, instead, for that pure place of Transcendent Wisdom,

***Yomogiu** no fukaki kusamura o wakete, bodai no makoto no michi o negawan.*
Parting the thick clumps of **Wormwood**, let us seek out the Way to the truth of enlightenment.

*Nani zo Mida no sonyō o utsushite, **Eawase** to shi,*
And might we not enter a rendition of the honored visage of Amida in the **Picture Competition**,

***Matsukaze** ni gosshō no **Usugumo** o harawazaran?*
Thus allowing the **Wind in the Pines** to blow away the **Thin Clouds** of hindrance?

Shō, rō, byō, shi no ***Asagao*** *no hikage o matan hodo nari.*[53]
Birth, aging, illness, and death last only as long as the **Morning Glory** awaits the sun.

Rōshō no sakai, ***Otome*** *ga* ***Tamakazura*** *kaketemo nao tanomigatashi.*[54]
Even the **Maiden** who has only just adorned her hair with the **Tendril Wreath** can hardly be certain whether old or young shall die first.

Tani uchiizuru uguisu no, ***Hatsune*** *mo nani ka mezurashikaran. Fugan en'ō no saezuri ni wa shikaji.*
What is there so wondrous in the **First Song** of the warbler that darts out from the valley? It is no match for the call of the drake, the wild goose, the mandarin ducks.[55]

Magaki ni tawabururu ***Kochō*** *mo, tada shibaraku no tanoshimi nari. Tennin shōju no asobi o omoiyare.*
The **Butterflies** that disport themselves by the fence offer but a moment's pleasure. Set your thoughts instead on the music of the heavenly host and the assembled saints.

Sawa no ***Hotaru*** *no kuyuru omoi,* ***Tokonatsu*** *nari to iedomo,*
Our smoldering regrets, so like **Fireflies** on the marsh, though they last **Summer Long,**

Tachimachi ni chie no ***Kakaribi*** *ni hikikaete,*
In an instant may be transformed into a blazing **Watch Fire** of wisdom,

Nowaki *no kaze ni kiyuru koto naku;*
Never to be extinguished by the winds of the **Storm**;

Nyōrai Kakuō no ***Miyuki*** *ni tomonaite,*
Then joining the **Royal Progress** of that Monarch of Enlightenment the Buddha,

Jihi ninniku no ***Fujibakama*** *o, jōbon rendai ni kokoro o kakete,*
We don the **Purple Trousers** of compassion and forbearance, set our hearts on the highest of the high among lotus thrones,

Shippō shōgon no ***Makibashira*** *no moto ni itaran.*
That we may arrive at the base of that **Cypress Pillar** so splendidly adorned with the Seven Treasures.

Umegae *no nioi ni kokoro o tomuru koto naku,*
Content yourself not with the fragrance of a **Branch of Plum,**

Jōdo no ***Fuji no uraba*** *o moteasobubeshi.*
But delight instead in the **New Leaves of Wisteria** in the Pure Land.

Kano sentō sennen mo kyūji ni wa, ***Wakana*** *o tsumite sennin ni kuyō seshikaba, jōbutsu tokudō no in to nariniki.*
Because he who was once King [*sentō*], throughout his thousand years of servitude, plucked **Young Sprouts** and gave them in offering to the Seer [*sennin*], this became the direct cause of his mastery of the Way and his attainment of Buddhahood.[56]

Natsugoromo tachii ni, ikani shite ka hitoeda no ***Kashiwagi*** *o hiroite, myōhō no takigi to nashite, mushi kōgō no tsumi o horoboshi, hon'u jōju no fūkō o kagayakashite, shōju no ongaku no* ***Yokobue*** *o kikan.*
In the course of our own daily lives, slight as summer raiment though they be, would that we might somehow take up a branch of the **Oak Tree**, use it to fuel the fire of the wondrous dharma, whose flames would consume all our sins throughout time without beginning and illumine brilliantly the beauties of our original and eternal Buddha nature, that we might hearken to **The Flute** as it plays the music of the assembled saints.

Urameshiki kana ya, busshō no yo ni umarenagara, ie o ide, na o sutsuru migiri ni wa, ***Suzumushi*** *no koe furisutegataku,*
How lamentable! That despite being born into this world with the Buddha nature, even when we leave behind our homes and abandon fame, we still find it so difficult to forsake the song of the **Bell Cricket**,

Michi ni iri kazari o orosu tokoro ni, ***Yūgiri*** *no musebi haregatashi.*
And when we enter the Way and take the tonsure, we still can hardly avoid being choked with tears at the sight of the **Evening Mist**.

Kanashiki kana ya, ningen ni shō o ukenagara, ***Minori*** *no michi o shirazu shite kukai ni shizumi;*
How very sad! That despite being born a human, we should sink in the sea of anguish, never knowing the Way of **The Law**;

Maboroshi *no yo o itowazu shite seiro o itonamu koto shikaji.*[57]
Far better that one make one's way down the road of life knowing never an ill thought for this world of **Illusion**.

Tada Kaoru daishō no ka o aratamete, shōren no hanabusa ni omoi o some ***Niou Hyōbukyō*** *no nioi o hirugaeshite wa, kōno kemuri no yoso'oi to nari,*

Merely by altering the fragrance of Commandant Kaoru, we shall imbue our thoughts with the bloom of the blue lotus[58] and, transforming the scent of **The Perfumed Prince**, provide the smoke of offertory incense,

Takekawa *no mizu o musubite wa, bonnō no mi o susugi,*
Scooping up water from the **Bamboo River** shall we wash away our delusion,

Kōbai *no iro o utsushite, aichaku no kokorozashi o ushinaubeshi.*
And, draining the tint from the **Crimson Plum**, banish our attachment to the bonds of affection.

Matsu yoi no fukeshi o nagekiken Uji no ***Hashihime*** *ni itaru made, Ubasoku ga okonau michi o shirube nite,*
Onward until we reach Uji—where the **Maiden of the Bridge**, on those evenings when she waited, must have sighed that it had grown so late[59]—with the Way as practiced by the Novice as our guide,

Shii ga moto *ni tomaru koto naku, hokubō no tsuyu to kienan yūbe ni wa, gedatsu no* ***Agemaki*** *o musubi;*[60]
Halting not **Beneath the Oak**, but of an evening when we might vanish as the dew on Mount Mang to the north, let us tie the **Trefoil Knot** of release;

Tōtai no ***Sawarabi*** *kemuri to noboran ashita ni wa,*
And on a morning when we might rise up as smoke from the **Fern Shoots** on Mount T'ai in the east,[61]

Sendan no kage ni ***Yadorigi*** *to naran.*
Let us shelter in the shade of the sacred sandalwood, clinging to it like **Ivy**.

Tsukasa kurai o ***Azumaya*** *no uchi ni nogarete,*
We must flee office and rank, taking refuge in the **Eastern Cottage**,

Tanoshimi sakae o ***Ukifune*** *ni tatoubeshi.*
And liken the pleasures and successes of this life to a **Drifting Boat**.

Kore mo ***Kagerō*** *no yo nari.*
For these, too, are of a world as ephemeral as the **Mayfly**.

Aru ka naki ka no ***Tenarai*** *ni, ōjō gokuraku no mon o kakubeshi.*
Even at **Writing Practice**—though so desultory that we wonder, "Is it or is it not"[62]—we should write the words "rebirth in paradise."

Kare mo ***Yume no ukihashi*** *no yo nari.*
For that, too, is of a world as insubstantial as a **Floating Bridge of Dreams.**

Asa na yū na ni raigō injō o negaiwatarubeshi. Namu saihō gokuraku kyōshu Amida Nyōrai zenzei, negawaku wa kyōgen kigyo no ayamari o hirugaeshite, Murasaki Shikibu ga rokushu kugen o sukuitamae.

Morning and evening, let us ceaselessly pray that the Buddha might come and lead us to Paradise. Praise be to the Lord of the Western Paradise, the Buddha Amida, he who has gone on to the world of good beyond. And may those wild words and fancy phrases be transformed, so that Murasaki Shikibu may be rescued from the pain and suffering of rebirth in the six realms.[63]

When he had finished, he sounded the chime and pushed his lectern aside. Her Ladyship the nun was hard put to dry the tears that soaked her sleeve. Her gentlewoman, too, had to lower her eyes. Then from the pouch that held her amulet, she produced a hundredweight of gold dust wrapped in thin white paper, which she placed before him. Seeing this, the Prelate realized that these could be no common people. The gentlewoman had the carriage drawn up, and they departed.

The Prelate summoned one of his guardian monks and told him to find out where the carriage went. As the man followed them, taking care not to be seen, they came to the First Avenue and there turned in the direction of Shirakawa. As they proceeded eastward, passing north of the temple Hosshōji and on toward Hanazono, the sun began to set. At the crossroads east of Kusakawa, he saw them enter a south-facing double-door gate that appeared to be the main entrance to a high-gated palace. A resident of the neighborhood said it was the palace of the Honorary Empress.[64] The guardsman gave some thought to the matter and then reported what he had learned.

"If she is the daughter of Naka no Kampaku,"[65] the Prelate said, "it seems to me this would make sense. Even so, this is most unusual. I sensed from the start that she was no ordinary woman."

It was nothing new that the Honorary Empress thought Seikaku a superb preacher, but *this* she could hardly consider the work of a mere mortal. To recall, on the spot, all the chapters of *Genji* in their proper order,[66] with never a moment's hesitation or missing a single one—all the while drawing upon famous phrases and composing impromptu in elegant parallels—this seemed too miraculous to be the work of any ordinary man. I have heard that thereafter she summoned him whenever Buddhist rites were in order and that it was she who promoted him to the rank of *hōin*.

TRANSLATED BY T. HARPER

Notes

1. *Muryōjukyō*, T 360.

2. Taya Raishun, Ōchō Enichi, and Funahashi Issai, eds., *Bukkyōgaku jiten* (Kyoto: Hōzōkan, 1955), 234; *Kegonkyō*, T 278.

3. A contemporary description of the Society for the Advancement of Learning can be found in *Sanbō ekotoba* (SNKBT 31:172–74) and is translated in Edward Kamens, *The Three Jewels: A Study and Translation of Minamoto Tamenori's Sanbōe* (Ann Arbor: Center for Japanese Studies, University of Michigan, 1988), 295–98. Another, shorter description is found in *Eiga monogatari*, ed. Matsumura Hiroji and Yamanaka Yutaka, NKBT 75:450.

4. Daughter of Sugawara no Takasue, *Sarashina nikki*, NKBT 20:493.

5. Actually his granddaughter and probably the author of *Mumyōzōshi*.

6. Translated from Fujiwara no Tametsune, *Ima kagami zenshaku*, ed. Unno Yasuo (Tokyo: Fukutake Shoten, 1983), 2:519–34.

7. Edward Conze, *Buddhist Thought in India: Three Phases of Buddhist Philosophy* (Ann Arbor: University of Michigan Press, 1967), 238–49.

8. (J.) *Nehangyō*, T 374, 12:485a.

9. Vimaladattā's (J. Jōtoku) conversion of her husband, with the help of an impressive display of magic by her two sons, is the subject of chapter 27 of the Lotus Sutra.

10. *The Lion's Roar of Queen Shrīmālā: A Buddhist Scripture on the Tathāgatagarba Theory*, trans. Alex Wayman and Hideko Wayman (New York: Columbia University Press, 1974).

11. Hachi no Miya, the Eighth Prince.

12. Hachi no Miya's eldest daughter, Ōigimi.

13. The Suzaku Retired Emperor.

14. Chapter 12 of the Lotus Sutra, in which the Buddha relates how long ago he himself forsook his kingdom to seek enlightenment as the servant of a seer.

15. Probably referring to Vasubandhu's (J. Seshin; fl. fourth century) *Trimsikā vijnapti-kārikā* (J. *Yuishiki sanjū ronju*), T 1586.

16. Biographical information from Kuwabara Hiroshi, "Fujiwara no Saneki no haha," and Gotō Shigeo, "Saionji Kintsune," both in *Nihon koten bungaku daijiten* (Tokyo: Iwanami Shoten, 1984), 5:280–81, 3:3; and Higuchi Yoshimaro, "Saneki no haha shū," KT 7:817.

17. Hashimoto Fumio, "Gon Chūnagon Saneki Kyō no haha shū," in *Katsuranomiya-bon sōsho* (Kyoto: Yōtokusha, 1959), 10:29.

18. Translated from *Saneki no haha shū*, KT 7:358. The numbers are those assigned by the *Kokka taikan* editors. Another transcription of the collection is found in

Katsuranomiya-bon sōsho 10:201–303; for these five poems and their headnotes, see 219–20.

19. Poems 453–461 in *Saneki no haha shū*, KT 7:363. The numbers are those assigned by the *Kokka taikan* editors. On these nine poems, see Onoe Miki, "*Gon Chūnagon Saneki Kyō no haha shū no Genji monogatari* kanmei tsugiuta ni tsuite," in *Genji monogatari to ōchō sekai*, ed. Waseda Daigaku Daigakuin Chūko Bungaku Kenkyūkai (Tokyo: Musashino Shoin, 2000), 259–75.

20. Poems 662–671 in *Saneki no haha shū*, KT 7:365.

21. This translation follows the KT text, in which the headnote reads *kano bodai no tame ni* (for the sake of her [Murasaki Shikibu's] enlightenment). A variant, which reads *kano bosatsu no tame ni* (for the sake of this bodhisattva), is found in *Katsuranomiya-bon sōsho*, 10:219. For a discussion of the *Katsuranomiya-bon sōsho* reading, see Teramoto Naohiko, "Saneki Kyō no haha shū no 'Genji kōshiki,'" in *Genji monogatari juyōshi ronkō* (Tokyo: Kazama Shobō, 1970), 731–38.

22. The rain is that of the Buddha's teachings, as described in the central metaphor of "The Parable of Medicinal Herbs," chapter 5 of the Lotus Sutra.

23. Translated from the text in GR 15:192.

24. Translated from the text in KT 1:271.

25. The title of this proclamation is clearly one of convenience. In order to convey its full significance, it would have to be expanded to read "The Officiant's Proclamation for the Dedication of the One-Chapter-per-Person Copying of the Lotus Sutra on Behalf of the Author of *The Tale of Genji* and Her Readers."

A proclamation (*hyōbyaku*) is a statement of purpose often delivered by the officiating monk at the commencement of a Buddhist service. Although delivered orally, in its written form the *hyōbyaku* is one of the chief literary genres of Buddhist preaching.

26. Bo Juyi's celebrated formulation, "I vow to take the error of wild words and fancy phrases of my worldly literary enterprise in this life and transform it into the karma of praising the Turning of the Wheel of the Dharma of Buddha's Vehicle for ages and ages to come," is found in volume 70 of the *Collected Works of Bo Juyi* and was included in the *Wakan rōeishū*, the early-eleventh-century collection of Chinese and Japanese verse.

27. Such group projects, known as *ipponkyō*, required that each member of the group produce a single chapter (*ippon*) of the sutra.

28. This proclamation is found in three manuscripts: (1) the *Shūjushō* (*Selections from Collected Jewels*), owned by the Sanzen-in temple in Ōhara, Kyoto; (2) the *Sōanshū, fuju tō* (*A Collection of Drafts of Offertory Statements and the Like*), owned by the Shakamon-in cloister on Mount Kōya; and (3) the *Shonin zatsushuzen* (*Good Works of Various People*), owned by Ōkura Seishin Bunka Kenkyūjo in Yokohama. All three manuscripts are thought to be from the Kamakura era, but only the *Shonin zatsushuzen* is dated, Kenpo 4 (1216). The translation is based primarily on the Shakamon-in manuscript.

29. This annotation appears only in the Shakamon-in *Sōanshū, fuju tō* manuscript, where it follows the title of the item. The appellation In no Nyōbō Tosa no Naishi refers to the fact that Tosa served as a palace attendant, an official appointment, in the court of the child emperor Konoe (1139–1155), who was given the honorary title *in* (retired emperor) posthumously. Apparently stricken by the tragedy of

the child's death, Tosa took the tonsure. *Nyōbō* indicates that she was a lady-in-waiting, but if the proclamation was created in the latter half of the twelfth century, she may have been serving the GoShirakawa Retired Emperor. The ambiguity of the annotation makes it impossible to identify the painter or painters. Tosa may have created the paintings herself, but given the collective nature of *ipponkyō* projects, it seems more likely that each image was created by an individual contributor.

30. The Duke of Zhou is thought to have written the *Book of Etiquette and Ceremonial* (C. *Yili*; J. *Girai*) and *Institutes of Zhou* (C. *Zhouli*; J. *Shurai*) and to have contributed to the *Book of Changes* (C. *Yijing*; J. *Ekikyō*).

31. "Benevolence, righteous, propriety, and wisdom" are the four virtues that, according to Mencius, are inherent in all humans. See James Legge, trans., *The Chinese Classics*, vol. 2, *The Works of Mencius* (Oxford: Clarendon Press, 1895), 202–3, 402–3.

32. The phrase "this world and the next" is a translation of the compound *shusseken*, which has been interpreted in several ways but is translated as "worldly and supra-worldly" in Hisao Inagaki and P. G. O'Neil, *A Dictionary of Japanese Buddhist Terms: Based on References in Japanese Literature* (Kyoto: Nagata Bunshōdō, 1984), 280. The term also is used in Mujū Ichien's spirited defense of *waka* against the charge of being *kyōgen kigo*, in the *Shasekishū* (NKBT 85:223), in which Japanese verse is characterized as both *hōben* (expedient means) and *dharani* (incantation).

33. The Scribe of the Left, paired with the Scribe of the Right, was said to have served the emperor in ancient China, and it was the responsibility of the Scribe of the Left to record the events of the reign. One theory held that a Scribe of the Left was thought to have produced the *Zuo zhuan* (J. *Shunjū sashiden*), a canonical commentary on the *Spring and Autumn Annals*.

34. The wording of this couplet is taken from Bo Juyi's "A Mirror of a Hundred Refinings," in *Wakan rōei shū* 655.

35. All the tales listed here except *Ōgi nagashi* and *Ama no hagoromo* are known to have circulated in Heian times.

36. Several works contemporaneous to this pronouncement refer to the fact that *Genji* was composed of sixty books or scrolls, which appears to reflect the existence of now-lost chapters. The organization of the work into forty-nine chapters is more difficult to understand. But some early listings of the chapters in the tale combine more than one chapter title into a single unit in the table of contents, which may be the source of the number forty-nine.

37. This complex phrase echoes Ki no Tsurayuki's criticism of the use of *waka* for erotic purposes in his *kana* preface to the *Kokinshū*, NKBT 8:97.

38. "Turning the dharma wheel" refers to the preaching and propagation of Buddhism.

39. This attribution appears only in the *Shūjushō* manuscript and reads "officiant [*dōshi*], same as the previous." The previous item is said to have been composed by Ango [*sic*] Hōin Chōken (1126–1203). Since this *hyōbyaku* accompanies his "Waka mandokoro kechienkyō hyōbyaku" in two of the three manuscripts that contain this item, and the latter *hyōbyaku* is dated Eiman 2 (1166) in the *Shūjushō*, it is often assumed that this *hyōbyaku* was produced at roughly the same time as that which precedes it. Chōken, however, was not awarded the rank of *hōin* until 1183.

40. In Tendai tradition, his name is read Shōkaku, but in Jōdo tradition, it is Seikaku. No preference is expressed in this text, but since the lady who comes to call

on him complains of being distracted in her recitation of the *nenbutsu* and the proclamation is redolent of Pure Land doctrine, he is called Seikaku here. Concerning Chōken, see the introduction to "A Dedicatory Proclamation for *The Tale of Genji*."

41. Another proclamation composed in Chinese, "*Genji monogatari* ganmon," appears to have been translated, at least in part, from Seikaku's Japanese text. Many of the chapter titles are out of order, and the author's Chinese is considered inferior to Chōken's, but it is nonetheless of interest for its inclusion of a number of apocryphal and alternative chapter titles.

42. Translated from Ii Haruki, *Genji monogatari no densetsu* (Tokyo: Shōwa Shuppan, 1976), 215–31. The *Genji monogatari hyōbyaku* text with which it is occasionally compared is found in Abe Akio, Oka Kazuo, and Yamagishi Tokuhei, eds., *Genji monogatari*, Kokugo kokubungaku kenkyū shi taisei 3 (Tokyo: Sanseidō, 1960), 133–34. Minor variants are numerous, but only those significant enough to affect the translation are noted.

43. *Hōin* (Dharma Seal) is the highest of three ranks granted by the government, at first only to Buddhist clerics, but later to painters, sculptors, doctors, and *renga* masters as well.

44. The city branch (*satobō*) of Chikurin-in, a temple in the eastern precinct (*tōtō*) of Hieizan. "Agoin" is the pronunciation specified in this text. It was often abbreviated further to "Agoi" and "Agui." Modern scholarship generally prefers "Agui."

45. As a form of homage to the Buddha image in the hall, he circumambulates the veranda in a clockwise direction.

46. The remainder of this sentence is garbled.

47. The verb translated as "tore up" is *yaru*, the classical equivalent of modern *yaburu*. It is here taken to mean that the lady tore her text of *Genji* to shreds so that the scraps could be soaked to a pulp and then remade as new (though slightly darker) sheets on which to copy the Lotus Sutra. Another method of executing this very physical form of the nonduality principle (*bonnō soku bodai*) was to unbind (or unroll) the offending text, turn it over, and copy the scripture on the reverse side. Ii points out, however, that the verb *yaru* is used elsewhere (*Izumi Shikibu zoku shū*) in the phrase *yarite, kyōshi ni tsukase* (tore up and remade into sutra paper) (*Genji monogatari no densetsu*, 187). On the basis of this evidence, the first method is thought to have been employed here.

48. The editors of the nō play *Genji kuyō*, in which the same phrase occurs, suggest that the *waka* of "Wakamurasaki" may be a *kakekotoba* (play on words) for *waga*, so that the phrase may be read *waga murasaki no kumo no mukae . . .* (*our* welcome by those who come upon purple clouds. . .). See Itō Masashi, ed., *Yōkyoku shū*, SNKS, 2:58; and Nishino Haruo, ed., *Yōkyoku hyakuban*, SNKBT 57:336.

49. The *Genji monogatari hyōbyaku* text reads *satoran* in place of *satorite*.

50. The *Hyōbyaku* text reads *bukkyō* in place of *busshō*.

51. The *Hyōbyaku* text reads *manugaruru tameshi nashi* in place of *manugaraegatashi*.

52. In the *Hyōbyaku* text, this phrase reads *Shichi enmyō no akashi no ura ni mi o tsukushi* (Strive with all one's might on the shore of total understanding of the four modes of wisdom). This is a far more attractive way of weaving the "Miotsukushi" chapter title into the text, which also makes the following sentence sound more sensible. The temptation to emend has been resisted.

53. Modern scholarship insists that the *asagao* of the Heian period was not the "morning glory" but the "bellflower," which is now called *kikyō*. Seikaku clearly disagrees.

54. The *Hyōbyaku* text reads *otomego* in place of *otome ga*.

55. Waterfowl that inhabit the ponds of Paradise, which brim with waters of the eight virtues.

56. This passage recounts in abbreviated form a story that Buddha tells in chapter 12, "Devadatta," of the Lotus Sutra. In one of his previous incarnations, "countless kalpas ago," when he was a great king, he forsook his throne and, for a thousand years, served as a menial to a seer who helped him on the way to Buddhahood. Because this king has relinquished sovereignty, he is here called *sentō*, a term of respect for retired sovereigns. The Lotus makes no mention of "young sprouts," but they fit the context well enough. The *Hyōbyaku* text reads *seson* in place of *sennin*, "the Buddha" himself rather than "the Seer." The *Kuyō sōshi* text is more accurate, as *sennin* is precisely the term used in the Chinese translation of the Lotus.

57. The *Hyōbyaku* text punctuates this passage differently, placing a period after *koto* and making *shikaji* the first word of the next line.

58. For its pale blue clarity, a favorite metaphor for the eyes of the Buddha.

59. Probably an allusion to *Kokinshū* 689:

samushiro no koromo katashiki koyoi mo ya / ware o matsuran uji no hashihime

This evening, too, on a rough mat, her robe spread out for herself alone,
does she await me, the Maiden of the Bridge in Uji?

"Samushiro" is also the title of an apocryphal chapter of *Genji* that is no longer extant.

60. The *Hyōbyaku* text reads *nakare* in place of *naku*, and *nobe no awayuki* (light spring snow on the fields) in place of *tsuyu* (dew).

61. Fern shoots and smoke are frequent partners in poetry, principally because "sprout" (*moyu*) and "burn" (*moyu*) are homonyms, but encouraged as well by the agricultural practice of burning off the withered remains of the previous year's growth at about the time new fern shoots are sprouting. Mount Mang, to the north (of Luoyang), and Mount T'ai, in the east (Shandong), were the sites of famous graveyards, as a result of which "dew on Mount Mang" and "smoke rising from Mount T'ai" became favorite tropes in both Chinese and Japanese, frequently used in parallel constructions, as they are here.

62. In *Genji*, this phrase occurs not in "Tenarai" but in the last line of the previous chapter, "Kagerō," where it is used more traditionally in reference to the mayfly as a metaphor for the ephemerality of life. Commentators identify Murasaki's source as *Gosenshū* 1191 and/or 1264, but the same phrase is found in at least thirty other poems that predate the *Hyōbyaku*.

63. The *Hyōbyaku* text goes on to complete the parallel: *Namu tōrai dōshi Miroku jison, kanarazu tenbōrin no en to shite, kore o moteasoban hito o annyō jōsetsu ni muketamae to nari* (Praise be to our guide in future lives, the compassionate Miroku. And may this [*Genji*] without fail cause the wheel of the dharma to turn,

so that those who would enjoy it may be welcomed to that Pure Land of peace and sustenance).

64. *Jūgo* and, in the last paragraph, *jūgo no miya*: an honorary title whose grantees (both male and female) were awarded all the emoluments and privileges of the "Three Empresses" (Empress Grandmother, Empress Mother, and Empress Regnant).

65. The only historical figure ever known as Naka no Kanpaku (Middle Chancellor) was Fujiwara no Michitaka (953–995), so called because he held the office of chancellor between the tenure of his father, Kaneie, and his younger brother Michinaga. His daughter was Empress Teishi, whose early death ensured the ascendency of her rival, Michinaga's daughter Shōshi. It is thus chronologically—not to mention politically—impossible that the lady in the story could be Michitaka's daughter. The suggestion, made by Horibe Hisamitsu in 1930, that the author may have meant to refer to the daughter of Fujiwara no Motozane (1143–1166), whose sobriquet seems to have been Naka Dono and who briefly held the office of Middle Chancellor, was convincingly discredited by Gotō Tanji but still finds its way into some bibliographical descriptions of the work. A good summary of these arguments is found in Fujii Takashi, *Mikan otogizōshi shū to kenkyū* (Tokyo: Mikan Kokubungaku Shiryō Kankōkai, 1967), 4:117–25.

66. In modern *Genji* texts, "Kōbai" and "Takekawa" appear in reverse order. Some early catalogs of chapter titles, however, show them in the same order as Seikaku's listing.

Chapter 5

The Tale of Genji Apocrypha

THE *OXFORD ENGLISH DICTIONARY* defines "apocrypha" as works "of unknown authorship; not authentic, spurious; uncanonical; false." One or more of these descriptions would fit each of the texts in this chapter, but none of them is "apocryphal" in quite the same way as any of the others. "Sakurahito" and "Sumori" are the surviving fragments of chapters that were considered authentic by late-Heian editors of *Genji*; they may even have been written by Murasaki Shikibu, but were later rejected as noncanonical. "Yamaji no tsuyu" is a spurious "last chapter" of unknown authorship, but is not without an air of authenticity. The six "Kumogakure rokujō" are blatantly false. And "Tamakura" is an academic exercise in neoclassical composition by an eighteenth-century author who made no attempt to conceal either the nature of his project or his own identity. In short, these "apocrypha" constitute a diverse body of texts, written over a span of about seven centuries. What they share with one another, however, apart from their apocryphal character, is a direct relationship to the early textual evolution of *Genji*, the end product of which was the fifty-four-chapter *Genji* that we know today. To better understand the *Genji* apocrypha, therefore, we must first consider how the canonical *Genji* came into being.

The *Genji* that we read today is not the *Genji* that its earliest readers read. At the outset, there would have been only a few independent tales about a young nobleman, the Shining Genji, probably commissioned individually by wealthy courtiers for the amusement of their daughters (not to mention themselves). The price of paper was such that even the shortest chapter could not have been written without a substantial subsidy to cover the cost of materials.[1] As the number of these stories grew, so did the reputation of their author. As a result, she was taken into the service of Empress Shōshi and commissioned to compile a volume of these stories for presentation to the Ichijō Emperor in 1008. But this first *Tale of Genji*, a luxurious edition the compilation of which Murasaki Shikibu describes in her diary, would probably have been no more than half the length of the present *Genji*. Thereafter, the text continued to grow, by both accretion and emendation, for about two hundred years before consensus coalesced and the fifty-four-chapter *Genji* became the canonical *Genji*.

In the meantime, even as the text was expanding, readers who had access to it were copying it. Genji's famous discussion of the merits and demerits of fictions in the "Hotaru" chapter is set in the midst of a scene describing this activity in considerable detail. Elsewhere in the capital, in the palace of Princess Senshi, the High Priestess of Kamo, the copying of literary texts was an ongoing activity of such magnitude that the ladies of this court were organized, pseudo-officially, into two "bureaus," one led by a director and a deputy director of poetry (Uta no Kami and Suke) and the other by a director and a deputy director of romances (Monogatari no Kami and Suke). Small wonder that a legend of later years claimed that the High Priestess, through her friend Empress Shōshi, had commissioned Murasaki to write *Genji*.

One by-product of all this copying was that the text soon found its way out of the palaces, to circulate among the lesser ranks of the aristocracy. In the palace of the High Priestess, for example, "When Her Highness commanded that fresh copies of the romances be made and the old texts were distributed among the members of the bureau, the Director of Romances sent some to Minbu's place." From her reply, we know that Minbu was a gentlewoman, probably of a middle-ranking aristocratic family, who had served the High Priestess, perhaps as a member of the Bureau of Romances. Other recipients of worn copies may well have passed some of them on to their relatives living at home. Even more explicit is the *Sarashina* diarist's description of her experience after returning from the provinces in 1020. When her mother wrote to relatives to tell them of their arrival in the capital, one of them, Emon no Myōbu, a gentlewoman in service at the palace of the Sanjō Princess,[2] "sent us some lovely booklets that the Princess had given her, all packed in the lid of a writing box." A little later, an aunt "gave me the fifty-odd volumes of *Genji*, all in their own box, and *Zai Chūjō*, *Tōgimi*, *Serikawa*, *Shirara*, and *Asauzu* as well."[3]

Needless to say, the travels of these hand-me-down texts did not end in their new homes. Some of them would simply have been passed on, but many were lent to friends and relatives to be recopied, in a process that was repeated endlessly—copies producing copies producing copies—until the advent of commercial printing centuries later. But copied how? In the first place, errors crept in. But scribal errors were by no means the principal cause of textual variation. Many of the discrepancies probably were intentional. Every copyist had his or her own idea of what made good grammar, a good sentence, or even a good story. If one felt that the poem Utsusemi traces in the corner of Genji's letter is too abrupt an ending to the chapter, then one could add, "She wrote and let it go at that" (*tote yaminikeri*, 1:106.10). Or if he considered it excessive to have the Kiritsubo Emperor recall his lost love as "adorable and lovely, more pliant than a maiden flower bending in the wind, her looks and the very aura about her more lovely and adorable than a pink moistened with dew," then one might, as one editor did, pare that down to "he recalled how adorable and lovely she was" (1:17.7–9).[4]

Nor was copying the only process through which a text might evolve into something quite different from its original form. The *Genji* scholar Inaga Keiji (1928–2001) describes how illustrated fictions of the sort depicted in the *Genji monogatari emaki* (mid-twelfth century) were particularly susceptible to textual metamorphosis. Because these "special editions" were meant to be read aloud while the listeners looked at the pictures illustrating the text, individual "copies" of them probably were made up of three separate components: the text of the tale itself, a set of pictures illustrating the text, and a companion volume of what might be called captions, which the reader would use to explain the details of the pictures and how they relate to the text. Repeated use, however, would eventually render these captions unnecessary to both readers and listeners. The volume containing the captions might then be dismantled and the captions combined with the text of the tale to form a new volume that would be used for reading without the pictures—quite literally a cut-and-paste editing process.[5]

In an age when concepts of authorial integrity were, to say the least, highly amorphous, practices of this sort could be carried to considerable extremes. We know, for example, of at least two romances, *Torikaebaya* and *Sumiyoshi monogatari*, that were so drastically rewritten that they came to be called by separate titles to distinguish the originals from the revisions. And Inaga is convinced that *The Tale of the Hollow Tree* (*Utsuho monogatari*) as we now have it is an amalgam of the textual components of a once-illustrated version and that many other Heian tales may have similar origins. Nor was *The Tale of Genji* immune to such interventions. References abound to "the sixty chapters of *Genji*,"[6] and, indeed, the number of chapter titles listed in various catalogs totals nearly seventy. None of the texts of these chapters survives, and some titles may refer to chapters better known by other titles. Still, a sixty-chapter *Genji* was by no means an impossibility. Some of Murasaki's readers probably made not only minor amendments to their copies; they thought of themselves as her co-authors, and in that capacity they developed the story in new ways and filled in what they perceived as lacunae. In some cases, they went so far as to write whole new chapters. Thus in the second century of its life, *The Tale of Genji* circulated in several variant versions, some much longer than others and some markedly different from others.

During this same span of two hundred years, currents of history in the larger world of *Genji* readers brought changes that checked these expansive tendencies in the textual development of *Genji*. As warriors married into aristocratic families and usurped the court titles, functions, and emoluments that were formerly the birthright of court aristocrats, these losses affected not only the social standing but also the economic well-being of the aristocrats. In compensation, their expertise in one or another of the leisure pursuits with which they amused themselves came to be regarded as a source not simply of personal pride but of economic sustenance in the form of patronage. The ability to compose poetry, once considered merely an instrument of dalliance,[7] would become the focus of such intense practice that it came to be regarded as a "Way," and the study of the canon of classics on which all poetry must be based became virtually a profession. Eventually (though not at first), that canon came to include *The Tale of Genji*.

As we have seen in chapter 3, the defining moment in this process is generally thought to be Fujiwara no Shunzei's pronouncement in 1190 that "to compose poetry without reading *Genji* is simply inexcusable."[8] Such an attitude made it a matter of high priority to establish a definitive text. By this time, many aristocratic houses possessed at least one *Genji* text, and every one of these texts differed from every other, some of them considerably so, not only in lexical detail, but also in the number and ordering of chapters. There never was, and never will be, a single text that could be designated "the" *Genji*; there were only multiple *Genji*s. Some of these texts, however, had descended in lineages thought to trace back more closely than others to Murasaki's original. One, attributed to the renowned calligrapher Fujiwara no Yukinari (972–1027), a contemporary of Murasaki Shikibu, understandably carried particular authority, as did those of Yukinari's grandson (the *Nijō no Sotsu Korefusa* text), Michinaga's grandson (the *Horikawa Sadaijin Toshifusa* text), and the great-great-grandson of Murasaki Shikibu's husband (the *Reizei Chūnagon Asataka* text), to name but a few.[9] But none of these manuscripts, however authoritative, could stand alone as the definitive *Genji*. Murasaki herself had put at least two versions of the text into circulation, her draft and her revised fair copy. In addition, all texts were subject to the myriad pitfalls of the reproduction process. Thus we encounter mentions of texts riddled with errors; scholarly-minded editors reading variant manuscripts together in order to correct errors in punctuation, voicing, and *kanji* glosses; repeated collations of texts, comparing eight or even twenty-one different manuscripts; and interlinear and marginal notes from borrowed manuscripts being gathered in booklets.

Unfortunately, too little documentary evidence survives to sketch even the broad outlines of all this activity, much less identify its participants and date their work. The tumultuous times that had set in motion so many of these acts of canonization were not kind to their fragile paper products. The culmination of the process, however, was the production of two carefully collated texts, the descendants of which form the basis of all standard modern editions of *Genji*. The Aobyōshi-bon (Text in Blue Covers), completed in 1225, was the work of Fujiwara no Shunzei and his son Teika, two court nobles of the Mikohidari house known for their learning, their expertise as poets, and their judgment of literary excellence. The Kawachi-bon is so called because both of its principal compilers had once held the title of governor of Kawachi. It was completed in 1255 by Minamoto no Mitsuyuki and his son Chikayuki, members of a warrior house that had had a dangerous habit of choosing the wrong side in power struggles,[10] thus ensuring themselves, as long as they managed to stay alive, ample time for literary pursuits. The two families cooperated closely over a span of more than fifty years, sharing manuscripts with each other, consulting on philological problems, and making fair copies of texts for each other. Thereafter, their descendants carried on the work, expanding the notebooks their forebears had filled with marginal notes gleaned from the manuscripts they had collated into the massive commentaries of subsequent centuries.[11]

Such, then, is the context in which the *Genji* apocrypha must be situated. The apocryphal texts collected in this chapter are presented not in the order of their composition, since the dates of their creation are impossible to ascertain, but in the order in which they would appear if they were canonical chapters of *The Tale of Genji*.

T. HARPER

PILLOWED UPON HIS ARM, CA. 1750s
(Tamakura)

MOTOORI NORINAGA

"Pillowed upon His Arm" is the most recent of the *Genji* apocrypha, written by Motoori Norinaga (1730–1801) after his return from medical studies in Kyoto, probably in the latter 1750s while he was giving his first series of lectures on *Genji* in Matsusaka.[12] As Norinaga himself describes the work, it "fills in the omission of the beginning of the story of the Rokujō lady in *The Tale of Genji*, the language and all else being fashioned in imitation of that work." Ozaki Masayoshi (1755–1827), in his bibliographical compendium published in 1801, was more specific:

> Tamakura 1 volume Motoori Norinaga
> Describes the beginnings of Genji's affair with the Rokujō lady in a style modeled on that of the tale; written to fill the gap between the "Utsusemi" and "Yūgao" chapters.[13]

Over the centuries, many readers have felt that certain "gaps" in *Genji* needed "filling in," but before Norinaga no one had suggested that the Rokujō episode was one of them. Medieval commentators had noticed the omission, but far from perceiving it as a flaw, they took it as an instance of the author's consummate "narrative strategies" (*hippō*).[14] Norinaga, too, modestly disclaimed any necessity for the work:

> Genji's affair with the Rokujō lady is abruptly introduced in "Yūgao" with the words "about the time he was secretly visiting Rokujō. . . ." Nothing whatever is said of how the affair began. So consummately crafted is the work that one infers all of this from one thing and another as one reads along. This clumsy bit of writing, however, in which everything is made explicit, is not merely puerile, but positively presumptuous and painful to contemplate.[15]

Why, then, did Norinaga write "Tamakura"? In seeking an answer to this question, it is helpful to recall how different Norinaga's world was from that of his medieval predecessors and how different his involvement with *Genji* was from theirs.

Many of the so-called Old Commentaries were compiled in an age of incessant warfare, by noblemen of the imperial court who were living in much reduced circumstances, some of them even in exile. For these people, *Genji*, however much an object of classical learning they had made it, still retained some of its immediacy as a document of their class, a window on a world of magnificence that in better times they themselves might have inhabited. Norinaga's *Genji monogatari Tama no ogushi* (1796), the pinnacle of the "New Commentaries," was the work of a provincial doctor of plebeian origins living in the second century of the Pax Tokugawa. For Norinaga, *Genji* could only have been purely classic, almost as far removed from the realities of his own life, times, and class as the Chinese classics. It is hardly surprising, therefore, that in his approach to *Genji*, he preferred the rigorous textualism (*kobunjigaku*), current among certain schools of classical studies, to the wistful and sometimes snobbish opining (as he saw it) of dispossessed noblemen.

For scholars of this time, the practice of textualism meant not merely strict adherence to the ancient text and the rejection of intervening commentary. To grasp the full, true meaning of what the ancients wrote, they also had to learn to write as the ancients wrote. For adherents of Ogyū Sorai's school of Confucian studies, this meant writing Chinese poetry in the style of the *Tang Anthology* (J. *Tōshisen*). For the pioneering scholars of the National Learning school (*kokugaku*), Kamo no Mabuchi and Kada no Azumamaro, it meant writing *waka* (Japanese poetry) in the style of the *Man'yōshū* or the *Kokinshū*. For Norinaga, it meant something even more difficult, composition in the style of *The Tale of Genji*. As he himself says in an early work, *Kogen shinan*: "If you mean to write, then you must carefully study *Ise*, *Genji*, *Makura no sōshi* [*The Pillow Book*], and other early tales and acquire such mastery of their language that you comprehend it completely. If you do not master this language, you shall never be able to write."[16] As this remark suggests, to Norinaga and his contemporaries the literary merit of "Tamakura" lay not in its beauties as a piece of storytelling, but in the virtuosity and authenticity of its archaism.

Superfluous though it may be, "Tamakura" is a remarkable demonstration of Norinaga's mastery of the language of *Genji*. Hardly a single phrase in "Tamakura" is at variance with the language of *Genji* and other Heian texts,[17] an impressive achievement in a day when variorum editions and exhaustive indexes did not exist and all this language had to be drawn from memory. Moreover, Norinaga's usage of Heian vocabulary and grammar is finely nuanced and precise. He was alert, for example, to the fact that *-te* as an adversative (rather than a consecutive) particle occurs more frequently in *Genji* than in any other Heian text, and he was careful to use the adjective *wakawakashi* not simply to mean "young" or "youthful," as it was used in his own time, but "childish" as in Heian usage.[18]

Yet however technically accomplished, Norinaga's neoclassical style (*gikobun*) could never be mistaken for genuine Heian prose. One clue to the difference is that it is so easily understood. If you do not understand something, you simply look it up in the dictionary and there you will find the precise meaning; you need never grope for shades of meaning that lie somewhere in between or adjacent to the dictionary definitions. And when Norinaga employs Heian-style ellipses, it usually is obvious what he is omitting and where. His is the prose of study, analysis, and emulation rather than something rising from gut feeling and everyday speech.

Qualities of this sort make it easy to dismiss such an exercise as unoriginal, derivative, a mere pastiche. As Fujita Tokutarō (1901–1945) put it, "Norinaga's command of the classical language is masterful and graceful, but what he has to say is utterly commonplace."[19] The modern critic Maruya Sai'ichi is far less patient, finding Norinaga's neoclassical prose so repellent that he was unable to read "Tamakura" through to the end.[20]

In Norinaga's own day, his skill as a writer of Heian prose greatly enhanced his reputation as an interpreter of Heian prose, and justly so.[21] Many of the qualities that make his *Genji monogatari Tama no ogushi* such a superb commentary clearly derive from the same fund of knowledge that makes "Tamakura" so flawless an imitation of Heian prose. But unfortunately, little of the learning that informs Norinaga's imitation of *Genji* survives the process of translation. The reader thus must be at pains to compensate mentally for both the lack, in English, of the archaism that would have delighted Norinaga's eighteenth-century readers and the narrative banality that they would have overlooked.

T. HARPER

The Former Crown Prince, as he was then known, was a brother of the reigning Emperor. He had been invested as heir apparent at the very outset of the reign and had enjoyed, indeed deserved, wide esteem. With his brother he was on the very closest terms, while the rest of the court looked up to him as a promising successor. Yet for all the grandeur of his position and all the promise that it held, he had, for whatever reasons, grown weary of his lot.[22] It became his constant wish that he might somehow escape the painful restrictions of his position and spend the years that yet remained to him in some more fulfilling way: to lead a more leisurely, tranquil life, free from all the cares that now beset him. And in the end, he resolved he would do just that. He renounced his claim to the throne and took up residence at Rokujō-Kyōgoku.

His palace there was of a most delightful design, and the gardens possessed a particular charm. Lush groves abounded; there was a broad pond and, flowing into it, a sparkling brook. All in all, it was an exquisite palace, in the most refined taste and modern fashion.

While still Crown Prince,[23] he had been married to the favorite daughter of a Minister of State of that day, a match that had gratified the hopes of all concerned. Their affection for each other left naught to be desired, and before long, as if in token of their great devotion, a lovely little Princess was born. The child was a source of endless delight to both parents, and they spent their every waking moment in caring for her. Then, in the autumn of the Princess's fourth year, her father, the Prince, was taken ill. At first it seemed but a minor ailment, but then quite unexpectedly, he passed away. His sudden death while still in his prime came as an enormous shock to the Emperor; nor, indeed, was there anyone at court who did not lament his loss. Small wonder, then, that his consort was so utterly devastated and disconsolate that she hardly knew one day from the next. So extraordinary had been their reliance over the years on the bonds of their mutual affection that she could scarcely contemplate being left behind in this world, even if only for an instant. But such is life, short though it be, that it does not always comply with one's wishes; alas, there was no following him. The sight of the little girl, however, frolicking about in all innocence, at once compounded her grief and aroused fond memories.[24]

As the days and months passed and the child grew, there was hardly a moment when her mother's eyes were dry and no sigh of longing issued from her lips. Then, in addition to all else, her father, the Minister, died.[25] Now she was utterly helpless and forlorn. Had there been only herself, she would, with no regrets, have taken vows, then and there, and hidden herself away in some mountain retreat, far from capital and court. But there was the future of the young Princess to consider. Everyone she had depended on was gone, nor was there anyone of substance to look after the child's interests. If even her mother abandoned her, what hope would she have of holding her own in the world as she grew up? These were painful ties, and she could not bring herself to sever them. With no one to look after the child, it was too great a worry to leave her alone in the world, and so the months mounted into years as she wavered between one impossible choice and another. Her gentlewomen and servants were so touched by her rare solicitude that they all stood by her, hardly a one of them leaving to go elsewhere.[26] Outwardly, nothing was changed from of yore, but all too often one thing or another would leave her feeling helpless and lonely. Even the sight of the blossoms and the autumn leaves only brought back a stream of memories of times past when they had delighted together in "their fragrance and their hues."[27] The little Princess, who was becoming as beautiful a creature as ever they could have wished, was a constant comfort to her through these bitter days. She was determined that the child should be raised with the very best instruction she could give her, be it in writing, playing the koto, or whatever; and her women, for their part, were as conscientious as she was. Throughout her palace, refinement reigned.

In the palace of the Emperor, the late Prince was not forgotten. His Majesty remembered his brother fondly and never failed to send condolences on the appropriate days. And to Genji he had said, "The consort of the former Crown Prince is in low spirits; do pay her a visit now and again." As it happened, Genji had himself wished that he might meet this lady, for he had heard reports of her elegance and beauty. And so one day, toward evening, as if just stopping by on his way home from the palace, he set out for Rokujō.[28] The distance was great,[29] and the sun had long since set by the time he arrived. He had his carriage brought to a halt before the gate and sent a guardsman in to announce his arrival. While he waited, he leaned out just a bit, the better to peer inside. He could see a dark expanse of ancient trees, and he could not help but be struck by the air of quiet elegance about the place. Then, mingled with the moan of the wind in the pines, came the faint, almost inaudible, sound of music. It was no common touch, he quickly discerned, that could produce strains of such haunting loveliness. His pulse quickened. It was well known that the consort was a consummate mistress of all the arts; this could only be her koto. He listened, enrapt.

Within the mansion, his sudden and unexpected visit had set the household buzzing and bustling in a flurry of confusion, and the lady put her koto aside. What a great pity, Genji thought, wishing that he might hear more. But his guardsman had emerged, and Genji alighted from his carriage. The sheer perfection of bearing and the dignity of movement with which he walked through the gate were so incomparably beautiful, and the refinement he seemed to radiate so exquisite, that they all were quite bedazzled and overawed. There was an awkward moment when no one came out to receive him, and he was left standing at the foot of the stairway, looking aimlessly about. Finally, after a long interval, a gentlewoman, Chūjō, emerged. "I am afraid the unexpected visit with which you honor us has found us regrettably ill prepared to receive you properly. I do apologize," she said, offering him a cushion with an air of practiced ease. "Not at all, madam," he replied, "I have meant for some time now to inquire after Her Ladyship, but with one thing and another, I have refrained from doing so and thus have not yet been able to acquaint her with the degree of my concern. His Majesty, too, never ceases to remember the late Prince. He speaks often of Her Ladyship's plight and of what a lovely little girl the Princess must have grown to be." He spoke of the Emperor's uncommon concern and was most punctilious and feeling in offering the usual condolences. "Now that I have presumed this once to call on you, I trust we shall have the chance to meet again at greater leisure," he said, and for that evening he brought his brief visit to an end and departed.

Could she possibly have ignored the attentions he had paid her in going out of his way to visit her thus? Thereafter, he never failed to send his regards when the occasion called for it, nor, for that matter, to call on her in person—in the course of which, he found himself growing rather more interested than he might have expected. The air of utter refinement and serene nobility about her struck him forcefully, and he could not help but regret that he had allowed so many years to pass without giving her a thought, much less paying her a visit.

Now and again, however, he resorted to more amusing sorts of banter, and his letters, too, came to be dotted with suggestive repartee. The lady could not help but be pleased by the depth of his devotion, yet as he grew more persistent, it came to seem rather distasteful and disagreeable to her, and she hardly ever responded to him. In his impatience, Genji wrote more frequently than ever and dispatched Koremitsu and others in his entourage to see to the lady's more practical needs as well. After some two years, in spite of all. Her Ladyship gradually came to regard him as not so disagreeable at all; and when the season or the occasion seemed to call for it, she at least would not omit to exchange a friendly note with him.

The careless charm of these missives was unutterably elegant, as was the hand of their author genteel and dignified, dashed off with an accomplished ease that immediately caught the eye. Whenever he saw it, seldom though this was, he found himself thinking that this was someone too rare simply to dismiss. He never let pass any occasion by which he thought she might be touched—be it but the blooming of a frail flower or the coloring of a tree—to let her know how deep his feelings for her were. Yet Her Ladyship, friendly though her regard for him was, found this only more inappropriate; she remained firm in her resolve that it was only proper that she should answer him through intermediaries.

The New Year came, but the lady's heart, far from thawing in the spring breeze,[30] grew only more obdurate. Yet when he considered her standing, his every thought left him bewildered. For so exalted was she, and so much to be pitied, that he would never dare press her in any more forceful terms. All the while, at his wife's great mansion, his evening absences were becoming the cause of ever-increasing consternation. In the tedium of spring's tranquillity at the palace, when the days are long and it rains from morning to night, he could not help but lament the wretched state he was in, that he, too, was "a very thing of spring."[31]

oki hito ni misebaya sode no namidakawa / kyō no nagame ni masaru fukasa o

Oh to show my cruel one: this river of tears upon my sleeve,
like my love, deeper than the waters of today's long rain.

That evening, too, they awaited him at the mansion, but again he passed them by and made his way to another destination. He went in the strictest secrecy, with no outrunners whatever, and in the plainest garb and equipage.

As usual, it was Chūjō who came out to meet him, this time bearing a message from her mistress. "The kindness of your visits, so much more frequent than I deserve, and the extent of your rare goodwill over the years move me quite to wonderment. Yet I shan't myself be able to greet you this evening, as I am feeling so painfully out of sorts that I am unable to move near the veranda. Sometime, if I'm feeling a bit better, I shall take the time to offer you my apologies for these last years." Clearly, the lady was not much inclined to receive him.

"What a pity," Genji said. "It's been painful, you know, always to be kept outside these blinds. Of little consequence though I am, my feelings have been far from shallow, quite literally for some years now. Surely, in spite of everything, she must realize this? Were she to take into account all that I have endured in this time, could she yet keep me at such a distance? Were she only to say to me, and without an intermediary, 'poor thing,' what a comfort that would be in the depths of my affliction. It's most upsetting. I'm quite unused to this sort of awkwardness. Yet having learned what a painful illness she is suffering, I must at least offer her my condolences without an intermediary." And so saying, he pulled the blind aside, leaned under it, and entered. Her women, thinking it hard indeed that he should be left on the veranda, took pity on him and led him within.

It was a moment when her ladyship had come quite near the veranda and had not yet lowered her shutters. She sat gazing out at an enchantingly misted sky, where through a gap in the rain clouds the moon now shone. Genji, having thus contrived to gain entrance, stealthily approached her screens. "On such a perfectly lovely evening as this," he thought, "were I just to declare my feelings, surely even she could not fail to be moved." He had no intention of turning back now.

koyoi dani aware wa kakeyo asu wa yomo / nagaraubeku mo aranu tama no o
"Tonight at least, pray take pity upon me,
lest this flicker of life not last until the morrow.

Should I die of love, who then would be the one for long thought obdurate?"[32] So close was he when he spoke that it was as if his words were intended only for himself. This came as a shock to Her Ladyship. But, then, she had been in correspondence with him, albeit only indirectly, for some years now; it was not as if a total stranger had burst in upon her, which perhaps is why she was neither repulsed nor frightened.

ware ni shimo ayana na kake so taenubeki / midare ya yoso no ada no tama no o
"Pray blame nothing so unjust upon me; the tribulations
of this flicker of life about to expire are none of my doing.

Isn't this all a bit contrived?" she said, so softly she seemed hardly to speak at all. She seemed on the point of withdrawing discreetly, as if embarrassed to think what she had just said, when Genji softly pushed open the panel and, sliding forward, grasped the hem of her robe and held her back.

"I do beg your pardon for this intrusion," he said, "but when you've been accustomed to hearing from me for months, nay, years on end, how can you still treat me with such indifference? Surely what you will have heard of me should assure you that I have absolutely no amorous intentions of that capricious, shallow sort so common in this world. Without your gracious permission, never, never would I presume to any greater liberties than I have taken thus far. It is just that as things were, I had to convey to you some small hint of the anguish that is wasting me away."

Calmly and with seemly restraint, he told her of the many cares and feelings he had found so difficult to endure. So ineffably appealing, so elegant and attractive, was his manner that even for this lady there were not a few moments when she found herself moved. In this inconvenient state of things, she was no longer able to treat him with such severity.

A chill wind arose as the night grew late. With the shutters still open, they were starkly visible as the light of the moon grew brighter. Genji took a low screen that stood nearby and placing it between them lay down, as though but for a moment, beside her. All her people, assuming that it had at last "come to this," withdrew to a distance and went to bed.

Her ladyship was overwhelmed with gloom and resentment at the enormity of what seemed her ineluctable fate. That having come this far, her gentlewomen would now think her up to something so childish and unseemly—the shame was vexing enough to make her die. And in a world where not a word that anyone speaks ever remains a secret, she was surely doomed to a name for waywardness and frivolity. In such a state of agitation, the most she could manage was to drown her cares in tears, for there was no casting them off. This pitiable sight must surely have moved Genji to a great many deeply felt promises and reassurances.

The spring night, so short at the best of times, passed as in an instant, and as dawn drew near, the setting moon cast a forlorn and misty light upon them.

kawasu ma mo hakanaki yume no tamakura ni / nagori kasumeru haru no yo no tsuki

"Fleeting as a dream, this time of ours together, pillowed upon my arm while the misted moon yet lingers in the sky this spring night.[33]

And how do you see it?" he asked.

> *oboroge no mi no usa naraba haru no yo no / kasumeru tsuki mo tomo ni mimashi o*
> "Were this anguish of mine of some common sort, then gladly would I view
> together with you this misted moon of a spring night."

She clutched her robes to her face and refused even to look at [the moon]. Genji was tender and solicitous in comforting her. Hoping to gain one more glimpse of her before leaving, he said, "If you could just look at the sky while it is still so beautiful, in the same spirit as do I, it might bring some small solace to you in your woe. Really, you mustn't carry on so." His attempts to entice her to the veranda were fervent and persistent, and overwhelmed by shame though she was, she did inch forward just a bit. The poise with which she managed somehow to disguise her feelings in the light of the dawning sky, at once so eerily beautiful and dreadfully revealing, was, in its sheer perfection, utterly elegant and captivating. He fairly exclaimed at the sight of her in profile, so breathtaking with wisps of her hair illuminated in the soft light of the dawn moon. More riveted than ever, he hung back and could not bring himself to leave, but his retainers were raising their voices now. "Well, it's morning," one of them said, coughing impatiently to urge him on. Upsetting and irritating though this was, the excruciating shame that the lady was suffering was truly pitiable, and it would not be to his own advantage to remain longer. In the gray light while all was still indistinct, under cover of the dawn mist, he stealthily departed—so it is said.

TRANSLATED BY T. HARPER

THE "SAKURAHITO" FRAGMENTS

Scattered throughout the commentaries, catalogs, colophons, and documents from which scholars attempt to glean some sense of the early textual development of *The Tale of Genji* are a dozen or so titles of chapters that no longer survive. Some of them may be alternative titles for chapters (or portions thereof) that we now know by different names ("Tsubo senzai" instead of "Kiritsubo"); some probably existed in name only ("Kumogakure"); and some seem actually to be the titles of chapters that had found a place in late Heian- and early Kamakura-period texts of *The Tale of Genji.*

Most of these "missing" chapters we know only by name. Two of them, however, "Sakurahito" and "Sumori," have left behind tantalizing fragmentary evidence that they not only once existed, but were considered by knowledgeable readers to be the work of Murasaki Shikibu. It is clear, though, that during the winnowing process that eventually produced the fifty-four-chapter version that is today the definitive *Tale of Genji*—a process in which some chapters still considered spurious ("Niou Miya," "Kōbai," "Takekawa") found their way into the canonical text—these two no less "authentic" chapters were excluded.

The first of these rejected chapters, in terms of its position in the *Genji* narrative, is "Sakurahito," whose title probably alludes to an old song (*saibara*) by that name. We know of this chapter only because Sesonji (Fujiwara) no Koreyuki, sometime before his death in 1175, decided that it was worthy of annotation, and thus his brief notes on "Sakurahito" are included in his *Genji shaku.*[34] In this collection of marginalia, between the commentary on chapter 31, "Makibashira," and that on chapter 32, "Umegae," Koreyuki quotes thirteen phrases from "Sakurahito," following each of which he cites a poem to which he thinks that phrase alludes. This is all that survives of "Sakurahito," but it at least provides a foothold for some interesting speculation on the content of the chapter and the role it may have played in the textual evolution of *Genji.*

Judging from the volume of Koreyuki's commentary (thirteen lemmas), "Sakurahito" probably would have been a chapter of medium length, comparable, for example, to "Yūgao." And the fact that "Sakurahito" is not annotated in the earliest collection of Koreyuki's commentary suggests that his later decision to include it reflects a considered judgment of its authenticity and importance.[35]

When we venture beyond these broad generalizations, however, problems arise. First, we have no idea what to make of the title. The song from which it seems to derive is about a man who sets off to inspect his rice fields on another island, telling his wife that he'll be back the next day. Not likely, says she, for surely you've got another woman over there; you'll not be back tomorrow.[36] Was there a scene in which this song was chanted? Does one of the characters allude to it in a poem? Does it refer to a particular character, perhaps a man not on the best of terms with his wife, such as Higekuro? We have no idea and thus cannot translate even the title of the chapter.

Then there is the tentative caveat that follows the title: "There are some texts that include this chapter. It is not indispensable. It should follow 'Hotaru.'" Did Koreyuki himself write this? And regardless of who wrote it, what are we to make of it? Ii Haruki suggests that this may be Koreyuki's defense of his decision to include "Sakurahito" in his text while conceding that there would be no harm in omitting it.[37] For although Koreyuki accepts the authenticity of the chapter, he also points to the major problem of its placement in relation to the other ten chapters of Tamakazura's story. In the text that he is annotating, Koreyuki leaves "Sakurahito" where he finds it, following "Makibashira," but he himself feels it belongs elsewhere, following "Hotaru."

Of Koreyuki's successors, only the author of the list of *Genji* chapter titles in *Hakuzōshi* expresses an opinion on these matters. He dismisses "Saku[ra]hito," "Samushiro," and "Sumori" as "the work of later authors appended" to the canonical fifty-four chapters.[38] Everyone else whom we might expect to have read "Sakurahito" and been concerned to establish a definitive text of *Genji* is silent on the subject. Not until the middle of the twentieth century did scholars begin to take an analytical interest in why "Sakurahito" might have found its way into Koreyuki's text in the first place. By this time, they had only the thirteen fragments preserved by Koreyuki to work with.

Horibe Seiji (1913–1944) was one of the first scholars to attempt to explain Koreyuki's dissatisfaction with the placement of "Sakurahito." The chapter, he noted, appears to deal principally with Hotaru Hyōbukyō no Miya's amorous interest in Tamakazura. But by "Makibashira," the last of the Tamakazura chapters, Tamakazura already is married to Higekuro. To then revert to a tale about one of her previous suitors would make sense only as a retrospective lament. Yet to place "Sakurahito" immediately following "Hotaru," as Koreyuki's *Genji shaku* suggests, is to create calendrical contradictions. "Sakurahito" appears to be set in late spring "after all the cherry blossoms have fallen," whereas "Hotaru" is set in early summer during the long rains. To follow the summer chapter with a spring chapter would be to upset the strict seasonal progression that is maintained throughout the ten Tamakazura chapters. Horibe's analysis demonstrates clearly why Koreyuki should be troubled by the placement of "Sakurahito" in his manuscript, as well as by the problems that his recommended relocation of the chapter would entail. Beyond this, however, Horibe could only conclude that a scholar as careful as Koreyuki must have had good reasons for his misgivings that we can never know, now that the text of "Sakurahito" has been lost.[39]

Textual studies of *Genji* began to thrive as never before in the immediate postwar years, in the course of which Kazamaki Keijirō (1902–1960) made a chance discovery that led him to a tentative but highly plausible solution to the "Sakurahito" problems posed by Horibe. In attempting to resolve some chronological anomalies in the *Genji* text, Kazamaki found that between chapters 21 and 32, only one year passes in the life of Lady Murasaki: in "Otome" (chapter 21) she is twenty-seven, and in "Umegae" (chapter 32) she is twenty-nine. In the intervening ten chapters, however, four years pass in Genji's life. How can so great a discrepancy be explained? In the first place, Kazamaki notes, the ten intervening chapters are precisely those that tell the story of the discovery of Yūgao's long-lost daughter Tamakazura, the amorous interest that she arouses in her guardian Genji and his brother Hotaru Hyōbukyō no Miya, and ultimately her marriage to Higekuro. Both Yūgao and a certain prince (*miya*) are mentioned specifically in the "Sakurahito" fragments and most of the poems cited by Koreyuki are love poems, so it seems reasonable to speculate that "Sakurahito" may have described some of the same matters as do chapters 22 to 31, the "ten Tamakazura chapters." This further leads Kazamaki to suggest that "Sakurahito" was once the only chapter between "Otome" and "Umegae"; that the events it depicts take place in the space of a single year, Murasaki's twenty-eighth; and that later the story it tells in a single chapter was expanded to fill ten new chapters that span four years—a discrepancy that passed unnoticed until detected by Kazamaki.[40] This new hypothesis was so persuasive and so thoroughly in accord with the work of other textual scholars of the time[41] that it gained immediate acceptance. As Ii Haruki pointed out, reaffirming its validity half a century later, it no longer makes sense to consider the "ten Tamakazura chapters" as the "original" and "Sakurahito" as a forgery by some later author.[42]

Who, then, was the author of "Sakurahito"? Ii Haruki implies (but does not state) that it was Murasaki Shikibu; Hasegawa Kazuko maintains that it must have been written by "the same person who wrote the rest of *Genji*";[43] and Inaga Keiji, pointedly and repeatedly, states that it was the work of Murasaki Shikibu. But as we have seen, even Murasaki could not have undertaken such a project without the support of a wealthy patron. Again, the patron was probably Fujiwara no Michinaga, for as Saitō Masaaki argues, the "ten Tamakazura chapters" may well have been written for Michinaga's younger daughter Kenshi (994–1027) on her marriage to the crown prince who later became the Sanjō Emperor (976–1017; r. 1011–1016). It would have been the perfect gift, for these ten chapters directly follow the three "Hahakigi" chapters, which Michinaga himself had purloined from Murasaki's room and passed on to Kenshi.[44] "Sakurahito," then, is "apocryphal" only in the sense that Koreyuki and later editors of the *Genji* text failed to recognize that it had been rewritten and then discarded by its author as superfluous.

Myriad questions remain; we have only thirteen fragments with which to address them; and as Ii Haruki wistfully notes, the golden age of postwar *Genji* textual scholarship, which carried us this far beyond the oversights of the previous eight centuries, has by now "drawn its last breath."[45] The explication of the following translated fragments, therefore, attempts only to summarize the work of those few scholars who have ventured to speculate on the relationship between "Sakurahito" and the "ten Tamakazura chapters."[46]

T. HARPER

Sakurahito

kono maki wa aru hon mo ari.
nakutemo arinubeshi. hotaru ga tsugi ni arubeshi.
There are some texts that include this chapter.
It is not indispensable. It should follow "Hotaru."

1. *koke no tamoto wa kesa wa sobotsuru to yomite nao tachikaeru to aru wa*

Where it says, "'The sleeves of this mossy robe are this morning soaked with tears,' he/she recited, thinking back again . . .":

inishie ni nao tachikaeru kokoro kana / koishiki koto ni monowasure sede
How I long to return once again to the past;
for once one has loved one never forgets. [*Kokinshū* 734]

This first fragment poses a daunting problem. "Mossy sleeves" are those of a robe worn by a nun or a monk, but there is no nun or monk in the Tamakazura chapters who might long to "return once again to the past." Who, then, might be the speaker of this lower hemistich of the poem that Koreyuki quotes? Inaga Keiji (8–9) proposes a daring solution to this problem. Perhaps, he suggests, Ukon's discovery of Tamakazura was far less elaborately plotted in "Sakurahito" than in "Tamakazura." Perhaps Yūgao's nursemaid, rather than taking the child with her to Kyushu, simply remains in the western purlieus of the capital and, after her husband dies, becomes a nun. When Ukon discovers her there, it would be entirely natural for the nurse/nun to express her longing for her dead mistress in terms of tear-soaked mossy sleeves. For the writer, however, this more economical plot line could have proved to be a problem when she set out to expand the single chapter into ten. Readers of the elaborated version might begin to wonder why, in the intervening twenty years, the nurse never contacted the child's father and how so beautiful and obviously aristocratic a girl could escape attention that long. To forestall such objections, Inaga suggests, Murasaki Shikibu may have decided that she must remove both nurse and child from any possible contact with denizens of the capital, to which end she brought the nurse's husband back to life and had him appointed to a post in Kyushu, to which his wife and her charge accompany him. As a result, the "mossy sleeves" of "Sakurahito" are not found in "Tamakazura."

Ii Haruki (140–41) proposes another way around this problem. He takes the "mossy sleeves" to be a metonym for garments of mourning and suggests that because the verb is *yomite* rather than *yomitamaite*, the speaker may be Tamakazura, who is described at the beginning of "Fujibakama" as mourning her grandmother, Princess Ōmiya. This interpretation, too, presupposes a beginning to "Sakurahito" somewhat more somber than that of the present Tamakazura story. Yet if the "ten Tamakazura chapters" were indeed written for presentation to a future emperor, it would have been entirely appropriate to give them a new and more auspicious beginning.

2. *koi o shi koiba to aru wa*
Where it says, "If one but loves . . .":

tane shi areba iwa ni mo matsu wa oinikeri / koi wo shi koiba awazarame ya wa

Be there but a seed, a pine grows, even if from a crack in a rock;
if one but loves, can it be that one never meets one's love?
[*Kokinshū* 512]

This is the first of a number of fragments that seem to look forward to episodes—many of them love scenes—depicted in the "ten Tamakazura chapters." Although the speaker of this particular phrase is not identified, both Hasegawa Kazuko (120) and Inaga (9) speculates that it may be Genji hinting at his own fondness for Tamakazura by quoting from the *Kokinshū* poem cited by Koreyuki. Inaga also notes that some medieval commentators identify this poem as one source of Genji's bitter rebuke of the Third Princess in "Kashiwagi,"[47] suggesting that the story of the affair of Kashiwagi and the Third Princess had already formed in the author's mind when she wrote "Sakurahito." For further evidence of this, see fragment 13.

3. *ware ya kawaranu to aru wa*
Where it says, "Shall I not change?":

e zo shiranu yoshi kokoromiyo inochi araba / ware ya wasururu hito ya towanu to
Never can we know, yet let's give it a try; for as long as we have life, shall I ever forget you, shall you not care for me?[48] [*Kokinshū* 377]

Textual problems, as Hasegawa (120–21) points out, make this fragment particularly difficult to deal with. The verb *kawaranu* does not agree with the source that Koreyuki cites, which instead reads *wasururu*. Moreover, because the verb is cast in the negative, *kawaranu* is not an appropriate substitute for *wasururu*. Scribal errors may, of course, account for these discrepancies. Inaga (9–10), though, seems not to be troubled by them; even so, he suggests no more than that the three-word quotation, which seems to occur early in the chapter, may form part of a dialogue between Genji and Tamakazura.

4. *itodo mo keburu to aru wa*
Where it says, "ever more smoke rose . . .":

[A blank space follows.]

The blank space following this fragment probably indicates that although Koreyuki had not yet found a source poem for these words, he hoped that he might later turn up something to insert here. As Inaga (10) notes, however, even a thorough search of *Shinpen kokka taikan* does not yield a promising candidate. The space is likely to remain forever blank. Still, the ruling metaphor is clear: the smoke must rise from those "fires of love" (*omohi*) so often encountered in love poetry. In arguing that "Sakurahito" was originally placed between "Otome" and "Umegae," Kazamaki Keijirō (72) points to this fragment as a possible reference to Yūgiri's love for Kumoi-nokari, in which case it may have served to link those two chapters (see also Inaga, 14n.3). Inaga, however, thinks it more likely to relate to Genji's attempt to seduce Tamakazura in "Kagaribi":

kagaribi ni tachisou koi no keburi koso / yo ni wa tae senu hono'o narikere
Smoke from the fires of my love that rises with that of the watch fires:
these are flames that never, as long as I live, will burn out.
("Kagaribi," 14:249)

5. *wakare semashi ya to oshimikikoyu to aru wa*
Where it says, "'Should there then be these partings?' he lamented":

akatsuki no nakaramashikaba shiratsuyu no / okite wabishiki wakare semashi ya
Were there to be no dawn, would there then be no awakening in tears,
or ever these wretched partings as the clear dewdrops form?[49]
[*Gosenshū* 862; *Shūishū* 715]

The context of this fragment is clear: the dawn parting of two lovers. But we have no way of knowing who those lovers might be. Inaga (10) prefers Genji and Tamakazura to Hotaru and Tamakazura.

6. *harezu ya kiri no to iu wa*
Where it says, "Will it never clear, this mist?":

shirakumo no kakaru okabe no sumika ni wa / harezu ya kiri no tachiwatarubeki
Here in this dwelling, set on a hill, enveloped in white clouds,
will it never clear, this mist that rises to cover all? [source not identified]

Mist that covers all and fails to clear is a frequent metaphor for the anguish of unrequited love. There is no clue, however, as to who the lovers might be. Inaga (10) ventures no more than that this lover's lament may be in some way connected with the previous two fragments.

7. *michi o sae seku koso to iu wa*

Where it says, "Cuts me off even from the Way . . .":

kakarademo kumoi no hodo wa nagekishi ni / michi o sae seku yamaji naruran
Quite apart from all else, I lament my distance from that dwelling in clouds,
for this mountain road cuts me off even from the Way. [*Saigū no Nyōgo shū* 77?]

The source poem that Koreyuki cites no longer survives precisely as he quotes it, but Horibe Seiji has found a poem in *Saigū no Nyōgo shū* in which the upper hemistich is identical to Koreyuki's citation. In 981, when Prince Yukihira was about to enter holy orders, the High Priestess of Ise wrote to him:

kakarademo kumoi no hodo wa nagekishi ni / mienu yamaji o omoiyaru kana
Quite apart from all else, I lament my distance from that dwelling in clouds,
for my heart yearns for the mountain road I cannot see.

In other words, she regrets her isolation in Ise for many reasons, but particularly because it prevents her from performing her Buddhist devotions. But what can an allusion to such a poem signify in the context of what is essentially a tale of romance? Inaga notes that in secular terms, such an allusion could be taken as a lament that something or someone is beyond one's reach. Here, therefore, it might be Hotaru Hyōbukyō no Miya's lament that when Tamakazura becomes Chief Palace Attendant, she will be beyond his reach.

8. *hana mo mina chirihatete wazuka ni fuji zo nokoreru katabuku kage ya nagametamawan* [*-nu*?] *to aru wa*

Where it says, "All the blossoms had fallen and only the purple wisteria remained; in the waning light he gazed at it pensively" [or ". . . won't you gaze at it?"]:[50]

haru kaerite tomeenu chūchō su / shitō no kaka yōyaku kōkon
With the passing of spring, I lament that I cannot stop it
while in the shadow of the purple wisteria, dusk gradually gathers.
[*Hakushi monjū* 631; *Wakan rōei shū* 52]

Inaga points out that the diction of the Chinese poem cited by Koreyuki forms the basis of not only the fragment quoted from "Sakurahito" but also the depiction of Tō no Chūjō's reconciliation with Yūgiri in "Fuji no uraba," which echoes both *Hakushi monjū* and *Wakan rōei shū*. On the twentieth day of the Third Month, when "all the blossoms had fallen in profusion" ("Fuji no uraba," 14:424–25), Tō no Chūjō hints to Yūgiri of his change of heart. A few days later, at the beginning of the Fourth Month, "when the wisteria was blooming in glorious profusion" and "its color grew ever richer in the gathering dusk," he sends one of his sons to Yūgiri with an invitation to come view the flowers. His message contains the poem

waga yado no fuji no iro koki tasogare ni / tazune ya wa konu haru no nagori wo

My wisteria, its color richer still in the deepening dusk:
will you not come view it, this last memento of springtime? (14:426)

On the basis of the striking resemblance of the language of this scene to the quotation from "Sakurahito" and the poem that Koreyuki cites as its source, Inaga (3–4) concludes that the successful resolution of Yūgiri's suit must originally have been depicted in "Sakurahito." Accordingly, "Sakurahito" may once have been the final chapter of what we now call part 1 of *Genji*. Indeed, it may even have depicted the imperial progress to Genji's Rokujō mansion, and the crown prince's coming of age, now depicted in "Umegae," even though no evidence survives to support this latter hypothesis.

9. *Yūgao no mite no, ito aware nareba, ato wa chitose mo to aru wa*

Where it says, "The hand of Yūgao was touchingly beautiful, its traces [a memento for] a thousand years":

hakanaku mo fumitodomekeru hamachidori / ato wa chitose no katami narikeri

These traces, as delicate as the plover's faint print on the sand,
shall remain as a memento for a thousand years. [source not identified]

Horibe (164) derides the use of the honorific *mi-* with reference to the hand of someone as insignificant as Yūgao. Moreover, he argues, in doing so the author reveals her own ignorance, thus proving that she could not be Murasaki Shikibu. Indeed, as Hasegawa (125–26) points out, honorifics are never attached to her name in the "Yūgao" chapter. Genji finds her living in a hovel, and she dies before he can learn her ancestry. In "Tamakazura," however, Ukon reveals that Yūgao was in fact the daughter of a nobleman of the third rank and thus a lady entirely deserving of such respect. Hasegawa feels, too, that the description of Yūgao's hand as *aware* implies that Genji, who was once her lover, must be the subject of this fragment. In contrast, Ii (138–39) suggests that it would be entirely natural for Tamakazura to speak deferentially about her own mother's writing and raises no objection to her thinking of it as *aware*.

Inaga (138–39) notes three possible forms in which Genji (whom he, too, assumes to be the subject) might be viewing Yūgao's handwriting: (1) the fan, which he has kept for years as a keepsake; (2) Yūgao's letters in the possession of her nursemaid, which come into Genji's possession when he takes the women in at the Rokujō mansion; and (3) the letters that come to Genji via Saishō no Kimi (a daughter of Yūgao's uncle), who is introduced in "Hotaru."

Ii suggests yet another possible scenario, in which Genji may have shown Tamakazura the fan he has kept as a keepsake, perhaps somewhere in the vicinity of "Miyuki" when he tells her father, Tō no Chūjō, the truth about her.

10. *ware sae kokoro sora nari ya to uchiwaraitamaite, ayashi, tsuma matsu yoi nari ya to aru wa*

Where it says, "I, too, find myself quite distracted," he said smiling. "And of all times, on this evening when even *his* love awaits him":

ōzora o hitori nagamete hikoboshi no / tsuma matsu yo sae hitori kamo nemu[51]

Alone, gazing longingly at the heavens; even on this night
when the herder star's love awaits him, must I sleep alone?
[*Shinkokinshū* 313]

Because the *ware* of this fragment is not identified, we have no way of knowing who speaks and smiles. But Tsurayuki's poem, which Koreyuki cites, helps clarify what he means. According to the headnote in the *Shinkokinshū*, the poem was composed to accompany a folding screen depicting, month by month, the yearly round of festivals. Tsurayuki's poem would thus have been inscribed on a picture depicting the Tanabata Festival in the Seventh Month, which probably shows a man gazing at the Milky Way, lamenting that even on this one night of the year when the Ox Herder can lie with his love, the Weaver Maiden, he must sleep alone. As Inaga's (5) commentary makes clear, the ambiguities of language and culture make possible several interpretations of *tsuma matsu yo* (*tsuma* can be either male or female, and who awaits whom?), of which the translator can choose only one. The most plausible guess at the identity of the speaker is that of Ii (140), who takes him to be Genji venting his own chagrin at losing Tamakazura to Higekuro. Hasegawa (126) strongly supports this hypothesis.

11. *miya wa au o kagiri ni nagekasetamau to aru wa*
Where it says, "'That finally we shall meet,' the Prince sighed":

waga koi wa yukue mo shirazu hate mo nashi / au o kagiri to omou bakari zo
Ah, this love of mine! I know not where it shall lead or how it shall end;
my one and only hope is that finally we shall meet. [*Kokinshū* 611]

Ii (140) regards this as another instance in which a scene in "Sakurahito" seems to coincide with a scene in the Tamakazura chapters. "The Prince" here would be Hotaru Hyōbukyō no Miya, who, when he finally expresses his desire to marry Tamakazura, finds that she is already married to Higekuro. In the present Tamakazura chapters, this scene may have been the basis of the events depicted in "Makibashira."

12. *nado seshi waza zo to aru wa*
Where it says, "Why have I done such a thing?":

ukishima ya uki tabi goto ni nazo shima ya / nazo seshi waza zo kokorozukushi ni
Ukishima! With every dismal moment I ask, Why *this* island?
Why have I done such a thing? I wonder with all my heart. [source not identified]

Neither of the commentators (Hasegawa [127]; Inaga [6]) who discuss this fragment offers to paraphrase the strange poem that Koreyuki cites as its source, but both agree that its most likely function in "Sakurahito" is as an expression of Genji's annoyance with himself for having allowed Tamakazura to fall into Higekuro's hands.

13. *mizu ni yadoreru to kakitaru wa*
Where it is written, "that lies in water . . .":

te ni musubu mizu ni yadoreru tsukikage no / aru ka naki ka no yo ni koso arikere
Like the moonlight that lies in water scooped up in the palm of the hand:
does it exist or does it not? And just so is this world. [*Shūishū* 1322]

The quotation in this fragment is from a poem by Tsurayuki composed on his deathbed. It is highly unlikely that anyone's death is described in "Sakurahito," but as Inaga (6–7) suggests, this allusion may well be an expression of the grief of someone who feels that he might die of lovesickness: Hotaru Hyōbukyō no Miya, who has lost Tamakazura to Higekuro. Inaga also notes that the same poem is identified by some medieval commentators as underlying the description in "Yokobue" of the death of Kashiwagi. Could this fragment from a discarded chapter thus be, Inaga asks tentatively, the seed of a much later episode in which a young man actually does die of lovesickness?

TRANSLATED AND COMMENTARY BY T. HARPER

THE SIX "HIDDEN IN CLOUD" CHAPTERS (Kumogakure rokujō)

The six "Hidden in Cloud" chapters are the product of a mystery and have remained shrouded in mystery since their inception. But their origin and development could not be described more succinctly and accurately than in the words of Yamagishi Tokuhei: "Originally, the 'Kumogakure' chapters existed in neither name nor fact. Later they came to exist in name but not in fact, and ultimately in both name and fact."[52]

Perhaps the most easily explicable aspect of them is their number. To our great misfortune, the earliest readers of *Genji* never mentioned how many chapters their copies contained. To the *Sarashina* diarist in the 1020s, *Genji* was already a work of "fifty-some" chapters. And in the two centuries following her reading of the tale, the text continued to grow and evolve in ways of which we now have only the dimmest sense. By the latter years of the Heian period, if any number at all was associated with the chapters of *Genji*, it was most likely to be sixty. Thus we find *Genji* ipponkyō (ca.1166) speaking of a *Genji* "made up of sixty chapters," the narrator of *Ima kagami* (1170) marveling that Murasaki "wrote not just one or two scrolls but sixty chapters," and even the narrator of *A Nameless Notebook* (ca. 1200) assuring her friends that now they "can imagine how [moving] the remaining sixty chapters must be."[53] Although the titles of many more than sixty chapters survive, sixty was the number of volumes in the "Three Great Treatises" (*sandaibu*) of the Tendai school of Buddhism. Thus to readers at all piously inclined, it seemed natural that Murasaki Shikibu should wish her tale to have the same auspicious number of chapters.

Yet it was during the same decades, when "the sixty-chapter *Genji*" was becoming a term in common parlance and the connection with Tendai doctrine was coming to seem an item of common knowledge, that the first attempts to compile a truly definitive text of *Genji* were begun; and the results of those efforts, both the Aobyōshi-bon and the Kawachi-bon, consisted of only fifty-four chapters. The question was bound to arise: What became of the other six? Were they hidden or destroyed or lost? So little remains of the earliest attempts to explore this mystery that it is "now beyond the reach of scholarly inquiry."[54] The *Genji* text was still extremely unstable and in constant flux. Readers could compile their own lists of six additional chapters, picking and choosing from the titles (and, in some cases, texts) of *Genji* chapters written in the Heian period and still in circulation. But the quality of these peripheral chapters was so markedly inferior that no single list emerged that could command general acceptance. Clearly, a solution of a different sort was required.

That new way forward was found in a fortunate conflation of the search for the six unspecified "missing" chapters with the search for another "missing" chapter, "Kumogakure" (Hidden in Cloud), which was presumed to tell the story of Genji's death. This combination then came to be known as the "Six Kumogakure Chapters" (Kumogakure rokujō). Once they had a name, and thus a locus within *Genji*, the attempt to solve this two-pronged mystery gave birth to what was probably the most productive myth in the history of the reception of *The Tale of Genji*. At some point in the process, it also produced the only concrete textual product of the entire effort, the most obviously faked and ineptly executed of the *Genji* apocrypha, the "Six Kumogakure Chapters" translated here.

How did it happen, then, and when did it happen that this set of six imaginary "chapters" came to be called the "Six Kumogakure Chapters"? At the stage in the process when the six chapters "missing" from the sixty-chapter Genji came to have a name, it was natural that their collective title should be "Hidden in Cloud." For in the Genji text itself, at the end of "Maboroshi," Genji murmurs:[55]

monoomou to suguru tsukihi mo shiranu ma ni / toshi mo waga yo mo
kyō ya tsukinuru
While I, beset by cares, notice not the passing of the months and days,
shall my life, as well as this year, have run its course today? (15:536)

Immediately following which: "He commanded, so they say, that this year the New Year's season should be grander than ever and that the gifts he prepared for the Princes and Ministers of State, as well as his rewards to one and all according to their rank, should be without parallel" (15:536).

At long last, Genji is about to take the step he has so often claimed to wish he might take and turn his back on the secular world. Yet the momentous event itself is never once mentioned, much less described. The first line of the next chapter, "Niou Miya," "begins in the past perfect" (*kako ni nashite*) tense:[56] "After his radiance had been hidden, there were none among his progeny who could succeed to his brilliance." References to Kaoru's age reveal that eight years have passed between the end of "Maboroshi" and the beginning of "Niou Miya" (16:11), and there are tantalizing mentions of Genji's move to the "temple in Saga where he spent his last two or three years in seclusion from the world" ("Yadorigi," 16:385). But sometime during those eight years, Genji passed from the scene, probably died, and certainly was "hidden in cloud."

Nomura Hachirō suggests that the word describing Genji's demise (and the idea of a chapter so named) may have been lifted from one of Murasaki Shikibu's best-known poems, where it is used in its more literal sense:[57]

meguriaite mishi ya sore to mo wakanu ma ni / kumogakure ni shi yowa
no tsukikage
We chance to meet, yet before I can be sure that you're the one I've known,
the light of the moon, so late this night, is hidden in cloud.[58]

Whatever its source, the notion that there should have been a chapter (or set of chapters) called "Kumogakure" that filled the perceived gap between "Maboroshi" and "Niou Miya" must have taken shape at least by the middle of the twelfth century, for the name appears under the heading of "Set Twenty-Six" in the oldest extant list of Genji chapter titles, thought to date from 1176 and contained in *Hakuzōshi*.[59]

Opinion seems to have been divided, however, whether the text of such a chapter ever existed, or only a title. Those who held that only a title had ever been put to paper appealed to Tendai doctrine to support their claim. Murasaki, they maintained, had in mind those doctrinal treatises that were known only by name because their texts had never been transmitted from India to China and Japan. In like manner, she had alluded to Genji's death with the title "Kumogakure," but never actually described the event.[60] For having depicted the deaths of Yūgao, Lady Aoi, and Lady Murasaki in such heartbreaking detail, she may have thought it best to stop when Genji senses that he is near death, insert the title "Kumogakure," and move past his death to "Niou Miya."[61] Or, alternatively, the missing chapters of *Genji* could be seen as analogous to the six missing poems of the Chinese *Book of Songs*, once extant but now, tragically, lost.[62] The assumption that these chapters had once existed led further to the thesis that the story they told had inspired their readers to take the tonsure and seek enlightenment. Thus—citing the precedent of an early Chinese emperor who had buried alive all the Confucian scholars and burned their texts—it was commanded that every copy of "Kumogakure" in the land be burned. "An amusing story," Gyōa commented, "but hardly worthy of belief."[63]

Others, however, seemed very reluctant to give up all hope that someday they might actually read "Kumogakure." Even Sesonji (Fujiwara) no Koreyuki left an opening in his *Genji shaku* into which the missing chapter(s) might be inserted. He divides the chapters of *Genji* into thirty-seven sets (*narabi*) and lists "Minori" and "Maboroshi" as the twenty-fifth set and "Niou Miya," "Kōbai," and "Takekawa" as the twenty-seventh. He does not mention a twenty-sixth set, but leaves a place open should a text of "Kumogakure" ever turn up.[64] Minamoto no Chikayuki's younger brother, Sojaku (fl. mid-thirteenth century), insisted in his commentary *Shimeishō* that "the 'Kumogakure' chapter must survive somewhere. If we ourselves had a wizard (such as both the Kiritsubo Emperor and Genji yearned for), how should he fail to find it? The idea that it never existed seems to me deeply suspect."[65]

It is important to emphasize at this point that these strained attempts to explain why *Genji* no longer had sixty chapters—or even just fifty-five—

were not simply the playthings of naive, credulous, or superstitious readers of *Genji*. The very scholars who produced the definitive fifty-four-chapter texts of *Genji* were equally eager to solve this mystery. Minamoto no Chikayuki was sufficiently intrigued to "inquire of several learned scholars." None of them, apparently, was able to offer him a convincing explanation, but he reported the results of his inquiries, including some of the fables recounted previously, in his *Genchū saihishō*, a version of which we know Fujiwara no Teika to have read. Nor did the descendants of these scholars, the compilers of the massive medieval commentaries on *Genji*, seem to lose interest in whether "Kumogakure" had ever existed or to cease trying to explain why it could not be found.[66] None of these scholars, however, would be likely to resort to forgery. How, then, did the "Six Kumogakure Chapters," once they had come to exist in name, come to exist in fact?

Of the many flights of fancy that this fruitless search produced, one in particular seems to have been almost an invitation to compose a set of "Six Kumogakure Chapters." *Genji hiun wahishō*, a little-known work, claims that "Kumogakure" once consisted of six chapters,[67] but because it contained "untoward material that was a disgrace to the tale," the GoShirakawa Cloistered Emperor (1127–1192; r. 1155–1158) had ordered all copies to be burned. Before doing so, however, he had allowed their content to be revealed, as a secret oral transmission (*kuketsu*) to a select and trusted few. What this "untoward material" was we are not told, but it may well have referred to the powerful effect that "Kumogakure" was said to have had on its readers, inspiring them, "one and all," to forsake the secular world to seek enlightenment[68]—a trend that, if allowed to continue, could seriously destabilize aristocratic society.

Whether inspired by this report or not we shall never know, but at some time in the Muromachi period, someone seems to have decided to adopt the persona of one of those trusted few to whom the contents of the six chapters had been confided and to write down all that he "knew." He would make the "Six Kumogakure Chapters" exist in both name and fact, and restore the canonical fifty-four-chapter *Genji* to its intended sixty-chapter perfection.

Since forgers and fakers do not usually reveal their intentions, sources, and methods of deceit, it is no surprise that we know nothing about when and by whom the "Six Kumogakure Chapters" were composed. The bare bones of his method, however, are obvious. He took "Kumogakure" as the title not of a single chapter but of a set of chapters (*narabi*). There is ample precedent for this usage; it could even have been the intention of the author of the *Hakuzōshi* list to use it in this sense. The forger then chose five more titles of chapters that had been in circulation during the Heian period but, having been rejected as noncanonical, probably were no longer extant at the time of the forgery. Two of these, "Sakurahito" and "Sumori," we have already encountered as fragments of lost texts. For each of these authentic chapter titles, the forger then wrote an entirely new text that had no connection whatever with the original content of the chapter, but making sure to include a poem on which the chapter title could be based. In short, he "found" the missing "Kumogakure" chapter, resurrected the other five chapters of that set, explained in a colophon (of which more later) why they had been hidden for so long, and completed the sixty-chapter *Tale of Genji*.

How this "discovery" was received, we have no idea. The work is not mentioned in any of the commentaries of the Muromachi period, nor do any manuscript copies survive that predate the Edo period. In her commentary *Gyokuei shū* (1602), Kaoku Gyokuei (1526–after 1602) tells of six (unnamed) chapters that were secreted in the Uji treasure house (of the Byōdō-in) but had been destroyed in one of the many fires that ravaged that temple.[69] Another report tells of a set of six chapters (likewise unnamed) being burned in the fire that destroyed Fujiwara no Shōshi's personal temple, the Tōbokuin.[70] *Genji higishō* (fourteenth century?) lists "six Sumori chapters" that it attributes to Akazome Emon.[71] And Ichjō Kanera's (1402–1481) son Jinson (1430–1508) records almost the same list[72] in his diary *Daijōin jisha no zōjiki* (entry for 1478.7.28), but describes them as "additional chapters written by Sei Shōnagon."[73] The closest we come to any recognition of the existence of the forged "Six Kumogakure Chapters" is a list of titles in a work called *Genji hakoiri nikki* that corresponds precisely to the names of the extant six chapters, but it is prefaced, "Stored in the Ishiyama treasure house and not allowed out; this because they are secret."[74] Readers obviously remained fascinated by the mystery of the "Six Kumogakure Chapters," but no mention survives of anyone actually having seen them. On the face of it, it would appear that the newly recovered "Six Kumogakure Chapters" were themselves headed for oblivion. But such was not to be, thanks largely to the interest taken in them by the learned monk and prolific writer of popular books, Asai Ryōi (1612?–1691).

Entering the world of scholarship on the history of the "Six Kumogakure Chapters" leaves us with a strange sense of déjà vu. Things that we now see as patently false are discussed as though they might be true. A few skeptics voiced reservations, but, for the most part, they were ignored. And we end up with yet another forgery.

To begin with, there are two lines of manuscript texts of "Kumogakure rokujō." The only dated manuscript is identified as a 1739 copy of a manuscript dated 1618. Expert opinion considers all other copies to date from the early, middle, or late Edo period.[75] Both lines of texts are assumed to have had pre-Edo antecedents that no longer survive. The two lines of texts are obviously related, but they differ considerably in their details. Their chapter titles are the same; they are arranged in the same order; and there are many passages that, if not identical, at least closely resemble one another. Conversely, the chapters differ greatly in length; the poems differ greatly in number; and the wording often differs so much that one scholar claims it would be impossible to produce a variorum edition of the two texts.[76] Finally, the two lines bear totally different colophons identifying their origins. The fuller of the two texts is usually described as the "standard text" (*rufubon, futsūhon*) and the other as the "variant text" (*ihon, beppon*).[77] Concerning their origins, Yamagishi Tokuhei and Imai Gen'e say:

> It is impossible to determine whether or not the variant text derives directly from the standard text. It probably makes more sense to assume instead that they have a common ancestor. For then we may manage to infer something of the original form of those "Six Kumogakure Chapters" that had been the subject of legend since the latter years of the Heian period or, at least, gain some hint of it.[78]

It was not by means of these manuscript editions, however, that "Kumogakure" circulated most widely in the Edo period. Sometime before 1670, in Kyoto, Asai Ryōi published not only an illustrated edition of the text but also an extremely learned and detailed commentary on all six chapters.[79] This publication was such a success that it was reprinted in 1677, 1678 or 1679,[80] 1696, and 1709. In the meantime, sales of "Kumogakure rokujō" in Kyoto encouraged the Edo publisher Urokogataya to bring out yet another edition, illustrated by none other than Hishikawa Moronobu (d. 1694). These Edo editions date from 1676, 1681, and 1682. After centuries of obscurity, the "Six Kumogakure Chapters" had become both a best seller and a long seller.

But if we look a little more closely, as Yoshida Kōichi has done, we notice certain anomalies that invite suspicion.[81] As noted, the two lines of manuscript texts bear totally different colophons. The longest of the three versions of the variant colophon reads as follows:

Of the sixty chapters of *The Tale of Genji*, fifty-four circulate widely in the world. These six chapters, however, describe the death of Genji and, moreover, contain esoterica of the Buddhist law, for which reasons they have been secreted within the precincts of the palace and not revealed to the world at large. Now as it happens, there was a certain lady, a Chief Palace Attendant [Naishi no Kan (= Kami) no Kimi], who was the most accomplished poet of her age. And because the Emperor harbored a fondness for her, he bequeathed to her all the secrets of the Way of Poetry, including even these volumes. But there was a scandal,[82] and in the early years of the Tenbun era [1532–1555] she was banished to the Takaki District[83] in the province of Hizen. When she departed from the capital, she secretly took along these six volumes. After making the most earnest entreaty of her, I [was allowed to] copy them. Ye who may read them hereafter, regard them with due gravity! Keep them secret! Keep them secret!

The other two extant versions are slightly shorter, differ a bit in phraseology, and are more effusive in their praise of this lady's talents, declaring her "superior even to Komachi of old."[84] And one of them bears a notation that it had been copied in Genna 4 (1618) from "the text of Arima Etchū Nyūdō Tokuen." All agree, however, that the Chief Palace Attendant was banished to Kyushu in the early to middle years of the sixteenth century and took the "Kumogakure rokujō" with her.

We must not take this colophon at face value, but it probably would have seemed more plausible to a seventeenth-century reader than would the colophons of the standard text (both of which are translated in this chapter). Scandals involving even the emperor's women were not uncommon in those years of endemic warfare, when no one knew what horror the morrow might bring. Placing the emergence of the "lost" chapters in this context and in this age thus has a certain ring of authenticity.[85] Moreover, the copyist's note, which probably can be trusted, identifies this line of texts as unquestionably predating the published edition.

By contrast, the two colophons of the standard text line ask us to believe that Murasaki Shikibu herself bequeathed these texts to Ishiyamadera Temple, where, according to another myth, she had begun writing *Genji*; that they were first viewed by the superior of that temple in 1058; and that they then were miraculously transferred to the possession of an obsessed courtier in 1319 by the bodhisattva Kannon. Moreover, every colophon in this line of texts agrees verbatim with every other; no historical record exists of either the superior or the courtier named; and none of the texts in this line can be shown to predate the printed edition.

On the basis of this and other evidence, Yoshida Kōichi argues, most persuasively, that whereas the variant text may faithfully represent a version of the forged "Six Kumogakure Chapters" that survived from Sengoku into the Edo period, the standard text is in fact a major revision of the variant text, executed by Asai Ryōi himself in order to produce a work that would fare better in the book market of his day and create a vehicle for the display of his own vast knowledge. The manuscripts in the so-called standard text line are as uniform as they are because they were copied not from earlier manuscripts, but from Ryoi's printed edition. The standard text is indeed the standard edition of "Kumogakure rokujō," but the variant text would more accurately be termed the "earlier/older text" (*kohon*).

Ryōi probably was right to do what he did. It was a good business decision. It wasn't even immoral. His commentary is often extremely helpful and occasionally amusing—as in his discussion of authorship, when he compliments himself by saying that "there are some passages that might well be the work of Murasaki Shikibu." Yet despite the charm of the author, the reader must remain ever aware that the "Six Kumogakure Chapters" translated here are not simply a forgery, but a forgery of a forgery.

T. HARPER

1. Hidden in Cloud (Kumogakure)

It had seemed more than ample cause for new hope when Genji set forth his orders for the New Year's festivities so much more meticulously than usual.[86] But then, on the morning of the first day of the New Year, in the first quarter of the Hour of the Tiger,[87] he had departed from the mansion in a wicker carriage, the inner curtains drawn and so worn from use as to evoke memories of times past.[88] He had to speak with someone in the neighborhood of Tadasu,[89] he said. His only attendants were Koremitsu's son Korehide,[90] who waited on him more attentively than his own shadow, and a single guardsman, one Okabe.[91] They had thought it strange[92] that on this of all days, when one ought to shun any hint of the inauspicious,[93] he would set forth so suddenly in the dead of night. For he had been distracted and not at all his old self of late, his men could not but note to their distress. What might he be up to now? And what, they could not but worry, would be said when it was found that he had left with so meager an entourage? It was not their place to raise objections, however,[94] and they simply asked whither they might escort their lord.

"There is a matter I must discuss with His Majesty of the mountain temple,"[95] he [Genji] replied. "So it has come to this," Korehide thought to himself as they made their way thither. And, indeed, when they had come within sight of their destination, he [Genji] told them, "I have decided it is time I forsook this world. I shall go deep into the mountains and live a life of austerity as a hewer of wood and bearer of water,[96] as they say the Buddha himself once did. What further need have I for anyone to wait upon me? You must go back now."

"Yet of your many retainers, Your Lordship was pleased to choose us to escort you thus far. In your service we would follow you to the ends of the earth, to the plains where tigers lurk,[97] to far shores infested with crocodiles."[98] Both of his men were now in tears. "Even the Buddha himself, we are told, was attended by five of his retainers when first he forsook the world and secluded himself in the mountains,"[99] they protested.

"So indeed he was," he [Genji] replied. "Well then, dispose of the carriage somewhere. As the first of our austerities, so I understand, we must proceed on foot." They unhitched the ox and he stepped down.

It was still dark when they arrived. The Retired Emperor was astonished. "What brings you here at this early hour?"[100] he asked, delighted nonetheless to see him [Genji] after so long a separation. His austerities had left him gaunt, as slender, he [Genji] thought, as when he was a much younger man.[101] For a time they could only regard each other in a state of deep emotion.

"So you're making a clean break of it!" His Majesty then said, to which he [Genji] replied:

maboroshi no mi o shiru kara no kokoromote / yume chō yo oba
sugushihateme ya
"Once one knows this body we inhabit is naught but a phantasm,
can one still go on living in this world, so like a dream?

Once I had made up my mind, the months and days passed as slowly as they do for a child."[102] Whereupon [the Emperor]:

yume no yo to omoisomuru ya murasaki no / ne sae kareno wa kaze mo tamarazu
So now you see this world is but a dream? The Murasaki withers
to the root, leaving naught to block the desolate plain winds.[103]

Genji greets the Retired Emperor at his hermitage. (Waseda University Library)

What could have moved him [Genji] to such a drastic resolve? His Majesty's mind raced with thoughts, for even a rude mountain ascetic could not but be struck by the pity, the charm, the waste of this one man to whom the world had always looked for protection.

His Lordship was determined never so much as to mention Her Ladyship [Murasaki]; yet even now, as he [Genji] thought with regret of the undeserved taint his act would cast upon her name,[104] his eyes filled with tears. Such was the true depth of his devotion to her.

It need hardly be mentioned that his people at the Rokujō mansion searched frantically for him once his absence was discovered. That the man who had been a virtual father to the whole land should simply disappear, and on the first day of the New Year—this would suffice to turn heaven and earth on end. But their search was to no avail.

Had he simply fallen ill and died, they might have accepted his loss as normal; the flowers of forgetfulness[105] would soon grow. Or even if he had forsaken only public life, he would at least have announced his intention to go into retreat, a practice for which there was ample precedent both past and present—though they still might have wondered if it were not all "but a dream."[106] But *this* could only be a source of unforgettable grief that the Commandant [Yūgiri] and the [Akashi] Empress would never cease to lament.

The Reizei Retired Emperor's regard, not to mention his unspoken affection [for Genji], had always been profound, and for his part, His Lordship had always discharged his duties with particular diligence when the imperial command issued from this quarter. His Majesty had, after all, learned what had happened while in mourning for his late mother the Empress.[107] He had even hoped that he might somehow persuade His Lordship to succeed to the throne. He had failed, however, and now, it seemed, he was gone. His Majesty was anxious that he himself might follow in his father's footsteps without a moment's delay:

tarachine no oyama no mine ni iritsuki no / kage no nokoranu asaborake kana
Gone now is my parent, quite as the moon sets behind the mountain peak;
dark will be the dawn, in which no trace of his light remains.

What to do? If only he [the Emperor] might learn *which* mountain peak it was that concealed him. Whole days he passed in ceaseless anxiety. Unable to sleep, he lay listening to the constant chirping of the birds, which normally he found such a joy, when, while dozing, there appeared to him the image of a mournful figure at his devotions, in a place that appeared to be the temple of His Majesty of the mountain. Beside him knelt a woman of indescribable beauty and grace. It was she! She whom His Lordship never had been able to banish from his thoughts—Her Ladyship of the West Wing, her hair as luxuriant and lovely as ever. What an extraordinary woman she was indeed! Yet even as the thought crossed his mind, he awoke. "Had I but known it were a dream . . . ,"[108] he thought, despondently:

omoiki ya kono yo nagara ni wakaretsutsu / yume ni kokoro o kudakubeshi to wa
Would I ever have thought it: that having once been parted in this life
 my heart should again be broken seeing him in a dream?[109]

Off in the mountains, the two brothers were inseparable. In the capital, there may have been those to whom it seemed that the dew settled even more heavily on the flowers of care.[110] But for the Retired Emperor, Genji's constant companionship in his devotions was a source of great delight.

Twice a year, Genji would look in at the Saga temple[111] and the Rokujō estate, but never did anyone detect him.[112] The Nijō mansion, which Lady Murasaki had cherished as her very own,[113] he visited every month on the day of her death at the Hour of the Ox,[114] there to reminisce upon the shade of she who had once lived there.

In the three years that he [Genji] had resided there, the Retired Emperor's health declined pitiably. "This is hardly cause for wonder," the Emperor said, "but surely it must be depressing for you to be left behind, even for the briefest while:

kusa no ue ni shibashi todomaru shiratsuyu yo / moto no shizuku o aware
 to mo miyo
Oh clear dewdrops, you who must yet linger on the leaves of this flower,
 look with pity upon we droplets that fall from the stem."[115]

His Lordship the Holy Layman[116] replied:

kono hodo mo nani to ka wa mishi sue no tsuyu / kiete shizuku no mizu
 no aware o
"In all these years, what have you learned of the evanescence of this
 world?
 The dewdrop, too, will soon vanish, a mere droplet of water.

What is it that has occupied your thoughts through all these years and months since you turned your back on the world? Once one has left the world behind, what reason can there be to retain any sort of attachment to it? You speak in such terribly disturbing terms. It is but the natural course of things that the Five Elements disintegrate[117] and the spirit returns to dwell in the Void, where all is at one with the Dharma Realm. Only awaken to this truth, and there will linger in your mind not the least trace of attachment:

hito no yo wa nenu ni katsu miru yume no yume / matsu fuku kaze ni haraisamashitsu

This world of man, this dream of a dream that we dream without sleeping:
the wind in the pine sweeps it away and awakens us."[118]

A most saintly figure he was when two or three days later he died.

Now, with naught to distract him, His Lordship gave himself up totally to his devotions. Even the news that Prince Hotaru, the Minister Higekuro, and the Akashi lady had one and all passed away, rumors of which had somehow reached him, only impressed him anew how like the flow of a river is the evanescence of life in this world and made him even more anxious to take the final step.

The New Year came, months passed, and the seventh anniversary of the death of Her Ladyship of the Western Wing came around. He [Genji] now took the tonsure:

yo no hoka no yo ni sumu kai ya ariake no / tsuki yori akuru shinonome no sora

What profits it one to live in some world other than this mundane world?
With the dawn moon comes a light as of the sky at daybreak.

Most saintly he was as he intoned this prayer. Afterward, he never left the hermitage for any reason, except, once a month, to make a pilgrimage to the peak of Mount Hie.

This year was the thirteenth anniversary of her death. Having decided he would now enter final meditation[119] at a place called Shibafugatani[120] in Saga, he went to pay his respects at the grave of Her Ladyship of the Western Wing. He murmured softly to himself:

toshi goto ni oisou kusa no tsuyukeki o / haraeba itodo okimasaritsutsu

Though I brush the dew from these grasses that grow every year more profuse,
the droplets only gather in yet greater abundance.

Genji at Murasaki's grave. (Waseda University Library)

Never, it seemed, even in his present state, could he forget her. Now, when one takes vows and leaves this mundane world, what use is it to mortify oneself and dye one's robes black if one remains ignorant of the one great truth for the sake of which the Buddha made himself manifest to this world? Indeed, it might be most unseemly to do so, as if in this guise one were trying to conceal the sins one has committed. Yet conversely, for one who is so thoroughly enlightened, what does it serve to turn one's back on the world?

kuma no naki kokoro no tsuki no tokotowa ni / kumogakure to mo omooenu kana
Eternal and unchangingly bright the moon of an unobscured mind,
unthinkable that it might ever be hidden in clouds.[121]

Many were the ladies he had once cared for, including even Her Ladyship of the Western Wing, who were now but names, mementos of a vanished world.

Korehide, determined that he should not be left behind, went to his lord and humbly placed himself at his service.

"This world of man," His Lordship said, "amounts to no more than remains of the wind that blows through the pines." Even as he spoke, his form receded from view until he could no longer be seen. His retainers were struck speechless. And when they thought of how even birds that course the heavens slow their wings to wait for their young;[122] how even a beast that roams the earth,[123] while its mate flees will itself approach the hunter's torch; how even the wind, invisible to the eye, seems to come calling at one's lodging—at the thought of all this, the two men[124] wept and wept, their heads on each other's shoulders.[125]

Now that there was no one at all at the mountain temple, even those times now past evoked fond memories. He would go to the Reizei[126] Retired Emperor, Korehide decided, and having done so, he related respectfully all that had taken place. Once again, His Majesty's mind was in turmoil. "These ten years and more he lived on in this same world as I, and quite close by; yet never, even in a dream, did he tell me." That he should be overcome was more than natural. "And when the moment came, did he say anything?" he asked. "Tell me that much at least."

Korehide, respectfully reticent, hung back a moment before he spoke:

fuku kaze no ato mo tamaranu amatsusora ni / shibashi wa kumo no tatazumai shite
In the high heavens, where naught remains even of the rushing wind,
there lingers on, for but a little while, a trace of cloud.

2. Watching over the Nest (Sumori)

Now their days were filled with the unremitting grief of His Lordship's disappearance. The Reizei Retired Emperor in particular had not known a moment's respite. In the hope that he might somehow find a way to go wherever it was that His Lordship had gone, he was ever and unflaggingly at his prayers to the Buddha. He wished, of course, that he might simply forsake this world that he held in such contempt. But the First Princess[127] still had no guardian and then there were the young Prince and the Second Princess, his children by the Consort,[128] and both so lovely that his fondness for them made it difficult indeed to take the final step. "Oh dismal world," he thought,

> *monogoto no misutegataki ni hodasarete / ware zo sumori ni narinubeki kana*
>
> Bound by that and those I cannot bear to abandon, I, then, it must be:
> the unhatched egg left behind to watch over the nest.

Weak indeed was his resolve that he could still think this way. Well may the seed of Buddhahood lie in the heart of every man; but so long as it lay undiscovered, his deluded distraction must remain a source of shame before the world. How long, he wondered, could he carry on in such a wretched state? This way and then that, he turned the matter over in his mind, yet naught could dispel his melancholy. He could not help but liken himself to the proverbial thread that took on whatever color it was dyed.[129] Splendid indeed, though, was the way he strove to subdue these thoughts, still so incorrigibly subject to vacillation, and persevered in his quest until ultimately he could grasp in the very depths of his mind the principle of Fundamental Void.[130]

His Majesty summoned the Abbot from the mountain[131] and told him all that was on his mind. "Even for monks, who devote long years of austerity to the quest, it is rare to reach the level of enlightenment that Your Majesty's mind has attained. It is quite magnificent, what Your Majesty has achieved. Surely," the Abbot declared, a bit grandiloquently, "Surely this will bring tears of joy to the eyes[132] of all the Buddhas of the Three Worlds." At this, His Majesty took heart.

After all, having attained this highest of all ranks, he could not imagine that the sins he had committed could be too grievous.[133] Still, all things

The Tendai Abbot counsels the Retired Emperor. (Waseda University Library)

are relative to rank; for different transgressions committed by those of different degree may nonetheless be deemed equally blameworthy. Even those who were revered as Sage Emperors, we are told, were condemned to the agonies of hell for the merest misstep or two.[134] How much more so now, inferior creatures that we are, living in these defiled times, must the ties of delusion ensnare and deter us, thus thwarting the growth of the strong resolve we need to shun and break free from them. Once he [the Emperor] had attained this realization, his anxiety over the future of the Prince and Princesses vanished from his thoughts, and the Secretary Major[135] was quite mystified to see how repellent His Majesty seemed to find the sight of the Dame of Honor of whom he had once been so fond.

"Whence cometh man, and whither goeth he?" he would chant softly, day and night. He could see that as surely as dusk gives way to dawn, each new day marched vainly to its close. His own days, accordingly, were spent in silent meditation. When his meals were offered him, he showed no desire to partake of them, yet neither could anyone see any sign that he was wasting away. He then had a lock shaved from the top of his head and had the vows administered.[136] Waiting on him was the Secretary Major, who had donned the same humble black garb and was overcome with grief at what he saw. "What a joy it is," His Majesty told him, "to escape the flames of the burning house and find the jewel hidden in the lining of my own robe.[137] No cares whatever beset me now."

The Palace Minister [Kaoru] had at length retrieved the young lady from Ono and had even restored her to secular life. He himself, he said, had certain matters on his mind and so had entrusted her to the care of Her Ladyship [his wife, the Second Princess]. All the jealous resentment that had plagued him in the past had vanished; his mind now was quite at rest. "But what might he be up to?" the Emperor and Empress wondered. "If only our royal father were here." For they knew not a moment's peace in their fond concern [for their daughter] and their pity for her.[138]

And so the passing of the reign approached; yet the Second Prince hadn't the least desire to be named Crown Prince and succeed to the throne. More particularly, his attainments as a scholar of Chinese were, at best, faltering. "All things being equal," he said, "the Third Prince [Niou] should be named to succeed." "But how dare we violate the proper order of precedence?" His Majesty asked. "There are precedents even in foreign lands," the Prince replied, "and long ago, on the accession of the Seiwa Emperor, the First Prince [Koretaka] was ten years his senior.[139] Even so—not to fly in the face of fate, I suppose—he succeeded to the throne. In our case, moreover, there is no such disparity between us;[140] no matter which of us is appointed, who could object?"[141] And, indeed, if pressed on the matter, both the Emperor and the Empress would have admitted that this was exactly as they had for years hoped things would turn out. And so it was decided that the reign would pass to the Third Prince.

When Kaoru became Palace Minister and assumed control of the government, he commanded the devotion of those who served him to a degree that surpassed even that of His Late Lordship [Genji]. These were times, so it was felt, that would one day be seen as the very model of a prosperous reign.

On the evening of the passing of the reign, the mistress of the Nijō mansion [Nakanokimi] proceeded to the palace, where she was to be known as the Wisteria Court Dame of Honor. In the autumn of that year, in the Eight Month, when an Empress was to be appointed, it was this very lady of the Wisteria Court whom His Majesty named. Now, surely, she must have realized how extraordinary had been his regard for her all these years. The sixth daughter of the Minister of the Left [Yūgiri] was likewise accorded great distinction, she being made mistress of the Shōkyōden.

The daughter of the Prince Minister of Ceremonial was now in the service of the [Akashi] Empress Mother, where she was known as Miyanokimi.[142] When the present Emperor was still the Prince Minister of War, he had taken a fancy to the Princess; but the Palace Minister, at the time still Commandant, was determined to give him [Niou] a taste of the ire he had harbored for so long and had himself made advances to Miyanokimi. For the Prince this had been disheartening, but chastened perhaps by the memory of his own behavior, he bore his friend no great grudge. Unfortunately, the Princess had borne a child, which the Minister found a most unwelcome turn of events. What had begun as an affair with a woman he had never loved, meant merely to spite the Prince, had ended in a situation that was hardly a matter for jest.[143] It was in the midst of His Lordship's disturbing ruminations on these sordid events that the Third Prince had succeeded to the throne. As there was no one among the Prince's own gentlewomen who might serve as his Imperial Emissary,[144] His Lordship, of his own volition, took this opportunity to relinquish his own claim to Miyanokimi. Mortifying though it was, she assumed the position and was thereafter known as Her Ladyship of the Third Rank.

The Minister [Kaoru] conducted himself in the most exemplary manner, according equal rank and ceremonial precedence to both [his wife] the Second Princess and the young lady from the Eastlands [Uki-

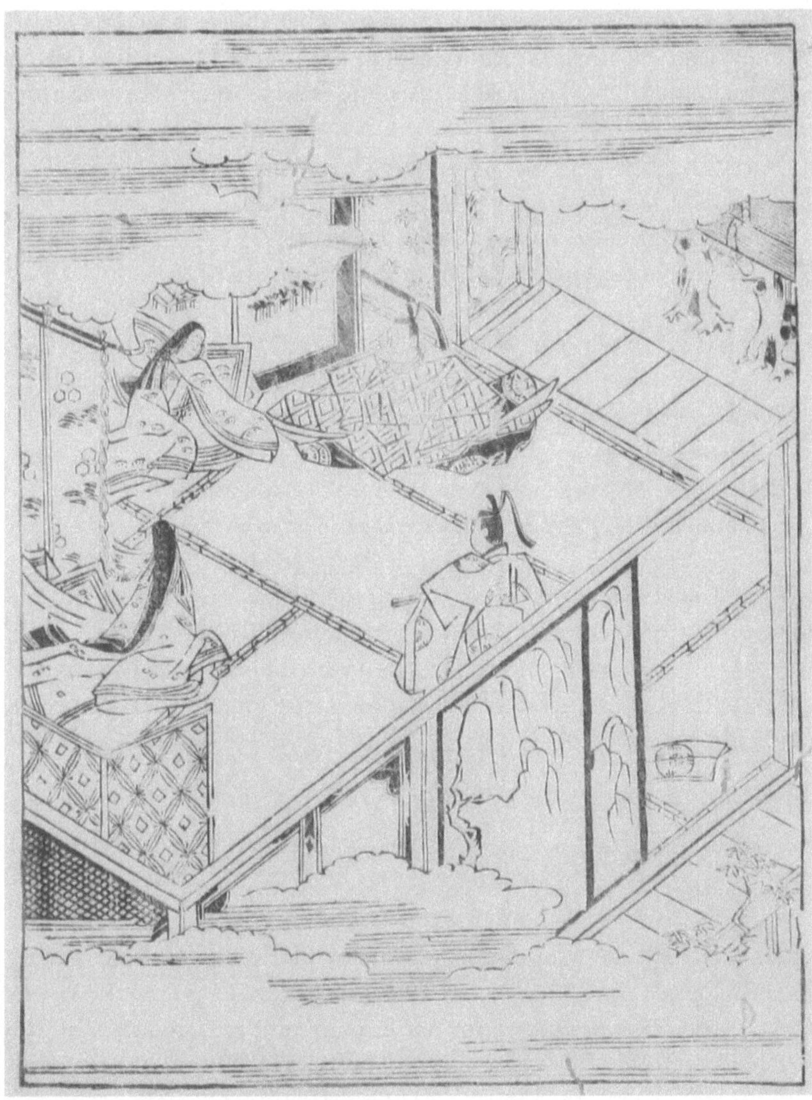

Nakanokimi comes to the palace. (Waseda University Library)

fune]. For this he was greatly esteemed by both high and low for his rare sensitivity. His guardianship of the Wisteria Court Empress [Nakanokimi], too, the Minister undertook to continue exactly as before, and he discharged his duties to her, both at court and beyond, with great dignity.

On some occasion, though I cannot say when, he went secretly to call at the Wisteria Court. As they talked, so easily and intimately, of times past, he found himself unable to resist the feelings that came over him:

tsukikage zo mishi yo no aki ni kawaranu o / yadoreru sode no sebaku mo aru kana
The moonlight differs not from that of another autumn we knew, yet this sleeve is too narrow to hold the tears that reflect it.[145]

Hearing this brought back fond memories, and she was deeply touched:

kumo no ue ni omoinoboreru sumika ni mo / mishi yo no tsuki no kage wa wasurezu
Even in this dwelling above the clouds to which I have aspired, never do I forget the moonlight we knew in times past.

And so it was, that even though both of them had prospered, from time to time he would still say, "If only Ōigimi were still alive . . . ," and never were his sleeves quite dry. Even the most ordinary people, they say, would speak with obvious emotion of what an exceptionally feeling man he always was.

3. Cherry Blossom Man (Sakurahito)[146]

Even after rising to such unanticipated eminence, never for a moment did the reigning Emperor [Niou] forget Lady Murasaki. "Ah," he thought, "if only she were still in this world, now that I can do as I would wish—then I would be able to care for her in truly proper fashion. Of all the royal children, and there were many of us, it was the Princess First Rank and myself, by far, of whom she was fondest and looked after the most solicitously. Young though we were, we knew her affection for us was something special, as deep and unchanging, it seemed, as Cathay crimson. During her illness, there was a time when the incessant prayers and incantations took effect and she seemed to revive a bit. But her affliction persisted, and she spoke sadly of her regret that she would not live to see me rise in the world. 'Think of me,' she said forlornly, 'when you see the blossoms at the Nijō mansion, and offer some of them to the Buddha.'[147] By then, she was already looking ahead to the next world." Even now, his faint memories of those times filled him with sorrow, and he sighed softly. Thinking it must be late, he at length had the shutters lowered, whereupon she appeared before him, no less beautiful than she had been in life—no dream was this!

"Even when you were young, I could see you were no ordinary child," she said. "What a joy it is, now that you have done so brilliantly, to know that my attentions—for I've never left your side—were of some avail and you have prospered precisely as I'd hoped you might:

> *kimi ga atari saranu kagami no kage soite / kumori naki yo o nao terasu kana*
> Ever at your side, as constant as is the image in a mirror,
> shall I continue to light this world of your flawless reign."

She seemed so alive to him, so much of this world, but all in vain; for as he reached out to grasp her sleeve, he awoke. And he had not spoken even a single word to her; the bitterness of that would be a source of unrelenting sorrow to him. Though he had been but a child when he was parted from her, he had only to think of those times to recall how delicately beautiful she had been; *that* was an image there would be no forgetting. ". . . they fall without surcease,"[148] he murmured softly in his grief at these recollections of times past. Yes, he decided, he would have the Eight Recitations performed at the Nijō mansion, which she had bequeathed to him. And sutras must be chanted at the temple in Saga.

Many of the prayers the Emperor himself chanted, which brought back poignant memories [of Murasaki]. Of late he had been thinking how much the Wisteria Court Empress [Nakanokimi] resembled her. Over the years, his memory of her had faded. In his dream, though, it all came vividly back to him, and he was drawn all the more to her. He went at once to the Wisteria Court. There he found her fussing tenderly over the Second Prince, who had grown to be such a beautiful boy. Flustered by His Majesty's unannounced approach, she blushed brightly. She was as delicately beautiful as ever, and quite apart from the fact that she was the mother of so many of his royal children, he was filled with a sense of how infinitely precious she was to him. His gaze fixed upon her, and the demure discomfiture that this caused her he found unspeakably lovely.

He called for Chinese kotos, which they were playing together when her gentlewomen announced that the Palace Minister waited upon Her Majesty. "Do show him in," she said. His accustomed seat of honor

The Emperor unexpectedly visits the Wisteria Court. (Waseda University Library)

inside the blinds was prepared, and he was ushered into the presence of Their Majesties. They fell to talking of times past in the most intimate detail. As close as they were to one another, there may well have been some unspoken ties of affection among them. But really, I have no idea what may have gone on in their minds.[149]

"Can it be true, what they are saying," His Majesty asked, "that you have found the girl who disappeared? In any case, I hope you'll not hold that against me now. I was dreadfully immature back then and had my mind set on something I ought never to have done. Ultimately it drove us both to our wits' end. But this lady here made such a deep secret of it all that I simply ached somehow to find out who that girl was. Jijū was only a child then, and when she came in saying she had a letter from out there, I snatched it and read it. That's what got me started. People shouldn't be so secretive as all that." He spoke so unreservedly of his own guilt in the matter that His Lordship forgave him. Yet even now it brought tears to his eyes.

Even as a much younger man, His Lordship had been so deeply thoughtful as to put others to shame, and he hardly ever gave vent to his own feelings. By now, life being what it is, he was even more aware what a frail and fleeting thing this body is, in which we take lodging for a time. He knew now what to think of all those moments in the past that had so charmed him, the good as well as the bad.[150] Indeed, he understood full well how profoundly sinful they had been, and to a degree that would put the most austere of monks to shame. To this affair, too, he now gave hardly a thought. His own lot had been but compensation for the considerable mental anguish that his father, for a time, had caused the lord of the Rokujō mansion [Genji].[151] He had been made to witness this with his own eyes, he was convinced, and thus not the slightest bit of the old bitterness remained. "What is the point," he said, "in condemning what is past? It was naught but the working out of fate." In the end he talked about this person and that and how superbly and beautifully they had played. "And now, alas, so many of them gone . . . ,"[152] he intoned. Today, in their talk of old times, he felt as if all the old transgressions had vanished, which brought him great comfort. "Until I have the honor of another audience . . . ," he said to Their Majesties as he took his leave.

"The Minister has been an incredible source of strength over the years, closer, indeed, than a real brother. Even so," His Majesty grumbled, "he is the sort of person who time and again has made me look so capricious that I'm still quite uncomfortable in his presence."[153] It rankled him to hear some of the older gentlewomen in his service whispering among themselves about "how very considerate a person the Minister always is."

Though the Minister [Kaoru] now proceeded to the palace in great splendor, never did he forget the old villa in the mountains.[154] As the years passed—for there is no halting them[155]—he held an imposing succession

Kaoru calls upon the Emperor and Empress. (Waseda University Library)

of the Eight Recitations—in the Eighth Month on the anniversary of the death of the Holy Layman, the [Eighth] Prince; in the Tenth Month for the Suzaku Retired Emperor,[156] and in the Eleventh Month for the Agemaki lady [Ōigimi]. This rare degree of devotion was regarded by all as a significant precedent.

The Governor of Hitachi, too, had been the beneficiary of the Minister's good offices and now held the title of Governor of Yamato. His wife, who in the past had been an object of derision, had now become a lady of some consequence. His Lordship, thinking it a blot on his own reputation that such a woman should be known as his mother-in-law, had installed her in a grand mansion that he had built in the northern quarter of his own estate. She declined to offer the Governor of Yamato quarters where he might live at his ease but treated him as a mere servant. This, of course, was because on rare occasions, the lady from Sanjō [Ukifune] would grace the mansion with her presence when forced to avoid directional taboos.[157]

The Major of the Left Bodyguards, though now over forty, remained a mere major, just as in the past. Kogimi, however, who had once seemed so far his inferior and still was only about twenty, had, through His Lordship's influence, become an Imperial Adviser Colonel and was a Privy Gentleman of considerable consequence. Both the Governor of Yamato and the Major now deeply regretted their past. Pure gold[158] she was, they now realized.

In the Second Month of that same year, hearing that the cherries, which were his keepsake of Lady Murasaki, were at their peak, His Majesty made an imperial progress there [to the Nijō mansion]. He gazed upon them [the cherry trees] in wonder, for indeed their beauty bore no resemblance to any ordinary blossoms, and their fragrance evoked fond memories.[159] "'And after they shall have fallen . . . ,'"[160] he mused,

naki kage no katami to omou hana nareba / katsu miru kara ni aware to
o shiru
Since to me these blossoms are a token of one no longer with us
merely to see their beauty is to be moved to sorrow.

Wistfully he beheld them, "oblivious to the darkening day . . . ,"[161] "the beauty [of the blossoms] unchanged,"[162] while his thoughts turned despondently to the past, wishing it "were something that might be turned back."[163] Suddenly, from the shadows beneath the blossoms, the shade from his previous dream appeared to him:

adashi yo to omoi na hate so sakurahito / hana no chiru chō koto no narai o
"Dismiss it not as a world of futility, cherry blossom man:
this eternal round of flowers that bloom only to fall again.

The Imperial Progress to Nijō. (Waseda University Library)

Even the Buddha, when he vanished into the clouds of his nirvana, as they say, did so but to teach us the nature of this world of mere mortals. Deep though the sea of life and death may be, and high though the waves of blind delusion may rise, still you must realize, it is all but a dream. In the end, rank and office, too, are of no avail. In this life, as well as in that to come," she meticulously counseled him, "turn your thoughts toward enlightenment to the True Way, and let that be your companion throughout the two worlds:[164]

moto yori mo mumarezariseba ima mo mata / tazunete kaeru furusato mo nashi

Were one never to have been born in the first place, then now one would have
no old home, once more to seek out and thither to return."

Then, from beneath the blossoms, her voice alone resounded to the heavens and, in a rush of wind, was swept far off into the clouds.

4. Teacher of the Law (Nori no shi)

With each passing month and day, the Palace Minister [Kaoru] grew ever more weary of life in this mundane world. Yet he now had a young son and a daughter by the Sanjō lady [Ukifune] and another son by [his wife] the Second Princess, in whom the Retired Emperor[165] had taken an extraordinary interest. His lot in life had left him no cause for regret, even he himself [Kaoru] had to admit. His son by the Lady of the Third Rank [Miyanokimi] was now a Chamberlain of the Fourth Rank and on very close terms with the reigning Emperor. He had grown to be a handsome gentleman, impressive for his prudence. "Though I suspect," he [Kaoru] had observed, "that the young gentlewomen at court may find it difficult to be at their ease in his presence."

The Fujitsubo Empress [Nakanokimi] had borne three sons, each one of whom was so impeccably and elegantly handsome as to invite comparison with foreign courts—as even their royal [father], to his own delight, had remarked. The First Prince had taken the place of the [former] Crown Prince, who had relinquished his claim to the throne. The Second Prince, in deference to past precedent no doubt,[166] had become Prince Minister of War, while the Third Prince, as Prince Minister of Central Affairs, enjoyed a very special place in the affection of the Emperor and Empress.

The tenth day of the Third Month had come and gone, and the cherry blossoms at the Southern Hall were more beautiful than ever before. "Too beautiful to let pass," the Emperor decided, and he commanded that there be a festival of cherry blossoms. The music and the gifts evoked times past,[167] and as they sang that old favorite, "My Great Lord,"[168] they enjoyed themselves riotously.

That same evening, the Third Prince fell ill, and the following morning, around the first quarter of the Hour of the Tiger,[169] he passed away, like the flame of a lamp that had flickered and failed. The shock left his people distraught and utterly forlorn, as if the world had lost all its color and been plunged into eternal darkness. The Emperor and Empress felt they might perish of grief at any moment, while for everyone else it was as if the earth had been pulled out from under their feet and their very breath cut off. This Prince, as it happened, had harbored a secret fondness for the Palace Minister's daughter by Kozaishō,[170] a young lady reputed to be a great beauty. The Minister thought this would make a highly desirable match and hoped that all would go as the young man wished. But his sudden death, following the briefest of illnesses, left His Lordship consumed with grief.[171]

In her grief, the Fujitsubo Empress [the Prince's mother] sighed that she wished she, too, might follow the same path, and only five or so days later, she herself passed away. So great was the shock to the Emperor that he was denied even the consolation of tears.[172] He would recall how in times past, in everything she did, she had been so graceful and charming. Though she knew full well how faithless he had been, she quite genuinely bore him no resentment and was determined to speak of him in only the best of terms. And if ever she did allow herself to weep, she did her best to disguise the fact and do so discreetly. There was a fetching beauty in the way that she bore her pain, for which none of the old tropes of birds and flowers offered any adequate description. If only there were some way he could see her again as she had once been. In foreign lands, it was said, there was an incense that could recall the spirits of the dead.[173] "But had anyone ever succeeded in finding it and bringing it back?" he lamented day and night. When he saw the young Princes, he would murmur to himself, "those ferns of remembrance . . . ,"[174] but to no avail. Even in lives to come, there would be no forgetting his despairing grief for her. His people were struck with admiration to hear his voice as he repeatedly chanted the scriptures.

Even had this never happened, the Palace Minister knew only too well what a dream this life is. And now that he had seen just how frail it could be, he felt he must no longer continue to vacillate, even for another moment. Then he sent to His Majesty a letter filled with talk of times past:

The Cherry Blossom Festival. (Waseda University Library)

aware yo no nageki wa izure kawaranu o / onaji keburi no sora ni
kuraben
Ah the pity! For whom are the world's sorrows any different?
And yet
we watch which wisp of this same smoke will rise first to the sky.

"How wretched indeed is fate,"[175] he thought as he wrote,

ochitagiru namida no kawa no hayaki se ni / okurete ima zo ware wa ukitaru
In the raging rapids of this torrential river of falling tears,
I am left behind, now but to float dismally about.

It must have pained him to go on this way, passing his days as if everything were perfectly normal. The Sanjō lady had once attained an exceptional degree of serenity, and yet, he explained to her, "I was so dissatisfied with the way things had turned out that I decided to go through with it, no matter how deep the sin it might plunge me into, and that is how it happened. But that stage in my life is now past. Such is this world, and so frail this body, that if one grows old in vain pursuits, one cannot even perform one's devotions with as much perseverance as one would wish. I want to enter upon the Way just as soon as I can." With no further ado he summoned the Prelate down from the mountain and talked to him at some length, even about his painfully complex personal ties.

"I had decided to concern myself no more with matters of this world, but hindrances of one sort and another arose—matters I simply could not neglect—which kept me from my goal. And now here I am. I even blocked the Way in which Her Ladyship here had reached an extraordinary level of enlightenment. I knew it was wrong, and yet I was painfully desperate to keep her with me that little bit longer. I simply could not banish the vision of what once had been, though I knew perfectly well how perverse this was. I did manage, despite myself, to calm my thoughts somewhat; yet even then, for some reason, I could not endure it, and so I did what I did just to be rid of the obsession. But now that I have seen with my own eyes such appalling disasters as these and know the ultimate extreme of grief, what is there to keep me in this world even one day longer? I've now come to feel that it would be just too painful to do so. I would become your disciple, as would Her Ladyship here, together with me."

"This is noble indeed," [the Prelate replied], "but His Majesty is deeply dependent upon you. And in times past, Her Ladyship carried such a load of resentment against certain people and the world at large that she became a nun and for a time went into seclusion. Yet as if to prove that the bond between you had not run its course, you were reunited, like the undersash in the poem.[176] Nor will the fact that you will now find it difficult to leave behind your noble children," he thought, "accord with the will of the Buddha."

"I have often spoken to her of this of late," His Lordship said. "But alas, the decision is ineluctable. Besides, if we remain together like this, we will only come to abhor what we did in the past. Not a trace of the old attachments now remains. If we persist in putting it off, myriad other hindrances are certain to arise."

And so he administered the vows. "Now then, you no doubt know the gravity of these vows from what I told you in that mountain village. Waver not in your resolve. For even if the dream of enlightenment leaves no trace of cloud in the dawn sky, how much more are the divigations of the mind mere figments of fantasy," he went so far as to tell them:

tōkaranu kokoro ni komoru nori no shi o / yama no oku made nani motomeken
That teacher of the Law, so near, secluded in your very own heart,
why was it that you sought him so deep in the mountains?[177]

No distance at all, he [Kaoru] realized upon hearing this. In the customary manner,[178] [the Prelate] shaved only a lock from the top of her head. All that remained of her hair she herself cut, and on the paper in which it was wrapped she wrote:

tokeyaranu kokoro no soko no midaregami / sashikushinagara kezuru matsukaze
This turmoil, deep in my heart, as untamed as untended tangled hair:
I cut away, combs and all; and feel the wind in the pines.[179]

The Minister was delighted that he should at last have had his way. That evening they went forthwith to Yokawa, where they took vows and lavished extravagant gifts on the temple.

"Do teach me the essentials of the easiest of the Ways. There remain a few questions that I would like to clear up."

"The True Way to which the Buddha was enlightened can never be reduced to words or described in all its fullness. But I do doubt the wisdom of seeking it outside one's own self. To what avail are one's devotions if even a mote remains in the depths of one's mind? You must realize that delusion and enlightenment alike are but as yesterday's dreams. If you will but probe the depths, is your understanding likely to be shallow?"

The Prelate counsels Kaoru and Ukifune. (Waseda University Library)

The Prelate counseled them in a fine resonant voice with frequent meaningful glances from his eyes.[180]

"Alas, what hope is there for me?" he [Kaoru] thought. "Why did I never come to that realization by myself?" He felt as if a bank of mist in which he had been shrouded had been cleared away:

yo no naka ni ari ya nashi ya to iu made wa / nao wasurarenu kokoro to o shiru
So long as I should even ask whether I be of this world or no—
 I see now I was still unable to forget it all.

With these words he made as if to step outside for just a moment—and vanished without a trace.

"What wearisome and painful experiences the man must have endured during his wanderings in this ephemeral world. And that his distaste should reach such heights that he would flee it all!" the Prelate mused, unable to resist a touch of envy. "What a saintly figure." If only, he thought, he might urge this example upon the many monks in his charge.

5. A Fledgling Lark (Hibarigo)

The world was in turmoil. So painful was the loss and so great their grief that many could think of naught but how keenly they wished he were still alive.[181] His Lordship, the Major [Shōshō no Kimi, Kaoru's son by the Second Princess], was a most attractive young man whose looks were a poignant reminder of [his father in] times past. Now that he had taken such a brotherly interest in the children left behind at the Sanjō mansion,[182] whose plight distressed him greatly, everyone marveled at his kindness as well.

It must have been about the middle of the Fourth Month when on his return from paying his respects at the temple in Saga,[183] he commanded his guardsmen to shoot arrows into the distance,[184] at which there came the faint cry of a lark as it ascended from the clumps of plume grass:

izuku o ka yado to sadamete hibarigo no / kono kusamura o nakite izuran
And where will you now call home, fledgling lark,
 as you flee, crying, from this tussock of grass?

Long ago, one very snowy day, when hawking on this moor, His Lordship [Kaoru] had recited a poem in which he referred to [something said by] the Commander of the Left Gate Guards, Tokishige:[185]

oshinabete tsumoru miyuki o nado sareba / wagami hitotsu to kikiwabinuran
When the snow falls equally on one and all
 why do you lament for yourself alone?

A guardsman's arrow rouses a flight of larks. (Waseda University Library)

"Had he lived, he [Kaoru] would not be of such an age that his looks would have deteriorated. Even people who are not good looking may appear quite presentable, even in their later years.[186] But what a blessing it would be if he who was so superlatively attractive were still alive." At this bitter thought, he [Shōshō] was suddenly choked with emotion, and his tears flowed without surcease. This came as such a shock to his retainers that they, too, were left with dampened sleeves. Just then there came the cry of wild geese passing overhead:

yukikieshi ato o hakanami ware nomi ka / kumoji mo ushi to kari zo naku naru

Do I alone find it sorrowful that he vanished without a trace?
Sad, too, is this way through the clouds, the wild geese seem to cry.

Even after he had returned home, he felt as if the shade were quite close to him, and a steady stream of memories, of times past and present, filled his thoughts and made him sadder than ever. Hoping perhaps for some respite from his relentless cares, he lay down and pillowed his head on his writing box when a figure in wondrously scented ecclesiastical robes and a surplice of what appeared to be Tōgyōkin brocade[187] awakened him gently.[188] Who could it be, he wondered, as he looked up, only to see that it was *he*, in no way less handsome than in life. In what seemed a reply to [his son's poem of] the hunt on the moor, he said:

oshinabete kari to shi kikaba suteshi yo ni / kokoro suzushiki michi motome seyo

If you accept that all is as transient as passing geese, seek then
serenity of mind in rejecting this mundane world.

But just when he wished to reply, he awoke from his dream. So he had been coursing the heavens above the moor where they had been hawking, he realized.[189] How marvelous that he should be watching over this mundane world even more than before! He wished ever so much that he could obey [Kaoru's] command to abandon this world as quickly as he could. Yet there were too many ties and cares to allow him rashly to retreat without a trace, the thought of which only made his sorrow more intense.

6. *Eight Bridges (Yatsuhashi)*

The reigning Emperor,[190] passing his days in a state of despondency, inquired of the Venerable Keikin:[191] "Numerous are the teachings of the

The Venerable Keikin counsels the Emperor. (Waseda University Library)

Buddha's dharma, each of which, in its own way, I find truly wondrous. But which of these Ways[192] in particular ought I to follow, so as to attain my goal forthwith?" The holy man is said to have replied:

nani sen ni sono yatsuhashi o motomubeki / hitotsu no mizu wa kumode naritomo

"How is it that you wish to choose among these eight different bridges,
though there be but one stream flowing in myriad channels?[193]

Whence are we born into this world? Wither lies the way by which we may return thither? So deign you to ask in your quest for that knowledge now lost to you. Yet I implore you, seek not that which lies within your good self in some place far removed from yourself.[194] The several teachings that the Buddha has bequeathed us, different one from another though they may seem, have, as he himself has taught us, but a single source. People's desires and aspirations are as different as their faces,[195] and thus the Buddha teaches through a variety of Expedient Means. Yet the Way by which one endeavors to attain enlightenment, whether one be of high station or low, can be no other than to penetrate to the very source of consciousness. The rain falls alike on all plants and trees; and though the season of their bloom may be early or late, all blossom forth in colorful splendor.[196] Likewise is it with the many different teachings of the Buddha; they are like the dewdrops, having but a single hue of their own, [but appearing to differ] because the cast of people's minds is not constant.[197] The body, be it that of one either deep in sin or one exalted in virtue, ends ultimately in the same form, as dew upon the mossy path. That which knows no limits, from the distant past into the future, which has neither beginning nor end, lies within your own honored mind. If it be tied by earthly cares and attachments, then never will it escape from the Three Worlds[198] but must wander aimlessly through the Six Realms.[199] In the dark of night, the three thousand greater worlds[200] are far removed and invisible to the Corporeal Eye.[201] Yet open the Mind's Eye[202] and that far-off world of enlightenment may be seen unobstructed. So you see, there is no need for you to become a monk and relinquish your reign. Even in your present exalted position, if you just set your mind upon it, you can attain enlightenment."

Lady Naishi no Kan:[203]

yukusue o fumishiru hito no kokoro yori / moto no michi o mo omoitorinuru
In the mind of one who walks with the knowledge of what is yet to come
lies likewise an understanding of paths trod in lives past.

These six Kumogakure volumes bring to completion *The Tale of the Shining Genji*. Despite this, Murasaki Shikibu, on the example of the *Shiki hyōrin*, gave them as a votive offering to the treasure house of Kannon.[204] They are thus the legitimate property of the Bodhisattva and a valued possession of this temple. Carelessly to reveal their contents would be to trifle with the intentions of Shikibu. Generation upon generation of Superiors have treasured them and kept them secret; let their example stand as a warning to future Superiors.

KŌHEI, FIRST YEAR (1058), FIRST MONTH, — DAY
SUPERIOR, ISHIYAMADERA
DAI-SŌZU SHIN'YŌ[205]

Having secluded myself in prayer and supplication at Ishiyamadera, in response thereto, at dawn, after six full days in retreat, this humble official was vouchsafed these six volumes in a miraculous vision. I thereupon read them in the treasure house. They complete *The Tale of the Shining Genji*, beginning to end, in every detail. How profound, how profound! Their wondrous words penetrate to the very marrow of one's bones. I, too, have kept them secret and have given them as a votive offering to the treasure house of Kiyomizudera.

GEN'Ō, FIRST YEAR (1319), NINTH MONTH, SECOND DAY
SECOND RANK SENIOR GRADE, ACTING MIDDLE COUNSELOR
FUJIWARA NO CHIKAKANE[206]
TRANSLATED BY T. HARPER

THE "SUMORI" FRAGMENTS

"Sumori" is the second of the two "lost" chapters, only fragments of which survive.[207] The "Sumori" fragments, however, are somewhat more substantial than the "Sakurahito" fragments. The title of the chapter appears in various sources; four poems from it were selected for inclusion in *Leaves in the Wind* (*Fūyōwakashū*, 1271), a massive anthology of poems drawn exclusively from works of fiction; and another three poems are found in what appears to be a fragment of a similar anthology (the "Horibe fragment"). In addition, some of the characters in the chapter are described in the "old *Genji* genealogies."[208]

From the poems alone, we can identify the main characters of the chapter as Niou and Kaoru, and we can reconstruct at least the outlines of one of the episodes it depicts. In the "Horibe fragment," Niou, true to form, slips into the carriage of a woman known only as Sumori as she leaves the palace, declares his undying (but unrequited) love for her (H-1), and spirits her away to the Shirakawa estate,[209] where he further protests her cruelty (H-2) and she in turn berates him for unfairly thinking such unkind thoughts of her (H-3). *Leaves in the Wind*, by a stroke of good fortune, also contains Niou's poem (F-2). The woman to whom it is addressed is not identified, but we at least can be certain that we are in the same chapter at the same time and the same place. Here, however, Kaoru is the focus of attention. He, too, visits the Shirakawa estate, ostensibly to view the late-blooming blossoms of the mountain cherry (F-1). Following Niou's poem, Kaoru addresses another poem to Sanmi, whom he has visited in a "mountain villa" (F-3), to which she responds quite favorably (F-4).

Unfortunately, these poems presuppose a reader who knows something of the story from which they are extracted, and thus they are introduced with only minimal reference to their context. Were it not for the "old genealogies"—through which we are able to reconstruct some of that context—we would have to guess, and many of our guesses would be wrong. For example, in 1943, Horibe Seiji, who seems not to have had access to the genealogies, identified Sumori with Nakanokimi, the younger daughter of the Eighth Prince in Uji. His guess was well founded, for in "Hashihime" (16:115), Nakanokimi addresses a poem to her father in which she describes herself as a *sumori* (unhatched egg):

naku naku mo hane uchiki suru kimi nakuba / ware zo sumori ni
narubekarikeru
Were it not for you, sheltering us under your wings, weeping all the while,
I should surely have been left in the nest, the unhatched egg.

And in *A Nameless Notebook*, there is a discussion of "Sumori no Nakanokimi" and "Sumori no Kimi," whom some commentators still take to be a daughter of the Eighth Prince.

From the genealogies, however, we know that Sumori no Kimi, or Sumori no Sanmi as she is called elsewhere, is the daughter of Gen Sanmi, a son of the Hotaru Prince Minister of War (G-1f, G-3g, G-5g), who may have been the boy, Jijū, who makes a brief appearance in "Umegae" (14:413) when his father sends him home to fetch some samples of calligraphy that he wants to show to Genji (G-1b, G-2b, G-3d). The genealogies further suggest that Sumori no Nakanokimi is the younger sister of Sumori no Sanmi

(G-1g, G-3h, G-5h), whom the young lady in *A Nameless Notebook* criticizes as "lustful" for preferring Niou to Kaoru. The elder sister, Sumori no Sanmi, as the granddaughter of a prince renowned for his talent as a lutenist, has inherited his skill on this instrument and is, moreover, a great beauty. These qualities earn her promotion to the third rank and a position as teacher of the lute to the Princess First Rank (G-1f, G-3g, G-5g). They also attract the amorous attentions of the princess's younger brother Niou, who at the time was having an affair with her younger sister (G-3h). Through the good offices of the sisters' younger brother, Sanmi no Jijū, he succeeds in seducing Sumori no Sanmi as well, for which the boy is rewarded with promotion to First Secretary Colonel (G-1e, G-5f). Ultimately, though, she is offended by Niou's frivolity: "The attentions of Commandant Kaoru being more sincere, her affections shift and she bears him a son. Thereafter, however, the Prince's persistent pursuit of Sumori makes her the object of suspicion, and she goes into seclusion at Ōuchiyama,[210] where the fourth daughter of the Suzaku Emperor dwells" (G-1f). There she takes the tonsure and spends her days with the Fourth Princess,[211] performing her devotions (G-3b, G-5g, G-5i). Her son by Kaoru is "the last of the Genji progeny" (G-5j).

In short, the old genealogies make it clear that the surviving poems from "Sumori" in *Leaves in the Wind* and the "Horibe fragment" depict Niou and Kaoru in pursuit of the same woman, Sumori no Sanmi, a granddaughter of Prince Hotaru. We have here another love triangle almost analogous to the Niou-Kaoru-Ukifune triangle, except that in this case Kaoru seems to be the more successful competitor. In the "Horibe fragment," we probably have the remains of an episode depicting Niou's persistence even after Sumori has rejected him in favor of Kaoru.[212] The first poem in *Leaves in the Wind* seems to depict one of Kaoru's advances, and the last two are an exchange between Kaoru and Sumori, probably after she has moved to the Fourth Princess's mountain retreat.[213]

How, then, does this fit into *The Tale of Genji* as we now know it? When, and by whom, was it written? Why does the whole chapter no longer exist? These questions are complex; the sources that can be brought to bear on them are meager and often equivocal, and very few scholars have made more than a cursory attempt to answer them. It is clear, nonetheless, that "Sumori" is in some way inextricably involved with the latter chapters of the canonical *Genji*, from "Niou Miya" through "Yume no ukihashi." Nakano Kōichi regards both "Sakurahito" and "Sumori" not as supplemental additions to *Genji* but as independent tales, some of the characters of which also appear in *Genji* and others are new creations.[214] Tokiwai Kazuko prefers to think of "Sumori" as the work of a reader-author who was dissatisfied with the latter chapters of *Genji*—in particular their inconclusive ending and their treatment of Kaoru—and who thus decided to rewrite this part of the work using many of the same materials that the original author used.[215] But the most concerted effort to deal with these and other fragments was made by the late Inaga Keiji, and it is the hypotheses that he has wrought from them that are the most convincing.[216]

Inaga's thesis is closely argued and covers many issues that would be impossible to discuss here without extensive quotations from the *Genji* text. Its broad outlines may be summarized as follows.

Inaga first discounts the notion, prevalent since *Hakuzōshi* and perpetuated by Horibe, that "Sumori" was "the work of a later author that was appended" to the canonical fifty-four chapters. Instead, he notes the close affinities among "Sumori" and "Kōbai" and "Takekawa": the young lady descended from a prince and highly skilled as a lutenist, Niou's amorous interest in her, and the role of the lady's younger brother in advancing this interest, all of which suggest that "Sumori" was written not as an afterthought but as a continuation of the plot already in progress in the "Niou Miya," "Kōbai," and "Takekawa" sequence of chapters.[217] And since the action of these chapters parallels that in the earlier of the ten Uji chapters (Inaga's *Hashihime monogatari*), the question then arises why these three chapters, which many scholars consider highly spurious, were included in the canonical *Genji* whereas "Sumori" was not.[218] The answer, Inaga suggests, lies in the even closer affinities of "Sumori" with the latter of the ten Uji chapters (Inaga's *Ukifune monogatari*). The love triangle involving Niou, Kaoru, and Sumori no Sanmi is so similar to that involving Niou, Kaoru, and Ukifune that the resemblance could hardly be coincidental. Added to which, the lady being pursued ends up retreating to the mountains and taking the tonsure, just as Ukifune does. None of this would make sense as an extension of the ten Uji chapters. What is far more likely is that "Sumori" was instead the source of the *Ukifune monogatari* and that it was dismantled and its components recycled in the composition of the last four chapters of *Genji*, after which, like "Sakurahito," it was discarded as superfluous.

In this case, however, Inaga is unwilling to venture that the author of "Sumori" might have been Murasaki Shikibu or even the author(s) of "Niou Miya," "Kōbai," and "Takekawa." What we can say, however, is that

"Sumori" was still found in many twelfth-century texts, that around 1200 the author of *A Nameless Notebook* regarded it as a canonical chapter of *Genji*, and that Inaga himself sees no reason to doubt that it was composed within or not long after Murasaki's lifetime.[219] Nor is this likely to be the last word on the subject. In 2008, the National Institute for the Study of Japanese Literature (Kokubungaku Kenkyū Shiryōkan) acquired a hitherto unknown "old *Genji* genealogy," which is both older and more detailed than any of the previously known genealogies.[220] And in 2009, Ikeda Kazuomi discovered two fragments of text that he believes were taken from a copy of the lost chapter "Sumori."[221] The unexpected appearance of these new materials has rekindled scholarly interest in "Sumori" and may yet add materially to our knowledge of this "apocryphal" chapter, which was by no means "apocryphal" to all readers in all times.

T. HARPER

The "Horibe Fragment"[222]

H-1. As Sumori is leaving the palace, the Prince slips quietly into her carriage. The Prince:

itou itou aware narikeru kimi ni yori / nadote inochi o oshimazariken
For you, my lovely one, who detests, yes, simply detests me so,
why am I nonetheless prepared to throw away my life?

H-2. They go directly to the Shirakawa estate, where he lies down. She talks of one thing and another, trying to evade his advances. He finds the sight alluring. The Prince:

tsurakarishi kokoro o mizu wa tanomuru o / itsuwari to shimo omowazaramashi
Had I never experienced the agony of your cruelty,
never should I think false these words that I would wish to trust.

H-3. In reply, the woman:

kotosara ni tsurakaran to wa omowanedo / ika ni ika naru kokoro ni wa mishi
Though never at all has it been my intent to treat you cruelly,
how can you even imagine me to have had such thoughts?

Leaves in the Wind (Fūyōshū)[223]

F-1. Composed when he went to view the cherry blossoms at the Shirakawa estate, where Prince Minister of War Niou was then present. Commandant of the Right Bodyguards Kaoru:

> *chirichirazu mite koso yukame yamazakura / furusatobito wa ware o matsutomo*
>
> Only after I see whether your blossoms scatter or not shall I leave,
> mountain cherry, though someone in the city awaits me.[224] [108]

F-2. The woman talked on, evading his advances, treating him coldly; once again she was trying to concoct an excuse, and so. . . . Prince Minister of War Niou:

> *tsurakarishi kokoro o mizu wa tanomuru o / itsuwari to shimo omowazaramashi*
>
> Had I never experienced the agony of your cruelty,
> never should I think false these words that I would wish to trust. [849]

F-3. Sent, after he had returned from the mountain villa,[225] to the woman who remained there. Commandant Kaoru:

> *akatsuki wa sode nomi nureshi yamazato ni / nezame ikani to omoiyaru kana*
>
> In the mountain villa where at dawn my sleeves were soaked, how fares she,
> I wonder; does she awaken sleepless in the night? [1393]

F-4. In reply, Sanmi of the house of the Princess First Rank:[226]

> *matsukaze o otonau mono to tanomitsutsu / nezame serarenu akatsuki zo naki*
>
> Ever hoping that he will come to call upon the wind in the pines,
> never comes there a dawn when I've not lain awake, sleepless. [1394]

G-1. SHŌKA (1257–1259) GENEALOGY[227]

a. Prince Minister of War Hotaru [Hotaru Hyōbukyō Shinnō]: Formerly known as the Viceroy Prince [Sochi no Miya]. Appointed Minister of

War on the occasion of the Emperor's progress to the Suzaku Palace in "Otome" [14:66].[228] His death is mentioned in "Kōbai" [16:33]. He was deeply in love with Tamakazura.

b. Chamberlain [Jijū]: In "Umegae" [14:413], he is the person dispatched from the Rokujō mansion by his father the Prince to fetch the calligraphic specimens.
c. Daughter of the Prince [Miya no on-kata]: Her mother is the Makibashira lady; daughter of Higekuro. After her father the Prince [Hotaru] dies, her mother takes her to live at the home of the Inspector Grand Counselor [Azechi Dainagon], Lord Kōbai [16:33]. Prince Minister of War Niou shows particular interest in her.

These next four persons do not appear in the standard text.

d. Gen Sanmi: An accomplished player of the lute, which he learned from his father the Prince. After his first wife dies, he lives an austere life. His present wife is a sister of his first wife. She was formerly the wife of the late Vice Minister Middle Counselor [Suke Chūnagon].
e. The First Secretary Colonel [Tō no Chūjō]: His mother is the daughter of the Fujiwara Middle Counselor [Tō Chūnagon], formerly Captain of the Palace Guards [Hyōe no Suke]. He was an intermediary in the affair between his elder sister Sumori no Sanmi and Prince Niou. He lives a most pitiable life. His present wife is a sister of his first wife. She was formerly the wife of the late Vice Minister Middle Counselor [Suke Dainagon] [*sic*].
f. Sumori no Sanmi: Same mother, enters the service of the Princess First Rank [Ippon no Miya], awarded the third rank for her accomplishment on the lute. The Prince Minister of War has an affair with her, but she is offended by his frivolity. The attentions of Commandant Kaoru being more sincere, her affections shift and she bears him a son. Afterward, however, the Prince's persistent advances make her the object of suspicion, and she goes into seclusion in Ōuchiyama, where the fourth daughter of the Suzaku Emperor dwells. She was a woman of beauty and a superb player of the lute.
g. Second daughter [Nakanokimi]: Gentlewoman to the Princess First Rank.

G-2. GENEALOGY ATTRIBUTED TO SHIMIZUDANI SANEAKI[229]

a. Prince Minister of War Hotaru: Formerly known as the Viceroy Prince, appointed Prince Minister of War on the occasion of the Emperor's progress to the Suzaku Palace in "Otome." His death is mentioned in "Takekawa" [16:105]. He was deeply in love with Tamakazura.
b. Chamberlain: In "Umegae," he is dispatched from the Rokujō mansion by his father the Prince to fetch the calligraphic specimens.
c. Sumori no Sanmi: A lute player. She appears in "Tenarai."[230]
d. Daughter of the Prince: Her mother is the Makibashira lady, daughter of Higekuro. After her father the Prince dies, her mother takes her to live at the home of the Inspector Grand Counselor, Lord Kōbai. Prince Niou shows particular interest in her.

G-3. EVERYONE, GREAT AND SMALL, IN *GENJI MONOGATARI*[231]

a. Prince Minister of War Hotaru: Formerly known as the Viceroy Prince. Appointed Prince Minister of War on the occasion of the Emperor's progress to the Suzaku Palace in "Otome." His death is mentioned in "Kōbai." He was deeply in love with Tamakazura.
b. Of the sons and daughters of the Suzaku Emperor, the Fourth Princess: When the Retired Emperor went into seclusion, she entered the service of the Reizei Emperor, but perhaps because he took little interest in her, she rejected the mundane world and went to live at Ōuchiyama.
c. Commandant Kaoru—his son: His mother is Sumori no Sanmi.
d. Gen Sanmi: In "Umegae," where he is called the Chamberlain, he is dispatched from the Rokujō mansion by his father the Prince to fetch the calligraphic specimens.
e. The young lady [Himegimi]: Her mother is the Makibashira lady, the daughter of Higekuro. After her father the Prince [Hotaru] dies, her mother takes her to live at the home of the Inspector Grand Counselor, Lord Kōbai. She is a "reserved" person, "but not at all timid in nature or manner."[232] Prince Niou shows particular interest in her.
f. The Colonel [Chūjō]: His mother is the first wife [of Gen Sanmi], the daughter of the Fujiwara Grand Counselor [Tō Dainagon]. He

was formerly known as the Captain of the Palace Guards [Hyōe no Suke].

g. Sumori no Sanmi: Same mother. After Prince Niou's clandestine visits, she enters the service of the Princess First Rank, [daughter of] the Akashi Empress. Because she plays the lute so marvelously well, she serves as a teacher to the Princess and rises to third rank. She is the object of Commandant Kaoru's affections.
h. Senji: Same mother. Formerly Chūnagon no Kimi. She, too, is a gentlewoman to the Princess first rank. She has an affair with Prince Niou, but when his affections shift to her elder sister, the Second Prince takes up with her.

G-4. ŌSHIMA GENEALOGY[233]

Fujiwara Major Counselor
Wife of Gen Sanmi: Mother of Sumori no Sanmi.
Princess First Rank: This is Senji.
Wife of the late Viceroy Middle Counselor [Sochi Chūnagon]: Same mother as the wife of Gen Sanmi.

G-5. A LITTLE MIRROR OF *GENJI* GENEALOGY[234]

Kiri[tsubo][235]

a. Prince Hotaru [Hotaru no Hyōbukyō]: The Fourth Prince, by Lady Shōkyōden. Called Prince Sochi [Sochi no Miya] when he sings "Autumn Winds" in "Momiji no ga."[236] At the time of the Emperor's progress to the Shujaku [*sic*] Palace in "Otome," he is called Minister of War. He is still alive in "Maboroshi" but dies in "Kumogakure." He has only three children.

Hotaru

b. Chamberlain Third Rank [Sanmi no Jijū]: An accomplished player of the lute, which he learned from his father the Prince. In "Umegae," he is dispatched from the Rokujō mansion by his father the Prince to fetch the scrolls.[237]

Hotaru

c. The two younger Princes, who thereafter dance "Myriad Years" at the rehearsals for the celebrations[238] in "Wakana, ge" [15:269].

They are the sons of the fifth daughter of the Nijō Minister [Tō no Chūjō].[239]

Hotaru

d. Apparently only the youngest of the young ladies [Himegimi] is a child of Makibashira. After her father the Prince dies, she goes with her mother to Kōbai's home. She was "reserved," it says, "but not at all timid in nature or manner." Prince Niou is interested in her and makes overtures through Taifu, her younger brother.[240]
e. Hotaru's three grandchildren are the Colonel [Chūjō], the elder sister [Ōigimi], and the younger sister [Nakanokimi], all children of the Chamberlain.

Chamberlain

f. Of these children, the First Secretary Colonel [Tō no Chūjō] was formerly a Captain of the Palace Guards [Hyōe no Suke], but through the good offices of Prince Niou he was made a Colonel of the Bodyguards [Chūjō].

Chamberlain

g. The elder sister enters the service of the Princess First Rank and becomes teacher of the lute to this lady, for which she is raised to third rank. Niou makes love to her, but she seems to have found his frivolity unseemly. Kaoru visits her in secret and her affections shift to him; she bears him a son. Depressed, however, by the gossip that Prince Niou's subsequent annoying attentions arouse, she goes into seclusion in Ōuchiyama, where the fourth daughter of the Suzaku Emperor dwells, and with whom she spends her time at devotions. This, it seems, is Sumori no Sanmi. She was a woman of beauty, it says, and a superb player of the lute.

Chamberlain

h. The younger daughter, the young Princess, was in the service of the Princess First Rank. Niou visited her secretly, but his affections shifted to her elder sister Sanmi. Thereafter, the Second Prince, a son of the reigning Emperor, visited her. She is the last of the progeny of Hotaru.

Su[zaku]

i. The Fourth Princess was a Dame of Honor [Nyōgo] to Renzei [*sic*], but he took little interest in her. Resentful of this treatment but telling no one, she went into retreat at Ōuchiyama and cut her hair. Her mother, too, it says, had been a Dame of Honor before she died.

The last of Genji's line is the reigning Emperor, a son of the Akashi Empress, followed by:

Gen[ji][241]

j. Kaoru's only son, it says, was borne by Sumori no Sanmi. He was the last of the Genji progeny.

TRANSLATED BY T. HARPER

DEW ON THE MOUNTAIN PATH
(Yamaji no tsuyu)

"Yamaji no tsuyu" is a noncanonical final chapter to *The Tale of Genji* in which a few loose ends of the plot, left hanging at the end of "Yume no ukihashi," are tidied up—at least partially. The narrator, however, in an introduction reminiscent of the opening lines of "Takekawa," insists that "Yamaji no tsuyu" is by no means a fictional sequel to *Genji*; that, in fact, it is an eyewitness account of what passed between the "real" Kaoru and Ukifune after he learned that his love was alive and living in Ono. "Yamaji no tsuyu" in no way advances the plot of *The Tale of Genji*. It nonetheless can be read with pleasure as a collection of imaginatively conceived and consummately executed vignettes depicting the reunion of Ukifune with her brother, her mother, Ukon, and Kaoru.[242]

As with most of the *Genji* apocrypha, we have no definite idea who wrote "Yamaji no tsuyu" or when. At first, the failure of the ladies in *A Nameless Notebook* (ca. 1200) to mention the title, as well as the absence of any poems from the work in *Monogatari nihyakuban utaawase* (1206) or *Fūyōwakashū* (1271), led naturally to the assumption that it postdated all those works. And the fact that the first mention of the title appears in a *Genji kokagami* attributed to Kasannoin Nagachika (d. 1429)[243] only strengthened this assumption. In 1802, however, in his bibliographical compendium *Gunsho ichiran*, Ozaki Masayoshi (1755–1827) mentioned a "tradition that this is the work of Sesonji [Fujiwara] no Koreyuki" (d. 1175). Masayoshi offers no source for or substantiation of this "tradition," nor has any been found since his time. But his brief mention of it inspired a twentieth-century scholar, Hon'iden Shigeyoshi (1908–1983), to explore its implications. Hon'iden found no evidence to suggest that Koreyuki himself was the author, but concluded that Koreyuki's daughter, Kenreimon'in Ukyō no Daibu (1157?–1233?), may well have written "Yamaji no tsuyu" around 1188/1189. If he is right, this raises the interesting possibility that "Yamaji no tsuyu," like *A Nameless Notebook*, is another work written by a woman who grew up in the house of a *Genji* scholar. As the descendant of the renowned calligrapher Fujiwara no Yukinari (972–1027), Koreyuki probably would have possessed a copy of the *Genji* text that was considered to represent most authentically that of Murasaki Shikibu, and his collected marginalia constitute the first "commentary" on *Genji*.[244] His daughter would have been well equipped to undertake a project of this sort. Hon'iden's thesis is based on numerous lexical and stylistic similarities between "Yamaji no tsuyu" and *Kenreimon'in Ukyō no Daibu shū* that he sets forth in detail in the introduction to his edition of the apocryphal chapter.[245] He notes, too, that Ukyō no Daibu would have experienced both life in Ono and a fire in the city like that described in "Yamaji no tsuyu."[246] None of this amounts to proof positive, of course, but as a circumstantial case, the evidence is quite persuasive.

Two lines of texts of "Yamaji no tsuyu" survive: the "printed text line" (*kanpon-kei*), so called because it was printed as a supplementary volume to *E'iri Genji monogatari* in 1654, and the "manuscript line" (*shahon-kei*).[247] The printed line is the fuller of the two and is generally considered to represent the original form of the work more accurately, whereas the manuscript line appears to be marred by the loss of a fold of two pages from a no longer extant text that later copyists have attempted, ineptly, to repair. Inaga Keiji, however, proposed a more complex and potentially interesting explanation of the discrepancies between the printed line and the manuscript line. He noted first that the earliest extant copy of "Yamaji no tsuyu" has an entirely different title, "Sumori."[248] As we have seen, this is also the title of a once canonical but no longer extant chapter (or set of chapters) that, Inaga suggests, may have been dismantled, rearranged, and expanded to form the basis of the present ten Uji chapters of *Genji*. The love triangle involving Niou, Kaoru, and a young lady (Sumori) descended from a prince resembles the story of Ukifune far too closely to be coincidental. In addition, the lady being pursued by these two men extricates herself from this impossible situation in precisely the same manner as Ukifune does. She retreats to the mountains and takes the tonsure. At this point in the narrative, *The Tale of Genji* ends. In the lost chapter, "Sumori," however, the story continues. The heroine in the mountains, now a nun, is visited by Kaoru, which is exactly what happens in "Yamaji no tsuyu." The fragments from which we know about this visit are too slight to prove a relationship between "Sumori" and "Yamaji no tsuyu." But the fact that the oldest copy of "Yamaji no tsuyu" is entitled "Sumori" strongly suggests that this may be an expanded version of the story of Kaoru's visit to Sumori, a reworking of materials left over from the Uji chapters that still bear the title of their source. Unfortunately, Inaga died before he was able to explore this hypothesis further. For the time being, then, the genesis of "Yamaji no tsuyu" must remain an open question, but one in which, one hopes, future scholars will take an interest.

T. HARPER

This that follows concerns the progeny of the Shining Genji, the Commandant Kaoru by name, which makes me painfully reluctant to reveal it lest this seem merely a sequel to that tale. In fact it is nothing of the sort. This is the testament of one who saw with her own eyes all that passed when the Commandant discovered his lady living in Ono, one so moved by their dreamlike moments together that she could not rest until she had somehow set it all down in writing. I doubt she had any intention of showing it to anyone else. But then, while briefly away from home, the lady herself passed away. In sorting through all the writings she had accumulated, trifles though they were, so as to have them remade into sutra scrolls for the benefit of the poor woman in lives to come, this was found. It is nothing of any great merit, yet it does reveal what ultimately became of the girl we have so long wondered about. For this, perhaps, it may have seemed sufficiently interesting to preserve.

He had not known a moment's peace since he had heard those whispered rumors of the whereabouts of his vanished drake fly.[249] Thereafter, he had several times sent her brother in search of her, but the boy had always returned no wiser than before.[250] In this pitiable state, more tormented than ever, he would rehearse yet again in his memory all that had passed, both before and after she had gone.

The depth of his affection for the departed elder sister [Ōigimi] had been anything but ordinary, so much so that at times the burden had become difficult to bear. Still, he had waited patiently in the hope that she might one day relent. The anguish he felt when those hopes were dashed would be difficult to forget even in lives yet to come. His only consolation was in those moments when he would yearn for a glimpse of her, even if only in the smoke of that incense so famous in foreign fable.[251] And then *her* face and form, so lovely and so like that of her dead sister, would sometimes make him wonder whether it was she whom he had loved. What had possessed him? he would wonder, as fondly he recalled those moments. Why, even now, was his longing still so painfully acute? Despite his best efforts, he knew he was powerless to help himself.

He had tried one way and another to quell these misgivings, but what was he to do? In the year or more that he had believed her dead, he had at least managed to carry on in the belief that nothing further could be done. Now, hearing this news, he found it excruciating to be unable to ascertain whether it was all a dream or, in fact, real. He resolved to go to her himself, in secret.

The taboo at the palace was to lift today. Dressed to perfection for his appearance, he proceeded to the quarters of [his wife] the Princess. She was wearing a russet gown lined in willow green and, over it, a robe of aster mauve, a combination she wore with great grace. There could hardly be a more elegant figure than she who reclined at his side, her hair flowing over her robes, not a strand out of place and impeccably trimmed at the tips. Yet her beauty only made more intense his memories of how easy and amiable had been the lady who had disappeared.

Her hair, too, had been at the very height of its beauty; and now it was cut short! She had weighed on his mind of late to the exclusion of all else. What, he could not help but wonder in bewilderment, had become of his resentment of that distasteful affair of hers? His feelings for her had never been shallow. But the shock of that incident, coming so unexpectedly, had made him doubt he could ever again trust her. Yet when she disappeared without a trace, the state of agitation in which he found himself was not one he could readily quell. There were, of course, encounters of various sorts with other women. But—was he still in the grip of that perverse attachment that had plagued him from of old?—these three sisters were the only ones for whom he felt any special attraction.

With the Prince's wife [Nakanokimi] he had remained on particularly close terms, while she for her part looked to him as a trusted friend. But over the years, both of them had risen to great eminence, and their prominence in the public eye now permitted them even fewer of those long evenings of reminiscence than in the past—which left him only the more inconsolable and unable to forget her of yore.

Yet why should he not have this one whose face so naturally reflected hers? Incorrigible, he had from time to time hinted casually at his feelings for this exquisite creature, only to be left feeling like the poet at Abandoned Crone Mountain.[252] There could hardly be another substitute, he realized, who resembled her as perfectly as this woman did. And the thought of that only exacerbated his bitter regret for his mistake of the past.[253]

At Ono, she had given herself over with unflagging zeal to her devotions, surpassing even those nuns who were several years her senior and developing a profound sense of dedication to her calling.[254] To the old nun, so moved by all she was seeing, it seemed that this indeed must be the life for which she was destined. She said as much to the Prelate when he came down from the mountain. He nodded and, after a moment, said, "This is indeed a rare accomplishment. In the case of the Commandant, even the most inept monks were inspired by the hope that they might emulate what they had seen in him. But a woman, pursued by a man of such intense devotion; well, I regret to say, I could not help but feel that, no matter how sincere the motives with which she sought us out, she was bound to regret the step she had taken. What a wondrous thing that her mind remains so untroubled. How touching this must be even to the Buddhas of the Three Worlds." She looked so young and so pretty as she turned away in embarrassment at his grandiloquence. Could she truly have been meant for this life of mortification? the old nun wondered to herself, trying to hide the tears that welled up as spontaneously as if she had been the girl's real mother.

No longer was she so downcast as she had been at the outset. The floating bridge of dreams, now behind her, had in the end withstood the winds. She had found the pearl in the hem of her own robe;[255] she had found tranquillity; and now, she realized, it had been her "guide to this village."[256]

As autumn deepened, the moan of the wind and the pale glow of the moon grew ever more affecting. Sleep anywhere would have been but fitful on these long lonely nights; but here, where gusts from the mountain beat against the brushwood gate and the deer cry longingly through the night for their mates, she was denied even the brief respite of dreams. Inevitably memories rushed back, but saddest of all were those of her mother. She had always striven to do at least as much for her as for an ordinary child, in return for which she had caused her endless disappointment and worry. How must she have felt when, just as all seemed about to go as she had hoped it might,[257] I disappeared without a trace? That she might learn, through some rumor carried on the wind, that *this* was what had become of her was too painful even to contemplate. And that he who had loved her[258] would now know everything—how wretched if that should be the cruel fate she would have to endure. Still, should she be permitted something to show for having lived as long as she had, she would wish that she might just once more see her mother. But she could never bring herself to come out and meet the messenger [her brother Kogimi] who had made his way over the mountain path. Nor could she even come up with words to compose a message for him to take back. Such was the state of despondency in which she passed the days. Yet it seemed that the boy *must* have known from the start. Why had *he* not told their mother? It was all too mysterious and unsettling.

The Commandant had not been well of late, and in the throes of the commotion caused by the frantic concern of his mother the [Third] Princess, his thoughts had for long been distracted from matters in that other quarter. The myriad elaborate incantations seemed to have taken effect, though, and his illness subsided apace. Still, he continued to take advantage of his lingering indisposition as a pretext for not venturing forth.

One pleasantly uneventful day, as he lay lost in thought in his private quarters, her little brother came to call. He summoned the boy to his side. "While I've been ill, there have been so many people about that it's been all but impossible to do anything, but it is terribly frustrating not to know where she might be. You must go out there straightaway. And this time, may I say, it would be most unspeakable if you were to return as ignorant as ever." Taking the letter that was proffered to him, the boy set out while the sun was still high in the sky. Yet though he rode as fast as his horse could be driven, it was already growing dark when he entered the shadow of the mountain.

Out there, with naught else to distract her, she was, as usual, sunk in reverie, when one of their people came into the room and whispered something to the nun, who was quite taken aback by such an unexpected turn of events at this hour. "Please," she said in a voice full of pity, "Please speak to him yourself. He's no one you have to behave formally with, and think how unpleasant it must be for him, left out there, at such a distance." At this, the others chimed in: "Poor thing, he'll never get to see enough of her, the wretched way she treats him,"[259] all of which made her feel perfectly miserable. And, indeed, when the nun sent someone to tell him, "This way, please," as she always did, he came forward and knelt at the edge of the veranda.

The nun moved out closer to him. "I'm sure it must be embarrassing to both of you to have to listen to a meddlesome old woman carry on about how you've come over the mountain path so many times with nothing to show for it. But for whatever reasons, it would distress her for anyone to discover her here, and it distresses me to see her in such a state." With almost pitiable charm he replied, "I've been told this time not to return without an unequivocal reply."

When the nun, speaking now in tones of great seriousness, relayed his appeal, the girl put her things in order.[260] Deeply reticent though she was, she nonetheless knew that with inquiries thus far advanced, her mother might soon learn everything, and it pained her to think how she might feel to find she had been kept in the dark by her own daughter. Often she had wished she could somehow get word to her before it came to this. Now she was quite beside herself.

"Do come in," the nun Shōshō was saying as she ushered the boy into the room. The other nuns slipped out of sight. The boy was overjoyed as he handed her the letter he had brought and gazed at her. Such an exquisitely slight creature she was and not in the least changed from the image of her he carried in his memory. And then he noticed her hair, which was *not* as it had been. Suddenly it all seemed a bitter dream, and he broke down in tears. The young lady, too, could not but recall all those events of the past that she had long forgotten. Above all, she longed to ask what had become of their mother, but she simply hadn't the words to express the wish.

Finally, after a time, she collected herself. "When I disappeared, everyone must have thought I was indeed dead, but this seems to be the cruel fate for which I was destined, for somehow, to my amazement, I survived. For days it felt as if I were in another world. But then, as one does, I gradually grew calmer, and as I did, I began to worry myself sick about Mother . . ." With which she broke off.

"After you disappeared, she was almost insane with grief. It looked very bad. But the Commandant did everything he could to console her. She is always saying what a comfort it is that he should deign to look after the likes of her as kindly as he does and that this is what saved her life. But of course she is still in a daze. She just doesn't seem her old self anymore. When I heard about you, I wanted to tell her immediately. But the Commandant warned me time and again that I mustn't tell anyone just yet. So I wasn't able to tell her." It was a sorrowful speech and spoken in so childlike a manner.

"Oh, how dreadful," she said. "I didn't want *him* to know, under any circumstances. How ever did he find out? This is just miserable. Tell him it turned out it wasn't me after all; make up something like that." That, he knew, was virtually impossible.

"But even in this wretched state," she went on, "I do want to see Mother again. Here, give this to her in secret." She took out a letter from beside her screen and handed it to him.

"But what will His Lordship say," he said as he inserted it in the fold of his robes, "if there is no reply to his letter? Do please let me have something to take back to him, even just a line or two."

"Oh, that's outrageous," she replied, a bit resentfully. "You've really changed this last year or so. Can't you bring yourself at least to conceal my shame from him and tell him there's been a mistake?" The boy lowered his eyes, utterly unable to speak.

She had never had much to say or been very forthcoming; that was just her nature. It was touching therefore that, to him at least, she was willing to reveal a bit of what she really felt, the result, no doubt, of their having been inseparable from the time they were children.

"How can you possibly return this evening?" said the same somewhat oversolicitous, and now commiserating, woman who had shown him in.

"Yes," the nun said, "how indeed? These mountain roads are steep and dangerous. Even someone who knows them well could easily go astray. Please, do stay over, at least this evening."

"How can I stay when His Lordship has told me to return as quickly as I can?" the boy said. "In the moonlight, the way will not be hard to find."[261] The other nuns were murmuring approvingly among themselves about how very grown up he was. And, indeed, he did inspire considerable confidence, having come with an escort of fully armed archers, in anticipation of a long night's journey.

The night was far advanced when he arrived, and all the gates had been locked. Well then, he would go home for the night, he thought; but that, he realized, could prove troublesome, for his mother was sure to ask where he had been. No, he had the good sense to realize, he should first report what he had heard from the girl and only then speak to his mother. Yet to knock at the gate would attract far too much attention. For a time he simply stood there, at a loss what to do, whereupon there arose a tumult of voices, apparently people in a great panic. Hardly had he time to wonder what might be the matter when flames burst forth and smoke billowed into the air. He was shocked to realize that the fire was very close by, in the immediate vicinity, and he set his men to beating on the gate.

The night duty gatekeepers, too, had just then discovered the blaze and were bustling around as quickly as they could, opening the gates.

"Why was this locked?" the boy demanded.

"His Lordship had forgotten that this was a day of abstinence," the man replied. "We had to lock up immediately." But now their precautions had come to naught. All the men in the guardhouse were up now. "Well, didn't *you* get yourself here in a hurry!" one of them said, which greatly amused the boy.

Word had spread of a fire near the mansion, and the night now reverberated with the din and bustle of the horses and carriages of those come to inquire after the safety of its occupants. The blaze had spread dangerously, but then suddenly the wind shifted to another quarter and the mansion was saved. Everyone marveled at what a miraculous escape it had been, and then, en masse, they departed.

The fire had been dreadful, but before very long, it had burned itself out. Calm returned, the crowds dispersed, and soon all was as still as if nothing had ever happened. Traces of dawn appeared in the sky, and His Lordship, drawn by its beauty, stepped out into the gallery. It was then that he sent for the boy.

"I waited up until late last night," he said. "When did you arrive?"

"It was during all that confusion that I came."

"How did it go? I can't bear to think that you might carry the same dismal answer."

In the boy's memory, there arose the image of his sister, so genuinely forlorn as she asked him to say that she was not to be found. Touched and disturbed, for a moment he hung back. But ultimately, he knew, the secret would come out. To lie would be wrong. He told every detail of what had happened.

His Lordship had lately heard reliable reports to the same effect, but somehow he could not bring himself to believe they were true. To learn that this was indeed how she felt both astonished and crushed him.

"She has become a nun," the boy said. "I hardly recognized her, she looks so different."

"Did she seem—distant?"

"She was—just the same." The boy was weeping, his face in his hands in an attempt to hide his tears. His Lordship was overcome with emotion at the sight.

"And the letter she told you to deliver?" The boy produced a small, tightly rolled bit of blue-gray paper, a strangely affecting sight in itself,[262] which made His Lordship only the more curious about its contents.

"I'm a terribly ill-mannered fellow, aren't I?" he said with a smile as he made to open the letter. "How is it that even I have come to stoop this low?"[263] It was clearly the same hand, but noticeably unsteady, the flow often broken.

itoitsutsu suteshi inochi no kieyarade / futatabi onaji ukiyo ni zo furu
This life I wearied of and tried to cast away refuses to perish;
again I go on living in this same dismal world.

mayowaseshi kokoro no yami o omou ni mo / makoto no michi wa ima zo ureshiki
Yet when I recall the darkness of the heart[264] in which I once wandered,
what a delight it is now as I travel the True Way.

It distressed him deeply to read this. Even as he struggled to control his feelings, tears welled up to wet his sleeves. In the pale glow of the dawning sky, he was unutterably handsome. The sight of him overcome with emotion was most fetching, and the boy gazed in wonder at the splendor of it. What a pity, he thought, and what a waste that she has done this pointless thing when His Lordship so obviously yearns for her.

"For the moment, I think, this can wait. I have something in mind. You can deliver it tomorrow or the next day," he said, still grasping the letter. "This may seem rash, but I will go to her tonight in secret. Have everything in readiness and report to me this evening." The boy winced as he thought of how his sister would feel, but of this he could say nothing. He bowed in assent and took his leave.

He would depart at dusk, in a woman's carriage of the most inconspicuous sort. Where the road entered the mountains, he switched to horseback. Shrouded in the evening mists, the way was very hard to find, but guided as much as anything by deep determination, he pressed on. He felt, strangely enough, that at this point there was little sense in what he was doing; yet driven by the desire at least to reminisce with her about those dreamlike times long past, he hurried on to his destination.

In a sky swept free of drifting cloud by the rushing wind, the moon rose bright and clear, lighting the way for his thoughts, he mused, as they raced on a thousand leagues ahead of him.[265] He was determined that he would leave no cause for regret. The farther into the mountains he went, the more dew drenched was the way, but it made a scene of great beauty as his outriders brushed away the dew, their garb, humble though it was, in perfect harmony with the setting.[266]

There at the foot of the mountain stood the tiny dwelling. First he sent the boy ahead to check on the state of things.

"The gate, such as it is, seems to be locked, but where the bamboo fence runs, there seems to be a path they use to go in and out. You can enter there; there's no sign of anyone nearby."

"Wait here a moment, and don't make a sound," His Lordship told them; then he went on alone.

The flimsily constructed brushwood fence, though much the same as any other, held for him a particular charm and attraction. The door to the veranda was open, from which he surmised that some of them might still be up and about. Keeping close to the rank growth in the garden, he drew near and hid himself in a thick clump of evergreens that stood almost under the eaves. His vantage seemed to be somewhere near the altar, for the scent of fine incense permeated the air and wafted out into the garden; and just inside the room, there seemed to be someone at her devotions. The soft rustle of a scroll being rewound, heard so close at hand, touched him with such poignancy that suddenly, without warning, he felt on the verge of tears. He watched, transfixed. Presently, she seemed to have completed her devotions, for he heard her say, as if to herself, "How bright the moonlight!" She lifted a corner of the blind and gazed enrapt at the face of the moon. The sight of her profile brought a fresh flood of memories of the girl as she had been in times past that overwhelmed him with emotion. In the moonlight that flooded in on her, she appeared, from what could be seen of her sleeves, to be wearing blue-gray over russet,[267] a captivating combination. And the gentle sway of her trimmed forelocks and her eyes;[268] they were exquisitely beautiful. Yes, he thought, she was in some ways even more delicately beautiful than before. To watch her was almost more than he could bear. She stayed a moment longer, gazing at the moon, and then went within. In a soft voice, suffused with tears, she spoke as if to herself:

sato wakanu kumoi no tsuki no kage nomi ya / mishi yo no aki ni kawarazaruran
The moon in the heavens that shines alike on each and every village:
can its light be the only thing unchanged from autumns past?

It was a scene so touching that even the most sober of men would have found it impossible to quell his emotions, and he replied:

furusato no tsuki wa namida ni kakikurete / sono yo nagara no kage wa mizariki
To the moon that shone on that village of old I was blinded by tears;
of the light it cast on the rest of the world I saw naught.

As he spoke, he moved swiftly to her side, which gave her such a fright that she thought he must be a ghost or a goblin. She recoiled in horror and attempted to flee into the house, but he caught her by the sleeve. At the sight of this tearful figure,[269] she realized that, yes, it was he, and her fear gave way to shame and chagrin. If indeed it had been some specter, it would at least have been beyond her power to save herself. But that *he* should discover she still lived! It was just too dismal. She had tried her best to think of a way to mislead him. Now she had been discovered, and there was no escaping him. Utterly helpless and touchingly forlorn, her tears began to flow.

How could he ever tell her of all his misery and anguish? Where should he begin? "I was in such a state when I heard, as I understood it, the news of your death that I was simply dumbstruck. Then later, to hear of the ghastly way it had happened—that was even more upsetting. Yet another instance of the uncertainty of this world, I took it to be. When I had only her [Ōigimi's] death to lament, I could still find some solace thinking of her as I gazed 'at the morning rains, the evening clouds.'[270] But with this new thing [Ukifune's death] to weigh upon my thoughts as well, I felt I could hardly go on living. Then someone told me everything that had actually happened. It seemed to be a dream. How could this be so? Now I was so perplexed that it seemed I was myself wandering in a daze, from dream to dream. But how was I to divine whether any of these dreams were true? Can't you comprehend at least a bit of the grief I endured? In any case, the gods and buddhas seem to have taken pity on me for making my way through the dew on that mountain path over which my yearning drew me—for never did I imagine I would again be talking to you as I am now. For once I am delighted to have gone on living this worthless life." He went on at some length, for he could never hope to convey all that he felt. She was, of course, deeply touched by much of what he told her, but to speak was more than she could do. She only wept, with great dignity and delicacy.

"Yes," he went on, "I must admit it hurts me terribly to be abandoned like this. I have for long known how fickle life can be. But given the depth of my own love for you, I was convinced there could be no one else so enamored of you, that I must be the only one, which no doubt only aggravates this foolish resentment that I feel." His veiled allusion to that painful incident[271] filled her with shame, and she felt more than ever at a loss for words. Yet to let it pass as if she hadn't even noticed would surely seem strange.

nagaraete aru ni mo aranu utsutsu oba / tada sono mama no yume ni nashite yo
This life that I still lead, living yet not living, real and yet unreal;
pray think of it as no more than in itself a mere dream.

Her subtle attempt to put him off made him think affectionately of how little she had changed. Perhaps it was the result of what she had learned from all she had been through, but he felt that she had grown more gracious and considerate than she had been in the past, more charming and mature. How very like the lady he had lost, he thought. But how perfectly extraordinary, that notion of hers! However excruciating the turmoil of these past months may have been, now that he was with her again, there was no way in the world he could force himself to consign her to the realm of dreams.

omoiidete omou dani koso kanashikere / mata ya ukarishi yume ni nasu beki
When I recall those times, if even the mere thought itself is painful,
how, then, can I now dismiss it as but a dismal dream?

His love for her was truly profound. Indeed, no one of even the slightest sensitivity could have remained unmoved by the sight of him trying to wipe away his tears as inconspicuously as he could.

His feelings for her were unchanged from of old, and the appeal of this she found so moving and so difficult to resist that, were she anyone but herself, she knew, she would not hesitate to heed the Prelate's advice.[272] Still, he made no attempt to go within. He sat there decorously and continued to converse tenderly of all that still filled his mind.

"For you to go on in your present state is a sin. Why couldn't you have remained as you were until we were able to meet just once more?" But of course, his attempt to change her mind only caused her pain.

From the peak that rose almost immediately before them came the eerie moan of the wind in the pines mingled with the cry of the hart. The dew-drenched clumps of grass in the garden at which they gazed glistened as if sprinkled with jewels while the moon that shone in the clear sky seemed to wear a look of sorrow at the advent of autumn, all of which, added to the waning cry of the insects, created a scene of almost overwhelming beauty.

Any meeting of lovers who meet but rarely is bound to be fraught with emotion, but what of one who has lost all hope of ever gaining a clear glimpse of his love in this life, even in a dream—and then finds himself face to face with her? How can his feelings be anything but overpowering? He was certain that no one could ever again feel as he did. From his sleeves as he wiped away the ceaseless flow of tears, rose a scent of unearthly fragrance. No words could describe the pristine beauty of the scene as the moonlight flooded in upon them.

Despite all she had been through, the woman understood well how he felt, and her replies were, for the most part, earnest and affectionate. Yet never once did he transgress the bounds of propriety, which struck her as rare indeed, and made her, if anything, even more susceptible.

Meanwhile the same old busybodies were peering pruriently at them from a crack in the shutters of the wing opposite.

"Whatever will he think of the way she looks?"

"After all that other dismal business, it *is* a pity she's got herself up in such a shabby way." He appeared to be sitting just inside the gallery door, for they could catch only a glimpse of the hem of his trousers protruding from beneath the blind. This threw them into a none-too-attractive flutter of delight.

"What a splendid figure, not like other young men nowadays. And how considerate of her he is."

"And that scent on the wind is uncanny, as if from another world."

"Yes, it must be the very scent of sandalwood that the Buddha tells us of in his sermon." Throughout the night, oblivious to the time, they lingered out of sight behind their shutters, whispering to one another.

"They're still right where they were."

"Oh, he does seem to love her so!" Their impertinences, it must be said, were quite disgraceful.

Sensing the approach of dawn, he prepared to leave.

"I try to tell myself that this dreadful depression and melancholy of yours is the recompense for my own wretched fate, but that makes it no less painful to endure. For long, I, too, have inclined in a religious way; thus your present state impresses me only the more. I do hope that in this new and very different intimacy between us, we shall not grow apart. But I must see to it that you are moved to some place less remote than this. When the [Eighth] Prince was still alive, I was quite attached to the old villa in the mountains; but after that dismal incident, the very name of the place became so repellent to me that I've let it fall to ruin as never before.[273] Never, though, has the dawn left me so worn with care as today. These sleeves soaked with dew in the depths of night—I wonder if you realize what makes them so?

omoiyare yamaji no tsuyu ni sobochikite / mata wakekaeru akatsuki no sode
Pray pity them, these sleeves soaked with dew on the mountain path,
and again
to be soaked as at dawn we part and I wend my way home."[274]

How could this expression of distress, or the depth of his emotion, ever have been feigned?

tsuyu fukaki yamaji o wakenu hito dani mo / aki wa narai no sode zo shioruru
Even so is it for one who plies not the dew-drenched mountain path;
tear-soaked sleeves are but the commonplace stuff of every autumn.

"Quite so," he said, "but you belittle my feelings. I mean to write to you in all sincerity, so this time you must answer and not leave me in suspense. That would be too distressing."

With this oft-repeated injunction, he hastily took his leave, lest he linger until too unseemly an hour. His hunting costume, though far beneath his station, he wore with such simple charm that surely she must have been touched as she watched him set off through the dew-drenched tufts of grass.

No sooner had morning come than the nuns who had been so curious about that intimate scene in the presence of the Buddha hurried around to the place where he had sat. The fragrance that lingered there set them raving with delight.

"It's a rare scent that permeates her purple trousers now that he's brushed them with his sleeve."[275] Their prattle, all of it terribly pretentious, was painfully irritating. But then, even people of the capital never ceased to marvel at how uncommon a scent it was. Small wonder that such minds—for whom so unremarkable a man as Chūjō, the nun's son-in-law, seemed the shining light of their village—should now be so astonished.

The young lady, vaguely embarrassed by all that had happened, did her best to seem absorbed in a sutra, no sooner than which, a letter arrived. As usual, she refused to look at it.

"Now that is a bit childish," said the nun, and she opened the letter and showed it to the girl. It was written on stiff, pale-blue Chinese paper.

tachikaeri nao koso madoe nagaki yo no / yume o utsutsu ni
samashikanetsutsu

"I return, yet wander still in the confusion of that long night's dream,
for never can I wake from it into reality.

I am more bewildered than ever this morning, yet despair of telling you all that I feel. At this point I would have expected a particular sensitivity of you. Yet you remain as cold as ever before, which seems to me anything but pure of heart."

She was extremely chary of replying precipitately and dismissed the matter from her thoughts, but the nun chided her sharply.

"It would be most inconsiderate when he has written to you in so seemingly sincere a manner. Indeed, it could seem to him that you are putting on airs." Hearing this, she broke down in tears. In the margin of his letter she scrawled:

sono mama ni mada waga tama no mi ni sowade / yume ka utsutsu ka wakare dani sezu

Quite the same as ever, my spirit resides no longer within me;
be this a dream or be it real, even this I know not.

It was in state of great emotion that he awaited her reply. Should she hastily choose a paper the color of which alluded pointedly to her changed condition, what then? Surely that would belie the truth of the matter. Then again, a delicate paper of a more alluring shade would, at this point, hardly make an appropriate impression. But the casual manner in which she dashed off her reply in fact reminded him that in the past, too, he had noticed with approval her attention to just such small details as these.

That past, he could now see to the delivery of her letter, which he still held.[276] "But how painful," he said, "to think of that old woman going into raptures of delight, with all her people there to hear everything."

Yet there *was* the woman known as Ukon. Although Jijū had gone almost immediately into the service of the Akashi Empress, Ukon, he had heard, remained stricken with grief and was living in seclusion in a poor quarter of the city. He had been touched by this, for he knew her to be a mature and dependable woman. He sent word that she should come quietly to him and, with his message, sent robes of fine fabric. Utterly delighted, she came immediately. In manner and appearance she had always stood out from her peers; yes, a comely woman, His Lordship thought.

The Ukon who had waited on Yūgao lacked even the presence of mind to respond to [Genji's] "smoke as clouds" poem.[277] This Ukon, however, not only was young and attractive, but also seemed never at a loss in matters of this sort. He gave not the least hint of the dreamlike news that he was to impart to her. But then, when no one was around, he seized the moment to summon her to him. What could compare with the feelings of his listener when he related his tale? Small wonder that she was utterly astonished.

"I, too," he said, "could hardly imagine what might have happened. At first I laid the blame entirely on the roar of the river; but then, the person who, by a strange stroke of luck, had discovered her told me that it must have been the work of a malign tree spirit and that she had suffered unremittingly long afterward.[278] That old estate, I thought, *would* be just such a place. But it appears from her letter to her mother that she herself had grown weary of life, yet, against her will, found herself wandering about, still alive. What actually happened, I've no idea. But surely one who saw what went on at the time would know better what to make of it."

"At first," she replied, "as I've told you, she was so distraught that she did nothing but weep night and day. From time to time she would get up and go to her devotions, so as to lighten the burden of sin she would carry to the next life. Then she would break down sobbing, 'How I wish I could die.' After she disappeared—without a trace, as I thought, and indeed until this very moment—I never doubted that she lay at the bottom of the river. Certainly the poem that she wrote on that scroll[279] gave the impression that she had finished with life. But yes, what did in fact happen?" she said, weeping bitterly.

"Mount Tsukuba[280] will be in hysterics. What a dreadful uproar there will be before she manages to get control of herself. The boy is by no means imprudent; still, I think it would be best if you were to go with him to keep her quiet, lest she spread the whole story around. It is difficult enough to keep any secret, even if one is careful to tell only one or two others. If this gets out to all and sundry, and the Prince [Niou] hears about it, then anything could happen, which at this point would do no one any good."

Straightaway she ordered her carriage, and in great haste they boarded it and set off. She stopped it a short way past the gate and told the boy, "You'll alight here, and this is what you're to say."

"Now what's all this," his mother said when he had spoken his piece, "announcing yourself as if you were some grand gentleman?[281] Just come on in." They went to the family's private rooms, which to eyes that had last looked on that splendid palace seemed utterly bereft of grace or charm. As it happened, the Governor, too, was at home.[282]

"To what do we owe the honor of so unexpected a visit?" the mother said. "I must say, you grow more handsome every time I see you. And when I think how kind His Lordship the Commandant has been, looking after all of us who were related to her. If she were still among us, I am sure we'd now see her settled in comfort. Oh, but it does break my heart!" She burst into tears, at which the Governor himself rambled on.

"We are most grateful for His Lordship's solicitude. The joy his favor brings us is far beyond anything we in our station have any right to expect, though I have neglected to say as much lest I seem presumptuous. If ever you have the opportunity, pray convey our very best to His Highness.[283] When I see how he goes out of his way to treat us so kindly, merely for the sake of our late young lady, I cannot help but marvel that we are still so privileged as to bask in the glow of his favor. How much more so might it be if she were still among us. It's such a great pity. And His Lordship the Commandant's gentlewoman, if I may say so, is looking very grand indeed. I would hardly have recognized you as the girl we once knew." He rambled on thus for some time and then left the room. From the way the mother and the Governor spoke, they seemed to pride themselves on the girl's connections even after her death.

By now, the others in the room had dispersed, and the conversation became somewhat more intimate. Ukon drew nearer.

"I've come because there is something I must tell you in confidence."

The woman flew into a panic. "Whatever might *that* be?"

"It was precisely to caution you against outbursts of this sort. The details of the matter Kogimi himself will tell you."

"Oh come now," she replied, "nothing my son might have to tell me is likely to be of any consequence."

The sheer absurdity of the woman brought a broad smile to Ukon's face. Without another word, she produced the letter and handed it to the woman. Mystified, she opened it as quickly as she could. But it was not at all the sort of thing the significance of which one might grasp in an instant, and she sat for some time staring at it blankly. But the hand was unchanged, and as she examined it, the truth gradually dawned upon her. Why of course, it was from—her! The shock of her discovery was beyond comparison.

"How can it be?" she said, and then collapsed in a heap on the floor. It was all exactly as she had anticipated, Ukon thought sadly.

"It would be very bad if the others were to hear you carrying on like this. His Lordship insisted that I warn you to be calm and act as if nothing had happened. This is why I have come to you." She tried every way she could think of to cajole her, and after a time the woman did manage to collect herself and sit up again. Still, it was hardly surprising that she should remain in a daze, wondering whether it were all a dream, or what.

The boy, for all his youth, gave his mother an excellent account of all that had happened, from the very beginning. She was stricken with grief, and her tears welled up until there was no containing them.

"So she is still alive! Then I simply must see her, now, without another moment's delay!" Small wonder she should be burning with agony.[284]

"Of course," Ukon replied, "but the girl is nowhere nearby. If suddenly you go rushing off into hiding without a word of where you are going, the Governor is sure to come looking for you. Be patient for just a day or two, and then make as if you are setting off on an ordinary pilgrimage to Hatsuse. The best thing would be for you to go to her sometime the day after tomorrow." Halfheartedly she nodded assent, though she could not begin to imagine how she might endure the anxiety of the next two days. A pitiful sight she was, with tears streaming from her eyes.

Her common old waiting women were aware, though only dimly, of the scene in the next room, but how could they have guessed what was actually afoot? Madam had been unpredictably prone to tears of late. It must have seemed likely to them that all this talk of the Commandant's kind concern had been enough to upset her yet again.

"I'll not fail to accompany you there," Ukon promised her repeatedly. "Indeed, I'd be dreadfully disappointed if you were to leave me behind." When she finally had to depart, the woman was left with the boy as her sole companion in conversation and source of consolation, and she kept him constantly by her side.

"Now tell me, how was she—everything you know. And how does the Commandant feel about all this?"

"His Lordship never indulges in idle talk or jest, yet never have I seen him as concerned as he is now. I could hardly believe my eyes when I saw him weeping so hard he couldn't take his sleeve from his eyes. For all your rolling about on the floor, I'm sure he is far more affected than you."

"Now see here!" She could not but smile at the boy, though it did nothing to diminish her painful sense of the futility of it all. Her daughter had become a nun. And that meddlesome old woman, her nursemaid, never did recover from her grief. In the end, she had become sick and, this past spring, died. If only she could have lived just a little longer, she thought back sadly.

As Ukon had instructed her, she told her people that she would be making a pilgrimage to Hatsuse. That same evening she sent for Ukon, and very early, even before the night had given way to dawn, they hastened on their way.

At Ono, they first sent in the boy [Kogimi] who had guided them to announce their arrival. The girl's mind was in such turmoil that she was helpless to do anything but weep. The nun, ever indomitable, tidied up an appropriate room for them and ushered them in. The young lady would have to appear in her habit, but she at least had her change into robes that were fresh and bright.

"I must say it's a sad sight to see these drab shades on a girl like you," she said, her own tears now beginning to flow.[285] "I shudder to think how someone who has never seen you in them before will feel." Yes, what would her mother think, the girl began to wonder, and she became so downcast she could scarcely move from the room.

"Come now," the nun urged her, "you wouldn't want your mother to think you don't want to see her." From the central sliding panel, before which stood a curtained screen, she emerged, inching forward on her knees.

Her mother, when at last she caught sight of her [daughter], was so overcome that she could hardly think and only sobbed uncontrollably. It had not been so very many months, but already the woman had wasted away to a mere shadow of her former self. Such a pleasant-looking woman she had been (if a bit too plump); now even her face was changed, almost beyond recognition. "And all because of me!" the young lady thought, and suddenly, filled with a sense of her own guilt, she wept bitterly. To Ukon, the sadness of the scene as she had imagined it now seemed as nothing before the sight she actually beheld, and her own eyes darkened with a fresh flood of tears.

It seemed an eternity before either was able to utter a word. At length, through stifled sobs, the mother spoke. "How I have managed to survive until now—on the verge of death as I've been—is a mystery to me. Had I died, I would never have seen you today. Why couldn't you have sent something—even just a hint on the wind—to let us know how you were? It's been so dreadfully painful! If I could have seen you just once as you were then, it would have been some consolation, but now that you've become a nun it upsets me more than ever." On she went until she collapsed on the floor. Well aware how right her mother was, the girl was too abashed and choked with tears even to reply.

Wanting to know everything that had happened from the very start, the mother turned to the nun and said, "I've come here so upset by this nightmarish situation; I do wish you'd be so kind as to tell me about it."[286]

Quite so, the nun thought as she faced the woman; it could hardly be mere chance that had brought them together this first time.

"So then," her guest said, weeping as she spoke, "how was it that you discovered her? In the wretched state she was in, she would surely have fallen to ruin. I shall never be able to tell you, in this life or the next, how grateful I am that you were kind enough to take her in." The nun proceeded to tell her, from the very beginning, though not in full detail, just what had happened.

"All through the Fourth and Fifth Months,[287] she hardly seemed alive. Indeed, we had all but given up hope. But just when we were thinking that any day we would see the poor creature die before our very eyes, our prayers and incantations seemed to take effect, for, praise be to the gods and buddhas, she came around as we see her now. Ever since then, the joy of looking after her has been a great solace to us in the dreary life we lead here. Yet we've never had even the slightest notion who she was or where she came from. Now and again, we would try to ask her what it was she was hiding, but this seemed to cause her such pain that we never pressed her.[288] We knew, to our constant distress, that such a lovely creature could hardly be any common person. But how terribly distressing that you have sought her out only to discover that she's become a nun."

The mother wept inconsolably. "I have several daughters, but this girl was different. From the time she was a child, she's had no one else she could depend on, and I've tried my best, day and night, to see that she should have as good a match as any of the others. And all for naught. She abandons me, doesn't leave so much as a body behind; so then what? Bereavement is something we all must experience, for such is the way of this world. But imagine, if you can, the agony of unknowing added to it all. To ignore all my best hopes and plans and hide herself away—and both of us still alive in this world—truly a case of 'not a fraction of the love a mother has for her child.' It made me feel so painfully bitter. I suppose it's only natural that she should turn in disgust from someone as worthless as me. All the same, it does seem a pity that I couldn't have seen her again as she was before. But what does all that matter now? Just the joy of seeing her again—and so unexpectedly—when I had thought her dead and gone. That makes up for everything." And on and on she went.

"Yes, indeed, how very much it must," the nun said, now in tears herself. "Even after she had recovered somewhat, she continued day and night in the most dreadful despond, with never a moment's respite from the torment. When she did speak, which was very seldom, it was only to drop some hint of—well, *this*. I always told her what a great shame, indeed how wrong it would be. But then, perhaps, she's only done what she's been fated to do. Since it was I who had looked after her from the very start, I decided I really must make a pilgrimage to Hatsuse to pray for her.[289] At the time, I suggested, very gently, that she might like to come along, but she seemed to feel it would be too much for her, and so, reluctantly, I left her behind. It was just then, as it happened, that my brother the Preceptor[290] came down from the mountain, and she pleaded with him, all in tears. Now, even for a monk he is a frightfully severe man, but it was he who granted her plea. When I saw what had happened, I was utterly aghast; I hardly knew where to turn or what to do. So I can imagine only too well how much it must grieve you. And the gentleman who came in search of her: he, too, it seemed to me, cared very much for her. It must have been a terrible disappointment to him to find her in this state." These women had a great deal to say to each other.

In the meantime, Ukon drew near to the girl and asked, "Just what was it that happened?"

"There was nothing I could do. I hardly felt I was alive, I was so dreadfully depressed," said the girl, who had never stopped weeping. Ukon was deeply touched. Even old and ugly women look wonderfully rejuvenated when they put on the habit, she thought. But it only made *her* seem even more helpless and frail, like a little child. And the sight of her hair—once so abundant and now cut short yet spreading more luxuriantly than a five-fold fan,[291] so that the tips were even lovelier than before—only plunged her into a dark depression.

"Why on earth did you do this?" Ukon asked. "When I was waiting on you, why, I never would have dreamed that you were contemplating anything so dreadful. And to think that you kept it all to yourself! From the time we were children, your Ukon has been utterly devoted to you; I would have followed you anywhere. And all for naught. If only you could have let me give him some small hint; that's what really hurts."[292] She was sobbing helplessly.

[Ukon] went on to talk about the Prince [Niou]. "He seems to have taken on in a way that was embarrassing to see. But before long, I heard, he was back to his old amorous ways, as much the rake as ever; it was pathetic.[293] His Lordship, however, took it all so calmly that he appeared positively chilly, but in fact it touched him so deeply that there was never a moment when you were out of his thoughts. He was even so good as to seek me out and take me in. And all, it seems, because he thought of me in connection with you. I'm terribly grateful to him. When no one was around,[294] he would summon me to his side and talk about all those things that still weighed on his mind. 'When she was alive,' he would say, 'I must not have inspired much confidence in her. Yet could anyone have been more steadfast? My feelings for her have remained the same throughout. But this habitual diffidence of mine can make me look terribly shallow in the eyes of others.[295] But no matter. Who is to tell her now? Were there some wizard who could convey my thoughts to her,[296] she might even now realize how I feel, but . . .' It was such a pitiful sight when I waited upon him in moments like this." The girl's mind was in turmoil, overwhelmed with both pity and shame. So in fact, his feelings for her *were* quite deep! How strange, she thought, that she could be so capricious as to be taken in, even slightly, by the Prince's outward charms. How utterly depressing. Ah well, this could hardly be the recompense for one life alone. What right had she to blame it on anyone else? It was her destiny to drift aimlessly through life, and that alone had been the cause of that sordid affair. All the misery that was now her lot, she concluded sadly, was simply the recompense for countless lives past; there was no escaping it.

Sitting here with someone from her old home, who had long thought her dead and gone, listening to tales that took her back to a world she had long since left behind, she felt as if she were listening to the story of a dream. How could it not but strike her as strange and sad? Yet as long as she might go on living, there were bound to be more and more of these encounters, which made it only the sadder to recall her old nursemaid, who had fretted over her right up until that very last evening, and then, heartbroken, had died.

Since their guest was to stay the night, the nun had an elegant basket of food prepared, full of fruits and nuts seldom seen in the capital, all beautifully arranged. Unable to sleep, the woman and her daughter talked on and on, and the long night passed in what seemed no more than a moment. Much still remained to be said, they both felt, when at dawn the lady had to leave.

"Despite the distance, we do, after all, inhabit the same world," her mother said, still in tears. "I really must see that you are moved someplace that will not be such a worry. Do you remember that rather rustic lodge [in Sanjō], where you hid yourself away from time to time in those days? It's quite a large place. I could have it done up nicely and move you there. But then His Lordship the Commandant says we're to keep this a secret; that does make one hesitate. But how is anyone to know? I think we can do it all very discreetly."

It was wrong, the girl knew as she listened, all wrong! But her tearful reply was only evasive. "I don't wonder that you find this depressing. But it would be most improper for someone in my condition to forsake this retreat in the mountains, which it's my duty to endure, and to go to live in plain sight of everyone again." Her profile as she averted her face was inexpressibly beautiful, yet to her mother only the more distressing to see.

"But even if it is in the capital, why would there have to be so many people about? I could have them do it up just like a place in the mountains." There was something touching in the woman's efforts to persuade the girl that all would be to her liking. She then produced a wealth of silks and damasks. Some, of course, were for the young lady's wardrobe, but to the nun, too, she gave extravagant gifts, which set her raving with delight. To a nun, unaccustomed to such largesse, who lived such a chaste life, gifts of this sort seemed dazzling.

"I am quite at a loss," the mother sent in to the nun, "to express my joy and my gratitude for all that you've done. But somehow, when next I make my way up this mountain path and my mind is more composed. . . ." The nun and all the lesser nuns soaked the sleeves of their dark robes with tears to think how touchingly regretful and sad the woman must feel.[297]

Ukon, for her part, wished to remain right there with her mistress.

"But how," the girl said, "how ever could you live shut away in such a forsaken place as this? No, it will never do!

> *aranu yo to omoinashitsuru yama no oku ni / nani tazunete kite sode nurasuran*
> In the depths of these mountains, this world apart where I have found refuge:
> why should you seek me out, only to soak your sleeves with tears?"

Ukon, deeply troubled, said:

> *tachikaeru nagori dani kaku kanashiki ni / nagaki wakare to omowamashikaba*
> If even the lingering regret of returning can cause such grief,
> how must I feel to think this may be the longest of partings?

"I wonder whether we shall ever again witness such extraordinary events," the nun said. "With so many such unexpected comings and goings, this mountain path may make quite a name for itself. And I can't help feeling that, all things being equal, it may 'grow only the more so.'"[298] As she spoke, the nun came out and slid closer. As their sleeves grew wetter, even the long road the mother had traveled came to seem quite unreal to her. Her joy, her astonishment, even what the nun had told her about what the malign spirit had said and about their guide on the road to Hatsuse, she treasured. Now weeping, now smiling, the mother chatted with Ukon on their way home.

Yet as they made their way down the road and she watched even the mountains that surround the place fade into the distance, she grew more and more forlorn. Back in Ono, an air of sadness lingered, and the young lady, to distract herself, gave herself over to the performance of her customary predawn devotions.[299]

At dusk, Ukon proceeded to her lord's mansion. It was a tranquil time when fewer of his people were around than was usual. He sat near the veranda, the blind rolled up, whiling away the time playing his flute. Then he caught the sound of her voice as she spoke softly with his gentlewomen. He summoned her by name and asked how it had gone. In reply, she related in great detail all that had taken place. And when she told him about the girl murmuring, "Why should you seek me out?" this touched him with particular poignancy, and tears welled up in his eyes. Yes, he thought, she would think that. Perhaps, were she still unchanged from of yore, he might not have been so stricken. But now he was only the more painfully moved. Not a moment went by when she did not weigh upon his mind.

The Prince, too, had never ceased to look back on those days. No, on many occasions he had mused, there could be but few like her in this world. Yet she was by no means the only one to occupy his thoughts. His old nature had again come to the fore,[300] and it had not been long before he had gone in pursuit of Miyanokimi. As always, their affair blossomed for a time, but lately he seemed to have lost interest in her. His affection for the mistress of his own mansion was as strong as ever, so much so, indeed, that it must have inspired the admiration of everyone. His Lordship the Commandant, too, was as constantly attentive and considerate of this lady as ever in the past. A rare thing, she knew well.

The young Prince grew steadily more handsome. Even in a large family, he would have had special attention, but in all this time there had been no others, and he had become the sole object of his parents' hopes and affection. His future seemed assured. The Emperor and Empress had expressed their desire to see their grandchild, but the young Prince being still childishly shy, his father had not yet presented him to Their Majesties.

Oh, and yes: His Lordship, having been promoted Commandant of the Left Bodyguards and, at the same time, appointed Palace Minister, seemed more radiant a figure than ever. The Princess, his wife, however, had been feeling out of sorts. Her nurses and gentlewomen knew at once what this meant, and when they told their lord, the news brought at least a small measure of cheer to brighten his joyless existence. His mother [the Third Princess], needless to say, was delighted, and she added forthwith to her round of devotions a plethora of prayers for safe delivery.

At Ono, the endless succession of dreary days dragged on, and then it was winter. Even in the capital, there had been a great deal of snow and hail, while here it had "snowed upon snows not yet thawed."[301] As she gazed out at eventide toward the road that wound through peaks buried in layer upon layer, the wisps of smoke that trailed ever so faintly above the snow left her with a feeling of inexpressible loneliness and desolation. No "peak of Fuji"[302] this, but yes, these must be those mountain folk, the charcoal makers of whom one hears.[303]

sumu hito no yado oba uzumu yuki no uchi ni / keburi zo taenu ono no sumigama
From amid the snow that buries the very homes of those who live here,
the smoke of the Ono charcoal kilns rises without surcease.

It was a time when the dark gloomy days, so familiar in this season, had lingered longer than usual, and even the footprints of the mountain woodcutters had vanished from the scene. Then came the sound of the shoes of a messenger who, to their amazement, had somehow forced his way through to them. Her people went out to see who it might be.

"In these days," he had written, "when even the capital wears an air of gloom, I wonder how you fare?

ika bakari nagame waburan kakikurashi / yuki furu koto no ono no yamabito
How downcast they must be as they gaze out at the falling snow
that darkens their lives these days, the mountain folk of Ono."

That he should send someone all this way, and at just this time, deeply touched her. She took some care with her reply.

tou ni koso ato oba mitsure shirayuki no / furiuzumitaru mine no kayoiji
Only because you sent to inquire could I even see it was there,
the road through the peaks buried far beneath white falling snow.

Her feelings, expressed so openly, moved him almost to tears. He sat gazing at her letter, unable to put it down.

Well then, just how was he to manage this? Her situation was entirely of her own choosing. And yet, even now he wished he could do something for her, if only to console himself for all that time spent devoid of any joy worth remembering. But she herself seemed unwilling to consider any dwelling that might be frequented by great numbers of people. Indeed, even in times past when no one could have objected, she had remained in that forsaken place [Uji] lest there be talk. If now she were to come out in the world, the gossip would in every way be devastating. Yet how excruciating to have her shut away in that hermitage up in the mountains. What should he do? He had had his heart set on building a proper retreat in the hills nearby and moving her there secretly. But with everyone making such a fuss over the Princess, and the countless prayers and incantations that went with it, none of his most competent stewards from any of his estates had a moment to spare. It was an awkward time; even the slightest hint of his plans might arouse an uproar of criticism, he told himself, as incurably cautious as ever.

As the year drew to a close, bustle and confusion prevailed, leaving no one any time to regret its passing; but His Lordship, at least, was unruffled by it all. He had written to the lady in the mountains, lest she feel forgotten, and had sent, in the guise of gifts from Ukon, great quantities of everything he thought she might need for the New Year. To the nuns, living as frugally as they did, this seemed more convincing evidence of his concern than the fact that he had not failed to think of them in their most trying moments and had sent his messenger through snow and hail to inquire after them. For the lady herself, it was painful to hear them go on so.

Her mother, too, had overlooked nothing and had sent gifts to the nuns as well, who regarded this with properly reverent joy, as succor for the poor sent at the behest of the Buddha himself. One can imagine, then, how their humble servants raved about the munificence of their lady and rushed about doing whatever they could for her.

The nun, too, busied herself night and day looking after the girl, for to her this was a source of solace in her life and a ray of light in her mountain retreat. But this largesse, so munificent that it might fill Treasure House Mountain, she could explain only as the Buddha providing for her, far beyond her needs, in both this life and the next.

On a quiet evening His Lordship the Commandant went to call on the Prince Minister of War. The Prince, he was informed, had just gone to Rokujō,[304] and so he proceeded instead to call upon the mistress of the mansion [Nakanokimi]. To the soft rustle of robes, a sound that never failed to delight him, he was offered a cushion.

"Since when," he sighed, "am I not allowed within the blinds? Bitter compensation, this, for my years of devotion." Someone must have reported what he said, for he then heard the voice of Shōshō.

"You are quite right not to let this error of an ignorant person pass unchastised. I would hope, though, that on 'the hunting ground of Ono,' I should instead get to know you better."[305] She then lowered the blinds of the main hall and ushered him in.

"That was a bit harsh," he said. "And your admonition is quite uncalled for. I am always asmolder." The faint smile that came over his face as he spoke was infinitely alluring.

Presently, there were signs that the Princess was about to appear, and he adopted a more formal posture.

"It is a pity," he said, "that the Prince is out just now. But I did hope that I might be granted the honor of, as the common folk seem to call it, a 'once yearly audience.'[306] What a delightful opportunity His Highness's absence provides."

"Yes, it does seem a bit forlorn, doesn't it, when the end of the year finally . . ." Her subtle evasion charmed him into wishing he might hear what else she might have to say.

"And how futile," he replied, "the way we rush about, ushering out the old year and seeing in the new, as if we were oblivious to where it all leads as they pile up upon us." He drew close to her, and they talked, as always, in the most intimate detail of times past and present, but he revealed nothing about the hermitage at Ono.

Ultimately, though, they would have to talk to each other about her. Were he to say nothing whatever and she were later to find out, it would create a distance between them that could prove painful. She herself could not have been ignorant of those strange goings-on at the time of her sister's disappearance, yet she acted as if she knew nothing. For him, too, there were certain matters he was loath to discuss. Were he to try to pass it off lightly, pretending that there had been only some distressing little incident, that would hardly strike her as credible. This wasn't the sort of thing he could satisfy her with vague hints of. If once he were to start, it all would have to come out. Yet even if he were to tell her as a matter of confidence and she were not carelessly to reveal it, still, if he were to speak openly of it in the Prince's own household, what if someone hidden from them should happen to hear? In his reluctance to speak lingered some of the old enmity, still unresolved.

TRANSLATED BY T. HARPER

Notes

1. For a hypothetical reconstruction of the nature of such patronage, see Konishi Jin'ichi, "*Utsuho monogatari* no kōsei to seiritsu katei," *Nihon Gakushi'in kiyō* 12 (1954), in *Nihon bungaku kenkyū shiryō sōsho, Heian monogatari II* (Tokyo: Yūseidō, 1974), 61–94.

2. Princess Shūshi (997–1050), eldest daughter of the Ichijō Emperor and Empress Teishi.

3. *Zai chūjō, The Ariwara Colonel,* is an alternative title of *Ise monogatari.* The other works no longer survive.

4. These examples are taken from Murasaki Shikibu, *Taikō Genji monogatari shinshaku,* ed. Yoshizawa Yoshinori (Tokyo: Heibonsha, 1954), 1:205, 106, 17, and lines 4, 10, 7–9, respectively. This edition combines the *Kogetsushō* version of the Aobyōshi-bon with the Owari Tokugawa version of the Kawachi-bon in such a way that the reader can see at a glance all the differences between the two.

5. Inaga Keiji, "'Yamaji no tsuyu' no nikeitō to kyōtsū sokei no seikaku: honmon seiritsu to bamen no 'bunkatsu,' 'tōgō' kinō," in *Chūsei ōchō monogatari zenshū* (Tokyo: Kasama Shoin, 2004), 8:340–54.

6. For example, *Imakagami* and *Mumyōzōshi.*

7. For the best-known example, see the "Kana Preface" to the *Kokinshū,* NKBZ 7:54.

8. *Roppyakuban utaawase,* round 13, "Sear Fields."

9. For a concise description of these and other such texts, see Ikeda Kikan, ed., *Genji monogatari jiten* (Tokyo: Tōkyōdō, 1960), 2:26–28.

10. Mitsuyuki was sentenced to death for his support of Emperor GoToba (1180–1239; r. 1183–1198) in the Jōkyū rebellion but was spared at the last moment through his son's entreaties. Chikayuki was removed from office for his part in a plot to have Ichijō Sanemasa (d. 1228) appointed shogun.

11. See, for example, Minamoto no Chikayuki's description of his father Mitsuyuki's collaboration with Shunzei, in Sojaku, *Explicating Murasaki,* translated in chapter 3 of this volume.

12. Concerning the origins of "Tamakura," Norinaga himself says only that he wrote it at the behest of "a certain person." Who that person was and when he completed the task, he does not say. Many reference works date the work to 1763, based on a chronology of Norinaga's work by Ban Nobutomo (1773–1846), which states, under the heading of that year, that "'Tamakura' [was] by then complete." See Motoori Norinaga, *Suzunoya Okina ryaku nenpu hosei,* in *Motoori Norinaga zenshū,* ed.

Motoori Seizō (Tokyo: Yoshikawa Kōbunkan, 1927), 1:17. Ōkubo Tadashi and Ōno Susumu, editors of MNZ, estimate that it was written sometime between 1758 and 1763.

13. Ozaki Masayoshi, *Gunsho ichiran* (Osaka: woodblock ed., 1801), 3:54b–55a.

14. As, for example, does Nakanoin Michikatsu (quoting *sen*) in *Mingō nisso* (1598), GMKS 11:239.

15. Motoori Norinaga, postscript to the printed edition of "Tamakura" (Nagoya: Eirakuya, 1792).

16. MNZ, 14:648. The manuscript of *Kogen shinan* is not dated, but Ōkubo Tadashi, editor of this volume of MNZ, estimates that it was written sometime between 1758 and 1763.

17. Nakagawa Tadamoto found only one infelicitous usage in the entire text of "Tamakura": the word *isagiyoshi*, which never appears in *Genji* but is frequently used in Buddhist texts ("Norinaga no *Genji*-gaku: 'Tamakura' ni tsuite," *Matsusaka joshi tanki daigaku ronsō* 24 [1987]: 18). A detailed comparison of Norinaga's phraseology with identical or highly similar phrases in *Genji* is found in Nakanishi Miyako, "'Tamakura' to *Genji monogatari*," *Seijō kokubungaku* 8 (1992): 57–67.

18. Tahara Nanken, *Genji monogatari Norinaga hosaku: Tamakura no kenkyū* (Sasebo: private publication, 1968), 166, 212. I am deeply indebted to the meticulous work of this little-known scholar, without which translating "Tamakura" would have been far more difficult and far less pleasant a task.

19. Fujita Tokutarō, *Genji monogatari kōyō* (Tokyo: Furōkaku, 1928), 271.

20. Ōno Susumu and Maruya Sai'ichi, *Hikaru Genji no monogatari*, 2 vols. (Tokyo: Chūōkōronsha, 1989), 1:52–53.

21. It could also get him into trouble. In 1772, Arakida Rei (1732–1806), who lived in the nearby town of Yamada, where her male relatives served as priests of the Inner Shrine at Ise, completed her historical tale, *Nonaka no shimizu*, and a copy was sent to Norinaga, probably by his friend Arikida Tsunemasa. Norinaga returned the manuscript covered with corrections and derogatory comments. An angry correspondence ensued, and the Arakida family seems never to have spoken to Norinaga again. See MNZ, 22:23–25, 343–86; and Ishimura Yasuko, "Motoori Norinaga no bunshō hihyō ni tsuite: Arakida Reijo no sakuhin *Nonaka no shimizu* o megutte," *Nihon bungaku* 7, no. 8 (1958): 45–55.

22. Tahara suggests that Norinaga here alludes to a scheme by the Minister of the Right to have the new son of his daughter, the Kokiden Dame of Honor, appointed crown prince. Rather than become involved in a power struggle, the emperor's brother simply—and decisively—abdicates (*Tamakura no kenkyū*, 52).

23. Tahara notes that in Genji's time, they could not have married during his tenure as crown prince, as he thus would have abdicated when he was about thirteen and the Rokujō lady about nine (*Tamakura no kenkyū*, 64–69).

24. In the printed edition of this work, Norinaga appends notes at the end of the volume identifying the four poems to which he alludes in the text. The phrase "aroused fond memories" (*nakanaka no shinobugusa nameri*), he says, alludes to *Gosenshū* 1187:

> When the mother of Kanetada Ason died, it was decided that Kanetada would go to the house of the [now] late Biwa Minister of the Left, and her daughter

would be placed in the service of the Empress, and I was sent along at the outset to take them both to the Biwa house. The nursemaid in the service of the mother of Kanetada Ason:

musubiokishi katami no ko dani nakariseba / nani ni shinobu no kusa o tsumamashi
Were not at least this child left behind as a keepsake,
what then would there be by which to remember her?

25. As Tahara points out, there is no explicit mention of the death of her father in *Genji*. Norinaga may, however, have found a clue in a passage in "Sakaki" (13:85) in which the Rokujō lady recalls her father as she boards her palanquin to pay a last visit to the palace before her departure for Ise (*Tamakura no kenkyū*, 82).

26. A claim possibly based on a passage in "Miotsukushi" (13:307) describing the dispersal of the household after the death of the Rokujō lady herself.

27. Possibly an allusion to *Kokinshū* 38:

Sent to someone with plum blossoms he had plucked. [Ki no] Tomonori:

kimi narade tare ni ka misemu ume no hana / iro o mo ka o mo shiru hito zo shiru
If not you, then to whom might I show these plum blossoms,
for only one who knows will know their hue and fragrance?

28. The translation here follows Tahara's rather subtle but convincingly argued interpretation of *tote* as suggesting a certain disingenuousness in Genji's setting off in the direction of his wife's home when in fact his principal interest lay elsewhere (*Tamakura no kenkyū*, 92).

29. It is approximately 2.5 miles (4.3 km) from the Kiritsubo to the Rokujō-in. Tahara estimated that to travel this distance by ox-drawn carriage at an unhurried pace would take about one hour and twenty minutes (*Tamakura no kenkyū*, 94).

30. "In the spring breeze," Norinaga tells us, alludes to *Kokinshū* 2:

sode hichite musubishi mizu no kōreru o / haru tatsu kyō no kaze ya tokuramu
The frozen waters that once wet my sleeve
may well melt in the breeze of this first day of spring.

31. Norinaga notes that "a very thing of spring" alludes to *Kokinshū* 616 (and *Ise monogatari*, 2); that is, Genji is comparing himself with the lovesick Narihira:

On the first day of the Third Month, after a secret conversation with a certain person as rain poured down, he sent this to her. Ariwara no Narihira no Ason:

Oki mo sezu ne mo sede yoru o akashite wa / haru no mono tote nagame kurashitsu
Having passed the night neither rising nor sleeping,
I spend the day in reverie, a very thing of spring.

32. Norinaga identifies "the one for long thought" obdurate (*nagaku ya hito o*) as an allusion to *Kokinshū* 624:

awazu shite koyoi akenaba haru no hi no / nagaku ya hito o tsurashi to omowamu
Should day break after this night kept apart from her, then for long, as long as this spring day is long, I shall think her obdurate.

Norinaga cites no source for the preceding phrase, "should I die of love" (*koishinaba*). Of the numerous possibilities (thirty in KT alone), Tahara suggests a variant of *Kokinshū* 603 (*Tamakura no kenkyū*, 185):

koishinaba ta ga na wa tataji yo no naka no / tsune naki mono to ii wa nasutomo
Should I die of love, whose name shall then be sullied;
protest though you may that it be but the uncertainty of life?

33. As Tahara points out, the mist that obscures the lingering moon hints at tears in Genji's eyes in his reluctance to leave (*Tamakura no kenkyū*, 216). Compare *Senzaishū* 961 / *Hyakunin isshu*:

In the Second Month on a bright moonlit night, when a number of people spent the night sitting up and talking, the Palace Attendant Suō, reclining, said as though to herself, "How I wish I had a pillow." Hearing this, Dainagon Tadaie slipped his arm [*kaina*] under her curtains and said, "For your pillow." She then composed this poem. Suō no Naishi:

haru no yo no yume bakari naru tamakura ni / kai naku tatamu na koso oshikere
To pillow upon someone's arm as briefly as a spring night's dream—
a pity indeed the ill fame one should gain for so little.

34. Shibuya Eiichi, ed., *Genji monogatari shaku*, GMKS 16:266–69.

35. Ii Haruki, "Tamakazura jūjō no shudai," in *Genji monogatari kenkyū shūsei*, ed. Masuda Shigeo, Suzuki Hideo, and Ii Haruki (Tokyo: Kazama Shobō, 1998), 1:135. Another possibility, mentioned though not preferred by Katō Masayoshi, is that Koreyuki's *Genji* text did not include "Sakurahito" and that the notes to this chapter in *Genji shaku* were added by a later writer whose text did include this chapter ("*Genji monogatari* 'Sakurahito' no maki no san'itsu o megutte," in *Monogatari no seisei to juyō*, ed. Kokubungaku Kenkyū Shiryōkan [Tokyo: Kokubungaku Kenkyū Shiryōkan, 2006], 55).

36. Text in NKBT 3:396–97.

37. Ii Haruki, *Genji monogatari chūshakushi no kenkyū* (Tokyo: Ōfūsha, 1980), 66–67.

38. Hashimoto Shinkichi, "*Renchūshō* no ichi ihon *Hakuzōshi* ni tsuite," in *Denki tenseki kenkyū, Hashimoto Shinkichi Hakase chosaku shū* (Tokyo: Iwanami Shoten, 1972), 12:317–38.

39. Horibe Seiji, "'Sakurahito,' 'Samushiro,' 'Sumori' kō,'" in *Chūko Nihon bungaku no kenkyū: shiryō to jisshō* (1943; repr., Tokyo: Kuresu Shuppan, 1999), 155–91.

40. Kazamaki Keijirō, "*Genji monogatari* no seiritsu ni kan suru shiron: shinkyū no toshidate, narabi no maki, gojūyon-chō no hoka no maki" (1950/1951), in *Kazamaki Keijirō zenshū: Genji monogatari no seiritsu* (Tokyo: Ōfūsha, 1969), 42–78.

41. In particular, Ikeda Kikan (1896–1956) and Takeda Munetoshi (1903–1980).

42. Ii, "Tamakazura jūjō no shudai," 141–42.

43. Hasegawa (Tokiwai) Kazuko, *Genji monogatari no kenkyū* (Tokyo: Tōhō Shobō, 1957), 134.

44. Saitō Masaaki, *Genji monogatari seiritsu kenkyū: shippitsu junjō to shippitsu jiki* (Tokyo: Kasama Shoin, 2001), 222–32.

45. Ii, "Tamakazura jūjō no shudai," 131, with particular reference to that demanding branch of textual scholarship that attempts to reconstruct the composition of *Genji*.

46. These comments are based principally on Hasegawa (Tokiwai), *Genji monogatari no kenkyū*; Horibe, "'Sakurahito,' 'Samushiro,' 'Sumori' kō"; Ii, "Tamakazura jūjō no shudai"; and Inaga Keiji, "San'itsu 'Sakurahito' to Tamakazura monogatari—'Sakurahito' no maki no fukugen to narabi no maki tsuika: Tamakazura monogatari seiritsu no kasetsu—," in *Yasuda Joshi Daigaku Daigakuin hakushi katei kaisetsu kinen ronbun shū* (Hiroshima: Yasuda Joshi Daigaku, 1997), 1–14. The page numbers of the comments by these scholars are in parentheses.

47. "Kashiwagi," 4:314:

ta ga yo ni ka tane wa makishi to hito towaba / ikaga iwane no matsu wa kotaen

Should anyone ever ask him who planted the seed, and in what reign,
what shall he answer, this little pine growing from the rock?

48. NKBZ and NKBT read *ima* for *yoshi*.

49. Although the interlinear variant *mono wa omowa[shi]* occurs in many other poems, it does not seem to be an alternative for *wakare semashi ya* in extant texts of this particular poem.

50. The alternative transcription and translation enclosed in brackets are based on Inaga's suggestion that . . . *ya* . . . *tamawamu* may be a mistake for . . . *ya* . . . *tamawanu*. In this case, the diction would be analogous to that of Tō no Chūjō's poem to Yūgiri.

51. NKBT and NKBZ read *ware mo* for *hitori*.

52. Yamagishi Tokuhei and Imai Gen'e, eds., "Kaidai," in *Yamaji no tsuyu: Kunaichō Shoryōbu-zō Aobyōshibon Genji monogatari* (Tokyo: Shintensha, 1970), 77.

For the first draft of this translation I followed the transcription of the standard text in Yamagishi Tokuhei and Imai Gen'e, eds., *Yamaji no tsuyu, Kumogakure rokujō* (Tokyo: Shintensha, 1970), 73–91. In preparing the final version, I followed Asai Ryōi's annotated edition of the same text in Yasuda Takako and Yoshida Kōichi, eds., *E'iri Genji monogatari no maki* (Tokyo: Koten Bunko, 1990), 245–437. I was also fortunate to have access to Ii Haruki's version of the text, "Kumogakure rokujō" (manuscript, 1990), for which I am extremely grateful. More recently,

I consulted Imanishi Yūichirō's annotated edition in *Suma ki; Sei Shōnagon Matsushima nikki; Genji monogatari Kumogakure rokujō*, ed. Chimoto Hideshi, in *Nihon koten gisho sōkan* (Tokyo: Gendai Shichō Shinsha, 2004), 2:97–131. The latest recension is Ogawa Yōko, "*Kumogakure rokujō* kōhon," in *Genji monogatari kyōjushi no kenkyū* (Tokyo: Kasama Shoin, 2009), 540–641. My thanks, too, to Ii Haruki for providing glossy photographs of the illustrations to this text before they were digitized.

53. *Mumyōzōshi*, ed. Kuboki Tetsuo, SNKBZ 40:205. The comment follows her description of the Kiritsubo Emperor's grief after the death of Genji's mother.

54. Imai Gen'e, *Genji monogatari no kenkyū* (Tokyo: Miraisha, 1962), 305.

55. Actually there is no verb to indicate whether he voices this poem in any way, or merely thinks it.

56. *Genchū saihishō*, in *Mikan kokubun kochūshaku taikei*, ed. Yoshizawa Yoshinori (Tokyo: Teikoku Kyōikukai Shuppanbu, 1936), 11:75.

57. Nomura Hachirō, "Kumogakure hiteisetsu," *Kokugo to kokubungaku* 2 (1925): 181–82.

58. *Murasaki Shikibu shū* 1; *Shinkokinshū* 1497.

59. Hashimoto, "*Renchūshō* no ichi ihon *Hakuzōshi* ni tsuite," 336–37.

60. *Genchū saihishō*, 75.

61. This comment is attributed to Chikayuki's grandson Gyōa. See *Genchū saihishō*, 75.

62. Ii Haruki, ed., (*Matsunaga-bon*) *Kachō yosei*, GMKS 1:272.

63. Reported in *Genchū saihishō*, 76.

64. Horibe, "'Sakurahito,' 'Samushiro,' 'Sumori' kō," 189n.5.

65. Quoted in Ii Haruki, *Genji monogatari no densetsu* (Tokyo: Shōwa Shuppan, 1976), 114.

66. An excellent overview of these materials is found in Ii, *Genji monogatari no densetsu*, 101–49.

67. Ii speculates that this text may have been instrumental in defining "Kumogakure" as a set of six rather than a single chapter (*Genji monogatari no densetsu*, 113).

68. Reported in *Genchū saihishō*, 76.

69. Kaoku Gyokuei, *Gyokueishū*, ed. Ii Haruki, in *Gengo kenkyū shiryō shū*, Hekichūdō sōsho 87 (Ōbuchō, Aichi-ken: Yanase Kazuo, 1969), 125.

70. Ii, *Genji monogatari no densetsu*, 134.

71. Ii, *Genji monogatari no densetsu*, 138.

72. Jinson's list includes "Sakurahito," whereas *Genji higishō* lists a third "Sagano no Miya" chapter in its place. See Ii, *Genji monogatari no densetsu*, 138.

73. In a handwritten endnote to his copy of "Kumogakure," Ōta Nanpo (1749–1823) says that this list appears at the end of Kanera's genealogy. See Yamagishi and Imai, eds., *Yamaji no tsuyu, Kumogakure rokujō*, 91.

74. Quoted in Ii, *Genji monogatari no densetsu*, 125.

75. Yamagishi and Imai, eds., *Yamaji no tsuyu, Kumogakure rokujō*, 132–33.

76. Yoshida Kōichi, "'Kumogakure rokujō' shōkō," in *E'iri Genji Kumogakure no maki*, ed. Yasuda and Yoshida, 449.

77. Yamagishi and Imai, eds., *Yamaji no tsuyu, Kumogakure rokujō*, 134.

78. Yamagishi and Imai, eds., *Yamaji no tsuyu, Kumogakure rokujō*, 134.

79. Both text and commentary are undated. The terminus ante quem is established by their mention in a catalog entitled (*Zōho*) *Shoseki mokuroku*, published in 1670. This work also identifies Asai Ryōi as author of the commentary. Complete bibliographical details of all printed editions are given in Yasuda and Yoshida, eds., *E'iri Genji Kumogakure no maki*, 439–46.

80. We know of this printing only because the location of the date of publication was moved from one volume to another without changing the date itself. See Yasuda and Yoshida, eds., *E'iri Genji Kumogakure no maki*, 443.

81. The following argument is based principally on Yoshida, "'Kumogakure rokujō' shōkō," 447–95, and particularly its section "Rufu hanpon 'Kumogakure rokujō' wa, Genji shō to tomo ni Asai Ryōi no saku ka," 490–95.

82. The phrase used is *koto no tagaime arite*. Normally, this would be translated as "something went amiss" or the like, referring to something that had gone wrong but had not been done intentionally. Somewhat stronger language is used here both because the severity of the lady's punishment suggests that her offense was no mere misdemeanor and because in Heian usage, the word could refer euphemistically to sexual misconduct. Kashiwagi, for example, describes his adulterous affair with Genji's wife, the Third Princess, as *isasaka naru koto no tagaime arite* . . . (there was this little mishap . . .) ("Kashiwagi" 4:306).

83. Glossed thus in the manuscript but now pronounced "Takaku." In local dialect, however, it still may be pronounced "Takagi" or "Takaki," according to Yoshida Tōgo, ed., *Zōho dai Nihon chimei jisho* (Tokyo: Fuzanbō, 1967), 4:280.

84. All textual variants are listed in Yoshida Takako and Mitadera Atsuko, eds., "Beppon 'Kumogakure rokujō,'" in *Setsurin* (Aichi: Aichi Kenritsu Joshi Daigaku, July 1960), 6:74–81.

85. For a detailed description of the most famous of these contretemps, the "dragon scale scandal" (*gekirin jiken*) of 1609, see G. G. Rowley, *An Imperial Concubine's Tale: Scandal, Shipwreck, and Salvation in Seventeenth-Century Japan* (New York: Columbia University Press, 2013).

86. This first sentence is a paraphrase of the last sentences of "Maboroshi," 4:536, quoted in the preceding introduction.

87. About 3:00 A.M.

88. Genji used carriages of similar description to conceal his identity when going to a secret tryst. The carriage in which the Rokujō consort, who wishes to remain incognito, goes to the Aoi Festival is described in precisely the same terms ("Aoi," 13:16).

89. Tadasu no Mori, the wooded point at the confluence of the Kamo and Takano Rivers through which one passes on the way to the Lower Kamo Shrine.

90. Signifying, perhaps, that Koremitsu is dead?

91. No one by this name appears in *Genji*, but Asai Ryōi offers an interesting suggestion as to who Okabe might be: "In the *Genji monogatari* there are six guardsmen, none of whom are named. Of these, the Okabe of this passage may be the one who was made to chant 'lost in the mists' when Genji, returning at dawn from Murasaki's home, passed the house of someone with whom he was having an affair ["Wakamurasaki," 12:321]. It may have been because of this that he was chosen to serve as an attendant on this occasion." Here Ryōi refers to the morning, shortly before Genji spirits Murasaki away to Nijō, when he passes the gate of one of his

current lovers. A knock on the gate produces no reply, and so he orders "a retainer of good voice" to chant the following poem—twice:

> *asaborake kiri tatsu sora no mayoi ni mo / yukisugigataki imo ga kado kana*
> Lost though I am in the mists that rise in the dim first light of day,
> I am loath to pass it by, this gate of my beloved. ("Wakamurasaki," 12:321)

This elicits a warm welcome from the lady, which he regrets having to pass up, but dawn is approaching, and in the end he decides he will go home. See Asai Ryōi, *Genji shō*, in *E'iri Genji Kumogakure no maki*, ed. Yasuda and Yoshida, 322–23, 317–437. This and all subsequent references to Ryōi's commentary are identified by the page numbers in this edition.

92. Where the standard text reads *to iu o kiku*, the variant text reads *to ibuseku*. Because the former looks suspiciously like a mistaken rendition of the latter, the translation here follows the variant text.

93. Ryōi is more specific. This is the day of the "Four Beginnings": Beginning of the Year, Beginning of the Months, Beginning of the Days, Beginning of the Hours. One should therefore avoid anything so inauspicious as a departure in the dark of night (*Genji shō*, 323–24).

94. Imanishi Yūichirō suggests emending this sentence, replacing *tayutawaruru osa mata mōsubeki naraneba* with *tayutawaruru o samatage mōsubeki naraneba* (it was not for them to raise objections). See Imanishi Yūichirō's annotated edition in *Suma ki, Sei Shōnagon Matsushima nikki, Genji monogatari Kumogakure rokujō*, ed. Chimoto Hideshi, in *Nihon koten gisho sōkan* (Tokyo: Gendai Shichō Shinsha, 2004), 2:103.

95. The Suzaku Emperor. He builds his temple in "Wakana, jō," 15:12, and moves there in 15:68. He is first referred to as *yama no mikado* in "Wakana, ge," 15:256. As Ryōi points out, "The villa in Katsura, which had been the property of the grandfather of the Akashi nun, was inherited by the Akashi lady. Adjacent to this, the retired emperor built a temple. Another theory says it is in Nishiyama" (*Genji shō*, 325).

96. A striking resemblance to the "hewers of wood and drawers of water" in Joshua 9:21, but in this case the phrase is from the Lotus Sutra 12, "Devadatta."

> At that time there was a seer who came to the king and said, "I have a Great Vehicle text called the Sutra of the Wonderful Law. If you will never disobey me, I will expound it for you." When the king heard these words of the seer, he danced for joy. At once he accompanied the seer, providing him with whatever he needed, picking fruit, drawing water, gathering firewood, setting out meals, even offering his own body as a couch and seat, never stinting in body or mind. He served the seer in this manner for a thousand years, all for the sake of the Law, working diligently, acting as a provider, and seeing to it that the seer lacked for nothing. (Burton Watson, trans., *The Lotus Sutra* [Columbia University Press, 1993], 183)

To many, however, the phrase was better known as the lower hemistich of a poem attributed to the Nara-period monk Gyōgi (668–749):

hokekyō o waga eshi koto wa takigi kori / na tsumi mizu kumi tsukaete zo eshi
The Lotus Sutra have I attained! Serving as a hewer of wood,
a gatherer of greens, a drawer of water have I attained it. (*Shūishū* 1346)

The substitution of "hew" for "gather" suggests that the "Kumogakure" author's most immediate source is the latter.

97. This phrase seems to derive from one of the better-known legends of the Buddha's previous lives, in which he allows himself to be eaten by a starving tiger so that the beast might nurse its young. By a curious process of association, this legend seems to have inspired a sub-subgenre of Japanese poetry devoted to the expression of a lover's passion for another man's wife. In this slightly naughty analogy, the lover (Buddha) declares his determination to abandon himself on the plains (the wife) where tigers (the husband) lurk. Ryōi (*Genji shō*, 325) cites *Shūishū* 1227:

Sent by a man who was deeply enamored of a woman who had a husband. Kunimochi:

ari tote mo iku yo ka wa furu karakuni no / tora fusu nobe ni mi o mo nageten
Though one lives, how many reigns does one survive? I shall abandon myself
on that plain in far Cathay where the tiger lurks.

Elsewhere in the same anthology (*Shūishū* 508):

Sent by a man who was deeply enamored of a woman who had a husband. Author unknown:

inishie no tora no tagui ni mi o nageba / saka to bakari wa towamu to zo omou
Should I throw myself before the tiger, as did Shaka long ago,
then, I trust, you will understand and ask after me.

And in *Kokin rokujō* 2978:

hitozuma wa mori ka yashiro ka karakuni no / tora fusu nobe ka nete kokoromimu
That other man's wife: is she a grove, a sacred shrine, a plain in far
Cathay where the tiger lurks? Let me sleep with her and see.

Whether or not Ryōi is right to identify this as the source of *tora no fusu nobe*, it must have seemed strange phraseology to anyone who knew these poems. The poems just quoted by no means exhaust the genre.

98. The translation follows Ryōi in taking the *wani* to be a crocodile (*Genji shō*, 325–26). Ryōi cites a sixth-century Chinese Buddhist work that purports to recount the propagation of the faith in Ceylon (now Sri Lanka), which describes the beast

as an aquatic creature "more than twenty feet long, having four legs, and resembling a turtle. Its teeth are extraordinarily sharp. Should a beast enter the water, its bite will crush its carcass." Many scholars, however, identify the *wani* of Heian and medieval usage not as a crocodile but as a shark. Also, the phrase *tora fusu nobe, isana yoru ura* (*Taiheiki* 4, cited in NKD, s.v.) (plains where tigers lurk, shores frequented by whales) suggests at least the possibility that the *Kumogakure* author could have had a fish of some sort in mind rather than a reptile. For a detailed discussion of this word, see *Kadokawa kogo jiten* (Tokyo: Kadokawa Shoten, 1999), 5:1009.

99. Ryōi names them and notes that they later become the Buddha's first five disciples (*Genji shō*, 326). His list differs markedly from those given in the principal sources of this legend but agrees almost exactly with that in *Konjaku monogatari*, suggesting that his source is not scriptural, as he claims, but literary.

100. Ryōi takes this to mean not early in the day but early in life, "at an age before that at which one would normally consider taking vows" (*Genji shō*, 327).

101. Ryōi takes this to mean that both men are gaunt, Suzaku from austerities and Genji from despondence (*Genji shō*, 327–28).

102. Ryōi cites a Chinese poem: "The mountains were still, as in antiquity; the days were long, as in one's youth" (*Genji shō*, 329).

103. In the variant text, a different poem, more direct in its reference to Murasaki, is attributed to Suzaku:

murasaki no ue oku tsuyu ni odorokite / hajimete yume no yo o ya shiruran
Awakened by the dew that forms upon the *murasaki*, then,
for the first time, you must have known that this is a world of dreams.

104. Genji will be criticized for leaving the world on her account, and she will be blamed as the cause of his weakness. As Ryōi puts it: "It says in the *Hokkekyō* that 'the seed of Buddhahood rises out of one's individual circumstances.' There may be a multitude of reasons for entering upon the Way of the Buddha; but what a shame for Genji's sake, the Retired Emperor thinks, that they should say he did so because he lost a woman" (*Genji shō*, 331).

105. Another name for the day lily, whose beauty was reputed (in China) to banish the grief of bereavement or (in Japan), the pangs of unrequited love.

106. *Ise* 83; *Kokinshū* 970. An allusion to Narihira's poem composed when he visited Prince Koretaka, who had taken vows and gone into retreat at Ono:

wasurete wa yume ka to zo omou omoiki ya / yuki fumiwakete kimi o min to wa
When I forget myself, it all seems but a dream. Would ever I have thought it:
that I should trudge through the snow to visit my lord?

As Ryōi points out, this allusion deftly contrasts Narihira, who was at least able to visit his lord, with Genji's people, who have no idea where he has gone (*Genji shō*, 333).

107. He learns that he is actually the illegitimate son of Genji in "Usugumo," 13:439–42.

108. Alluding to *Kokinshū* 552, by Ono no Komachi:

omoitsutsu nureba ya hito wa mietsuramu / yume to shiriseba
samezaramashi o
Was it because I fell asleep longing for him that he appeared to me?
Had I but known I dreamed, I should not have awakened, but. . . .

109. In the variant text, *kudakubeshi* is replaced by *nagusamen* (that I should find consolation in a dream?).

110. The dew of tears on the flower of cares (*omoigusa*) is a common image in post-Heian poetry. This flower is now better known by its early Edo-period and, alas, more appropriate name of "Dutchman's-pipe" (*nanban kiseru*). But in earlier times, apparently, it was thought to resemble a beautiful woman weighed down by the woes of care; hence its name in poetry.

111. The building of this temple is mentioned in "Eawase," 13:383, and "Matsukaze," 13:389. In "Yadorigi," 16:385, Kaoru mentions to Nakanokimi that Genji had lived there during his last two or three years after taking vows.

112. Ryōi takes this detail to indicate that the severity of Genji's austerities has changed him beyond recognition (*Genji shō*, 337–38).

113. As Ryōi reminds us, this is where she grew up (*Genji shō*, 338). She is described as thinking of it as her own in "Minori," 15:481.

114. The Hour of the Ox is 1:00 to 3:00 A.M.

115. Compare *Shinkokinshū* 757, by Sōjō Henjō:

sue no tsuyu moto no shizuku ya yo no naka no / okuresakidatsu tameshi
naruran
The dewdrop on the tip of the leaf or the droplet on the stem?
Whichever falls first, or last, 'tis but the way of this world.

116. Ubasoku no In. As Ryōi points out, "In the Buddhist scriptures, a man who leaves his home and practices the Way of the Buddha without taking the tonsure is called an *ubasoku*. This refers to Genji. He is described thus because he has yet to take the tonsure" (*Genji shō*, 338).

117. The text says only *itsutsu no mono* (the five objects). The translation follows Ryōi in specifying them as the five elements (earth, water, fire, wind, and air), whose coalescence is birth and whose disintegration is death (*Genji shō*, 339).

118. The retired emperor's poem. Ryōi conjectures that it was composed on his attainment of enlightenment as a result of Genji's admonition.

119. The term used is *nyūjō*, meaning simply "entering meditational trance" but also used as a euphemism for death. In the case of a very eminent monk, however, like Kōbō Daishi (774–835), it may suggest that he had not in fact died but is resting in his mausoleum in an extremely deep trance. The variant text states explicitly that Genji does the same as Kōbō Daishi.

120. No such place-name is found in the surviving records. The variant text says Ōjōgatani, likewise unknown.

121. The poem, Ryōi suggests, exemplifies the doctrine of non-duality, according to which the cycle of birth and death itself is tantamount to nirvana (*Genji shō*, 344).

122. The pheasant, crane, and swallow are the birds most renowned for their selfless defense and care of their young.

123. In this case, the stag.

124. Korehide and Okabe.

125. As Ryōi puts it: "In spite of all these instances of consideration in the subhuman world, Genji has gone, where they do not know, without a trace, without a sign, without a sound" (*Genji shō*, 348).

126. The variant text prefers Reisen (or perhaps Reizen).

127. His only child by the Kokiden Dame of Honor, a daughter of Tō no Chūjō.

128. The daughter of Higekuro and Tamakazura.

129. Ryōi cites *Enanshi* as the source of this allusion: "Mencius, seeing a skein of thread, wept because it could be made either yellow or black" (*Genji shō*, 354). That is, His Majesty's thoughts are not steadfast, as they must be to attain enlightenment, but take on the hue of whatever whimsy happens to cross his mind.

130. *Honrai kū*, the doctrine that all phenomena are devoid of substance.

131. The Tendai abbot from Mount Hiei. Ryōi identifies him as the abbot whose ministrations were needed when Aoi no Ue gave birth to Yūgiri ("Aoi," 13:35; *Genji shō*, 355–56). But because Yūgiri is in his thirtieth year by the end of the "Maboroshi" chapter and "Sumori" begins at least thirteen years later, at this point in the narrative this particular abbot would be a very old man—perhaps even impossibly old.

132. A more literal rendition would be "roll their eyes in delight."

133. Although this sentence as it stands is clearly affirmative (*obosaredo*), Ryōi's gloss indicates that he reads it as negative (*obosanedo*), which does indeed make more sense (*Genji shō*, 356). Imanishi follows his lead, as does this translation (*Genji monogatari Kumogakure rokujō*, 2:111n.20).

134. Ryōi identifies the Kōgyoku Empress (594–661; r. 642–645) and the Daigo Emperor (885–930; r. 897–930) as the "sage kings" of Japan. The legend that the emperor was condemned to hell is recounted in *Taiheiki* and *Kitano Tenjin engi*. See Imanishi, *Genji monogatari Kumogakure rokujō,* 2:111n.21.

135. Kurōdo no Shōshō, a son of Tō no Chūjō, and thus a brother of the lady in question.

136. No officiant is named, but Ryōi suggests that it is the Tendai abbot who administers the vows (*Genji shō*, 361).

137. The parable comparing this mundane world to a burning house is found in chapter 3 of the Lotus Sutra, "Simile and Parable," and the parable of the jewel hidden in the lining of the poor man's robe, in chapter 8, "Prophesy of Enlightenment for the Five Hundred Disciples."

138. The text is corrupt here. Ii suggests that the principal object of imperial concern is the Second Princess, the daughter of the reigning emperor ("Kumogakure rokujō," 6–7). Imanishi speculates that *uchi* maybe a mistake for *chichi*, and thus the emperor here wishes that his father were still alive (*Genji monogatari Kumogakure rokujō*, 2:112). Ryōi interprets the passage similarly, except that he has the emperor wishing that Genji were still alive, thinking that he might be able to deter Kaoru from this strange pattern of behavior, but of course this interpretation completely ignores the word *mikado* (emperor) (*Genji shō*, 363–64). The translation here owes something to all these interpretations.

139. In 858, Prince Korehito, son of the empress and grandson of Fujiwara no Yoshifusa, succeeded to the throne as the Seiwa Emperor in place of his elder brother Prince Koretaka, whose mother was only a Mistress of the Wardrobe.

140. Because they all are children of the same mother, the Akashi Empress.

141. Readers will have noticed that the current crown prince's views on this subject are not mentioned. Ryōi, too, notes that "these seem to be the words of the Second Prince" and speculates that this must be because the crown prince likewise has no desire to become emperor and both brothers agree that Niou is far more talented than either of them (*Genji shō*, 365).

142. Her sobriquet makes it clear that she is a princess (*miya*) whose straitened circumstances have forced her to become a lady-in-waiting.

143. As Ryōi (*Genji shō*, 371–72) notes, this phrase appears to derive from *Kokinshū* 1025:

arinu ya to kokoromigatera aimineba / tawaburenikuki made zo koishiki
Can I survive without her? I wondered, yet when I stopped seeing her,
  I yearned for her so, it was hardly a matter for jest.

These "sordid events" are described in "Kagerō."

144. This vaguely defined office (*senji*) was held by a woman of high rank whose nominal duty was to transmit the emperor's commands to his private secretary (*kurōdo*). It was often held jointly by one of the palace attendants (*naishi*).

145. Kaoru's poem echoes one that Hanachirusato addresses to Genji when he visits her immediately before he leaves for Suma:

tsukikage no yadoreru sode wa sebakutomo / tometemo mibaya akanu hikari o
Narrow though they be, these sleeves of mine wherein dwells the light of the moon,
  how I wish they might stay its glow, of which I never tire. ("Suma," 13:167)

Because narrow sleeves are a euphemism for poverty, insignificance, and the like, it is interesting that Kaoru uses this metaphor to acknowledge Nakanokimi's new status as empress.

146. Ryōi notes that "in some texts there is a chapter entitled 'Hanami' [Blossom Viewing], which may be the same as this chapter. But variant texts are rare and thus this cannot be confirmed" (*Genji shō*, 376). The title does survive in some lists of *Genji* chapters, and modern scholars agree that it may have been a variant title for the now lost but once canonical chapter "Sakurahito." It is unlikely, however, that "Hanami" ever was a variant title for the apocryphal "Sakurahito." As the title of a once canonical chapter, "Sakurahito" was untranslatable, as in that context it was unclear whether *-hito* was a man or a woman. In this apocryphal chapter, however, the context makes it clear that "Sakurahito" is a man, Emperor Niou.

147. "Minori," 15:488–89.

148. The phrase is from *Kokinshū* 923, by Narihira, composed at Nunohiki Waterfall:

nukimidaru hito koso arurashi shiratama no / ma naku mo chiru ka sode no sebaki ni
Someone, it would appear, has loosed them; for the white jewels, in disarray,
fall without surcease, though my sleeves be too narrow for them.

149. Ryōi suggests that this "authorial intervention" (*sōshiji*) refers to Kaoru's clandestine visit to Nakanokimi in the previous chapter and hints at the possibility of an affair between them (*Genji shō*, 385).

150. The variant text is helpful here, specifying that "delights of the past, whether good or bad, all result from sins committed in previous lives" (Yasuda and Mitadera, eds., "Beppon 'Kumogakure rokujō,'" 68).

151. Ryōi suggests that Kaoru's "own lot" refers to Niou's affairs with both Ukifune and Miyanokimi (*Genji shō*, 386).

152. *Shūishū* 1299, by Tameyori, lamenting the loss of so many he had once known:

yo no naka ni aramashikaba to omou hito / naki ga ōku mo narinikeru ka na
Those friends of whom we think, "Were they but still among us in this world . . . ,"
and now it has come to this, alas, so many of them gone!

153. Ryōi takes this to mean that Kaoru was a source of strength to Niou, but it also was Kaoru who at times himself appeared capricious. The variant text, however, specifies that it is to the empress (*kisaki ni wa*), rather than Niou, that Kaoru has been such a source of strength and that the person thought capricious is Niou himself (*maro o*). See Yasuda and Mitadera, eds., "Beppon 'Kumogakure rokujō,'" 68.

154. At Uji.

155. Ryōi (*Genji shō*, 389) cites *Kokinshū* 897 as a possible source:

toritomuru mono ni shi araneba toshizuki o / aware ana u to sugoshitsuru kana
Since one cannot, after all, put a stop to them,
the months and years I pass simply sighing, "Ah how wretched."

156. The variant text prefers Shujaku.

157. Ukifune is her daughter by the Eighth Prince, with whom she had a brief affair before she married. Because her husband is of far inferior birth, she considers him unworthy to share the same roof with her well-born daughter.

158. *Kuchinu kogane*, more literally, "incorruptible gold," which, of course, refers to Ukifune.

159. Ryōi (*Genji shō*, 394) cites *Kokinshū* 851:

iro mo ka mo mukashi no kosa ni nioedomo / ueken hito no kage zo koishiki
Their beauty and their fragrance radiate with a redolence of old,
yet how I long to see the face of she who planted them.

160. Ryōi (*Genji shō*, 394) cites *Kokinshū* 6:

sakura iro ni koromo wa fukaku somete kimu / hana no chirinamu nochi no katami ni
Let me wear a robe dyed deeply the color of the cherries
as a keepsake of their blooms after they shall have fallen.

Compare *Kokinshū* 67, by Mitsune, sent to a person who had come to view his cherry blossoms:

waga yado no hana migatera ni kuru hito wa / chirinamu nochi zo koishikarubeki
He who came to call by way of viewing the blossoms in my garden
after they shall have fallen, then surely shall I miss him.

The phrase "after they shall have fallen" was repeated countless times in later poetry, sometimes even referring to plum blossoms and autumn leaves.

161. Imanishi (*Genji monogatari Kumogakure rokujō*, 2:134n.31) suggests an (anachronistic) allusion to a poem in the *Iwashimizu Wakamiya utaawase* of 1232:

tazunemiru hana mo nagori ya shitauran / kururu mo shirazu niou yamazakura
Do even these blossoms we come to view lament their passing beauty,
these mountain cherries, oblivious to the darkening day?

162. *Kokinshū* 90, by the Nara emperor (Heizei):

furusato to narinishi nara no miyako ni mo / iro wa kawarazu hana wa sakikeri
Even in the capital of Nara, now become our home of old,
the cherry blossoms again have bloomed, their hue unchanged.

163. Ryōi (*Genji shō*, 394–95) cites the following but does not identify the source:

torikaesu mono ni mogana ya yo no naka o / arishinagara no waga mi to omowan
How I wish that this world we live in were something that might be turned back,
that I might once again be what I had been in the past.

164. Many of the metaphors in this passage occur frequently in Buddhist scriptures, a few examples of which Ryōi quotes in his commentary (*Genji shō*, 395–97).

165. Son of the Suzaku Emperor who becomes the "reigning emperor" from the "Wakana" chapters to the end of the tale. He is the father of Kaoru's wife, the Second Princess, and thus is her child's grandfather.

166. His father, Prince Niou, also had been the Prince Minister of War.

167. Referring, of course, to the Cherry Blossom Festival in "Hana no en."

168. From the Saibara "Waie" (My Home): "In my home the curtains of her chamber are hung. Come, my great lord, you shall be my son. And what shall we serve you with your drink? Abalone, turbo, sea urchin—just the thing! Abalone, turbo, sea urchin—just the thing!" As befits a party turned riotous, all these delicacies are shellfish thought to resemble a woman's sexual organs.

169. The first quarter of the Hour of the Tiger extends from about 3:00 to 3:30 A.M.

170. Kaoru's liaison with this lady is mentioned in passing in "Kagerō," 17:234–35, 245; and in "Tenarai," 17:352–55, although nothing is said about a child being born of their union.

171. Translation of this passage follows Imanishi's emendations, based on the variant text (*Genji monogatari Kumogakure rokujō*, 2:122nn.3–4). The standard text omits Kozaishō's description of Kaoru's daughter, which leads Ryōi to regard Kaoru as the subject of *shinobishinobi no on-kokorozashi*, which in turn suggests to him the possibility that this phrase is a veiled hint that the deceased Third Prince was in fact the illegitimate son of Kaoru and the empress, conceived at the time of their meeting described in the previous chapter, "Sumori" (*Genji shō*, 402). Ryōi thus may have been misled by his own inadvertent error in the process of reworking the variant text.

172. Ryōi notes that the *Records of the Historian* describes Empress Lu's grief at the death of the Han emperor Gaozong as similarly so great that her tears failed to flow.

173. This refers to the legend that Emperor Wu of the Former Han dynasty (156–87 B.C.E.) was able to recall the ghost of his beloved Lady Li from the netherworld by burning a magical spirit return incense (*hangonkō*).

174. Ryōi (*Genji shō*, 406) cites *Shūishū* 1310:

ikani semu shinobu no kusa mo tsumiwabinu / katami no mieshi ko dani nakereba

What am I to do? When desolate, I pluck the fern of remembrance
without even a child to serve as a keepsake of her?

Niou does, of course, have a child by Nakanokimi, but even so, he will never forget her.

175. Ryōi takes this and the next poem to be Niou's words (*Genji shō*, 407). This translation follows Imanishi in assigning them to Kaoru, which seems more natural in the overall context of the narrative (*Genji monogatari Kumogakure rokujō*, 2:123nn.13–14).

176. *Kokinshū* 405:

shita no obi no michi wa katagata wakarutomo / yukimeguritemo awan to zo omou

Though the road parts, and like the undersash, we go our separate ways;
however we may wind about, surely we'll meet again.

177. The speaker of this poem is not identified. Ryōi believes it is Kaoru (*Genji shō*, 415); Imanishi, Ukifune (*Genji monogatari Kumogakure rokujō*, 2:134n.40); and Ii, the prelate. This translation follows Ii's interpretation in "Kumogakure rokujō," 13.

178. In the same manner as the prelate had done when she first took vows in Ono. The act is described in almost the same words in "Tenarai," 17:286–87.

179. Ryōi notes that the decorative combs (*sashigushi*) in this poem may indicate that this is the same chapter that elsewhere is referred to as "Sashigushi" (*Genji shō*, 416). Such a chapter title does appear in some lists of *Genji* chapters, but it is hardly likely that this is the text that once went with it.

180. This sentence is not entirely clear. The translation follows Ryōi's division of the words (*Genji shō*, 420), which Imanaishi also seems to accept (*Genji monogatari Kumogakure rokujō*, 2:125).

181. Ryōi points out that this sentence is open to two interpretations, the first being that in the translation and the second that there were many people recently passed away whom one would wish were still alive (*Genji shō*, 424–25).

182. Kaoru's children by Ukifune.

183. Genji's temple.

184. Probably to raise prey for their hunting hawks.

185. Ryōi suggests that this person might be the son of Niou's trusted factotum Tokikata (*Genji shō*, 427). In the variant text, this poem's situation is described in greater detail: "Long before, one very snowy day when hawking on this moor, His Lordship [Kaoru], on hearing Commander of the Left Gate Guards Toshishige remark that the snows [of age] seemed to fall only on him, recited a poem." On this basis, Imanishi suggests that this passage may have been inadvertently omitted from the standard text (*Genji monogatari Kumogakure rokujō*, 2:127n.15).

186. As Ryōi notes, "When you live at close quarters with such persons and see them every day, you tend not think of such things" (*Genji shō*, 427)

187. Brocade patterned with figures in red on a white ground, originally imported from Annam via China and later produced in Japan as well.

188. Literally, "saying *yaya*." The word is a gentle interjection, comparable to modern *chotto*.

189. Ryōi interprets this sentence as meaning that Shōshō no Kimi has heard that Kaoru went directly from Yokawa to Kōyasan and there ascended to the heavens (*Genji shō*, 429). Imanishi repeats this interpretation (*Genji monogatari Kumogakure rokujō*, 2:128n.6). The translation follows Ii's interpretation, which follows the text more closely, both semantically and syntactically ("Kumogakure rokujō," 15).

190. Niou.

191. Although Ryōi identifies this person with the Kitayama prelate (*Genji shō*, 430), he has no textual basis for doing so.

192. The variant text asks this question more specifically: "Which of the eight schools should I follow?" The Eight Schools are those that Gyōnen (1240–1321) singled out for explication in *Hasshū kōyō* (1268): the Kusha, Jōjitsu, Ritsu, Hossō, Sanron, Tendai, Kegon, and Shingon. See Kamata Shigeo, ed., *Hasshū kōyō* (Tokyo: Kōdansha, 1981).

193. The Eight Bridges (Yatsuhashi), made famous by Narihira's acrostic poem in *Ise monogatari* 9, are here a metaphor for the Eight Schools of Buddhist doctrine listed in the previous note.

194. As Ryōi notes, the argument here is based on the doctrine of the dharma nature, which underlies all phenomena and from which all phenomena are "born" (*Genji shō*, 432–33). Although this nature is inherent in all creatures, distracted as we are by the five desires, our knowledge of it is lost to us. In order to attain enlightenment, therefore, we must find our way back to the dharma nature that all along has been inside us. See the parable of the jewel hidden in the lining of the poor man's robe in chapter 8 of the Lotus Sutra, "Prophesy of Enlightenment for the Five Hundred Disciples."

195. Ryōi (*Genji shō*, 433) cites the *Zuo Commentary*: "People's minds are not all the same, just like their faces."

196. From chapter 5 of the Lotus Sutra, "The Parable of Medicinal Herbs."

197. Ryōi (*Genji shō*, 434) cites *Kokinshū* 257:

shiratsuyu no iro wa hitotsu o ikani shite / aki no ko no ha o chiji ni somuran
The clear dew has but a single hue; how then does it
dye the autumn leaves their myriad colors?

198. The worlds of desire, the material, and the immaterial into which the not yet enlightened may be reborn, depending on the degree of their progress toward enlightenment.

199. The six levels of existence through which the unenlightened wander in the cycle of birth, death, and rebirth.

200. In Buddhist cosmology, the billion worlds, each presided over by a buddha, the world we inhabit being but one of them.

201. *Nikugen*, the least of the Five Eyes of Buddhist doctrine, the other four being the *tengen* of heavenly beings; *egen*, the eye of wisdom; *hōgen*, the dharma eye of the bodhisattva; and the *butsugen* of the Buddha.

202. *Shingen*, the vision of transic meditation.

203. This lady appears nowhere else in the standard text. A lady holding the same office, said to have lived in the sixteenth century, is mentioned in the colophon of the variant texts, one version of which is translated in the introduction to this translation. What the connection between these Naishi might be, no doubt only Ryōi knows. For the Japanese text, see Yasuda and Mitadera, "Beppon 'Kumogakure rokujō,'" 73.

204. *Shiki hyōrin* is a Ming-dynasty commentary on the *Records of the Historian*, completed in 1576. Ii suggests that in contemporary lore, this work may have been thought to have been dedicated to a temple (*Genji monogatari no densetsu*, 123). In any case, it postdates *Genji* by more than five hundred years, so could not have been known to Murasaki Shikibu.

205. No record of this person exists.

206. No record of this person exists. An earlier Fujiwara no Chikakane, descended from Michinaga's elder brother Michitaka (953–995), died in 1246. This second colophon is omitted from editions published in Edo.

207. The texts translated here are conveniently collected in Tokiwai Kazuko, *Genji monogatari kokeizu no kenkyū* (Tokyo: Kasama Shoin, 1973), 303–8. Other versions of the texts are cited in notes to the individual texts. Yet another genealogy that includes characters from "Sumori," but had not been published at the time Tokiwai's book appeared, is in the collection of the Tsurumi University Library. This text, now known as the *Tsurumi Genealogy*, has since been briefly introduced in two exhibition catalogs: *Geirin shūyō: Tsurumi Daigaku Toshokan shinchiku kinen kichō toshoroku* (Yokohama: Tsurumi Daigaku Toshokan, 1986); and *Kotenseki to kohitsugire: Tsurumi Daigaku zō kichōshoten kaisetsu zuroku* (Yokohama: Tsurumi Daigaku, 1994). More recently, the section of the *Tsurumi Genealogy* dealing with characters from "Sumori" was reproduced and its distinctive features analyzed in Inaga Keiji, "Sumori monogatari to Hakuga Sanmi—*Genji monogatari* no bōryū kōsō no jinbutsu settei to moderu," in *Yasuda Joshi Daigaku Daigakuin hakushi katei kansei kinen ronbunshū* (Hiroshima: Yasuda Joshi Daigaku, 1999), 1–12; and Kuboki Hideo, "*Genji monogatari* Sumori no maki kanren shiryō saikō," in *Heian bungaku no shin kenkyū: monogatari-e to kohitsugire o kangaeru*, ed. Kuge Hirotoshi and Kuboki Hideo (Tokyo: Shintensha, 2006), 255–85.

208. So called because they predate that completed by Sanjōnishi Sanetaka (1455–1537) in 1488.

209. In *Genji monogatari kokeizu no kenkyū*, 295, Tokiwai cites an article by Nakano Kōichi, "Sumori monogatari oboegaki," *Bungaku gogaku* 12 (1959): 83–93, in which she points out that the Shirakawa estate (Shirakawa no In) could not be Niou's estate because it had always been owned by the Fujiwara regental house or their close relations, and thus Niou would have had no claim to it. Sumori, however, because she was a Fujiwara, might well have had access to it.

210. *Sengenshō* locates this mountain "in the vicinity of Ninnaji" (1381). See Inaga Keiji, *Genji monogatari no kenkyū: seiritsu to denryū* (Tokyo: Kasama Shoin, 1967), 497.

211. We know of this princess's existence only through a brief mention in "Wakana, jō" (15:2): *onnamiyatachi namu yotokoro owashimashikeru*. On why the Fourth Princess may have been so dissatisfied as to leave the palace and take vows, see Inaga, *Genji monogatari no kenkyū*, 497–99.

212. Tokiwai, *Genji monogatari kokeizu no kenkyū*, 294.

213. Higuchi Yoshimaro, ed., *Ōchō monogatari shūka sen* (Tokyo: Iwanami Shoten, 1989), 2:316.

214. Nakano, "Sumori monogatari oboegaki," 92.

215. Tokiwai, *Genji monogatari kokeizu no kenkyū*, 300–301.

216. Inaga, *Genji monogatari no kenkyū*, 413–523.

217. Inaga, *Genji monogatari no kenkyū*, 496.

218. Inaga, *Genji monogatari no kenkyū*, 505–6.

219. Inaga, *Genji monogatari no kenkyū*, 489–90.

220. Katō Masayoshi and Kuboki Hideo, "Kokubungaku Kenkyū Shiryōkan zō Hikaru Genji keizu: kaidai, chūkai," *Heian bungaku no kochū to juyō* 2 (2009): 2–10; Katō Masayoshi and Furuta Masayuki, "Kokubungaku Kenkyū Shiryōkan zō Hikaru Genji keizu: honkoku," *Heian bungaku no kochū to juyō* 2 (2009): 11–16.

221. Ikeda Kazuomi, "*Genji monogatari* ni wa gojū-yon-jō igai no maki ga atta—San'itsu shita Sumori no maki no ko-shahon dankan," *Jissen Joshi Daigaku bungei shiryō kenkyūjo nenpō* 29 (2010): 48–62.

222. Text also in Horibe, "'Sakurahito,' 'Samushiro,' 'Sumori' kō," 173. Horibe's interpretation of this fragment follows on 180–83.

223. Text also in Nakayama Yasumasa, ed., *Kōchū kokka taikei*, vol. 23 (Tokyo: Seibundō, 1934); Higuchi Yoshimaro, ed., *Ōchō monogatari shūka sen*, vol. 1 (Tokyo: Iwanami Shoten, 1987); and Horibe, "'Sakurahito,' 'Samushiro,' 'Sumori' kō," 172.

224. Compare *Shūishū* 49, a poem by Lady Ise, written to be inscribed on a folding screen of the High Priestess of Kamo, the scene depicting a person walking along a mountain road:

chirichirazu kikamahoshiki wo furusato no / hana mite kaeru hito mo awanan
I should like to ask whether or not they scatter; would that I might meet someone who returns from viewing the blossoms in the old capital.

Tokiwai points out that *chirichirazu* might be taken as Kaoru's indirect way of expressing his concern whether a certain woman would "submit or not," but given the nonchalance of the poem as a whole, as well as the fact that it is placed in the "Spring" chapter of *Fūyōshū*, she thinks it safer to take it at face value (*Genji monogatari kokeizu no kenkyū*, 295).

225. Probably Ōuchiyama. See Higuchi, ed., *Ōcho monogatari shūka sen*, 2:316.

226. Probably the First Princess, daughter of the Akashi Empress and the reigning emperor. See Horibe, "'Sakurahito,' 'Samushiro,' 'Sumori' kō," 185–86.

227. Text also in Murasaki Shikibu, *Genji monogatari taisei*, ed. Ikeda Kikan (Tokyo: Chūōkōronsha, 1953–1956), 7:499–500. A photograph of the manuscript of the passage translated here appears in the unnumbered pages of the front matter of Ikeda's book.

228. It would probably be more accurate to say that he had been promoted by the time of the progress. The text says only, "the present Prince Minister of War, formerly known as Prince Sochi."

229. Gon Dainagon, Jūni-i (d. Ōei 27.4.21 [1420]).

230. In extant texts, she does not appear in "Tenarai."

231. Also discussed in Ikeda, ed., *Genji monogatari jiten*, 2:79a.

232. Quoting "Kōbai," 16:37.

233. Text also in *Genji monogatari taisei*, ed. Ikeda, 7:201; photo on 7:200.

234. *Genji keizu kokagami.*

235. The following headings indicate the father of the person(s) described.

236. Extant texts do not identify the Fourth Prince as Prince Sochi, and he dances rather than sings "Autumn Winds" (12:387). The identification of this Fourth Prince as Prince Sochi/Hotaru was first advanced in the medieval commentary *Kakaishō.* Although some scholars now regard Sochi/Hotaru to be the third son of the Kiritsubo emperor (Ikeda, ed., *Genji monogatari jiten*, 2:394, 418), others continue to follow *Kakaishō* (Inaga, *Genji monogatari no kenkyū*, 462–67).

237. Conflates Gen Sanmi and Jijū?

238. In honor of the fiftieth birthday of the Suzaku Emperor.

239. Current consensus identifies this lady as a daughter of the Minister of the Right. See Ikeda, ed., *Genji monogatari jiten*, 2:395, 419.

240. Meaning her stepbrother, the son of Kōbai.

241. Probably referring to the Genji lineage rather than Hikaru Genji the individual.

242. The principal texts I consulted in making this translation are Ikeda Kikan, ed., *Kohon Yamaji no tsuyu*, in *Genji monogatari*, ed. Ikeda Kikan (Tokyo: Asahi Shinbunsha, 1955), 7:243–92; Hon'iden Shigeyoshi, ed., *Genji monogatari Yamaji no tsuyu* (Tokyo: Kasama Shoin, 1970); Yamagishi and Imai, eds., *Yamaji no tsuyu, Kumogakure rokujō*; Inaga, "Yamaji no tsuyu," 261–354; and Ogawa Yōko, "Yamaji no tsuyu kōhon," in *Genji monogatari kyōju-shi no kenkyū* (Tokyo: Kasama Shoin, 2009), 326–538. A detailed bibliography listing texts, commentaries, and scholarship on "Yamaji no tsuyu," compiled by Oka Yōko, is included in Inaga, "Yamaji no tsuyu," 336–39.

243. Most modern reference works render this gentleman's surname as "Kazan'in." Contemporary sources, however, are unanimous in pronouncing it "Kasannoin."

244. Now known as the *Koreyuki shaku* or the *Genji shaku*.

245. Hon'iden, ed., *Genji monogatari Yamaji no tsuyu*, 21–26.

246. Hon'iden, ed., *Genji monogatari Yamaji no tsuyu*, 26–28.

247. They are also referred to as the number-one line (*daiichi-rui*) and number-two line (*daini-rui*), respectively.

248. This text was published by Ikeda under the title *Kohon Yamaji no tsuyu*. See especially his brief introduction, 245–47.

249. Compare Kaoru's poem in "Kagerō," 17:264, on which that chapter's name is based:

ari to mite te ni wa torarezu mireba mata / yukue mo shirazu kieshi kagerō
There it is, yet I cannot take it in my hand; again I see it,
only for it to vanish without a trace, this drake fly.

250. "Yume no ukihashi," 17:370.

251. In the smoke from the incense burned by Emperor Wu of the Han dynasty, he saw the image of his deceased love Lady Li.

252. *Kokinshū* 878:

waga kokoro nagusamekanetsu sarashina ya / obasuteyama ni teru tsuki o mite
Utterly inconsolable was my heart, there in Sarashina,
gazing at the moon that shone on Abandoned Crone Mountain.

Later commentary suggests that the poem may have been composed by someone who had abandoned a grandparent on the mountain or by an old person who had been so abandoned. Neither notion has any known basis in fact.

253. His mistake in relinquishing Nakanokimi to Niou.

254. The translation of this sentence follows an emendation suggested by Hon'iden, who speculates that *kokoro-okure* may be an error for *kokoro-okite*, in *Genji monogatari Yamaji no tsuyu*, 37–38n.16. In support of this hypothesis, he cites a phrase in *Genji* describing Kaoru's determination to take vows in identical terms.

255. The pearl of Buddhahood, famous from the parable in the Lotus Sutra, chapter 8, "Prophecy of Enlightenment for Five Hundred Disciples."

256. *Kokinshū* 727, by Ono no Komachi, alluded to in "Shiigamoto," 16:198:

ama no sumu sato no shirube ni aranaku ni/uramimu to nomi hito no iuramu

Though I be no guide to this village where fisherfolk live,
everyone seems to be saying, "Let us tour this shore."

257. With Kaoru coming to take Ukifune to the capital. See "Ukifune."

258. Textual problems make it unclear whether Ukifune means the man who loved her or the man she loved. See Inaga, "Yamaji no tsuyu," 312n.16.

259. *Kokinshū* 683:

ise no ama no asa na yū na ni kazuku chō/miru me ni hito o aku yoshi mo ga na

Like the "see" weed for which the fisherfolk of Ise dive day and night,
how I wish I might "see" her as often as I should like.

260. The manuscript line is more specific: *shidokenaki kichō o hikinaoshi* (she straightened out her curtained screen, which was in disarray).

261. Perhaps an allusion to *Kokin rokujō* 371:

yūyami wa michi tadotadoshi tsuki machite/kaere waga seko sono aida ni mimu

In the dusk the way will be hard to find; so await the moon, my dear,
before you return, and in the meantime let us make love.

262. Probably because its color marks it as coming from a nun.

263. Hon'iden suggests that this sentence can also be taken to mean "Someone out there seems a bit lacking in taste [for encouraging Ukifune to write to her own mother on such somber paper,]" he said with a smile as he opened it. "Or could she herself have been this downcast?" (*Genji monogatari Yamaji no tsuyu*, 158, suppl. note to 49). But since this interpretation requires the reader to ignore the absence of any honorific language in reference to Ukifune, this translation follows the dictates of grammar and assumes that Kaoru is the subject.

264. Hon'iden notes that in *Genji monogatari*, "darkness of the heart" invariably refers to a parent's concern for a child but that Ukyō no Daibu, whom he considers the author of this work, uses the expression in a broader range of senses, including the cares of love (*Genji monogatari Yamaji no tsuyu*, 49n.11).

265. Both Ikeda (*Kohon Yamaji no tsuyu*, 262n.3) and Hon'iden (*Genji monogatari Yamaji no tsuyu*, 158, suppl. note to 50) suggest a possible source in a Chinese poem included in *Wakan rōei shū*.

266. Recalling Genji's visit to Suetsumuhana in "Yomogiu," 13:337–38.

267. Both suitably ecclesiastical colors.

268. The manuscript line is more specific. It is her eyebrows and not her eyes that he finds alluring, for now that she has become a nun they would have grown back.

269. Inaga suggests that alternatively, *sekitomegataki* (unstoppable) might be taken to refer to Kaoru himself rather than his tears ("Yamaji no tsuyu," 313n.28).

270. Hon'iden suggests that this is an allusion to a Chinese poem by Sō Gyoku (*Genji monogatari Yamaji no tsuyu*, 159, suppl. note to 54).

271. Her affair with Niou. See "Ukifune."

272. To return to secular life. Hon'iden notes that although the text of the letter in which the prelate makes this recommendation is ambiguous and difficult to pin down precisely, the author of *Yamaji no tsuyu* clearly takes it to mean this (*Genji monogatari Yamaji no tsuyu*, 160–61, suppl. note to 57).

273. Compare "Kagerō," 17:225: "Ever since he had first felt the attraction, he had traveled on this steep mountain road, but now he could hardly bear to hear the name of the village." Uji, the name of the village, is a near homonym of the adjective *ushi*, meaning "dismal, miserable."

274. The poem from which the title of this "chapter" obviously is drawn.

275. The nuns' remark borders on overt indecency, for it strongly suggests, through reference to the *Kokinshū*, that Kaoru removed Ukifune's trousers during that "intimate scene in the presence of the Buddha":

nanihito ka kite nugikakeshi fujibakama / kuru aki goto ni nobe o niowasu
Who is it that comes and takes off his purple trousers, then hangs them up,
thus scenting the fields with the coming of every autumn? (*Kokinshū* 239)

nushi shiranu ka koso nioere aki no no ni / ta ga nugikakeshi fujibakama zo mo
A scent the bearer of which I know not pervades; yet who is it
that takes off his purple trousers and hangs them up in the fields? (*Kokinshū* 241)

276. Ukifune's letter to her mother, which Kaoru had taken from Kogimi.

277. Compare Genji's poem in "Yugao," 12:262:

mishi hito no keburi o kumo to nagamureba / yūbe no sora mo mutsumajiki kana
If I think of these clouds as smoke from the pyre of my love,
then even this cloudy evening sky seems lovely.

278. "Yume no ukihashi," 17:362. The Yokawa prelate tells Kaoru the story of the discovery of Ukifune and her sojourn in Ono.

279. "Ukifune," 17:187. On a scroll listing the names of the sutras and the number of times they had been chanted, she wrote:

kane no oto no tayuru hibiki ni ne o soete / waga yo tsukinu to kimi ni tsutaeyo
To the fading echo of the bell, pray add the sound of my weeping,
to carry the word to her that my life has run its course.

280. A large mountain in the province of Hitachi, thus a fitting nickname for Ukifune's mother, wife of the (vice) governor of Hitachi. The original coinage is Ukon's, in "Kagerō," 17:222. Elsewhere it is used to refer more generally to the family of the governor, including his adopted daughter Ukifune. See "Azumaya," 17:11.

281. The manuscript line reads "as if you were a stranger."

282. In fact, he is the vice governor of the province of Hitachi (Hitachi no Suke). But since he is always referred to as *kami* in the "Yamaji no tsuyu" text, he is designated as "the governor" throughout this translation.

283. The verb used is *kei su*, which normally indicates humble speech directed to an empress, a dowager empress, or (rarely) an emperor. As Hon'iden notes, its use here, to refer to speech addressed to Kaoru, is inappropriate (*Genji monogatari Yamaji no tsuyu*, 67n.15). Perhaps the author means to illustrate yet another aspect of the governor's rustic manners?

284. The translation follows the emendation suggested by Inaga, replacing *momikogaeru* with *modaekogareru* ("Yamaji no tsuyu," 316n.54).

285. Ikeda assigns these words to the mother, but their larger context makes attribution to the nun more plausible, as suggested by the interlinear notes in the printed line (*Kohon Yamaji no tsuyu*, 277).

286. The translation of this sentence follows the emendation proposed by Inaga, based on the reasonable assumption that the repetition of *-mahoshiki* twice in the same sentence distracted the copyist, thus causing the omission of the mother's speech to the nun ("Yamaji no tsuyu," 316n.60).

287. "Tenarai," 17:280.

288. "Tenarai," 17:287–88, 297–98.

289. "Tenarai," 17:311.

290. That is, Ajari. In fact, her brother had long since been promoted from Ajari to Sōzu, and thus in the last two chapters of *Genji* ("Tenarai" and "Yume no ukihashi"), he is known as the Prelate of Yokawa.

291. Compare the description of her hair, as seen by the peeping Chūjō, in "Tenarai," 17:338. The meaning of "fivefold fan" is obscure.

292. Compare the scene depicted at the beginning of "Kagerō," 17:191–93.

293. For Niou's return to form, see "Kagerō," 17:254–56.

294. In reading *nodoyaka naru* for *nodoyaka naku*, this translation follows Ikeda, *Kohon Yamaji no tsuyu*, 282, and Hon'iden, *Genji monogatari Yamaji no tsuyu*, 79. As Ikeda points out, this reading echoes an analogous passage in "Yūgao" describing Genji and the Ukon, who waits upon Yūgao.

295. This translation follows the emendation of *tayumashiki* for *tayumajiki*, suggested by Hon'iden, *Genji monogatari Yamaji no tsuyu*, 165, suppl. note to 79.

296. An allusion to the "The Song of Everlasting Sorrow," the same poem to which the Kiritsubo Emperor alludes after the death of his beloved Mistress of the Wardrobe in "Kiritsubo," 12:111.

297. This and the next paragraph beginning "I wonder if" are translations of material from the manuscript line that Inaga added to the printed line. He explains his reasons for doing so in "Yamaji no tsuyu," 340–54.

298. Compare *Kokinshū* 24:

tokiwa naru matsu no midori mo haru kureba / ima hitoshio no iro masarikeri
Even the everlasting green of the pines, with the coming of spring,
takes on a shade that has grown only the more so.

299. *Goya no okonai. Goya* is the last of the "six hours" into which the day of a religious is divided.

300. "Tenarai," 17:311.

301. Editors suggest possible allusions to *Kokinshū* 333:

kenu ga ue ni mata mo furishike harugasumi / tachinaba miyuki mare ni koso mime
Upon snows not yet thawed, snow again; for once the spring mists have risen,
rare indeed will be the chance to see such deep snows again.

and to *Gyokuyōshū* 963:

shita kōru miyama no yuki no kenu ga ue ni / ima ikue to ka furikasanuramu
Upon snows fallen deep in the mountains upon snows not yet melted
how many more layers will fall to cover them over?

302. Editors suggest a possible allusion to *Shinkokinshū* 1132:

fuji no ne no kemuri mo nao zo tachinoboru / ue naki mono wa omoi narikeri
Higher still than the peak of Fuji rises its smoke
and even higher than them all burn these flames of passion.

303. Editors suggest possible allusions to *Shūishū* 1144:

miyamagi o asa na yū na ni koritsumete / samusa o kouru ono no sumiyaki
Night and day, cutting and gathering wood from the mountains,
hoping all the while for cold weather, the charcoal makers of Ono.

and to *Horikawa hyakushu*:

ōhara ya ono no sumigama yuki furite / kokorobosoge ni tatsu kemuri kana
Ōhara! Snow falling on the charcoal kilns of Ono
while their smoke rises up forlornly.

and to *Shokugoshūishū* 497:

towabaya na ono no sumigama onozukara / kayoishi michi wa yuki fukakutomo
I would ask of you, charcoal kilns of Ono,
how fares that road I once traveled, deep though the snow may be?

304. Where his other wife, the daughter of Yūgiri, lives.
305. *Shinkokinshū* 1050:

mikari suru kariba no ono no narashiba no / nare wa masarade koi zo masareru
As with the twigs of oak on the imperial hunting ground at Ono,
our intimacy fails to progress while my passion only mounts.

306. The expression is not attested elsewhere. Hon'iden speculates that it might be a colloquial way of referring to a tryst with a lover whom one can meet only rarely but whom one hopes to meet at least before the year is over (*Genji monogatari Yamaji no tsuyu*, 91n.11).

Chapter 6
Medieval Commentary

"BY WHAT MEANS DO WE ATTRIBUTE VALUE to works of art, and how do our evaluations affect our ways of attending to them?"[1] In the case of *The Tale of Genji*, the short answers to this double-edged question would be that the most voluminous of all such means was exegetical commentary and that this "form of attention" encouraged readers to regard *Genji* in ways that hitherto had been considered more appropriate to the Chinese classics or the Buddhist scriptures than to anonymous fictions written in prose.

As we have seen in previous chapters, in its earliest years *Genji* was treated principally as a romance, written "by a woman, for women, and about women."[2] This form of attention was a bountiful source of percipient and witty responses to *Genji*, though far too few of them were recorded. It was also completely compatible with that attitude to noncanonical texts, prevalent in manuscript cultures, in which each copyist feels free to make creative (or corrective) contributions to his or her own copy, uninhibited by the notion that the work in question might be regarded as in any way inviolable. Sei Shōnagon does lament how humiliating it is for the author of a tale when someone copies it badly or, worse, notes in the margin that something had to be "corrected" or, worse still, "left as is."[3] But for the most part, creative copying and even radical rewriting were regarded as literary acts just as legitimate as original authorship. With the application of commentarial modes of thinking to *The Tale of Genji*, all this changed.

If attitudes to noncanonical works can be described as creative or even forward-looking—in the sense that they mean to improve on the received text for the benefit of future readers—then commentarial thinking can only be described as conservative and retrospective. Commentarial tradition advances not by introducing new ideas and theories, but by looking to the past, not only to preserve the text as it was originally written, but also to consult previous commentary, on which to build further contributions to the study of the work in question. We may regret the loss of the spontaneity, daring, and wit of the ladies in *A Nameless Notebook*, and lament some of the outlandish notions that come from delving too deeply into obscure corners of the past. But neither can it be denied that in virtually every one of the multitude of commentaries compiled over the past eight hundred years there lie nuggets of observation and discovery that remain indispensable to our contemporary understanding of *Genji*. A glance at the annotation appended to almost any modern edition of *Genji* shows that exegetical commentary neither has outlived its usefulness nor will cease to be a major form of *Genji* scholarship in years to come.

Unfortunately, exegetical commentary is also the most difficult form of attention to illustrate concisely and does not lend itself to easy summary. The vastness of the corpus alone makes it impossible to convey a full sense of its riches with a few random samples, however judiciously chosen. And many of the annotations that might be offered as exemplars of the art, when torn from their context and translated, may seem either so cryptic as to demand further commentary of their own or so prolix as to conceal their virtues in verbiage—cryptic because they were not written to be read but to serve as aides-mémoires for an author who used them as lecture notes, and prolix because commentary is cumulative and its compilers often quote extensively from previous commentaries and other texts in the course of elaborating their own contributions to the discourse.

Commentary, then, is a very mixed bag. It presumes, in the first place, that you have a text of *Genji* on your desk alongside it and that you will immediately apply its comments to that text. Then, too, commentary is almost never neutral. It intends not only to remove obstacles to the understanding of the text to which it applies, but often to lead the reader to a "proper" understanding of that text—an understanding that may go beyond what the author actually states but that the commentator feels certain she must have meant.

Our introduction to the wealth of medieval commentary on *Genji* must therefore attempt to negotiate a compromise between the impossibility of fullness and the inconclusiveness of random illustration. No compromise is ideal, but the one we have chosen is this: we first briefly introduce the major mainstream commentaries, the salient features of each, and its place in the development of the tradition. Then we sample a few works that are anomalous to the tradition, yet of great importance in their own right. One is a commentary by the *renga* (classical linked verse) master Sōgi (1421–1502) devoted entirely to the famous "rainy night ranking of women" in the "Hahakigi" chapter of *Genji*. Another introduces the work of Kaoku Gyokuei (1526–after 1602), one of the very few women known to have written commentary on *Genji* in the medieval era. Finally, we translate a short passage from Kitamura Kigin's (1624–1705) *Kogetsushō*, the last of those works that in the Edo period came to be called the "Old Commentaries." The net result of this compromise is a rather short chapter on the most voluminous form of attention ever paid to *The Tale of Genji*, but one that, we hope, will suggest both the breadth and the depth of this rich tradition.

Tracing the development of this tradition, from its origins in textual criticism and simple glosses into a massive body of exegesis, is itself one of the many rewards of studying *Genji* commentary. The elements of the process had long been familiar to the educated in Japan, having been transmitted from China first via the Korean Peninsula and then through direct contact with the mainland. As in China, the principal objects of commentary in Japan were the Confucian classics and the Buddhist scriptures. At first no one felt any need to explicate *Genji*. It was written in the language of its day, about the people of its day. Nor had it any pretensions whatever to philosophical or doctrinal authority that might require further elucidation. As we have seen, almost two centuries were to pass between the first compilation of the *Genji* text and the *Roppyakuban utaawase* (1193), in which Fujiwara no Shunzei was to insist that "to compose poetry without having read *Genji* is inexcusable."[4] This declaration is rightly seen as signaling a turning point in attitudes to *Genji*.

The subsequent growth of a tradition of exegetical commentary is often linked to the increasing difficulty of understanding the language of *Genji* that came naturally with the passage of time. No doubt this was a contributing factor, but far more important was the growing sense, clearly evident in Shunzei's pronouncement, that *Genji* should be required reading for any person of culture, that *Genji* was becoming canonical, a classic. And in the cultural milieu of East Asia, the intellectual traditions of which were, and are, so predominantly exegetical, it was inevitable that *The Tale of Genji* should become the object of commentary. What, then, was the process by which this nascent attitude to *Genji* burgeoned into a tradition of exegetical commentary?

The attitude articulated in Shunzei's dictum of 1193 had begun to manifest itself in various forms well before the turn of the thirteenth century. Both Shunzei and his son Teika were collating several texts of *Genji*, with the aim of establishing an authoritative recension, an "ideal" text that would approximate as closely as possible the no longer extant text written by Murasaki Shikibu. And they were joined in this activity by Minamoto no Mitsuyuki and his son Chikayuki, with whom they regularly shared their knowledge and their manuscripts.[5] It was these two houses that were to produce the two texts of *Genji* that have remained the most authoritative to the present day. In describing their efforts, these collaborators mention many other texts that they consulted—a text in the hand of Fujiwara no Yukinari, the Koreyuki manuscript—most of which survive only in fragments, if at all. Comparison and analysis were the most important aspects of this particular project, but it was from this work that the first sprouts of a commentarial tradition grew.

Related to the quest for an authoritative text was the quest for a deeper understanding of *Genji*. Like readers everywhere, the readers of *Genji* sometimes wrote little notes to themselves in the margins and between the lines of their texts. Most of these marginalia have been lost with the texts in which they were written. But in two cases that we know of, some were preserved. Sesonji (Fujiwara) no Koreyuki (d. 1175), for reasons he does not explain, decided to collect the marginalia from his own text in a separate volume that now, under the title *Genji shaku* or *Koreyuki shaku*, is considered the earliest extant commentary on *The Tale of Genji*. Koreyuki seems to have been concerned primarily to identify the literary sources, both Japanese and Chinese, to which Murasaki alludes in the tale. And so, in transferring his notes from text to notebook, he would usually preface them with a summary of the context in which they occurred. He also seems to have conceived his project as ongoing, for in later versions of his work some entries have been considerably expanded. For example, in the Maeda text:

> In the "ranking of women" passage where it says, "Choose this one, and there you are; if she measures up in one way, she'll be lacking in another . . ."

shika areba to areba kakari kaku sureba / ana iishirazu au sa kiru sa ni
If you choose thinking "there is this," but then if you decide on that . . .
I hardly know what to say. Having the one, she'll lack the other.[6]

In the later Shoryōbu text, this is expanded to read:

> In the "rainy night ranking of women" passage (Uma no Kami's story) where it says, "When you give some thought to the one woman you must choose to be the mistress of your house, you realize how many important matters there are that can go wrong if she is not equal to the task. Choose one, and there you are: if she measures up in one way, she'll be lacking in another . . ."

shika ~~ari to~~ [*shikari tote*; *-reba* in variant texts] *to sureba kakari kaku*
sureba / ana iishirazu au sa kiru sa ni

If you choose thinking "there is this," but then if you decide on that . . .
I hardly know what to say. Having the one, she'll lack the other.[7]

Thus begins the long line of medieval commentaries on *Genji*. A reader happens on a phrase that he recognizes from another context. It is made up of two noncontiguous *ku* from a variant version of a poem in the *Kokinshū* (no. 1060), and in a discussion of the difficulties of choosing a wife, the allusion lends a lightly ironic touch of humor to the speaker's lament. Koreyuki, the reader, appreciates this and jots down the source poem between the lines of his text, next to the phrase that draws on it (or perhaps in a margin or on slip of paper that he glues to the margin). Or he may jot down something gleaned from a note in a borrowed manuscript. As these marginalia accumulate, he decides that it would be more convenient to transfer them to a separate notebook, at which time he notes, along with the poem, the phrase in the text with which it belongs. Thereafter, in a new, and presumably larger, notebook, this same information is augmented with a fuller citation of the passage in *Genji*, which also identifies the speaker as well as variant versions of the source poem.

This is only one of the hundreds of notes that Koreyuki scribbled into his text of *Genji*. Elsewhere he identifies Murasaki's many allusions to the "Song of Everlasting Sorrow" (J. Chōgonka) in "Kiritsubo," and he points out another such reference in "Suetsumuhana," in which Genji slyly notes that of the "three companions"—music, poetry, and wine—the last would not be at all appropriate for a princess. As this meager sampling of examples suggests, Koreyuki's principal interest lies in elucidating the sources of the sense of depth that a sensitive reader of *Genji* detects. His project never reached completion, for some entries consist of only a word or a phrase followed by "to be investigated." Nonetheless, his *Genji shaku* was a brilliant start to this long tradition.

And just to make the picture complete, we should also point out that while Koreyuki was busy with his textual and commentarial work, his daughter, whom we know as Kenreimon'in Ukyō no Daibu, may well have been busy with a *Genji* project of her own, the composition of an apocryphal "last chapter" to the tale: "Yamaji no tsuyu."

That other readers were annotating their texts of *Genji* in similar fashion, we know from Koreyuki's mention of them in his own compilation. Beyond this, we have no idea how widespread the practice was or what the fruits of it were. More than sixty years were to pass before the appearance of another such compilation, Fujiwara no Teika's *Endnotes* (*Okuiri*, ca. 1236). Teika, too, it seems, had been collecting marginalia from the texts that friends had lent him. But instead of recording them in the margins or between the lines of his text, he jotted them down in the empty spaces at the end of each chapter. There they might have remained, as a set of random notes to each of the fifty-four (or more) booklets that constituted his text, had it not been for the malicious gossip of some of his fellow readers. Just as others had lent Teika their texts of *Genji*, Teika had agreed to their requests to borrow his, whereupon word filtered back to him that some of the recipients of his generosity were making unkind comments about his notes. No names are named and no examples are given, but Teika himself tells us that he was so incensed that he decided to rip the notes out of each chapter and make a separate volume of them, which, presumably, he would *not* lend.

Like Koreyuki, Teika took advantage of this rewriting to expand some of his notes. And like Koreyuki, his main interest was identifying Murasaki's sources, particularly in poetry. At the beginning of his notes to "Hahakigi," for example, under the heading "Koreyuki Ason," he simply lists ten of the poems that Koreyuki cites in *Shaku*, including *Kokinshū* 1060, mentioned earlier, but omits the explication that Koreyuki appends to these poems. Apparently, he felt no need to repeat what he could readily consult in Koreyuki's work. On the whole, therefore, Teika's *Endnotes* is a somewhat leaner work than Koreyuki's *Shaku*. When he felt it necessary, though, he was willing to quote Chinese poetry at considerable length.

It must not be thought that Koreyuki and Teika interested themselves *only* in the identification of Murasaki's poetic sources. Their notes also touch on the grouping of chapters within the text (*narabi*), the identification of places the names of which had changed (for example, Nakagawa), the titles of the three classics and the five histories mentioned by Tō Shikibu no Jō in the "Hahakigi" chapter, and the like. But the first truly comprehensive commentary on *Genji*, in terms of both mass and breadth of interest, no longer survives and is known from only scattered fragments and quotations. This is a work known as *Suigenshō* (*The Wellspring Commentary*), and it, too, originated in a collection of marginalia and interlinear notes, though on a much grander scale than Koreyuki's and Teika's collections.

As we have seen, Minamoto no Mitsuyuki and his son Chikayuki spent years collating texts of *Genji* in a project that produced the text we now call the Kawachi-bon. And like Koreyuki and Teika, they collected annotations from the texts they had assembled and copied them into their personal texts. But their own contributions to this store of lore, knowledge, and interpretation seem far to have exceeded those of their predecessors. Not only did they include many more such annotations, but to judge from surviving quotations, they also seem to have reached into new areas of interest, such as orthography and textual interpretation. Mitsuyuki and Chikayuki seem, too, to have initiated the practice of setting aside their most valued nuggets of knowledge as "secrets" to be shared only with the select. Fortunately, these secrets survive under the title *Genchū saihishō*, a work that affords us at least a glimpse of the lost but much larger whole. At some point, Mitsuyuki, like his predecessors, decided to collect his notes in a separate volume, but the task was daunting and he died before finishing the work. It was completed by his son Chikayuki in about 1265. Beyond this, not much can be said with certainty, except that the *Suigenshō* was extremely influential and probably served as a model for the large-scale commentaries compiled in later years.

The honor of being the first major commentary to survive the ravages of time and medieval warfare must go to the *Shimeishō*, compiled by Sojaku, a younger brother of Minamoto no Chikayuki, and completed in 1294. But by far the most valuable of the early commentaries was the *Kakaishō*, compiled around 1362 to 1367 by Yotsutsuji Yoshinari (1326–1402). The Edo-period scholar Motoori Norinaga (1730–1801) describes Yoshinari's work as follows: "The *Kakaishō* ranks first among the commentaries. There are others that precede it, but they are limited in scope and lacking in detail, whereas this work draws on a wide range of sources, Japanese and Chinese, Confucian and Buddhist. Everything in the tale, almost without exception, is explicated here."[8] Coming from a man who was more inclined to denigrate his medieval forebears than to commend them, this is high praise indeed. It also pinpoints the two features of the work that make it so distinctive: the vast variety of sources on which it is based and the great breadth of the author's concern for what should be annotated. *Kakaishō*, of course, perpetuates Koreyuki's and Teika's interest in the sources of Murasaki's poetic allusions and regularly cites *Genji shaku* and *Okuiri*. But Yoshinari's own contributions to our understanding of the *Genji* are grounded in more than three hundred other works, including not only Chinese and Japanese collections of poetry, but also fictions, histories, diaries, scriptures, and the Chinese classics. And the uses to which he put this vast corpus opened many new lines of inquiry in the study of *Genji*, a number of which survive into the present day.

One of these that merits special mention is Yoshinari's investigation of the historical basis of *Genji*. No doubt many early readers felt they could detect echoes of history in the plot of *Genji* and the shades of past notabilities in the characters. The subject is touched on tangentially as a topic of debate in *Kōan Genji rongi* ("What place is 'a certain estate' modeled on?"), but *Kakaishō* is the earliest record of an attempt to demonstrate precisely what those connections might be. Yoshinari is quite precise. In his prologue, he writes:

> The age in which the tale is set is that of the three reigns of the Daigo, Suzaku, and Murakami Emperors. The Kiritsubo Emperor reigned in the Engi era [901–923], the Suzaku Retired Emperor in the Tenkyō era [938–947], and the Reizei Retired Emperor in the Tenryaku era [947–957]. The Shining Genji corresponds to the Nishinomiya Minister of the Left [Minamoto no Takaakira, 914–982].[9]

Throughout the entire work, Yoshinari draws on his panoply of sources to illustrate exactly how the *Genji* text relates to the historical record and how Murasaki Shikibu used that record in crafting her fiction. The fact that this subject remains a flourishing field of research is testimony to the lasting value of Yoshinari's work.

A century was to pass before the appearance of another major commentary on *The Tale of Genji*. This was *Kachō yosei*, compiled by Ichijō Kanera (or Kaneyoshi, 1402–1481) and completed in 1474. Kanera's stated purpose in compiling this work was simply to augment Yoshinari's work with commentary on items he had passed over and to correct some of what Kanera thought to be Yoshinari's errors. In the broadest sense this is exactly what he does. He builds on foundations laid down by Yoshinari and proceeds by much the same methods, citing, as Yoshinari does, literally hundreds of works of many sorts in evidence of his opinions. Close comparison of the two works, however, suggests that *Kachō yosei* is not merely an extension of *Kakaishō*. Kanera seems far less interested in demonstrating the historicity of *Genji* than in explicating the language of the text. It was Yotsutsuji Yoshinari who pioneered the semantic and syntactic explication of *Genji*, but in following Yoshinari's lead, Kanera carried this line of inquiry to heights far beyond those achieved by his predecessor. Take, for example, the first sentence of the "Hahakigi" chapter:

> The Shining Genji. The name itself was awe inspiring; yet many, it was said, were the misdeeds whispered about behind his back. And thus, lest his escapades of this sort be made the talk of age upon age to come and gain him a name for frivolity, he himself was at pains to keep them secret. Really, it was quite spiteful of whoever spread those tales about.

In *Kakaishō*, Yoshinari comments:

> This means that the name "Shining Genji" *sounds* imposing but what the man *did* was often whispered about behind his back. It must be understood that this sentence breaks after "the name itself was awe inspiring" and that "whispered about behind his back" refers only to his deeds. To read it as a single syntactic unit misrepresents the meaning. The text in the hand of Kyōgoku Kita no Mandokoro [Reishi, junior first rank] introduces a full stop after "awe inspiring." This, it seems to me, makes good sense.[10]

This is a useful warning to readers that the adverbial inflection of "awe inspiring" should not tempt them to assume that Genji's name as well as his deeds were "whispered about behind his back." Yoshinari then singles out the word *sukigoto* (here translated as "escapades") and cites the kanji (characters) with which this word is written in the *Nihongi*, as well as a phrase from *Hakushi monjū* in which it is used. Apropos of the phrase "spiteful of whoever spread those tales about," Yoshinari cites a poem he attributes to the *Kokinshū* (correctly the *Shūishū*) in which the same phrase appears. From this, it is apparent that Yoshinari's concern does not extend beyond the sentence itself, whereas Ichijō Kanera situates its meaning in a much larger context. In *Kachō yosei*, Kanera comments:

> *The Shining Genji*. . . . These first words hark back to the end of the "Kiritsubo" chapter, where it is written: "It is said that the name 'Shining Lord' was bestowed upon him in praise by the physiognomist from Koma."
>
> . . . *whispered about behind his back*. . . . There were probably many things, some true, some false, that were whispered about behind his back because of the mother of the Crown Prince, who was not at all well disposed toward this lord. There is a theory that *sukigoto* refers to his romantic escapades, but judging from the phrasing of this passage, it does not appear to be so. Here *sukigoto* refers to the name Shining Genji. In what follows, the things that might "gain him a name for frivolity," and thus "he was at pains to keep them secret," are just what the physiognomist from Koma divined in him. The details of those secrets are to be found in the "Kiritsubo" chapter. The "talk of age upon age to come" that might "gain him a name for frivolity" actually refers to present-day gossip.[11]

Clearly, some of Kanera's interpretations would no longer be accepted by modern scholars or not even, perhaps, by Yotsutsuji Yoshinari. But it is equally clear that he advanced the explication—and our understanding and appreciation—of the *Genji* text in a major way. His accomplishment is even more impressive when we think of the circumstances under which he worked, as a refugee in Nara, deprived of his library, fleeing from the ravages of the Ōnin Wars in Kyoto.

At this point in our overview of the commentarial tradition, it would be well to touch briefly on the role of familial factionalism in the development of this tradition. Such factionalism was nothing new. We have seen how various aristocratic houses collated their own familial texts of *Genji*, and one need only glance at the development of other forms of artistic endeavor in the medieval era—poetry in particular, but also music and even kickball—to see that the esoterica of these, too, were highly prized and jealously guarded as family property. Moreover, all the major commentaries discussed so far have been paired with companion volumes containing secret interpretations: *Suigenshō* and *Genchū saihishō*, *Kakaishō* and *Sango hishō*, *Kachō yosei* and *Gengo hiketsu*. In such an environment, it was entirely natural that one familial faction should emerge as the foremost authority on the interpretation of *The Tale of Genji*. That authority was finally claimed by the house of Sanjōnishi Sanetaka (1455–1537), and all subsequent major commentaries before the *Kogetsushō* (1673) are the work of Sanetaka, his descendants, and their allies among the leading *renga* masters who were instrumental in establishing the Sanjōnishi ascendency.

The *Kogetsushō* cites four commentaries from this school of scholarship, and they are best considered as a group, for being the work of a unified school they are far more like peas in a pod than were their predecessors. Present-day scholars tend to characterize them all as "carrying on" (or "advancing" or "deepening") the traditions of Sanjōnishi *Genji* studies, which is unquestionably true but not terribly helpful. A more notable characteristic of the Sanjōnishi school is its willingness to criticize, revise, and even refute earlier commentary. This is not to say that they write in opposition to Koreyuki, Teika, Yoshinari, and Kanera. They routinely cite their forebears and continue to add to the store of poetic allusion, historical precedent, explication, and interpretation found in earlier commentary. But they also attempt to refine it as they build on it. A quick comparison of their comments on the opening sentence of "Hahakigi" with those already examined offers at least a glimpse of this attitude in action.

Rōkashō (1476) is very much a joint effort. The *renga* master Sōgi had given a series of lectures on *Genji* that were attended by his disciple Shōhaku (1443–1527). Shōhaku then wrote out his lecture notes, no doubt augmenting them with his own thoughts as he did, and then lent his notes to Sanjōnishi Sanetaka, who further augmented them with his own contributions. On the sentence in question, they (for it is impossible to tell with whom this originates) comment:

> *The Shining Genji. The name itself was awe inspiring.* . . . This was written in continuation of the last words of the previous chapter. It goes without saying that this means his name was imposing, but there were many things about which people whispered behind his back.
>
> . . . *his amorous escapades, which he kept secret.* . . . Genji's amorous escapades differ from those of Zai Chūjō [Narihira] and others, in

that he maintains a facade of rectitude behind which he hides his amours.[12]

Sairyūshō (1528), though long thought to have been compiled by Sanetaka's son Kin'eda (1487–1563), has been shown to be the work of Sanetaka himself, who speaks here in his own voice:

> *The Shining Genji. The name itself was awe inspiring. . . .* The *Kakaishō* [correctly *Kachō yosei*] says that this sentence should be read as coming to a halt at this point. This is all well and good, but neither is there any harm in reading it continuously on into the next clause. Those who are inclined to be critical will whisper behind the back of anyone of any note whatever. This is simply the way of the world. [*Kachō*] says that he is whispered about by the Kokiden lady, but this should probably be attributed simply to the world of the court. His "misdeeds" are amours, but the same would be true of any others.
> *. . . his amorous escapades. . . . Sukigoto* are amours. *Kachō yosei* says that the name Shining Genji is a *sukigoto*. I have my doubts about this; rather, they are the things he keeps hidden. *Kachō* also says that the physiognomist from Koma divined this, but this, too, I doubt.[13]

Mōshinshō (1575) was compiled by a grandson of Sanetaka, Kujō Tanemichi (1507–1594), who comments:

> *The Shining Genji. The name itself was awe inspiring; yet . . .* [*he was*] *whispered about behind his back.* It is said that this should be read with a break after "whispered about behind his back [*sic*]," but it should be read continuously.
> *. . . many were the misdeeds. . . .* Those inclined to criticize will speak ill of both good and bad deeds, and those inclined to praise will speak glowingly even of evil deeds. *Kachō yosei*'s interpretation is wrong. It refers only to his amorous escapades.[14]

Tanemichi then quotes the entire commentary of *Kachō yosei*, after which he remarks that if Kanera meant to say that "criticism of Genji's amorous escapades, that being simply the way of the world, comes only from the Kokiden lady, then this is contrary to the purport of the tale." Concerning "his amorous escapades," Tanemichi first quotes (without attribution) Yotsutsuji Yoshinari's kanji glosses and then goes on to say:

> *Sukigoto* are probably just amours. . . . *[L]est his escapades of this sort be made the talk of age upon age to come and gain him a name for frivolity, he himself was at pains to keep them secret. Really, it was quite spiteful of whoever spread those tales about.* This means that although Genji was of an amorous disposition, he maintained a facade of rectitude and kept his amours hidden. Thus we know that it is Murasaki Shikibu herself who speaks of "whoever it was that spread those tales about."[15]

Tanemichi then offers as his "personal opinion" (which, of course, it is not):

> *Kachō yosei* says that the name Shining Genji is a *sukigoto.* This is wrong.
> . . . *his secrets that he kept concealed* . . . *Kachō yosei*'s interpretation of this is very wrong. I need not elaborate. *Rōkashō*: Genji's amorous escapades differ from those of Zai Chūjō [Narihira] and others, in that he maintains a facade of rectitude behind which he conceals his amours.[16]

Mingō nisso, the last in the lineage of "Sanjōnishi *Genji* scholarship," is in many ways the most impressive work in this line. Its author, Nakanoin Michikatsu (1556–1610), a great-grandson of Sanetaka, compiled the work at Tanabe-jō, the remote retirement castle of the warrior Hosokawa Yūsai (1534–1610), during a nineteen-year period of banishment from the capital. Michikatsu's aim was not so much to add another link to the Sanjōnishi chain but to produce a summa of previous commentary on *Genji.* By its very nature, then, it was destined to be a massive work: four closely printed volumes in the most recent modern edition. In elucidating the first clause or two of "Hahakigi," Michikatsu cites five previous explications of this passage. First he quotes the preceding *Kakaishō* and *Kachō yosei* comments. He then notes that

> Sōgi says that it was meant as praise to say that the name, the Shining Genji, was awe inspiring; but that to say many were the misdeeds whispered about behind his back simply shows that it is the way of

> the world to whisper behind the backs of those of renown who are praised.

Michikatsu next quotes his maternal grandfather, Sanjōnishi Kin'eda (Shōmyōin), to the effect that "*Kakaishō* says that the clause breaks after 'awe inspiring,' but it can just as well be read continuously," and that "those who are inclined to criticize will whisper behind the backs of anyone. This is just the way of the world. *Kachō yosei* says that he is criticized by Kokiden; but it is simply those in the world at large who whisper behind his back."[17] To that, Michikatsu adds that his uncle Sanjōnishi Sanezumi (Saneki; 1511–1579) "agrees with this." Then, under the heading "the name itself," he notes that in this context in one of his lectures, Sanezumi cited both the *Laozi* and the *Analects*, both of which Michikatsu quotes here in the original Chinese, following which he offers his own explanation of their significance:

> Because even Genji's name was noised about in so exaggerated a manner, his was a name well known in the world. As is said here, "having a name is the mother of all things."[18] And having a name that was noised about in so exaggerated a manner, it generated an infinitude of flaws. It is for this reason that this passage is cited. The reason the *Analects* is cited is to show that attitudes of the people of the world are not all the same. There is good, and there is evil. And thus when Zigong asks Confucius, "What would you think of a man if everyone liked him?" he answers, "This is not enough." And when he asks, "What if everyone disliked him?" again the answer is, "This is not enough."[19] Ultimately, to regard the good as good and the evil as evil is the Way of the Sages. Though people may make much of Genji's failings, that is just the way of the world. Yet when one is in quest of overall excellence, one does not quibble over every trifling flaw, for most good people are not without minor shortcomings. As for Genji's "misdeeds that were whispered about behind his back," it is precisely because he was so highly praised that people found fault with him. These "misdeeds" are said to be amorous escapades, but this is wrong. The foregoing is the significance of these citations.[20]

Michikatsu then moves on to the phrase "escapades of this sort," noting that the matter of Genji's amours begins here and that Sanezumi has said that "if his 'faults' were all of an amorous sort, then there would be no need to use the word 'amours' [*sukigoto*] here." And then Michikatsu continues:

> Since despite being praised so highly as the "Shining Genji" people still found fault with him, he realizes that if he were to be more open about his amours, they would only find fault with him all the more. Here we can see the spirit of discretion that is one aspect of Genji's character.

Next we are shown which characters were used to write *sukigoto* in the *History of the Han Dynasty*, that Kanera's commentary on this word in *Kachō yosei* is questionable, and that Sōgi's commentary says that Genji is of an amorous nature but that he maintains a facade of rectitude beneath which he conceals his amorous inclinations. Finally, in his own voice, Michikatsu adds, "Because his many failings are whispered about behind his back, he has good reason for being discreet about his amours."[21]

> *Really, it was quite spiteful of whoever spread those tales about.*

Michikatsu first notes that *saganashi* (here translated as "spiteful") can be written with the characters for "not good" and that it can mean "evil" or "horrid":

> And inasmuch as these clandestine activities are passed down to us in writing, we know that it was Murasaki Shikibu herself who wrote about them. But the author of the tale writes as if to make us think that these are things others have said and that it was bad of them to spread them about.[22]

The foregoing survey amounts to no more than a droplet in a vast sea (a favorite metaphor of medieval exegetes). Nonetheless, some of the more salient characteristics of the genre do emerge, even from so cursory a glance. We see the growth of a vigorous tradition from scribbled marginalia to massive tomes of exegesis, as well as new ways of reading *Genji* and new standards of judging the tale. We also see some of the faults that so irritated Motoori Norinaga in the eighteenth century: the inattention to accuracy and the perverse citation of esoteric sources that have nothing to do with *Genji*. But then we see as well a new awareness of the narratological structure of *Genji*, which Sōgi termed *sōshiji* and which remains a fertile field of research to this day. In short, whatever its shortcomings and excesses, the exegetical commentary of the medieval era is not only the most voluminous "form of attention" ever paid to *Genji*, but also a rich and deep vein of valuable scholarship that is only just beginning to be mined.

T. HARPER

NOTES ON THE RAINY NIGHT'S DISCUSSION, CA. 1485

(*Amayo danshō*)

SŌGI

Notes on the Rainy Night's Discussion, completed in or before 1485 and also known by the title *Hahakigi betchū*, is a detailed commentary on "The Broom Tree" (Hahakigi), chapter 2 of *The Tale of Genji*.[23] It cites and discusses each line or passage from the first several pages of the text and is of interest as the medieval era's only commentary that focuses on a single chapter and glosses it extensively. Another aspect of historical interest is its attention to rhetorical and grammatical usage, an aspect it shares with Ichijō Kanera's seminal work *Kachō yosei* (1472). *Notes on the Rainy Night's Discussion* also is the first commentary to introduce the term *sōshiji*. This is a technical term, literally meaning "the ground of the book," that is used widely in later commentaries on *Genji* to refer to passages of narrative commentary or authorial intervention, analogous to the use of parabasis in classical Greek drama or the use of comments from author to reader in, for example, novels by Henry Fielding and William Makepeace Thackeray. Sōgi (1421–1502) distinguishes *sōshiji* from other, similar terms, such as *sakusha no kotoba* (the author's words) or *Murasaki Shikibu no kotoba* (Murasaki Shikibu's words), though the distinction does not always appear to be rigorous.

LEWIS COOK

The chapter is titled "The Broom Tree" because when Genji uses a directional taboo as a pretense for going to spend the night at Nakagawa and Utsusemi refuses [later] to meet him, treating him coldly, Genji sends her the poem, "Not knowing the mind of the broom tree, how I have lost my way on the paths of Sonohara,"[24] to which the woman replies, "In the sadness of the humble dwelling of my station, I am at once there and not there."[25] The chapter title is taken from these poems. The poems are based on a poem by Sakanoue no Korenori: "The broom tree growing in Fuseya in Sonohara seems to be there, yet I do not find you."[26] This is taken to mean that while Utsusemi is indeed there, she will not meet [Genji] and thus seems to be there but is not there.

Even though this is the name of this one chapter, it extends to the entire fifty-four chapters of the tale. The reason is that this tale is a made-up work and thus a fiction, yet is composed of traces of events that happened in the past. To begin with, the three reigns of Emperors Kiritsubo, Suzaku, and Reizei are patterned on those of Engi [901–923], Shōhei [931–938], and Tenryaku [947–957].[27] Hikaru Genji is modeled on the Nishinomiya Minister of the Left Lord Takaakira[28] and his removal to Dazaifu. In addition, Genji's exile evokes the eastern expedition of Shū Kōtan [Zhou Gongdan][29] and the case of Hakurakuten[30] in China, and, in our land, the case of Sugawara no Michizane.[31] In addition to these, other instances of modeling on historical precedents are innumerable.

Throughout the whole fifty-four chapters of the tale, because things that appear real are not, and things that appear unreal are in fact real, this title, "The Broom Tree," suffices to name the whole work. Among the Four Gates [of Existence] propounded by Tendai doctrine, the Gate of Both Existing and Empty [of reality or essence] applies to this tale. "The Floating Bridge of Dreams" [Yume no ukihashi], too, though it is the title of a single chapter, likewise serves as a title for the whole tale. How so? All the actions of the characters in the tale, whether of high, middle, or low station, are nothing more than charades in a dream. Compare, for example, Zhuangzi's knowing not whether he has dreamed of being a butterfly or is a butterfly dreaming of being Zhuangzi.

It is difficult to decide whether this tale is a dream of past times or the reality of those of us living now in this world: both are passages across a floating bridge of dreams, the reality or not of the broom tree. Thus the shades of Murasaki Shikibu's brush are deep, their meaning beyond fathoming.

Now, the opening words of this chapter, beginning with "The Shining Genji" through "would have been laughed at by the Katano Lieutenant" are those of the author of this tale herself. Many of Murasaki Shikibu's words are inserted here and there throughout.

The name alone was impressive.

These are words that praise the name "Shining Genji" as awe inspiring.

He was blamed for many faults.

This refers to the commonplace that even people of high repute, those honored for their adherence to the Way, are often disparaged in the world of society.

Fearing that his amorous affairs might be talked of for generations to come, earning him a reputation for frivolity, he always was discreet, but even those affairs he did his best to conceal became the talk of the town. Such is the meanness of gossips.

This is to say that although Genji was a person of an amorous nature, he made a show of outward seriousness while in his inmost heart he was inclined toward the pursuits of love. With this in mind, Murasaki Shikibu thus asks who it was, after all, that passed on stories of the affairs that Genji conducted with such discretion?

Indeed, in his caution about appearances and insistence on prudence, he refrained from risqué or flirtatious behavior to the degree that he would have been mocked by the Katano Lieutenant.

Beneath the surface he was given to amorousness but put on such a show of seriousness that he appeared prim and thus lacking the true instinct of the amorous, and at that the Katano Lieutenant would have laughed, so Tō no [Murasaki] Shikibu thought and so she wrote.

Although there are various interpretations of the matter of the Katano Lieutenant, what is known is that a certain Katano Lieutenant was a character in a fictional tale, one who was notorious for his amorous ways. Although Hikaru Genji and the Katano Lieutenant were not contemporaries, Murasaki Shikibu matched them and wrote about them in this way. To contrast one character of a fictional tale with another is an interesting literary technique.

The foregoing serves as the introduction to this one chapter.

While Genji was still a Captain . . .

In this chapter Genji is sixteen years of age and holds the rank of Captain. In the chapter "A Celebration of Autumn Leaves" [Momiji no ga] he becomes a Consultant, although here and through

"The Cherry Blossom Festival" [Hana no en] he remains a Captain. Since throughout this chapter he must, of course, be a Captain, to write "while he was still a Captain" [as though he were soon to be promoted] must appear odd. Nonetheless, there is a reason for this. In composing this tale, Murasaki Shikibu did not write as though she were inventing the story but as though she were merely recording accounts of past events she happened to have heard passed down to her, records she then gathered to make up a single work. This is indicated in the concluding words to several chapters. Since it is about events that took place in the past, there can be no doubt about the use of the [past particle] *shi* in the expression "while he was still a Captain." . . .

He spent his time entirely in the palace, only rarely visiting the Minister's residence.

Genji became the spouse of the Minister of the Left's daughter Lady Aoi at the age of twelve. At the time, Lady Aoi was sixteen. Because Genji was not very attached to her, he spent almost all his time in the palace and only rarely visited the Minister's residence.

Some people seem to have suspected a case of "hidden feelings entangled."[32]

This means that Aoi's attendants suspected that Genji's coolness toward their mistress must be due to some entanglement with this or that woman in the palace.

But his nature was such. . . . He had no interest in superficial, impulsive, or trifling affairs of the heart.

While some may have suspected otherwise, Genji was not one to be drawn to a woman easily seduced, so it was not, after all, such an entanglement. The ellipsis after "But his nature was such" carries the sense that he was not indeed entangled [in some superficial affair]. Such use of ellipses is common in the writing of this tale and creates a sense of subtlety [*yū*].[33]

Yet on rare occasions he did, unfortunately, yield to an inclination toward affairs fraught with difficulty and anguish, leading him to behavior most unbecoming.

The phrase "on rare occasions" means that while by nature he was averse to the easy liaison and seemed above such dalliances, sometimes one who resisted his attractions appealed to him, leading him to compromising behavior and affairs that gave rise to rumors.

The early summer rains were falling without end.

It was just around the Fifth Month.

As Genji's seclusion went on and on and he stayed indoors [at the palace], some at the Minister's residence became resentful, even though all manner of clothing and furnishings were forthcoming.

"Seclusion" refers to confinement within the Inner Palace. Such confinement [*monoimi*] was practiced when malicious forces threatened, and the characters for *monoimi* were written on [a slip of paper that was attached to] a blind. Going out was avoided in observance thereof. . . .

His sons spent all their time in Genji's quarters [in the palace]. Among them, the Captain, who was the son of the Princess, was on especially close terms with Genji.

"His sons" means those of the Minister [of the Left]. "The son of the Princess" refers to Tō no Chūjō. He attains the rank of His Excellency, the Chancellor, in the "Wakana" chapters [chapters 34 and 35], where he is called *chichi no otōdo*. The younger sister [Princess Omiya] of the Kiritsubo Emperor was taken in marriage by the Minister of the Left and bore two children. One was Lady Aoi and the other was this Captain, Tō no Chūjō, who was thus a cousin of Genji. This accounts for their affinity and their sharing, more closely than others, both their studies and their amusements.

While this son was treated with great care by the Minister of the Right, he, too, found his residence there quite oppressive and was fond of romantic adventures abroad.

"Kiritsubo" [chapter 1 of *Genji*] states that Tō no Chūjō is a son-in-law of the Minister of the Right. The phrases "he was treated with great care" [but] "found his residence there quite oppressive" refer to the fact that while Tō no Chūjō was married to the Minister of the Right's fourth daughter, his heart was not drawn to her. The words "this son" [*kono kimi*] recall that likewise, Genji was not attracted to Lady Aoi and thus imply that he also was fond of romantic adventures.

While keeping Genji company throughout his comings and goings, sharing both their studies and their diversions, he hardly fell behind Genji in either.

Thus Genji and Tō no Chūjō were best friends and kept none of their feelings in reserve. The preceding serves as the preface to the "Rainy Night's Discussion."[34]

While sitting close to the lamp, reading texts, Tō no Chūjō could not restrain his curiosity and took out some multicolored papers from a cabinet nearby.

"Reading texts" refers to their study of [Chinese] textbooks. Writings on "multicolored papers" would be love letters.

"I'll let you see some of those that don't matter. Not those that could be embarrassing . . ." "But it's just those that let slip things that might be embarrassing that I'm curious about. Even I exchange a few letters, nothing of possible interest to you, with ladies of various ranks. Those worth reading are the ones written in moments of anger, or perhaps at dusk by someone awaiting a visit." When he so complained [enzureba]. . . ."

From "I'll let you see," the exchange of words between Genji and Tō no Chūjō is expressed directly. A reply from Genji that should [grammatically] follow "so complained" is elided, and Tō no Chūjō continues speaking instead. The [conditional] particle *-ba* in *enzureba* is [thus] difficult to parse. That said, words left hanging in this unaffected way are one of the commonplaces of this tale, so this could be regarded as an example.

Since those from exalted writers would be hidden away, hardly left scattered around on a cabinet shelf, these letters must be from correspondents of only lesser interest.

The subject is Tō no Chūjō's reading of Genji's love letters, and the sense is that only those letters that Genji would not feel embarrassed to let others see would be left lying around unconcealed. *Ni no machi* [of only lesser interest] refers to paddies or fields of second-rate yield. Also, the words from the phrase "Since those from exalted" to "only lesser interest" might be identified as *sōshi no ji* [literally, "the ground of the book": narratorial commentary or metanarrative, as opposed to narration per se]. If so, that would seem to resolve the problem of the ellipsis after *enzureba* [when he so complained].

Of women there are very few whom one can expect to be flawless, so I have come to learn. Those who display some superficial sensibility, write a flowing hand in appropriate response to letters, and seem capable of rising to the occasion—there are enough of these when you look around, but to discover one who is truly without imperfections, one who should not be missed, this is difficult indeed.

The words from "Of women . . ." to "so I have come to learn" are those of Tō no Chūjō. Even though Tō no Chūjō is young, he nonetheless has learned much about women in society. "A flowing hand" refers to women's epistolary style; "in response to letters" refers to composing poems in reply; "capable of rising to the occasion" means those who are not necessarily able to write a fluent hand or to compose poems well. Here follows the "ranking of women" [into three grades]. This consists of assembling accounts of a number of women from society and presenting their dispositions [*kokoro*] to Genji by way of relating, for his benefit, that there are in this world women of such minds. Tō no Chūjō is not well acquainted with the ways of the world, but because he is a little ahead of Genji in regard to knowing the ways of women, he takes the lead here. Overall, this chapter ["The Broom Tree"] might seem difficult to understand. It might be compared, for example, to the way elderly persons in our present age, talking of their experiences over the past fifty or sixty years, might say that such and such a person's disposition [*kokoro*] was, after all, like this or like that. In this respect, the minds of people of the present might be seen to resemble those of persons of the past. If you take this principle as the basis [for reading the chapter], matters can be understood without difficulty.

TRANSLATED BY LEWIS COOK

KAOKU GYOKUEI

Within the flood of exegetical commentary on *The Tale of Genji* that poured forth between the twelfth and twentieth centuries, we know of very few works written by female commentators. One of those was Yūrin (fl. 1450), described by her contemporaries as a *Genji-yomi bikuni*, a nun who traveled around reading aloud sections of the text and explicating them for her audience.[35] Yūrin's digest-cum-commentary, *Hikaru Genji ichibu uta* (*The Complete Poems of the Shining Genji*), was completed in 1453.[36] Another female commentator was Kaoku Gyokuei (1526–after 1602), whose surviving oeuvre reveals a lifelong engagement with *The Tale of Genji*. A narrative picture scroll (*emaki*) in six scrolls dated 1554 has been attributed to her,[37] and works signed with her name include a copy of an account of the origins of *Genji* that she made for a niece who was in the service of Nei

(1548–1624), wife of the military hegemon Toyotomi Hideyoshi;[38] a set of fifty-four poems on the chapters of *Genji*, dated 1589;[39] and two commentaries: *Kaokushō* (*Kaoku's Gleanings*, 1594), and *Gyokuei shū* (*Gyokuei's Collection*, 1602).

The details of Gyokuei's biography have yet to be established.[40] What is clear from her commentaries is that they were written for a female audience. As other texts in this anthology reveal, women recalled their reading of *Genji* (in *Sarashina Diary*, ca. 1059), they recorded their discussions of *Genji* (in *A Nameless Notebook*, ca. 1200), and they advised their daughters to memorize *Genji* (in *The Nursemaid's Letter*, ca. 1264). But Gyokuei seems to have been the only woman in the medieval period to have written commentaries on *Genji* specifically for other women readers of the text.

Gyokuei accommodated *Genji* to her female audience in various ways. First, she advocates reading *Genji* for pleasure and not as an adjunct to some other pursuit, such as the composition of poetry. She encourages women to read the fifty-four chapters straight through. Second, this kind of reading demands a different level of knowledge from that provided by the mainstream commentaries. Anyone who has studied the earlier commentaries that she cites approvingly—*Shimeishō*, *Kakaishō*, and *Kachō yosei*—must be struck by the vast distance between them and Gyokuei's work. Commentaries written by men are larded with citations to Chinese sources, "proof" that *The Tale of Genji* was a classic that could bear comparison with other classics, both Buddhist and Confucian. Such citations also demonstrated that the compiler of the commentary was engaged in a serious, scholarly, and properly masculine enterprise, and thus served to legitimate the interest of men in a mere tale. Gyokuei obviously was familiar with these earlier commentaries, and as the notes to the following translated passages reveal, she was not averse to borrowing from them when they could be of use to her.[41] In her own commentaries, however, she cites no Indian or Chinese examples, proofs, or precedents. Rather, she selects only what she believes to be important to an understanding of *Genji*, simplifying and reducing as she goes along.

Gyokuei's third set of accommodations to her female audience are those of language, style, and tone. Both *Kaokushō* and *Gyokuei shū* are written principally in hiragana. Gyokuei frequently translates words or phrases from *Genji* into contemporary sixteenth-century Japanese. She also is particular about how words ought to be pronounced. Her concern with pronunciation suggests that at this time, the ability to read *Genji* aloud, to "perform" the text for listeners, was still as necessary a skill for aristocratic women, especially those employed as gentlewomen, as it had been three centuries earlier when Abutsu (d. 1283) achieved renown for her accomplishment.[42] Throughout both works, Gyokuei's tone is conversational, almost chatty.

Gyokuei's discussion of theories of authorship is another distinctive feature of her writing. In both her commentaries, Gyokuei explains that the phrase *murasaki no yukari* (related to Murasaki) at the beginning of the "Takekawa" chapter refers to Murasaki Shikibu, not the character Murasaki. This interpretation enables her to entertain the possibility that the chapter was written by someone other than Murasaki Shikibu.

G. G. ROWLEY

KAOKU'S GLEANINGS, 1594 (*Kaokushō*)

The oldest surviving manuscript of *Kaoku's Gleanings* is in the collection of the Hōsa Bunko, formerly the library of the Owari branch of the Tokugawa family, and is dated 1603. There are no woodblock-printed editions; the text was first published in 1936.[43] In identifying her work only by her style, "Kaoku," Gyokuei implicitly declines to associate it with the great mainstream commentaries, which were compiled by male scholars and whose titles were drawn from Chinese sources. Such commentaries typically begin with a preface in which the commentator describes the origins of the text to be discussed, summarizes previous scholarship, and situates his own commentary within a particular scholarly lineage. Gyokuei chose not to provide her commentary with a preface and opted instead for a modest afterword in which she explains her reasons for compiling the work. *Kaokushō* thus launches straight into a discussion of "Kiritsubo" and then proceeds through the remaining fifty-three chapters. The following are complete translations of Gyokuei's commentary on the "Kiritsubo" chapter, her remarks on the authorship of the "Takekawa" chapter, and her afterword.

G. G. ROWLEY

Kiritsubo

The name of this chapter is taken from the text [of *Genji*]. "Kiritsubo" refers to the Paulownia Court within the Shigeisha, which is one of the residences [*goten*] of the Inner Palace. It should be understood that it is used as the name of the residence. Among the residences are the Plum Court, the Paulownia Court, the Wisteria Court, the Bamboo Court, the Pear Court, and the like. Each residence takes its name directly from the tree that grows in its courtyard. It should be understood, therefore, that the Shigeisha and the Kiritsubo are the same place.[44] Thus it is that, although the palace quarters of Genji's daughter, the Akashi Princess, are the Paulownia Court, in the "Wakana" chapters and elsewhere she is mentioned in connection with the Shigeisha. This chapter describes the events between Genji's birth and his twelfth year.

In which reign was it?
Refers obliquely to the reign of the Engi Emperor.[45]

[Not] of the highest rank
Means that [the Kiritsubo Consort] was not the daughter of a Minister of State. That is why she is not called a *nyōgo*, but a *miyasundokoro*. This was a source of anguish, and she grew sickly and weak.

Otagi
Present-day Toribeno.[46]

Now she is gone
[No commentary given.]

The Bodyguards of the Left announcing their arrival for duty
The Bodyguards of the Left go on night duty at the Hour of the Rat [11:00 P.M.–1:00 A.M.]. From the Hour of the Ox [1:00–3:00 A.M.] until the Hour of the Tiger [3:00–5:00 A.M.], the Bodyguards of the Right are on night duty. That is why it says this. When the Bodyguards of the Left turn over the watch to the Right, they call out, "Who goes there?" and relieve them on night duty. That is why it is called "announcing night attendance."[47]

Dais service
Refers to the meal served to the Emperor in his day room.

The Uda Emperor's admonition

The father of [the Emperor regnant during] the Engi era. Because there had not been much hesitation about having physiognomists from foreign lands enter the palace, and even make pronouncements concerning the Crown Prince, [the Uda Emperor] warned against having them called to the palace.

Kōrokan

At Seventh and Shuja[ku] Avenues.[48] A place where envoys from foreign lands were received.

He has the signs of one destined to become the father of his people and to achieve the Sovereign's supreme eminence[49]

That Genji becomes the father of his people means that he is destined to attain the title of Honorary Emperor in Retirement [*daijō tennō*].

When I see him in that position, I wonder if it might not lead to disorder and suffering

Means that he is destined to be exiled to Suma Bay.[50]

Japanese physiognomy

This is the Japanese way of doing physiognomy.

Maternal relatives of an unranked Prince

Imperial Princes are ranked from first to fourth rank. Those lower still are not called fifth rank but are known as unranked Princes.

Unsupported by maternal relatives

This means that Genji's familial connections through his mother's line are not as they ought to be. Because he lacks solid support, he should not be set adrift as an unranked Prince with no one he can depend upon. *Gesaku* is how it is written in kana. One should pronounce it *geshaku*.

For sukuyō, *read* shukuyō

This refers to fortune-telling.

Three reigns of court service

This refers to the three reigns of the Kōkō [884–887], Uda [887–897], and Daigo [897–930] Emperors.

To an exceptional degree

This word means to an extent that was unsurpassed.

Disrespectful

The same as "apparently disrespectful" [*nanmege*]. Means to treat someone lightly.

Imperial granaries
The imperial storehouses [*mikura*].

[The Emperor had his] throne placed
Something on which he would be seated.

Juvenile
This means to be childlike.

The duty [room]
The waiting [room].[51]

Rice balls
This is called wrapped rice [*tsutsumi-ii*]; when all the lower-ranking servants and the like are fed, they are given rice that has been wrapped up rather than made into a meal served on a tray. In the present day, for example, this is what we would call "bird's egg rice balls" [*torinoko*].

Without reserve
Ostentatiously [*yōyō nari*].[52]

Takekawa

According to some people, this chapter was added by Murasaki Shikibu's daughter Daini no Sanmi.[53] Other people say that it is the written record of tales told by old women who had been in Higekuro's service. But I wonder how certain it is that Sanmi wrote it. [The sentence that begins] *murasaki no yukari nimo* means "although this does not resemble anything related to what Murasaki Shikibu has written, I am just writing down what I have heard."[54]

(Afterword)

The three commentaries on *Genji*—*Shimeishō*, *Kakaishō*, and *Kachō yosei*—are the source of the work called *Sangen ichiran*, which dispels the darkness like a clear mirror, leaving not a shadow of doubt.[55] After this, many other works of various sorts were compiled, giving free rein to their authors' intellect. All these, however, are but displays of their authors' erudition and cleverness. Often they are unintelligible, and often they have little basis in *Genji*. Such stuff is beyond the reach of a beginner.

On an evening in the Fourth Month as our young lady gazes out at the darkening sky, longing for the lost vestiges of the cherry blossoms of spring, or, in summer, when recalling the story of he who gathered fireflies as they flitted past his window,[56] she draws to herself this tale. And how much more so when she would seek consolation of an autumn evening as the tints that move her so deeply one after another fade away; as the insects cry; as the evening sky, so beautiful she could die, all but breaks her heart. Or of a long winter's night, when she turns the lamp up high close to her bed or, next to the hearth, spreads out the tale, [at such times] what our young lady wants is just to enjoy herself—to read through the fifty-four chapters easily, entirely on her own, with nary a doubt, for *this* is the most important thing. After all, the reflection of the light of the moon in the waters of a shallow well is no different from that in a deep spring.

And so for the sake of us foolish women, I have written this work and bound it in four volumes. Of an autumn evening or a snowy morning, as you think back and your heart goes out to [*Genji*], you can consult this in conjunction with the text. Lest there remain any little points of doubt—for this is meant only for girls and women [*osanaki hito, onnadochi*]—I have glossed some of the kanji with kana.[57] Insignificant as it is, I entitle it simply *Kaokushō*. Rather like something a cuckoo might do.[58]

TRANSLATED BY G. G. ROWLEY

GYOKUEI'S COLLECTION, 1602
(*Gyokuei shū*)

Gyokuei's Collection, like Gyokuei's earlier commentary *Kaoku's Gleanings*, circulated solely in manuscript. The mimeograph version, transcribed by Ii Haruki and published in 1969, remains the only printed edition.[59] *Gyokuei shū* begins with a preface, though it is not announced as such. The remainder of the text can be divided into three sections. In the first, Gyokuei explains the origin of each chapter title; in the second she provides interpretations of difficult-to-understand poems; and in the third, she lists unfamiliar words and phrases with short explanations of their meaning. Throughout, Gyokuei remains determined to facilitate women's reading of *Genji* in the original. Her deprecation of digest versions of the tale is, as Tsutsumi Yasuo suggests, typical of the aristocratic readership she represents.[60] Complete translations of Gyokuei's commentary on the "Kiritsubo" chapter, taken from the first two sections of the text, follow the partial translation of the preface. Her remarks on the authorship of *Genji* from the "Takekawa" chapter are also included.

G. G. ROWLEY

(Preface)

As a rule, I would not be inclined to prattle on about matters concerning *The Tale of Genji*, but there are those who, knowing not the first thing about it, consider it merely another storybook [*monogatari sōshi*] along the lines of *The Tale of Sumiyoshi* [*Sumiyoshi*], *The Distant Isle* [*Tōjima*], and *The Single Chrysanthemum* [*Hitomotogiku*]; lament bitterly the fact that the language is so difficult to follow; and wish that somehow they might understand it.[61] Thus, with the intention of putting an end to their longing for *Genji* by instructing them in the basics, reluctant though I am to prattle on about such things, I have taken up my brush to make these notes to *Genji*.

. . . *Genji* is no amusement for the lower ranks. Because it is a work with which poets of the palace and the Retired Emperor's palace busy themselves, it never occurs to them that large numbers of people might not know the language of *Genji*, and thus they think, "No need to comment on this minor point." They comment only on matters that people at large could hardly be expected to know. As the world lapses into decline, knowledgeable people pass away, and therefore things that people of the past thought nothing of knowing, nowadays no one knows. So it is that *Genji*, too, has become an extraordinarily unfamiliar work.

Many and various are the works compiled by recent commentators that tell one about even those things concerning which there is no doubt whatsoever. Some have eleven chapters, some twenty, others fifty-four. . . . These people are only showing off their store of knowledge, endlessly adducing Chinese and Indian precedents in order to elucidate things that are of no particular use to a reader of *Genji*. As a result, gentlewomen are unable to make any sense of them, and in the end, their desire to know what the commentary is saying remains unsatisfied. I think all this is totally unnecessary.[62]

Section 1

The [title of the] first chapter, "Kiritsubo," is taken from the text. It is the name of a residence within the Greater Palace [*daidairi*]. On the east, the upper limits of the Greater Palace extended to the area of present-day Yōkandō; the lower limits were bounded by Shijō and the pond of the Shinsen'en Imperial Gardens; all this was contained within the Greater Palace. There were twelve gates facing the four directions; so enormous were gates like the Rashōmon that they were the dwellings of demons and the haunts of evil tricksters.[63] One commonly encounters such goings-on. During the Hōgen era [1156–1159] the Greater Palace was destroyed by fire; after that it was never rebuilt, and it fell into ruin. There was a great deal of land devoted to residences, and these were indications of rank. The one with a paulownia tree was called the Paulownia Court; the one with a wisteria vine was called the Wisteria Court; the one with the plum tree was called the Plum Court; and so on. A cherry tree was planted in the garden of the Southern Hall, and when the flowers were in bloom, the Emperor and Empress would grace them with their presence morning and evening. The Paulownia Court [Kiritsubo] was within the Shigeisha; in the Inner Palace [*dairi*] of later years, because it was close to the Emperor's day rooms, he installed this consort there and she came to be called the Kiritsubo Consort. Because the Emperor, too, was so often present there, he is known as the Kiritsubo Emperor. These [characters] are the inventions of the *Genji* author. In the days when the Greater Palace still existed, there was no Emperor known as Kiritsubo. He, too, is a fiction. Since the disappearance of the Greater Palace, the old names of the residences are no more.

[. . .]

This chapter ["Takekawa"] is an exceptional one, both the language and the spirit of which are totally different [from the others]. It is said that after the death of Murasaki Shikibu, her daughter Daini no Sanmi wrote [this chapter] and added it [to the text of *Genji*]. Another theory suggests that it was composed by Sai'in no Senji.[64] There are also a variety of theories suggesting that the Uji [chapters] were composed by [Daini no] Sanmi. Which of these might be correct? The language of the Uji chapters is the same as the rest of *Genji*. The "Takekawa" chapter is exceptional, and so it may well be true that Daini no Sanmi created it. It is difficult to know. That the chapter begins "Although this does not resemble anything related to what Murasaki has written . . ." is entirely appropriate. There is also the theory that Sai'in no Senji wrote it because she was envious of Murasaki Shikibu's having composed *Genji*; but realizing that it would be difficult to improve on it, she instead wrote the ten [Uji] chapters.[65]

Section 2

There are a total of 796 poems in *Genji*. As requested, I list here those poems that are difficult for a beginner to understand.

In the "Kiritsubo" chapter:

> *kagiri to te wakaruru michi no kanashiki ni / ikamahoshiki wa inochi narikeri*
>
> In my grief, now that the end has come and I tread this path that parts us, far more do I wish that my destination were life. ["Kiritsubo," 12:99]

i(ka)mahoshiki means "I want to go on living."[66]

Toward the end of section 2 is a lengthy digression on the subject of insects, prompted by Gyokuei's discussion of the famous poem from the "Kagerō" chapter.[67] She concludes:

To have described this, [the *kagerō* (mayfly),] in such great detail is, in truth, foolish. Yet I realize that many works in this world are simply riddled with errors, and since my work is different, I thought it might just serve as a point of comparison, so I wrote this down when I came to it.

There are a variety of works that discuss all manner of peripheral topics in *Genji*; I can by no means set right all their errors.[68] It is best not even to look at these works, so worthless they are, when you are in no position to tell what is right and what is wrong in them. Thus it is that those who know say, "Never show a *Genji Small Mirror* [*Genji kokagami*] to a beginner! Once you do, they'll come down with the *Genji* disease [*Genji yamai*]." How true this is! They go about with a know-it-all look on their faces, thinking, "So that's the original verse [*honka*]!" but they are wrong. They are worse off than if they had never seen it. This you simply have to realize.

Gyokuei shū *concludes as follows.*

To have gone into such detail may well be excessive, but in response to requests from beginners I've simply told what I know as it happened to come out. Mark my words! Mark my words! Read this through by yourself, whenever you have time on your hands, to while away the tedium. And thereafter, throw it in the fire. You really must!

ari to miru nashi to mo miru na minamoto o / kokoro na kakeso yume no ukihashi

Regard it not as being, nor, again, as being not; nor concern yourself whither it might have come, this floating bridge of dreams.[69]

TRANSLATED BY G. G. ROWLEY

THE MOONLIT LAKE COMMENTARY, 1673 (*Kogetsushō*)

KITAMURA KIGIN

Kitamura Kigin's (1624–1725) *The Moonlit Lake Commentary* is usually described as the last of the "Old Commentaries." That designation can be misleading, however, for the "newness" of the "New Commentaries" of the Edo period was not a newness of format and presentation, but a newness of attitudes and allegiances. Keichū's *Genchū shūi* (1696), Mabuchi's *Genji monogatari shinshaku* (1758), and Norinaga's *Tama no ogushi* (1796), the vanguard of the New, are visually indistinguishable from the Old Commentaries: lemma after lemma cited from the *Genji* text are followed by the commentator's explication of them. Only upon careful examination of those explications does the reader discover what is new about them: their rejection of moralistic, didactic, and (to some extent) historicist modes of interpretation; their refusal to be influenced by aristocratic familial factionalism; and their rigorous adherence to higher standards of evidentiary scholarship.

Kigin's *Kogetsushō*, by contrast, is instantly distinguishable from its predecessors, without reading a single word of it. In the first place, it incorporates a complete text of *Genji*, and all commentary is keyed to that text. Upon closer scrutiny, readers see that commentary and text are paired in several different ways, some of them highly innovative. Old-style commentary (lemma plus explication) survives here as headnotes, in which every comment that applies to a word or phrase on a particular page is placed at the top of that page; and whenever a commentary threatens to outrun the text, the text on that page is halted short of the margin, allowing the commentary to run the full length of the page. This is why many pages give the impression of a block of text "framed" by commentary. Moreover, between the lines of the text itself are further comments that Kigin feels would be more useful standing immediately adjacent to the words or phrases to which they apply. Sometimes these notes are lexicographical, providing a concise definition of a word, a modern (Genroku) translation of a phrase, or the kanji version of a potentially ambiguous word written in kana. Others identify the speaker of the passage in question. Still others supply an earlier commentator's interpretation of a particular phrase. And the entire text is punctuated. Many of these annotations and interlinea are provided by Kigin himself, but others are drawn from whichever of the Old Commentaries Kigin deemed most apposite to the text in question.

The need for a summa of this sort had been felt since at least a century earlier, when Nakanoin Michikatsu compiled *Mingō nisso*, which remained the most comprehensive compilation of *Genji* commentary well into the twentieth century. But the radically innovative formatting of *Kogetsushō*—combining text, commentary, and modern language glosses in a single work—was to make it the most widely used *Genji* for the next two centuries and more. Even Motoori Norinaga, despite his generally unfriendly attitude toward the Old Commentaries, used *Kogetsushō* as the basis of both his lectures on *Genji* and his own commentary, *Genji monogatari Tama no ogushi*. Still later, Arthur Waley (1889–1966) made the first complete English translation of *The Tale of Genji* using Kigin's *Kogetsushō*. Indeed, a close comparison of Waley's translation with *Kogetsushō* reveals several passages that Waley translated not from the *Genji* text itself but from Kigin's interlinear version of the text. This is why many of Kigin's annotations, read in translation, seem almost redundant.

Kigin's mission, then, was not to take issue with the "Old Commentators," but to present the finest fruits of their labors in a new format that

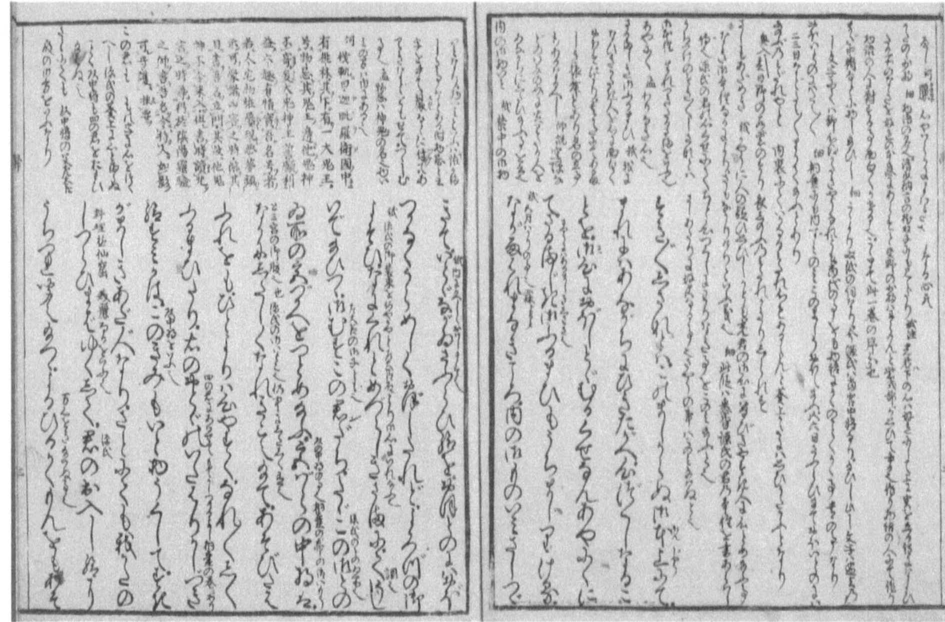

Two pages from Kitamura Kigin's commentary on "Hahakigi" in *Kogetsushō*. (Waseda University Library)

would be immediately useful to readers of his own day as an aid to deciphering an ancient text. In this he was extremely successful. Just as *Mingō nisso* had become indispensable to scholars of *Genji*, *Kogetsushō* became indispensable to readers of the tale.

For obvious reasons, the following excerpt from the "Hahakigi" chapter of *Kogetsushō* is based on Waley's translation of *The Tale of Genji*.[70] It also attempts to approximate the formatting of Kigin's text, insofar as is possible when translating from a vertically written language into a horizontally written one. For the sake of clarity, the annotations that appear in the original as headnotes are here rendered as footnotes, and the passages in the *Genji* text to which Kigin's interlinea refer are given in boldface type. Material taken from earlier commentaries is identified either by the short title of the work from which it is drawn (*Mōshin* = *Mōshinshō*) or by the name of its author (Yasoku = Nakanoin Michikatsu).

T. HARPER

still dear
It was on a [**quiet**] night when the rain never ceased its **dismal** downpour.
Mōshin: the Paulownia Court
There were not many people about in the palace and **Genji's rooms**
a short lampstand
seemed even quieter than usual. He was sitting by **the lamp**, looking at
Sōgi: scholarly texts *Sairyū*: love letters on colored paper
various books and papers. Suddenly he began pulling **some letters** out
a cabinet
of the drawers of **a desk** which stood near by. This aroused
Genji's words. He will show Chūjō only
he wants to read them those letters he has no objection to showing
Tō no Chūjō's curiosity. "**Some of them I can show to you**," said Genji,
Tō no Chūjō's words
"but there are others which I had rather . . ." "**It is just those** which I want to see. Ordinary, commonplace letters are very much alike and I do
Chūjō speaks of his own experience
not suppose that **yours differ much from mine**. What I want to see are
Sairyū: just as they themselves then feel
passionate letters **written in moments of resentment**, letters hinting consent, letters written at dusk . . . [These are the ones most worth looking at,"]

"***when the rain never ceased***" This follows the previous statement, "It was the season of long rains." (**Yasoku**) The author captures vividly the mood of this one day among many, when the rain falls without letup, thus quite enhancing the fascination of the story she is about to tell.

"***others I would rather . . .***" Among them are some that might prove embarrassing. He implies that he will keep the most interesting ones secret.

"***written in moments of resentment [just as they themselves then feel]***" ***Kakaishō*** gives kanji for "they themselves" as well as another rendition of the same from the *Nihongi*; it also cites a poem from *Shūishū* in which the word is used. **My Mentor explains**: Letters expressing the resentment a woman feels just at that moment, as well as letters written at dusk when she awaits her lover, are the most interesting, and Tō no Chūjō resents not being shown these.

---

meaning he spoke bitterly

He begged so eagerly that Genji let him examine the drawers. It was not

letters that he valued and thus

felt should be kept secret

indeed likely that he had put any very important or **secret documents** in

Sairyū: 大惣

meaning "commonplace"

the **ordinary** desk; he would have hidden them away much further from

these letters were of

sight. So he felt sure that the letters in these drawers **would be nothing**

secondary importance | Genji's feelings

to worry about. After turning over a few of them, "What an astonishing

as Chūjō reads the letters

variety!" Tō no Chūjō exclaimed and began guessing at the writers' names,

by guesswork | mostly

and made **one or two good hits**. **More often** he was wrong, and Genji,

Genji's feelings

amused by his puzzled air, said very little but generally managed to lead

Genji's words addressed to Chūjō

him astray. At last he took the letters back, saying "**But you too must have a large collection**. Show me some of yours,and my desk will open

Chūjō tells Genji he has no letters that
Genji would be likely to find interesting

to you with better will." "**I have none that you would care to see**," said Tō no Chūjō, and he continued:

"***he begged so eagerly***" **My Mentor explains:** Immediately afterward, Genji says he will let him see the love letters. Often in this tale, a person's intentions are conveyed in just such an offhand manner.

"***any important or secret documents***" Here the author speaks in her own voice in describing the love letters in his desk that he shows to Tō no Chūjō.

"***the letters in these drawers would be nothing to worry about***" ***Sairyūshō*** says: These are not likely to be letters of primary importance, which he would keep hidden; they are of secondary importance.

"***a few of them***" From here on, Tō no Chūjō speaks as he reads the love letters.

"***guessing at the writers' names***" Because love letters have no specific names or addresses, Chūjō has to guess on the basis of whose handwriting it might be, and the like.

---

from here forward is Chūjō's speech
"**I have at last discovered** that there exists no woman of whom one can say 'Here is perfection. This is indeed she.' There are many who have
Mōshin: on the surface only *Mōshin*: be skilled in calligraphy
the **superficial** art of writing a **good running hand**, or if occasion requires
in conversation or poetry Sōgi: though accomplished to this extent,
of making a **quick repartee**. But there are few who will **stand the ordeal**
they are not expert calligraphers or poets Sairyū: thinking only of themselves and no one else, a common failing in women
of any further test. Usually **their minds are entirely occupied** by
Mōshin: a sense of self satisfaction denigration of others
admiration for their own accomplishments, and their **abuse of all**
describing girls raised by
rivals creates a most unpleasant impression. Some again are **adored by**
indulgent parents kept since infants and until grown behind
over-fond parents. These have been **since childhood guarded behind**
closed windows only the slightest bit
lattice windows and **no knowledge** of them is allowed to reach the outer-world, save that of their excellence in some accomplishment or art;
the feelings of the man who hears something of her such a girl
and this **may indeed sometimes arouse our interest**. **She** is pretty and
Mōshin: meaning "serene"? lived with her parents and done nothing else
graceful and has **not yet mixed at all with the world**. Such a girl by
endeavor, strive
closely copying some model and **applying herself with great industry**
the koto, poetry, and suchlike
will often succeed in really mastering one of **the minor and ephemeral**
her intermediaries hide her bad points and emphasize her good points
arts. Her friends are careful to say nothing of her defects and to exaggerate her accomplishments, and while we cannot altogether
Mōshin cites kanji from *Kakai*
cannot imagine they lie not likely to be so
trust their praise **we cannot believe** that their judgment is **entirely astray**.

Sairyū: we find they do not

But when we take steps to test their statements, **we are invariably**

measure up to what we have heard, for in any case,

he moans, there are no perfect women in all the world

disappointed."

"***no woman of whom one can say, 'Here is perfection'***" Chūjō, on the basis of the experience of women he has accumulated, says he has at length come to realize that there is hardly a one in whom you cannot find some fault.

"***this is indeed she***" ***Sairyūshō*** says: He puts the emphasis on *this*. ["Indeed"] is an emphatic interjection. *Kachō yosei* divides this conversation into four sections.

"***the superficial art***" From here forward, the author lists one by one the deficiencies of feeling in women. Murasaki Shikibu's purpose in writing this "Ranking of Women" is to advise her readers that no woman in all the world is faultless, and thus if a woman at least gives no cause for major misgivings, one should be willing to marry her and tolerate a few minor flaws in her.

"***since childhood guarded behind lattice windows***" Kept inside since birth. Kanji is given for "since birth." *Okuiri* quotes the *Song of Everlasting Sorrow*: "In the house of Yang they had a daughter, raised throughout life within deep windows, and unknown to anyone without."

"***no knowledge of them is allowed to reach the outer world***" ***Sairyūshō*** says: Fragments of rumor may get out that she composes poetry, plays the koto, or writes a good hand. For the most part, this "Ranking of Women" describes people in general, without reference to any particular individuals. But to a certain extent, we can apply what it says to certain characters in the tale. Here, for example, we are reminded of how Genji is attracted to Suetsumuhana when he hears of her skill at the koto.

Rōkashō: Tō no Chūjō's attitude

He paused, **seeming to be slightly ashamed**[71] of the cynical tone which

Genji's thoughts. He has experienced nothing so

he had adopted, while Genji, **though his affairs had not been so**

extreme as Chūjō describes, but . . .

all-encompassing as this, seemed to have had some similar experiences,[72]

Genji's words: Are there any so completely

and he asked, smiling: "**And are there any who lack even one**

hopeless? Tō no Chūjō's words: if there were anyone so completely lacking

accomplishment?" "**No doubt, but in such a case** it is unlikely that anyone would be successfully decoyed. The number of those who have

these are words of praise

nothing to recommend them and of those in whom **nothing but good**

meaning "both are few"

can be found **is probably equal**. I divide women into three classes.[73]

even their

Those of high rank and birth are made such a fuss of and **their weak**

most minute flaws are hidden

points are so completely concealed that we are certain to be told that

of exceptional excellence

they are **paragons**. About those of the middle class everyone is allowed

there are many distinctions to be made

to express his own opinion, and we shall have **much conflicting evidence**

we pay no attention to them

to sift. As for the lower classes, **they do not concern us**."

"***seeming to be slightly ashamed***" In revealing to Genji that he, too, has been deceived by the lies of such go-betweens, Chūjō, even as he speaks, must begin to feel a bit ashamed of himself.

"***but in such a case***" A woman with something to commend her will, of course, be praised by her friends, and even I myself might be deceived and make advances toward her. But who would ever be deceived by a woman who has nothing whatever to commend her?

"***those who have nothing to recommend them***" ***Sairyūshō*** says: Those of the very lowest quality and those of the very highest quality are few in number. It is in the middle ranks that one can observe the gradations of quality that distinguish one from another.

"***those of high rank and birth***" ***Mōshinshō*** says: From here forward, women are divided into upper, middle, and lower ranks, beginning the discussion with those of high birth.

Chūjō's clear-cut classification of women

The completeness with which Tō no Chūjō disposed of the question

Genji's words. *Sairyūshō*: Genji asks, Who is to be placed

amused Genji, who said, "**It will not always be so easy to know into which**

in these three classes? people of

of the three classes a woman ought to be put. For sometimes **people of**

Rōkashō: yet another sort;
good birth who fall commoners; not of noble birth
high rank sink to the most abject positions while **others of common birth** rise to be high officers, wear self-important faces, redecorate the inside
making it difficult to distinguish these two classes
of their houses and **think themselves as good as anyone**. How are we to deal with such cases?" At this moment they were joined by Hidari no Uma no Kami and Tō Shikibu no Jō, who said they had also come to the Palace to keep the fast. As both of them were great lovers and good talkers,
Chūjō lets them speak
Tō no Chūjō **handed over to them** the decision of Genji's question, and
these are the author's own words
in the discussion which followed **many unflattering things were said**.

"***sink to the most abject positions***" ***Kakaishō*** says: Even in the Statute of Appointments, the word "abject" is used to describe those of low rank.

"***others of common birth rise to be high officers***" *Sairyūshō* says: For example, stewards of noble houses may prosper and rise to become ranking nobles themselves.

"***as good as anyone***" **My Mentor explains**: Refers to making distinctions.

"***Hidari no Uma no Kami and Tō Shikibu no Jō***" In the midst of their discussion these two gentlemen appear. There are no genealogies that indicate who they might be.

"***great lovers***" The great rakes of their day.

GENJI TEXT TRANSLATED BY ARTHUR WALEY;
COMMENTARY TRANSLATED BY T. HARPER

Notes

1. This question is borrowed from Frank Kermode's inquiry into "the processes by which we establish the high opinion of a work or of an artist which normally precedes the most energetic efforts of criticism and interpretation—that is, the nature of the historical forces which certify some works but not others as requiring or deserving these special forms of attention" (*Forms of Attention* [Chicago: University of Chicago Press, 1985], viii).

2. Tamagami Takuya, "Onna no tame no onna ga kaita onna no sekai no monogatari," in *Genji monogatari kenkyū* (Tokyo: Kadokawa Shoten, 1966), 432–40.

3. *(Nōin-bon) Makura no soshi* 262, in Sei Shōnagon, *Makura no sōshi*, ed. Matsuo Satoshi and Nagai Kazuko, NKBZ 11:415.

4. *Roppyakuban utaawase*, ed. Kubota Jun and Yamaguchi Akiho, SNKBT 38:187.

5. See, for example, the passage from *Genchū saihishō* in the headnote to Sojaku's *Explicating Murasaki*, translated in chapter 3 of this volume.

6. Abe Akio, Oka Kazuo, and Yamagishi Tokuhei, eds., *Genji monogatari*, Kokugo kokubungaku kenkyūshi taisei 3 (Tokyo: Sanseidō, 1960), 41. The passage

discussed (*to areba kakari, au sa kiru sa ni*) can be found in "Hahakigi," 1:138. Koreyuki's version of the *Kokinshū* poem (1060) is inexact.

7. Abe, Oka, and Yamagishi, eds., *Genji monogatari*, 85.

8. Motoori Norinaga, *Genji monogatari Tama no ogushi*, ed. Ōno Susumu, in MNZ 4:180.

9. Yotsutsuji Yoshinari, *Kakaishō*, ed. Tamagami Takuya, in *Shimeishō, Kakaishō*, ed. Tamagami Takuya, Yamamoto Ritatsu, and Ishida Jōji (Tokyo: Kadokawa Shoten, 1968), 186.

10. Yoshinari, *Kakaishō*, 214.

11. Ichijō Kanera, *(Matsunaga-bon) Kachō yosei*, ed. Ii Haruki, GMKS 1:21–22.

12. *Rōkashō, fu Genji monogatari kikigaki*, ed. Ii Haruki, GMKS 8:18.

13. Sanjōnishi Sanetaka, *(Naikaku Bunko-bon) Sairyūshō*, ed. Ii Haruki, GMKS 7:15.

14. Kujō Tanemichi, *Mōshinshō*, vol. 1, ed. Nomura Seiichi, GMKS 4:36. The [*sic*] refers to the fact that earlier commentaries actually say that it should be read with a break after "The name itself was awe inspiring," not after "whispered about behind his back," as Tanemichi has it here.

15. Tanemichi, *Mōshinshō*, 36–37.

16. Tanemichi, *Mōshinshō*, 37.

17. Nakanoin Michikatsu, *Mingō nisso*, vol. 1, ed. Nakada Takeshi, GMKS 11:92.

18. *Lao-tzu*, 1. Arthur Waley translates this passage,"It was from the Nameless that Heaven and Earth sprang; / The named is but the mother that rears the ten thousand creatures, each after its kind" (*The Way and Its Power: A Study of the Tao Tê Ching and Its Place in Chinese Thought* [New York: Grove Press, 1958], 141).

19. This translation of Michikatsu's paraphrase of the *Analects*, 13–24, is based on Simon Leys's translation of the Chinese original in *The Analects of Confucius* (New York: Norton, 1997), 64. Simon Leys was the nom de plume of the renowned Sinologist Pierre Ryckmans (1935–2014).

20. Michikatsu, *Mingō nisso*, 92–93.

21. Michikatsu, *Mingō nisso*, 93.

22. Michikatsu, *Mingō nisso*, 93.

23. Translated from *Genji monogatari kochūshaku sōkan*, ed. Nakano Kōichi (Tokyo: Musashino Shoin, 1980), 4:615–38, esp. 615–19. The text of *Genji* cited in the commentary is in SNKBT 19:32–34 and NKBZ 12:129–32.

24. *Hahakigi no kokoro wo shiranu sonohara no / michi ni ayanaku madoinuru kana* (SNKBT 19:76).

25. *kazunaranu fuseya ni ouru na no usa ni / aru ni mo arazu kiyuru hahakigi* (SNKBT 19:76).

26. *sonohara ya fuseya ni ouru hahakigi no / ari tote yukedo awanu kimi kana* (*Kokin rokujō*, 3019).

27. Much internal evidence in *Genji* implies that the tale is set during approximately these three historical eras, a period that by Murasaki Shikibu's time had come to be regarded as a "golden age" of relatively direct imperial rule.

28. Takaakira (914–982), a son of the Daigo Emperor, was forced into exile in 970 by the Fujiwara hegemons.

29. Zhou Gongdan, the Duke of Zhou, brother of King Wu (who founded the Zhou dynasty [1045–256 B.C.E.]), and regent to King Cheng, King Wu's son. He conducted a successful military expedition against rebels, led in part by the duke's two brothers, in areas east of Zhou. One of the duke's brothers was killed and the other exiled.

30. Hakurakuten, or Bo Juyi (772–846), a Chinese poet esteemed by Japanese readers during and after the Heian period, was demoted and exiled in 815 after arguing with the emperor.

31. Michizane (845–903), Minister of the Right and a distinguished scholar and poet of Chinese, was a victim of political factionalism and forced into exile in 901 to Dazaifu.

32. An allusion to the first poem in *Tales of Ise* (ca. 900), in which the hero expresses his feelings in response to a glimpse of two charming sisters.

33. The term *yū* here may be taken as synonymous with *yūgen*, conventionally used to refer to an aesthetic of subtle or obscure beauty.

34. A term adopted by *Genji* readers and commentators to refer to the discussion of the qualities of various "types" of women and their suitability for courtship. It extends through the first half of "The Broom Tree" and is the primary object of Sōgi's commentary here.

35. Yūrin is so described, for example, in *Yasutomi-ki*, the diary of the low-ranking courtier and scholar of Chinese Nakahara Yasutomi (ca. 1394–1457), which covers the years 1417 to 1455. See entry for Kyōtoku 3/1454.7.5, cited in Ii Haruki, ed., *Genji monogatari chūshakusho, kyōjushi jiten* (Tokyo: Tōkyōdō Shuppan, 2001), 441, 497.

36. For a printed edition, see *Yūrin: Hikaru Genji ichibu uta*, ed. Imai Gen'e, GMKS 3.

37. The manuscript is in the Spencer Collection of the New York Public Library.

38. Kaoku Gyokuei's "*Genji monogatari* no okori" (manuscript, 1587 and 1593) is in the collection of Senshū University, Tokyo. For a discussion, see Niimi Akihiko, "Kaoku Gyokuei to 'Chaa,'" in *Heian bungaku no kochūshaku to juyō*, ed. Jinno Hidenori, Niimi Akihiko, and Yokomizo Hiroshi (Tokyo: Musashino Shoin, 2009), 2:120–42.

39. For a transcription of the holograph, see Ii Haruki, "Kaoku Gyokuei ei '*Genji monogatari* kanmei waka' ni tsuite," in *Genji monogatari to sono kenkyū sekai* (Tokyo: Kazama Shobō, 2002), 1055–60.

40. For a summary of the research, see G. G. Rowley, "*The Tale of Genji*: Required Reading for Aristocratic Women," in *The Female as Subject: Reading and Writing in Early Modern Japan*, ed. P. F. Kornicki, Mara Patessio, and G. G. Rowley (Ann Arbor: Center for Japanese Studies, University of Michigan, 2010), 41–49; rebutted in Niimi Akihiko, "*Kaokushō* kaidai," in Kaoku Gyokuei, *Kaokushō*, ed. Ishikawa Hajime et al. (Tokyo: Musashino Shoin, 2010), 502–3.

41. Numerous examples of Gyokuei's borrowing from earlier commentaries are offered in Nakaba Yoshiko, "*Kaokushō* no chūshaku taido: 'Osanaki hito, onnadochi' no tame ni," *Kokubungaku* 80 (2000): 17–30. The most detailed discussion of Gyokuei's commentarial attitudes is in Tsutsumi Yasuo, "*Genji monogatari* chūshakushi jō no jidai kubun ni tsuite (ge): Kochū sekai e no hangyaku to sono tassei," *Kokugakuin zasshi* 89, no. 8 (1988): 36–52.

42. See Abutsu, *The Nursemaid's Letter*, translated in chapter 2 of this volume.

43. Translated from Kaoku Gyokuei, *Kaokushō*, in *Mikan kokubun kochūshaku taikei*, ed. Yoshizawa Yoshinori (1936; repr., Tokyo: Teikoku Kyōikukai Shuppanbu, 1969), 384–448. Page numbers follow each passage.

44. The Shigeisha is now understood to be simply the Sino-Japanese designation for the pavilion known more familiarly as the Kiritsubo.

45. That is, the Daigo Emperor (884–930; r. 897–930); the Engi era lasted from 901 to 923. Gyokuei here borrows just the first sentence of the commentary on the phrase *izure no ohon-toki ni ka*, from *Kakaishō*. See Yoshinari, *Kakaishō*, 189a.

46. This is the place where Genji's mother is taken to be cremated.

47. Gyokuei here glosses a phrase that begins *Sakon no Tsukasa* (Bodyguards of the Left) in her commentary, but this seems to be an error—either hers or a later copyist's—for the *Ukon no Tsukasa* (Bodyguards of the Right) given in texts of *Genji*, "Kiritsubo," 12:112.

48. The text reads "Shujaka," surely a copyist's error for Shujaku. Gyokuei borrows the sentence *Shichijō Shujaku ni ari* from the entry for Kōrokan in *Mōshinshō*. See Tanemichi, *Mōshinshō*, 26–27.

49. Murasaki Shikibu, *The Tale of Genji*, trans. Royall Tyler (New York: Viking, 2001), 13.

50. This and the previous note closely follow Kanera, *Kachō yosei*, 16.

51. Gyokuei quotes just the first sentence of Kanera, *Kachō yosei*, 18. Present-day commentators understand the *shimo-saburai* (anteroom) referred to here in the text of *Genji* to be a room south of the *tenjō no ma* (waiting room) in the Seiryōden of the Inner Palace. Gyokuei's comment suggests that she thinks both are the same room.

52. Gyokuei, *Kaokushō*, 385–86.

53. Daini no Sanmi Fujiwara Kataiko (999–1082?), daughter of Murasaki Shikibu and Fujiwara no Nobutaka (947?–1001). Daini no Sanmi served as wet nurse to the GoReizei Emperor (1025–1068; r. 1045–1068) and was noted for her poetry, which is collected in the *Daini no Sanmi shū* (*Tō Sanmi shū* [*Collected Poems of Daini no Sanmi*, after 1068]).

54. Gyokuei, *Kaokushō*, 436. Recent scholars take the opposite view and understand *murasaki no yukari* to mean "tales told by gentlewomen in the service of [the character] Murasaki." See "Takekawa," 16:53n.4.

55. *Sangen ichiran*, completed in 1496, is a commentary on *The Tale of Genji* in which the compiler, Tominokōji Toshimichi (d. 1513), combined interpretations from the three earlier commentaries *Shimeishō*, *Kakaishō*, and *Kachō yosei*. There is no complete printed edition, but selections can be found in Abe, Oka, and Yamagishi, eds., *Genji monogatari*.

56. A reference to a story from the *Meng Qiu* (J. *Mōgyū*), a Tang-period primer in which rhyming four-character compounds are used to help students remember key stories about historical and legendary figures. The family of Che Yin of the Qin "was often too poor to buy oil for lamps, and so in the summer months he would fill a gauze bag with several dozen fireflies and use it to light his books, thus continuing his studies far into the night" (Burton Watson, summary, in Li Han, *Meng Ch'iu: Famous Episodes from Chinese History and Legend*, trans. Burton Watson

[Tokyo: Kodansha International, 1979], 120). Gyokuei's source may be the *Mōgyū* itself, which had long circulated in Japan, or one of the many Japanese versions of the text. Murasaki Shikibu herself alludes to this very story in the "Otome" chapter of *Genji*, 14:20; see *Tale of Genji*, trans. Tyler, 383.

57. *Manna o erami isasaka nimo kana o tsukehaberu nari.* In the text of *Kaokushō* translated here, Gyokuei does not gloss kanji with kana; instead, she omits most of the kanji and renders almost all words in kana.

58. Gyokuei, *Kaokushō*, 447–48. In comparing *Kaokushō* to the *hototogisu* (translated here as "cuckoo"), a bird that lays its eggs in the nests of other birds, Gyokuei may be suggesting that her commentary is no more than an interloper in the nest of legitimate *Genji* commentaries. The simile is modest, too, in a different way, since the word *hototogisu* can be written with characters that read *funyo*, meaning "unworthy of comparison."

59. Translated from Kaoku Gyokuei, *Gyokuei shū*, ed. Ii Haruki, in *Gengo kenkyū shiryōshū*, Hekichūdō sōsho 87 (Ōbuchō: Yanase Kazuo, 1969), 121–62. Ii's transcription is of an undated manuscript in the collection of Yanase Kazuo (1912–2008).

60. Tsutsumi Yasuo, *Genji monogatari chūshakushi ronkō* (Tokyo: Shintensha, 1999), 258–59.

61. Both *Sumiyoshi monogatari* (mid-tenth century) and *Hitomotogiku* (Muromachi period) are "stepchild stories" (*mamako monogatari*). *Sumiyoshi* is mentioned in *The Tale of Genji*, but extant versions of the text are thought to be Kamakura-period rewrites. So far, it has proved impossible to identify *Tōjima*; *The Distant Isle* is a tentative translation of the title.

62. *Gyokuei shū*, 121–22.

63. The Rashōmon was the principal gate to the city of Heian-kyō, located a considerable distance south of the Suzaku Gate to the Greater Palace. The Rashōmon was rebuilt several times during the mid-Heian period, but after its collapse during a storm in the Seventh Month of 980, it was never reconstructed, and by the time of *Genji*, only its foundation stones remained. See "Rashōmon," in *Kokushi daijiten* (Tokyo: Yoshikawa Kōbunkan, 1979–1997), 14:501–2.

64. There are two possible *senji* (imperial emissaries) to whom Gyokuei may be referring here, as suggested in Inaga Keiji, *Genji monogatari no kenkyū: seiritsu to denryū* (Tokyo: Kasama Shoin, 1967), 439–40. One is a *senji* in the service of the Daisai'in Princess Senshi (964–1035), the daughter of the Murakami Emperor (926–967; r. 946–967), who served as High Priestess of Kamo for fifty-seven years, from 975 to 1031. The story that the High Priestess asked the Jōtōmon'in Empress (Fujiwara no Shōshi) for stories "to while away the tedium," that Shōshi summoned Murasaki Shikibu and asked her to write something, and that "in response to the command she wrote *Genji*" is related in *A Nameless Notebook* (*Mumyōzōshi*), translated in chapter 2 of this anthology. The other *senji* (ca. 1020–1092) was wet nurse to a later High Priestess of Kamo, the Rokujō Sai'in Princess Baishi (1039–1096), and is the author of *Sagoromo monogatari* (ca. 1060).

65. *Gyokuei shū*, 125–26, 136.

66. *Gyokuei shū*, 141. This is the Kiritsubo Consort's poem to the emperor, recited just before she is given permission to leave the palace.

67. *Gyokuei shū*, 155–56; *Tale of Genji*, trans. Tyler, 1073. The poem is

ari to mite te ni wa torarezu mireba mata / yukue mo shirazu kieshi kagerō
There it is, just there, yet ever beyond my reach, till I look once more,
and it is gone, the mayfly, never to be seen again. ("Kagerō," 17:264)

68. The text is corrupt here, and one phrase in this sentence could not be translated.

69. *Gyokuei shū*, 156, 162.

70. *The Tale of Genji: A Novel in Six Parts, by Lady Murasaki*, trans. Arthur Waley (1935; New York: Modern Library, 1960), 21–23.

71. Modern commentators take this to mean that Genji is flabbergasted rather than that Tō no Chūjō is ashamed. Waley, of course, follows the *Kogetsushō* interpretation. Both commentary and translation are thus left unaltered.

72. Waley translates this as Tō no Chūjō's speech ("I know my experience is not large, but that is the conclusion I have come to so far"), whereas both the *Kogetsushō* and modern commentators take it to represent Genji's thoughts. In this one sentence, therefore, it has been necessary to correct Waley's translation to agree with Kigin's interlinear paraphrase of it. Otherwise, Waley's rendition has been transcribed verbatim.

73. This sentence does not appear in the *Genji* text.

Chapter 7

Edo-Period Treatises

BY THE END OF THE EDO PERIOD, it had become common practice to distinguish the *Genji* commentaries of that era from those of the medieval era. The former were called the "New Commentaries" and the latter, the "Old Commentaries." But what was so "new" about the New Commentaries or, for that matter, "old" about the Old Commentaries? At first glance, the last of the Old Commentaries, Kitamura Kigin's *Moonlit Lake Commentary* (*Kogetsushō*), actually *looks* newer than anything by Keichū, Kamo no Mabuchi, or Motoori Norinaga. As we have seen, it contains a complete text of *The Tale of Genji*, as well as a whole panoply of aids to help the reader understand the text. On closer scrutiny, however, we find that despite surface resemblances, there are good reasons for considering the New Commentaries strikingly newer and better than the Old. Here is how Hagiwara Hiromichi, the first commentator to make this distinction, defines that difference:

> Now, *Kakaishō*, *Kachō yosei*, and most of the other [early] commentaries were written by ranking gentlemen of the court nobility, and they date from an age nearer to antiquity than our own. One might well wonder, therefore, how they could be [so inaccurate]. But let us consider the reasons. These learned gentlemen of the past had one unfortunate failing: whatever they learned they kept secret. Even the most insignificant bits of knowledge were kept secret. As a result, these commentaries would be transmitted secretly to no more than one or two persons. Not only was there no custom of sharing their work, but they were lax about the collection and collation of ancient texts and the study of evidence. In many cases they would simply decide that such-and-such was the case and compose their annotation from memory. . . .

> Of course, if we know all there is to know about something, there is no need for anyone to write a commentary on it. But the amount of detail that remains unknown, despite this plethora of commentary, is extraordinary, which makes it difficult to trust anything they have to say. For this reason, the *Kogetsushō* and all commentaries before it I call the "Old Commentaries," and I do not, as a rule, cite them.

In contrast,

> *Genchū shūi* [*Gleanings of Commentary on Genji*, 1696], by the monk Keichū, is a fascinating and magnificent work. On the basis of an extensive investigation of ancient texts, the author demonstrates the failings of the aforementioned Old Commentaries and rectifies their errors. The author is an extraordinarily learned man. In his interpretations of the poetic anthologies, he is never bound by the views of [previous] commentary. He makes not a single unfounded assertion; indeed, he is the pioneer scholar of modern "critical philology" [*kōshōgaku*]. His *Genchū shui* totally changed the nature of commentary on this tale. For this reason I set it and those that follow it apart and call them the "New Commentaries."[1]

For Hiromichi, then, the distinction between old and new is as much a social as a scholarly distinction. The Old Commentaries were compiled principally by aristocrats of the imperial court and a few lesser mortals, like Sōgi, who had been granted entrée to court society. By contrast, none of the authors of the New Commentaries were aristocrats or even hangers-on at court. Nor was it simply that the baton had passed to a new generation. There was a decided sense of opposition between the two camps. For example, Lord Karasumaru Mitsuhiro confided to one of his worshipful disciples that "the honored houses of the nobility deign not to consult" *Bansui ichiro*, a commentary compiled by a provincial *renga* master, while Motoori Norinaga was at pains to point out that "the work of someone of a certain [noble] house may be of no worth whatever, whereas it often happens that someone of the most humble birth will produce surpassingly fine work."[2] And as James McMullen notes in his introduction to *Discursive Commentary on Genji* (*Genji gaiden*), even Kumazawa Banzan, a samurai who collaborated with a ranking aristocrat in his study of *Genji*, wanted "to liberate the tale from courtly patronage and to claim it as a text of universal relevance." Their success in this endeavor must be counted a major accomplishment of the New Commentators and their contemporaries.

The rigor of their scholarship and their social sensibilities aside, however, commentators and critics of the Edo period continued to be exercised by some of the same moral issues as their medieval forebears: *Genji*'s value as a fictional narrative; the overt eroticism of the tale; and, particularly, Genji's secret liaison with his own father's empress, which, in the eyes of some, constituted a "taint" (*mono no magire*) to the hitherto unbroken line of emperors descended directly from the gods. As the title of this chapter suggests, even those scholars whose principal purpose was exegesis prefaced their commentary with lengthy treatises in which they developed quite a variety of solutions to these problems. Whereas medieval commentary might interpret the depiction of "flaws" of this sort as moral homilies, justifiable by resort to the Buddhist concept of Expedient Truth (*hōben*) or, alternatively, as Confucian object lessons, Edo-period scholars were more inventive.

For Kumazawa Banzan, *Genji* was essentially a work of history, depicting the "fine style" of ages past, which, unless recorded, might deteriorate and "be lost in vulgarity." But Murasaki Shikibu was well aware that her good intentions might come to naught if her work did not last. So the amours that she depicts are meant to serve the important function of attracting readers to the tale, thus ensuring the long life of the lessons that were her main purpose in writing it.

Andō Tameakira, too, treats the same moral issues, including the troublesome "taint" to the imperial line, but he insists that the exemplary personal character of Murasaki Shikibu is ample assurance that her motives can be only admonitory. In Tameakira's view, *The Tale of Genji* serves the important Confucian function of encouraging good and chastising evil (*kanzen chōaku*), but it does so subtly, through the depiction of "human feeling" (*ninjō*) and the "ways of the world" (*setai*). Having read *The Tale of Genji*, readers will see the consequences of the social transgressions that Murasaki depicts, particularly Fujitsubo's great lapse (*mono no magire*), and thus will be more cautious and circumspect in their own behavior. Significantly, Tameakira cites the *Murasaki Shikibu Diary* as proof that Murasaki Shikibu was both highly educated and a morally upright woman who, for example, rebuffs the amorous advances of Fujiwara no Michinaga. In this implicitly biographical criticism, the author's own impeccable morality stands as proof of the tale's moral integrity.

Perhaps the most famous defense of *Genji* against charges of moral turpitude was that of Motoori Norinaga. Though not totally dismissive of either the medieval commentators or his more immediate predecessors Banzan and Tameakira, Norinaga rejected absolutely all arguments based on Buddhist or Confucian doctrine. Although there are, he says, "points of chance resemblance and accord with Confucian and Buddhist texts, it will not do to seize on these as characterizing the work as a whole. Its overall import differs sharply from works of that sort." Readers do not read fiction in search of moral instruction. Nor did Murasaki Shikibu write *Genji* in order to teach moral lessons. "The main purpose of the tale," Norinaga insists, "is the depiction of the workings of the emotions [*mono no aware*]." In support of this claim, he explicates in great detail the passage in the "Hotaru" chapter generally taken to represent Murasaki's own views on the writing of fiction. No commentator in the previous eight hundred years had ever identified the primary importance of this passage, much less analyzed it in such detail.

Hagiwara Hiromichi, the last scholar represented in this chapter, displays an entirely different form of originality. Whereas the work of his predecessors was in one way or another driven by ideology, Hiromichi is eclectic and open-minded; he seeks not to displace but to synthesize, to bring together the best work of past commentators and combine it with a new and more authoritative text of *Genji*. Unfortunately, Hiromichi's health failed, and he died after completing only the first eight chapters of his commentary. But his introductory treatise remains a model of scholarly magnanimity, and his commentary on the early chapters of *Genji*, from "Kiritsubo" through "Hana no en," leaves the reader regretting that there could not have been more.

T. HARPER

DISCURSIVE COMMENTARY ON GENJI, CA. 1673
(*Genji gaiden*)

KUMAZAWA BANZAN

Kumazawa Banzan (1619–1691) was born into a samurai family that had suffered a decline during the final phase of Japan's unification, yet retained proud traditions of imperial ancestry and ownership of land. Banzan himself was employed by the daimyo of Okayama, Ikeda Mitsumasa

(1609–1682), who valued him both for his qualities of leadership and administrative ability and for his knowledge of Confucianism. As a young man, Banzan also studied briefly under the Ming-dynasty Wang Yangming scholar Nakae Tōju (1608–1648). From Tōju he learned Shingaku (Learning of the Mind), a tradition within Neo-Confucianism that valued the individual's conscience as the highest moral authority. Banzan is traditionally associated with a period of enlightened Confucian-style administration in the Okayama domain. In fact, however, his success was largely limited to a period of reconstruction following a disastrous flood that afflicted the domain in 1654. He fell victim both to the hostility of senior hereditary vassals of the Ikeda house and to his own ill health.

In 1657, Banzan retired from active feudal service. He moved to Kyoto, where he cultivated a circle of court nobles (*kuge*) and pursued the study of music. Among his friends was the monk and litterateur Gensei of Fukakusa (1623–1668), with whom Banzan seems to have begun the systematic study of *The Tale of Genji.* Another friend was the court noble Nakanoin Michishige (1631–1710), a member of a senior court lineage long associated with the study of *Genji.* But Banzan's activities in Kyoto aroused the shogunate's suspicion, and he was expelled from the city in 1667. He settled eventually in Akashi, the site of Genji's own exile in the tale. It was in Akashi that he began a remarkable and secretive collaboration with Michishige on a joint commentary on *Genji.* The basic procedure was for Michishige to send Banzan copies of his own drafts. Banzan responded by inserting his own interpretations into Michishige's manuscripts. At a later stage, Banzan's contribution was excerpted from the joint work to form an independent commentary. This work, known as *Genji gaiden* (*Discursive Commentary on Genji*), is the main source of his views on the tale.[3]

Banzan had come late to court culture, and he read *Genji* from a fresh, albeit provincial, perspective. His reflex was to liberate the tale from courtly patronage and to claim it as a text of universal relevance. Unlike most of his Confucian contemporaries, who condemned the work for its "debauched morality," Banzan saw it as a highly serious historical record of a phase of history in which Japan still retained many features of the ideal Confucian government that, he believed, had characterized the world in the remote past. Banzan recovered from the tale a society of high culture and manners or, as he termed it, "style," which contrasted with the military and authoritarian society of his own times. Society was, he believed, still articulated by "ritual" and music; authority still resided in the court and was exercised through virtue rather than law or coercion; the family was respected; women were conceded dignity and importance, especially as mothers; and society had not yet been divided into the separate estates of courtier and warrior. At the same time, a modest level of consumption preserved Japan's pristine, forest-clad mountains from deforestation. Perhaps most of all, this was a society in which the good and the cultivated could, irrespective of their hereditary status, as Genji's own ascendancy demonstrated, rise to positions of political influence. Banzan insisted, furthermore, that the tale should form the basis for the reconstruction of Japanese society. But he also found negative features, signs of incipient decline, in the world of *Genji*. The tale, in fact, described a society already in transition: the delinquent lack of interest in the personal administration of emperors and the oligarchic exercise of power by the kindred of the Minister of the Right were symptoms of the approaching end of the "royal age" (*ōdai*). Thus Banzan was able both to exploit the tale as embodying an ideal and to put it to admonitory and cautionary purposes for his contemporaries.

The problem of the salacious nature of the tale remained. Banzan constructed an elaborate set of arguments to explain this. In his introduction (translated here), he insists that superficial appearances notwithstanding, this was basically a historical narrative. The erotic license that it depicted was simply a device to ensure that the work attracted readers and thus survived. Properly understood, *Genji* was a text of universal relevance, an invaluable national resource, a witness to the high moral and cultural achievements of Japan in the age before the ascendancy of the warrior state and the associated instability that had characterized Japanese history ever since, and Genji himself, though not without flaw, was an exemplar of human potentiality.

JAMES MCMULLEN

Introduction

A certain lady said, "Among the various books from former times that contain teachings for men, there must be lessons for women, but for the unlettered [in Chinese texts], they are hard to read and interpret. So we have no alternative to reading just the kana stories that have been passed down in written form from the past and gaining some slight understanding from them. Even among these, there do not appear to be any that offer reliable teachings. *The Tale of Genji* is a fictional account dedicated to amorous matters, but since it is the work of such a very clever woman, and perhaps because the style is easy or because it is suited to the same feminine minds, reading its multifarious incidents offers much that is readily accessible. Would even a work of that kind, by any chance, possibly provide lessons for foolish women?"

The reply: On the surface, *The Tale of Genji* describes amorous events, but the reality is different. For this reason, among those who are fond of reading *The Tale of Genji* are people who are excessively fastidious. The motive for writing this tale is that the author lamented that, since her whole age was proceeding to its end, the fine style of the remote past was deteriorating and would be lost in vulgarity. Yet people would shun and keep away from an overtly proper book. Since it would have few readers, it would not be universally available. Although a given book may be educational, when the language is stiff and people are alienated, it does not long survive. Or even if it survives, since it lacks readers, it is as good as lost. So, judging that it would be to no avail were she to leave [a book of that sort], she deliberately did not display a didactic style. She simply treated [her narrative] as an amorous amusement and thereby bequeathed a detailed account of the courtly fine style and attitudes of past times. With no understanding of its original [purpose], people think of [*Genji*] as a wholly fictitious tale. Praising its telling and style, they conceive of it as a tale from the mouth of an ordinary narrator. This is because people of shallow views are unfamiliar with Japanese and Chinese books. In fact, [*Genji*] belongs to the same category as Zhuang Zhou's apologue;[4] it sometimes identifies this with that, speaks of the circumstances of the people of past times as though they concerned contemporaries, and writes of Chinese matters as Japanese. But with regard to the reality [behind them], all matters are supported by evidence. Therefore a man of old said that with regard to its factuality, [*Genji*] is in the style of Sima Qian's *Shiji*.[5] It must be that in order to disguise matters concerning people of recent times, she improvised the name of the amorous man Lord Genji; treated [his story] like a fictitious tale; and, gathering together stories ancient and modern, Japanese and Chinese, even down to things of her own age, attributed them to him. It also is said that Murasaki Shikibu's father, Tametoki, was an erudite and talented man and left a draft with the intention of writing a sequel to the national histories and that Shikibu got hold of this and rewrote it in the form of this tale. Thus the Ichijō Emperor as well, reading this tale, is reported to have said that [the author] was well read in the *Nihongi*.[6]

So then, a would-be reader of this tale should not be concerned with the amorous and immoral content but pay attention to the author's inner motive and be concerned with the good aspects of the book. Devoted readers ignorant of this approach suffer much detriment and derive little benefit.

Now the reason that the Royal Way of Japan has long endured is because rites, music, and literature have not been lost or fallen into vulgarity. The excessively hard and strong do not last long, but the generous and soft endure. Such phenomena as the teeth being hard but quickly dropping out; the tongue being soft but lasting till the end are all-pervasive principles. The military houses may on occasion grab power over the realm through the awesomeness of their great strength, but like teeth falling out, they do not last long. Royalty dwells in submissiveness but does not lose its position. However, when it combines softness with a lack of virtue, people's respect for it is slight. When it lacks the capacity to inspire people to shame and respect in its presence, even though it exists, it is as though it did not. In the end, it verges on extinction. Only in this tale does there survive the means to revive what has become extinct and to afford a vision of rites, music, and literature. Therefore, what one should first pay attention to in this tale is the fine style of the remote past. The way in which rites were correct and gently paced and music was harmonious reflects the fact that men and women alike were courtly and constantly played court music and were not demeaned in spirit.

Next, the descriptions of human feelings in the book are detailed. Ignorance of human feelings frequently results in loss of the harmony of the five human relations. When one contravenes these relationships, the state is not well governed nor is the house in order. For this reason, the preservation, even in the *Maoshi*, of the debauched style[7] is in order to familiarize [readers] with human feelings both good and bad. Were the people of a state all superior men, administrations and punishments would serve no function. The Way of Government is simply to teach ordinary men and so is impossible without knowledge of human feelings and historical change. This being the case, in this tale, too, by the use of various transpositions, she [Murasaki] provides an exhaustive account of human feelings and, further, gives a good description of how times progressively change. Beginning from the poetry right down to the least significant prose passages, there are descriptions of the temperaments of the respective characters as though painted in pictures. Therein lies the great marvel of the comprehension of human feelings in this tale.

As far as the poems are concerned, their language is deep and mysterious, and they are difficult to understand unless one is qualified in the field. Furthermore, with regard to the composition of verse, the people of the past related the feelings in their hearts much as the people of the present write letters. However, [since that past] the hearts and language of people have gradually approached closer to the vulgar; a dichotomy [between speech] and verse has resulted; and with the coming into being of what is called "the Way of Poetry,"[8] matters have become vexatious. Were this trend to continue, the elegance of the language of the people of the past would, in future times, become hard to understand, and [language] would become more and more lost in vulgarity. So one should select those passages where the text is admirable and where the old language is hard on the ear and understanding and should concentrate on them. Thus the people of the past also said that to resolve uncertainties about language, nothing can rival *The Tale of Genji*.

In general, this tale was written basically to transform style. In this context, she [Murasaki] gave a particularly detailed account of the Way of Music. The pastime of strings and woodwinds is the activity of superior men. Therefore, when there is ignorance of the pastime of woodwinds and strings, the courtly style and customs die out and are lost in common feelings. The reason for this is that the hearts of people are living things and so are always in motion. Music is the correct and beautiful form of pastime. Therefore, when one relies on pastimes that contain this correct Way, people become courtly of their own accord, and their style and customs become noble and elegant. However, a person who is a stranger to the Way of Music is unattractive. When he grasps its spirit a little, [it is found to be] supremely delicate and attractive. Delicacy without satiety is perfection. There is an ancient saying, too, that the relations of a superior man are delicate like water.[9]

Music is the object of the affections of the superior man who takes pleasure in the Way; it is thus an activity that anyone of a little sensibility cannot afford not to know. For this reason, long ago, from farthest Tsukushi as far as the end of Michinoku, anyone of a little sensibility, whether man or woman, played music. Still less was there anyone among the court nobility ignorant of it. But with the arrival of recent times, the pastimes of the courtly have been lost in vulgarity; tasteless things are done; people devoted to and knowledgeable of musical matters have become rarer and rarer; and houses in various respective fields have been formed. In the end, a state of barely maintaining performances has resulted. As they have become the occupation of respective houses, the pastimes of the superior man have degenerated into [mere] techniques. Since [the practitioners] feel like functionaries, matters have become progressively shallower; a selfish concern with establishing rival houses has resulted; and contrary [to its true purpose], music has become the resort of the affections of small men. Although there are some people dedicated to their Way, since they do not release it beyond their own houses on the grounds that it is an esoteric treasure, people who know it subsequently become rare. Scarcity of people with the requisite knowledge leads, in the end, to extinction. The Way of the superior man is for universal dissemination among men, so there is nothing at all to make an esoteric treasure. Though he wishes to inform people of it and to preserve a written record for universal dissemination, the superior man takes it as a matter of sadness that those in the know simply become progressively rarer. Thus, although setting up esoteric treasures looks like valuing a Way, in most cases it derives from the small man's profiteering and competitive spirit of self-satisfaction and self-assertion. Had she [Murasaki] not recorded the Way of Music in this tale, with the arrival of the present age there would be no one with knowledge of it. [Such practitioners as there are] would not be deeply versed in their Way, and it would be hard for them to gain understanding of their tradition.

With all Ways, the loss of the *furi* is difficult to repair. Therefore in this tale, there is a great deal written to record the *furi*. *Furi* refers to the style of performance. Even this tale finds it hard to express comprehensively on paper the esoteric and oral traditions of the various houses of the time. They are recorded in outline to "await the superior man of the future."[10] Since Ways in all cases proceed from the superior man, even in later ages a true superior man will, on obtaining a little clue, understand its significance and be able to revive what has been abandoned. It is said that "to change style and alter customs, there is nothing better than music."[11] This is the reason that in this tale, [Murasaki] paid special attention to music in writing her account. By exhausting the way of transforming style, people naturally gain inspiration. This is why the tale is useful for the Way of administration.

In all cases, the manners of remote antiquity were pure, bountiful, and noble. The usages of a terminal age are extravagant, depleted, and base. She [Murasaki] lamented the fact that teachings of rites and music were deteriorating in each successive age, that the elegance and beauty of manners and customs were progressively changing as time wore on, that the residual style of the Ninefold [Palace], too, with the advent of the terminal age, was lost in vulgarity, and that the manners and customs of the court noble houses were on the verge of extinction. In accordance with the saying "catching a fish and forgetting the trap,"[12] with this tale, she made a fishing line of the amorousness that people naturally have a predilection for, and provided universal entertainment to people of the world. [The resulting work reflects] her ambition to preserve [the inheritance of the past] until an enlightened lord should arise. So, without this tale, how might one behold and know the style bequeathed by the royalty of remote ages? Therefore, the Juntoku Emperor also left a description of this tale as the supreme treasure of Japan.[13] The profound significance of its quality as a supreme treasure, however, is not accessible to people of mediocrity and below[14] who are not versed in the Way of Rites and Music.

The lady said: "From listening to you, I understand its meaning. Although one hears that [*The Tale of Genji*] is a fictional tale, reading it does not give that impression at all. This must be because it disguises matters that [actually] happened."

TRANSLATED BY JAMES MCMULLEN

SEVEN ESSAYS ON MURASAKI SHIKIBU, 1703
(*Shika shichiron*)

ANDŌ TAMEAKIRA

Andō Tameakira (1659–1716) was born in Kyoto as the second son of Andō Sadatame, whose great-grandfather was a Fushimi no Miya prince.[15] Together with his older brother Tamemitsu, Tameakira served Tokugawa Mitsukuni (1628–1701), lord of the cadet branch of the Tokugawa house in Mito. For a time, Tamemitsu was the acting director of the Shōkōkan, the research institute established by Mitsukuni for the study of historical texts, and during his fourteen years in Mito, Tameakira was one of the many people who worked on the compilation of the *Dai Nihonshi* (*History of Great Japan*) and contributed to a commentary on the *Man'yōshū*.[16] He also received instruction from Nakanoin Michishige (1631–1710) as well as Keichū (1640–1701).

Seven Essays on Murasaki Shikibu (*Shika shichiron*),[17] completed in 1703, relies heavily on Tameakira's reading of Murasaki Shikibu's diary, which, he maintains, provides irrefutable proof that she was a virtuous woman of great intelligence. He argues that although *Genji* scholars had always spoken of her superior intellect (*sai*), they never studied her memoir and thus did not comprehend Murasaki's true nature, which was, above all, that of unyielding feminine virtue (*futoku*). Failing to understand the author, they also failed to understand her intent in writing *The Tale of Genji*, which was to provide moral instruction for her readers.

According to Tameakira, although the tale was written to admonish women, it could serve just as well to educate men. As he writes in Essay 6, the most important lesson to be learned from *Genji* is found in the clandestine affair between Genji and Fujitsubo. Although earlier scholars had shied away from speaking openly of this "incident" (*onkoto*), Tameakira maintains that there is no disruption of the imperial line, since the child born to Genji and Fujitsubo, who becomes the next emperor, is in fact a blood descendant of the preceding emperor. According to Tameakira, this episode serves to warn future emperors against possible temptations and shows Murasaki's desire to avert any problems of this sort that might arise in the future.

Because of his insistence on the tale's didactic function, Tameakira is often seen as adhering to conventional Confucian readings of *The Tale of Genji*. But he actually emphasizes that the tale was not meant to influence people to adopt the Ways of either Buddhism or Confucianism. Thus although Motoori Norinaga deplored *Shika shichiron* in *Genji monogatari Tama no ogushi* (1796) for extolling Murasaki's Confucian ideology, Tameakira did not in fact write a simplistic Confucian apologia for *The Tale of Genji*.

According to his epilogue, Tameakira completed *Shika shichiron* after discussing *The Tale of Genji* with Keichū and being encouraged by the similarity of their interpretations of the tale.[18] However, *Shika shichiron* diverges considerably from Keichū's *Gleanings of Commentary on Genji* (*Genchū shūi*, 1696), which highlights the beauty of the text over any possible instructional utility.[19] Nonetheless, their shared attention to historic detail and their willingness to debunk previous theories may well be attributed to their mutual respect for the diligent study of historic records. Tameakira's use of the *Murasaki Shikibu Diary* to correct previous theories of dating and the like underscores his complete trust in it. For him, the diary is a sincere, unfiltered record of her thoughts and actions. Tameakira's *Seven Essays* also gave rise to the first commentaries on the *Murasaki Shikibu Diary*.[20]

SATOKO NAITO

Essay 1: Possessing Both Intellect and Virtue

As a rule, intellect and virtue are seldom found combined in a single individual, even in men. In women it is even rarer, both in Japan and China. Those who have discussed *Genji* have spoken only of the superior intelligence [*eisai*] of Murasaki Shikibu, without mentioning her true virtue [*jittoku*], which not only obscures the true significance of the tale but also is an insufferable affront to Murasaki Shikibu.

I, Tameakira, have carefully read *The Tale of Genji* and the *Murasaki Shikibu Diary*. Considering her character and pondering the truths of her life, I find that in Japan there exists no one who can even compare with Murasaki. She was a sagacious woman [*kenpu*] of both intellect and virtue.

Now, if I were to cite one or two examples [of this intellect and virtue] in the tale, there is Lady Murasaki, who is gracious and magnanimous, yet mature and prudent; the Akashi lady, proud and yet possessing great reserve; Hanachirusato, never one to envy; the Fujitsubo Empress, who is quick to repent her errors and takes vows early in life; Asagao, who deeply values her good name; Tamakazura, who cleverly deflects the amorous advances of various men; and the Agemaki lady, who vows to live in accordance with her father's last wishes. Such are the several female virtues [*futoku*] depicted in the tale. In particular, in the Ranking of Women scene [in the "Hahakigi" chapter], frivolity is scorned and true virtue is praised. These frequent admonitions, though they represent the beliefs of Murasaki herself, are related as if they all were tales of the time. But because she does not make an overt display of her wisdom, those who read the tale think it is simply composed of gossip. This may be compared to the puppets of the theater: the audience remains unaware of the talents of the puppeteers maneuvering them. A reading of Murasaki's diary reveals this same general principle.

Tameakira here quotes passages from her diary in which Murasaki Shikibu speaks against criticizing others and laments the unflattering reputation that precedes her.[21]

To those who had not yet met her, Murasaki Shikibu had the reputation of being lascivious, a poetaster who enjoyed showing off her scholarship, a woman who could be expected to speak ill of others. But upon meeting her, to their surprise they found her a truly gracious and thoroughly modest woman. These traits can also be inferred from various passages in *The Tale of Genji.*

> Her Majesty too has often remarked that she had thought I was not the kind of person with whom she could ever relax, but that now I have become closer to her than any of the others. I am so perversely standoffish; if only I can avoid putting off those for whom I have genuine respect.[22]

Because Shikibu was such a gentle and placidly serene person, the Empress became very close to her as well. Those who only feigned goodness and gentility were likely envious and vexed by her.

> The key to everything is to be pleasant, gentle, properly relaxed, and self-possessed; having this as the foundation, grace and composure will naturally follow.[23]

This passage merits the most careful consideration. Virtue is the foundation; intellect, what follows.

Tameakira praises her humility in refraining from writing even the simplest Chinese characters so as not to appear to flaunt her learning. He also urges "both men and women to take note of her discretion [yōi]."[24]

In studying the several foregoing passages, we find that they concur with the admonitions set forth in the Ranking of Women scene. The good manners and prudence of Lady Murasaki and other characters in fact represent the standards that Shikibu herself adhered to, yet her tale appears as if she were portraying people of the past. From this we may infer that Shikibu herself was a virtuous woman.

Moreover, after [her husband] Nobutaka died in Chōhō 3 [1001] and Murasaki Shikibu was living as a widow, because she was an intelligent woman she was summoned to serve both Jōtōmon'in [Shōshi][25] and Takatsukasa-dono. And while she was at court, we can see how Shikibu tactfully evaded Michinaga's amorous advances.

Tameakira quotes a famous series of exchanges, said to have taken place between Michinaga and Murasaki Shikibu, comparing her favorably with Gen no Naishi no Suke and claiming that if unhindered by practical concerns, she would have taken vows as Utsusemi did.[26]

Again, [Murasaki's] diary says in Kankō 6 [1009]:

> His Excellency happened to see that Her Majesty had the *Tale of Genji* with her. Out came the usual comments, and then on a piece of paper that held some plums he wrote:
>
> It is well known to be a sour fruit,
> but who could pass or stay his hand who saw such ripeness here?
>
> And he handed it to me.
>
> Who is it who can be so glib
> about the reputation of a fruit that has not yet been tasted?[27]

Indeed, Shikibu has no intention of being "plucked" [*orarumajiki*] by any man other than her husband, Nobutaka. Again it says:

> One night as I lay asleep in a room on the corridor, there came the sound of someone tapping at the door. I was so frightened that I kept quiet for the rest of the night. Early next morning I received:
>
> All night long I cried and cried
> Even louder than the water rail tapping at your door.
>
> To which I replied
>
> Apparently insistent, the water rail
> just tapped an instant; how galling to have opened it![28]

As the months and years passed, Michinaga's advances never ceased. We can well imagine how in such an unpleasant situation, she must have longed to take vows. We must both respect and pity her for her constancy. Those who have not carefully studied her diary surmise that she was Michinaga's mistress; this is despicable. It is a world of slander and lies we live in. This shows Shikibu's womanly virtues.

For her intellect, there has been much earlier praise, but it all refers only to the tale and does not consider the author's diary, so here I shall at least show an example.[29]

Tameakira cites accounts of her reading Chinese texts as well as her nickname "Lady Chronicles" [*Nihongi no mitsubone*].[30]

Were she a man, she would have been a scholar without rival, past or present.

> Then Her Majesty asked me to read with her here and there from the *Collected Works of Po Chü-i* [Bo Juyi], and, because she evinced a desire to know more about such things, we carefully chose a time when other women would not be present and, amateur that I was, I read with her the two books of Po Chü-i's "New Ballads" in secret; we started the summer before last.[31]

We know from this diary that Shikibu left the neck [of her kotos untouched,] propped up between the cabinet and a pillar in her study, and instead read Chinese texts. She understood well the *Nihongi, Records of the Historian* [*Shiji*], and Bo Juyi's *Collected Works.* Aside from these, she was familiar with the details of the Three Histories and Five Classics, the sutras and commentaries of the Buddhists, various families' records [among which it seems that she carefully read the records of Prince Shigeaki],[32] collections of Japanese poetry [from the *Kokinshū* and various family collections], old romances [*Utsuho, Taketori*], incense blending, drawing, sewing, and other womanly accomplishments. This we can infer from her diary and also from the content of her tale. Noting how much brighter she was, to an unusual degree, than her brother Nobunori, we realize what a brilliant and studious young girl she was, gifted with natural intelligence. Those stacks of books that filled those two great cabinets—what were they? We would very much like to know. This tale, written by a brilliant woman possessed of both virtue and wisdom, ought not to be lightly overlooked.

Essay 2: The Seven Characteristics That Determine Her Nature

In Essay 2, Tameakira outlines what he regards as the seven defining characteristics of Murasaki Shikibu's character: (1) her father, Tametoki, was a high-ranking scholar; (2) her brother was also a poet; (3) she read both Japanese and Chinese and practiced music and the arts; (4) she was versed in the full range of court ceremonials; (5) she was born in neither great antiquity nor the degenerate age of later years; (6) she visited an exceptional number of famous places and historical sites; and finally, (7) she was a woman of the middle rank.

If *The Tale of Genji* had been [written] by a man, neither the conception nor the wording of the text as a whole would have been as complex as they are. Because she was a woman, she could write about things no man would ever think of. Even among women, those of the highest classes know nothing about the ways of those in the lower ranks. Even more so, how could those of the lower class possibly imagine the lives of those above them? Because Shikibu happened to be born into the middle ranks, no corner of life lay beyond the reach of her imagination. This is the seventh point.

Because Shikibu possessed all seven of these characteristics in combination, she was able to produce this tale even without the divine support of the deities of Ishiyama Temple.[33] The myth that she was an incarnation of the Bodhisattva Kannon is likewise a foolish notion made up by people of later times, of whom it must be said that they did not understand Shikibu. It is extremely rare to find anyone with all seven of these characteristics, which is why there has never existed, before it or since, a tale as excellent as *The Tale of Genji*.

Essay 3: Chronology Corrected

The diary says, in the entry for the Eleventh Month of Kankō 5 [1008]:

> Commander of the Gate Guards of the Left Kintō poked his head in.
> "Excuse me," he said. "Would our little Murasaki be in attendance by any chance?"
> "I cannot see the likes of Genji here, so how could she be present?" I replied.[34]

From this passage, it is apparent that the tale was completed before this time, that it already was in circulation among members of the court, and that it was also read by men. Kintō refers to Shikibu as "little Murasaki." Again, in the sixth year it says: "His Majesty was listening to someone reading *The Tale of Genji* aloud."[35] As this was added to the record later, from here forward it becomes difficult to determine the year [in which the incidents recorded occurred]. Again in the same year, it says: "His Excellency happened to see that Her Majesty had *The Tale of Genji* with her."[36]

The *Kakaishō*[37] says that the tale was written at the beginning of the Kankō era [1004–1013]; this must be based on the preceding passages. In any case, it was likely written at the end of Chōhō [999–1004] or the beginning of Kankō, after Shikibu had been widowed, returned to her [father's] home, and had time on her hands. In Kankō 5, when Michinaga was forty-three years old, he made amorous advances toward Shikibu, and in the following year he knocked on the door of her room on the corridor, lamenting [her coldness]. Considering this, she could not have been very old at this time. Conversely, as she herself claims that she has aged, neither can it be that she was a young woman in her prime. We must keep in mind, however, that in *A Tale of Flowering Fortunes* [*Eiga monogatari*], in the "Tenjō hanami" chapter, Empress Takeko [999–1036], at age thirty-one or thirty-two is said to have "passed her prime."[38]

In both Japan and China, it has always been that those of incisive intelligence can accomplish anything very quickly, and so this tale, too, must have been written with greater ease than might be imagined. The obtuse nature of later people led them to think there was something strange and mysterious [about this accomplishment] and to formulate such foolish notions as that she was the Bodhisattva Kannon, that her father, Tametoki, had helped her [write *Genji*], or that Michinaga revised the tale. None of these people knew Shikibu, and careful consideration of what they wrote requires us to declare it nonsense.

I was asked: "In the 'Ura ura no wakare' chapter of Chōtoku 2 [996] in *A Tale of Flowering Fortunes*, it is written, in praise of the good looks of the Palace Minister Korechika [974–1010], that 'the Shining Genji, too, must have looked like this.'[39] Thus this tale must have been written and in circulation at court before the Chōtoku period [995–999] for Akazome Emon to have compared Korechika with Genji. What do you say to this?" In reply, I say: "It is precisely because there are so many passages of this sort that I maintain that Akazome Emon is not the author of *Flowering Fortunes*. This work would appear to have been compiled by a person living in an age later than both Akazome and Murasaki, someone who gathered old records and patched them together with interstitial additions to make a single whole. The 'Hatsuhana' chapter was pieced together from fragments lifted directly from Murasaki's diary. The diary contains critiques of Akazome Emon, Sei Shōnagon, Izumi Shikibu, Sai'in no Chūjō, and others; these cannot have been be divulged during their lifetimes. Besides, how could Akazome ever have purloined the diary of a contemporary colleague and then used it, just as she found it, to write the 'Hatsuhana' chapter? We must consider this carefully. What is more, the 'Nunobiki no taki' chapter [of *A Tale of Flowering Fortunes*] records the reign of the Horikawa Retired Emperor [1079–1107]. Had Akazome been alive then, she would have been a hundred and ten years old. I have yet to hear of anyone living such a long life. Although there is much further evidence that Akazome did not write the *A Tale of Flowering Fortunes*, [to recount] it would be tediously long, so I will omit it. Instead of being led astray by unfounded theories and false transmissions, we should simply read with close attention." When I said this, my questioner departed with a perplexed look on his face.

Essay 4: Writing Like No Other[40]

Both the poetry and the prose of *The Tale of Genji* are far different from those of the old style found in the *Man'yōshū*, *Kokinshū*, *Ise monogatari*, *Taketori*, and the like. Serene and easily graceful, *Genji* epitomizes the refinement of this land. No one who reads it could ever weary of it. Indeed, nothing surpasses *Genji* in all of Japan's literature. The work as a whole has that air of gentility possessed by those of wealth and rank, and it is written in the refined language of the court. Nonetheless, throughout it we encounter those who have taken Buddhist vows and retreated to mountain temples, and we are shown the marketplace and the countryside as well as poverty and sorrow. Every chapter depicts the myriad emotions of women. Such are the portrayal of human feeling and the descriptions of scenery that we feel as if we are face to face with that very person and as if we were visiting that very place.

In overall form, the tale is a narrative, and thus there is the introductory style, the conclusive, the descriptive, the analytical, and the epistolary [styles]; we can find in *Genji* these various different styles. In particular, the Ranking of Women scene in "Hahakigi" is uncannily well done. In the past, when I was examining the several divisions of this passage, [I found that] it employs a number of Chinese narrative devices. Following an introduction, there is refutation, acquiescence, discussion of essentials, and discussion of tangentials. It moves from the coarse to the detailed and ranges from the mundane to the refined; from the complex it reverts to the simple, and there are "great changes and sudden obstacles" and "retroactive reflection and foreshadowings." The flow of the text is measured and magnanimous, its force smooth and tactful. These qualities are found not only in the Ranking of Women passage but also throughout the entire text. It is similar to the *Record of the Historian*, the *Zhuangzi*, and works by Han Yu [768–824], Liu Congyuan [773–819], Ou Yangxiu [1007–1070], and Su Shi [1037–1101]. For something written by a woman, it is extraordinary and wondrous; Shikibu must truly be deemed a brilliant woman, without peer, past or present.

It has long been the custom to speak of Murasaki and Sei Shōnagon as two of a kind. But Sei Shōnagon's talent is so narrow and slight and her intellectual pretensions so obvious that her work is often distasteful. These two women can hardly even be compared. . . .

A certain person said to me, "Shikibu's writing does not convey historical fact; instead, she has left us a useless work of fiction. It is by no means unthinkable, is it, that at worst it may well incite lasciviousness?"

In answer I say: "This is an unfortunate problem that would not exist were she a son of Tametoki. Had she been a man, she would have compiled a comprehensive national history, which would have served as a model for myriad ages to come. Although a woman, she was of great intellect, and therefore, being unable to accomplish what she wished, she instead wrote a tale of a sort appropriate to a woman, which teaches the proper ways and prudent behavior of a woman's world; this is precisely what Shikibu did. To judge from a careful reading of both her tale and her diary, it was not in Shikibu's character to do anything excessive. She disdains displays of cleverness. Had she written anything resembling a historical record, it would have been deemed unseemly for a woman. It would have been excessive. That would have been a willful display of cleverness. It would have been at odds with the modesty that is her nature. Yet if one insists on a historical record, then her diary is precisely such a record. The 'Hatsuhana' chapter of *A Tale of Flowering Fortunes* is lifted almost entirely from this diary, which must once have comprised volumes that spanned several decades, but unfortunately they no longer exist. I believe the diary that survives today is but a fragment of the whole."

Again, this person said, "Those who read this tale and grasp its meaning may well reconsider their own behavior and, be they men or women, themselves may become wantons." Yet if we are to call this tale lewd, must we then bring the same charge against the love poems included in our own land's anthologies? The encouragement of good and the chastisement of evil is one of the very virtues of poetry; yet though our forebears have taken great pains to teach us this, we seem to find it difficult, feeble-minded as we are, to grasp their admonitions. Fortunately, however, this tale does not hew to the ideals of Confucianism or Buddhism from far-off lands, but adheres to the familiar customs and feelings of Japan. In this way it praises and admonishes implicitly and, in its deeper sense, deplores wanton behavior, leaving an impression of profound seriousness. Those who do not know Shikibu wrongly accuse her of being lascivious. Those who do know her realize how obvious is the instructional nature of the tale. Thus this tale should be revered as a classic of the Way of Poetry. When I asked if this were not so, the person in question nodded in agreement and allowed that as *The Tale of Genji* is born of so frightfully flawless a person of our own land, it would be difficult to criticize it; that her gentle admonitions are like medicine to combat a disease, are indeed the true essence of the Way of Poetry.

Essay 5: The Author's True Intent

This tale portrays human emotion and the ways of the world, depicting the manners and customs of the upper, middle, and lower levels of society. Without openly expressing either praise or blame, it allows readers, through the medium of the amours it depicts, to discern for themselves what is good and what is bad. Although the principal aim of the tale is said to be the moral instruction of women, it also contains much that serves naturally to admonish men. I will cite one or two examples:

The Kiritsubo Emperor, placing love above all else, devotes excessive attention to his Mistress of the Wardrobe. Paying no heed to his people's warnings, he treats her in ways that could set a dangerous precedent. His behavior becomes a source of anguish for his courtiers and others of high rank, as well as for everyone else in the land. Doesn't the author depict this shameful lack of virtue on the part of the Emperor as a lesson for future Emperors?

The same Emperor thinks of Genji as his own private treasure. From the time of his coming-of-age ceremony, he treats him as if he were in no way inferior to the Crown Prince and even hints that he might name him his heir apparent. Is this not unseemly behavior for an Emperor?

In her overbearing and arrogant manner, Kokiden purposely takes no notice of the Emperor's grief [following the death of the Kiritsubo Mistress of the Wardrobe]. Where in this is the imperial virtue that we expect of an Empress? All women who read this, from the rank of Empress on down, should reflect on their own manners and mores, lest they, too, earn the reputation of a "wicked Empress."

The entire Ranking of Women scene in the "Hahakigi" chapter is an admonition for women, which every woman who calls herself a woman should be made to read and put into practice. And clearly there are lessons to be learned from the "Utsusemi" chapter, from the way Nokiba no Ogi plays go with her robes untied in the inner chambers and in her propensity to oversleep. Utsusemi, however, is so uncompromisingly chaste that she is determined to remain unaffected [by Genji's advances] throughout; in this, she represents Shikibu's own beliefs. And then that poem that Yūgao writes with such casual charm on the fan that she favors—this is in many ways open to criticism for amorous laxity. Because she is so excessively pliant, naive, and deficient in deep consideration, she is ultimately led to ruin. Any woman who hears of this should ponder what it means to be loved by a libertine.

As for Genji, his unbridled frivolity leads him to dally with Yūgao and eventually cause her death, while he himself falls from his horse at the riverbank and suffers the utmost despair—a clear admonition against the furtive amorous activities of noblemen. Nor is the sin of Koremitsu, who accompanies him on all these adventures, at all light; those who serve in close attendance on their lords should ponder this. As we read the chapters that follow with this point of view in mind, we see the deeds and thoughts of the characters in all of them as if reflected in a mirror. Neither the good nor the bad is hidden, for this is no frivolous work; instruction in the ways of the world was the author's main purpose.

In particular, there is the incident in which Genji violates Fujitsubo and she bears his child, who then ascends the throne, allowing Genji to take control of the government. This story is truly a mirror for courtiers, which should send shivers of fright through those of the rank of Prime Minister and below. I shall discuss this further in the next essay. This being but a tale of times past, the teller incurs no crime; and if the people of the land are moved to reflect on it, it will serve as a gentle warning—as the old saying goes, like soft cotton used to strangle someone. As it says in the "Hotaru" chapter:

> It isn't that they describe the events of some person's life exactly as they happened. Rather, there are some things that happen as people go through life, be they good or bad, that one cannot simply see and let pass, or hear of and pay no heed to. One cannot shut all these away in one's heart, but wants to pass them on to subsequent generations—and so sets out to tell a story.[41]

This appears to reflect Shikibu's own opinions, presented in the guise of a discussion of old romances; her tale, therefore, cannot be deemed naught but a fiction. Throughout, it depicts the lives of people who lived in that world, during which it conveys praise of the good and admonition of the bad. Those who fail to recognize its true intent and see *The Tale of Genji* as lascivious literature are the lowest of the low. And those who appreciate it only for the pretty poems and flowery phrases are like those who praise only the decorations on the hilt of a sword and fail to mention the keenness of the blade. Taken as a whole—with all its fine writing and its cautionary qualities—it is a poetic work endowed with both beauty and benefit. Given this, it would be no exaggeration to term it a "Golden Classic of the Way of Poetry."

Essay 6: The Crux of the Entire Work[42]

Regarding the incident [*onkoto*] involving the Reizei Emperor: there are some who say, "*Genji* is just a fiction; don't even bother discussing it." Others say this is a very delicate matter and do their utmost to conceal it. Still others say it is such an unseemly subject that no part of the tale should be read at all. And none of them has any inkling of Shikibu's true intent. I, Tameakira, shall set forth my own views here and await the opinions of later scholars regarding their merits and demerits.

In "Kiritsubo" it says:

> Genji was not free to live at home [at his father-in-law's residence], for His Majesty summoned him too often. In his heart he saw only Fujitsubo's peerless beauty. Ah, he thought, she is the kind of woman I want

> to marry; there is no one like her! His Excellency's daughter was no doubt very pretty and well brought up, but he felt little for her. . . .[43]

In this way, the author foreshadows what she will finally describe further on as an illicit affair. In the "Wakamurasaki" chapter, [Fujitsubo's] pregnancy is revealed; in the "Momiji no ga" chapter, the child is born; in the "Aoi" chapter, he is named Crown Prince; and in "Miotsukushi," he ascends the throne and thereafter is known as the Reizei Emperor. Then in the "Usugumo" chapter, the monk in night attendance upon him secretly reveals to him for the first time that he is in fact Genji's child. Yet having no one whom he can ask, he himself decides to investigate past precedents [in the histories]:

> [H]e plunged into his studies more ardently than ever in order to peruse all sorts of works. These taught him that while in Cathay there had been many such irregularities, some open and some concealed, no example of the kind was to be found in Japan. And even if something like that happened, how, if it was kept well hidden, could knowledge of it have been passed on?[44]

In the latter "Wakana" chapter, when Genji finds out about Kashiwagi's clandestine meetings with the Third Princess, he ponders the matter thus:

> In early times as well there were those who might violate an Emperor's wife, but that was different. No wonder liaisons like that may occur, when there are so many people in palace service waiting on the Sovereign. What with one thing and another it must happen quite often. Even a Consort or an Intimate may err for this reason or that. They are not all as serious as they might be, and strange things happen, but as long as no obvious lapse comes to light the man can carry on as before, and it may be ages before anyone finds out. . . . When a woman wearies of giving her service meekly and all too respectably, even to the Emperor himself, she may yield after all to urgent pleas, love where she is loved, respond when she feels she must. . . . He realized bitterly that despite his fury he could not afford to show it, and he thought of his father, His Late Eminence. Did he really know all the time and just pretend not to? That, yes, that *was* a fearful and a heinous crime![45]

Considering the manner in which she writes this, Shikibu seems to be describing her own feelings about what she has seen and heard, whether they were events of the past or of more recent times. The significance of these finely nuanced reflections is far from shallow; the reader should not dismiss them lightly. Such women as the Nijō Empress in *Ise monogatari* [who is visited by the Middle Counselor Narihira], Kyōgyoku Miyasundokoro in the *Gosenshū* [who had an affair with Prince Motoyoshi], Lady Kazan in *A Tale of Flowering Fortunes* [who was amorously involved with Lord Sanesuke], Lady Reikeiden, and Lady Shōkōden [both of whom were said to have been involved with Lord Yorisada] all were women who lacked a steadfast heart and allowed themselves to be swayed by their own desires. But fortunately—it gives me great pleasure to record—there is no evidence that this led to any untoward consequences [*mono no magire*] for our land.

Tameakira next cites the case of Emperor You (J. Yūō, 795–771 B.C.E.) of Zhu (J. So), who was rumored to have been illegitimately conceived.[46]

Although this occurred in another land, it is nonetheless upsetting. It need hardly be said that in this country of ours, from the time we were vouchsafed this divine land down to the present day, there has been one continuous imperial line through all the myriad ages, without a single aberrance. Yet in ages to come, among the Dames of Honor [*nyōgo*] and Mistresses of the Wardrobe [*kōi*], there may well be some who lack strength of will and could thus cause a disruption in the imperial line. In thinking so far ahead and seeing the need gently to warn against this, Shikibu, though a woman, in the beauty of her character combined with the strength of her scholarship, displays a degree of perspicacity equal to that of the greatest Confucian scholars.

And then, the way in which the principle of heavenly retribution is demonstrated in the case of Kaoru is identical to what is seen in *Helinyulou* [J. *Kakurin gyokuro*, ca. 1252]. As this single incident is the crux of the entire work, those who discuss this tale must grasp its significance. Some say that discussing a tale written as casually and lightly as this in terms of such profound principles goes against Shikibu's intentions. In reply I would say: In the Ranking of Women scene it says, "Why should anyone, just because she is a woman, be completely ignorant of what matters in this world, public or private? A woman with any mind at all is bound to retain many things, even if she does not actually study."[47] This is a salutary bit of writing.

If even a single generation of our imperial line were tainted by Ariwara or Fujiwara blood, it would be a tragedy for our land of the sort that moved Lu Zhonglian [J. Ro Chūren] to throw himself into the Eastern Sea. Genji's clandestine affair with Fujitsubo, resulting in the birth of the Reizei Emperor, was indeed a transgression that should never have taken place. Yet though the sin of Genji's licentiousness is great, still it did not in any way disrupt the imperial line. Genji and Reizei are the legitimate son and grandson of the Kiritsubo Emperor; they both are of the bloodline of the Jinmu Emperor. They are thus to be worshipped at the Imperial Shrine in Ise, as is the populace of the entire realm obliged to submit to their rule. Even so, Reizei's son is passed over and the reign is returned to the proper line of the Suzaku Emperor—a majestic piece of writing, is it not? After all, which is the graver, and which is the slighter sin: a momentary moral misstep or a long-term disruption of the imperial line? Even though it was likely a difficult decision, speaking as subjects, we must be delighted that [the Emperor] chose to pretend ignorance of Genji's sin so that the imperial line could continue undisrupted. Shikibu's principal intention here merits careful consideration. Would someone as profoundly prudent as Shikibu, in a tale that would circulate in the court at that time, have written of such things without due consideration? This fictional admonition, so very carefully crafted, must have served to prevent in advance any future disruptions, for it was not impossible that such dubious things could happen. It is frightening, is it not, to call to mind such clandestine affairs as that of the Nijō Empress in *Ise monogatari*? Genji's infatuation, mentioned earlier, is entirely the work of Shikibu, who is determined to demonstrate in full detail the consequences of a clandestine affair. Seeing the incident with Kaoru, any loyal subject should be on his guard. In China, there have been many such untoward incidents. For example, we see in *Records of the Historian* the often-repeated rumor that Qin Shihuang [J. Shikōtei, 259–210 B.C.E.] was in fact fathered by a minister, Lü Buwei [J. Ryōfui, d. 235 B.C.E.].

In [Murasaki Shikibu's] diary, it says, "The key to everything is to be pleasant, gentle, properly relaxed, and self-possessed; having this as the foundation, grace and composure will naturally follow."[48] We should also note how in the tale the clandestine affair between Genji and Fujitsubo at first is described in gentle terms, but ultimately is shown to be a frightful transgression that should never have been committed. What is more, we see in her descriptions of the womanly virtues of several characters throughout the tale, as well as her appraisal of Akazome, Shōnagon,

Izumi, and others in her diary, that Murasaki is a woman whose character is marked by prudence and dignity. This tale being the product of such a mind, those who see it as no more than something agreeable but inconsequential fail to understand Murasaki. Without searching out the tale's true intent, its attractions amount to no more than pretty poems and fine phrases. Although its true intent is meaningful instruction, it is skillfully wrought in a feminine style, written as though it were but a smooth piece of storytelling. One is reminded of what Jakuren [d. 1202] once said, that even a ferocious wild boar may seem a gentle creature when described in a poem as being asleep in its nest. I was then asked, "If what you say is true, then it would appear that the teachings of earlier scholars concerning how one should read *Genji* are soundly conceived and not ill written, wouldn't it?' I replied, as before, that this tale is a classic of the Way [of Poetry] and a treasure to those poets who compose *waka*. The person in question again nodded his head in agreement.

Essay 7: Some Mistaken Traditions Rectified

Since times long past, there has been no authoritative explanation of how this tale came to be written, just one person after another mouthing one notion after another as it happened to occur to him. It is no wonder that the commentaries question which of these theories might be correct. As I, Tameakira, consider them carefully, it seems to me that none are true and all are false.

First of all, there is the story that Tametoki constructed the larger outline and had his daughter fill in the details. This is the notion of some hopeless person who knows nothing whatever about literary structure. An examination of the content of the several chapters [of *Genji*] reveals many things that no man could ever have thought of. Not only is it thoroughly feminine, but the flow of the prose is such that the whole could have been written by only one person. Anyone who reads the work in its entirety with attention to detail will not be misled on this score. Furthermore, as I noted earlier, the author is a woman of superior intellect and virtue, who possesses the seven characteristics [listed in Essay 2], given which, it is clear that she could easily have composed this tale without any help from her father. What is more, her diary is a work written entirely on her own, with no assistance from her father, and yet its prose is in no way inferior to that in the tale. Those who read her diary carefully should be even less tempted by these blind theories. . . .[49]

In reading the tale and the diary, we come to understand Shikibu's personality and can calculate the time [when she was in service at court]. We note then, for instance, that when the High Priestess requested a new work and the Empress summoned Shikibu and asked what they might offer, the newly arrived Shikibu, rather self-importantly, apparently replied that they had nothing interesting and she herself would write something new. It is said that she then took it upon herself to compose this tale. This story can only be the blind notion of someone who has no idea how humble a person Shikibu was, someone ignorant of how she pretended she could not even write the number "one." It was only after the early death of her father, Tametoki, and the death of her husband, Nobutaka, that she went to court. She remained at home as a widow, and to while away the tedium of those days, she began writing the tale. When word of this reached the court, she was summoned to service, after which she came to be known as Murasaki Shikibu.

Tameakira then criticizes the Kakaishō *for its account of the myth that Murasaki Shikibu began writing the "Suma" and "Akashi" chapters on the fifteenth night of the Eighth Month at Ishiyamadera.*

The *Kakaishō* was written by a gentleman of exalted rank, so it is rather worrying that he would write passage after passage of groundless fabrications. But because he is such an exalted personage, those who read his text trust it. Whereas whatever I myself might have to say, even if once in a hundred times I am right, is likely to be dismissed as slipshod. Still, one must say what one thinks—otherwise one's stomach feels so bloated that it might burst—so I shall just let my brush do its work.

Murasaki Shikibu would have been too young to have known Takaakira before he was banished from the capital; she may not even have been born by then. The legend that her retreat to Ishiyama coincided with the period in life when she was suffering from the loss of her friend cannot be true.

Even if the scenes in the novel had appeared to her, as if out of the blue, and she had begun writing "Suma" and "Akashi" so that she would not forget them, how could anyone living in a later age know what went on in Murasaki's mind? This is simply laughable. It should be obvious that the tale was written beginning with the "Kiritsubo" chapter. When I was young, I believed the story told in the *Kakaishō*, and wishing to see the copy of the *Hannyakyō* in her own hand, I went to stay with a monk I knew at Ishiyama. When I questioned him about this matter, he told me immediately that it was false. So whose idea was it, and when was it that they decided to call [one of the rooms in the temple] the "Genji Room," display a portrait of Shikibu there, and install a desk and inkstone in the style of her time?

Tameakira also denounces the Kakaishō's *claim that Michinaga contributed an epilogue to* The Tale of Genji, *as well as the* Sairyūshō's *foolish attempt to demonstrate that the tale covers the historical period beginning with the Daigo Emperor.*

This nitpicking manner of reading is inappropriate to fictional tales. It might be suitable to a discussion of *A Tale of Flowering Fortunes*, but we can hardly countenance such an understanding of *The Tale of Genji*.

Then, too, it says, the author's intent was to lead people to the path of benevolence, reason, and the five constant virtues, and ultimately to enlighten people concerning the principle of the Middle Way and the nature of True Existence, thus establishing the root of renouncement of this world. This, too, is impossibly pretentious. And in various other commentaries, it says that the tale is based on the homilies of the *Zhuangzi*, that it derives from the *Records of the Historian* or the *Commentary of the Scribe of the Left* [*Zuo zhuan*], that it is modeled on the sixty volumes of the Tendai treatises, or that it adheres to the Four Noble Truths. The various schools of Confucianism and Buddhism each hew to their own doctrines and try to make Shikibu conform to them in ways that she never intended. There are, indeed, many points in which, by chance, *Genji* happens to conform to the principles of Confucianism or Buddhism, or may call to mind earlier legends from either China or our own land. But her true intent was not to illustrate the Ways of Confucianism and Buddhism. Nor was it to provide a historical record. This should be understood by anyone who holds forth on the subject.

Regarding the Hōbutsushū's *account of Murasaki Shikibu appearing in peoples' dreams:*

This is naught but a hallucination within a dream; it is a waste of ink even to discuss it. But among the Buddhist poems in the *Shinchokusenshū* [no. 602], we find:

> Upon sending "The Parable of Medicinal Herbs" to be dedicated at rites of bonding with the Buddha, for the benefit of Murasaki Shikibu.
>
> ACTING GRAND COUNSELOR MUNEIE

nori no ame ni ware mo nuren mutsumashiki / wakamurasaki no kusa no yukari ni

By the rain of the dharma, would that I, too, might be blessed, for my close
affinity with the tender young *murasaki* sprouts.

It seems that this poem was composed as an offering during a day of copying sutras for use in rites of dedication. Also written at this time were what are called "Proclamations" [*hyōbyaku*]. There were those who believed that these evanescent dreams indeed represented reality and thus charged Shikibu's tale of instruction and admonition with the sin of Falsehood.[50] This is indeed despicable and stems from the delusion of shallow-minded people.

Although the various commentaries set forth such theories, I have cited only one or two as examples of the rest. *Uji Dainagon monogatari* is an old text, but even this is full of blind myths, while those theories that were developed later are even more replete with unreliable matter. Yet if, as we must, we first consider [Murasaki Shikibu's] character as it is reflected in the tale and then ascertain the facts as they are set forth in her diary, we shall not often go wrong.

TRANSLATED BY SATOKO NAITO

THE TALE OF GENJI: A LITTLE JEWELED COMB, 1799
(*Genji monogatari Tama no ogushi*)

MOTOORI NORINAGA

Motoori Norinaga's (1730–1801) preface to *The Tale of Genji: A Little Jeweled Comb* is one of those texts so central to its culture that its influence extends far beyond the small community of those who have actually read it.[51] For its compelling critique of *The Tale of Genji*, scholars rightly deem it one of the most original works of criticism in the history of Japanese literature. Its wider renown, however, grows not out of the argument of this critique but out of the informing premise on which it is founded, Norinaga's *mono no aware ron*. As the locus classicus of this well-known phrase, *Tama no ogushi* has become a major contributor to the store of concepts—and clichés—that the Japanese nation as a whole draws on in construing and defining itself. *Tama no ogushi* is thus a work with a double identity: its importance is determined as much by what it has been imagined to say about the Japanese people as what it actually says about *The Tale of Genji*.

How, then, are we to explain this appeal to two so widely disparate audiences, this capacity to serve two so widely disparate ends? We are often told that the character of a thinker and the character of his thought are intimately related, and it is true that Norinaga was a man capable of both rigorous academic reason and monomaniacal chauvinist passion. Why these two traits should appear in such an unhomogenized blend in *Tama no ogushi*, however, is probably better explained in terms of the accidents of its textual history than the psychology of its author.[52]

Norinaga's interest in *Genji* extended throughout his literate life, yet it was only in his early years as a scholar that he wrote on the subject; it never became the principal focus of his scholarly activity. When Norinaga first read *Genji* is not recorded. He may well have begun while still in his teens, for the first written evidence of his reading it, a miscellaneous collection of memoranda on the meaning and orthography of words in *Genji*,[53] dates from his twentieth (1749) or twenty-first year (1750). Thereafter, during his years in Kyoto (1752–1757), where he had been sent to study medicine, he records the copying and purchase of a few works of criticism of and commentary on *Genji*. And finally, just before he returned home to Matsusaka, he invested the substantial sum of 1 *ryō*, 3 *bu*, 210 *mon* in a complete twenty-five-volume set of Kitamura Kigin's *Moonlit Lake Commentary* (*Kogetsushō*). This text, which survives, replete with interlinear, marginal, and appended annotations, is the text he used in teaching *Genji* throughout his career.

Norinaga's career as a teacher and a scholar began almost immediately after his return to Matsusaka. In 1758, aged twenty-nine, he began his first series of lectures on *Genji*, which met nine times a month and continued with interruption through the next eight years. It was probably in the same year that he completed his first treatise on poetry, *Ashiwake obune*, and composed the very short treatise *Aware ben*, in which he adumbrates his later use of the term *aware*.

Over the next five years, Norinaga's scholarly activities seem to have continued along the same paths, for in 1763, aged thirty-four, he completed two more substantial treatises: *Isonokami sasamegoto*, on the art of poetry, and *Shibun yōryō*, on *Genji*. These two early works were not to be harbingers of his subsequent career, however, for shortly after their completion Norinaga experienced something of an epiphany upon meeting the renowned scholar Kamo no Mabuchi (1697–1769), who happened to pass through Matsusaka on his way to the Great Shrine at Ise. Norinaga presented himself at the inn where Mabuchi was lodged, and the grand old man granted him an audience, during which he urged the young scholar to take on a task that he himself was now too old to begin: the study of the ancient chronicle *Kojiki*. So overwhelmed was Norinaga that thereafter he made the *Kojiki* the principal object of his scholarship, a life's work that culminated in 1798, only three years before his death, in the completion of his massive commentary *Kojiki den*.

Throughout these thirty-five years, however, Norinaga continued to lecture to his disciples on *Genji* with undiminished diligence and frequency. His second series of *Genji* lectures was begun in 1766, barely a month after the conclusion of the first, and continued through 1774. The third series, begun immediately after the New Year festivities, lasted from 1775 until 1788. At the time of Norinaga's death 1801, the fourth series had advanced as far as the "Wakana" chapters. *Genji* was still very much on his mind, but had it not been for another fortuitous encounter, he might never again have written on the subject.

Matsudaira Suō-no-Kami Yasusada (1747–1807), lord of the Hamada domain in the province of Iwami, was a daimyo with a strong scholarly bent. How he had learned of Norinaga's work is not recorded, but his interest was sufficiently aroused to send one of his vassals, an accomplished Confucian scholar named Ozasa Mino (or Min; dates unknown) to Matsusaka to study directly under Norinaga. Ozasa's reports must have been favorable, for while en route to the Great Shrine, Yasusada himself summoned Norinaga to his lodgings and talked with him "into the night." Three days later, on his return from the shrine, Yasusada again summoned the scholar. This time, Norinaga arrived at midday, lectured to Yasusada on the "Hatsune" chapter of *Genji* throughout the afternoon, and thereafter the two conversed until about ten that night. Norinaga found his lordship to be "a staunch devotee of ancient studies [*kogaku*] and a diligent scholar." Yasusada, too, must have been favorably impressed, for during this long meeting, he seems to have offered to finance the publication of a commentary on *Genji*, which he asked Norinaga to compile "as quickly as possible." This was an offer he could not refuse, yet neither was he willing to devote so much time to the project that it would prevent him finishing his commentary on the *Kojiki*. Norinaga's solution to this problem was to cobble together a commentary on *Genji* from bits and pieces already at hand, some of them written more than thirty years earlier. In this way he was able to complete the manuscript of *Tama no ogushi* within a year of Yasusada's original offer.

Chapters 1 and 2 of *Tama no ogushi*, his general introduction to the "new" commentary, are revised versions of the two volumes of *Shibun yōryō*, first written around 1763 and modified in minor ways, mainly for stylistic reasons, sometime before 1779. Chapter 3 is a chronology of *Genji*, consisting of a schematic diagram and a chapter-by-chapter listing of indicators of the passage of time and the ages of the characters. This work originally was entitled *Genji monogatari nenki kō* and was probably begun shortly after Norinaga's return from Kyoto. Chapter 4 is a list of textual emendations to the *Kogetsushō*, which he compiled in the course of two collations of his teaching text in 1763 and 1772. Chapters 5 through 9, constituting about three-fifths of the work, are made up of commentary on the fifty-four chapters of *Genji*. The sources of this material cannot be identified with complete certainty. "Kiritsubo" and "Hahakigi" are annotated quite extensively; the notes to these two chapters alone fill all of chapter 5 and half of chapter 6. The remainder of chapter 6 is devoted to "Utsusemi," "Yūgao," and "Wakamurasaki," following which Norinaga appends a note explaining that

> in annotating the foregoing five chapters I have omitted nothing whatever that I have thought should be said, but the several chapters that follow are extremely long. With so much else to do, I am unable to carry on and, for the time being, must stop here. It distresses me terribly that I must do something so unseemly, but I am nearing seventy and know not but what I may die today or tomorrow. Here at the end of my years, the chief work in my life, my commentary on the *Kojiki*, remains unfinished.[54]

It is hard to know what moved him to insert this lament, but it appears to indicate that his annotations to "the foregoing five chapters" were composed at some earlier date, and it explains why the remaining forty-nine chapters of *Genji* are annotated so sparsely. Many of the entries for subsequent chapters appear to be drawn directly from slips of paper pasted into the copy of the *Kogetsushō* that Norinaga used in his lectures.

How, then, does this history of the compilation of *Tama no ogushi* affect the way we read Norinaga's criticism? Above all, it means that we must keep constantly in mind that the ideas Norinaga expresses in *Tama no ogushi* were formulated in the earliest years of his study of literature and remain substantially unchanged in the finished version of his *Genji* commentary. This is particularly true of the idea for which *Tama no ogushi* is best known, the so-called *mono no aware ron*. This term, which most often appears as an element of the phrase *mono no aware o shiru*, is so closely associated with Norinaga and so central to his critique of *Genji* that it is often taken for granted that he is the author of the concept, or at least was the first to use it in the senses that he assigns to it. Hino Tatsuo (1940–2003) has demonstrated, however, in a series of brilliant articles, that the phrase *mono no aware o shiru* was widely used in the popular literature of Norinaga's day and that popular usage corresponds precisely with the sense in which Norinaga uses it, meaning "to empathize or sympathize with the feelings of others."[55] Hino notes, moreover, that after 1763, when Norinaga completed *Shibun yōryō*, he never again used the term until he refurbished this early work to serve as the prefatory chapters of *Tama no ogushi*. We can only speculate what might be the significance of these thirty-some years of neglect. But as Hino points out, Norinaga was very tenacious of his pet ideas and hammered them home with relentless repetition. It may simply be that *mono no aware* no longer seemed as important or as relevant to his current interests as it once had, that in Norinaga's mind it was a youthful fancy that he had outgrown and to which he returned only as a matter of urgent editorial necessity.

If, then, the phrase that expresses the formative principle of *Tama no ogushi* did not originate with Norinaga, and apparently failed to interest him sufficiently to apply it in his later work, what is left to justify the high regard in which the work is still held? Attempts to explicate Norinaga's *mono no aware ron* have mostly been of two sorts: endeavors to flesh out the denotational meaning of the term, and enumerations of the ways in which it is applied. Both unquestionably are needed.

Norinaga's own definition of *mono no aware* is too cursory to serve as the foundation of a well-reasoned theory of literature. *Aware*, he tells us, derives from two ancient expletives, *aa* and *hare*, uttered in moments of overwhelming emotion, whether of sadness or joy, dejection or elation, disappointment or satisfaction. And *mono* is an affix that "broadens the reference of the word to which it is attached" (*hiroku iu toki ni soeru kotoba*), as in *monogatari*, in which "speaking" becomes "conversation" or "storytelling," or *monomi*, in which "looking" or "seeing" becomes "gazing" or even "sightseeing." To say that *The Tale of Genji* is a work of *mono no aware* identifies it unambiguously as a work of the literature of feeling. That claim, however, takes on significance only in specific contexts. Norinaga provides a vast array of examples, some highly judicious and some in which logic is stretched to the point of contradiction, and non sequiturs abound.[56] His insistence that *Genji* is a work of *mono no aware*—written only to depict the varieties of human emotion (*mono no aware*), to acquaint the reader with the workings of human emotions (*mono no aware o shirashimuru koto*), and to depict people who are deeply sensitive to human emotions (*mono no aware o shiru hito*)—is often linked to counterclaims concerning what *Genji* is not. *Genji* is not a moral homily written to illustrate Buddhist or Confucian moral principles. *Genji* is not a guide to good governance. *Genji* is not a tale of moral dissolution to be kept out of the hands of impressionable young boys and girls. *Genji* is not a seditious work, depicting a taint to the imperial line of the sort that should never even be contemplated, let alone mentioned. These claims are a refreshing antidote to the views of *Genji* often voiced in the medieval commentaries that Norinaga so deplores. Yet, as Hino points out, when Norinaga goes on to assert that *Genji* was written to show readers the sensitivity to emotion to which they themselves should aspire, he in fact contradicts his own claim that the author has no didactic motives; he simply replaces one form of didacticism with another. But is this all there is to *Tama no ogushi*: a mixed bag of timely and intelligent observations given a certain thematic unity by gathering them under the rubric of *mono no aware*? I think not.

Norinaga can lay claim to yet another significant accomplishment, little noted in modern scholarship but that emerges with greater clarity in a comparative context. In eighteenth-century England, the era of "the rise of the novel,"[57] there arose a recognition of prose fiction as "a new species of writing,"[58] a distinct genre as worthy of consideration as epic, drama, or poetry. In the words of Norinaga's near contemporary Samuel Johnson (1709–1784), the distinguishing feature of the genre is that it "exhibit[s] life in its true state, diversified only by accidents that daily happen in the world, and influenced by passions and qualities which are really to be found in conversing with mankind," as opposed to "the wild strain of imagination" of earlier ages.[59] Johnson did not go so far as to give this "new species" a new name, but by the end of his century, a clear distinction had developed between the older sort of fictions and the newer—and better—sort. The former continued to be called "romances" or "old romances," and the latter, in recognition of their supposed novelty, became "novels." The differences between them were described succinctly and precisely by Clara Reeve (1729–1807), in *The Progress of Romance*:

> The Romance is an heroic fable, which treats of fabulous persons and things. —The Novel is a picture of real life and manners, and of the time in which it is written. The Romance in lofty and elevated language, describes what never happened nor is likely to happen. —The Novel gives a familiar relation of such things, as pass every day before our eyes, such as may happen to our friend, or to ourselves; and the perfection of it, is to represent every scene, in so easy and natural a manner, and to make them appear so probably, as to deceive us into a persuasion (at least while we are reading) that all is real, until we are affected by the joys or distresses, of the persons in the story, as if they were our own.[60]

In the light of these developments on the far side of the world, it is fascinating to note that every shift in literary perception and opinion that accompanied "the rise of the novel" is echoed in Norinaga's treatise. The recognition of prose fiction as a discrete genre of literature (*hitokusa no fumi*), the distinction of a newer version from the old, the advocacy of a more appreciative attention to these fictions—they are all there in Norinaga, and then some. Individual elements of his argument may be foreshadowed (albeit faintly) in earlier commentary, but his deployment of them in concert as a unified theory, which he expounds at length and proposes as an alternative to previous characterizations of *Genji*, is totally unprecedented.

The very first words of the introduction to *Tama no ogushi* read: "In the Heian period [*nakamukashi*] there was a form of writing called *monogatari*, or 'tales.' These *monogatari* are what we would now call 'stories' [*hanashi*], or 'tales of times past' [*mukashibanashi*]." Further on, at the beginning of his discussion of"Larger Purposes," he continues: "As I mentioned briefly at the outset, these tales [*monogatari*] possess a nature [*omomuki*] uniquely their own.... What the nature of all these tales is and why people read them can be learned from passage upon passage in chapter after chapter of *The*

Tale of Genji." Norinaga then cites a number of these passages, in which Murasaki Shikibu describes her characters as reading old romances to while away the tedium, to learn more about the world and the people who live in it, to experience vicariously what they could never do in real life—but decidedly not, Norinaga adds, for moral homilies and admonitions of the sort found in Confucian and Buddhist treatises. In this, Norinaga was a step or two ahead of the protagonists of "the rise of the novel," for while Johnson still grounds his approval of the newer "familiar histories" in their ability to "convey the knowledge of vice and virtue with more efficacy than axioms and definitions," Norinaga explicitly rejects this line of argument and appeals instead to the psychological processes of reading. In reading the old romances, he says, "readers put themselves into a situation from the past and enter into the emotions that moved people of the past [*mukashi no hito no mono no aware o mo omoiyari*]. They liken their own circumstances to those of the past and thus come to comprehend these emotions [*mono no aware o shiri*]. In this way, they find some solace in their melancholy." Moving on from the satisfactions that fictions afford their readers, Norinaga proceeds to describe Murasaki Shikibu's underlying motives in writing this greatest of all Japanese fictions. Here again, he bases his argument on the author's own words and in a way that seems never to have occurred to any previous commentator.

In the "Hotaru" chapter of *Genji* is a remarkable passage often described as Murasaki's "defense of the art of fiction."[61] It is, of course, integral to the dramatic structure of that chapter and not a piece of literary criticism. But so revolutionary is its argument, that the worth of fictions lies not in their service to any external goals but in their intrinsic qualities and the effects of these qualities on their readers, that it is usually—and probably rightly—taken to represent Murasaki's own views on this subject. Almost equally remarkable, however, is the fact that for nearly eight hundred years, none of the countless commentators on *Genji* ever paid much more than minimal attention to this passage. Norinaga changed all this. He not only identifies the passage as one of great significance, but also quotes it in its entirety and explicates it "sentence by sentence," devoting most of the section "Larger Purposes" to the project. Norinaga, of course, takes Murasaki's declaration that "among these fabrications, some show us people's feelings in so real a manner as to convince us that so life may well be" as a description of "the very essence of *The Tale of Genji*." His logic is not impeccable; Murasaki's aims here are nowhere near as grandiose as Norinaga's.

But elsewhere in his exposition of this fascinating passage, he makes scant reference to *mono no aware* and is judicious and untendentious in his reading of Murasaki.

This, then, is where Norinaga's true genius lay: he listened to his author, recognized that her understanding of fiction was dramatically different from that of anyone before her time, and saw that no one before his own time had ever taken more than cursory notice of this. He then molded what he had learned from Murasaki into a theory of fiction that was unprecedented in eight hundred years of previous *Genji* commentary.

Unfortunately, however, it was with divided attention that he set about this task. *Shibun yōryō*, his source text, is not only an exposition of Murasaki Shikibu's views on fiction, but also an elaboration of Norinaga's conviction that "all Japanese poetry springs from a sensitivity to human emotion [*mono no aware o shiru koto yori izuru*], while *Ise*, *Genji*, and other such tales all depict these emotions [*mono no aware o kakinosete*], thus enabling us to comprehend them [*hito ni mono no aware o shirashimuru*]." The two concerns become intertwined and confounded; Murasaki is called on to corroborate Norinaga's *mono no aware ron*, on the strength of which, *mono no aware* is identified as the essence of *The Tale of Genji*—an argument that is both circular and illogical. Even so, the results of this confusion are not as disastrous as might be imagined. The concept of *mono no aware* proved to be a convenient rubric under which a number of important but otherwise unrelated observations on the art of fiction could be grouped, and very little damage was done to Murasaki's vision. But in attempting to unify all that he had to say under the rubric of *mono no aware*, Norinaga indelibly identified his entire treatise with that rubric; his extraordinary exposition of Murasaki's even more extraordinary vision was all but lost in the shadow of *mono no aware*. Perhaps Norinaga himself came to realize this, for he concludes *Shibun yōryō* with an impassioned plea to the reader not to condemn him for the roughness of his writing, and in the years thereafter he ceased to mention *mono no aware*. Thirty-some years later, *mono no aware* reappears, but only as a reincarnation of its former self. Now in his late sixties, Norinaga's priorities had shifted, and he was unwilling to spare the time to do more than edit what he had written as a much younger man. The preface to *Genji monogatari Tama no ogushi* thus remains, like its predecessor *Shibun yōryō*, a flawed masterpiece, a work of double identity, but nonetheless well worth our attention and admiration.

T. HARPER

Chapter 1

sono kami no kokoro tazunete midaretaru / suji tokiwakuru tama no ogushi zo
To untangle the tousled strands; to seek out, set straight, and know aright
the minds and hearts of times past: this little bejeweled comb.[62]

TALES IN GENERAL

In middle antiquity [*chūko*] there was a form of writing called *monogatari*, or tales. These *monogatari* are what we would now call "stories" [*hanashi*], which is to say "tales of times past" [*mukashibanashi*]. In the *Annals of Japan* [*Nihongi*], the character 談, "converse," is read *monogatari*. Perhaps the first piece of writing to be entitled thus was [*The Tale of*] *the Bamboo Cutter* [*Taketori* (*monogatari*)], for in the "Eawase" chapter [13:370] we read that "the progenitor of all tales, *The Old Bamboo Cutter*, was matched against 'Toshikage' of *The Hollow Tree* [*Utsuho*]."[63] When and by whom this story was written, we do not know, but it does not appear to be of great antiquity. Probably it dates from the Engi era [900–922] or later. It is said that a great many of these old romances existed before the time of *The Tale of Genji*. The titles of several are known to us, but most of them seem to have been lost in later times. Quite a number from around the time of *Genji* and thereafter survive even today. In the "Keburi no nochi" chapter of *A Tale of Flowering Fortunes* we read of a *monogatari*-matching competition: "New works by twenty people were divided into two groups, Right and Left, and then were matched against each other. How fascinating it was!"[64] From this we see that even then, tales continued to be written in great numbers.

Now, although they may differ in their particulars, all tales, of whatever sort, purport to relate actual events from the past. Some are based in minor ways on actual events that are altered in the writing. Some conceal the names of the persons concerned, or change them. Some are total fabrications; and once in a great while, one may describe an event exactly as it happened. Of these several sorts, however, the greatest number are fictions.

What, then, is the nature of [these tales], and why do we read them? Tales depict the myriad aspects of life: the good and the bad, the fantastic and the amusing, the intriguing and the moving [*aware*]. Some may even include illustrations of such scenes. In our idle hours they amuse us. When our hearts are troubled and we are beset by worries, they console us. They help us understand our lives in this world and the workings of the emotions [*mono no aware o shiru*].[65] That tales treat principally of relations between men and women is for the same reason that we find so many love poems in the anthologies of every age: nothing so deeply engages human feelings as does love. I shall have more to say about these matters further on.

THE AUTHOR OF *THE TALE OF GENJI*

That this tale was written by Murasaki Shikibu is a matter of common knowledge. Since evidence of this is found even as early as in her own diary, there is no disputing the fact. There are, nonetheless, a variety of theories on this subject. First of all, in *Uji no Dainagon no monogatari* it says, "*Genji* was written by Tametoki, the Governor of Echizen, after which he had his daughter Shikibu fill in the details." Even *Kachō yosei* quotes this, but the idea is unacceptable. Even the aforementioned commentary does not claim this as a certainty, but asks, "Which [theory] might be correct?"[66] Moreover, in the *Kakaishō* we find, "The Chancellor [Michinaga] added a colophon in which he wrote, 'This aged monk has made emendations.'"[67] This, too, is in error, the reasons being as argued in some detail by one Andō Tameakira in his *Shika shichiron*.[68] There are various other theories, but they are nothing but the inventions of men of later ages. In the end, it is difficult to accept any of them, other than that maintaining that Murasaki Shikibu wrote [*The Tale of Genji*]. There is also the theory that the ten Uji chapters were not written by Murasaki Shikibu, but this, too, is in error. It is obvious that they were written by the same person. And then there is the "Hidden in Clouds" [Kumogakure] chapter: owing to Shikibu's sensitivity, we are told, only the title exists but no text; yet nowadays, we have even the chapter itself. This is the work of some later person—a wretched thing, hardly worth looking at. There is also "Dew on the Mountain Path" [Yamaji no tsuyu], which takes up where "The Floating Bridge of Dreams" [Yume no ukihashi] ends. It is somewhat better written than "Hidden in Clouds," but still, it is the work of a later person and cannot compare with the work of Shikibu. She has no superior.

The genealogy of Murasaki Shikibu can be found in any of the several commentaries. Her father, Tametoki, is referred to variously as the Governor of Echigo or the Governor of Echizen. He appears as the Governor of Echigo in the headnote to a poem by Shikibu's elder brother Nobunori in chapter 8 of *Goshūishū* [466]. His transfer from the governorship of Echigo to that of Echizen is mentioned in chapter 9 of *Zoku yotsugi*.[69] He was thus first the Governor of Echigo and subsequently became the Governor of Echizen.[70] [Murasaki's] husband, Nobutaka, was descended in the fifth generation from [Fujiwara no] Yoshikado and was the founder of the Kajūji house. That Shikibu herself was a lady-in-waiting to Jōtōmon'in is indisputable, but I cannot imagine what evidence there might be that she was ever in the service of [Michinaga's wife] Takatsukasa Dono. The notion that she was Michinaga's mistress is utter nonsense.[71]

Now, the name Murasaki Shikibu is not her real name. As a rule, the names of gentlewomen—Shikibu, Shōnagon, Ben, Ukon, and the like—are all what we call "sobriquets." I mention this at the outset for the benefit of beginning scholars. The real name of this particular person has not been handed down. Neither, as a rule, are the real names of most well-known gentlewomen of the past anywhere to be found. Even in the anthologies, they are designated by their sobriquets. Likewise, among those called Shikibu are those known by such names as Murasaki [Shikibu], Izumi [Shikibu], and Koshikibu. So many are called Shikibu that it becomes confusing; therefore, they are distinguished one from another in this way. They are so designated on the basis of their surname, the office held by their father or husband, or the name of their mother. Sei Shōnagon and Gō Jijū have the surnames Kiyowara and Ōe. Izumi Shikibu is the wife of Izumi no Kami Michisada. Koshikibu is the child of Izumi Shikibu. Ise no Taifu is the daughter of Ise no Saishu Sukechika. Daini no Sanmi is the wife of Dazai no Daini Nariakira. Thus Murasaki Shikibu, too, was originally called, after her surname, Tō Shikibu. Gō Jijū, too, should be read similarly, just as with Sei Shōnagon. They should not be read "Fuji Shikibu" or "E no Jijū." With men, too, such names as Gō Sotsu, Tō Dainagon, and Zai Chūjō should all be read in their Sino-Japanese pronunciation.

Now then, as to the reason she should also be called Murasaki, the *Kakaishō* says: "According to one theory, she was originally called Tō Shikibu, but because this lacked resonance, it was changed to Murasaki for this word's associations with the color of the wisteria flower." Upon present consideration, this explanation seems but conjecture based on the fact that she is called Murasaki. How is it lacking in resonance to call her by her surname? *Fuji* is a word of exceptional elegance! Moreover, in Lord Kiyosuke's *Fukurozōshi*, it says: "Concerning the name Murasaki Shikibu, there are two theories. According to one, she acquired the name as a result of the great profundity of her writing in the 'Wakamurasaki' chapter. According to the other, she was a child of the nursemaid of the Ichijō Emperor. And so when he sent her into the service of Jōtōmon'in, he said, 'She is very close to me, please take good care of her,' hence the name, which derives from the 'Musashino' poem."[72] Of these two theories, all the commentaries follow the first. Even in the *Kakai*[*shō*], it says: "Because her characterization of Lady Murasaki is far superior to that of all the others, in place of Tō Shikibu she was dubbed Murasaki Shikibu." Upon present consideration, it seems indeed the case that "her depiction of Lady Murasaki is far superior." But I fail to grasp how it could be "the result of the great profundity of her writing in the 'Wakamurasaki' chapter." How is it that only the "Wakamurasaki" chapter is so exceptionally profound? Now it may well be that because she was the daughter of the Ichijō Emperor's nursemaid, he said, "She is very close to me." This does not have the ring of conjecture from hindsight. Shikibu's mother appears in the genealogies as "the daughter of Hitachi no Suke Tamenobu." I wonder, though, if any document says that this person was the nursemaid of the Ichijō emperor? This bears investigation. Now, when the Ichijō Emperor says that "she is very close to me" because she is the daughter of his nursemaid, this would mean that they were brought up as brother and sister by the nursemaid. "Derives from the 'Musashino' poem" means that [her name] derives from the poem in the *Kokinshū*, Miscellaneous I:

murasaki no hitomoto yue ni musashino no / kusa wa minagara aware to zo miru
For the sake of this one sprig of Murasaki, I look with fondness
on all the plants that grow upon the moors of Musashi. [*Kokinshū* 867]

From this it became the practice to refer to *murasaki* as [a symbol of] close relationship. In the *Diary of Murasaki Shikibu*, it says, "Saemon no

Kami «Lord Kintō»[73] inquired, 'I beg your pardon, but is little Murasaki in attendance hereabouts?' Hearing this, I thought, 'I don't see anyone who resembles Genji; why, then, should that lady «Lady Murasaki» be here?'"[74] In the light of the text of this diary, the close relationship theory seems to me the more attractive. The reason is this: according to the close relationship theory, the name Murasaki [Shikibu] has no connection with Lady Murasaki, and thus it becomes humorous to refer to her as if it did. As a rule, a jest is humorous precisely when one refers to something in a novel way when it is least expected. But if her name were the result of her superior characterization of Lady Murasaki, what would be so novel about a jest that calls her little Murasaki?

CIRCUMSTANCES OF COMPOSITION

It is difficult to ascertain definitely the circumstances under which this tale was written. One story has it that when she was in the service of Jōtōmon'in, the High Priestess [of Kamo] asked whether they had "any interesting stories," whereupon [Murasaki] wrote [*Genji*] for Her Ladyship. It is difficult to accept this, the reasons being as argued in some detail in the aforementioned [*Shika*] *shichiron*. Then, too, there are chronological contradictions in the claim that she knew Lord Nishinomiya [Minamoto Takaakira] well when she was young. The claims that she wrote it while in retreat at Ishiyamadera or that she wrote it on a copy of the *Daihannya kyō* are nonsense. The "fair copy by Lord Yukinari" was probably invented because of this man's reputation as a calligrapher. And it is utterly impossible to accept the claim that when she was in retreat at Ishiyama, the reflection of the full moon on the lake, on the fifteenth of the Eighth Month, so suffused her mind that the plan of the tale came to her, and she began writing the "Suma" and "Akashi" chapters—this being the reason that it says in the "Suma" chapter, "Then they realized that it was the night of the full moon" [13:194]. But if the sentence "It was the night of the full moon" is to be taken as proof that she wrote it on the fifteenth, then is the sentence "Today was the Day of the Rat" in "Hatsune" [14:139] to be taken as being written when the first day of the New Year fell on the Day of the Rat? This is positively puerile. And the "Genji Room" at Ishiyamadera, as well as the image of [Murasaki] Shikibu and her writing desk and inkstone that are kept there—these all are the inventions of some overly ardent enthusiast who believed this story. Although Genji may well be modeled on the Nishinomiya Minister, the claim that Lady Murasaki is modeled on Shikibu herself is simply ridiculous. How could she ever have come up with such a presumptuous notion?

TIME OF COMPOSITION

In the *Kakaishō*, it says, "This tale was completed at the beginning of the Kankō era [1004–1011] and was in general circulation by the end of the Kōwa era [1099–1104]," and this has been accepted by several [subsequent] commentaries. To judge from the *Diary of* [*Murasaki*] *Shikibu*, it must indeed have been completed at the beginning of the Kankō era. These matters are considered in some detail in [*Shika*] *shichiron*, which says, "Its completion must surely have been either at the end of the Chōho era [999–1004] or the beginning of the Kankō era." Yet there are those who say that because the passage in the "Uraura no wakare" chapter of *A Tale of Flowering Fortunes* that says, "I expect the Shining Genji must have looked just like this" dates from the second year of the Chōtoku era [996], the tale must have been in circulation before this time, and that to say that it was written at the beginning of the Kankō era is an error. This claim is itself incorrect. Had *Flowering Fortunes* been written by the second year of the Chōtoku era, then one might indeed make such claim, but since *Flowering Fortunes* was completed after the Kankō era, what problems does it pose? What, then, about its being "in general circulation by the end of the Kōwa era"? In the *Diary*, it is apparent that [the tale] was already in wide circulation within the palace while Shikibu was still in service at court. And what, too, about the theory that it found particular favor from the time of Lord Shunzei [1114–1204] and Lord Teika [1162–1241] onward? This is but another instance of unbridled conjecture, based on Lord Shunzei's judgments in the *Poetry Contest in 600 Rounds* and Lord Teika's words of praise.

THE TITLE OF THE TALE

Judging from the titles of the several tales [that still survive], most take their titles from the name of the principal character. The same is true of this tale. Since it depicts mainly Genji the Shining Lord, it is called *The Tale of Genji*. This lord is referred to by the name of "Hikaru" in "Kiritsubo," where it says, "So incomparably radiant was his beauty that people called him the Shining Lord" [12:120], and "The name Shining Lord, it is said, was given him as a token of admiration by the Korean" [12:126].

It is wrong, I think, to regard these as two [contradictory] explanations. It simply means that the name Shining Lord by which people referred to him was given him originally by the Korean. And so it is that in chapter after chapter, the appearance of this lord is often praised using the word *hikaru*. In "Momiji no ga": "His face seemed to shine with a radiance even greater than usual" [12:384], and "He emerged with the same radiance" [12:401]. In "Aoi" [13:18]: "They were overwhelmed by his radiance." And there are many more. At the beginning of "Niou Miya" [16:11], this lord's death is described as "after his radiance had been hidden." In contrast, Kaoru is often praised with reference to his fragrance.

Now then, Genji is this lord's surname. We see in "Kiritsubo" where he is made a member of the Genji [clan] at the time of his initiation ceremonies. In the tale, the words "Shining Genji" are found in combination in several chapters, such as at the beginning of "Hahakigi" [12:129], in "Wakamurasaki" [12:283], "Tamakazura" [14:123], "Kōbai" [16:42], and "Takekawa" [16:85]. And so there are those who say that the title of the tale should be *The Tale of the Shining Genji* and not simply *The Tale of Genji*, but this is not the case. As early as in the author's own journal, it is called simply *The Tale of Genji* [*Genji no monogatari*].

HISTORICAL BASIS

Various commentaries claim that this tale is founded upon historical fact. Some say, for example, that although there never lived an actual Hikaru Genji, the character is modeled on the Nishinomiya Minister of the Left, Lord [Minamoto no] Takaakira [914–983]. But not every event in the life of every character depicted in a tale is patterned on an actual event. Most of them are fictional, with some among them based on a shred of fact whose particulars have been reshaped in the writing. Nor are the lives of people in them ever drawn on a one-to-one correspondence [with historical models]. Events in the life of Genji can be traced to events in the lives of several different persons of the past, both Japanese and Chinese, from each of whom the author has drawn some bit of information, according to no fixed plan. This "basis in history," then, consists mainly of fragments of information in the mind of the author, not all of which can be identified precisely though subsequent research. Be that as it may, I make these few general remarks only because for ages the matter has been a topic of discussion.

In passing I might add that the "relics" one hears about, such as that of Yūgao in the Fifth Ward [of Kyoto], Genji in Suma, or Tamakazura in Hatsuse, are the work of antiquaries who failed even to realize that the tale is fictional. This is extremely naive and likely to mislead no one. I mention it merely for the benefit of beginning scholars, to put them on the alert.

MISCELLANEOUS MATTERS

The theory that describes this tale as "*Genji* in sixty chapters," and says that it was patterned after the sixty Tendai volumes, is mistaken. Though this tale does have fifty-four chapters, there is no evidence that it ever had sixty; most likely it was the attempt to force a correspondence to the Tendai texts that led some to assert that it did. And even if it were to have sixty chapters, the matter of the Tendai texts would still be far [from proven].

It also is said that the arrangement of the several chapters follows that of the "Annals," "Hereditary Houses," and "Biographies" of *Records of the Historian*, but this, too, misses the mark. As a rule, when one speculates retrospectively concerning such matters, one is bound to find resemblances and correspondences, but this is mere coincidence; to argue that the one is based upon the other totally misses the mark.

The arrangement of chapters in synchronous groups and consecutive groups [*tate yoko no narabi*] is of no great use, but as this has been a matter of discussion since ages past, one should be familiar with it in a general way.

One should commit firmly to memory the genealogies of the characters of the tale. If one does not know the genealogies of the characters, one will frequently confuse them and fail to grasp the finer points of the work. But in the genealogies that have come down to us, there are many omissions and occasionally even errors. As readers have been confused by this, some of these have been corrected in later commentaries, but even now they are far from perfect. On account of this, I have long wished to study these matters in greater detail and construct new genealogies, but I've not had time to finish the job. Although a work of fiction, [*Genji*] has been composed so that the ages of the characters and the chronological progression of the chapters all jibe with one another; these matters thus must be set aright. This has been a subject of discussion since ages past, and thus we have the chronology drawn up by Lord Go-Jōonji.[75] But this work is fraught with errors throughout, and in the Uji chapters his errors are particularly numerous. [Some] have been corrected in subsequent commentaries, but since mistakes still remain, I too have set down my own ideas, elaborating on them in some detail. I have also constructed a chart as an aid to ready comprehension of the chronological progress of the chapters.

It is said that in the past there were, broadly speaking, two lines of texts: the Kawachi-bon and the Aobyōshi. From among them, out of no consideration for its merits or demerits but simply because it is the text of Teika no Chūnagon, all of the more recent commentaries adopt the Aobyōshi. Now what is one to make of this? Any text whatever should be adopted or rejected strictly on the basis of its merits or demerits. The choice should never be made because of the person who compiled it. As it happens, each of the numerous texts now extant, whether printed or in manuscript, differs here and there in some small way from each of the others, and each has its own merits and demerits. I have collated several of these texts and, wherever they differ, selected the best version and noted it down. These notations are collected in a separate section further on [in the volume]. Each and every ancient text written in kana that has been handed down to the present day contains numerous scribal errors and omissions, and hence many passages are difficult to decipher. But this tale, perhaps because it has enjoyed such deep appreciation and wide favor with age upon age of readers, in comparison with lesser works, contains very few scribal errors. This is not to say, however, that no passages whatever appear mistakenly copied.

COMMENTARIES

The *Kakaishō* [ca. 1362–1367] ranks first among the commentaries. There are others that precede this work, but they are limited in scope and lacking in detail, whereas this work draws on a wide range of texts, Japanese and Chinese, Confucian and Buddhist. Everything in the tale, almost without exception, is explicated here. There is also the *Kachō yosei* [1472], which treats items either omitted or in error in the *Kakaishō*; this is in many ways an extremely useful work. These two commentaries are absolutely indispensable, yet they do often err. Their definitions of terms, in particular, are replete with errors and are not to be relied on.

Following these come the *Rōkashō* [1510] and *Sairyūshō* [ca. 1510–1513], which set right the errors in the *Kakaishō* and *Kachō yosei* and also present new ideas of their own. In addition, we have the *Myōjōshō* [ca. 1552], *Mōshinshō* [1575], *Mingō nisso* [1598], *Bansui ichiro* [1652], *Kogetsushō* [1673], and others. These contain a multitude of headnotes and other materials of various sorts, but all of them draw on the several earlier commentaries; they differ slightly one from another but present no new information.

Of these, the most widely used today is the *Kogetsushō*. This commentary draws extensively and judiciously from several commentaries of several sorts and cites this information in headnotes and interlinear notes, together with the author's own theories and those of his teacher.[76] And it is formatted in a manner that makes it extremely convenient to consult all this information.

There is also the *Genchū shūi* [completed 1698], a work in eight volumes by the monk Keichū [1640–1701]. This is not an exhaustive commentary, but a work that treats a variety of matters either omitted or in error in the other commentaries. The author, a man of uncommon brilliance, has many unusual new ideas. In all his writings he accepts none of the irresponsible notions of more recent times, but goes directly to the ancient texts for documentation, and in this way has achieved many new insights.

As mentioned earlier, there also is a volume called *Shika shichiron*. This work is not a commentary, but discusses the larger purposes of this tale; considers in some detail the genius and virtue of Murasaki Shikibu, citing evidence from her diary; and analyzes the many mistaken notions that have been handed down from the past. It is an unusual and individual work and should definitely be read. By and large, however, the author thinks only in terms of precedent from the works of Chinese writers and gives no consideration to the nature of these works we call tales. He fails to realize that tales are written principally to depict human emotion [*mna*]. Rather, he views tales as homilies, in the same spirit as do the Confucianists.

My own teacher, [Kamo no] Mabuchi [1697–1769], has also written a *Shinshaku* [completed ca. 1758] on this tale. I have known of this work for some time but so far have been unable to read more than the first volume, the "General Discussion," in which his ideas resemble those of Keichū and Tameakira. It also cites material from [his own] *Shinshaku*.

There is also *Genji gaiden* by Kumazawa Ryōkai [Banzan], but this work is so thoroughly of the Confucian mentality that it is of no use in understanding the tale.

Besides these, there are doubtless other, lesser-known works. Of such guidebooks, there are many, but their treatment of the broader aspects of the tale aside, they seldom penetrate to the finer nuances of the language or the deeper aspects of the author's intentions. So one ought not to depend only on commentaries for the general sense and content oneself with that. To probe more deeply into its intricacies is to find this a work of inexpressible savor.

"ALLUSIONS TO POETRY"

Those passages in the tale that quote a single phrase [*ku*] of poetry in order to convey the sense of an entire poem or to convey the sense of the words that follow that line are called "allusions to poetry" [*hikiuta*]. Most of these poems are identified in the *Kakaishō*, and those few that were missed appear in *Kachō yosei*. Those quoted in the later commentaries are taken from the *Kakaishō* and *Kachō yosei*. Of the allusions cited in the *Kakaishō*, however, some are mistaken and a great many are quoted incorrectly, while some confuse one poem with another, and some cite a spurious poem that is neither ancient nor identifiable. On the whole, [these citations] are extremely careless. As Keichū, too, has pointed out, it appears that whatever came to [the author's] mind, whether mistaken or otherwise, he just jotted it down. And in subsequent commentaries, they simply cite the *Kakaishō* with no further consideration. This, too, is careless scholarship. One must always consult these works with great caution. Now, in the *Kakaishō* and other commentaries, there are passages marked "allusion unidentified," whose source poems are not known. One hopes that these will be studied further and identified.

THE *KOGETSUSHŌ*

Among the numerous texts of this tale currently in circulation, most people find it convenient to read it in the *Kogetsushō* edition. In this connection, certain cautions are in order. In the first place: although for the most part the text given in this commentary is good, occasionally there occur passages that are corrupt or from which words are missing.

I have collated [the *Kogetsushō*] with another text and noted all of these; they are as recorded further on [in volume 4]. Moreover, the punctuation of this commentary is extremely unreliable throughout and often mistaken. Frequently the meaning of the sentence is seriously distorted by its punctuation. One must be alert to this as one reads. There also are many errors in the indication of voiced and unvoiced syllables. The fact that kana spellings are invariably incorrect hardly calls for special mention, as this has become the norm in recent years.

What is more, many passages marked as "allusions" [*hikiuta*] are in fact not allusions. An "allusion" is a passage based on an old poem and is absolutely unintelligible without reference to that poem. Yet this commentary frequently fails to distinguish these from passages cited in the *Kakaishō* or *Kachō yosei* not as "allusions" but simply as quotations from old poems. It regards them all as allusions and marks them as such.

Furthermore, in the annotations, those that should be marked as deriving from the *Kakaishō* or *Kachō yosei* are invariably cited as quotations from some later commentary and are marked as deriving from the *Rōkashō* or *Sairyūshō*. It should be understood, therefore, that many explanations quoted from the *Rōkashō* or *Sairyūshō* derive originally from the *Kakaishō* or *Kachō yosei*.

I note here only these one or two points as they happen to come to mind. The reader may infer from them what further problems there may be. Owing to its convenience as the most widely read text, I have in most cases followed the *Kogetsushō* faithfully in compiling this [*Tama no*] *ogushi*, as, for example, in the page numbers cited in the several chapters [of this commentary].

LARGER PURPOSES

From of old, there have been various interpretations of the intentions of this tale. All, however, fail to take into account the nature of these works we call tales. They argue entirely in the idiom of Confucian and Buddhist texts, which is not what the author intended. Although there are, as it happens, points of chance resemblance and accord with Confucian and Buddhist texts, it will not do to seize upon these as characterizing the work as a whole. Its overall import differs sharply from works of that sort. Tales possess a nature uniquely their own. And, as

I mentioned briefly at the outset, *Genji* stands out from the old romances as a work composed with more than ordinary seriousness. This matter will be discussed in detail later.

Now, the nature of these tales, as well as the reasons that people read them, can be learned from passages found in the various chapters of *The Tale of Genji*. Let me cite some of these and say a few words about each by way of explanation.

In "Yomogiu" [13:320], it says:

> Frivolous old poems and romances and other amusements of that sort might have helped her to dispel the tedium and reconcile herself to such a life; but . . .[77]

"Such a life" is the forlorn and lonely life of Suetsumuhana. The reason such a person would find it comforting to read old romances is that in reading descriptions of others like oneself one finds it consoling to think that there are those in this world in just such dismal straits as one's own.

In "Eawase" [13:368]:

> His travel journals . . . were so touching they might have brought tears to the eyes of anyone of the least sensitivity, even someone seeing them for the first time with no knowledge [of the circumstances]. How much more so . . .

The "travel journals" are Genji's journals from the time of his sojourn at Suma. "Seeing them for the first time with no knowledge" means that even someone with no knowledge of the events of the time, but now, seeing only the journal for the first time [would be moved]; how much more so the feelings of a reader who did know [the circumstances of Genji's exile] and had lived through [those times].

In "Kochō" [14:175]:

> In her reading of old romances she had gradually been learning something about what people and the world were like. . . .

Since tales generally depict events of this world and the various thoughts and deeds of human beings, in reading them one naturally gains a good knowledge of life and comes to understand better the deeds of people and the workings of their emotions. This is the principal aim of those who read tales.

In "Hotaru" [14:202]:

> The rains this year had persisted much longer than usual, and the ladies of the household were amusing themselves whole days at a stretch with illustrated romances.

And again [14:206]:

> "My but these are very well drawn," she said, looking at the pictures of the *Tale of Komano*.[78] The scene of the little girl peacefully napping reminded the lady of herself in times past.

The "lady" is Lady Murasaki. "Times past" refers to Murasaki's own childhood, which she here recalls.

In "Makibashira" [14:364]:

> One knows from reading old romances that even the most loving parent, when his affections shift and he comes under the sway of another woman, may do the most heartless things. But this man. . . .

Here they learn about life and the world from reading tales.

In the latter "Wakana" chapter [15:203]:

> As always on nights when he was not at home, she stayed up late and had her people read tales to her. In all these old stories,[79] these stores of worldly wisdom—indeed, even in those that tell of the most fickle and wanton men, and of women who take up with faithless lovers—everyone ultimately settles down with someone they can depend upon. How strange that I should continue to lead such an uncertain life.

The passage that begins "In all these" describes Murasaki's feelings on having tales read to her. *Kayō* should probably be read *waga yō*, the *wa* having been missed out.[80] "How strange" refers to her own situation.

In "Yūgiri" [15:401]:

> Sometimes in the old romances, even if some outsider should learn the secret, they are still able to hide it from their parents.

In “Hashihime” [16:132]:

> When he had heard his young ladies reading old romances, there would always be some story of this sort, and he had dismissed them impatiently, thinking that such things could never actually exist; but now it must have struck him that there were indeed truly affecting little scenes to be found in hidden corners of this world.

In “Agemaki” [16:256]:

> . . . if anyone ever wants to tell a tale of warning for posterity, ours will do nicely as an instance of the sort of woman they invariably depict as such fools in the old romances.

And again [16:214]:

> It made them realize what a help these old turns of phrase [*furukoto*] are in giving vent to a person’s feelings.

“Old turns of phrase” here refers to poetry, but the same is true of old romances.

In “Yadorigi” [16:401]:

> She had always been puzzled, in both reading old romances and hearing the experiences of others, why women in such a predicament worried so dreadfully about it. Now that it had happened to her, she realized that in fact it was no trifling matter at all.

Here the younger daughter from Uji, through experiences in her own life, comes to understand events in the old romances and realizes that such things can indeed happen. The “predicament” is that of a woman who frets over the infidelity of a man.

And further [16:404–5]:

> Such festive and gay occasions as this are indeed a delight to behold, which is why they are described with such particular prominence in tales.

In "Kagerō" [17:199]:

> She recalled that in the old romances there were instances of just such strange goings-on as this.

And again [17:248]:

> He could not help but liken his own situation to that beautifully drawn scene from *The Serikawa Commandant*, in which Tōgimi, of an autumn evening, despondent with yearning for the First Princess, sets out for her home. If only his own lady were as compliant, he thought to himself with chagrin.

These are Kaoru's thoughts about the First Princess.

In "Tenarai" [17:300]:

> "It seems like something out of an old romance," he said.

In "Yume no ukihashi" [17:362]:

> "I recalled the story in an old romance of someone who had been placed in a mortuary [coming back to life] and wondered, in amazement, whether just such a thing might have happened here. . . ."

This, by and large, is the frame of mind in which tales are read. Readers put themselves into a situation from the past and enter into the emotions that moved these people of the past [*mukashi no hito no mna o mo omoiyari*]. They liken their own circumstances to those of the past and thus come to comprehend such emotions [*mna o shiri*]. In this way, they find some solace in their melancholy.

Thus we can see, from the foregoing descriptions in chapter after chapter, that the attitudes of those who read the old romances were the same as the attitudes of present-day readers of *The Tale of Genji*—and that these differ markedly from the attitudes in which most Buddhist and Confucian works were read.

Now then, Murasaki Shikibu's intentions in writing this tale are set forth quite clearly in "Hotaru" [14:202–6]. She does not, however, state them outright, but speaks through Genji as he discusses old romances with Tamakazura, her underlying intention being to express the aims of her own tale. But the commentaries contain many errors, and the author's underlying meaning is not readily apparent. Therefore, as a guide to readers of the tale, I will here quote this particular passage in its entirety and explicate it sentence by sentence so as to make clear its underlying meaning. The passage reads as follows:

> There were a number of young gentlewomen who were no mean hands at the art and had collected all sorts of astonishing stories of people's lives. Whether they were fact [*makoto*] or fiction [*itsuwari*] she had no idea, yet in none of them, it seemed to her, was there anyone who had experienced anything like what she had been through.

These are Tamakazura's feelings as she reads the old romances.

> The young lady in *Sumiyoshi*,[81] at the time of her adventures, needless to say, and even in the present day, seemed still to be held in high regard; and her narrow escape from the Superintendent of Finance [*Kazoe no Kami*] did remind her of the ferocity of that Kyushu First Secretary [*Gen*].[82]

She reads the *Tale of Sumiyoshi* and compares it with events in her own past.

> His Lordship could not help but notice all these things scattered here and there around the room.

"His Lordship" is Genji. "These things" are the texts of old romances.

> "My, what a mess! You women seem to have been born only to be deceived by people, and without your ever even raising a complaint."

From here forward, Genji is speaking to Tamakazura. These trifling tales, so full of lies, are a nuisance even to look at, he says; but you women, far from regarding them a nuisance, are quite fond of them. Indeed, you seem to have been born for the very purpose of being deceived. At first he teases her, belittling the old romances.

Now, from here on, the author's underlying intent is to adopt the viewpoint of a reader of *The Tale of Genji*. At first, as in the belittling manner of this passage, her attitude is critical; then she then goes on, now praising, now belittling, while one after another she states the reasons why, ultimately, it would be difficult to do without these tales.

> "You know perfectly well that there's very little truth in any of these, and yet here you are, captivated and deceived by all this nonsense, copying away as if you were quite unaware that it is a stifling hot day in the middle of the rainy season and your hair is all in a tangle." He smiled, but then went on.

From the fact that he "smiles," we know that these words are spoken partly in jest. Thereafter, from "but then," the argument takes a new turn. The underlying intent here is at first to find fault with *The Tale of Genji*: it is a trifling tissue of lies; to be taken in by it and to read it is but a waste of time.

> "Yet without these old stories, how indeed would you while away this interminable tedium?"

His initial belittlement was just in jest; indeed, he says, if it were not for these old romances, there would be no way to while away the tedium. With the word "indeed," he takes the part of those who enjoy tales. The underlying intent here is to respond to his previous criticism.

> "For among these fabrications are some that show us people's feelings in so real a manner as to make us feel that, yes, this is life as it really is. One thing follows another so plausibly that, although we know it to be sheer nonsense, still, for no good reason, we are deeply moved. And so we may see some lovely little lady stricken with grief and, in one corner of our minds, find ourselves quite caught up in her woes."

Tales, Genji says, are for the most part fabrications, yet in them we find what strikes us as life as it really is. And though we know it to be a fabrication, still we find it affecting, and our feelings are moved. "For no good reason" refers to the futility of being moved by reading a piece of fiction. This is the same as when the preface to the *Kokinshū* speaks of [being moved by] "looking at a woman in a painting."[83] The "lovely little lady" is one seen in an illustration of such a scene in an old romance. To be "caught up" means much the same as to be "moved."

The underlying meaning here is as follows: The passage "It shows us people's emotions in so real a manner as to make us feel that, yes, this is life as it really is" describes the very essence of *The Tale of Genji*. This tale was written principally with the purpose of revealing to us, in just this way, the workings of the emotions [*mna o shirashimuru koto*]. I shall have more to say of this elsewhere. And from these words we realize that it is mistaken to claim that this tale was written to "encourage virtue and castigate vice." I shall have more to say of this, too, further on.

> "And then there are those tales of things we know could never happen, but that are told with such grandiloquence that they quite dazzle us. Upon a calmer hearing, we would only find them irritating, and yet how vivid are those scenes that do somehow chance to excite our interest."

This describes yet another sort of old romance. Previously, we had the sort that describes "life as it really is," to read of which we find moving, while here we have the absurd, of which we read only in wonderment. We are "dazzled," she goes on to say, and they "somehow excite our interest." "See" and "hear" in this passage amount to the same thing; we either read to ourselves or are read to by others. Generally, when something is just too outlandish or incredible, we are irritated when we read or hear of it again in a calmer frame of mind. Still, such things do have a certain fascination.

The underlying intent here is to divide the events depicted in *The Tale of Genji* into two sorts and to explain their significance. One sort is that discussed previously—"life as it really is"—which moves the reader's feelings and reveals the workings of the emotions [*mna o shirasetari*]. For one's "feelings to be moved" [*kokoro ugoku*] means one reacts to the emotional quality of a thing or situation [*mna ni kanzuru*]. Now, the second sort is the outlandish event described in this passage. The former, of course, is the principal concern of the tale; the latter sort is occasionally used merely to arouse interest. Thus in saying that "upon a calmer hearing, we would only find them irritating," she is saying, in effect, that in this tale such absurd and astonishing events are extremely rare, whereas those that show us the workings of the emotions [*mna o misetaru suji*] are numerous. And those in this world who prefer books depicting the strange and unusual, and find uninteresting those that calmly depict the workings of the emotions [*mna o misetaru*], are insensitive dolts.

> "Lately when I have stopped to listen to our young [Akashi] lady's gentlewomen reading to her,"

Illustrated tales were considered a frivolous amusement for young girls—nothing a man would normally take the time to read. And so the author speaks here of his [Genji's] stopping to listen to the women read. In reality, however, such was not strictly the case. Men, too, commonly read tales—so avidly, in fact, that they would even cite old romances on points of precedent. We see examples of this here and there, even in this tale. This is a bit of self-deprecation on the author's part.

> "I have been struck with what extraordinary tellers of tales we have these days. Such stuff could have come only from someone thoroughly accustomed to lying [*soragoto*], it seems to me, but am I perhaps wrong?"

Am I wrong, Genji asks, to think that a person who can write about something that we know does not exist and yet make us feel that it is so real that we are moved, or write about something we know never could have happened and yet arouse our interest in it, must be someone accustomed to lying and quite skilled at it? "But am I perhaps wrong?" means that although one might think this, such perhaps is not the case. The underlying intent here is to voice the doubts of a reader. The question posed is answered after this next passage.

> "Isn't it rather that it takes a person who is accustomed to lying even to imagine such things?" she said, pushing her inkstone away. "I myself accept them as completely true."

These are Tamakazura's words. The habitual liar, she says, as a matter of course doubts everyone and assumes everything they say to be a lie. Incidentally, the commentaries that say that this statement refers to Genji are mistaken.[84] If she were speaking of Genji, she would use the deferential verb *tamau*, but because she uses the verb *haberu*, we know that she is speaking only of people in general. The words "I myself" are blurted out in a fit of petulance. She "pushes her inkstone away" because previously he had chided her for "copying away quite unaware that your hair is all in a tangle." This is a part of her petulant manner.

> "That was rude of me to run them down so, wasn't it? As they say, everything that has gone on in the world since the age of the gods is recorded in them. The histories of Japan are really very one-sided. But these tales must be full of practical little details," he said with a smile.

Here Genji speaks again. When Tamakazura says petulantly, "I believe they all are true," he responds playfully, "Why, yes, indeed." His attitude is clear from the fact that he smiles. The underlying intent here is to forestall the derision of those who might think that in praising tales too extravagantly and saying only good about them, she considers *The Tale of Genji*, with all its "practical little details," superior to the official histories.

> "It isn't that they describe the events of some person's life exactly as they happened. Rather, there are some things that occur as people go through life, be they good or bad, that one cannot simply see and let pass, or hear of and pay no heed to. One cannot shut all these away in one's heart, but wants to pass them on to subsequent generations—and so sets out to tell a story."

The transition from "he said with a smile" to this passage seems a bit abrupt. Perhaps this is due to the loss of a few words in between. Whether or not this is the case, the force of the transition would be clearer if one were to add a few words, such as "I spoke only in jest, of course, for in fact . . ." In any case, Genji's previous denigration of tales does not at all represent his true feelings. He sees Tamakazura utterly absorbed in copying and reading tales and, just to be perverse, speaks ill of them. His jest extends only thus far; the passage from "the events of some person's life" forward is intended as a genuine critique of tales. There are many, many tales of many different sorts, most of which are pure fabrication, but here, in order to make clear her motives in writing *The Tale of Genji*, Murasaki Shikibu speaks of it as a work depicting things that actually happened. "Be they good or bad . . . ," as with all mentions of good and evil, requires special attention. The subsequent reference to [description] in a "favorable" and an "unfavorable" manner is of the same sort. I shall discuss this matter in detail further on. The "things that one cannot simply see and let pass or hear of and pay no heed to" are those events one sees and hears of and cannot bear to shut away in one's heart. All the things one sees and hears and experiences in this life, of whatever sort—be they joyous, delightful, strange, ridiculous, fearsome, irritating, distressing, or sad[85]—when one is deeply moved and struck by them, they cannot simply be shut away in one's heart. We wish to tell someone or write them down and show them to someone. This sets our hearts at ease as nothing else does, and when the listener or reader is moved to feel as we have felt, our relief is even greater.

In "Kiritsubo" [12:106], it says:

> "I should like very much to talk with you again, for it always clears away at least a small part of that darkness of a parent's cares that we find so hard to bear; so please do visit me privately sometime when you are at leisure."

In "Sawarabi" [16:338, 340]:

> His Lordship the Middle Counselor [Kaoru] was longing to tell someone the woes pent up in his heart and so set out to call upon the Prince Minister of War [Niou]. . . . Now comforting him so as to dispel the grief that burdened his heart, now soothing his overwrought feelings, [Niou] commiserated with him . . . so that bit by bit he [Kaoru] did in fact reveal to him the pent-up woes that seemed to choke his very heart, and he felt such comfort and relief as he had never known before.

In "Yadorigi" [16:413]:

> "I [Nakanokimi] was so pleased to hear of all that you [Kaoru] did on my behalf the other day that it would be most regrettable, I thought, if I were to keep this to myself, as I usually do, and you were not to know at least some small part of the gratitude I feel."

In "Tenarai" [17:328–29]:

> She [Ukifune] had never been the sort who could put her thoughts into words when talking with others; much less was there anyone here close enough to confide in. She could only turn to her inkstone and, when her grief seemed more than she could bear, write down as best she could—as in writing practice—whatever came to mind.

From examples of this sort, the point should be clear. "Writing practice" here means amusing oneself by writing down with no forethought whatever comes to mind.

Now, the difficulty of shutting away in one's heart anything whatever that has made a deep impression upon one remains the same in the present day, even for ordinary people with the shallowest of minds. For instance, when we see or hear of something marvelous or strange, even something that has nothing to do with ourselves, we are not content simply to muse, "how strange, how marvelous." Invariably, we want to tell someone else as quickly as we can. The telling is of no benefit whatever, either to ourselves or to the other person, yet when we do so, spontaneously, we feel relieved. Such is simply the innate nature of human feeling—for which reason we are also moved to compose poetry.

The underlying sense is this: the previous passage that speaks of those "thoroughly accustomed to lying" is critical of this tale, but from here forward her intent is to answer that criticism. Murasaki Shikibu states clearly her own intentions in writing *The Tale of Genji.* This tale, she says, is indeed a complete fiction [*soragoto*], but it is not groundless nonsense. Although she does not state actual names or describe events as they actually happened, they all are events such as one sees or hears of every day in this world—events, be they good or bad, that so move us that we "want to pass them on to subsequent generations." And since she cannot bear to shut these away in her heart, she writes them out in the form of a tale. We must realize, therefore, that fiction though it is, false it is not [*soragoto nagara soragoto ni arazu*]. One may wonder, thus, if these are all events that Murasaki Shikibu herself saw or heard of in her own time and wrote down, concealing only those persons' names. But these are not necessarily particular persons or particular events precisely as they happened, but merely such things as one sees or hears of every day in this world, things that deeply moved her and that she could not bear to let pass into oblivion. Using them, she would create certain persons and events, assign thoughts and words to those persons, and thus express her own feelings.

> Should one decide to describe someone favorably [*yoki sama ni*], one may select every good quality imaginable.

The tale being a fictional creation, when the author sets out to speak well of a person, she may select all the good qualities in the world, assign them to a single character, and speak of him only in the best of terms.

In its underlying sense, this passage applies to Genji—to his deeds and thoughts, needless to say, but also to his looks and appearance, his station and rank, and his brilliant career. She attributes to him every good thing in the world. This she does to deepen his emotional potential and thus move the reader more deeply [*mna o fukaku shite yomu hito o fukaku kanzeshimen*].

> "Or instead one may defer to the tastes of others . . ."[86]

Considering the phrase that follows, we might expect the author to say here, in contrast to her remarks about the portrayal of a good character, "and should one decide to speak ill of someone. . . ." But she does not. This is an interesting example of Murasaki Shikibu's discretion. Generally it is best not to speak pointedly of people's faults. Thus, without taking it upon herself to speak ill of anyone, she describes those things that are judged by others to be bad in accordance with that judgment. "Defer to the tastes of others" means she speaks not from her own inclinations but in accord with what others say. A similar use of the expression is found in "Momiji no ga" [12:412]: "He [Genji] deferred to his companion [Gen no Naishi] and exchanged playful jests with her."

> ". . . and gather in all manner of evils and marvels [*ashiki sama no mezurashiki koto*]."

"Evil" does not necessarily mean evil deeds as described in commonplace Confucian and Buddhist works. This matter will be discussed in detail further on.

In its underlying sense, this passage applies to such characters as Suetsumuhana and Ōmi no Kimi, and encompasses as well everything described in unfavorable terms. This the author does, not with the intent of pointing out people's faults and criticizing them; it is simply that in order to arouse the reader's interest she from time to time writes of "evils and marvels." Her intent we know from the phrases "defer to the tastes of others" and "marvels."

Now, the two categories [of writing] mentioned previously, the one that "shows us people's feelings in so real a manner as to make us feel that this is life as it really is" and the other, "told with such grandiloquence," correspond to the present categories of "good" [*yoki sama*] and "evil" [*ashiki sama*]. The former category describes the spirit in which tales are read and the latter, the spirit in which they are written. When we consider all these in combination, we realize that the depiction of "all the good qualities imaginable" is for the purpose of "showing us people's feelings in so real a manner as to make us feel that this is life as it really is" and thus to move the reader, whereas the "evils and marvels" are not integral to the tale, but are only occasional amusements. This we know from her previous statements that such things may "dazzle us," but "upon a calmer hearing we would only find them irritating, and yet how vivid are those scenes that do somehow chance to excite our interest."

But in neither case will these depart from the realities of this world we live in. Everything the author writes, be it good or be it evil, will be about the ordinary stuff of life, and not that which could never happen in this world.

> "In other courts, their scholarship and their styles of writing differ from our own . . ."

"Other courts" means foreign lands. "Scholarship" means the learning a person acquires. In most tales, such learning is called "scholarship" [*zae*]. "Styles of writing" refers to the composition of their literature. The single word "differ" applies to both "scholarship" and "styles of writing." To interpret this as meaning "that which is written by a person of learning" is contrary to the sense of this sentence.

Now, with regard to these differences in scholarship and differences in styles of writing: the nature of the scholarship and the styles of writing of foreign peoples, the author says, differ drastically from the nature of our own tales and the style in which they are written. For the most part, foreign writings run to stern, carping arguments over questions of good and evil, right and wrong. They probe into the principles of things, every man disputing against every other, and all of them affecting airs of omniscience. We speak of their tradition of poetic elegance and refinement, but it differs totally from the poetry of our own land. The innermost corners of the heart are left hidden and unspoken; they merely embellish the surface and carry on in a self-important manner. The tales of our own land, however, describe life in this world and the human emotions just as they are, with the result that they are often frivolous and insubstantial. But never are they pompous, pedantic, or overbearing. In this respect, their "styles of writing" differ from that of foreign lands.

> "while even within this same land of Yamato, those of old are bound to differ from those of the present day."

Texts that read "because" [*nareba*] in place of "while even" [*naredo*] are in error.[87] Nor it it simply that Chinese books differ [from our own], but that even books of this same land of ours differ from past to present in their styles of writing. In saying "are bound to" [*naru beshi*], she means that these differences are no doubt the result of differences between times past and the present. The Japanese books of the past to which she refers are probably the aforementioned official histories and other works of that sort. These were written in Chinese, and the matters they describe are quite different from those in tales. "Those of the present" are tales, for by comparison with the ancient histories of Japan, even the old romances would have been works of a recent age. In its underlying sense, "those of the present day" refers to *The Tale of Genji*, which she was then in the process of writing.

> "To be sure, there is a distinction to be drawn between deeper language and shallow language";

In both instances, "language" [*koto*] means "writing." "Deeper language" refers to foreign texts as well as to the official histories of Japan and other works of that sort—works written in Chinese, which young women find difficult to understand. "Shallow language" refers to tales, which are written casually in everyday language just as it is spoken, using women's script. Since she does not simply say "deep" and "shallow," but specifically mentions "language," we know that she speaks [only] about the language in which these texts are written.

> "yet to dismiss these [tales] totally as empty fabrications surely misses the point."

"Misses the point" means much the same as the colloquial expression "mistaken." In its underlying sense, everything from "It isn't that they describe the events of some person's life . . ." down to this point is in response to the previous criticism that tales are "empty fabrication" [*soragoto*]. This passage thus concludes that response. The passage that follows cites examples as evidence that tales should not be dismissed totally, even though they are fictions.

> "Even the holy law that the Buddha in his beneficence has expounded for us contains what we call Expedient Truths [*hōben*]."

"Beneficence" signifies what in colloquial speech we would call "righteousness." In the holy law that the Buddha in his righteousness has expounded to us, we should hardly expect to find untruths [*soragoto*], yet even there we find Expedient Truths. Why, then, she says, should not mere mortals, depending on the situation, fabricate events that never happened as a means to an end [*hōben*]? Although in a sense untruth and Expedient Truth may amount to the same thing, they differ in spirit. Untruth is what we call "falsehood" [*mōgo*], the utterance of which is harmful. Expedient Truth is meant to benefit the hearer. The underlying sense of the passage is: In the previous reference to "empty fabrication" [*soragoto*], the word was used to speak ill of tales. In reply, the author says that this tale cannot be called utterly untrue. It depicts all manner of things, both good and evil, for the purpose of revealing the workings of human feeling [*mna o shirashimen tame*], and thus is comparable to the Expedient Truths of the Buddha.

> "which, owing to contradictions that occur here and there, the unenlightened doubtless view with suspicion."

Those who lack the wisdom to understand the true nature of Expedient Truths in the teachings of the Buddha will be skeptical of the inconsistencies between what is taught in one place and what is taught in another. The underlying intent here is merely to pose an objection to this tale.

> "In the Vaipulya sutras [Hōdōkyō] these are quite numerous";

Expedient Truths, she says, are particularly numerous in the Mahāyāna [Hōdōbu] scriptures.

> "yet in the final analysis they all share a single aim."

Expedient Truths may appear to differ from the true teachings, yet ultimately they amount to the same thing.

> "The disparity between enlightenment and delusion, you see, is comparable to the difference between good and evil in these people."

The "single aim" is mentioned with reference to the "enlightenment" and "delusion" in this passage. The Buddha's Law contains a variety of Expedient Truths, and though here and there these appear to contradict one another, in the final analysis they are the same as the true teachings and share the single aim of explaining the difference between enlightenment and delusion. From the phrase beginning with "these," the foregoing illustration is applied to tales.[88] "These," then, refers to tales. "People" are the people in tales. As for the "difference": the depiction of the difference between good and evil in the people in tales is like the explanation of the disparity between enlightenment and delusion in the teachings of the Buddha. Someone once asked me: "In that case, since tales, too, illustrate good and evil in people, ultimately this amounts to encouraging virtue and castigating vice, the same as in Chinese writings. Why then, do you say that tales differ so drastically from Confucian and Buddhist writings?" I answered: "As I said earlier, the good and evil depicted in tales are in many ways unlike the virtue and vice, right and wrong, described in Confucian and Buddhist writings, and thus they differ drastically in nature." The underlying meaning here is precisely as it appears on the surface.

> "Given its fair due, then, nothing whatever is utterly bereft of benefit, is it?" He made quite a case for tales as something of particular value.

"Given its fair due" means that although one might think of tales as trivial and worthless, when one considers the case in all fairness, one sees that this is not so. "Something of particular value" means that they are not trivial amusements but something indispensable. Although tales may be the playthings of young women, mere trivial amusements, Genji maintains, we could not get by without reading them. The underlying sense of this conclusion, from "tales" forward, has been carefully crafted by Murasaki Shikibu. Previously she has spoken of *The Tale of Genji* as if it were of some worth, yet in truth, she says, it is frivolous and worthless. With this humble touch, she sets her brush aside. The significance of this passage should be savored carefully until it is understood. As I have said repeatedly, this section of "Hotaru," in its underlying sense, describes the author's attitude toward writing this tale. And the manner in which she does this—with no proclamation of her general purpose at either the beginning of the book or the end, but by revealing it subtly and unobtrusively in a passage of no particular prominence—is simply magnificent.

Now the commentaries over the years have merely skimmed over this passage, explicating only its surface meaning without making clear the author's underlying intent. They are fraught with errors throughout, but most particularly in their comments on the passage comparing tales with the teachings of the Buddha. This they explicate in the most pretentious manner, but only as it relates to the scriptures; not one of them hits on the significance of the comparison as it is cited here. Yet if the meaning of this passage is not made clear, neither will the import of the entire *Tale of Genji* be clear. I shall therefore point out just a few of the errors in these commentaries.

First of all, the passage that speaks of "the Buddha in his beneficence" is annotated with grandiloquent references to the Buddha illustrated with quotations from the scriptures, but all of them miss the point. In the tale, the word "beneficent" is used in its everyday sense of "righteous"; what more profound meaning than that might it have?

And then there is Expedient Truth. In the doctrines of the Lotus school, it may be perfectly correct to speak of the Lotus Sutra as Ultimate Truth and all previous scriptures as Expedient Truth. But to take this as the basis for construing the Expedient Truth of this passage as meaning the Lesser Vehicle of Buddhism is an egregious error. The Expedient Truths spoken of here are the sort found in all the scriptures. They are parables fabricated for the salvation of the masses. Discussion of the Greater and Lesser Vehicles, the Four Teachings, [and] the Five Ages is irrelevant here and quite out of place.

Furthermore, the expression "the unenlightened" can be used to refer to those who during the Buddha's lifetime attended his meetings and listened to his sermons, but here it simply means those in this latter age who read or listen to the Buddha's teachings. This we know from the inflection *-beku*, "doubtless [view with suspicion]."

"In the final analysis they all share a single aim" is interpreted as meaning "the teachings of the Five Ages all lead to the single truth of the Lotus," or "ultimately all is Void," or "the myriad dharmas are but a single Absolute." All these are totally irrelevant to this context.

And concerning the passage that reads "the disparity between enlightenment and delusion," they cite the story of the dragon girl who attained Buddhahood,[89] and then claim that there is no distinction between enlightenment and delusion. This interpretation directly contradicts the statement that there is a "disparity," and thus is a gross mistake. The "disparity between enlightenment and delusion" is likened to the "good and evil" of the people in the tale. But to claim that there is "no distinction" amounts to saying that there is likewise no distinction between the good and evil of the people [in the tale], does it not? In any case, this disregard for the meaning of the text, while interpreting it pretentiously only in terms of the scriptures, is utterly irresponsible.

The notion that Murasaki Shikibu was in receipt of a dispensation from the Tendai sect, was deeply learned in its doctrines, and thus wrote everything in accordance with the scriptures of Tendai is complete nonsense. This attempt to lavish praise on Shikibu only betrays her purposes. She herself had a strong distaste for women who boasted of their learning and affected airs of wisdom. We see evidence of this in chapter after chapter of *Genji*, and she often mentions it in her diary as well. Why, then, would she herself behave with such pomposity? More particularly, would Genji cite such frightfully abstruse points of Buddhist doctrine in a conversation with as young a lady as Tamakazura? Surely [the author] would never have written anything so inappropriate in this tale.

In the passage from "Hotaru" just cited, in which it speaks of "things that happen as people go through life, be they good or bad"; or "Should one decide to describe someone favorably, one may select every good quality imaginable. Or instead one may defer to the tastes of others, and gather in all manner of evils and marvels"; or the "good and evil in these people [in tales]"—the "good" and "evil" mentioned here and in a number of other passages in the tale are unlike the good and evil as usually described in Confucian and Buddhist texts, and thus, in many cases, it would be a mistake to understand the good and evil in tales strictly in Confucian or Buddhist terms.

First of all, good and evil extend to all manner of concerns and, even with regard to people, need not apply only to thoughts and deeds. There are good and bad in rank and social position, the noble being regarded good and the lowly, bad. In tales, those of high rank are called the "good people," while even in colloquial speech we speak of "good family" or of "good or bad standing." Needless to say, we speak also of good and bad looks or bearing. Again, long life, wealth, and prosperity and the acquisition of property all are good things; whereas short life, poverty, failure, loss of property, as well as illness, disaster, and the like are all bad things.

Nor is this so only in human affairs. Clothing, furniture, houses, and countless other such things all have their good and their bad. These [qualities] are by no means limited to the realm of human thoughts and deeds. Moreover, good and evil may change, depending on the thing, the time, or the situation. For example, an arrow is good if it penetrates its mark, while armor is good if it is impenetrable. On a hot summer day, that which is cool is good, while in the cold of winter, that which is hot is good. One traveling at night will consider darkness bad, but one seeking to conceal himself will consider moonlight bad. And so it goes in all matters.

Thus it is that even good and evil in human thoughts and deeds, although the contrast may not be so marked, will nonetheless differ according to doctrine. What Confucian doctrine considers good, Buddhist doctrine may consider bad; while what Buddhist doctrine considers good, Confucian doctrine may consider bad. And just as there is no absolute agreement here, some things in tales are considered good or evil, but do not accord with standard Confucian and Buddhist concepts of good and evil.

What sorts of thoughts and deeds, then, are considered good and evil in tales? Generally speaking, those who know what it means to be moved [*mna o shiri*], who have compassion, and who are alive to the feelings of others are regarded as good; whereas those who do not know what it means to be moved, lack compassion, and are insensitive to the feelings of others are regarded as bad. That said, there may appear to be no great difference from the good and evil of Confucianism and Buddhism; but to put the matter more precisely, there are many cases in which sensitivity or insensitivity to the feelings of others do not accord with Confucian and Buddhist concepts of good and evil. Moreover, even when the tale treats good and evil, it does so in gentle and moderate terms, rather than with utter obstinacy, as in a debate among Confucian scholars.

The main point of the tale being emotional sensitivity [*mna o shiru*], it often stands in opposition to the teachings of Confucianism and Buddhism. When one is moved by something, whether for good or bad, right or wrong, one's feelings may run counter to reason. Improper though it may be to be moved, one's feelings do not always follow the dictates of one's mind. They cannot be suppressed, and one is moved despite oneself. For instance, Genji's attraction to Utsusemi, Oborozukiyo, and Fujitsubo, and his affairs with these ladies, are, from the point of view of Confucian and Buddhist doctrine, immoral deeds of the worst sort. No matter how good he might be in other respects, he could hardly be called a "good person." Yet in the tale his immoral deeds are given no particular prominence; rather, his great depth of feeling [*mna no fukaki kata*] is described again and again. Genji is depicted as the very model of the "good person," possessing every good quality imaginable. This being the main point of the tale, the good and evil it depicts differ distinctly from those of Confucian and Buddhist writings.

Yet neither does it depict such immorality as good. The evil in Genji's deeds would be plain to see even if it were never mentioned. There are books enough discussing sins of this sort; there is no need to seek such stuff so far afield as in a tale. Tales do not teach us that we must abandon earthly lust so that we may attain enlightenment or that we must regulate our lands, our households, and our persons, as do the stern teachings of the Confucian or Buddhist Ways. They are simply stories of life in this world and so leave aside questions of good and evil. Rather than concern themselves with such matters as these, they celebrate the virtues of understanding what it means to be moved [*mna o shireru kata*].

In this respect, the tale may be likened to a person who wishes to cultivate and enjoy the lotus flower, and so must keep a store of muddy water, foul and filthy though it may be. It is not the mud—the illicit love depicted in the tale—that we admire; it is the flower that it nurtures—the flower of the emotions it inspires [*mna no hana*]. Genji's conduct is like the lotus flower, which grows up from the muddy water yet blooms with a beauty and fragrance unlike any other in the world. Nothing is said about the water's filth; the tale dwells instead on Genji's deep compassion and his awareness of what it means to be moved [*nasake fukaku, mna o shireru kata*] and holds him up as the model of the good man. I need hardly say more, but if I may cite one or two more examples:

In "Suma" [13:176], when Genji departs for that shore:

> It was lamented by everyone; and some secretly reviled the court for it.

In "Akashi" [13:241]:

> That year portents were frequently seen at court, and there was often great unrest. On the thirteenth day of the Third Month, on a night when thunder roared and lightning flashed and a violent rainstorm arose. . . .

And again [13:251]:

Since the previous year, the Empress Mother [Kokiden] had been tormented by malign spirits, and there had been frequent portents and disturbances.

And again [13:251]:

The Emperor's eye ailment had lately grown much worse.

In "Yomigiu" [13:324]:

He was pardoned and would be returning to the capital; the whole land was in a tumult of joy.

In "Makibashira" [14:367]:

His Lordship, who had never been criticized by anyone. . . .

We see from the "Akashi" passages that even the gods took pity on Genji. If the author had intended to convey a Confucian or Buddhist moral, why would she write about the gods, the buddhas, and the heavens taking pity on a man guilty of such grievous immorality?[90]

Again, three women are singled out as examples of good people: the Fujitsubo Empress, Lady Murasaki, and the Asagao High Priestess. Fujitsubo, for example, is praised in "Usugumo" [13:437, 438]:

Even among those ranked as the most exalted, she was remarkable for her unstinting kindness toward everyone, for there will always be those who, in the name of their own might, will bring grief to others. Never, however, was she guilty of the slightest license of this sort, nor would she allow anything to be done for her that might bring pain to the people. . . . Even the most ignorant mountain ascetics mourned her loss, and when the time came for her funeral, there was universal lamentation, for there were none who were not grieved.

If all this were meant in the same spirit as that of Confucianism and Buddhism, surely the author would not have depicted such a fine person in such an immoral situation as her affair with Genji, nor would she have cited her as an example of a fine person. Thus we can see how great the difference is between the good and evil in the tale and the good and evil of Confucianism and Buddhism. And when we consider along with this the case of Kashiwagi, which I shall cite further on, we realize that the main purpose of the tale is the depiction of the workings of the emotions [*mna*]. But our savants, one and all, down through the ages, have been so totally in thrall to notions taught in those severely dogmatic and doctrinaire texts of Confucianism and Buddhism that everything they think or say is twisted in some outlandish way. Never does it occur to them to investigate the nature of the tales themselves. Why, I wonder, did none of them perceive this thing I call *mono no aware*? The details of *mono no aware* I shall discuss in the next chapter.

Chapter 2

MORE ON LARGER PURPOSES

As to this "sensitivity to the power of things to move one" [*mna o shiru*]: first of all, speaking in general terms, *aware* originally was a cry of emotion such as we utter when we are moved by something we see, hear, or experience, just as in present-day colloquial speech we still exclaim *aa!* or *hare!* For example, when we are moved by the sight of the moon or the cherry blossoms, we may say, "*Aa*, what beautiful blossoms!" or "*Hare*, how magnificent the moon!" *Aware* is the combination of this same *aa* and *hare*; likewise, in Sino-Japanese texts, the characters 嗚呼 are read *aa*. The same *a-* is found in such ancient [exclamations] as *ana* and *aya*. And the *wa* of *wa ya* and *wa mo* is the same as the *ha* of *hare*. In the speech of later ages, the word *appare* expresses the feeling *aa hare* and amounts to the same thing. For as time passed, the *ha* of *ahare*, through a process of euphonic change, came to be pronounced *wa*. In ancient times, however, in all such occurrences, *ha* was pronounced according to its original [sound value], as in [the Chinese characters for] "leaf" or "tooth." This was, of course, the case with the word *ahare*, since it was an interjection formed from the combination of *aa* and *hare*. The explanation given in *Kogo shūi* [807], that "the meaning of *aware* is *ame hare*" [天晴], is quite mistaken.[91] But from this text we can at least ascertain that in earlier times *hare* was pronounced the same as 晴. Thus in ancient poetry, *aware* is a direct expression of emotion, the simple cry *aa hare*, as, for example: "The lone pine, *aware* . . ." [*Nihon shoki*, 24]; "*Aware*, the song of the bird . . ." [*Man'yōshū* 1756]; "*Aware*, this lodging of mine for these several nights . . ." [*Kokinshū* 984]; "*Aware*, he that in ancient days . . ." [*Kokinshū* 1003]. This is the origin of the word. Likewise with "'*Aware, aware*,' I sighed in an excess of grief . . ." [*Kokinshū* 1001], and "'*Aware*, how dismal,' I sighed as the days passed . . ." [*Shinzokukokinshū* 2038].

> *aware chō koto o amata ni yaraji to ya / haru ni okurete hitori sakuran*
> Is it because they would not share this word *aware* with the many,
> that they bloom all by themselves, long after springtime has passed?
> [*Kokinshū* 136]

The sense of this poem is that *these* cherry blossoms do not wish to share the words *aa hare* with the other blossoms; they want this said only of themselves, which perhaps is why they alone bloom after all the other blossoms have scattered.

From the foregoing, we can ascertain the basic sense of the word *aware*. Then, in slightly extended usage, we have expressions like *aware to miru*, "to be moved by the sight of . . ."; *aware to kiku*, "to be moved at the sound of . . ."; and *aware to omou*, "to be moved at the thought of . . ."; which mean that one reacts with the feeling *aa hare* to something that one sees, hears, or thinks. And an expression like *aware nari* indicates something of which one happens to feel *aa hare*. Then, too, in such expressions as *aware o shiru*, "to be susceptible to emotion"; *aware o misu*, "to show one's feelings"; and *aware ni taezu*, "to be overcome with emotion," *aware* is used to designate a situation of any sort whatever about which one may feel *aa hare*. And thus when one encounters something that by all rights should move one to exclaim *aa hare*, and one does indeed apprehend this emotional quality, we say of this *aware o shiru* that one is susceptible to emotion. The expression *mono o awarefu/-mu*, too, originally referred to the exclamation *aa hare*, as we know from phrases such as that in the Preface to the *Kokinshū*, *kasumi o awarehi/-mi*, "to be moved by [the sight of] the mist."

In more recent times, *aware* has come to be written with the character 哀[92] and tends to be associated exclusively with a sense of deeply felt sadness [*hiai*]. But *aware* is not restricted to deeply felt sadness. Whenever one happens to feel *aa hare*—be it in joy, fascination, pleasure, amusement—this is *aware*. Hence it is used in combinations like *aware ni okashiku*, "touchingly amusing," and *aware ni ureshiku*, "touchingly joyous": one is moved by something amusing or joyful to feel *aa hare*, and this is described as *aware ni*. Now, the reason *aware* is often contrasted with joy, amusement, and the like is that of the many emotions experienced by human beings, joy and amusement are not deeply felt, whereas sorrow, misery, longing—any of the emotions experienced when things do not go as one would wish—are felt with particular poignancy. Thus these deeper feelings are distinguished as quintessentially *aware*. This also accounts for the fact that in common usage, [*aware*] refers only to deeply felt sadness. In "Wakana, jō" [15:65], for example, there is an analogous usage: "How I should like to see the plum blossoms [*ume no hana*] alongside the [cherry] blossoms [*hana*] at their peak." The plum blossom is, of course, a blossom, but the cherry is contrasted to it as *the* blossom par excellence.

Now, in common usage the expression "to be moved with emotion" seems to be used only with reference to good things, but this, too, is incorrect. In dictionaries of Chinese characters, "emotion" [*kan* 感] is defined as being "moved" [*dō* 動], meaning that one's heart is moved. Whenever one's heart is moved, whether by something good or something bad, and one responds *aa hare*, then one is "moved to emotion," which makes this character a highly appropriate rendition of *aware*. In Chinese, there is the phrase "to cause the demons and spirits to be moved with emotion" [感鬼神],[93] which also appears in the Chinese preface to the *Kokinshū*. And when translated into Japanese in the Japanese preface, it is rendered as "to cause the demons and spirits to feel *aware*," from which we know that *aware* means to be moved to emotion. From the foregoing one can grasp in a general way the origins of the word *aware* and the development of some of its extended usages.

The expression *mono no aware*, then, means much the same thing. The *mono* is the *mono* that is added in order to generalize the reference of a word—as when *iu* [speak] becomes *mono iu* [discuss], *kataru* [tell] becomes *monogatari* [tale], or, in *monomōde* [pilgrimage], *monomi* [observation], *monoimi* [abstinence].

Now when a person is confronted with a situation of any sort whatever that might be expected to move him to emotion, and he apprehends the emotional quality of this situation and is indeed moved to emotion, this is described as being "sensitive to emotion" [*mna o shiru*]. But when a person's heart remains unmoved and he experiences no emotion, even in a situation that by all rights should move him, this person is described as "insensitive to emotion" [*mna o shirazu*] or "heartless" [*kokoro naki hito*]. By their very nature, persons of discernment cannot help but be moved by that which is moving, whereas when people are not so moved, it is precisely because they lack discernment and are insensitive to things that by rights should move them. Thus in the *Gosenshū*:

> At a certain person's house, outside the bamboo blinds, I was chatting about this and that when I heard from inside the voice of a woman who had been listening, and she said, "My, what extraordinary airs of sensibility [*mna shirigao*] this old gentleman affects."
>
> TSURAYUKI

aware chō koto ni shirushi wa nakeredomo / iwade wa e koso aranu mono nare

That little word *aware* may produce no discernable effect,
yet never to utter it can in no wise be endured. [*Gosenshū* 1272]

The sense of this poem is that to exclaim *aa hare* may avail one nothing, yet when one experiences something that is by rights moving, one can hardly bear not to exclaim so. Thus is it in any situation whatever for a person of sensibility [*mna o shireru hito*].

Now, as I have said, people's emotional reactions to things are of many sorts, and this tale is notable for its depiction of every variety of moving situation and its demonstration of its emotional qualities [*aware o misetaru*]. To begin with, it depicts public and private life in all its fascination, splendor, and magnificence, and it describes in the most exquisite manner the changing scenes of spring, summer, autumn, and winter—the blossoms, the birds, the moon, the snow—all of them things that move the heart and inspire emotions [*aware to omowaseru*]. And when cares weigh heavily upon one's mind, the appearance of the sky and the tints of plants and trees work with particular effect to arouse emotion [*aware o moyōsu*]. Thus, for example, in "Kiritsubo" [12:111], it says: "At the sound of the wind or the cry of an insect, he would be plunged into melancholy. . . ." In "Hahakigi" [12:180]: "Whether the patterning of the heartless heavens appears gorgeous or threatening depends solely upon the viewer." In "Aoi" [13:44–45]: "In the pale light of dawn, when all was shrouded in mist . . . [she wrote], 'the sky as it looks just now moves me to grieve . . . the brevity of her life.'" And again [13:48–50]: "As the wind blew ferociously, driving the autumn rains . . . he was inclined to imagine that even the Asagao Princess, despite all, must understand how he felt today [*kyō no aware*]. . . ." In "Matsukaze" [13:393]: "Now that autumn had come, her feelings [*mna*] seemed to weigh more heavily upon her mind." In "Asagao" [13:465]: "The rustling of the leaves brought back touching memories of times past [*suginishi mna*], and they recalled how charming and moving [*okashiku mo aware ni mo*] had been the concern he had time and again shown for her." In "Kagerō" [17:208]: "When something is troubling me, be it only the slightest little thing, even the cry of a bird flying across the sky is enough to move me to grief."

Then, too, there are occasions when one is moved by a person's good looks. In "Kiritsubo" [12:114–15], it says: "Such was the figure he cut that not even the fiercest of warriors or the bitterest of enemies could look at him without breaking into a smile. . . ." In "Hahakigi" [12:175]: "Even a demon would hardly have taken offense at his manner; much less could she [Utsusemi] be so crude as to raise the alarm that someone was here [in her room]." In "Yūgao" [12:223]: "Much less could those in a position to exchange poems with him and look upon his beauty with their own eyes, if they were possessed of the least sensibility, have any but the highest regard for him." In "Momiji no ga" [12:385]: "Had she perhaps found it impossible to overlook such dazzling beauty?" And further on [12:387]: "The glittering beauty of his 'Waves upon the Ocean Blue' . . . even the heavens seemed to appreciate." And again [12:387]: "Even ignorant menials, if possessed of the slightest sensibility, shed a tear."[94] In "Suma" [13:161]: "His elegance and his beauty as he pondered his fate, only the more apparent in the bright clear light of the setting moon, would have moved even a tiger or a wolf to tears." In "Yūgiri" [15:457]: "He was approaching the peak of his manhood and had grown remarkably handsome of late. Even if he were guilty of some such dalliance, surely no one could criticize him; indeed, the gods and demons themselves would be moved to forgive his transgression. . . ." In "Ukifune" [17:182–83]: "So handsome was he that even if he had been a bitter foe transformed into a demon, she could not have taken her eyes from him." As the foregoing examples suggest, not to be moved by human beauty is to be more insensitive than a tiger or a wolf.

One also finds numerous instances, in chapter after chapter, of being moved by a person's rank or position. This is something different from calculated obsequiousness or sycophancy toward the powerful and the rich; it is a natural and ineluctable sense of awe before a person of exalted station, of the sort when Utsusemi ["Hahakigi," 12:187] "forced herself to feign indifference and ignore [his tenderness], though it pained her to think how pretentious he must consider her." Her feelings are an emotional response to Genji's rank and position. In "Suma" [13:195]: "When they heard the music of his koto carried from afar on the wind, the beauty of the place, the exalted station of the player, and the sadness of the tune combined to move all those of any sensibility to tears." This combination of several moving things causes them to weep. The mention of "those of any sensibility," however, suggests that those who are insensitive and impervious to emotion [*kokoro naku mna o shiranu hito*] remain oblivious even to this combination of touching things and are not moved. Compare this, for example, with the quotations from other chapters cited earlier, referring to "those possessed of the slightest sensibility."

Apropos of the fact that insensitivity [*mna o shiranu*] was considered bad, it says in "Kiritsubo" [12:111–12]:

> At the sound of the wind or the cry of an insect, he would be plunged into melancholy. But the moon was beautiful, and from the quarters of the Kokiden lady, who had not waited upon His Majesty in his chamber for some time now, there came the strains of music far into the night. She was terribly haughty, a lady with an abrasive side to her, and determined, apparently, to behave as if nothing at all were amiss. His Privy Gentlemen and Gentlewomen, who were witness to his condition of late, listened to this in horror.

Such then is the manner of a person who is impervious to emotion [*mna o shiranu hito*]. At a time when the Emperor "at the sound of the wind or the cry of an insect would be plunged into melancholy," could any person of sensibility [*kokoro aramu hito*] find beauty in the moon, much less make music? After all, as has been said, whether the moon "appears gorgeous or threatening depends solely on the viewer." In this passage, "the moon was beautiful" is a description based upon Kokiden's feelings. Her behaving "as if nothing at all were amiss" describes her lack of concern for the Emperor's sorrow. "His condition of late" refers to the sorrow of the Emperor.

In "Sakaki" [13:94], it says: "As long as the old Emperor was still alive, she behaved with restraint; but the Empress Mother had a vile temper, and now she seemed bent upon avenging all the grudges she had been suppressing." And again: "As she grew older, she grew steadily more disagreeable, until even the [Suzaku] Emperor found her company more than he could endure" ["Otome," 14:69]. This passage, too, refers to the Kokiden Empress Mother. In the same chapter where the Empress Mother and her father the Minister denounce so bitterly the affair between Genji and Oborozukiyo ["Sakaki," 13:138–39], her father, "a quick-tempered and disagreeable" man, is described thus:

> Even though she was his own child, he should have known that this would embarrass her, for a man of his standing really ought to exercise some discretion. But the Minister was a quick-tempered, intolerant man and not guided by good sense. . . . It was not in his nature to hold back anything that was on his mind, added to which he had grown quite crotchety in his old age.

And the stepmother of Lady Murasaki is described in "Makibashira" [14:368] as "that lady, who was most disagreeable," and in the latter "Wakana" chapter [15:155] as "that most disagreeable lady."

For the most part, then, this tale tends not to dwell upon Genji's amorous indiscretions, nor does it speak of them in particularly unfavorable terms. Rather, as in the foregoing citations, it condemns those who bear ill will toward Genji and his friends and treat him badly. As shown, all these people are depicted as insensitive [*mna o shirazu*] and evil. This is because Genji, being sensitive [*mna o shirite*], is considered a good person. If judged by the standards of Confucianism such as prevail in our own time, the Fujitsubo Empress would have to be considered worse than the Kokiden Empress Mother, yet she is depicted as the very model of the supremely good person, whereas someone like Kokiden, who carried on no illicit affairs, is depicted as an extraordinarily evil person. This is precisely because the tale is chiefly concerned with sensibility to what is moving [*mna o shireru kata*] and considers this quality a virtue. In depicting the affair between Yūgiri and Kumoinokari, her father the Minister's harsh restrictions and admonitions are treated as excessively heartless, whereas Yūgiri and Kumoinokari are never described in unfavorable terms. Yet here, too, if judged by currently prevailing standards, the admonitions of her father the Minister are quite correct, and Yūgiri and Kumoinokari are culpable. As one reads through the several chapters, one cannot but realize that good and evil are distinguished according to whether a person is sensitive or insensitive to what is moving [*mna o shiru to shirazaru to o mote*]. It is never stated explicitly that this is good or this is evil, but the distinction between what is regarded as good and what is regarded as evil is clear from the manner in which things are described.

Now then, monks are often described as creatures insensitive to what is moving [*mna o shiranu mono*]. In "Kashiwagi" [15:312], it says:

> "I beg you to take pity on me" [*aware to obose*], he said. "I have heard," she replied, "that those in my condition are insensitive creatures [*mna mo shiranu mono*], and it is only the more so for one who has always been that way."

This scene takes place after the Third Princess has cut her hair and taken vows. Genji says: "Even though you have become a nun, pray do have some consideration for my feelings," to which the Princess replies, "I have heard that everyone who has forsaken the world as I have is insensitive to what is moving, but it is only the more so for someone as hopeless as myself, who has always been insensitive. So what can I say to you?" This remark is based on the fact that monks were commonly said to be insensitive to all that is moving.

Now, the reason monks are described as insensitive is, first of all, because, in the Way of the Buddha, one must forsake utterly the bonds of affection with those to whom one is most attached—father, mother, wife, and children; mortify one's own cherished flesh; abandon home and possessions and seclude oneself in a mountain forest; renounce the savor of fish and meat, the delights of song and women—all of which are among the most difficult things for the human heart to endure. If one is frail of spirit and susceptible to emotion [*kokoro yowakute mna o shirite wa*], they are not easily accomplished. To practice this Way, therefore, one must force oneself to become a creature firm of spirit and insensitive to all that is moving [*aware shiranu mono ni narite*]. In addition, it is difficult to guide others in the Way when one's own thoughts are on the emotions of this life [*kono yo no mna o omoi*] and one's resolve is weak. Thus [the monk] may, on the face of it, appear insensitive to emotion [*aware shiranu yō*], but his doctrines urge compassion for those who wander in the long darkness of delusion. By the standards of the Way, he is in fact deeply sensitive [*mna o fukaku shireru*]. In "Shii ga moto" [16:181], it is written, "They found the stubborn devotion of the Preceptor distastefully painful." When the Eighth Prince dies and his daughters are beside themselves with grief, the Preceptor, with never a thought for the tender feelings between parent and child, preaches sternly to them to abandon their feelings of attachment in accordance with the spirit of the Way of the Buddha. This they find excessively resolute and distastefully painful. In most cases, it is for reasons of this sort that monks are described as insensitive to feeling [*mna o shiranu*]. Of course, a deeply devout monk is very much a stranger to worldly concerns and may quite genuinely be unmoved.

Now, then, to affect a sensibility to what is moving [*mna no shirigao o tsukurite*] and make a show of feeling is considered highly reprehensible. For this sort of thing is not genuine sensitivity, but only the affectation of its outward appearances, and is most irritating. In "Hahakigi" [12:165, 166], it says:

> It is a pity, but a general rule, that the worst people, men and women alike, will try to show off every last scrap of what little they happen to know. . . . In any situation, any moment of doubt whatever, it is always more seemly for the undiscriminating not to affect airs of refinement. Indeed, one should always pretend not to know what one may know perfectly well and omit a thing or two that one might wish to say.

This is what is meant in "Kochō" [14:170] where it says:

> As a rule, when a woman fails to exercise discretion and surrenders to the impulse to affect airs of emotional sensitivity [*mna mo shirigao tsukuri*] and aesthetic discernment, this—if she persists in it—can grow tiresome.

Among frivolous people, such as the "Winter Winds" woman,[95] there are many of this sort. Usually such expressions as "affected" [*keshikidatsu*], "with an air of refinement" [*yoshibamu*], and "sensitive seeming" [*nasakedatsu*] describe those who put on outward airs and make a show of feeling.

Now, then, the fact that "an excess of susceptibility to emotion" [*mna o shirisugusu*] is deemed a bad thing is not to say that profound sensitivity to emotion [*mna o shiru koto no fukaki*] is excessive. "Exceed" here means that it is excessive to behave with seeming sensitivity [*aware o shirigao naru*] toward all things, even those hardly deserving of it, or to be so readily acquiescent to others as to seem frivolous. Thus the expression "with moderation" [*yoki hodo ni*], too, signifies that an excess of feigned sensitivity [*shirigao no sugitaru*] is bad, and not that profound sensitivity [*fukaku shiru*] is bad. In "Usugumo" [13:454], it says: "The Dame of Honor felt a twinge of shame that she had replied with such airs of sensitivity [*mna o shirigao ni*] to the emotions of autumn." The "Dame of Honor" is the Akikonomu Empress. Here she has in mind her reply when Genji asks whether she prefers spring or autumn [13:452]: "There's really no saying which, but one does hear about the 'strange beauty' of autumn evenings." In the same chapter [13:433–34], it says:

> "I knew it was hardly likely I should escape this year, but I was not that frightfully ill, and so I was reluctant to carry on as if I knew my life were coming to an end, for people would have thought that appallingly exaggerated."

This, too, is in the same spirit. These are the words of Lady Murasaki, who is ashamed even to speak as if she knew this were the end of her own life.[96] In "Minori" [15:487], it says: "There were many matters that occupied the lady's thoughts, but she was not one to make knowing pronouncements about 'after she was gone.'" Here, too, the same lady would be ashamed to speak so knowingly of this or that "after she is gone."

Considering all this, then, it seems that women of the best sort regard even such behavior as this shameful. How much more so the affectation of sensibility and the display of it [*aware shirigao o tsukurite, misemu*]! And as we reflect on the attitude of Lady Murasaki, who is described here as the very model of excellence among women, [we recall] the passage in "Hotaru" [14:207] concerning illustrated romances in which "the lady [said], 'It is painful even to read of such simpleminded behavior.'"[97] "The lady" is Lady Murasaki, and these are the words she speaks. "Behavior" refers to that in tales. It says this because they are written in imitation of the lives of people in this world. "Simpleminded" describes the behavior of frivolous women. "Painful" denotes what in colloquial speech we would describe as "excruciating." When she says "even to read," we realize how much more painful she would find such women in real life.

> "The daughter of Lord Fujiwara in *The Hollow Tree*[98] is a very prudent and capable person and seems never to make a mistake Yet her very firmness, and the want of anything womanly in the way she speaks, do seems excessive,"[99] she [Murasaki] said.

"Firm" here means lacking in tender and winning qualities. "Womanly" means as a woman should be. "Excessive" means tending to one extreme. This refers to a character in *The Tale of the Hollow Tree*; she is succinctly described in *Kachō yosei*.[100] For further details, one should read the tale. This person stands in contrast to those described as "simpleminded." She is cold and pays no heed to the pleas of her many suitors, some of whom die of their bitter disappointment, yet she is not at all moved [*aware to mo omowazu*]. Such a woman, who by the prevailing standards of the Confucianists would be praised as "fervently chaste," is here described as "excessive." Of the same sort are those described in "Suetsumuhana" [12:339–40]:

> "The cold, resolute ones, so incomparably unfeeling in their earnestness, seem to lack all sense of proportion."

In response to what Lady Murasaki said, Genji says ["Hotaru," 14:207]:

> "There would appear to be just such people in real life. Each persists in her own predilection, and none exercises any moderation."

"People in real life" refers to living people, as opposed to characters in the old romances. "Just such" means "of just that sort." "Each" refers to those such as the daughter of Lord Fujiwara who, in making such a point of their own personal chastity, differ from the ordinary run of people. His casual mention that "none exercises moderation" carries the implication that, in agreement with what the Lady Murasaki said, this is indeed "excessive." In "Hahakigi" [12:166–67], it says:

> Through it all His Lordship was thinking to himself of that one person. "She lacks nothing, she is guilty of no excess." Her very rarity . . .

Genji goes on to say ["Hotaru," 14:207–8]:

> "When parents who are themselves not lacking in qualities endeavor to raise a daughter who has at least some childlike charm about her, and despite their pains she turns out deficient in any number of ways, then even the parents' efforts come into question. 'What sort of upbringing can they have given her?' people ask, and that is a great pity."

"Deficient in any number of ways" may also extend to her accomplishments in the polite arts, but following as it does the foregoing reference to deficiencies in emotional sensitivity [*mna o shiru koto*], it would refer principally to these. This we may also ascertain from the passage in "Yūgiri," cited further on.

> "That said, however, when she gives the impression that '*she* is the very image of those people,' that is rewarding and certainly something to be proud of." ["Hotaru," 14:208]

"That said, however" means, in colloquial speech, "Indeed, she is in every way all that one would expect of a daughter of those people." "Rewarding" means rewarding of the parents' endeavors to raise her properly. "Be proud of" refers to the rightful pride of the parents.

In "Yūgiri" [15:442], when Genji hears about the affair between Commandant Yūgiri and the Second Princess, and he tells Lady Murasaki that he worries how she will feel after he is gone, Lady Murasaki's thoughts are described thus: "There is nothing so constricting, so afflicting as the self-restraint a woman must exercise." This means that nothing could be more trying, more fraught with emotion [*mna naru koto no arubeki*] than the self-restraint a woman must exercise. The reason this is so is that if she acts as compassion [*mna o mishiritaru kokoro*] dictates, she will inevitably be the object of criticism, and her cares will tend to weigh upon her mind, thus increasing extraordinarily the burden on her emotions [*mna naru koto*]. These words merit close attention.

> Those affecting things, those fascinating moments—if she just ignores or suppresses them as if she had no knowledge of them, how is she to savor the joys of living in this world or beguile the tedium of this ephemeral life?[101] [15:442]

Concerning "ignores or suppresses them as if she had no knowledge of them": when something works on a woman's feelings and she finds it poignantly touching [*sechi ni aware naru*], she will shrink from letting her feelings show openly, lest she seem guilty of feigned emotion [*shirigao o tsukuri*] or an excess of susceptibility to emotion [*mna o shirisugusu*]. In the course of which, unable to let her feelings show, she will repress and contain them, as though she did not feel what she does indeed feel [*shiritemo shiranu sama ni*], with the result that they weigh heavily on her mind with intense emotion [*musubōrete aware wa fukaki*]. It is precisely the exercise of this self-restraint that is "so constricting, so afflicting." This being the case, then, "how is she to savor the joys of living in this world or beguile the tedium of this ephemeral life?" The very mention of "this ephemeral life" would seem to imply that, life in this world being insubstantial and of no great duration, it would be a pity not to have some source of comfort to the feelings. If this were not the case, the word "ephemeral" would be superfluous.

Now, as to letting one's feelings show openly, in "Suetsumuhana" [12:348–49], it says:

> When a person who leads such a life from time to time lets her feelings show in clever references to the ever changing plants and trees and to the patterns of the sky and thus affords one an inkling of her character, *that* is touching [*aware naru*].

As this suggests, in moments of emotion [*mna naru toki*], it is consoling to compose a poem or write a letter referring to the plants and the trees and such and send it to someone, thus revealing to him the feelings in one's heart [*kokoro no aware*]. Further, in "Yomogiu" [13:320–21]:

> Quite undeliberately, but just as a natural thing, at times when no urgent concerns were pressing upon them, they would carry on a casual exchange of notes and poems with others of like mind, and in these references to the plants and trees, her young people were able to amuse themselves.

Here again she speaks of young women living in dismal circumstances with no means of support. "Quite undeliberately" is to say that the deliberate exchange of notes and poems referring to the plants and trees is to affect airs of emotional sensitivity [*mna shirigao tsukuru suji*] and is unattractive. For this reason, it is described as "just a natural thing." This means "They do so without premeditation, but. . . ." In "Yūgiri" [15:442], Lady Murasaki continues to muse:

> Yet if she should turn out to be one of those utterly hopeless creatures, with no sense at all of the significance of things, then are not the parents who raised her, too, greatly to be pitied?

A "sense of the significance of things" means to be possessed of emotional sensitivity [*mna o shiru*]. The insensitive are described as "utterly hopeless creatures." Note this carefully. It should be considered in conjunction with what I said about the passage from "Hotaru" quoted earlier, that "deficient in any number of ways" refers principally to deficiencies in emotional sensitivity [*mna o shiru koto*]. Lady Murasaki continues [15:442]:

> How dispiriting it is to shut things away in one's heart, like the mute prince of those old homilies that our monks relate so mournfully, who, though he knew full well what was bad and what was good, buried it all in himself.

The mute prince is annotated in *Kakaishō*.[102] "What is bad and what is good" is the good and evil discussed previously in detail. To see this and comprehend its meaning is to have some sense of the significance of things [*mono no kokoro o shiru*] and to apprehend their emotional quality [*mna o shireru*]. "How dispiriting it is . . . to bury it all" is what is meant in the preceding passage by "she ignores or suppresses them as if she had no knowledge of them." In this passage, Murasaki Shikibu surely suggests some of her own intentions in writing this tale. This tale is something she wrote because she found it dispiriting to bury and shut away in her heart all that she knew about the good and the evil in this world. Again [15:442]:

> "How then is one to maintain a proper balance, even within one's own heart?" Her musings now were only on behalf of the First Princess.

"A proper balance" should be considered in conjunction with the phrase in "Hotaru" [14:207] quoted earlier: "none exercises any moderation." "How is one to maintain . . ." is her musing on the difficulty of maintaining such a proper balance. This is why "there is nothing so constricting, so afflicting as the self-restraint that a woman must exercise." "Her musings now were only on behalf of the First Princess": the lot in life of Lady Murasaki herself had long since been determined; she had passed the prime of life and now was in every way at peace with herself. Yet her concern for the upbringing of the First Princess was still a matter of great importance to her.

Studying the foregoing passages, we learn, of course, that people who are inconstant are bad; and, apart from that, so are those who make an excessive display of feigned emotion [*mna shirigao no sugitaru*] bad. The inconstancy of a person who is easily swayed by the blandishments of others may appear sensitive [*mna o shirite*] and feeling, but in fact it is not. In the final analysis, inconstancy is actually unfeeling [*mna shirazaru*]. Such people shift their affections from this person to that person precisely because they are fond [*aware to omou*] of neither the one nor the other. If one *is* fond of one particular person, one is not likely to shift one's affections to another. And yet Genji becomes enamored of a great many women, one after another, not through inconstancy, but because he cannot resist feeling affection [*mna o sugushigataki*] for each of them. His feelings can best be appreciated by reading the tale. It is difficult to generalize.

For there are some surpassingly fine people [*yoki hito*] who fall prey to their own emotions [*mna shinobigataki*], like the Fujitsubo Empress, who, against her own better judgment, enters into an affair with Genji. In a seemingly similar situation, the Oborozukiyo lady is deemed a frivolous and inconstant person, whereas the [Fujitsubo] Empress is deemed in every way to be a fine, indeed superior, person. Consider this distinction and you will grasp the essence of the tale. Then, in "Hahakigi" [12:184–85], describing the character of the Utsusemi lady, it says:

> It was not that she did not recall how extraordinary she had thought his manner and mien, which she had so faintly perceived, "but even if I were to show an interest in him," she thought anew, "what could come of it?"

And again [12:186–87]:

> In her mind she knew that if she had never been consigned to such a horrid station in life as this but still was in her old home, filled with the memory of her dead parents, and could await his visits there, however rare they might be, this would be such a delight. Now she must force herself to feign ignorance and ignore him; how presumptuous he must think her. It was her own choice, but a painful one. Her thoughts were in turmoil.

And again [12:187]: "Of course the woman, too, lay sleepless." In "Utsusemi" [12:191–92]:

> There were no more letters from him. He has thought better of it, she thought; but should he be so heartless as to break with me, here and now, how *that* would hurt. Yet if this impetuous, albeit winsome, behavior of his were not to stop, that too would be distressing. I must put an end to it while the opportunity yet remains, she thought; but still it was no easy matter, and she continued to agonize over it.

From "impetuous" to "she thought, but still" must be understood as a continuous whole. The thought appears to end with "that too would be distressing," but it does not. It continues, meaning "because that would be distressing, I must put an end to this. . . ." And further [12:204–5]:

> Only thus did this coldhearted lady manage to maintain a calm exterior, but his attentions, which certainly did not seem shallow, made her long to be as she had been in days past. But there is no turning back time, and bearing up as best she could, she wrote on a corner of that paper:

utsusemi no ha ni oku tsuyu no kogakurete / shinobi shinobi ni nururu sode kana
Like dew on the wings of the cicada's shell, hidden amid the trees,
wet, so wet are my sleeves with secret, the most secret, tears.

In "Yūgao" [12:220], in a similar vein, it says:

> Of course, she thought that if he were to forget her entirely, that would be unspeakably hurtful, and in her replies, as this occasion or that demanded, she spoke amiably. . . .

This woman's character is such that she is extremely sensitive [*mna o yoku shirite*], and she exercises due moderation.

Another woman who is described as the model of a certain sort of superiority is the Asagao Princess, about whom it says in "Aoi" [13:13]:

> When she heard about these things, the Asagao Princess resolved that she would never end up like the others; and never was there even the

most casual sort of reply. Yet neither did she treat him in an offhand manner that might make him think ill of her, while he, for his part, continued to regard her as an exceptional woman indeed.

"Never end up like the others": Of all the women at court, there are hardly any who do not submit to Genji, but she is determined she will not be like these ordinary women. In this, the Princess is superior to the others. But then, the passage "Yet neither . . ." shows how emotionally sensitive [*mna o shiritamaeru*] she is. As it says in "Suetsumuhana" [12:339–40] about "the cold, resolute ones, so incomparably unfeeling," a woman who insists that she "shall not be like the others" invariably, like the daughter of Lord Fujiwara in *The Hollow Tree*, turns out to be somehow warped. But this Princess does not, and because she is of such rare character, even Genji considers her to be "exceptional." In "Asagao" [13:477], it says:

She was by no means unaware how grand and sensitive a gentleman he was, but, she thought, "If I ever let on that I appreciated these qualities, I would then be thought but another of that common throng who have only admiration and praise for him. And then he would suppose that he had seen through me and knew how frivolous my intentions really were, which would shame me in the eyes of so fine a gentleman as he is." It made no sense whatever, she decided, to show any sort of feeling that might encourage intimacy. She would not cease to reply to his other communications; she would go on answering him properly, through an intermediary, saying nothing that might be misinterpreted.[103]

This, too, describes the feelings of the same Princess as she decides what she will do with regard to Genji; her attitude here is precisely the same as that in the "Aoi" chapter just cited. "How grand . . . a gentleman" refers to Genji's high rank and surpassing good looks and manner; "sensitive" refers to the sensitivity of his compassion. "She was by no means unaware" means that her feelings were touched by his rank and his looks and his manner and touched by the sensitivity of his compassion. "Let on that I appreciate these qualities" means that "if she were to reveal her own feelings, so as to show Genji the extent to which they are touched . . ." "Common throng": Genji being a person whom no one at court does not admire, she too might be thought but another of that common throng of women. Here, again, she is thinking "never shall she end up like the others." The phrase "and then he" [*katsu wa*] merits particular attention. Although Genji deeply resents her coldness, he would then look down on her as frivolous. Most occurrences of *katsu* are of this same sort. Present-day people use the word where one should say *mata*, which is incorrect. "Shame me": Genji, being a gentleman of deep feeling who in every way puts one to shame, to be regarded as frivolous by him would be shameful. "Feeling that might encourage intimacy" refers to any display of feeling on her part that might encourage him to feel attracted to her. The *-te* of *uchitaete* [cease] is unvoiced, and the phrase continues from there: "not in such a manner that she would cease and there would be misunderstanding." As we see, then, this Princess is a person of extreme sensitivity to matters emotional [*mna o yoku shirite*], in which she yet exercises moderation to the very end—a true rarity, well worthy of regard as a model for women. And precisely because she is so, Genji finds her exceptionally charming and is only the more attracted to her.

And so, from our study of the several passages from the chapters just cited, we know that Murasaki Shikibu, in one way and another, is concerned principally with emotional sensitivity [*mna o shiru*]; that the lack of sensitivity is, needless to say, unfortunate; and that even behavior that smacks too much of sensitivity can be tediously distasteful and, depending upon the situation, may well verge on indecency. It thus is important that one be deeply mindful of this and behave in such a way that [one's feelings] are expressed with duly considered moderation. Such is the larger concern of this tale.

Now, the author, observing carefully with her own profoundly sensitive faculties [*fukaku mna o shireru kokoro ni*] the nature of all there is in this world—the good people and the bad, their thoughts and their deeds—and being moved by much that she sees and hears and experiences, has found it difficult to confine this to the secret musings of her own heart. And so, she writes it all down in minute detail, presenting it as the lives of the characters she creates. Those things she herself thinks good or bad, those things she herself wants to say, she causes her characters to think and say, thus giving vent to her own smoldering anxieties. Of the entire range of emotions [*mna no kagiri*] in this world, there are none not to be found in this tale; and in order to impress deeply on the reader's mind that "this is how it really is," she describes everything in painstaking depth and with remarkable skill. To read this tale, therefore, is just as if one were to meet Murasaki Shikibu and in her presence one were to hear her relate in full detail all that she thinks about things. And when one studies carefully the deeds and thoughts of the people, both good and bad, that appear in the tale, one comes to know that when they see or hear of such-and-such a thing, it will be regarded thus; that their feelings when faced with such-and-such a situation will be thus; that the deeds and thoughts of a good person will be thus; and a bad person thus—and in this way one comes to understand well all such situations in this world, as well as the feelings in the deepest recesses of the minds of all people. As a means of acquiring a thorough knowledge of what Chinese books describe as "human feeling and the ways of the world [*ninjō setai*]," I doubt there is anything to equal reading this tale.

Of all those things that move the human heart, there is none to surpass love [*koi*].[104] Thus it is that those emotions that are the most deeply affecting and difficult to bear occur most frequently in love. And in poetry, ever since the age of the gods and through age upon age thereafter, poems expressing these feelings have been the most numerous, and many of the most deeply felt and finest of poems are love poems. Likewise, the fact that even the songs sung by lowly mountain rustics of the present day are mostly on the subject of love is entirely natural and true to the human heart.

Love, then, is a state in which, depending upon the circumstances, there are moments of anguish and sorrow, moments of spite and anger, moments of amusement and elation—virtually every sort of emotion experienced by the human heart is to be found in love. And so, this tale having been created in order to inventory the full range of life's emotional experiences [*mna no kagiri o kakiatsumete*], thereby moving the reader deeply, the manifold nuances of feeling in the human heart, the savor of the extreme depths of emotion, could hardly be expressed without touching on the subject of love. For this reason, episodes treating principally this subject occur with particular frequency, while the divers thoughts and deeds of those who love, as well as the manifold aspects of their feelings [*toridori ni aware naru omomuki*], are described with extraordinary precision, illustrating the entire range of human emotion [*mna o tsukushite misetari*]. This matter will come up again later, but the following poem by Shunzei of the Third Rank expresses precisely the essence of this tale.

koi sezu wa hito wa kokoro mo nakaramashi / mono no aware mo kore yori zo shiru

Were one never to love, neither could such a one possess a heart,
for only through love can we comprehend human feeling. [*Chōshū eisō* 351]

Concerning this state in which the emotions of love are particularly profound and unendurable, it says in "Kiritsubo" [12:107]:

> "I can't imagine even the slightest thing I might have done to hurt another's feelings, but on this particular person's account, I am the object of considerable undeserved resentment. . . ."

These are thoughts the Emperor deigns to think. "This person" is the Kiritsubo Mistress of the Wardrobe. Again [12:93, 94]:

> His treatment of her—for he could no longer heed the reproof of his people—was certain to set a bad example for the world. . . . Eventually it became a cause of distress for people throughout the land.

And [12:113]:

> When it reached the point where, heedless of the reproof and resentment of so many of his people, he seemed to have lost all reason with regard to this matter and now had even forsaken his responsibility for governance of the realm. . . .

In the same chapter [12:113–14]:

> Come the spring of the following year, when a Crown Prince was to be named, he wanted to pass over [his eldest son in favor of Genji], but there was no one who might serve as his backer, nor was the court likely to accept this. On the contrary, it would be dangerous, and he eschewed the thought, giving no hint of it whatever.

As we see in the foregoing passage, this Emperor is a circumspect and unusually astute sovereign, but when it comes to love, he breaks down and goes astray. In "Aoi" [13:66, 68]:

> "My [Genji's] feelings of fondness for her [Murasaki] in years past were not even a fragment [of what I now feel]. . . ." Thereafter, even on his shortest calls at court or at the palace of the Retired Emperor, he found himself longing for her so restlessly that her face seemed to appear before him. "How strange that I feel this way," he thought, to his own chagrin.

These events refer to the time when Genji first sleeps with Lady Murasaki. In "Usugumo" [13:454]:

> "Yes, that old recklessness, that wild obsession is still there," he had to admit, despite himself.

After the Reizei Emperor learns about Genji and the Fujitsubo Empress, Genji, though frightened, is unrepentant, and this time makes advances toward the Akikonomu Empress. These are his own reflections on this. In "Kochō" [14:168], it says: "On the mountain [road] of love, even Confucius may stumble."[105] This is a popular saying to the effect that there is no one who, when in love, will never go astray. The *Kakaishō* gives as a source poem:

> *ika bakari koi no yamaji no fukakereba / iri to irinuru hito mayouramu*
> How deep into the mountains winds the road of love;
> he who follows it, ever onward, must surely go astray.[106]

In "Yūgiri" [15:440–41], it says:

> Whenever he had seen or heard of others who were the thralls of such passions, he found it irritating and thought they must have lost their minds, but now that it was happening to him, he found that it was indeed quite an unbearable experience. "How strange!" he thought in retrospect. "Whatever could have made me feel this way?" But there was nothing he could do about it.

These are Yūgiri's thoughts. When he had seen or heard of others who were the thralls of love, he could hardly believe they were in their right minds. He found it irritating and highly improper, but now that he himself is in love, he realizes that it is "indeed quite an unbearable experience."

This should be considered in conjunction with the poem by Shunzei quoted earlier. When experiencing the unbearable passions of love, one naturally comes to feel compassion for the feelings of others in myriad matters not of this magnitude and thus to comprehend human emotion. And again: "Indeed, in matters of this sort, it appears to be impossible to heed either the admonitions of others or the promptings of one's own heart" [15:455]. These are the words of the same gentleman. On the road of love at least, they say, one "heeds neither the admonitions of others nor the promptings of one's own heart," and now that he finds himself in that situation, he says, he realizes that so it is indeed. Even to as earnest a man as he, this can happen. I wonder whether something is missing after "the admonishments of others"?

From such phrases in the foregoing passage as "'How strange that I feel this way,' he thought, to his own chagrin" and ". . . he thought in retrospect. But there was nothing he could do about it," we see how profound and insuperable are the emotions of this Way [of love (*kono michi no mna*)]. And thus it is that such situations give rise to unthinkable transgressions, in the natural course of which things are done that defy all reason. In Genji's case, there are the Utsusemi affair, the Oborozukiyo affair, the Fujitsubo Empress affair, and their ilk. For in love, the emotions of such rash and reckless behavior are only the more profound, and thus [the author] purposely writes about illicit love, showing us the depth of emotion in such relationships. This we know from what it says in "Sakaki" [13:104] about the affair between Genji and the Empress:

> Even the most ordinary affairs, to those as close as this, are fraught with emotion, they say, and it was only the more so in so unparalleled a situation.

Even in the most ordinary, casual relationships between people of no great emotional depth, it is normal that such escapades will be particularly affecting; but how much more is this so of the liaison between these two, both possessed of such extraordinary emotional depth. So utterly overwhelmed is the man, she is saying, that their passion is without parallel.

Again, in "Kashiwagi" [15:281], in the poem composed by the Gate Guards Commander when, on account of the Third Princess, he falls ill, grows steadily worse, and is on the verge of death:

ima wa tote moemu keburi mo musubōre / taenu omoi no nao ya nokoran
Even then when the end is come and smoke rises from my burning pyre,
these unquenchable flames of yearning surely shall remain.

The Princess's reply [15:286]:

tachisoite kie ya shinamashi uki koto o / omoimidaruru keburikurabe ni
How I wish I too might die, that my smoke might rise together with yours;
then could we compare whose flames of sorrow burn the brighter.

Of all the many loves in this tale, and of all the emotions of the Gate Guards Commander that are so particularly moving, this scene when he is on the verge of death, this exchange of poems, is one of the most profoundly moving. When I read that passage in which he says, "This smoke, this will be the sole memento of my life" [15:286], I feel I could break down in tears. Ultimately he does pass away, concerning which it says in the same chapter [15:314]:

> That so proud and fine a figure should bring about his own ruination, leaving behind only this secret little keepsake that he could never reveal to his parents, despite their lamentation that there might "at least be a child"—this he found so sadly affecting that he quite forgot how mortified he had felt and could not help but heave a sigh of sorrow.

These are thoughts Genji thinks about Kashiwagi when he sees Kaoru. As it says, "He quite forgot how mortified he had felt and could not help but heave a sigh of sorrow." So it was with people of emotional sensitivity [*mna o shiru hito*]. And again [15:330]: "At the Rokujō mansion, with every passing day and month, fond memories of him recurred only the more often." And [15:330]:

> There was no one, high or low, who did not lament his loss, for apart from all that one takes for granted in such a person, he was a man of uncanny sensitivity. Even court officials and elderly gentlewomen, of whom one would hardly expect it, spoke of him with fondness and sorrow. And above all, whenever there was music, the Emperor would immediately recall him and think of times past. "Ah, the Gate Guards Commander . . . !" Such a set phrase was it that never was there no one who said it.

In “Yokobue” [15:333], it says:

> Many mourned the late Acting Grand Counselor as though their grief at his sudden passing would never cease. All the more so was this of Rokujō-in [Genji], whose nature it was to sorrow over the deaths of good people he had known in even the most casual way, for in this case he had been constantly close to him and had been fonder of him than anyone else. To be sure, there was that matter that he recalled with displeasure, yet so much was there to be fond of that he was often in his thoughts. On the anniversary of his death, he went to great trouble to arrange a chanting of the scriptures. And as he looked at the guileless child, its face so utterly innocent, he was so strongly affected that he determined secretly he would give yet another hundredweight of gold.

The “Acting Grand Counselor” is Kashiwagi. The “guileless child” refers to Kaoru. The “hundredweight of gold” he gives as Kaoru’s contribution to the chanting of additional scriptures for the benefit of Kashiwagi. In “Suzumushi” [15:371–72], it says:

> As they played together, the strains of their kotos blending beautifully, he said, “An evening of moon viewing, whatever the season, is never unaffecting; but truly, the beauty of this evening’s new moon in so many ways sends my thoughts flying beyond this world of ours. Now that the late Acting Grand Counselor is gone, I find myself missing him again and again; no matter what the occasion, public or private, it feels as if its radiance has been lost. He was so perceptive of the song of the birds and the beauty of the blossoms and spoke so discerningly of such things; but now. . . .” The strains of the koto he himself was playing [brought tears to his eyes sufficient to] wet his sleeves. Though with one corner of his mind he was wondering if this had caught the ear of her within the blinds and made her listen, yet above all else it was the man himself he missed on such musical evenings as this, as did His Majesty as well.

From “an evening of moon viewing” are Genji’s words. “Her within the blinds” is the Third Princess. “With one corner of his mind” refers to his feelings of spite. “Above all he misses him” is Genji [thinking] of Kashiwagi.

What the Gate Guards Commander does, then, comes down to this: having committed an act of immorality, he proceeds to do away with himself. No matter how fine a gentleman he may be, when judged by the prevailing standards of the world, this is not something deserving of sympathy; and yet [Murasaki Shikibu] describes it here in the most moving terms. Again and again, she speaks of how he is missed at court and how even Genji misses and pities him, which is to say that on the road of love, emotions run deep, and that among the best people, deep are their feelings of sensitivity [*aware o shiru kokoro*]. We see here the degree to which the essence of this tale lies in its depiction of emotions of one sort or another.

In "Hashihime" [16:151], it says: "'Truly, even were I to hear it told of a complete stranger, it would seem a touching old story [*aware narubeki furukotodomo*].'" These are Kaoru's thoughts when at Uji he first hears Ben no Kimi tell of Kashiwagi. These words merit attention. Anyone who reads this tale yet fails to be moved by the story of Kashiwagi is simply a person without a heart. Again, in "Umegae" [14:416]:

> "In matters of this sort, I was not much inclined to follow even his august advice, so I am loath to lecture you, but . . ."

These are among Genji's words of admonition to Yūgiri. "Matters of this sort" refers to matters of love. "His august advice" is the august admonition given to Genji long ago by his father the Emperor. "I was not much inclined to follow" means not that he purposely determined not to follow it, but that he found it difficult to behave in accordance with the august advice. As it happens, this admonishment of Yūgiri is very long and is entirely a warning against lust. That a parent should counsel his child is entirely natural. In saying, "Now in the past I, too, felt I could not abide by his august advice, and so now I am loath to lecture you one way or another on matters of this sort, but . . . ," he is saying that everyone, when young, is impatient in matters of this sort and errs in untoward ways, but this is nothing that we who feel we've grown old and wise should reproach. Such are the feelings of persons of sensibility [*mna o shireru hito no kokoro*], who are lenient and not intolerant. In "Yūgiri" [15:457]:

> He had heard of this matter, but thinking "why should I appear to have heard?" he kept his peace and looked straight at him. Wonderfully handsome he was, and, lately in particular, it seemed to him, quite

grown up and in his prime. Though he had committed that indiscretion, he showed no sign that it was something people might hold against him; indeed, so radiant was he in the freshness and beauty of the prime of youth that even the demons and deities must forgive his transgression. Why, these things are only to be expected, for he is no callow youth, after all, but perfectly grown up and with no glaring faults. "Were I a woman, could I fail to love him? When he looks in the mirror, could he fail to feel a little proud of himself?" His own child though this was, such were his thoughts.

"That indiscretion" refers to the matter between Yūgiri and the Ochiba Princess. From "wonderfully handsome" forward are the thoughts Genji's thinks as he looks at Yūgiri. Although in his previous admonitions, he warns him severely against lust, in his heart he thinks it "only natural." In "Usugumo" [13:454]:

"This is most unseemly. I'm sure I've committed many far more frightfully grievous sins, but those lusts of the past I trust the buddhas and gods will have forgiven as the errors of a thoughtless time of life."

These are Genji's thoughts. "This" refers to his own advances toward the Akikonomu Empress. "Frightfully grievous sins" are what he now considers his past trysts with the Fujitsubo Empress. As one grows older, in myriad ways one grows more deeply thoughtful, so now, upon reflection, he thinks his advances toward the Akikonomu Empress "unseemly." And yet, in this respect, there remains a part of him that he is unable to restrain, for even after this, he does not cease trysting secretly with the Oborozukiyo lady. As the text says ["Wakana, jō," 15:83]: "Though on reflection he felt strongly how improper this was, he was powerless to act accordingly." Such are the passions of love. In "Sakaki" [13:115–16]:

He had heard word to the effect that the affair with Kan no Kimi [Oborozukiyo] was not yet at an end, and on occasion had himself seen signs of it. "But what of it?" he said to himself. "If this had only just begun, well yes, but in a relationship of some standing, surely it is nothing unseemly that they should still be fond of each other." He did not hold this against them.

"The affair with Kan no Kimi" is Genji's trysting with the Oborozukiyo lady. It is the Suzaku Emperor who "hears" about this. His attitude is the same as Genji's when he shows pity for Kashiwagi.

Then, too, the way that Ukifune gives in so easily to Niou, while keeping Kaoru in reserve, is just too frivolous and faithless, even a bit despicable, one feels. Yet when one reads that long description of the emotions she experiences thereafter, one cannot help but be touched. The way she feels is described in "Ukifune" [17:134–36]:

> "How can I possibly receive him?" she thought, so stricken with fright that even the skies seemed to reproach her. Then, as the sight of that man who had been so dashing suddenly manifested itself to her memory and she imagined meeting this man again, she grew desolate in the extreme. "You know," he had said, "I feel as if I've lost interest in all the other women I've been seeing these past years." And indeed, she had heard that thereafter it was said that he was unwell, that there had been no sign of his usual activities anywhere at all, and that a great fuss was being made with chants and prayers and whatnot for him, which made the thought of what he might think if he were to hear of this extremely painful. This man, too, cut an attractive figure, having an air of considerable thoughtfulness about him. Of that long period of neglect he said but a few words and nothing at all to suggest that he had missed her or had suffered. Yet he was that sort of person whose genteel professions of the pain of loving someone he cannot often see were such that anyone would have to find them more affecting than some more ardent outburst. Quite apart from his good looks, his was a disposition in which one might place far greater trust over the long run. "If ever anyone should let on what a strange turn my feelings have taken, that would be simply dreadful. That I should be attracted to someone so obsessed that he hardly seems in his right mind—how very wrong this is and how frivolous! Were I to be thought despicable by this man and he were to forget all about me, I know full well how desolate I should be. . . ." He had said he was thinking that "sometime this spring, if it is convenient, I'd like to move you there," which called to mind that only yesterday that man had told her, "I've made plans for a place where you can live quietly." "All of which he must be thinking while quite unaware of these developments," she thought, and attractive though he was to her, she determined that she "mustn't be drawn

> any further in that direction." Yet no sooner had she thought that than the image of him as he had been appeared to her thoughts, and despite herself she thought, "Oh, what a wretched predicament," and she broke down crying.

"How can I possibly receive him?" refers to Kaoru. "That man who had been so dashing," "someone so obsessed," "that man," and such refer to Niou. "This man" always refers to Kaoru. It is Niou who spoke of "these past years." And again [17:148–49]:

> Though in her own mind she knew that "this is just as I've wished it, just what I've been hoping for from the very start," still whenever she recalled that impetuous man, in that instant there would appear some image of him—the sight of him reproaching her, his words as he spoke to her. And should she doze off even for a moment, he would appear to her in a dream. All in all, it made her feel quite miserable.

And again [17:149–50]:

> In the feelings of one so young and not particularly mature, this sort of thing was bound to arouse still greater passion. And yet he who had loved her from the start—he, after all, was a man of great depth and estimable character, and was it not precisely because he was her first love that he should seem so? "What would my life be if he were to hear of this sordid business and lose interest in me?" she thought. "And Mother, too, as worried as she is about when all this will come good—I'd surely be rejected by her as someone shockingly awful. And this man—obsessed with me as he is, I only hear how faithless he is. . . ." "If for the delinquency of my own affections, I were to be rejected by that man, that would be dreadful," she thought, her mind in a turmoil.

And again [17:178–79]:

> "But if he comes looking like that, I won't be able to speak to him again, and they'll send him away without my even seeing him. What chance would I have then to invite him in, even for just a moment? And the sight of him leaving, having come all this way for nothing, and so angry with me!" Whenever she imagined the scene, his image would again appear to her. Hopelessly forlorn, she pressed his

> letter to her face, and although for a moment she tried to hold back, she wept uncontrollably.

And again [17:184–85]:

> "Pray forgive my sin of preceding my parents in death" was her only thought. She took out the pictures from that time and looked at them, and the flow of his hand and the glow of the faces made her feel as if he were there with her. "Yes, it's even worse, not saying a single word to him on the last night," she thought. "And that man who was always talking about how we would live a quiet life together, for ever and ever—what is he going to think?" she thought pityingly. . . . She missed her mother; she even missed her rather unattractive brothers and sisters, whom normally she never even thought of. And then she recalled the Princess [Nakanokimi], whereupon she found herself wishing she could see any number of people just one more time.

The degree of emotion in such passages as these is truly so affecting as to make even a tiger or a wolf weep.

To say that the main aim of this tale is to encourage virtue and castigate vice [*kanzen chōaku*], that above all it is an admonition against lust, is a grave error. The author's intentions are nothing of the sort. Neither is the reader at all likely to take it as such an admonition. The reason, in the first place, is that Genji is depicted as in all things peerless, the very model of the superior person. The reader, therefore, is bound to perceive every deed and thought of this gentleman as superior. And yet, this man is guilty of frequent misconduct, particularly in matters of the heart [*koi no midare*], and even commits an act of unparalleled immorality. The reader, however, is most likely to be struck by the thought that if even so superior a person does such things, how can they be wrong? As for women, the Fujitsubo Empress is praised as a particularly fine person. Any woman who reads about her is likely to find her character attractive and wish to emulate her, but what then is she to make of the passages describing her affair with Genji? Common sense tells us that this might actually arouse feelings of lust. How is this to serve as an admonition?

Now, the depiction of people who do good as having good fortune and people who do evil as meeting with ill fortune—this, to be sure, is "encouraging virtue and castigating vice." One may well consider Kashiwagi and Ukifune to be examples of this, for both, through the passions of love, bring ruin upon themselves. But what can one say about Genji? Here is a man guilty of frequent misconduct in affairs of the passions, who has sullied even the august imperial line of succession. Judged by prevailing principles, the gods themselves should utterly abominate him and he should meet with horrendous misfortune, yet he prospers splendidly throughout his life. He has children who become Emperor, Empress, and Minister of State, and he himself attains the title of Honorary Emperor in Retirement. Who, seeing how nothing in this world is denied this man and how even his progeny prosper, will be inspired to abstain from lust? The fact that he suffers a temporary setback in midlife[107] is attributed to a sinister plot on the part of the Kokiden Empress Mother, and the episode is described as one in which all the world grieves for him and even the gods and buddhas condemn her.[108] This hardly qualifies as an admonition against lust, and in no sense whatever does it "castigate vice." Indeed, pushing this argument to its logical extreme, is it not the case that he becomes Honorary Emperor in Retirement precisely by means of lust? Can even this be called "castigating vice"?

Speaking further of how unlikely this is to serve as an admonishment against lust, in "Yūgao" [12:218] it says:

> He had never paid much attention to these ordinary sorts of women, but since the discussion on that rainy night, his interest in all those other varieties that had piqued his curiosity seemed to burgeon.

This describes how after listening to that discussion, Genji's thoughts grew even more lustful. Just reading this, one realizes that it could never serve as an admonition. In "Suetsumuhana" [12:343]:

> "It is in just such places as this that those touching scenes in the old romances are set," he was thinking. "Shall I say something and perhaps make a move on her?" he wondered, but. . . .

In "Agemaki" [16:294]:

> Looking at the picture depicting the scene in *Tales of Zaigo* in which the man gives his younger sister a koto lesson and says, "Were another to bind them . . . ,"[109] he said, "for people of the past who were prop-

erly related as we are, it was quite normal that no barriers should separate them."

Consider these examples! This, by and large, is the spirit in which people of the past read the old romances. One sees no sign here of anyone inspired with an urge to abstain from the passions of love. We may assume that the attitudes of present-day readers will be much the same. Thus, in "Hotaru" [14:207]:

> "Pray don't read any of these love stories to our young lady. She's hardly likely to find scheming girls of that sort attractive, but it would be dreadful if she should come to think such affairs commonplace," he said.

Present-day readers of *The Tale of Genji*, seeing so many passages describing the passions of love, are likely to think such affairs abundantly commonplace. If this tale were really intended as an admonition against lust, would it relate such things as this? There are, in its several chapters, numerous instances of instruction and admonition against lust, for the work discusses a vast variety of subjects. It stands to reason, therefore, that in the midst of all this, such instances will quite naturally occur. In the latter "Wakana" [15:243]:

> There were points of style that were clear and unmistakable. The words with which he described how he had longed for her for years, how his hopes were realized so unexpectedly, and his apprehension thereafter, were quite eloquent and touching. "But must one write everything out so clearly? That such a fine man should write so thoughtless a letter! In the past, I myself was well aware what can happen when letters go astray, and even when I might well have been this explicit, I was terse and evasive. But it is difficult for people to exercise due discretion," he thought, somewhat contemptuous of the man.

These are Genji's thoughts as he contemplates the letter he has found that Kashiwagi sent to the Third Princess. If one regards [*Genji*] as entirely a work of moral instruction, then here we have a lesson in how to write love letters, which thus could serve to encourage the conduct of love affairs.

Scholars down through the ages, no matter what texts they might be annotating, have neglected to study carefully the overall import of those texts, but have succumbed totally to the teachings of Confucianism or Buddhism, which they then have attempted to apply forcibly to the texts they are explicating, thus distorting their meaning. This has been a habitual failing of scholars of this land since times long past, and not one of them is there who has not succumbed to Confucianism or Buddhism. And thus, in the same forcible manner, this tale too is dragged within the ken of Confucian and Buddhist doctrines.

And so, even events that, with an understanding of human emotion [*mna o shirite*], are described as good but do not conform to the spirit of those doctrines, are forcibly misinterpreted and construed as bad. This is a lesson in such-and-such; this is an admonition against such-and-such, they insist. When passages of this sort are interpreted as castigating vice, their depth of feeling [*mna no fukaki*] vanishes, which of course means that in most cases the author's original sense is entirely lost. To interpret tales entirely in terms of Confucianism and Buddhism is but envious pandering to the moral pretensions of those texts and the sagaciously grandiloquent fine phrases of their sharply argued disquisitions on good and evil, right and wrong. It is all mere sophistry.

Each and every text, of any sort whatever, has its own individual purport [*omomuki*]. So what does it matter that some, inevitably, should be at odds with the spirit of Confucianism or Buddhism? To take a tale that was written in order to exhibit the varieties of human emotion [*mna o misemu*] and make a moral homily of it is like cutting down a cherry tree planted for the beauty of its blossoms and breaking it up it for firewood. We could not live without firewood, even for a single day; it is a valuable substance and there is nothing wrong with it. But there are many other trees that make perfectly good firewood. To cut down a treasured cherry tree can only be deemed a heartless deed.

Furthermore, although sensitivity to human emotion [*mna o shiru to iu koto*] differs in nature from the doctrines of Confucianism and Buddhism, in the broadest sense it embraces even the Way of regulating oneself, managing one's household, and governing the state.[110] Were they to empathize with [*aware to omoishiraba*] all the thoughts and deeds that constitute a parent's love for a child, surely there would be no unfilial children in this world. And were they to empathize with all the labors of the peasantry and the travails of their servants, surely there would be no inhumane lords in this world. But the fact that there are inhumane lords and unfilial children in this world, in the final analysis, is because they are insensitive to human emotion [*mna o shiraneba*]. Thus when we understand that tales are texts that exhibit the varieties of human feeling and we read them principally for that purpose, they may often serve naturally as moral instruction in all manner of ways; but when we read them, having decided from the start that they are moral homilies, we can go terribly wrong. Consider what it says at the end of *The Tale of Sumiyoshi*:

> In the past as in the present, this is what malicious people are like. Anyone who has seen or heard of such things should be at pains to be kind to others.[111]

These words are critical of the insensitive [*mna o shirazarishi*] behavior of the stepmother of the Sumiyoshi lady. [The story] shows how the stepmother comes to a bad end and describes the young lady in splendid terms—how she meets Shōshō and, though guilty of an affair of passion, in the end prospers. This is clearly intended as an admonition that "encourages virtue and castigates vice," but it admonishes only against insensitivity to human emotion [*mna o shirazaru*], which is quite a different matter from the usual Confucian and Buddhist admonishments. *The Tale of Genji* should be understood in like manner.

As I said at the outset, tales have a nature of their own that is unique to tales; they should not be discussed in terms of Confucian and Buddhist texts, which are quite irrelevant and unrelated, all the while ignoring evidence that is close at hand. One argument of this sort, however—that tales illustrate the principle that "those who rise must inevitably fall and those who meet must invariably part"—often seems to make sense, and there is some justice to this claim. In the first place, the Way of the Buddha, as we term it, is a Way that categorically renounces human emotion [*mna oba sutsuru michi*]. Its doctrines are far more rigorous than those of the Confucian Way, and it is a Way meant, in every respect, to be far removed from human feeling. Yet despite this, it is readily attractive to the human mind. Even ignorant mountain folk, even women and children, strange to say, are deeply moved by it; and in any predicament whatever, their thoughts turn habitually to this Way. In fact, neither the affairs of this world nor the events of this life are of the slightest concern to that Way. But it is a Way that propounds its principles attractively and powerfully, so that people far and wide will be persuaded to alter their garb and look to the afterlife. And so the minds of everyone everywhere, accustomed as they are to hearing such things, be they high or low, wise or foolish, are permeated with these doctrines. Thus it is that someone in the prime of life, struck by the insubstantiality of this world or overwhelmed by the anguish of his own life, may mortify himself in the black garb of a monk, seclude himself deep in the mountains far from all civilization, and devote himself to the practice of austerities.

And since such scenes are so replete with deep emotion [*mna no fukaki koto*], this tale describes every person of profound sensibilities, from Genji on down, as in one way or another attracted to the Way of the Buddha. This is just the way things were in that world, and these are the varieties of feeling experienced by people [*hito no nasake no mna*] who lived in a world in which such customs prevailed. Thus the many references to the Way of the Buddha, in chapter after chapter, are in no way meant to propagate its doctrines; they simply depict the emotions [*aware o misetaru*] that arise in such a milieu. If they were for the purpose of propagating the principles of the Way of the Buddha, they would, without fail, depict the decrepitude of Genji in old age, and they would surely depict his death as well. But they depict neither the decrepitude nor the death of this gentleman; they stop short of that and depict only the full panoply of his virtues. From which we know that this is not a lesson in the principle that "those who rise must inevitably fall." Though the commentaries maintain that such is the case, who could read this tale and thereby be persuaded of this principle? Reading those scenes here and there that depict someone entering the Way of the Buddha, someone of a Confucian turn of mind may conclude that Murasaki Shikibu is of the Buddhist persuasion, or some monk may maintain that she writes in order to turn us to the Way. But readers of this sort are merely indulging the prejudices of their own chosen Way. This tale does not participate in any such prejudices. The Way of the Buddha occupied the minds of everyone who lived in that world; the innumerable scenes of this sort are simply descriptions of the world as it was then. How then can one attribute [Buddhist] motives to the author?

Moreover, Mr. Kumazawa, whom I mentioned previously, states at the beginning of his *Discursive Commentary* on this tale:[112]

> *The Tale of Genji* on the surface would appear to describe lascivious matters [*kōshoku*], but in fact, it is not a lascivious work. Thus it is that

> even among readers who delight in this tale, there are those who are overly fastidious. What motivated the author to write this tale was her grief that, in every way, as the end of the age drew nigh, the beauteous ways of times past should decline and lapse into vulgarity. Yet people would shun and shy away from an overtly proper work, so that it would have few readers and thus would not circulate widely. There are many works written to set forth certain doctrines, but because their language is stiff and people find them off-putting, they do not last for long. Or if they do survive, they will have no readers and thus might as well not exist. And so, judging that it would be useless to write such a work, she [Murasaki] took great pains not to write in a didactic style. She simply fashioned an amorous amusement, in the course of which she has left us a detailed description of the fine manners and thoughtful ways of the ranking aristocracy of long ago. People who, having no idea of its true nature, describe it as a mere fiction, albeit well told and well written, or consider it just another story, written down exactly as it came from the author's mouth—such people only display the paucity of their knowledge of Japanese and Chinese literature. . . . Only in this tale do the means survive to observe the rites, music, and fine writing of times past. Therefore, what one should first of all attend to in this tale are the beauteous ways of antiquity. That is, rites performed properly and placidly, music played with harmony and grace, the courtliness of both men and women, the way they constantly delight in courtly music, their caring manners so free of meanness. Second is the detail with which human feelings are depicted in this work. For ignorance of human feeling frequently results in a loss of harmony in the five human relations. . . . In short, this tale was written with the basic aim of moral reform. In particular, it describes in great detail the Way of Music. . . . It is said that for the modification of manners and the improvement of customs, there is nothing better than music. This is why, in this tale, the Way of Music is described with such particular attention.

I, Norinaga, will now discuss these points. First of all, [Kumazawa] says that "even among readers who delight in this tale, there are those who are overly fastidious." This is something that will depend entirely on the person in question. Of course, this may well be true of a pure-minded person who believes deeply that lasciviousness is evil, but then, might not a deeply lascivious reader just as well be incited to become even more so?

And then [Kumazawa] says: "What motivated the author to write this tale was her grief that, in every way, as the end of the age drew nigh, the beauteous ways of times past should decline and lapse into vulgarity." Since by comparison with the crude customs of later ages, the manners and attitudes of people of the past are elegant indeed, one might well come to such a conclusion, but the author's intentions have nothing to do with this. It takes a Confucian mentality to think that in that age she should be minded to do such a thing. This tale does indeed afford us a glimpse of the courtly ways of the past, but that is for readers of later times to say; the book was not from the very start written in order to illustrate such things.

And then [Kumazawa] says that "people would shun and shy away from an overtly proper work . . . [and so] she simply fashioned an amorous amusement." Such an attitude is indeed in evidence, but it is mistaken to consider her [Murasaki's] description of amorous matters a "mere amusement." As I have said time and again, her principal concern in writing is the varieties of human feeling [*mna*]; and since for depth of feeling, nothing surpasses the passions of love, she writes giving prime importance to these matters with particular frequency. Thus the degree to which her depiction of the condition and feelings of those who love is anything but mere amusement should be perfectly plain; to insist that it is otherwise is the same old Confucian mentality.

And then [Kumazawa] speaks of "the detail with which human feelings are described in this work." This is indeed the case. There is nothing to compare with it in the literature of either Japan or China. But when he says that "this tale was written with the basic aim of moral reform," once again this is the same old Confucian mentality. Neither is it true that "in particular, it describes in great detail the Way of Music." The musical performances that one frequently encounters are much the same as when present-day people enjoy playing the shamisen, chanting *jōruri*, or the like; they are simply descriptions of the way things were in ages past and what they enjoyed. To say that "for the modification of manners and the improvement of customs, there is nothing better than music" is a typically twisted Confucian notion that has nothing whatever to do with tales.

In short, harsh pronouncements and misinformed interpretations of this sort are precisely the same as those of the buddhistically inclined when they go on about how "those who rise must inevitably fall" and the like. Neither have any thought for any ideas other than those in the texts that they themselves are accustomed to, and both are ignorant of the fact that tales have a different nature entirely their own. This *Discursive Commentary* extracts short fragments of text, one after another from chapter after chapter of the tale, and interprets them in whatever manner the author, as a Confucianist, wishes to, with no regard for what that text might mean. Occasionally an interesting idea turns up among them, but for the most part, they are utterly outrageous. Again, in the *Seven Essays* it says:

> Just as in China, Sima Qian and others, in consequence of their own suffering, gave vent to their rage in writing and, in doing so, created a unique voice of their own. Shikibu, too, having lost her father, Tametoki, and having been widowed by her husband, Nobutaka, and having no means of support with which to raise her two daughters, in this time of privation wrote this tale, describing each and every aspect of her world, setting them down as satire and as homilies and, in doing, so dispelled her melancholy.[113]

This, too, is but speculation of a Confucian bent and cannot be considered the essence of the tale. And when he [Tameakira] takes the Reizei Emperor's taint to the imperial line [*Reizei no In no mono no magire*][114] to be a moral allegory, claims that it is the "crux of the entire work" [*ichibu daiji*], and discusses his reasons for doing so, this too is Confucian thinking, totally obsessed with precedents in the literature of China and ignorant of the basic nature of tales. In his discussion of the clandestine affair between Genji and the Fujitsubo Empress, he says: "Observe that at first this is described in a most graceful manner and in the end as a most frightful and improper transgression." He insists upon making a moral allegory of this, but even if Genji does later come to feel that it was "most frightful and improper," what is one to say about his subsequent clandestine trysting with the Oborozukiyo lady, such as we see in the previous citation from "Usugumo" [13:454]?[115] Were it the author's [Murasaki's] intent to assert that his affair with the Fujitsubo Empress was a "most frightful transgression," would she really describe such goings-on again later? If this was meant as a moral allegory, having once warned against it, surely she would then back away and move on.

Again, in "Miotsukushi" [13:276], it says: "With the accession of the present Emperor, he was delighted that all was just as he wished." These are Genji's thoughts. "The present Emperor" refers to the Reizei Emperor. If all were as argued in [Tameakira's] essay, then when the Reizei Emperor acceded to the throne, should she [Murasaki] not have described Genji as feeling even more fearful and as deploring his defilement of the imperial line [*kōin no magirenuru koto*], rather than as she does here, "delighted that all was just as he wished"? There is much more that misses the mark in this discussion of the secret of the Emperor's birth [*mono no magire*], but since it is such a delicate subject, I shall refrain from discussing it further. In any case, this is not something that can be singled out as a moral allegory.

After all, defilement of the imperial line [*mono no magire*] is now, and long has been, a matter of unparalleled importance. But tales being tales, they do not depict matters of such magnitude in the real world as the "crux of the entire work." [*Genji*], too, being a tale, this is but a single episode in a story. What, then, one may ask, was [the author's] intention in depicting such an affair? As stated earlier, she did so above all in order that through this affair with the Fujitsubo Empress, she might exhibit in their fullest possible depth all the emotions of passionate love [*mna . . . o misemu*]. For here we have a man and a woman, both possessed of all the finest qualities, a couple superior to all others in their sensitivity to emotion [*mna o shiritamaeru*]; and since the emotions of love aroused in an illicit relationship of this intensity are even deeper than usual, [the author] purposefully depicts these people involved in a love affair of the most thoroughly improper sort, thus gathering together a full array of the very deepest emotions.

Then, too, the Reizei Emperor's taint to the imperial line [*Reizei no In no mono no magire*] is depicted as a means of furthering Genji's rise to success. For in every tale, there is a main character who is described in the most favorable terms and to whom are attributed all the best things in life. Since personal success is the ultimate human good, as a rule most tales depict this character as fortunate in all things, ultimately rising to the highest station in life. This tale, too, describes Genji's rise to success, yet since the pinnacle of human success is to become Emperor, even a Minister of State, as a commoner, must still harbor some lingering dissatisfaction, and thus [the author] decides to bestow upon him the title of Honorary Emperor in Retirement. Yet without some plausible reason for doing so, this would only seem unnatural, in fact shallow and contrived. This is why this disruption [*mono no magire*] is described, in order to make [Genji] the father of an Emperor. Thus it is that this gentleman can become Honorary Emperor in Retirement, for he is the son of an Emperor, he has as children an Empress and a Minister, and in addition to all this, he is even the father of an Emperor. It is in this manner that he rises to the peak of honor, splendor, and personal success.

Further evidence for claiming that this was done in order to facilitate the bestowal of the honorary title is found in "Usugumo" [13:440–41], in the words of the monk on night duty, who has long known about the tainted succession [*mono no magire*] and decides to inform the <<Reizei>> Emperor secretly:

> "This is a matter of great importance, as much so to the future as it was in the past, but that might well leak out and instead prove detrimental to all concerned—the late Emperor and Empress, as well as the Minister who currently governs the land. But what has an old monk like myself to regret, no matter what misfortune may be my lot? What has been vouchsafed to me in a revelation from the Buddha I humbly relate to you. . . ."

The "matter of great importance, as much so to the future as it was in the past" refers to the fact that the Reizei Emperor does not know who his true father is. Now, to inform him of this, so that he does know his true father and can perform his filial duties, is a very fine thing indeed. And yet [the monk] speaks of how it might "instead prove detrimental" to the Kiritsubo Emperor, the Fujitsubo Empress, and Genji were word of it to leak out. If, then, we take this to mean that he describes the tainted succession [*mono no magire*] as a matter of great importance, it does not jibe with his statement that it might "instead prove detrimental." If he refers to the tainted succession [*mono no magire*], then of course it is detrimental to all these people, so why would he say "instead" [*kaerite*]? By paying close attention to this word "instead," we can grasp the correct meaning of this passage. The [objective] particle *o* in the phrase *haberu koto o* connects to the clause beginning "from the Buddha." This matter of great importance, vouchsafed to me in a revelation from the Buddha, he says, I humbly relate to you.

Upon hearing what is humbly told him, the Emperor says in reply to the monk [13:442]: "Had I gone on in ignorance of this, I would have carried the guilt into my next life. . . ." Had he gone on in ignorance of the fact that Genji was his real father, this means. With these words, the meaning of the foregoing passage becomes clearer. If the matter in question were the tainted succession [*mono no magire*], the Reizei Emperor would bear no guilt whatever, even if he knew nothing about it. And then the monk says [13:442]:

> "The repeated omens that appear in the heavens and the unrest that pervades the realm are all manifestations of this. It was one thing when you were young and could not have reached the age of discretion, but now, as you've grown steadily more mature and become fully cognizant of everything, they are making their displeasure known. All things begin in the days of one's parents. . . ."

"A revelation from the Buddha," "I would have carried the guilt into my next life," "the repeated omens that appear in the heavens . . . are manifestations of this," and "they are making their displeasure known"—all these result from his ignorance of who his true father is. If they were due to the tainted succession [*mono no magire*], then guilt would fall, for the most part, on Genji, but note that it is described as falling entirely upon the Reizei Emperor. In "Hashihime" [16:154], when Kaoru, in Uji, first learns from Ben no Kimi that his real father is Kashiwagi, he says: "If we had not had this conversation, I would have gone through life bearing a heavy burden of sin." Comparison with what is said here, too, should make this clear. "All things begin in the days of one's parents" means that the fate of a child, whether for good or for ill, is in recompense for the good and evil done by its parents. In saying this, [the monk] means that Reizei's rise to his current position as Emperor, ruler of all under heaven, has come to pass in recompense of the myriad virtuous deeds of his father, Genji; and thus it is all the more imperative that he know that Genji is his father. But if one takes his guilt to be the guilt of the tainted succession, then the text should read, "All things are repaid in the days of the child." One must pay careful heed to the text. By the same token, as we know from the foregoing text, it makes quite a difference whether it refers to the parent or the child. And in the text that follows ["Usugumo," 13:445–46], it says:

> He pursued his studies even more assiduously . . . and found several instances of those who within their lifetime had been [of the] Genji [clan] and then, after becoming Counselors and Ministers of State, had gone on to become Imperial Princes and had even succeeded to the throne. Should he perhaps, giving as his reason [Genji's] personal acumen, abdicate in his favor? the Emperor mused in the course of his

> myriad meditations. In the autumn promotions, he certainly must be made Grand Minister [*daijō daijin*].

"He pursued his studies even more assiduously" because he wished to find some precedent that would allow him to make Genji the Emperor. This we know because he "found several instances." Finally, thinking to relinquish the throne to him, he first of all will make him Grand Minister of State.

One must consider carefully the process by which the taint [*mono no magire*] in this tale, beginning several chapters before this, has been mentioned repeatedly and, having come this far, concludes with the Emperor deciding that he will make Genji the Emperor. So if we assume that the author is intent on describing this gentleman's rise to success, then the fact that she might have gone one step further and raised him to the rank of Emperor, but instead stopped short at Honorary Emperor in Retirement, is an example of her profound attention to detail. The Commandant in *The Tale of Sagoromo*, who is ultimately made Emperor,[116] is patterned after Genji in this tale and then is raised even further [than Genji], but raising the Commandant to the rank of Emperor with no good reason for doing so actually seems rather contrived, indeed silly. But Murasaki Shikibu is well aware of this and so refrains from making [Genji] the Emperor, and since even Honorary Emperor in Retirement would seem too abrupt if there were no good reason, she begins laying the groundwork from the very start, with the words of the Korean physiognomist in "Kiritsubo" [12:116]:

> "He has the signs of one destined to become a father to his nation and rise to the supreme rank of Emperor; yet when I read them as such, I somehow fear unrest and affliction."

Then in depicting the taint to the succession [*mono no magire*], she proceeds to describe him as one who ought to be given an honorary title. When we come to "Usugumo" [13:446], at the point where [the Emperor] wants to appoint him to the throne, she has this gentleman [Genji] say:

> "Though the late Emperor was disposed to favor me over his many other sons, never did he consider relinquishing the throne to me. How could I betray his wishes and rise to a rank to which I am not entitled?"

Although he ought to rise to the rank of Emperor, she says, that last step is purposely omitted. These words signal the author's underlying intentions, as well as the extraordinary depth of care that went into the creation of this work. Careful consideration of the thrust of the foregoing quotations should make it clear that, throughout, her depiction of the tainted succession [*mono no magire*] was for the purpose of advancing the rise to success of this gentleman.

Furthermore, *Sagoromo* is in every way patterned on this tale. Among many things that have been altered only slightly is the Commandant who carries on a clandestine affair with the Second Princess, and the child whom she bears is falsely passed off as the son of the Saga Emperor. When it is decided that this "Prince" will be appointed Crown Prince, the Commandant, in consequence of a revelation from Amaterasu Ōmikami, is raised to the rank of Emperor.[117] This is patterned totally on the Reizei Emperor's taint on the succession, and the author has done so for the same reason as in this tale, in order to advance the rise to success of the Commandant by appointing him to this rank. Thus the intentions of the former are made clear by comparison with the latter.

MISCELLANEOUS MATTERS

Among the multitude of tales, this tale [*The Tale of Genji*] is one of particular excellence and magnificence. Neither before it nor after it are there any at all to compare with it. In the first place, the old romances that precede it are in no sense profound, nor do they seem to have been written with any care. They are utterly prosaic, filled with outlandish goings-on, mainly with the aim of astonishing the reader. Not one of them has any depth or detail in matters of human feeling [*mna naru suji*]. Of those that follow [*Genji*], the [*Tale of*] *Sagoromo* seems to be modeled entirely on this tale; yet despite the effort expended, it is utterly inferior. None of the others is any different. It need hardly be said that this tale [*Genji*] alone is of surpassing excellence, a work of particular depth, and written with every possible care, so that the language is in every way magnificent. The panorama of people as they go through life; the passing scenes of nature, even the very plants and trees in spring, summer, autumn, and winter; everything is splendidly described. But in particular it is the differentiation of the people, the distinct manner and character of each and every one, be they men or women. Even the terms in which they are praised are not uniform but in every case are distinguished according to the manner and character of this person or that, so one can picture them as if one were meeting real people. This is nothing any ordinary writer could hope to achieve.

But more magnificent than all else is this: first of all, Chinese writings, even those regarded as the finest of them all, although they do depict in cursory fashion the feelings of people as they go through life, are but crude and shallow works. This thing we call the human heart is by no means as utterly uncomplicated as it is made out to be in Chinese writings. Faced with a problem that engages the feelings deeply, [the human heart] wavers this way and that, tediously and effeminately, confusion vying with confusion in so many different gradations that it can hardly come to any firm conclusion. And in this tale, these divers gradations, none excepted, are depicted in minute detail and particularity; it is like gazing into a mirror in which all is reflected with total clarity. I doubt there is another work, in either Japan or China, past or present or future, that can match the manner in which it delineates human feeling. Moreover, in none of its several chapters is there anything of a sort to astound, horrify, or shock. From beginning to end, it treats but the selfsame theme, the uneventful flow of ordinary life. Though it is a very long book, one neither grows impatient nor wearies of reading it but, rather, wishes only to know what comes next. From early on, I have several times explicated this tale for the benefit of my students. With lesser books, even those that are not very long, there are moments when one wearies of teaching them. But with this book, long though it is, years and months may pass and still one never wearies of it, not even slightly. Every time it seems so fresh and wonderful that I feel as if I were reading it for the first time and realize anew how superior it is, how truly magnificent!

Someone asked: "I must say that the conciseness with which *Tales of Ise* is written, the way it packs its meaning into just a phrase or two, and the overall economy of words, is truly superb. But isn't this tale, by comparison, extraordinarily wordy and long, tending far too much to excess of detail? How do you explain this?"

I answered: "In the first place, the standards of stylistic criticism as practiced by the Chinese, which as a rule value linguistic economy and concision in writing, are entirely correct, and the very same holds true for the writings of this land. *Tales of Ise* is indeed splendidly economical of words, and in this it surpasses other tales. But to consider this tale [*Genji*] inferior to *Tales of Ise* because its sentences are long and complex is to judge it without reference to the quality of the text, but only according to the length or brevity of its periods, which is but blind adherence to the standards of Chinese style. That the wordiness of bad writing is bad goes without saying. Conversely, one cannot conclude categorically that length is bad. Be it ever so short, bad writing is bad; be it ever so long, good writing is good. The writing in this tale is wordy, but not a word is wasted; its lengths are appropriately so and, even when it goes on at great length, is only the more splendid for its length. *Tales of Ise* is written in an entirely different style. It must not be held up as a standard by which to judge the merits and demerits of a text that makes no attempt at economy and concision but strives instead to write in meticulous detail."

Concerning the poems in tales: since many of those in *Tales of Ise* are old poems, many are good; but those that appear to be newly written by the author are not good; and among them are some that are indescribably bad. In most other old works of fiction, all the poems are bad. But in *The Tale of Genji*, since all of them are written by the author, one seldom finds a bad poem, and mixed in among the good ones are some that are superb. There are those who say that when it comes to poems, those in *Sagoromo* are better than those in *Genji*, but this is not so. Compared with the poems in other old romances, those in *Sagoromo* are very good indeed, but they do not surpass those in *Genji*.

In this tale, everything about everyone who is deemed a good person, from Genji on down, is praised in glowing terms, except only that the poems they compose are never once praised, and here and there, one notes that, in contrast to a person's excellence in other ways, his or her poems may be described as bad. This is because all the poems by the characters in the tale are composed by Murasaki Shikibu herself; for her to praise them would be to praise herself.

In "Kiritsubo" [12:110], she says of "harsh winds . . .":

> "Such a shambles it was, but considering how upset she was at the time,
> the Emperor surely will overlook that."

In "Yūgao" [12:233], of "lives past . . .":

> "In matters of this sort, too, she seems, in fact, rather ill at ease." "Ill at ease" refers to her [Yūgao's] incompetence in the composition of poetry.[118]

In "Sakaki" [13:81–82]:

> "Was it perhaps because of the tumult of confusion in her mind that words failed her? 'Though even an ordinary autumnal farewell. . . .'"

And again [13:92], of "broad being the shadow . . .":

> "It was nothing at all special, but given the occasion, the Commandant found it touching, and his sleeves grew positively damp with tears."

And again [13:92], of "the glistening expanse . . .":

> ". . . he said, which was only what chanced to come to his mind. Too juvenile, really."

In "Asagao" [13:466], of "autumn ends . . .":

> "It was in no way interesting, but. . . ."

In "Hatsune" [14:140], of "after parting . . .":

> "It was just a jumble of words, whatever came into her child's mind."

In "Kochō" [14:164–65], of "in the flower garden . . ." and "by the butterflies . . .":

> "This was what they wrote. It would appear that even the most worthy and practiced sometimes found this sort of thing more than they could manage, for these compositions certainly bear no resemblance to what we would expect of them."

In "Nowaki" [14:275], of "winds rage . . .":

> "Yet he produced a strangely stiff, indeed dreadful, composition."

In "Makibashira" [14:379], of "deep within the palace . . .":

> "It was nothing out of the ordinary, but it seemed splendid, I suppose, while they were gazing at the fine face and figure of the Emperor."

In "Yūgiri" [15:437], of "wisteria robes . . .":

> "It was not good, but the occasion and the suppressed emotion in her voice made it sound good to him."

In "Hashihime" [16:115], of "how is that . . .":

> "It was not good, but given the occasion it was touching."

In "Agemaki" [16:265], of "no barrier between . . .":

> "It was very ordinary, but the man who had awaited it was genuinely touched by the unaffected feeling he saw in it."

In "Yadorigi" [16:471–72], of "him most high . . . ," "through ages eternal . . . ," "for the sake of my lord . . . ," and "of common sort . . .":

> "As you see, there were none of any particular interest."

In "Azumaya" [17:77], of "how utterly . . ." and "in this dismal world . . .":

> "They expressed their feelings in this exchange of perfectly commonplace poems."

In "Tenarai" [17:306], of "late in the night . . .":

> "Of this lame string of words. . . ."

Passages like these are all expressions of self-deprecation on the part of the author. How is it that, from of old, no one has ever noticed this and these poems were annotated as if they were indeed bad?

With regard to Murasaki Shikibu's own character, when one studies this tale and her diary, one notes here and there how thoroughly she deplored women who pride themselves on their learning and affect airs of intelligence and intellect and that she herself was profoundly cautious lest she be thought by others to do so. The passage in "Hahakigi" [12:165–66] beginning with "As a rule, the foolish ones, whether men or women . . ." and continuing to "and even of those matters one might particularly wish to mention it may be best to omit one or two" demonstrates her disdain for any pretension to learning and her determination to do no such thing herself. In the same chapter [12:165], it says: "Why should not even a woman . . . in the natural course of things see and hear a great deal?" This is to say that since anyone, even a woman, should know at least this much, it is nothing to take pride in. This shows the lack of any sense of pride in [Murasaki Shikibu] herself. Again, in the same chapter [12:161–64], she describes how, when Shikibu no Jō tells the story of the professor's daughter, the young gentlemen snap their fingers in disgust at such unpleasantness. When we consider this woman's manners, we see no reason to speak so ill of her; but in order to show her own repugnance for the affectation of learning, Murasaki Shikibu goes out of her way to describe her deeds as most disagreeable. And again, in "Otome" [14:17–20] where she describes the behavior, the attitudes, and the speech of the Academy people as exceedingly vulgar, entertaining though it is, she makes a particular point of deriding the inelegance of those who purposely pride themselves on their learning. Although it is normal that people lavish praise on anything and everything that they themselves esteem, [Murasaki Shikibu], despite her own particular partiality to learning, nonetheless describes it as though it were unworthy. In this there is a profound discretion that sets her apart from others.

Someone asked: "Whenever one reads descriptions of the thoughts of Genji and others in this tale who are considered 'good people,' they never seem to be manly and forthright, nor are they able to decide matters resolutely. They vacillate this way and that; they are feminine, weak willed, and faltering. What about this?"

I replied: "When you probe the innermost depths of people's true feelings, you find that everyone, quite frequently, is feminine and faltering.

What may seem to be masculine wisdom is often the result of conscious reflection and pretense, affected in order to preserve appearances. For when one converses with another person, one chooses [one's words] carefully so as to present the best possible exterior; things do not come pouring out just as they are. For example, a stalwart warrior, in time of battle, dies bravely for the sake of his lord and his domain. When one describes such an act in writing, one depicts his deeds and thoughts as truly dauntless [*daijōbu*], for one imagines that within his own heart the man was indeed gallant. And yet if one were to describe in full detail his innermost feelings at the time, surely he would also have yearned for his father and mother in his ancestral home; and surely he would have wished to see, just once more, the faces of his wife and children. How could he not, in some small measure, regret the loss of his life? These are the ineluctable true feelings that all human beings invariably possess, and if they say that a man, by virtue of his dauntlessness, is not the slightest bit subject to such feminine feelings, then he must be more akin to a heartless rock or log. Yet the usual run of books in the Chinese mold—both in relating the author's feelings and even in praising others—describe only those outer manifestations of feeling, the pretense of which we are careful to preserve, and omit to mention any unseemly inner recesses. And so, at first glance, one is impressed with their wisdom, manliness, and integrity. And under the preconceptions that come with a familiarity with books of this sort, fictional tales will seem, by comparison, frivolous and feminine. Tales, after all, are not written to teach moral principles; they describe people's feelings just as they are so as to illustrate the workings of their emotions [*mna naru suji o misemu tame ni*]. And of all tales, this one is particularly meticulous; it depicts the state of people's feelings in the most scrupulous detail. And since the best of these people tend to be profoundly sensitive [*mna o shiru kata fukakereba*], descriptions of the emotions that they experience will often sound feminine and fainthearted."

Another question: "The initiation of relations between men and women [in *Genji*] is not proper and orderly, as in China, but somehow indecent—and not merely in their clandestine affairs but even when they marry with the permission of their parents. What about this?"

I answer: "This is something in which the past differs from the present, and when you view the matter from the standpoint of modern

Chinese custom, the past may well seem indecorous. In all things, whatever they may be, China is China, and our realm is our realm; the present is the present, and the past is the past. But the Confucianists and their ilk judge things entirely on the basis of Chinese custom, and present-day people, being accustomed to present-day practice, look askance at the past. This is, in every way, unfair. In the past, after all, when men and women met, a stranger would not so much as approach a woman's blinds, and even fairly close acquaintances would be separated by blinds as well as a curtained screen. Even brother and sister would often be separated by a curtained screen, and she would not show her face openly. As a rule, a woman would be reluctant even to let a man hear her voice. Viewed in the light of these customs, present-day customs, as well as the customs of China are indecorous in the extreme. Likewise with the etiquette of the initiation of marital relations. In the past, it was the man who went daily to the home of the woman, whereas now we have adopted the Chinese custom, in which the woman goes to the home of the man. Strictly speaking, then, when the proper way was for the man to go, one may well wonder why the woman should now go first. If the tables could be turned and people of the past could observe the customs of the present day, they would probably describe them as indecent and improper."

Another question: "In the tale, at the mere mention of illness, they say, 'It's a malign spirit, a malign spirit,' and frantically offer prayers and incantations. Even in the case of a severe affliction, they rely entirely on monks and appear never to consult a physician or take medicine. Isn't this foolish?"

I answer: "This, too, is just the way things were in those days. It is a mistake, however, to assume that they did not take medicine in earlier times just because one finds no mention of medicine. From of old, there occur mentions of medicine in ancient texts, and illness is referred to as a 'medicinal matter' [*kusuri no koto*]. In 'Wakana' [15:98], [the old nun] is described as 'looking just as if you were a doctor [*kusushi*],' and in 'Yadorigi' [16:432] [Kaoru suggests to Nakanokimi that he might be allowed to] 'wait upon her as one of her doctors,' from which we know that both medicines and physicians were employed. Yet in writing they make no mention of physicians, but instead speak often of summoning wonder workers [*genza*]—because faith in the miracles of the gods and buddhas and reliance on the power of wonder workers rings touchingly frail and trusting, whereas calling a physician and taking medicine somehow seem pretentious, a bit distasteful, and not at all touching. Thus we see in *A Tale of Flowering Fortunes* that when Lord Higashi Sanjō no In [Fujiwara no Michinaga] was ill, they did not consult a physician.[119] Given the ways of times past, when anything and everything had to be elegant and lofty, it was only natural that such a man would not be permitted to approach a woman of high rank. Consider, for example, how the woman in 'Hahakigi' [12:163] who 'imbibes a potion of garlic' is deplored as being dreadfully repellent. This is why medicine is not called 'medicine,' but simply 'hot water.' In passages describing the ill, the mention of 'hot water' would seem in most cases to refer to medicine. But even though the word is the same, it must not have sounded so bad to refer to illness as a 'medicinal matter,' whereas to speak of 'taking medicine' would have sounded vulgar. Throughout this tale, there are countless cases in which great importance is attached to such fine distinctions. Thinking as we do in the present day, we may well wonder what could possibly be vulgar about the mention of taking medicine, but these are things that change with the times. For example, words like *kashiratsuki* [the look of a person's head] and *tsuratsuki* [the look of a person's face; countenance] are nowadays extremely vulgar words. In the past, however, they must not have been, for in tales they are often used when praising the looks of people of high station. Here again, one must realize that every successive age has its own ways. As always, a good knowledge of the ways of the age is a prerequisite to the reading of tales."

The usual question: "If this tale describes anything and everything that exists in this world, then it ought to describe in some detail the lives of people of the lower orders, but it describes only the upper classes and hardly mentions the lives of the humble. What is the significance of this?"

I answer: "Such is the world we live in that every age, every rank of persons, every region, every group is a world unto itself. In antiquity, there was the world of antiquity; in the present, the world of the present. Those of high rank have their world of the high. Humble people have their world of the humble. Warriors have their world of warriors, farmers their world of farmers, merchants their world of merchants; and the thoughts that normally occupy their minds are for the most part thoughts of their own individual worlds. Now tales, whatever they may be in the present day, in the past were not normally read by humble people of the lower classes. They were for the amusement of upper-class people, and thus they dealt mainly with goings-on in the world of the upper classes. This is simply because anything that does not directly concern us, that we do not constantly see and hear of, is unfamiliar to us, and our interest in it is slight. When you think how coarse a creature Tsukushi no Gen is and how rough and boorish Ukifune's stepfather Hitachi no Suke is, how could those of yet lower station possibly possess qualities attractive to the upper classes?[120] In 'Yūgao' [12:222], they speak of the 'unfeeling mountain folk,' and in 'Momiji no ga' [12:387], of the 'uncomprehending menials and their ilk.' In the 'Ongaku no maki' chapter of *A Tale of Flowering Fortunes*, in describing the construction of the Hōjōji, it says of the old moat digger who composed a poem, 'it was touching that such a creature should be so sensitive.'[121] In 'Suma' [13:205–6], Genji hears the fisherfolk lamenting the condition of their lives and looks on them with pity, thinking 'of their unintelligible chatter that "the vicissitudes of their feelings must be much the same as mine."' From such passages as these, we can see just how alien to them the lower orders were. Moreover, since the author Murasaki Shikibu herself was by no means a person of hopelessly humble station, the things she habitually saw, heard, and thought of would seem to be entirely of the upper classes and not at all of the lower."

If you would know something about those states of mind conducive to the composition of poetry, you should read this tale regularly and carefully. The matters described in this tale, the deeds and feelings of the people in it, are one and all the very stuff of poetry. Why do I say this? In the first place, it is said that human feelings [*hito no kokoro*] never change, whether past or present, high or low; yet they are not without slight differences among them, resulting from differences in the worlds that each and every individual inhabits, such as the customs of their age and their station in life. And likewise with poems: as works composed in response to the feelings that things arouse, by rights they too should never change, whether past or present, high or low. Yet, while such may well have been so in antiquity [*kamitsuyo*], poems from the Heian period [*naka-mukashi*] onward by no means describe only the feelings of the moment, exactly as they were felt. This being an art learned by emulating the poems of the past and composing after their manner, it is an art that cannot be practiced without knowing well the ways of the world of the past and the feelings and deeds of those who lived then. Still, in the process of learning from the past, we leave out of consideration the poems of the *Man'yōshū* and earlier, for their subject matter is unfamiliar and their style extremely antiquated. For the most part, therefore, we imitate [the poems] of the *Kokinshū* and later. Yet none of the poems of these successive ages was composed by hopelessly humble mountain folk. And so, emulating the poems of the past is not something one can do without knowing something about the feelings and deeds of people of middling court rank and above and of the world in which people of those ranks lived. In the present day, there is no better way to attain a detailed knowledge of these than to read this tale. And even with these old poems, if one reads only the poem itself, one still knows none of the details of the original feelings from which that poem arose, and thus there remain aspects of it too unfamiliar to imitate. Yet if one makes a practice of reading this tale night and day, it is just as if one could mingle with courtly people possessed of all the finest qualities—foremost among them Genji himself—observe with one's own eyes their manners and their appearance, and listen to their conversations, so that one grows familiar with all their activities and learns every detail of their innermost feelings. It is as if one could observe before one's very eyes, as in present reality, every conceivable courtly thing—that world above the clouds in times past, the round of ceremonies at court, and even the private goings-on in the houses of the highest nobility. In this way, you see, one acquires a thorough knowledge of the circumstances and feelings that originally gave rise to these poems by people of the past; one comes to know precisely that a poem of this particular sort arises from such-and-such a moment and that the writer's feelings on that occasion were of such-and-such a sort. It is for this reason I say that everything described in this tale, the deeds and feelings of the people in it, one and all, conduce to the composition of poetry.

Now if I might discuss in yet more detail this matter of composing present-day poems in imitation of those of the past: in the first place, this thing we call poetry originally was simply the act of expressing in words something felt in one's own heart, and not an imitation of thoughts and words expressed by someone else. Yet although this may well have been so in antiquity, since the Heian period this has not been the only way [the art was practiced]. Moreover, since all poetry is meant to reveal one's feelings, either to the gods or to other people, the desire to compose as well as one can is genuinely felt and not false affectation after the fact; but you will never be able to compose good poems if you do not learn to imitate the best poems of the past.

Now, in learning from the past, you will find many things that differ from the present day. Matters of little consequence in the present day were often taken very seriously in the past and were made the subject of a great many poems. And just as often, matters that present-day people make much of were never even mentioned in poems of the past. In such cases, we usually ignore present-day practice and concentrate on following the example of the past. In both the depth of their admiration for the moon and the blossoms and the intensity of the emotions that these feelings could arouse in them, people of the past far surpassed people of the present day. Present-day people do, in a general way, regard the blossoms as beautiful and the moon as affecting [*aware nari*], but not to the extent that it deeply permeates their feelings. In poetry, however, one must compose as if one were just as deeply touched as were people of the past. To describe the feelings of a present-day person just as they are would only be deficient in feeling [*aware asakarubeshi*]. After all, when people who never travel write travel poems and people who have never loved write love poems, are not they, too, simply imitating the past?

As in all things, of course, sometimes the poet's actual feelings, even those of a person of the past, were nowhere near as intense as those described in the poem, for in attempting to describe accurately something that is felt poignantly, there is a natural urge to exaggerate the truth. As [Genji] says ["Hotaru," 14:204], "Should one decide to describe someone favorably, one may select every good quality imaginable." Poetry, too, is an art that describes deep emotions [*mna o fukaku iite*] and attempts to move deeply those who read and those who hear it. Thus even if poems of the past do exaggerate the truth, this is nothing to quibble about. Simply learn from the feelings they express and the situations that gave rise to them.

So then, if regularly you read this tale and transport your mind to the world of the people in the tale, then when you compose poetry, your feelings will naturally be imbued with the courtliness of the past and will far surpass the feelings of people in this mundane world, and your experience of viewing the same moon and blossoms will be infinitely more deeply moving. Be that as it may, people of recent times, even though they may study the poems of the past, know nothing of the world of the ancients and are unfamiliar with their feelings; they simply write whatever occurs to their modern minds, and thus, in most cases, end up producing something quite crude and unlike anything of the past. Nor is this true only of poems. In reading the introductory notes [*kotobagaki*] in the old anthologies, a person who is unfamiliar with this tale, since he has no precise knowledge of that world, will feel himself to be in terra incognita and will find many passages incomprehensible. Yet when one reads this tale with care and becomes familiar with the way things were in the world of the past, then not only the old poems but also the introductory notes, which one reads off in only a line or two, will come to feel intimately familiar, like something one sees or hears in the world of the present day, in one's own native village. Then, of course, their emotional quality [*mna*] will be that much greater. As I have said again and again, the person who composes poetry, as well as the person who harbors a yearning for the courtly world of the past, should make a particular point of reading this tale with great care.

TRANSLATED BY T. HARPER

FROM BLOSSOMS TO MOONLIGHT, 1818
(*Kagetsu zōshi*)

MATSUDAIRA SADANOBU

Matsudaira Sadanobu (1758–1829) is a name associated principally with the political history of Japan. Born a grandson of the eighth shogun, Tokugawa Yoshimune (1684–1751; r. 1716–1745), he was at one time himself a potential candidate for the office of shogun, but was thwarted in that ambition through the machinations of his archenemy, Tanuma Okitsugu (1719–1788). Subsequently, however, as lord of the northern domain of Shirakawa, presiding officer of the shogun's Council of Elders, and author of the Kansei Reforms, Sadanobu earned a distinguished reputation as a statesman of great intellect and high integrity. After resigning from the Council of Elders in 1793, he devoted much of his time to artistic and literary pursuits, in the course of which he copied the entire *Tale of Genji* seven times in his own hand.[122] Not surprisingly, Sadanobu's reading of *Genji* is profoundly political, but the acuteness of observation and depth of knowledge that he displays in these two short excerpts from his miscellany, *From Blossoms to Moonlight*,[123] make it seem only the more unfortunate that he wrote no more about *Genji*. Sadanobu's last paragraph, in particular, is a salutary reminder that beneath the emotional sensitivity and aesthetic sensibility, which Norinaga so rightly focuses upon, there is also a strong current of ruthless political ambition that runs throughout the tale.

T. HARPER

The Profundity of The Tale of Genji

Of the many meticulously crafted episodes in *The Tale of Genji*, some are particularly impressive. One of these is Genji's sojourn in Suma. This is an event of major importance in his life, but its origins trace back to the "Hana no en" chapter. How mysterious are the workings of the human mind! Just as one is wondering, "How can he possibly not realize what he is doing?" —Ah, she tells us: "There seemed to be hardly anyone around. The inner door, too, was open and there were no sounds of people. 'This is just the way one gets into trouble,' he thought as he stepped up and peered inside."[124] *This*, I must say, is magnificent writing.

A Critique of The Tale of Genji

In *The Tale of Genji*, Genji is first attracted to the Usugumo Empress [Fujitsubo] when he hears that she resembles his mother, and thus from an early age begins to feel an indefinable fondness for her. The way this is drawn is simply superb.

And then there is the way that his indiscretion, committed that night of the Cherry Blossom Festival while tipsy from saké, leads ultimately to his fall from power. At first, all heaven and earth tremble before his might, but by the time we reach "Sakaki," he is in decline. Everything he does goes wrong and only hastens his downfall. And this, too, is set down in a manner that makes it all seem inevitable. Even as he departs for Suma, he still speaks as if he were blameless and behaves as if he were somehow wronged; but the punishing wind and waves of that shore make it clear that the heavens are unforgiving. He is distracted momentarily when messengers bring news of torrential rains in the capital, but then lightning strikes his kitchens. It is quite ingenious the way he is made to see that this [the wrath of the heavens] is directed solely at Suma.[125]

And again, when Genji returns [to the capital] once more, and we reach "Eawase," she [Murasaki] relates how he flaunts his power as Ministers of State vie with one another for supremacy. Subsequently, he rises to the very highest rank, and we think, "What misfortune could possibly befall him now?" Then comes the business of his guardianship of the Third Princess, and he ends up failing to achieve perfection. This I find particularly impressive.

The spirit that attacks the Third Princess might better have been identified as the living spirit of Kashiwagi, but since people were unaware of this affair, the author does not name him but shows how, because memories of the Rokujō lady remain, people think "ah yes" and take this to be her.[126] This is simply superb.

At a time when the Fujiwara were at the peak of their power, she describes, fearlessly, the contempt with which the mighty treat the Emperor. Genji, a Minamoto, is made a Minister of State; he quells his Fujiwara opponents; Yūgiri is enrolled in the Academy; and in depicting these events, the author suggests that she herself thinks that such is as all things ought to be. This is highly admirable.

It is truly an incomparable tale. Every time I read it, I am struck by the author's profundity. Yet although she is well versed in the Way of the Buddha, she knows little of the True Way [Confucianism]; and in her ignorance of the Way, she errs in her depiction of the scene in which the Reizei Emperor first learns that he is the son of the Shining Genji.[127] This one episode, it seems to me, is dangerous, for if women and children should read it, it might well lead them astray. That Usugumo [Fujitsubo] and Oborozukiyo violate the Way of Humanity should be obvious even to children; I cannot imagine that [these episodes] would mislead anyone. It is superb, too, the way that the author, who treats all matters relating to the Buddha with the utmost awe and respect, nonetheless mentions no fewer than three times the gratuitous tattling of the monk on night duty.

Motoori's thesis is interesting—that this tale is but an exposition of the varieties of human feeling and is not meant to exemplify any philosophical principle. But there can be no doubt that here and there she writes with some more particular purpose in mind.

TRANSLATED BY T. HARPER

A CRITICAL APPRAISAL OF GENJI, 1854–1861
(*Genji monogatari hyōshaku*)

HAGIWARA HIROMICHI

In 1845, Hagiwara Hiromichi (1815–1863) resigned his position as a low-ranking samurai in the service of the Ikeda daimyo house and moved from Okayama to Osaka to devote his full attention to the study of literature. After establishing himself as a poet and critic, he next embarked upon an extremely ambitious project. He would compile a new treatise and commentary on *The Tale of Genji*, to be published in combination with a revised text of all fifty-four chapters of the tale. In 1854, Hiromichi published the first installment of *A Critical Appraisal of Genji* (*Genji monogatari hyōshaku*), which includes an overview of previous *Genji* scholarship and a comprehensive analysis of the tale, followed by the text and detailed commentary on the first four chapters.[128] Soon thereafter, palsy affecting the right side of Hiromachi's body became so severe that he was forced to write with his left hand. An acquaintance wrote about this period that despite the obstacles of ill health and financial difficulty, Hiromichi continued to work on his magnum opus "with the devotion of a Buddhist ascetic."[129] By 1861, he had managed to publish the second installment of *A Critical Appraisal*, covering up to the eighth chapter of *Genji*. Two years later, aged forty-nine, he died, leaving his revisions to the text and his commentary on the rest of the tale incomplete.

Clearly, it was Hiromichi's aim to build on the success of Kitamura Kigin's *Kogetsushō*. In doing so, he not only emulates the format of commentary and analysis combined with a complete text of *Genji*, but also provides an even greater array of interpretive aids than Kigin did, including commentary gleaned both from the distant past and from the "New Commentaries" by Keichū, Mabuchi, and Norinaga, as well as interlinear notations to indicate structural breaks, shifts in narrative voice, syntactic flow, and even the widely separated components of *kakari-musubi* constructions.

Hiromichi's primary emphasis on literary style and internal textual evidence, however, reveals a profound analytical shift that sets his work apart from Kigin's hugely successful edition of *Genji*. Hiromichi avoids reproducing annotation that is contradictory or extraneous to a thoroughly literary reading of the text. In particular, he mediates long-standing ideological disputes by integrating interpretive theory from both national studies (*kokugaku*) and Confucian studies in an attempt to resolve issues of interpretation rather than perpetuate ideological dispute. Concerning the question of Murasaki Shikibu's intentions in writing *Genji*, he cites both Tameakira and Norinaga, but rather than take the side of either, he notes that both made positive contributions to the debate. The result is a complex and completely constructive critical analysis that transcends many of the limitations of previous scholarship.

Hiromichi brought a wide-ranging knowledge of literary styles and genres to the task of compiling *A Critical Appraisal of Genji*. In his own day, he was best known as a poet and judge of poetic composition. After Takizawa Bakin's death in 1848, Hiromichi was commissioned to produce a conclusion to Bakin's unfinished but highly successful novel, *Daring Adventures of Chivalrous Men* (*Kaikan kyōki kyōkakuden*, 1832–1835). Typically, so that he could compose a conclusion faithful to the original, Hiromichi undertook a detailed study of the vernacular prose fiction in Chinese that had inspired Bakin's novel. This study was also to form the basis of one of the most innovative aspects of *A Critical Appraisal*.

In a section of his comprehensive analysis, "Principles of Composition," Hiromichi develops what might be called a "rhetoric of fiction," designed to help the reader distinguish the universal constants of literary composition at all levels of *Genji* and thus better appreciate both the beauties of the text and the consummate skill of its creator. In arguing the benefits of such an interpretive strategy, Hiromichi cites both Tameakira's and Mabuchi's earlier resort to Chinese concepts and techniques. Hiromichi, however, had access to the more sophisticated scholarship of Jin Shengtan (1608–1661), and his own experience as the writer chosen to complete Bakin's unfinished novel had made him a master of this newer mode of textual analysis. This enabled Hiromichi to provide a map to guide readers in exploring and comprehending the complexities of Murasaki's narrative, rather than reduce the entire *Genji* to a single meaning, as so many earlier commentators had done.

Hiromichi rightly anticipated that the application of his eclectic interests in Chinese vernacular fiction and Confucian studies to the interpretation of *Genji* would invite the criticism of scholars dedicated to promoting the superiority of Japanese literature. In his introductory remarks, he moves to deflect such attacks by emphasizing the superior sophistication of the tale's elegant prose over that of its Chinese antecedents. He also confronts the issue head-on by informing readers that "zealous scholars of our country [*kokugakusha*] are apt to be displeased that I even suggest that *Genji* is in some way similar to Chinese literature. There are those who would accuse me of a crime for saying as much, but I must emphasize that this is simply a working theory." Hiromichi's confidence in the persuasive power of this generous, all-embracing approach seems to have been misplaced, as scholarship for many decades thereafter favored Motoori Norinaga's ideologically driven treatise, *Tama no ogushi*, over Hiromichi's more systematic and comprehensive literary analysis.

A Critical Appraisal of Genji was widely reprinted immediately after its first publication in the mid-nineteenth century. However, with the opening of Japan to Western influence only a few years later, this attempt by an Edo-period scholar to promote a classical text received only sporadic scholarly attention in the Meiji and Taishō periods. Studies of the history of *Genji* commentary may go so far as to describe *A Critical Appraisal* as a work of finely detailed analysis and innovative interpretive theory, but they fail to delineate Hiromichi's accomplishments other than in such generalities.[130] Not until the 1980s, when Noguchi Takehiko published his laudatory reappraisal of *Genji monogatari hyōshaku*, was Hiromichi's accomplishment given its due by modern scholarship.[131] Nonetheless, the 1909 Kokugakuin edition of *Hyōshaku* remains the most recent recension of his work. Yet despite these years of unwarranted neglect, Hiromichi has left an indelible mark on the way we talk about *Genji* commentary, for it was he who first distinguished between pre- and post-*Kogetsushō* commentaries, calling the former *kyūchū* (Old Commentaries) and the latter *shinchū* (New Commentaries).

PATRICK CADDEAU

Principles of Composition

Praise for this tale requires no exaggeration on my part. The more one reads *Genji*, the more difficult it becomes to express how exceptional it is. I believe that this tale was not written in an ordinary manner, but that it was thought out and composed with various "principles of composition" in mind from the very beginning. I have yet to find anything in Japanese literature that I could say corresponds exactly to these "principles of composition." Where these principles might originate, I cannot say, but they do speak of "principles of composition" in the literature of China, and these, for the most part, are not so different from those in *Genji*. So, initially, might we say that these principles are based on Chinese models? The practice of identifying "principles of composition" in Chinese literature dates from a much later period, however, than the composition of *Genji*. No one is going to maintain that what we find in *Genji* can be attributed to Chinese techniques alone. But then, even in China the first people to write things down did not discuss such principles. Rather, later generations saw the remarkable qualities of those early works and attached provisional names to the more noteworthy passages so they might learn from the way they had been composed. "Principles of Composition" evolved from this process. The identification of particular principles was simply a means to an end. Texts of ancient times were not originally composed with these principles in mind; rather, passages were labeled as such at a later date to facilitate their appreciation and interpretation. These principles make it possible to specify the remarkable qualities of a text. To claim that such principles exist is not mere conjecture.

The author of the *Genji* did not deliberately apply these principles of composition to her writing. She was an extraordinarily learned woman and had read widely in Chinese texts, and thus could not have failed to absorb these principles, indeed from early on. Nor can it be said that Sima Qian's [b. 145 B.C.E.] *Records of the Historian* [*Shiji*; J. *Shiki*] also contains such principles of composition. However, *Genji* and *Records of the Historian* are vastly different in both language and content, so I do not assert that the author of this tale modeled her story on the *Records of the Historian.*

While I say that we cannot assume Murasaki Shikibu emulated the work of Sima Qian, zealous scholars of our country [*kokugakusha*] are apt to be displeased that I even suggest that *Genji* is similar in any way to Chinese literature. There are those who would accuse me of a crime for saying as much, but I must emphasize that this is simply a working theory. In ancient times, as everyone knows, there was no written language of our land, so classical Chinese was used to record everything except only sacred Shintō prayers [*norito*] and certain imperial decrees [*semmyō*]. Elegant prose [*bunshō*] written in Japanese appeared for the first time with the composition of *Genji*. Tales before *Genji* told stories merely by stringing together words. More precisely, they were not worthy of being called elegant prose. *Genji* marks the birth of elegant prose written in Japanese.

Originally, *bunshō* corresponded to what was called "elegant words" [*aya kotoba*], indicating a technique by which the material being recorded was embellished so as to cause the reader to experience an exceptional sense of satisfaction. This is different from writing in which things are expressed just as they would be in conversation. The character *bun* in *bunshō* means to have a sense of beauty or design. The character *shō* means to possess elegance. One should keep this in mind.

Our country has never followed the Chinese practice of attaching exaggerated names of this sort to language. However, the sacred prayers and imperial decrees composed in Japanese that I mentioned earlier do contain elegantly composed expressions with a unique vitality. They are unlike the words we utter in conversation. It is said that excessive adornment of language is not a good thing, but if a sentence isn't constructed with care and lacks the quality to move the reader, it cannot be called elegant prose. Although the term "elegant prose" is borrowed from the Chinese, a similar concept has always existed in Japan. Sacred prayers and imperial decrees have such qualities. The elegant prose found in *Genji* probably is not a direct imitation of *Records of the Historian*, but we can say that it was written by someone who had read such elegant prose, and in trying to write an interesting story, she would naturally have been influenced by it.

When one compares *Records of the Historian* and *Genji*, one discovers great differences in subject and style, so it is clearly a mistake to say that *Genji* was written in imitation of *Records of the Historian*. But who would deny that *Genji* is the first work written in Japanese worthy of being called elegant prose? In any case, when one sets out to evaluate the prose in *Genji* and to describe its wonders, one naturally assigns names to those principles, for if one does not name those wonders, by what other means is one to describe them? It would be a simple matter, of course, to create a whole new terminology; but since the Chinese terms have already been transmitted to Japan, even if one does change the wording, who could say we have nothing to learn from them? And so, rather than dwell on pointless matters that lead only to misunderstanding, I have simply appropriated those principles, as delineated in recent Chinese treatises, that can help one interpret the text. Dear reader, please keep this in mind and do not hold it against me.

I am not the first person to suggest that such principles of composition can be found in *Genji*. Andō Tameakira noticed it early on and made the following remarks in his *Shika shichiron*:

> The work as a whole has that air of gentility possessed by those of wealth and rank and is written in the refined language of the court.

And yet throughout it we encounter those who have taken Buddhist vows and retreated to mountain temples, and we are shown the marketplace and the countryside as well as poverty and sorrow. Every chapter depicts the myriad emotions of women. Such is the portrayal of human feeling and the description of scenery that we feel as if we are face to face with that very person and as if we were visiting that very place.

In overall form, the tale constitutes a Narrative [伝], and thus, naturally, an Introductory style [序], a Conclusive [跋], a Descriptive [記], an Analytical [論], [and] an Epistolary [書] style; one can find in *Genji* these various different styles. In particular, the Ranking of Women scene in "Hahakigi" is uncannily well done. In the past, when I was examining the several divisions of this passage, [I found that] it employs a number of Chinese narrative devices. Following an Introduction, there is Refutation [論破], Acquiescence [論承], Discussion of Essentials [論腹], [and] Discussion of Tangentials [論尾]. It moves from the coarse to the detailed and ranges from the mundane to the refined; from the complex it reverts to the simple, with "great changes and sudden obstacles" [波瀾頓挫] and "[retroactive] reflection and foreshadowings" [照応伏案].[132] The flow of the text is measured and magnanimous, its force smooth and tactful. These qualities are found not only in the Ranking of Women passage but also throughout the entire text. It is similar to *Records of the Historian*, the *Zhuangzi*, and works by Han Yu [768–824], Liu Congyuan [773–819], Ou Yangxiu [1007–1070], and Su Shi [1037–1101]. For something written by a woman, it is extraordinary and wondrous; Shikibu must truly be deemed a brilliant woman, without peer, past or present.

It has long been the custom to speak of Murasaki and Sei Shōnagon as two of a kind. But Sei Shōnagon's talent is so narrow and slight, and her intellectual pretensions so obvious, that her work is often distasteful. These two women can hardly even be compared. [Hiromichi notes that these comments are from Tameakira's introduction to the "Rainy Night Ranking."]

Kamo no Mabuchi also interpreted *Genji* based on such teachings in his *Genji monogatari shinshaku*. As with Tameakira, I believe Mabuchi tried to write an interpretation based on certain "principles of composition." I will now quote from passages in his interpretation in which he attempts to explain his application of that technique:

To explain the meaning of "elegant prose," one needs to consider the following terms: To bring up in advance things that are not yet finished is called "foreshadowing." There is a slight difference between the two terms used for "foreshadowing" [*chōhon* and *fukuan*], but in general they mean the same thing. There are also cases where an event that happens early on in the story and a later event correspond to each other. This is called "retroactive reflection" [*shōō*]. In some instances, things are suddenly cut off in the telling of the story. And then, quite apart from those instances in which two characters address each other, there are those in which the author intervenes to criticize events in the story. This is called "authorial speech" [*kisha no go*]. [Hiromichi notes that in common terminology, this is called "authorial intrusion" (*sōshiji*).] There are also passages in which it isn't clear who is being addressed. In my comments I note who is being addressed in such passages, indicating Genji or Murasaki, for example. I mark where to end sentences with a period to the side of the text and where to break sentences in the middle with commas. The comma mark [*tō*] indicates a phrase. I indicate the division between distinct portions of text with a small square. To distinguish breaks of greater significance, I add an L-shaped box. By "breaks of greater significance," I mean the conclusion of a larger event in the story. Although there is no precedent for this practice in Japanese texts, I've done it here simply to make it easier to understand the tale. There are other techniques that I have employed, but you should be able to understand them as they appear in the main text, so I will limit myself to these representative examples. For the most part, these are things that differ from the practice of recent commentaries; the reader should pay close attention to them.

This partially covers what Mabuchi wrote on the subject. In Norinaga's *Tama no ogushi* as well, it says that in reading *Genji*, "one must examine the details of the text in depth [Hiromichi's gloss for the term *shaku* (commentary)] and savor the author's scrupulous care in the construction of the tale" [Hiromichi's gloss for the term *hyō* (criticism)]. I took Norinaga's oft-stated principle regarding criticism and commentary [*hyō* and *shaku*] and embraced it fully. Having pored over the text with this in mind, I have discovered things I never expected to find. I noted with surprise the great importance of these principles of composition [*nori*] found in the text. I added to the principles first applied by Mabuchi and put together this commentary that I call a "critical appraisal" [*hyōshaku*].

Let me then describe these principles of composition. Some principles apply to the entire tale, and others concern individual chapters. Some apply to a specific section or scene in the text, and others are relevant only to a particular passage or phrase. Even minute details can be governed by principles of composition.

An example of the type of compositional principle that applies to the tale as a whole would be the pattern that emerges to form the overall design of the narrative through the lengthwise threads of the passage of time and the crosswise threads of events in the lives of the characters. These two elements intersect and overlap to form the grand design of the tale. In terms of the passage of generations and the times, as I mentioned briefly before, we have the passage of imperial reigns from the Kiritsubo Emperor to the Suzaku Emperor to the Reizei Emperor and on to the present Emperor in the tale. Within this pattern, there are always spans of time that remain blank. This type of ellipsis is a principle of the tale. The approximately fifty years of Genji's life from the time of his birth are described in the fifty-four chapters of the tale. The correspondence between divisions in the rise and fall of Genji's fortunes and the passage of imperial reigns just mentioned is a principle of composition. The passage of time in the tale is such that the lives of various characters can generally be compared and their relative ages calculated. This, too, is a principle of composition. In the Uji chapters, one can determine Niou's age based on what one knows about Kaoru's age. This also is a principle of composition. The narrative strands intertwined with the base threads of the passage of time are embellished in ways that add to the design of the story, again following certain principles of composition.

The main character of the tale, Genji, is referred to as the Shining Genji [Hikaru Genji], and his counterpart, Lady Fujitsubo, is called Her Radiant Highness [Kagayaku hi no Miya]. This establishes these two, one shining and one radiant, as corresponding characters in the story. However, Murasaki, Fujitsubo's niece, is introduced because the relationship between Genji and Fujitsubo is based on a secret incident. Murasaki thus serves as a substitute for Fujitsubo. This is why Murasaki always appears with Genji but Fujitsubo does not. This is a brilliant pairing. Establishing a connection between the shining one and the radiant one in this way is ingenious. It is probably the finest example of the deliberately composed quality of the tale.

In the later chapters, the names of the characters Kaoru [the Fragrant Commandant] and Niou [His Perfumed Highness] convey physical beauty, indicating that they are vestiges [*nagori*] of Genji's enduring presence in the tale. Kaoru and Niou complement each other as principal and supporting characters [*seifuku*]. In combination they appear as Genji's shadow in the tale, thus serving as a pair corresponding with him. Similarly, Tō no Chūjō serves as a foil to Genji, and this type of relationship, too, is that of principal and supporting characters [*seifuku*], as is that of the Minister of the Right [Udaijin] and the Kokiden Empress Mother as they relate to Genji. Genji's family, associated with the Minister of the Left [Sadaijin], has strained relations with the family of the Minister of the Right. This animus between left and right works as a seed [*kusawai*] of the tale's plot. This relationship between left and right is also one of oppositional pairs [*shukaku/hantai*].

Lady Murasaki is described as the story's most attractive central female character. Conversely, Suetsumuhana is somewhat backward and not good looking. Their contrasting colors of purple, for Murasaki, and red, for Suetsumuhana, set them apart as well. Together they illustrate the compositional principle of oppositional pairs.

Individuals in the tale are distinctively portrayed without stock characterizations. Among them the description of Lady Rokujō is particularly noteworthy. The narrative of the "Yūgao" chapter begins when "Genji had been secretly visiting the Sixth Ward [Rokujō]. . . ." This description of his going to visit the woman in the Sixth Ward [Lady Rokujō] leads the reader to imagine that there must be some connection with the subsequent scene in which an apparition [*henge*] appears, [causing Yūgao's death], but it is impossible to specify what that connection might be. Much later, in the "Aoi" chapter, we learn for the first time that this apparition [responsible for both Yūgao's and Aoi's deaths] is the widow of the former Crown Prince, Lady Rokujō, who now resides in the Sixth Ward. This description is completely unexpected and provides a most delightful narrative flourish. It is an excellent example of the compositional principle known as "foreshadowing" [*fukusen*]. Another example of foreshadowing is the reference to Asagao in the "Hahakigi" chapter. As with the foreshadowing of Lady Rokujō, Asagao is mentioned only briefly in passing, when the maids at the home of Utsusemi discuss Genji's reputation. Additional details are gradually revealed. In the case of Lady Rokujō, we learn that she is accompanying her daughter, who is to become the High Priestess of the Ise Shrine. Asagao herself, however, is the one who becomes the High Priestess of the Kamo Shrine. In both cases, the foreshadowing is implemented in a way that connects these characters with two opposing but affiliated shrines. Furthermore, in the "Aoi" chapter, the shrines of Kamo and Ise continue to be relevant. Lady Aoi is the victim of Rokujō's jealous spirit because she was in attendance at the Kamo Shrine carriage fracas [*kuruma arasoi*] in which Rokujō's dignity was offended. This fracas arouses Lady Rokujō's angry spirit, causing Lady Aoi's death. Genji's aversion to Rokujō stems from this, and she, feeling rejected, ends up retreating to the Ise Shrine in the "Sakaki" chapter. Thus the locations of Ise and Kamo as well as the events of the "Aoi" and "Sakaki" chapters, correspond to each other.

I also believe it is possible to see the author's careful design in the case of the illicit affair between Genji and Fujitsubo, which she depicts despite the extreme delicacy of the incident. It is due to these events that Genji is accorded the rank of Honorary Retired Emperor [Daijō Tennō] and is described as attaining glory unsurpassed in this world. As a result of Genji's earlier indiscretion in the story, the Third Princess, Genji's wife in later chapters, is unfaithful to him and has an affair with Kashiwagi. Her betrayal exemplifies both the compositional principle of analogous events [*shōtai*] and the principle of retribution [*hōō/mukui*] for Genji's actions earlier in the tale. The Prelate on night duty, therefore, intimates to the Reizei Emperor that he is the child of Genji and Fujitsubo's illicit relationship. And likewise, the lady-in-waiting known as Ben no Omoto informs Kaoru that he was conceived as a result of the Third Princess's betrayal of Genji. The way that the corresponding relationship between these two events is revealed is evidence of this tale's meticulous composition. Kashiwagi is deeply troubled by the illicit affair and eventually dies as a consequence. After his death, Kashiwagi's wife, Princess Ochiba, has an affair with Yūgiri [Genji's son by his first wife], and Kōbai, descended from Tō no Chūjō, is appointed Minister of the Right. All these events are vestiges of the retribution following from Genji's actions.

Other examples of the tale's deliberate composition include Yūgao and Ukifune, who correspond to each other [*shōtai*] in that neither had anyone on whom she could rely. The "certain estate" [*nanigashi no in*] where Yūgao is taken by Genji and the house at Uji where Ukifune is hidden by Kaoru are parallel settings. On the one hand, Yūgao is caught between two characters: Genji and Tō no Chūjō. On the other, Ukifune is caught between Kaoru and Niou. In terms of timing, Yūgao is taken by Genji from Gojō on the fifteenth night of the Eighth Month [which is inauspicious according to the lunar calendar], while Ukifune is taken by Kaoru from the house in Sanjō on the evening of the thirteenth day of the Ninth Month [also inauspicious]. In both cases, the women are taken by carriage. These details are a clear indication that they are structurally parallel. And then one of them is fatally possessed by a malign spirit [*henge*], and the other is abducted by a tree spirit [*kodama*], making them parallel characters on this account as well. By employing the same narrative technique, the author implies that an unsavory fate awaits women without firm moral fiber. Tamakazura [daughter of Yūgao and Tō no Chūjō] inherits Yūgao's disposition and also serves as a character corresponding to Ukifune. Tamakazura is from the west and Ukifune is from the east; the two men who pursue them are parallel characters; and the locations to which they retreat, the temple in Hatsuse and the hermitage in Ono, can also be seen as structurally parallel.

Another example is Genji's move to Suma, which serves to depict his brief fall from power. Genji's exile is foreshadowed early on in the "Wakamurasaki" chapter, when at Kitayama, Yoshikiyo is made to mention the Akashi lady in preparation for writing the "Suma" and "Akashi" chapters further on. Seeing how the author had foreshadowed these events in the earlier "Wakamurasaki" chapter, one cannot help but laugh at how foolish the old theory must be that Murasaki Shikibu began the tale by composing the "Suma" and "Akashi" chapters at Ishiyamadera. And in the "Hana no en" chapter, Genji reaches the peak of his youthful rise to power during the reign of the Kiritsubo Emperor. Under the misty moon and the radiant cherry blossoms of spring, Genji begins an illicit affair with the Oborozukiyo Chief Palace Attendant. There [in Suma], the Akashi Novice comes to fetch him and cares for him most graciously. In the third year of his exile, Genji returns to the capital under the autumn moon and presents himself at the palace under the full moon of the fifteenth night of the Eighth Month. Readers are thus made to realize that this incident, which begins with the flowers of spring and reaches its conclusion with the moon of autumn, portrays the inevitability of Genji's rise and fall by employing the compositional principle of symmetry between cause and effect [*shubi sōō*].[133]

Other examples include the lascivious old woman Gen no Naishi and that rather coarse chatterbox the lady from Ōmi, who stand in contrast with the daughter of the professor whose academic pretensions reflect those of the Confucian scholars in the Academy. Even these comic scenes are informed by the principles of composition. Specific examples are addressed in the commentary as they appear in the main text of the tale, so I will mention only a few of the principal instances here.

An outstanding example of compositional principles is the "Kumogakure" chapter, of which only the chapter title appears and the text of the chapter is omitted. There is no other example of such a rare and wonderful technique being put to use in all of Japanese or Chinese literature, past or present. This is a most remarkable example of the principle of ellipsis [*shōhitsu*]. Nonetheless, several earlier commentaries cite totally irrelevant Buddhist doctrine to support their groundless theories, which unfortunately contribute nothing whatever that would explain the "Kumogakure" chapter. Those who cobbled together a worthless chapter of their own in place of the missing "Kumogakure" show even less understanding of the author's intentions than a single drop of water in the ocean, which I find quite painful to endure.

The tale begins in the "Kiritsubo" chapter with the Emperor lamenting the death of Kiritsubo, following which he composes a poem alluding to the legend of Yang Gueifei:

tazuneyuku maboroshi mogana tsute nite mo / tama no arika o soko to shirubeku
Would that there were a wizard to go and seek her out that I might know,
if only by report, the place where her spirit resides. [12:111]

Genji's rise to prominence ensues and continues until the death of Murasaki in the "Minori" chapter. Her death marks the passing of a main character in the tale and prepares the reader for the moment when Genji himself will be "Hidden in Cloud" [Kumogakure]. The following chapter, "Maboroshi," spans an entire year, during which Genji's anguished recollections are poignantly depicted in terms of the changing seasons, from the First Month to the Twelfth, suggesting that Genji himself will soon die. In the course of this, Genji sees the wild geese flying through the clouds and composes a poem

ōzora o kayou maboroshi yume ni dani / miekonu tama no yukue tazuneyo
O wizard, you who course the heavens, pray find where she has gone,
whose spirit never appears to me, even in my dreams. [15:531]

In giving the title "Maboroshi" to this chapter, she brings to a close the story begun in "Kiritsubo."

Even if this theory is not correct, the author's construction of this sequence of events leaves no doubt that she had no intention of depicting Genji's death. At the end of the "Maboroshi" chapter, Genji recites a poem:

> *mono omou to suguru tsukihi mo shiranu ma ni / toshi mo waga yo mo kyō ya tsukinuru*
>
> In my sorrow I've lost count of the passing days and months. Can it be that today is the end of the year and my own life, too? [15:536]

indicating that this is his parting poem and that he soon will be "Hidden in Cloud."

The "Kumogakure" chapter marks the passage of some years, after which the "Niou Miya" chapter begins, "His radiance was gone, and none among his progeny could compare . . . ," succinctly explaining the connection of Genji to his offspring. This is an inexpressibly wonderful passage, the likes of which cannot be found anywhere else. In all the fictional tales of the world, whether in Japan or China or elsewhere, the main character achieves unlimited fortune and success and there the story ends. Such a pattern is quite artless and contrived, yet it is what one usually finds in tales.

In the case of *Genji*, however, the pinnacle of Genji's fortunes is described in the "Fuji no uraba" chapter, and thereafter follows a description of the inevitable consequences of his earlier actions. Yet because the ending is concealed or omitted, it doesn't seem at all contrived. It seems to be something that really happened, which is indescribably wonderful. And again, as the older commentaries say, if a description of Genji's death were included, it would be extremely overwrought to describe all the grief of all the other characters at Genji's passing, and so such a scene was omitted. The "Maboroshi" chapter depicts Genji's grief at Murasaki's death. This is a wonderful use of a principle of composition. Dear reader, please take this into consideration and savor the great depth of the tale.

The end of the last chapter, "Yume no ukihashi," when the narrative abruptly ends, is also indescribably wonderful. The Uji chapters begin with the tale of Kaoru and Niou followed by the "Hashihime" chapter and then the story of the Eighth Prince. The narrative here is somewhat different from the earlier chapters describing Genji's life. It is extremely subdued and moving. Inescapably human feelings are described with passion and extreme skill in these chapters. There is the case of the Eighth Prince, who has grown weary of society and removes himself to Uji. This is followed by the death of his wife, leaving his daughters without a guardian. As a result, he cares for them, and his appreciation for the Way of the Buddha deepens. And then there is the case of Kaoru, who learns the unhappy fate of his father, Kashiwagi, grows weary of his place in society, and ends up becoming deeply involved in the Way of Buddhism. He travels to Uji on the pretext of devoting himself to the Way of the Buddha. We also have the story of the Prince's eldest daughter, Ōigimi, who somehow tries to make her sister Nakanokimi happy and, in doing so, forsakes her own happiness. All these are very sad cases that are very moving. Reading these stories makes one's eyes brim with tears. . . .

In general, Genji's character is described as tending to be somewhat self-centered, but he [nonetheless] is very sensitive to the feelings of others, a figure both captivating and substantial. He is the mainstay of this tale, and his progeny are depicted as two vestiges of his character. Kaoru is depicted as more serious and sensitive than Genji, while Niou is more frivolous and sensual. The characters' names—Shining Genji, Fragrant Kaoru, and Perfumed Niou—all indicate something different about their characters. The author entered deeply into the minds of the characters and wrote from their perspectives, and because of this, her description is rare and indescribably wonderful.

At the end of the tale, Ukifune becomes a nun and secludes herself in Ono. Kaoru hears of this and uses the son of Hitachi no Suke, Kogimi, as his messenger and sends him to Ono. Ukifune, being a nun and feeling humiliated, cannot bring herself to meet him. Kogimi, unable to deliver his message from Kaoru, returns to Kaoru, whereupon Kaoru considers several possible outcomes, and there the tale ends. The narrative expertise of this episode would dazzle even a demon. Precisely because of this, *Genji* is something that one simply cannot forget, even after reading the whole thing. There are so many things that remain to ponder and appreciate even after one finishes reading. One can read it over and over again and never tire of it. There is no limit to the fascination one finds in this tale. It is no wonder that the person who wrote and appended "Dew upon the Mountain Path" [Yamaji no tsuyu] should have felt dissatisfied and wished to know more, but it betrays a lack of comprehension of the author's wisdom to have added this chapter.

The author has used the technique of omitting details, but not because it would have been troublesome to have written them. Instead, she has consciously omitted passages because she felt they were best left out. The text of this tale is very detailed and complete. To put it more simply, it is written in a way that allows the reader to scratch in all the places that itch. While the tale is quite long, the ending is succinct, and the omission of further detail is surprisingly resolute. The way the "Kumogakure" and "Yume no ukihashi" chapters end is unique even among the abundant works from China. From the beginning, the story is crafted with care and in great detail, and its being cut off in the middle in this way may seem perplexing. As I mentioned previously, however, the tale includes a description of Genji's ascent to the height of his fortunes, and the "Kumogakure" chapter marks the conclusion of his life. The Uji chapters then mark Genji's absence from the tale, providing a complete description of the lives of his progeny, so there is no reason to feel the story lacks a conclusion. It goes without saying that a text this sublimely evocative [*yojō no kagiri naki*] is without precedent. . . .

Among the many aspects of narrative excellence in this tale, five noteworthy points tend to go unnoticed by less experienced readers. Two of these have been mentioned earlier. One is that the "Kumogakure" chapter is not missing but, rather, was omitted by design, and the other is that the "Yume no ukihashi" chapter is perfect as it is. The remaining three points are as follows:

1. Many characters lack a fixed name, and so readers often don't appreciate that there is no confusion among them whatever.
2. Readers often fail to realize that Lady Rokujō is implicated in the death of Yūgao because although the text in the "Yūgao" chapter indicates that Genji is visiting the Sixth Ward [Rokujō], it does not specify that he is going to see Lady Rokujō. This is revealed only many chapters later.
3. There is an ellipsis between the "Fujibakama" chapter and the "Makibashira" chapter.

The first two points have been explained elsewhere, but I should elaborate on the third. The "Makibashira" chapter begins in a particularly wonderful way. Among the many suitors to pursue Tamakazura, Prince Hotaru stands out for his sincerity. Accordingly, Tamakazura becomes well disposed toward him. In the "Fujibakama" chapter, Tamakazura becomes a Chief Palace Attendant, and in the next month, when she enters the palace, she receives many letters of proposal. She responds only to the letter from Prince Hotaru, and there the "Fujibakama" chapter ends. However, the story resumes in a different way at the beginning of the next chapter, "Makibashira." Commandant Higekuro, whom she seemed greatly to dislike in the previous chapter, has already taken Tamakazura as his wife. Without any explanation, the chapter begins "Genji warned Higekuro that 'I would not like His Majesty to hear of this. It is best that you keep this to yourself for now.'" Readers are stunned by this very unusual way to begin a chapter. At first, they have no idea what has happened. But as they read on, it becomes clear what Higekuro has managed to do. The technique is clever and wonderful. Without revealing anything specific, the narrative proceeds to the Eleventh Month, whereupon it is noted that "Tamakazura was assigned to serve in the Hall of the Sacred Mirror, and Higekuro, much to her dismay, was always nearby." This is an extremely adroit way of revealing what has happened between Tamakazura and Higekuro.[134] This is an excellent example of the compositional principle of narrative reversal [*hanpuku*]. It demonstrates how an attractive and gentle woman managed to create a narrative powerful enough to scare away tigers and wolves and dazzle the fiercest spirits. Many similar examples can be found in my commentary on the main text. For the most part, however, the foregoing are the most exceptional examples.

Commentaries of the past contain a great deal of useless information and fail to call attention to the matters I have mentioned. I have found this quite disappointing. While I hardly need to mention it again, I would like to emphasize that clearly there are principles of composition in this text. At the risk of sounding arrogant, I must emphasize this point to my readers. There is much more to be said about the text. I will limit myself to the preceding examples of the principles of composition, since I include more detailed information in my commentary. Please use these points as a guide to what follows. Some principles of composition are peculiar to an individual chapter or section. I include commentary in the relevant passage in the main text and omit such examples from the foregoing discussion.

Virtually no critical analysis of elegance in prose style can be found in works written in Japanese. Most of the interpretive points that I raise are found here for the first time, for which reason I follow the Chinese practice just described. I have given provisional names to these critical terms and described them in a general way. These terms are only for beginning students of *Genji*. Some terms are taken directly from the Chinese, some from previous *Genji* commentaries. Some are developed by me and are used here for the first time. All of them are designed to make it easier to understand the text and are not conceived in slavish imitation of the Chinese. Dear reader, please keep this in mind, and do not be suspicious of my methods.

"Major and minor" characters [*shukaku* 主客]: When there are two characters [who regularly appear together or in corresponding circumstances in the story], the more important character is referred to as the host [*shu*], and the secondary character is called the guest [*kaku*]. The importance of this principle varies from one section of the text to another. Chapters and paragraphs sometimes correspond to each other in accordance with this principle as well. One should be aware of this when reading the text.

"Lead and secondary character" [*seifuku* 正副]: This is analogous to the military ranks of general and vice general. The main character is considered to be the general [*sei*]. The one who is subordinate to the general is the vice general [*fuku*]. The prominence of this principle varies from one example to the next.

"Corresponding" or "contrasting" characters [*seitai* 正対]: Characters or objects of equivalent importance in the narrative, without one being superior to the other, are called corresponding or contrasting characters. This pairing is distinct from the next category, "opposing characters," in which characters stand in opposition to each other rather than being equivalent or parallel in nature.

"Opposing characters" or "character foils" [*hantai* 反対]: This relationship is defined by the oppositional quality of the characters or events in relation to each other. For example, one scene in which it is raining versus another in which it is fine, or daylight versus nighttime. While they are not equals, the two characters or elements are related to each other as are the front and back sides of the same object.

"Retroactive parallel" and "retroactive reflection" [*shōtai* 照対 and *shōō* 照應]: These two are largely the same, but retroactive parallel denotes the appearance of analogous events. These events are similar just as the light of the sun and the moon are similar, yet they are rivals just as the light of the sun comes from the east and the light of the moon appears in the west. Retroactive reflection, in contrast, denotes the conclusion of a matter that appeared earlier but for some reason lingers on in the story or has not yet come to a resolution. The narrative thread of this matter reappears and can be understood as corresponding to the meaning or significance of a previous event. This is similar to the way the moon and stars reflect light from the sun.

"Narrative interlude" [*kankaku* 間隔]: Sometimes the uninterrupted description of a single point would be too long and distracting to the reader. To avoid irritating the reader, other details are inserted into the narrative using the device of an interlude in the narration. One might think of this technique as similar to the effect produced by inserting clouds or mist into a scene of distant seas or mountains so that the view becomes even more magnificent. This technique is often used in the middle of chapters.

"Foreshadowing" [*fukuan* 伏案 and *fukusen* 伏線]: These two are largely the same. The technique of *fukuan* takes into consideration the outcome of something while quietly revealing parts of it, but hiding the general facts of the matter. *Fukusen* is written with a character with the radical for thread, and as such, the thread is buried up to a distant point while revealing itself from time to time. When you reach the outcome, it is as if you have pulled on the end of the thread to reveal how all the different stitches are connected. This technique is also called "plotting" [*shitamae*, alternatively read as *kekkō*]. Plotting more broadly refers to the placement of details that the author has planned in advance.

"Narrative modulation" or "diminuendo and crescendo" [*yokuyō* 抑揚]: Diminuendo [*yoku*] is a technique of modulated description that is used to suppress details, and crescendo [*yō*] is the use of this technique to emphasize details. This principle imbues the text with dynamism. One might think of this technique in terms of the operation of a rice husker: to make the mallet head go up, the pedal is pressed firmly so that when one aspect of the story is to be emphasized, a different component is deliberately suppressed.

"Narrative tempo" [*kankyū* 緩急]: The technique of narrative tempo involves making things go quickly or slowly. That is, calm passages rely on a slow narrative tempo. For example, a slow narrative tempo is used to depict a maiden walking through a field on a warm spring day, whereas a fast narrative tempo suits the description of treetops violently swaying in the wind of a gathering typhoon. The technique of setting a narrative tempo changes according to the nature of the passage.

"Reversal" [*hanpuku/uchikae* 反覆]: This technique is used to surprise the reader. A reversal in the narrative comes unexpectedly like a sudden shower in the middle of a calm evening. Circumstances change drastically, causing the story to suddenly change direction. The author does this specifically to surprise the reader with something unanticipated. One might think of this technique as producing something similar to the experience of a calm, clear evening when the light of the moon is abruptly obscured, it begins to thunder loudly, and a rain shower suddenly begins.

"Ellipsis" [*shōhitsu* 省筆]: In some cases a full description of events would be too long, so the description is shortened, and only the beginning and the end are told, thereby making the reader guess at what happened in the interval. A second type of ellipsis is having a character talk about something that has already happened in order to inform the reader of an event. In another case, the author may wish to avoid discussing something disturbing. These all are examples of ellipsis.

"Lingering presence" or "resonance" [*yoha* 余波]: Following the description of a major event in the story, lesser remnants of that event linger in a way that conveys a reluctance to let it fade from the narrative. After writing the description of a grand scene, the author regrets allowing the scene to disappear, so she extends the description. One might think of this technique as similar to the small, shallow waves and bits of foam that linger after a great wave has come crashing ashore.

"Narrative device" or "seed" [*shushi* or *kusawai* 種子]: A narrative device or seed is sometimes employed when there is a gap between stories that is difficult to bridge. Examples of the use of this narrative device include the appearance of Wakamurasaki's sparrow [in the "Wakamurasaki" chapter when the perspectives of Genji's and Wakamurasaki's attendants are integrated as they both observe her crying over a lost sparrow], and the Third Princess's Chinese cat [which connects unrelated events in the "Wakana, jō" and "Wakana, ge" chapters].

"Retribution" [*hōō* 報應]: This technique introduces retribution or punishment that arises from certain actions. The events described are the consequences following from a character's behavior. The resulting event is the logical outcome of the earlier action.

"Parable" [*fūyu* 風諭]: A parable allows real events to be inserted into the fictional narrative. By including such an event in the story, the author can show readers the consequences of an action. Retribution and parable allow us to speculate about the intentions of the author.

"Context" [*bunmyaku* 文脈 and *gomyaku* 語脈]: Context is the narrative fiber or thread that joins one sentence [*bun*] or one word [*go*] with the next. The meaning of the story flows through these narrative veins in the same way that blood circulates throughout the human body. The term "fiber" or "thread" also is used in reference to foreshadowing but refers to a different type of connection.

"Narrative symmetry" or "beginning and end" [*shubi* 首尾]: This term indicates a place in the text where the beginning and end of an event or story are symmetrical, so it should really be called "symmetry between cause and effect" [*shubi sōō*]. But it has always been referred to in *Genji* commentary simply as *shubi* [literally, "beginning and end"] so that is how I refer to it here.

The names for the following terms are given just as they appear in Old Commentaries.

"Textual parallelism" or "intertextuality" [*ruirei* 類例]: Textual parallelism refers to events or words for which similar or parallel instances can be found in another work or works. This can also refer to quotations from poems. All such instances are referred to as textual parallelism. Textual parallelism constitutes an entire category of commentary on *Genji*.

"Planning" or "narrative design" [*yōi* 用意]: This is when the author's thoughtful planning of events or details in the story makes the narrative work well. In general, this is what constitutes narrative design. An example of narrative design is the scene in the "Utsusemi" chapter in which Utsusemi [quietly leaves as Genji enters her room in the dark, leaving Nokiba no Ogi to be seduced by Genji in her stead], which one can say was a masterful planning of events.

"Authorial intrusion" [*sōshiji* 草子地]: [This is] a thought or utterance that originates outside the narrative. Because the language is that of the person narrating the tale, the narrator is considered to be the author herself. However, bear in mind that even though it represents the author's utterance, it represents temporarily the language or feeling of the narrator as if she were also a character in the story. Close attention should be paid to these passages.

"Aesthetic aftereffect" and "aesthetic satisfaction" [*yokō/nioi* 余光 and *yojō* 余情]: The term "aesthetic aftereffect" [*yokō*] should be read according to the Japanese pronunciation for the word "fragrance" [*nioi*]. It is a term used to express praise for a passage that defies appreciation in words. The term "aesthetic satisfaction" [*yojō*] refers to the conclusion of an event in the story in which a sublime sense of poignancy is evoked by the text and is felt by the reader. It is not possible to pinpoint the source of such evocative power in the text, but in some places I indicate that an abundance of this type of expression, which cannot be explained in words, is to be found in the story.

TRANSLATED BY PATRICK CADDEAU

Notes

1. Hagiwara Hiromichi, *Genji monogatari hyōshaku*, ed. Muromatsu Iwao (Tokyo: Kokugakuin Daigaku Shuppanbu, 1909), 36–37.

2. For a more detailed discussion of this distinction, see Thomas Harper, "*The Tale of Genji* in the Eighteenth Century: Keichū, Mabuchi, and Norinaga," in *Eighteenth Century Japan: Culture and Society*, ed. C. Andrew Gerstle (1989; repr., London: Routledge, 2000), 106–23, and in *Critical Readings in the Intellectual History of Early Modern Japan*, ed. W. J. Boot (Leiden: Brill, 2012), 2:549–65.

3. Translated from *Genji gaiden*, in *Zōtei Banzan zenshū*, ed. Masamune Atsuo, Taniguchi Sumio, and Miyazaki Michio (Tokyo: Meicho Shuppan, 1978), 2:419–23.

4. "Yuyan" (J. Gūgen), the title of book 27 of the *Zhuangzi*. Burton Watson translates the term as "imputed words," in *The Complete Works of Chuang Tzu* (New York: Columbia University Press, 1968), 303.

5. Sanjōnishi Kin'eda compares *Genji* and *Shiji* in *Sairyūshō*, in *(Naikaku bunkobon) Sairyūshō*, ed. Ii Haruki, GMKS 7:9.

6. Nakanoin Michikatsu, *Mingō nisso*, ed. Nakada Takeshi, GMKS 11:10, 15, based on Murasaki's diary. The text Michikatsu cites is in *Murasaki Shikibu nikki*, ed. Nakano Kōichi, in *Izumi Shikibu nikki. Murasaki Shikibu nikki. Sarashina nikki. Sanuki no Suke no nikki*, ed. Fujioka Tadaharu et al., SNKBZ 26:208. See also *Murasaki Shikibu: Her Diary and Poetic Memoirs*, trans. Richard John Bowring (Princeton, N.J.: Princeton University Press, 1982), 137.

7. Referring to the "licentious" odes of Zheng and Wei, included in part 1, books 5 and 7, of the canonical *Book of Poetry*.

8. Compare "Therefore, only when Tao is lost does the doctrine of virtue arise" (*Daodejing*, chap. 38, in *A Source Book in Chinese Philosophy*, trans. and ed. Wing-tsit Chan [Princeton, N.J.: Princeton University Press, 1963], 158). Banzan's point is that the loss of spontaneity in verse composition resulted in a codified set of practices.

9. "The friendship of a gentleman, they say, is insipid as water" (*Complete Works of Chuang Tzu*, trans. Watson, 215).

10. Compare "[The path proper to the Sage] waits for the proper man, and then it is trodden" (*Doctrine of the Mean*, chap. 27, v. 4, in *The Chinese Classics*, trans. James Legge [1893; repr., Hong Kong: Hong Kong University Press, 1970], 1:422).

11. *Book of Filial Piety*, chap. 12, trans. James Legge, in *Sacred Books of the East*, ed. F. Max Müller (Oxford: Clarendon Press, 1899), 3:481–82.

12. "The trap exists because of the fish; once you've gotten the fish, you can forget the trap" (*Complete Works of Chuang Tzu*, trans. Watson, 302).

13. Ichijō Kanera, *(Matsunaga-bon) Kachō yosei*, ed. Ii Haruki, GMKS 1:9.

14. "The Master said: 'To those whose talents are above mediocrity, the highest subjects may be announced. To those who are below mediocrity, the highest subjects may not be announced'" (*Analects*, 6:19, in *Chinese Classics*, trans. Legge, 1:191).

15. Fushimi no Miya, Prince Kunisuke (1513–1563). Biographies of Andō Tameakira's ancestors are included in *Kokugakusha denki shūsei* (Tokyo: Dai Nihon Tosho, 1904). See also Orihara Atsuko, "Andō Tameakira to Mitogaku," in *Heianchō bungaku kenkyū: sakka to sakuhin*, ed. Waseda Daigaku Heianchō Bungaku Kenkyūkai (Tokyo: Yūseidō, 1971), 358–59.

16. In 1657, Mitsukuni ordered the compilation of a *kanbun* history of Japan. After some debate about its title and direction, it eventually came to be called *Dai Nihonshi* and was finally completed in 1906. It covers the period from the (mythical) Jinmu Emperor to the GoKomatsu Emperor (1377–1433; r. 1382–1412). For the beginnings of the project, see Bitō Masahide, "Mitogaku no tokushitsu: Mitogaku to *Dai Nihonshi* hensan jigyō," in *Mitogaku*, ed. Bitō Masahide et al., Nihon shisō taikei 53 (Tokyo: Iwanami Shoten, 1977), 562–70. In addition to the *Man'yōshū* and *Genji*, Tameakira published studies of *Eiga monogatari* and *Utsuho monogatari*.

17. The work is also known as *Shijo shichiron*, *Genji monogatari shichiron*, *Genji monogatari kō*, and *Genji shichiron*. The *ka* (*ie*) of this title may indicate emphasis on Murasaki Shikibu as a scholar. See Orihara Atsuko, "*Shika shichiron* no daimoku oyobi genkei ni tsuite," *Bungei to hihyō* 2, no. 5 (1967): 49–59. Information about Tameakira and *Shika shichiron* is compiled from the entry in Ii Haruki, ed., *Genji monogatari chūshakusho, kyōjushi jiten* (Tokyo: Tokyōdō Shuppan, 2001), 369–71; Orihara, "Andō Tameakira to Mitogaku," 358–73; Kubota Osamu, "Andō Nenzan no gakuteki keizu," *Kokubungaku* 8 (1952): 34–41; and Seki Michiko, "Andō Tameakira to *Shijo shichiron*," *Gakuen* 6, no. 10 (1939): 33–60. This translation is based on Andō Tameakira, *Shika shichiron*, in *Kinsei shintō ron, zenki kokugaku*, ed. Taira Shigemichi and Abe Akio, Nihon shisō taikei 39 (Tokyo: Iwanami Shoten, 1972), 422–41. I am indebted to Thomas Harper for his help with this translation.

18. In the epilogue, Tameakira also states that his interest in *Genji* was aroused by lectures by students of Nakanoin Michimura (1588–1653), Michishige's grandfather.

19. Sugita Masahiko, "Monogatari no yō—Kōyōshugiteki *Genji monogatari* kan to kokugakusha tachi," in *Kōza Genji monogatari kenkyū 1: Genji monogatari no genzai*, ed. Ii Haruki (Tokyo: Ōfū, 2006), 124–49; Shigematsu Nobuhiro, "Keichū oyobi Andō Tameakira no kenkyū," in *Shinkō Genji monogatari kenkyūshi* (Tokyo: Kazama Shobō, 1961), 311–22; Hisamatsu Sen'ichi, "Keichū to Tameakira," *Kokubungaku: kaishaku to kyōzai no kenkyū* 14, no. 1 (1969): 46–47.

20. There are three known Edo-period commentaries on Murasaki Shikibu's diary. The first, *Murasaki Shikibu nikki bōchū* (1729), by Tsuboi Yoshitomo, is an annotated text that provided the whole diary for the first time. Adachi Inao's *Murasaki Shikibu nikki kai* (ca. 1819–1821) was the first full commentary and study of the diary and was followed by Shimizu Noriaki's *Murasaki Shikibu nikki shaku* (1833).

21. The quotations from *Murasaki Shikibu nikki* are from *Murasaki Shikibu*, trans. Bowring, 131, 131, 135. Corresponding passages are found in *Murasaki Shikibu nikki*, ed. Nakano, SNKBZ 26:200, 202, 204. In the following notes, the page numbers are from both the Bowring translation and the SNKBZ edition.

22. *Murasaki Shikibu*, trans. Bowring, 135; *Murasaki Shikibu nikki*, ed. Nakano, 206.

23. To emphasize the relationship of the two parts of the sentence, this translation is adapted from *Murasaki Shikibu*, trans. Bowring, 135–37; *Murasaki Shikibu nikki*, ed. Nakano, 206.

24. *Murasaki Shikibu*, trans. Bowring, 139, 129; *Murasaki Shikibu nikki*, ed. Nakano, 209, 198, 199.

25. Shōshi (988–1074), Fujiwara no Michinaga's daughter and the Ichijō Emperor's empress.

26. *Murasaki Shikibu*, trans. Bowring, 45, 75; *Murasaki Shikibu nikki*, ed. Nakano, 125, 151, 152. Gen no Naishi first appears in the "Momiji no ga" chapter as a woman in her late fifties who enjoys relationships with both Genji and Tō no Chūjō. Utsusemi first appears in "Hahakigi," in which she is approached by Genji but avoids entering into a relationship with him. She appears again in "Sekiya," when her husband dies and she takes Buddhist vows.

27. *Murasaki Shikibu*, trans. Bowring, 145; *Murasaki Shikibu nikki*, ed. Nakano, 214.

28. *Murasaki Shikibu*, trans. Bowring, 145; *Murasaki Shikibu nikki*, ed. Nakano, 214–15.

29. This passage, beginning with "This shows," does not appear in the Nihon shisō taikei text but is found in a version included in *Genji monogatari shinobugusa*, ed. Sekine Masanao (Tokyo: Fuzanbō, 1926), 259, and in at least one very early manuscript. This passage is included here because of the smooth transition it provides between discussions of Murasaki's virtue and intellect.

30. *Murasaki Shikibu*, trans. Bowring, 133, 139; *Murasaki Shikibu nikki*, ed. Nakano, 203, 204, 208, 209.

31. *Murasaki Shikibu*, trans. Bowring 139; *Murasaki Shikibu nikki*, ed. Nakano, 209–10.

32. Shigeaki (906–954), son of the Daigo Emperor (885–930; r. 897–930).

33. The story that Murasaki Shikibu wrote *Genji* at Ishiyamadera is recounted in Essay 7.

34. *Murasaki Shikibu*, trans. Bowring, 91; *Murasaki Shikibu nikki*, ed. Nakano, 165.

35. *Murasaki Shikibu*, trans. Bowring, 137; *Murasaki Shikibu nikki*, ed. Nakano, 208.

36. *Murasaki Shikibu*, trans. Bowring, 143; *Murasaki Shikibu nikki*, ed. Nakano, 214.

37. *Kakaishō* (ca. 1362–1367), by Yotsutsuji Yoshinari (1326–1402).

38. *Eiga monogatari*, ed. Yamanaka Yutaka et al., SNKBZ 33:195.

39. *Eiga monogatari*, ed. Yamanaka Yutaka et al., SNKBZ 31:248.

40. For a translation and discussion of parts of Essay 4, as well as a valuable discussion of Hiromichi's analysis of Andō Tameakira and Motoori Norinaga, see Patrick W. Caddeau, *Appraising Genji: Literary Criticism and Cultural Anxiety in the Age of the Last Samurai* (Albany: State University of New York Press, 2006), esp. 90–91.

41. "Hotaru," 14:204; SNKBT 20:439.

42. For a translation and analysis of parts of this essay, see Caddeau, *Appraising Genji*, 57–59.

43. Murasaki Shikibu, *The Tale of Genji*, trans. Royall Tyler (New York: Viking, 2001), 17; SNKBT 19:26–27.

44. *Tale of Genji*, trans. Tyler, 357; SNKBT 20:237–38.

45. *Tale of Genji*, trans. Tyler, 660–61; SNKBT 21:384–86.

46. Tameakira cites the *Doushiguanjian* (J. *Dokushikanken*).

47. *Tale of Genji*, trans. Tyler, 35; SNKBT 19:59.

48. This is repeated from Essay 1.

49. Tameakira provides a rough time line of the Chōhō (999–1004) and Kankō (1004–1013) eras, providing references from the diary. For example, in Chōhō 1 (999), Michinaga's daughter Shōshi enters court service, and in the Ninth Month of Kankō 5 (1008), her son is born. Tameakira is certain that Murasaki Shikibu began court service in the second or third year of Kankō.

50. See Chōken, "A Dedicatory Proclamation for *The Tale of Genji*," translated in chapter 4 of this volume.

51. Translated from Motoori Norinaga, *Genji monogatari Tama no ogushi*, ed. Ōno Susumu, in MNZ 4:173–242. One of the best guides to reading *Tama no ogushi* is Norinaga's own *Shibun yōryō* (1763). The roughness and prolixity of this earliest version of *Tama no ogushi* are often, paradoxically, helpful to the reader in passages that have been severely edited in the final version. The edition in *Motoori Norinaga shū*, ed. Hino Tatsuo, SNKS 60 (Tokyo: Shinchōsha, 1983), is particularly useful for the editor's extensive analytical annotation.

52. This account of the textual history of *Tama no ogushi* and Norinaga's *Genji*-related activities is based principally on Ōno Susumu, "Kaidai," in MNZ 4:5–39.

53. *Genji monogatari oboegaki*, in MNZ 4:571–79.

54. Norinaga, *Genji monogatari Tama no ogushi*, in MNZ 4:396.

55. Hino Tatsuo, "Norinaga-gaku no seiritsu made," in *Motoori Norinaga*, ed. Yoshikawa Kōjirō, Satake Akihiro, and Hino Tatsuo, Nihon shisō taikei 40 (Tokyo: Iwanami Shoten, 1978), 565–91; "Norinaga izen no mono no aware," *Kokugo kokubun* 51, no. 8 (1982): 1–19; "Kokugaku izen: sobyō," in *Kojima Noriyuki Hakushi koki kinen ronbun shū: Koten gakusō*, ed. Itō Haku and Ide Itaru (Tokyo: Hanawa Shobō, 1982), 128–45; and "Kaisetsu: 'Mono no aware o shiru' no setsu no raireki," in *Motoori Norinaga shū*, ed. Hino, 505–51. All the foregoing are conveniently collected in Hino Tatsuo, *Norinaga to Akinari* (Tokyo: Chikuma Shobō, 1984).

56. Abe Akio, "'Mono no aware' no ron," in *Genji monogatari no monogatari ron: tsukuribanashi to shinjitsu* (Tokyo: Iwanami Shoten, 1985), 133–213. In this excellent analysis of the argument of *Tama no ogushi*, Abe points out a number of inconsistencies and contradictions in Norinaga's logic.

57. Ian Watt, *The Rise of the Novel: Studies in Defoe, Richardson, and Fielding* (Berkeley: University of California Press, 1962).

58. Samuel Richardson (1689–1761), describing his epistolary novel *Pamela* (1740).

59. Samuel Johnson, "The Modern Form of Romances Preferable to the Ancient," *The Rambler*, no. 4, March 31, 1750, 20, 21.

60. Clara Reeve, *The Progress of Romance* (1785; repr., New York: Facsimile Text Society, 1930), 1:111.

61. See Murasaki Shikibu, *The Tale of Genji*, translated in chapter 1 of this volume.

62. Norinaga probably takes his title from a poem by the Akikonomu Empress in "Wakana, jō," 15:37:

sashinagara mukashi o ima ni tsutaureba / tama no ogushi zo
kamisabinikeru

As I wear it in my hair, it brings back times past, just as once they were,
this little bejeweled comb, now so very worn and old.

63. The first chapter of *Utsuho monogatari*.

64. *Eiga monogatari*, ed. Matsumura Hiroji and Yamanaka Yutaka, NKBT 76:471, probably referring to the tale-matching contest (*monogatari awase*) sponsored by Princess Baishi (1039–1096), the High Priestess of Kamo, in 1055.

65. All phrases containing the term *mono no aware* are given in their original form following their translations. In these references, *mono no aware* is abbreviated as *mna*.

66. *Uji no Dainagon no monogatari* is no longer extant. The passage quoted here is known only through Kanera, *Kachō yosei*, 9.

67. *Shimeishō, Kakaishō*, ed. Tamagami Takuya (Tokyo: Kadokawa Shoten, 1968), 186.

68. Portions of this work are translated earlier in this chapter.

69. *Zoku yotsugi* is another title for the work now most commonly known as *Ima kagami*. See *Ima kagami, Masu kagami*, ed. Kuroita Katsumi (Tokyo: Yoshikawa Kōbunkan, 1965).

70. Actually the reverse is the case.

71. Murasaki Shikibu is described as the "mistress of the Regent Michinaga" (*midō kanpaku Michinaga no mekake*) in the genealogy *Sonpi bunmyaku* as well as in the first chapter of Norinaga's base text, the *Kogetsushō*.

72. Sasaki Nobutsuna ed., *Nihon kagaku taikei* (Tokyo: Kazama Shobō, 1956–1965), 2:68.

73. All notes enclosed in double angle brackets are Norinaga's own notes that appear in his original text.

74. *Murasaki Shikibu nikki*, in *Izumi Shikibu nikki. Murasaki Shikibu nikki. Sarashina nikki. Sanuki no Suke no nikki*, ed. Fujioka Tadaharu et al., NKBZ 18:201–2.

75. Referring to *Genji monogatari toshidate*, by Ichijō Kanera/Kaneyoshi (1402–1481).

76. Minokata Joan (dates unknown).

77. The *Genji* text goes on to say, ". . . but she was a bit slow-witted for such diversions."

78. Current editions read "Kumano."

79. Current editions read *mukashigatari* for *mukashi monogatari*.

80. Current editions accept the text unemended.

81. *Sumiyoshi monogatari*, no longer extant. A newer version with the same title dates from the Kamakura period.

82. A high-ranking official in the Dazaifu hierarchy from whom Tamakazura herself escaped only narrowly.

83. "Sōjō Henjō shows a mastery of form, but his poetry lacks veracity. It is as if one were to lose one's heart in vain to a woman painted in a picture" (*Kokinshū*, NKBZ 7:57).

84. In *Kogetsushō*, for example, Kigin cites his teacher Minokata Joan's theory that Tamakazura here vents her resentment of Genji's false claim that she is his daughter, a lie he tells because he has amorous designs on her.

85. Norinaga expects the reader of this procession of adjectives to note the distinction between *okashi* and *wokashi*, translated here as "delightful" and "ridiculous." In *Tamakatsuma* 26, Norinaga praises his disciple Tanaka Michimaro (1730–1784) for identifying the distinct etymological origins of these two words and deplores the orthographical confusion that has resulted in the loss of this distinction (MNZ 1:49). Modern scholarship seems not to accept Michimaro's etymology.

86. Many modern commentators take the word *hito* in this passage to mean "readers (of tales)." Norinaga, however, takes it to mean *yo no hito*, so it is translated here in accord with his interpretation.

87. This is but one of several textual variants in this short sentence. This translation, of course, follows Norinaga's text and his interpretation of it. Modern editors have yet to agree on a preferred version.

88. In translation, unfortunately, the word "these" (*kono*) comes near the end of the phrase.

89. The Lotus Sutra (T 262), chap. 5.

90. Compare Matsudaira Sadanobu's opposing view in *Kagetsu zōshi*, translated in this chapter.

91. *Kogo shūi*, ed. Yasuda Naomichi and Akimoto Yoshitoku (Tokyo: Gendai Shisōsha, 1976), 45.

92. Norinaga himself writes *aware* with this character in *Shibun yōryō*.

93. Probably referring to the "Great Preface" to the *Book of Poetry*.

94. Here and elsewhere, Norinaga's quotations differ markedly from those in the NKBZ edition of *Genji* to which these translations are keyed. This seems to be not simply because he quotes from the *Kogetsushō* text, which he used in teaching. Perhaps some of these discrepancies are the result of misquotation from memory? Whatever the reason, the translations given here represent the text that Norinaga cites and not the NKBZ text. When Norinaga's interpretation of the text differs from that of modern scholars, this translation follows Norinaga's interpretation.

95. So called for her poem that begins *kogarashi ni*. See "Hahakigi," 12:155.

96. One of Norinaga's rare errors. These are Fujitsubo's words, not Murasaki's.

97. This translation follows Norinaga's interpretation of the passage. More recent commentators take it to mean that Murasaki finds it painful even to observe

as a bystander those who ape the thoughtless behavior of characters in tales. See "Hotaru," 14:207.

98. Referring to Atemiya, the peerless but ill-fated heroine of this tale.

99. Again, the translation follows Norinaga's interpretation of the text. Modern commentators take *hitoyō* to mean not "excessive" but "equally (reprehensible)." That is, the capable but obdurate Atemiya is no better than the flighty young ladies mentioned previously.

100. Kanera, *Kachō yosei*, 184–85.

101. The editors of the NKBZ text of *Genji* (15:442n.2) point out that *Sairyūshō* annotates this passage using language remarkably similar to Norinaga's: "If she behaves in a manner that seems deficient in emotional sensitivity [*amari mna o shiranu yō*], people will wonder what sort of upbringing her parents have given her, but if she feigns sensitivity [*aware o shirigao*], she will be thought frivolous. Either way, this is matter of some importance."

102. *Shimeishō*, *Kakaishō*, ed. Tamagami, 515.

103. Here, again, the translation follows Norinaga's interpretation of the passage quoted, which differs slightly from that of modern commentators.

104. Although *koi* is translated here as "love," in reading Norinaga's thoughts on the matter, it is well to keep in mind that the many meanings of these two words overlap only partially. *Koi* adequately describes the passionate and visceral aspects of "love," but the caring and compassionate aspects of the Western concept are usually described with a different word, *ai*. By far the most frequent use of the word *koi* in *Genji* (seventy-eight occurrences) is in the compound verb *koi-kanashimu*, which might be translated "to suffer the pangs of love." As one writer aptly put it, "If you're happy, it's not *koi*."

105. The phrase "Confucius may stumble" appears in a Heian-period collection of sayings, *Sezoku genbun* (ZGR 30, II), compiled by Minamoto no Tamenori (d. 1011). See Tamagami Takuya, *Genji monogatari hyōshaku* (Tokyo: Kadokawa Shoten, 1965), 5:250. Tamagami suggests that the location of the sage's misstep may be Murasaki Shikibu's contribution to this little joke. No Chinese source has yet been identified.

106. This poem is not cited in modern editions of *Kakaishō*.

107. Referring to Genji's period of banishment in Suma and Akashi.

108. Perhaps referring to Kokiden's being troubled by malign spirits and the Suzaku Emperor's eye ailment?

109. A quotation from *Ise monogatari* 49 (NKBT 9:139):

> *uchi wakami neyoge ni miyuru wakakusa o / hito no musubamu koto o shi zo omou*
>
> These new sprouts, so very young and so inviting a place to sleep;
> yet if another were to bind them to make a traveler's bed. . . .

110. In his notes to *Shibun yōryō*, Hino Tatsuo suggests that Norinaga probably added this passage, stressing the social and political importance of emotional sensitivity, because the patron for whom it was being rewritten was a daimyo, Matsudaira Suō-no-Kami Yasusada. See *Motoori Norinaga shū*, ed. Hino, 165n.5.

111. *Ochikubo monogatari, Sumiyoshi monogatari*, ed. Fujii Sadakazu and Inaga Keiji, SNKBT 18:403.

112. The following excerpt translates Norinaga's quotations from *Genji gaiden*. Banzan's original is translated by James McMullen at the beginning of this chapter. For a discussion of Norinaga's critique of Banzan, see James McMullen, *Idealism, Protest, and The Tale of Genji: The Confucianism of Kumazawa Banzan (1619–91)* (Oxford: Clarendon Press, 1999), 400–405, 449–50.

113. This quotation does not appear in extant texts of *Shika shichiron*.

114. In modern scholarship, the phrase *mono no magire* is often used to refer not only to the break in the imperial line caused by the succession of the Reizei Emperor but also to any of the illicit sexual liaisons in *The Tale of Genji*, including not only Genji's clandestine affair with the Fujitsubo Empress but also the affairs of Onnasannomiya and Ukifune. In every case, it is, of course, a euphemism, the fundamental sense of which is illustrated by the use of *mono no magire* in "Sakaki" (13:137) to describe the "confusion" in the household of the Minister of the Right during the violent storm in the aftermath of which Genji is discovered lying in Oborozukiyo's curtained bedchamber. Norinaga's use of the phrase is thus translated, equally euphemistically, as the "taint to" or "disruption of" the imperial line. Note that Tameakira, against whom Norinaga writes, is more forthright than Norinaga, referring explicitly to *kōtō no magire* and *kōin no magire*, the "imperial succession" and the "imperial bloodline."

115. Another of Norinaga's rare errors. The citation from "Usugumo" in fact refers not to the Oborozukiyo lady but to Akikonomu.

116. These events are described in the fourth and final chapter of the work. See *Sagoromo monogatari*, ed. Mitani Eiichi and Sekine Yoshiko, NKBT 79:422–32.

117. *Sagoromo monogatari*, 422–32.

118. Modern commentators do not follow Norinaga in taking *kayō no suji* as referring to the composition of poetry but as referring to the Buddhist notions of karmic bonding alluded to in Genji's poem. In this interpretation, Yūgao is not as ill at ease in composing her poem as with Genji's grandiose promises. See "Yūgao," 12:233n.18.

119. Described in chapter 30, "Tsuru no hayashi." See *Eiga monogatari*, ed. Matsumura and Yamanaka, 319–28.

120. Taifu no Gen is described in "Tamakazura" and recalled in "Hotaru." Hitachi no Suke appears in "Yadorigi," "Azumaya," "Ukifune," and "Kagerō."

121. *Eiga monogatari*, ed. Matsumura and Yamanaka, 61.

122. Matsudaira Sadanobu, *Kagetsu zōshi*, ed. Nishio Minoru and Matsudaira Sadamitsu (Tokyo: Iwanami Shoten, 1939), 179n.116.

123. Translated from Matsudaira, *Kagetsu zōshi*, 113, 128–30. For a detailed discussion of these excerpts, see Miyakawa Yōko, "Rakuō to *Genji monogatari*," *Bungaku* 7, no. 1 (2006): 140–51.

124. "Hana no en," 12:426.

125. In fact, because lightning destroys the gallery (*rō*), Genji is moved to the kitchens (*ōhidono*). Note that Sadanobu's interpretation of this passage is strengthened by the fact that the lightning strike immediately follows a long and fervent prayer by one of Genji's retainers protesting his lord's innocence ("Akashi," 13:216–17). Norinaga, of course, argues for precisely the opposite interpretation: "If the author

had intended to convey a Confucian or Buddhist moral, why would she write about the gods, the buddhas, and the heavens taking pity on a man guilty of such grievous immorality?" (*Genji monogatari Tama no ogushi*, in MNZ 4:199).

126. "Kashiwagi," 15:300.

127. "Usugumo," 13:439–42.

128. Translation based on Hagiwara Hiromichi, *Genji monogatari hyōshaku*, "Sōron" (1854), in *Hihyō shūsei Genji monogatari*, ed. Akiyama Ken (Tokyo: Yumani Shobō, 1999), 2:275–367. Hiromichi's preface is not included in this typeset edition but can be found in the entry for Hiromichi in Ii, ed., *Genji monogatari chūshakusho, kyōjushi jiten*, 318.

129. Yamazaki Katsuaki, "Hagiwara Hiromichi ryaku nenpu kō," *Kokubun ronsō* 17 (1990): 88. For a detailed biography and analysis of Hiromichi's work on *Genji*, see Caddeau, *Appraising Genji*.

130. For examples, see Ikeda Kikan, ed., *Genji monogatari jiten* (Tokyo: Tōkyōdō, 1960), 2:91; Fujita Tokutarō, *Genji monogatari kenkyū shomoku yōran* (Tokyo: Rokubunkan, 1932); and Shigematsu Nobuhiro, *Genji monogatari kenkyūshi* (Tokyo: Kazama Shobō, 1961).

131. Noguchi Takehiko, *Genji monogatari o Edo kara yomu* (Tokyo: Kōdansha, 1985).

132. Shuen-fu Lin translates *zhaoying* as "retroactive reflection," which appears as *shōō* in Japanese, in "The Chapter Comments from the Wohsien ts'aot'ang Edition of *The Scholars*," in *How to Read the Chinese Novel*, ed. David L. Rolston (Princeton, N.J.: Princeton University Press, 1990), 250.

133. Hiromichi's reference to the symmetry between the moon appearing in the scenes when Genji begins his exile in Suma and when he has his first audience with the emperor after returning two years later to the capital on the fifteenth night of the Eighth Month is a detail that continues to attract the interest of commentators in modern editions of *Genji*. See, for example, "Akashi," 13:263n.11.

134. Tamakazura has acquiesced to Higekuro's advances, against her better judgment. The gentlewoman Ben's dismissal from Takamazura's service early in this chapter suggests that the failure of Tamakazura's attendants to protect her from Higekuro's pursuit led to her discharge.

Chapter 8
Modern Reception

WHEN JAPAN ENTERED THE FRAY of global politics at the end of the nineteenth century, its new nation builders were convinced that a national literature, which presupposed a common and continuous national language, would be indispensable to the construction of a unified nation-state. In this context, *The Tale of Genji* was to become a crucial text.

From a global perspective, the publication in 1882 of an English translation of *The Tale of Genji* was an epoch-making event. The translation was an abridged version of the first seventeen chapters of *Genji* by Suematsu Kenchō (1855–1920), who lived in England from 1878 to 1886 as a secretary to the Japanese legation in London and a student of law and literature at the University of Cambridge.[1] Clearly Suematsu's underlying concern was political, an attempt to impress European nations with Japan's social and cultural achievements, including the high position of women in the past.[2] Suematsu stressed that "we [Japanese] had once made a remarkable progress in our own language quite independently of any foreign influence, and that when the native literature was at first founded, its language was identical with that [of the] spoken [language]."[3] In many ways, his evaluation of *The Tale of Genji* (written in English, excerpts from which are included in this chapter) anticipated later Meiji views of the *Genji*.

In Japan, Tsubouchi Shōyō's (1859–1935) *The Essence of the Novel* (*Shōsetsu shinzui*, 1885–1886) introduced a new concept of the novel that strongly influenced the development of critical discourse on literature in Japan. Achievement in fiction (*shōsetsu*), Shōyō argued, was an important indicator of a nation's level of civilization, and he proposed a "reform of fiction" as part of an urgent national agenda to make Japan an "advanced," "civilized" nation in the eyes of Western powers. Under the influence of Herbert Spencer's social Darwinism, Shōyō traced the "development of fiction" from mythology through romance/fable/allegory to the novel and proclaimed that the most advanced "true novel" is the "realistic novel" (*mosha shōsetsu*), which depicts all aspects of "human feelings and social conditions" (*ninjō setai*) just as they are, unconstrained by didactic purposes.

On the one hand, Shōyō describes *Genji* as a representative romance of Japan (in the evolutionary lineage from mythology to romance to the novel). On the other hand, he considers *Genji* to be a "contemporary, social" novel, depicting the upper-class court society of its time, and an early Japanese predecessor of the modern realistic novel. *The Tale of Genji* appears prominently in the central section of *Essence of the Novel*, "The Main Purpose of the Novel" (Shōsetsu no shugan, excerpted here), in which Shōyō argues that the "true novel" depicts all aspects of life in contemporary society, particularly the innermost feelings of a variety of people. He clearly regards *Genji* as a masterpiece for its emotional content, realistic descriptions, and refined classical Japanese style. Shōyō also considers *Genji*'s literary language to be based on the actual colloquial language (*zokugo*) of the Heian court aristocracy. *Genji* thus came to be regarded as an early antecedent of the realistic and artistic modern novel that describes contemporary society in the vernacular language of the present.

In the 1890s, the first modern literary histories as well as the earliest modern anthologies of classical Japanese literature were published by graduates of the Japanese literature departments in the newly reconstituted Imperial University. All of them considered literature (*bungaku*) to be both a "reflection of the human mind/heart" and a "reflection of national life." Accordingly, they illustrated, using concrete literary examples, the "development of the mentality of the nation" in order that "the nation's people [could] deepen their love for the nation," that "the national spirit" [could] be elevated, and that "social progress and development of the nation [could] be advanced."[4]

Following the lead of Hippolyte Taine's (1828–1893) *History of English Literature* (1864; English trans., 1872), Mikami Sanji (1865–1939) and Takatsu Kuwasaburō's (1864–1921) two-volume *History of Japanese Literature* (*Nihon bungakushi*, 1890) characterized Japanese literature in terms of the Japanese national character. To them, the Chinese "value proper decorum"; the English are "calm and practical"; the French are "gallant and emotional"; and the Japanese "revere their gods" and are "loyal to their lords." Since a nation's literature reflects its people's character, Chinese literature is "grand and heroic"; Western literatures, "precise, detailed, and exhaustive"; and Japanese literature, "elegant and graceful."[5] This belief persisted in subsequent literary historiography and had a lasting impact on Japanese views of their literature and national character, with *The Tale of Genji* as the foremost representative of Japan's national literature.

Mikami and Takatsu's discussion of *Genji* introduces its author, Murasaki Shikibu, as a virtuous woman and a talented writer; outlines the basic plot, with the Shining Genji and Lady Murasaki as the hero and the heroine; and lists the major commentaries and critical treatises. Kitamura Kigin's *Moonlit Lake Commentary*, Andō Tameakira's *Seven Essays on Murasaki Shikibu*, Motoori Norinaga's *The Tale of Genji: A Little Jeweled Comb*, and Hagiwara Hiromichi's *A Critical Appraisal of* Genji are recommended as four indispensable works for understanding *Genji*. Mikami and Takatsu disparage Buddhist and Confucian allegorical readings as slighting the rich intertextuality of *Genji*, a "predecessor of the realistic novel," as well as praise its "exquisite," "subtle," and "precise" language; its "fertile imagination"; and its "careful design and compositional structure." Echoing Hagiwara Hiromichi's *Critical Appraisal* as well as Shōyō's *Essence of the Novel*, Mikami and Takatsu reposition *Genji* and its earlier commentaries in the developing Meiji discourse on the novel and literature.

Japan's national literature was defined in the context of two competing concepts of literature. On one hand was the Confucian idea of learning, which had been the traditional conception of literature in Japan, augmented by the Western idea of literature as humanities in general. On the other hand was the new, nineteenth-century European conception of imaginative literature defined primarily in terms of aesthetics: beauty, imagination, and moral elevation. As a result, the position of *Genji*, now defined as a novel, remained unstable until the early twentieth century. After the end of the Russo-Japanese War in 1905, the field of literature rapidly became an independent cultural realm in which the specialized notion of aesthetic literature came to prevail, with the novel assuming a central position. In this context, *The Tale of Genji* came to be regarded as unquestionably the masterpiece of Japan's national literature. Sassa Seisetsu's (1872–1917) preface to *A New Exegesis of The Tale of Genji* (*Shinshaku Genji monogatari*, 1911–1914), translated here, exemplifies this view. Paradoxically, however, the institutional promotion of the new colloquial language and the aggressive separation of the new literary language from the old literary language led to a clear separation between "modern literature" and "classical literature," making *Genji* the "greatest national *classic*," written in a language that modern literary writers could no longer employ.

In this literary and cultural milieu, Yosano Akiko (1878–1942) published *A New Translation of The Tale of Genji* (*Shin'yaku Genji monogatari*, 1912–1913), the first complete modern colloquial translation of *The Tale of Genji*. Akiko had become established as a celebrated *tanka* (modern *waka*) poet and the leader of the Myōjō poetry coterie, and her *tanka* collection *Tangled Hair* (*Midaregami*, 1901) had a decisive impact on the aesthetic direction and popularity of the literary magazine *Myōjō* (1900–1908). But in the early twentieth century, both *tanka* and *wabun*-based prose were relegated to a secondary position by the rise of the colloquial novel as the central literary genre of the new age. From 1906 onward, although Akiko wrote a number of essays and short stories in the new colloquial style, it was her modern translation of *Genji* that allowed her to fully explore the new fictional form and language with the authority of a mediator between the (now feminized) classical language and the new colloquial language.

From its inception in the late 1880s, the notion of "national literature" in Japan, as in other modern nation-states, existed in a symbiotic relationship with "world literature." Japanese scholars of classical literature stressed the value of *The Tale of Genji* as the "world's earliest sophisticated, realistic novel" and as "required reading for everyone in the nation." But even though the view that Japanese literature was ready to participate actively in world literature began steadily growing in the 1910s, it was not until the mid-1920s that *The Tale of Genji* suddenly became a fresh object of contemporary literary attention. This was the result of the publication between 1925 and 1933 of an English translation of *Genji* by Arthur Waley (1889–1966), as well as the international recognition accorded the work in the review by Virginia Woolf (1882–1941) of Waley's first volume.

In 1922, the intellectual historian Watsuji Tetsurō (1889–1960) published three articles on Heian literature—*The Pillow Book*, *mono no aware*, and *The Tale of Genji*—in the newly established journal *Shisō* (*Thought*). In his article "On *The Tale of Genji*," now considered a pioneering work of textual criticism, Watsuji suggests that *Genji* was not written in the current order of the chapters and that Murasaki Shikibu may have been only one of several authors of the text. In the latter part of this essay, Watsuji expresses his "long-held uncertainty with regard to the artistic value of *The Tale of Genji*." "I hesitate to call it a masterpiece," he complains; "it is monotonous, repetitive, and even its partially beautiful scenes are clouded by the dull tedium of the whole."[6]

In 1926, Masamune Hakuchō (1879–1962) made a similar complaint in his essay "On Reading the Classics," also translated here. Hakuchō found the style of the original *Genji* text to be "sluggish and loose" and "hard to read," a style "that continues like a stream of jellyfish," and "prevents us from being impressed by the truth of life." From the mid-1920s, however, particularly after the first volume of Arthur Waley's English translation was published, *The Tale of Genji* as "world literature" acquired new significance, and the novelist Tanizaki Jun'ichirō (1886–1965) praised the very stylistic characteristics that Watsuji Tetsurō and Masamune Hakuchō had criticized.

In his essay "On the Defects of the Modern Colloquial Written Style" (1929), Tanizaki argued that the modern colloquial style, which had developed since the middle of the Meiji period, was an artificial written language based on a "translation style" (*hon'yakutai*), a "half-breed" (*konketsuji*) of Japanese and Western languages, mixing Western syntax and new Chinese loanwords as substitutes for Western words, and that this hybrid had strangled the beauty and uniqueness of the Japanese language. This Westernized language, Tanizaki maintained, may be better suited for the clear, precise, and rational writings of science or philosophy, but not necessarily for literature, for which the original Japanese language had unique advantages.[7] In his *Manual of Style* (*Bunshō tokuhon*, 1934), Tanizaki divides both classical and modern Japanese literature into two opposing types: the *wabun*-based style versus the *kanbun*-based style; the misty type versus the lucid type; the sluggish type versus the brisk type; the flowing, elegant type versus the solid type; the feminine type versus the masculine type; and the emotional type versus the rational type. These dichotomies, Tanizaki claimed, "could most simply be summed up as the *Genji monogatari* type versus the non–*Genji monogatari* type" and noted that while he, too, had been interested in the *kanbun*-based style in his younger years, he had become increasingly drawn to *Genji*'s *wabun*-based style.[8] Beginning in the late 1920s, Tanizaki embarked on a series of stylistic and narratological experiments, during which he found in older Japanese literary styles fresh possibilities for exploring modernist fiction. In 1935, at the behest of the president of the Chūōkōron publishing company, Tanizaki began translating the entire *Tale of Genji* into modern Japanese, which was published between 1939 and 1941. His own account of the inception of his first translation and his working methods is translated in this chapter.

Beginning in the early 1930s, all primary- and secondary-school textbooks included selections from *Genji*, which was popularized through both these textbooks and modern colloquial translations. Several different modern translations appeared in this period, including Yosano Akiko's revised translation (1938–1939).

In the postwar period, when the militaristic narratives associated with wartime Japan were removed from the school curricula, *The Tale of Genji* was recanonized as the cultural treasure of a new, nonmilitaristic, peaceful nation. Old translations were reprinted and new ones commissioned. As Japan rejoined the international community of nations in the 1950s, *The Tale of Genji* was held up as a cultural symbol for overseas consumption. For a middle-school textbook published in 1951, the leading *Genji* scholar Ikeda Kikan (1896–1956) wrote a brief biography of Murasaki Shikibu, in which he remarked:

> This novel is said to be the oldest, the grandest, and the greatest novel in our country. It has been admired by many people in all times, and recently it has been translated into several foreign languages and has been praised throughout the world as one of the world classics.[9]

By the 1970s, *Genji* had been popularized through new adaptations, free translations, and new media (film, *manga* [comics], *anime* [animation]), all supported by a continuing tradition of *Genji* scholarship that has produced numerous new annotated editions, making it the most studied text in all of Japanese literature. Its continued importance as world literature, too, is attested by the appearance of several new foreign-language translations, including two new (and complete) English translations, by Edward Seidensticker in 1976 and Royall Tyler in 2001. In addition, excerpts from *Genji* now are included in almost all English-language anthologies of world literature.

TOMI SUZUKI

INTRODUCTION TO *GENJI MONOGATARI: THE MOST CELEBRATED OF THE CLASSICAL JAPANESE ROMANCES*, 1882

SUEMATSU KENCHŌ

Although it is not widely read or known today, Suematsu Kenchō's (1855–1920) translation of the first seventeen chapters of *The Tale of Genji*, published in London in 1882 as *Genji Monogatari: The Most Celebrated of the Classical Japanese Romances*, was a literary sensation at the time. Extensively reviewed in important newspapers and magazines, it was also translated into German; partially rewritten in French; and reprinted, rewritten, or anthologized in English, in full or in part, no fewer than five times between 1882 and 1934.[10] In an age when Europe and the United States were seized, as one observer wrote in 1881, by "the modern craze for things Japanese, which has converted grocer's shops into Japanese art depositories, and flooded the country with penny fans and inferior porcelain," it should come as no surprise that Suematsu's translation attracted considerable attention.[11]

Suematsu lived in England from 1878 to 1886, and his introduction to *Genji* indicates that by 1882 he was thoroughly acquainted with Victorian views of literature.[12] This is evident, above all, in his decision to market the work as a "classical romance" and a "true romance." On the one hand, this reverberated with the contemporary distinction between "romances, or the stories of individual life, and chronicles, or stories of the nation's life."[13] On the other hand, it also distanced *Genji* from the genre of "sensational romances" that then were so popular and so reviled.

Suematsu's motivation for translating *The Tale of Genji* is unclear. On the eve of his departure for England, Suematsu had been instructed to study English and French historiography, so much of his own interest in the text must have been historical. At the same time, his political intentions become evident when he notes that readers "will be able to compare [classical Japan] with the condition of mediaeval and modern Europe." Japan's foreign minister, Inoue Kaoru (1836–1915), had arranged a series of meetings beginning in January 1882 between representatives of parties to the "unequal treaties." As Suematsu hoped to see the treaties revised, the timing of the translation's publication could not have been better.

MICHAEL EMMERICH

Genji Monogatari, the original of this translation, is one of the standard works of Japanese literature. It has been regarded for centuries as a national treasure. The title of the work is by no means unknown to those Europeans who take an interest in Japanese matters, for it is mentioned or alluded to in almost every European work relating to our country. It was written by a lady, who, from her writings, is considered one of the most talented women that Japan has ever produced. . . .

Many Europeans, I daresay, have noticed on our lacquer work and other art objects, the representation of a lady seated at a writing-desk, with a pen held in her tiny fingers, gazing at the moon reflected in a lake. This lady is no other than our authoress. . . .

In fact, there is no better history than her story, which so vividly illustrates the society of her time. True it is that she openly declares in one passage of her story that politics are not matters which women are supposed to understand; yet, when we carefully study her writings, we can scarcely fail to recognize her work as a partly political one. This fact becomes more vividly interesting when we consider that the unsatisfactory conditions of both the state and society soon brought about a grievous weakening of the Imperial authority, and opened wide the gate for the ascendency of the military class. This was followed by the systematic formation of feudalism, which, for some seven centuries, totally changed the face of Japan. . . .

I may almost say that for several centuries Japan never recovered the ancient civilization which she had once attained and lost. . . .

Another merit of the work consists in its having been written in pure classical Japanese; and here it may be mentioned that we had once made a remarkable progress in our own language quite independently of any foreign influence, and that when the native literature was at first founded, its language was identical with that spoken. Though the predominance of Chinese studies had arrested the progress of the native literature, it was still extant at the time, and even for some time after the date of our authoress. But with the ascendency of the military class, the neglect of all literature became for centuries universal. The little that has been preserved is an almost unreadable chaos of mixed Chinese and Japanese. Thus a gulf gradually opened between the spoken and the written language. . . .

Again, the concise description of scenery, the elegance of which it is almost impossible to render with due force in another language, and the true and delicate touches of human nature which everywhere abound in the work, especially in the long dialogue in Chapter II, are almost marvellous when we consider the sex of the writer, and the early period when she wrote.

Yet this work affords fair ground for criticism. The thread of her story is often diffuse and somewhat disjointed, a fault probably due to the fact that she had more flights of imagination than power of equal and systematic condensation; she having been often carried away by that imagination from points where she ought to have rested. But, on the other hand, in most parts the dialogue is scanty, which might have been prolonged to considerable advantage, if it had been framed on models of modern composition. The work, also, is too voluminous.

In translating I have cut out several passages which appeared superfluous, though nothing has been added to the original. . . . The authoress has been by no means exact in following the order of dates, though this appears to have proceeded from her endeavor to complete each distinctive group of ideas in each particular chapter. In fact she had even left the chapters unnumbered. . . . It has no extraordinarily intricate plot like those which excite the readers of the sensational romances of the modern western style. . . .

I notice these points beforehand in order to prepare the reader for the more salient faults of the work. On the whole my principal object is not so much to amuse my readers as to present them with a study of human nature, and to give them information on the history of the social and political condition of my native country nearly a thousand years ago. They will be able to compare it with the condition of mediæval and modern Europe.

THE ESSENCE OF THE NOVEL, 1885–1886
(*Shōsetsu shinzui*)
TSUBOUCHI SHŌYŌ

The critic, playwright, and novelist Tsubouchi Shōyō (1859–1935) is perhaps best known for his translation of Shakespeare's complete works into Japanese between 1884 and 1928. His *Essence of the Novel* is widely considered to be the first substantial work of literary criticism in Meiji Japan.[14] Shōyō attended lectures in philosophy taught by American instructors at

Tokyo University and was familiar with a variety of contemporary Western authors and critics. In his own writing, he attempted to integrate what he loved in traditional Japanese fiction with what he found worthy of emulation in Western literature, but he was rarely satisfied with the results. At the height of his career, frustrated with his own attempts to develop a literary language and style for the modern novel, he abandoned his efforts to succeed as a novelist.

Shōyō's lifelong infatuation with traditional literature and his desire to imbue contemporary Japanese fiction with the finest qualities of Western literature are apparent in the references he makes to both *The Tale of Genji* and modern fictional prose in the following excerpts from his pioneering treatise on the novel.[15] He devotes the first volume of *The Essence of the Novel* to a general discussion of "the art of the novel." He combines examples from Western literature and history with those from China and Japan in an attempt to trace the development of prose from early chronicles and epics like the *Iliad* to didactic texts like *Aesop's Fables* and the *Zhuangzi*.

In the second selection translated here, "The Main Purpose of the Novel," he concludes that *Genji* can be used to illustrate his point that great prose fiction is about more than moral didacticism. In the third selection, Shōyō concludes that the novel is the most sophisticated form of prose fiction to arise from this tradition because it allows realism to trump didacticism. He argues that the novel is the literary form of the future and urges Japanese authors not to slavishly emulate the works of the Edo-period writers Kyokutei Bakin, Tamenaga Shunsui, and Ryūtei Tanehiko when they can follow the path of such great novelists as Sir Walter Scott, Edward Bulwer-Lytton, Alexandre Dumas, and George Eliot.

PATRICK CADDEAU

Introduction

Our nation can boast of a most remarkable legacy in the composition of prose fiction [*monogatari*]. Looking to the distant past, we find *The Tale of Genji*, *The Tale of Sagoromo*, *The Tale of Hamamatsu Chūnagon*, and *The Tale of Sumiyoshi*. Later, one finds Ichijō Zenkō's popular fiction followed by such works as Ono no O-Tsū's *The Tale of Jōruri in Twelve Episodes*.[16] Closer to our own era, we have [Ihara] Saikaku [1642–1693], Ejima Kiseki [1666–1735], Hiraga Gennai [1728–1780], and [Santō] Kyōden [1761–1816], all of whom wrote prose fiction and, in seeking ever greater repute in their own day, contributed to the increasing popularity of the novel [*shōsetsu*]. Talented writers of the day strove to compose historical romances [*haishi*]. Others sought to imitate the comedies of [Shikitei] Sanba [1776–1822] and [Jippensha] Ikku [1765–1831]. Others attempted to write love stories [*ninjōbon*] in the style of the famous Tamenaga Shunsui [1790–1843]. [Ryūtei] Tanehiko [1783–1842] became famous for *An Imposter Murasaki and a Rustic Genji*, and [Kyokutei] Bakin's [1767–1848] reputation rests on his *Satomi and the Eight Dogs* [*Hakkenden*, 1814–1842]. But popular writers temporarily stopped publishing with the changes wrought by the Meiji Restoration, leading to a decline in the novel's popularity. Today the situation has greatly improved, and writers now seem to be publishing prose fiction again. . . . While there is no shortage of so-called writers of popular fiction, nearly all of them should really be considered as producing adaptations, for not a single one is worthy of the title of author. . . . This is most unfortunate. . . . For this reason, I offer my own views concerning the reform and improvement of the novel in our country in an attempt to educate readers while also enlightening authors. It is my hope that in my doing so, we will see the prose fiction of our nation surpass the European novel so that it takes its rightful place among the arts of painting, music, and poetry.

The Main Purpose of the Novel

In *A Little Jeweled Comb*, Motoori Norinaga argues as follows concerning the main purpose of *The Tale of Genji*:

> From olden times, there have been various interpretations of the intentions of this tale. All of them, however, fail to take into account the nature of those works that we call tales. They argue entirely in the idiom of Confucian and Buddhist texts, which was not what the author intended. Although there happen to be points of chance resemblance and accord with Confucian and Buddhist texts, it will not do to seize on these as characterizing the work as a whole. Its overall import differs sharply from works of that sort. Tales possess a nature uniquely their own.

The preceding quotation from Motoori Norinaga clearly explains the main purpose of the novel. His is truly a work that addresses the nature of prose fiction. I understand that many lesser scholars of classical literature have mistakenly lectured on such far-fetched topics as the notion that *Genji* is in fact a work of didactic intent. How terribly mistaken they are.

In the second volume, Shōyō talks about specific techniques and principles relating to the composition of prose fiction. In discussing literary style, he refers to Genji *as the finest example of the classical Japanese language and praises Murasaki Shikibu's style for its ability to evoke the culture of her time. In the section "Compositional Techniques of the Novel," he returns to* Genji *for an example of ideal structure and composition. He begins by arguing that when considering the design of the novel, it is best to avoid the monotony of a single compositional approach. For example, humor should be complemented by sadness. Likewise, tragic novels will bore the reader if they contain nothing but tragedy. It is particularly important that the conclusion be written in a simple and understated style.*

Compositional Techniques of the Novel

Murasaki Shikibu, in hinting to the reader of Genji's passing simply by creating the chapter [title] "Kumogakure," displays her true genius as a great writer.

["CONSTRUCTING A MAIN CHARACTER"]

The "main character" [*shujinkō*] is the character who is the focus of the novel, what might be called its "main object of worship." . . . Without a main character, it [*Genji*] probably would lack logical continuity.

There are two schools of thought regarding construction of a main character: the realist approach and the idealist approach. The main difference is that the realists take as their model people as they exist, while the idealists take as the basis for a character what society says ought to exist. Take, for example, Hikaru Genji in *The Tale of Genji*. In Murasaki Shikibu's time, there must have been many men of a rank similar to Genji's who were like him. For this reason, ignorant men among the scholars of classical literature have argued that *Genji* is an allegorical work in which each man and woman represents someone who was alive at that time. Nothing could be further from the truth. They simply have failed to recognize that Murasaki Shikibu was a writer belonging to the realist school.

TRANSLATED BY PATRICK CADDEAU

PREFACE TO *A NEW EXEGESIS OF THE TALE OF GENJI*, 1911 (*Shinshaku Genji monogatari*)

SASSA SEISETSU

One of the many consequences of the rise in literacy during the Pax Tokugawa was the attempt to wrest the riches of Heian literature—and particularly *The Tale of Genji*—from the control of their aristocratic custodians and make them available to a burgeoning national readership. As we saw in chapter 7, the task was begun by Edo-period scholars of national learning, who compiled a number of commentaries based less on aristocratic familial traditions than on the model of Chinese "critical philology" (*kōshōgaku*). Far more effective as means of bringing Heian-period texts into the public domain, however, were the commercial publication of printed editions and vernacular translations. The first complete translation of a classical text into modern Japanese was the vernacular version of *Tales of Ise* in seventeenth-century Japanese: *Tales of Ise in Plain Language* (*Ise monogatari hirakotoba*, 1678). By the end of the eighteenth century, two complete translations of the *Kokinshū*, one by Motoori Norinaga and the other by Ozaki Masayoshi (1755–1827), had been completed and published. Despite their colloquial character, the purpose of these translations was explicitly didactic: to enable the beginning student to experience the courtly language of antiquity as "a part of his own being."[17] At this stage, translations did not replace commentaries; rather, they supplemented them.

Bibliographies reveal that during the Edo period, more than a dozen attempts were made to render *Genji* into the contemporary vernacular.[18] None were ever published complete, and the only Meiji-period attempt to produce one was terminated after two volumes. This was *A New Exegesis of The Tale of Genji* (*Shinshaku Genji monogatari*, 1911–1914). The first volume contained the eight chapters from "Kiritsubo" to "Hana no en," and the second volume included another six chapters, bringing the work up to the end of "Miotsukushi."

A New Exegesis provides an edition of *Genji* with headnotes similar in format to those in Kitamura Kigin's *Moonlit Lake Commentary* (*Kogetsushō*,

1673). The compilers also included summaries of each chapter, as well as separate sections of commentary and a modern Japanese translation. Each section of translation is preceded by the original text and followed by commentary. In *Shinshaku Genji monogatari*, translation performs essentially the same function as commentary: it is to be read as an adjunct to and not as a substitute for the original text.

The four compilers of *Shinshaku Genji monogatari* were students at the Imperial (Tokyo) University between 1890 and 1900: Fujii Shiei (1868–1945), Sassa Seisetsu (1872–1917), and Nunami Keion (1877–1927) graduated from the Department of National Literature; and Sasakawa Rinpū (1870–1949), from the Department of National History. All went on to earn their living teaching Japanese literature at high schools and universities. All were also *haikai* (popular linked verse) poets, and members of the Tsukubakai poetry society founded by Imperial University students in 1894. An understanding of *Genji* had always been a prerequisite of *haikai* composition, and the fact that the compilers of *A New Exegesis* chose to list themselves by their *haikai* pen names suggests that they still saw themselves as part of the "old" world of *haikai* as well as the new world of literature in the service of the nation.

In a grandiloquent preface to the initial volume, Sassa Seisetsu explained the mission that underlay the translation project and, in doing so, articulated the agenda of virtually his entire generation of national literature scholars.[19] His mantra-like repetition of the term *mono no aware* (emotional sensitivity) to encapsulate the Japanese "national character" is noteworthy. Clearly, he wanted to mitigate the image of Japan as a nation of battle-hungry samurai driven by the code of the warrior (bushido). In arguing for the preeminence of the culture delineated in and exemplified by *The Tale of Genji*, Sassa and his colleagues were attempting to resituate Japan in the world.

G. G. ROWLEY

Whether or not they know the characters with which the words are written, no one with even the slightest knowledge cannot call to mind the title of *The Tale of Genji*. Yet most have only a vague sense that it is the greatest treasure of our national literature. They know not one thing about its style, its structure, or the thought that informs it. Many have read through two or three passages or a chapter or two in a "history of national literature" or a "national language reader" and admired the fluid style. Many have become familiar with the general structure of the plot through *Shinobugusa* [*A Reminder* (of *The Tale of Genji*)] or *Osana Genji* [*A*

Child's Genji] or another of the various digests or adaptations.[20] But when it comes to people who have read it through from beginning to end, even if one searched among the ranks of those who lecture on contemporary literature, one would not find one person in one thousand one hundred. Indeed, we have no hesitation in asserting that even among specialists in language and literature, most have only read as far as [the twelfth chapter] "Suma." Why is it, then, that the name of *The Tale of Genji* is bandied about so noisily when so few have actually read it? Probably because, first, people have been troubled by the difficulty of understanding its words and phrasing and, second, it is dismissed as a mere curiosity and people do not realize that it is a book that everyone in the nation should read.

Our first task in this *Shinshaku*, therefore, was to make *The Tale of Genji* accessible and popular, and thus we have translated it into ordinary spoken language. The purpose of this book is simply to make *Genji* accessible. Accordingly, for those planning a more traditional study of the tale, this book, from the very outset, will not be the best. Conversely, as a Japanese, if you will be satisfied acquiring some sense of what *Genji* is and acquainting yourself with the rudiments of its style, its structure, and the thought that informs it, then this simple *Shinshaku* will probably serve you well. Our project, if it is not too much to hope for, is to make the incomprehensible *Genji* a thing of the past, once and for all. If at that point, readers still do not flock to *Genji*, then it can only be that they do not fully appreciate its worth, that they do not fully understand why it is a book that everyone in the nation should read. Anyone who attempts to make *Genji* easily understandable, therefore, has a duty to explain its true worth.

To begin with, *Genji* is the unrivaled treasure of the nation and, as such, is something we can boast about to the entire world. When we listen to what the people are saying at the present time, they are praising bushido; all the nations of the world together marvel at our bushido. Yet even many native Japanese forget that the beautiful bushido of the Kamakura period onward was rooted in the Heian court, with its culture of the purest refinement and sensibility. The concepts of firm will and devotion to duty were the strong points of bushido. Just as significant, however, was the graceful, elegant, and genial taste of the Heian court, without which our warriors would have amounted to no more than brutes from the north. If in an earlier age there had been no *Kokinshū*, no *Tales of Ise*, no *Tale of Genji*; if in the age of military government there had been no poetry and no linked verse; [and] if military men had never cultivated *mono no aware*, they would have been only heartless warriors, mere battle-loving barbarians.

Leaving aside for the moment the distant age of the gods, it is undeniable that after the heavenly ancestors of our race subjugated the central regions of the country, the culture that at long last flowered was nourished by the literature and art of Korea, China, and India. No matter how much superb art and literature survive today from the Asuka, Fujiwara, and Nara courts, the period up to and including Nara must be regarded as an era of importing culture from abroad, when literature, art, religion, and other elements from the outside had not been fully assimilated to our own literature and art. For that reason, the poems of the *Man'yōshū* are no more than the simple cries of joy and anger common to all primitive peoples. Two hundred years into the Heian period—what with the vogue for Chinese poetry, the diffusion of exoteric and esoteric Buddhism, and the rise of the purely Japanese in literature and art—imported literature, art, and religion were completely assimilated into and fused with native thought. In the natural development of our national character, this imported culture was fully absorbed and digested, whereupon the unique literature and art of our own nation came into full bloom along with the efflorescent glory of the Fujiwara clan. In the full maturity of peace, the most important accomplishments of ladies and gentlemen were poetry and music. Striving single-mindedly for refinement of sensibility and a richer appreciation of beauty, *mono no aware* was the foremost aesthetic, the highest moral; everything that a person did was always judged by this standard. Is this not the culture of the Heian court?

According to what we hear, Rome should be regarded as the epitome of a culture based on reason, whereas the culture of Greece is a culture of beauty and feeling. This, however, is no more than a comparative evaluation. When in the world, where in the world, has there been a culture like that of our Heian court, so utterly ruled by sensibility? Where in the world were the moon and the cherry blossoms so admired? In what period was there such fondness for *mono no aware*? The world misunderstands our bushido; they say that we are a war-loving people. Yet what is unique in the culture of our nation is this emotionalism, this love of beauty. In our opinion, the most refined culture in the world is the culture of our own Heian court, and our *Tale of Genji* is truly the epitome of this culture. Nonetheless, it must be said that the so-called bushido of the Kamakura period and later was sullied with the bloody dust of battles, and to a certain degree this hindered the development of a natural and harmonious national character. Be that as it may, those investigating our true national character must first of all look back to the Heian court and *The Tale of Genji.*

So refined indeed were their sensibilities that they were uninterested in tales of the weird or the supernatural. The ghosts and the living spirits of *Genji* are, almost without exception, paler than those of the superstitions of our own day. This vast work in fifty-four chapters never depends on strange and terrifying turns of plot to capture the reader's curiosity. Simply by setting down the things she observed, day and night, in the society of her own time, the author makes it impossible for the reader to set the work aside, a rare and extraordinary skill. When you note the period in which the work was composed, around the Kankō era [1004–1012], during the reign of the Ichijō Emperor, this turns out to be more than three hundred years and several decades before the age when Chaucer, whom Tsubouchi Shōyō called the English Murasaki Shikibu, first laid the foundations of English literature. Apart from the ancient literatures of Greece and Rome in the West and India and China in the East, this is a time when nowhere else in the world is any literature worthy of attention to be found. Indeed, in the Kankō era, which corresponds to the beginning of the eleventh century, not a single realistic tale [*shajitsu monogatari*] or novel depicting human emotion [*ninjō shōsetsu*] is to be found, in either the East or the West. *The Tale of Genji*, therefore, is not only the unrivaled treasure of Japanese literature; it should in fact be called an unrivaled treasure of world literature.

Given, then, that *The Tale of Genji* represents the very best in our national character, is the unrivaled treasure of our national literature, and, moreover, is an unrivaled treasure of world literature, how is it that we, the people of Japan, ignore it? Particularly since over the ages the scholars of our nation have made it the focal point of so much research and not a single work of our earlier literature has escaped its influence?

Even before it had been completed, *The Tale of Genji* was the talk of the court, and before long, men and women in both the city and the provinces were vying with one another to make copies of it. The earlier tales came to seem no brighter than stars before the moon. Countless authors of tales competed to produce adaptations and variations. Nor were poets and masters of linked verse behindhand in drawing on the landscape of *Genji* as poetic material. Later, with the development of the study that we now call poetics [*kagaku*], the most revered books after the *Kokinshū* were *Tales of Ise* and *Genji*. Every initiate in the traditions of the way of poetry known as the "secret teachings of the *Kokinshū*" [*Kokin denju*] was constantly engaged in the study of this tale. Accordingly, we find no other tale in our literature that has inspired more works of commentary and criticism than this one. To enumerate only the best known of these: from the Kamakura and Muromachi periods are the *Suigenshō*,[21] *Shigenshō*,[22] *Sengenshō*, *Kakaishō*, *Kachō yosei*, *Rōkashō*, *Rin'itsushō*, *Sairyūshō*, *Myōjōshō*, *Mōshinshō*;[23] at the beginning of the Edo period came the *Mingō nisso* and the *Kogetsushō*;[24] [and] following the revival of the study of the classics were *Genchū shūi*, *Shijo shichiron*, *Tama no ogoto*, and *Genji monogatari hyōshaku*.[25] Never for a moment did scholars, whether of traditional poetics or the new national learning, neglect the intensive study of *Genji*. Consequently, the vocabulary, the sources, the thought, and the structure of *Genji* exerted a ceaseless influence on their works. No matter what the endeavor, it is wasted effort for anyone who wishes to read Japanese prose, Japanese poetry, linked verse, and the like not to recognize *Genji* as the wellspring of them all.

And not just Japanese prose and poetry: as is well known, there are many *Genji* plays in the repertoire of that progenitor of our drama, the nō. Even among the popular songs of the age of the Northern and Southern Courts, an important source for nō drama, many derive from *Genji*. Furthermore, as a result of the masters of linked verse immersing themselves in *Genji*, its influence is plainly to be seen not only in linked verse proper but also in *haikai*. Thus from early Edo onward, the Teitoku school made *Genji* required reading, along with the *Kokinshū* and the *Tales of Ise*. Likewise, Kitamura Kigin, himself a poet of the Teitoku school, wrote a commentary on *Genji*, the *Kogetsushō*, and various *haikai* poets and literati such as Hinaya [Ryūho][26] and Kitamura Koshun wrote a number of digests and popularizations such as *Osana Genji*, *Jūjō Genji* [*A Genji in Ten Volumes*], *Shinobugusa*, *Hinazuru Genji* [*A Fledgling's Tale of Genji*], and *Wakakusa Genji* [*A Young Sprout's Tale of Genji*].[27]

It must have been at about this point that early modern writers of popular literature, even if they knew nothing about the original text, caught something about the general idea of *Genji* from either nō or digests and popularizations. Saikaku structured his *Life of an Amorous Man* [1682] as a story of a single man who has relations with numerous women. Chikamatsu's *Kokiden uwanariuchi* brings together the Kokiden Empress Mother and the Rokujō Consort.[28] There is a song, with koto accompaniment, about Oborozukiyo, and in the theater, Lady Aoi's vengeful spirit is portrayed. Then, after the resurgence of ancient studies [*kogaku*], when the literature of the past became somewhat better known, an adaptation of the entire tale appeared: *An Imposter Murasaki and a Rustic Genji*.[29] In the Bunka [1804–1818] and Tenpō [1830–1844] eras, this work was received with unprecedented acclaim. Such was its vogue that nothing—from color prints and drama to clothing and household furnishings—was untouched by it. This is but another example of the extraordinary influence of *Genji* itself.

An Imposter Murasaki and a Rustic Genji and its ilk are extraordinarily crude adaptations, which, needless to say, show a complete disregard for the sensibility of the original text. Even judged as one of Tanehiko's popular fictions, it is not a work of the first order. The only reason that it drew such praise, it seems to me, is that knowledge of our *Tale of Genji*, however vague, had, through the several literary arts, spread throughout society from top to bottom, and this in itself inspired boundless admiration for the work.

Ah! *The Tale of Genji*! Were we to lose it, the literary arts of the Heian court would lose most of their luster. Were we to banish its influence, we would lose half of all the literary arts since the Kamakura period. And this is but the prospect in the field of literary history. How immense would be the loss were we to dismiss it as a source for painting and the plastic arts. Ah! It is not simply as a major work of literature from the past that *The Tale of Genji* is the unrivaled treasure of the nation. For some eight hundred years, it has never ceased to exert a profound and widespread influence on our literature and arts while at the same time it has provided an unshakable basis for the sensibility and the thought of the people of our nation.

With our work on the *Shinshaku*—though in many ways we have not fulfilled our expectations—it is our earnest hope that we may bring a bit of clarity to our readers' vague knowledge of this tale. It is our earnest hope that we may give our fellow citizens an opportunity to reflect anew upon our national character.

TRANSLATED BY G. G. ROWLEY

UPON FINISHING *A NEW TRANSLATION OF THE TALE OF GENJI*, 1913
(*Shin'yaku Genji monogatari* no nochi ni)

YOSANO AKIKO

By the end of the first decade of the twentieth century, the descendants of Edo-period scholars of national learning were calling for a modern translation of *The Tale of Genji* that would help build a national identity both at home and abroad. The respect accorded novels in Europe also contributed to this perception: in *Genji*, it was felt, Japan had something comparable. To this end, Yosano Akiko (1878–1942) took a major step in 1912 to 1913 when she published her first translation of *Genji* into colloquial Japanese, *Shin'yaku Genji monogatari* (*A New Translation of The Tale of Genji*).

Yosano Akiko was born into a merchant-class family in the old port city of Sakai on the Inland Sea south of Osaka. She received a comparatively good education for a young woman of her class and time, completing primary school and going on to graduate from the Sakai Girls' School in 1892. *The Tale of Genji* was her favorite book: she once wrote that she could not count how many times she had read *Genji* before she turned twenty.[30] Romantic yearning became reality when in June 1901 she ran away from home to live with her lover, the poet Yosano Hiroshi (pen name Tekkan, 1873–1935), in Tokyo. In August of that year, her literary career was launched with the publication of *Midaregami* (*Tangled Hair*), a collection of 399 *tanka* that has remained her most celebrated work.

It is clear from the afterword to her first modern translation of *The Tale of Genji* that Akiko regarded *Genji* as a novel (*shōsetsu*) and Murasaki Shikibu as a novelist (*shōsetsuka*). Therefore, she had no compunctions about translating the language of the Heian-period "novel" into the novelist's language of her own time.[31] With her publisher, Kanao Tanejirō (1879–1947), Akiko originally planned a thousand-page translation that would be divided evenly into three volumes. At first she cut boldly, drastically rewriting the twenty-one chapters from "Kiritsubo" to "Otome." But readers wrote to say that they wanted a more complete translation. She complied, and the later chapters were translated more thoroughly—though by no means in their entirety—necessitating a fourth volume.[32] By reducing the length of the tale and translating freely, Akiko rewrote *Genji* in the language of the modern novel. She thus broke completely with an exegetical tradition grounded in the study of the Chinese classics and developed by generations of scholars for the interpretation of works in the native literary tradition. The *Shin'yaku* was designed to be read from cover to cover, not pored over piecemeal as a commentary would be. Although Akiko was quick to disparage her first translation, it was hailed as a landmark by Ueda Bin (1874–1916) and Mori Ōgai (1862–1922) and reviewed favorably by the major newspapers and literary journals of the period. It also was popular with readers and remained in print for twenty-five years until her second translation began to appear in October 1938.

G. G. ROWLEY

[. . .] Of all the classics [*koten*] of our country, *The Tale of Genji* is the book I have most loved to read. Quite frankly, when it comes to comprehending this novel [*shōsetsu*] in all its complexity, I have the stubborn confidence of a master.

My approach to translating this work has been much like that of beginning painters, who, in emulating the masterpieces of earlier ages, may produce rather free renditions of them. I have eliminated those details that, being far removed from modern life, we can neither identify nor sympathize with and thus only resent for their needless nicety. My principal aim has been to re-create as directly as possible the spirit of the original through the instrument of the modern language. I have endeavored to be both scrupulous and bold. I did not always adhere to the original author's expressions; [that is,] I did not always translate literally. Having made the spirit of the original my own, I then attempted a free translation.

Needless to say, I do not hold in high regard any of the existing commentaries on *The Tale of Genji*. The *Moonlit Lake Commentary*, in particular, I find to be a careless work that misinterprets the original.

For the first few chapters, from "Kiritsubo" onward, I have attempted a somewhat abbreviated translation. Since these chapters have long been widely read and offer few difficulties, I thought that little more was needed. Beginning with the second volume of this work, however, for the benefit of those who might find it difficult to read the original, I've taken care to translate the text virtually in its entirety.

The Tale of Genji can be divided into two large parts: the part in which Hikaru and Murasaki are the main characters, and the part in which Kaoru and Ukifune are the main characters. When we reach the ten Uji chapters in the second part, the sumptuous style of the first part, replete

Monks discover Ukifune under a tree in "Tenarai." (Woodblock illustration by Nakazawa Hiromitsu [1874–1964], in *Shin'yaku Genji monogatari*, trans. Yosano Akiko, vol. 4 [Tokyo: Kanao Bun'endō, 1913]. Private collection)

with glitter and refinement, gives way to a simpler and cleaner style, which imparts an air of freshness to the narrative. This sense of rejuvenation is the product of Murasaki Shikibu's genius, ever vigorous, at which one can only marvel. [Accordingly,] those who fail to finish the final ten Uji chapters when reading *The Tale of Genji* cannot be said to have read the whole of Murasaki Shikibu.

None of the principal characters in *The Tale of Genji*, neither men nor women, is given a name. Therefore, past readers have borrowed words from poems with which the characters are associated, using them as nicknames. For the sake of convenience, I have followed these customary appellations in this work. . . .

In conclusion, to commemorate this occasion, I wish to add that in the summer of last year, in Paris, I personally presented copies of the first two volumes of this work to the sculptor Auguste Rodin and the poet Henri de Régnier.[33] Rodin looked through the illustrations and, exclaiming all the while over the beauty of the Japanese woodblock prints, he said:

> The number of people in France and in Japan studying the language and thought of our two countries will gradually increase. I bitterly regret being unable to read Japanese, but I trust that one day in the future I shall be able to appreciate the thought of this book by means of a friend's translation.

The memory of his words is still fresh in my mind.[34]

TRANSLATED BY G. G. ROWLEY

AFTERWORD TO *A NEW NEW TRANSLATION OF THE TALE OF GENJI*, 1939
(*Shin-shin'yaku Genji monogatari*)

YOSANO AKIKO

Akiko was never happy with her first, abbreviated, translation of *The Tale of Genji* and always hoped to prepare a complete version. In the autumn of 1932, aged fifty-four, she began work; *Shin-shin'yaku Genji monogatari* (*A New New Translation of The Tale of Genji*) was published in six volumes between October 1938 and September 1939. It does not seem to have attracted the notice that had greeted the publication of *Shin'yaku* a quarter of a century earlier and, by all accounts, was a commercial failure. By 1938, Japan was at war. Moreover, Akiko's translation had a powerful competitor in Tanizaki Jun'ichirō's first modern translation of *Genji*, which began appearing in January 1939. Akiko's publisher, Kanao, could not afford to advertise extensively, and some people apparently thought that *Shin-shin'yaku* was merely a reprint of the earlier *Shin'yaku*. Only after the end of World War II was *Shin-shin'yaku* commercially successful. It was first reprinted as part of the Nihon no Bunko (Library of Japan) series during the Occupation—before the appearance of Tanizaki's second translation—and has since been republished several dozen times in a variety of formats.[35]

Akiko's "Afterword" to *Shin-shin'yaku* is a useful summary of her views on the structure and authorship of *Genji*.[36] In both these areas of research, Akiko was recognized by twentieth-century scholars as an important pioneer.[37]

G. G. ROWLEY

[. . .] I believe that *The Tale of Genji* is a work in two parts by two authors. I am unable, however, to set forth in detail my research on the matter here. It has long been said that the ten Uji chapters are the work of Murasaki Shikibu's daughter Daini no Sanmi.[38] Many Tokugawa-period scholars of national learning denied this. Previously, I too was so persuaded. In the Meiji period, when Dr. Kume Kunitake wrote in a nō journal that *Genji* appears to have been written by several people, I did not at all accept this, thinking that although Dr. Kume was a first-rate scholar of history, he was no scholar of literature.[39] It was some years before I began work on the *Shin-shin'yaku* that I realized that there were two authors of *Genji*. The work of the first author ends at "Fuji no uraba": everything is very auspicious, and after Genji becomes Honorary Emperor in Retirement [*daijō tennō*] all is tinted in gold. Undaunted, the second author begins to write about Genji facing a turn in his fortunes. The woman he loved best, Lady Murasaki, dies, and there also is Nyosan no Miya's [Onnasannomiya's] indiscretion. In preparation for the birth of Kaoru, the main character of the latter part, talk suddenly turns to the women of the court after the Suzaku Emperor retires. Suzaku's pathetic fondness for Nyosan no Miya prepares the way for Kaoru's bounty. The skill with which the novel is structured here surpasses that of the first part.

If one reads the original with care, one should notice that from the "Wakana" chapters onward, the text is constructed differently. What had without fail been *kandachime, tenjōbito* [senior nobles and privy gentlemen] becomes *shodayū, tenjōbito, kandachime* [stewards, privy gentlemen, and senior nobles].[40] This should be immediately apparent to those who read a recent movable-type edition rather than an old manuscript or woodblock-printed edition. The style is bad; there are fewer poems. And superior poems are exceedingly rare. The first part, written by Murasaki Shikibu, abounds in superb poems—not that there are none whatsoever by the second author.

me ni chikaku utsureba kawaru yo no naka o / yukusue tōku tanomikeru ka na
Ah, how trustingly I believed that what we had would last on and on,
when your feelings in this world shift and change before my eyes.[41]

obotsu ka na tare ni towamashi ika ni shite / hajime mo hate mo shiranu wagami zo
What can it all mean, and whom have I to question? What is my secret,
when I myself do not know whence I come or where I go?[42]

These poems closely resemble the first poem in the autumn section of the *Goshūishū* [1086] by Daini no Sanmi:

haruka naru Morokoshi made mo yuku mono wa / aki no nezame no kokoro narikeri
In the autumn, waking from sleep and opening one's eyes—that feeling
is like traveling all the way to far distant Cathay.[43]

This poem is very similar, is it not?

At the beginning of the "Takekawa" chapter, which is couched as a tale told by an elderly serving woman who had worked in the household of the late chancellor [Higekuro], it is written: *Murasaki no yukari koyonaki ni wa nizameredo*. This passage means "What follows will not be of the same quality as the foregoing written by Murasaki Shikibu," and it is wrong of commentators to interpret this passage as referring to Lady Murasaki in the novel.[44] It would be strange, would it not, to compare Lady Murasaki, who had no descendants, with those of a different household?

Previously, when I was doing this research, I calculated twenty-six years as the period between the writing of the first part [of *Genji*] and the writing of the latter part.[45] By then, the era of the Heian court had given way to an era in which provincial administrators using military force were beginning to gain power. One of these is the rich man who, having been governor of Michinoku, becomes the deputy governor of Hitachi.[46]

It still is possible to see a plaque in the hand of Emperor GoReizei [1025–1068; r. 1045–1068] in the temple next door to the Byōdō-in [in Uji]. *Kanbun* diaries kept by men of the period say that when GoReizei was crown prince [1037–1045], he often went to visit the mansion of [Fujiwara no] Yorimichi in Uji. Daini no Sanmi was Emperor GoReizei's wet nurse; she went often to Uji in his entourage and came to know the place well.[47]

The poems [in this part] are not as good as those of the author of the first part, but neither are they mediocre. Because this is a great novel from the hand of one who had distinguished herself as a poet at that time, I searched high and low for Daini no Sanmi's personal poetry collection, but it is no longer extant.[48] I carefully examined the *Daini Collection* [*Daini shū*], which is listed in the catalog of the Kōgakukan in Ise, but it is the work of Sanmi's daughter, the woman known [also] as Sanmi who served GoReizei's consort, and the compositions are far inferior to her mother's poems, let alone her grandmother's.

Ukifune already is a subject of discussion in the *Sarashina Diary* [*Sarashina nikki*], but because the diary, which begins with an account of the author's younger days, was written in her later years, it is possible that her memory is not entirely reliable. Although in my estimate of twenty-six years I took into account the year in which the *Sarashina* diarist returned to the capital, it may be that this gap is a little too long.[49]

The author whose style and narrative technique in the "Wakana" chapters are rough has become a splendid writer by the "Kashiwagi" and "Yūgiri" [chapters]. I say this because these chapters so abound in genius. From the "Azumaya" chapter on, her technique, as much as the content, is magnificent. The author of the first part, Murasaki Shikibu, was extraordinary as a novelist [*shōsetsu sakka*] and as a poet [*kajin*]; Daini no Sanmi, who wrote the second part, was, in my opinion, a great general practitioner of literature [*bungakusha*]. It is a shame that I do not have the time to expound this in greater detail. . . .

TRANSLATED BY G. G. ROWLEY

THE TALE OF GENJI: THE FIRST VOLUME OF MR. ARTHUR WALEY'S TRANSLATION OF A GREAT JAPANESE NOVEL BY THE LADY MURASAKI, 1925

VIRGINIA WOOLF

Arthur Waley's (1889–1966) translation of *Genji monogatari* was published in six volumes from 1925 to 1933. Although this translation was completed nearly half a century after the publication of a partial translation by the Japanese diplomat and journalist Suematsu Kenchō, Waley's work is often considered the first English translation of Murasaki Shikibu's tale. It was through Waley's translation that *The Tale of Genji* came to be recognized inside and outside Japan as a literary masterpiece with the potential of rivaling the great modern European novels. It was indeed the new understanding of this work as a "novel" that guided modern Japanese writers like Masamune Hakuchō and Tanizaki Jun'ichirō in their encounters with this work and led Jorge Luis Borges to call it a "psychological novel" in his review, published in 1938.[50]

A graduate of King's College, Cambridge, Waley began studying Chinese and Japanese while working in the Print Room of the British Museum, where he was appointed manager of the China and Japan collection. Waley began publishing translations of Chinese and Japanese poems in the late 1910s, and by the time he started to work on *Genji*, he had already published two books on Japanese literature: *Japanese Poetry: The Uta* (1919) and *The Nō Plays of Japan* (1921). Waley's introduction of the eleventh-century Japanese tale (based on the Hakubunkan edition of 1914) caused a stir in the English-speaking literary world, and the volumes were enthusiastically reviewed in leading literary journals such as the *Times Literary Supplement* and *The Nation*. Waley's translation was subsequently retranslated into many European languages, including Italian, German, Dutch, Swedish, and French.

Waley's liberal approach to translation is revealed in this reflection in 1958: "When translating prose dialogue one ought to make the characters say things that people talking English could conceivably say. One ought to hear them talking, just as a novelist hears his characters talk."[51] In the introduction to the first volume of the translation of *Genji monogatari*, Waley makes the author and text familiar to the reader by referring to contemporary British society:

> There is a type of disappointed undergraduate, who believes that all his social and academic failures are due to his being, let us say, at Magdalene instead of St. John's. Murasaki, in like manner, had persuaded herself that all would have gone well if her father had placed her in the highly cultivated and easy-mannered entourage of the Emperor's aunt, Princess Senshi.[52]

Waley's equation of Murasaki Shikibu with a male university student at a prestigious British institution provides an interesting juxtaposition to the review of his translation of *Genji* by Virginia Woolf (1882–1941), for whom women's exclusion from higher education was a crucial part of her feminist thinking. Soon after the publication of a book-length collection of essays, *The Common Reader* (1925), and her fourth novel, *Mrs. Dalloway* (1925), Woolf, who was an established literary critic and an emerging highbrow writer at the time, received an assignment from the British edition of *Vogue* to review the first volume of Waley's translation.[53] From the beginning of her career as a published writer and throughout the 1920s, Woolf's main source of income was literary journalism, primarily reviews of contemporary works. She was a regular reviewer for the *Times Literary Supplement* and other major literary journals, and it was largely for financial reasons that she wrote for the commercial magazine *Vogue*, to which she contributed a total of five signed articles in the 1920s.[54]

Drawing from Murasaki's own vision of the artist, Woolf characterizes the world of *Genji* as one of beauty, serenity, spontaneity, and perfection, in contrast to which the contemporary Western world appears crude and sordid, despite possessing richness, vigor, and maturity that eclipse this ancient Japanese work. Nonetheless, the evocative metaphor of Murasaki's poetry "break[ing] the surface of silence with silver fins" echoes Woolf's own artistic vision, which can be traced throughout her writings, and suggests that *The Tale of Genji* offered Woolf an inspiration for an ideal type of art that she was trying to create. While Woolf did not include Murasaki Shikibu among the "great storytellers of the Western world" (gendered as masculine), she later named her as one of the world's three great women writers in her feminist treatise *A Room of One's Own* (1929), thereby inducting the Japanese author into the canon of women's writing.

HITOMI YOSHIO

Our readers will scarcely need to be reminded that it was about the year 991 that Ælfric composed his Homilies, that his treatises upon the Old and New Testament were slightly later in date, and that both works precede that profound, if obscure, convulsion which set Swegen of Denmark upon the throne of England. Perpetually fighting, now men, now swine, now thickets and swamps, it was with fists swollen with toil, minds contracted by danger, eyes stung with smoke and feet that were cold among the rushes that our ancestors applied themselves to the pen, transcribed, translated and chronicled, or burst rudely, and hoarsely into crude spasms of song.

> Sumer is icumen in,
> Lhude sing cuccu

—such is their sudden harsh cry. Meanwhile, at the same moment, on the other side of the globe the Lady Murasaki was looking out into her garden, and noticing how "among the leaves were white flowers with petals half unfolded like the lips of people smiling at their own thoughts."

While the Ælfrics and the Ælfreds croaked and coughed in England, this court lady, about whom we know nothing, for Mr. Waley artfully withholds all information until the six volumes of her novel are before us, was sitting down in her silk dress and trousers with pictures before her and the sound of poetry in her ears, with flowers in her garden and nightingales in the trees, with all day to talk in and all night to dance in—she was sitting down about the year 1000 to tell the story of the life and adventures of Prince Genji. But we must hasten to correct the impression that the Lady Murasaki was in any sense a chronicler. Since her book was read aloud, we may imagine an audience; but her listeners must have been astute, subtle minded, sophisticated men and women. They were grown-up people, who needed no feats of strength to rivet their attention; no catastrophe to surprise them. They were absorbed, on the contrary, in the contemplation of man's nature; how passionately he desires things that are denied; how his longing for a life of tender intimacy is always thwarted; how the grotesque and the fantastic excite him beyond the simple and straightforward; how beautiful the falling snow is, and how, as he watches it, he longs more than ever for someone to share his solitary joy.

The Lady Murasaki lived, indeed, in one of those seasons which are most propitious for the artist, and, in particular, for an artist of her own sex. The accent of life did not fall upon war; the interests of men did not centre upon politics. Relieved from the violent pressure of these two forces, life expressed itself chiefly in the intricacies of behaviour, in what men said and what women did not quite say, in poems that break the surface of silence with silver fins, in dance and painting, and in that love of the wildness of nature which only comes when people feel themselves perfectly secure. In such an age as this Lady Murasaki, with her hatred of bombast, her humour, her common sense, her passion for the contrasts and curiosities of human nature, for old houses mouldering away among the weeds and the winds, and wild landscapes, and the sound of water falling, and mallets beating, and wild geese screaming, and the red noses of princesses, for beauty indeed, and that incongruity which makes beauty still more beautiful, could bring all her powers into play spontaneously. It was one of those moments (how they were reached in Japan and how destroyed we must wait for Mr. Waley to explain) when it was natural for a writer to write of ordinary things beautifully, and to say openly to her public, "It is the common that is wonderful, and if you let yourselves be put off by extravagance and rant and what is surprising and momentarily impressive you will be cheated of the most profound of pleasures." For there are two kinds of artists, said Murasaki: one who makes trifles to fit the fancy of the passing day, the other who "strives to give real beauty to the things which men actually use, and to give them the shapes which tradition has ordained." How easy it is, she said, to impress and surprise; "to paint a raging sea monster riding a storm"—any toy maker can do that, and be praised to the skies. "But ordinary hills and rivers, just as they are, houses such as you may see anywhere, with all their real beauty and harmony of form—quietly to draw such scenes as this, or to show what lies behind some intimate hedge that is folded away far from the world, and thick trees upon some unheroic hill, and all this with befitting care for composition, proportion, and the like—such works demand the highest master's utmost skill and must needs draw the common craftsman into a thousand blunders."

Something of her charm for us is doubtless accidental. It lies in the fact that when she speaks of "houses such as you may see anywhere" we at once conjure up something graceful, fantastic, decorated with cranes and chrysanthemums, a thousand miles removed from Surbiton and the Albert Memorial. We give her, and luxuriate in giving her, all those advantages of background and atmosphere which we are forced to do without in England today. But we should wrong her deeply if, thus seduced, we prettified and sentimentalised an art which, exquisite as it is, is without a touch of decadence, which, for all its sensibility, is fresh and childlike and without a trace of the exaggeration or languor of an outworn civilisation. But the essence of her charm lies deeper far than cranes and chrysanthemums. It lies in the belief which she held so simply—and was, we feel, supported in holding by Emperors and waiting maids, by the air she breathed and flowers she saw—that the true artist "strives to give real beauty to the things which men actually use and to give to them the shapes which tradition has ordained." On she went, therefore, without hesitation or self-consciousness, effort or agony, to tell the story of the enchanting boy—the Prince who danced "The Waves of the Blue Sea," so beautifully that all the princes and great gentlemen wept aloud; who loved those whom he could not possess; whose libertinage was tempered by the most perfect courtesy; who played enchantingly with children, and preferred, as his women friends knew, that the song should stop before he had heard the end. To light up the many facets of his mind, Lady Murasaki, being herself a woman, naturally chose the medium of other women's minds. Aoi, Asagao, Fujitsubo, Murasaki, Yugao, Suyetsumuhana, the beautiful, the red-nosed, the cold, the passionate—one after another they turn their clear or freakish light upon the gay young man at the centre, who flies, who pursues, who laughs, who sorrows, but is always filled with the rush and bubble and chuckle of life.

Unhasting, unresting, with unabated fertility, story after story flows from the brush of Murasaki. Without this gift of invention we might well fear that the tale of Genji would run dry before the six volumes are filled. With it, we need have no such foreboding. We can take our station and watch, through Mr. Waley's beautiful telescope, the new star rise in perfect confidence that it is going to be large and luminous and serene—but not, nevertheless, a star of the first magnitude. No; the lady Murasaki is not going to prove herself the peer of Tolstoy and Cervantes or those other great story-tellers of the Western world whose ancestors were fighting or squatting in their huts while she gazed from her lattice window at flowers which unfold themselves "like the lips of people smiling at their own thoughts." Some element of horror, of terror, of sordidity, some root of experience has been removed from the Eastern world so that crudeness is impossible and coarseness out of the question, but with it too has gone some vigour, some richness, some maturity of the human spirit, failing which the gold is silvered and the wine mixed with water. All comparisons between Murasaki and the great Western writers serve but to bring out her perfection and their force. But it is a beautiful world; the quiet lady with all her breeding, her insight and her fun, is a perfect artist; and for years to come we shall be haunting her groves, watching her moons rise and her snow fall, hearing her wild geese cry and her flutes and lutes and flageolets tinkling and chiming, while the Prince tastes and tries all the queer savours of life and dances so exquisitely that men weep, but never passes the bounds of decorum, or relaxes his search for something different, something finer, something withheld.

ON READING THE CLASSICS, 1926
(Koten o yonde)
MASAMUNE HAKUCHŌ

Standard literary histories typically describe Masamune Hakuchō (1879–1962) as an important minor author who stands slightly outside the center of the Japanese naturalist movement and emphasize his penchant for fiction steeped in nihilism, skepticism, and irony. He is also seen as a worshipper of the West, an impression that Tanizaki Jun'ichirō summed up nicely when he wrote in 1932 that "there can't be many authors over the age of forty writing today who are as skeptical of the value of their motherland's traditions and as partial to the literature of the West as Mr. Hakuchō."[55] In fact, Hakuchō continued writing for half a century after the naturalist movement petered out, and although the stories he produced in the first decade or so of his career do exhibit many of the characteristics associated with the naturalist style, this is by no means true of his work as a whole, which includes translations, plays, and a large body of extremely interesting criticism. The image of Hakuchō as a naive, uncritical devotee of all things Western is also, one might argue, greatly exaggerated.

If Hakuchō is remembered by literary historians for a handful of his early stories and for his critical writings about Dante and other Western writers, he remains infamous among scholars of *The Tale of Genji* for a series of four essays published between 1926 and 1955 that contain some unflattering descriptions of the text of *Genji* itself ("its sentences are like bodies with their heads chopped off, tottering unsteadily this way and that—maddening things to read")[56] but say very complementary things about Arthur Waley's English translation. The scholar Chiba Shunji went so far as to say that Hakuchō's statements on *Genji* and its English translation are the ultimate symbol of the "ironic" position that *Genji* has occupied in modern Japanese literature.[57] It is not difficult to see why many scholars of *Genji* might agree with this statement. At the same time, not all readers of Hakuchō's essays saw things in this way: a newspaper column in 1933 noted that "for us, living in the modern age, a text like *Genji* that's written in the old language is totally unreadable—it's only after we translate the thing into a foreign language that we can read it, even if we do have to keep consulting the dictionary . . . foreign countries are still closer than the past."[58] One might argue that Hakuchō's four essays on *Genji* encourage us to consider the ironic position that *Genji* scholarship—rather than the work itself—has occupied in modern and contemporary Japan. Hakuchō's essays, including "On Reading the Classics," push us contemporary readers to think more about what we are doing when we read *Genji*, what or whose standards we use in evaluating it, and how we define its relevance to our own times and lives.

"On Reading the Classics," which first appeared in August 1926 in the magazine *Chūōkōron* and was reprinted in a collection of critical essays, *Bungei hyōron* (1927), is the first of Hakuchō's four essays on *Genji*.[59] Hakuchō makes no reference to the English translation of *Genji* in this piece because he had no idea when he wrote it that one was being written (the second volume of Arthur Waley's six-volume *The Tale of Genji* was published in February 1926). Even so, translation figures prominently in this essay. "On Reading the Classics" contains what may be the single most infamous sentence ever written about *The Tale of Genji*: "Say what you like about the content, the writing is incomparably bad." It may surprise readers who have come across this phrase but never have seen it in context to learn that the essay in which it appears is not an attack on *Genji* but, rather, a nuanced, wide-ranging, and thought-provoking meditation on the potentials of translation and the importance of literary style.

MICHAEL EMMERICH

I started reading *The Dream of the Red Chamber*[60] and *The Tale of Genji*; then, partway through, I gave up. Unless at some later date I find myself with a great deal of time on my hands, I doubt that I will ever feel the urge to continue reading these two great and celebrated novels of the Chinese and Japanese traditions. . . .

At the same time that I was agonizing over the literal translation of *The Dream of the Red Chamber*, I was also reading *The Tale of Genji* and feeling disgusted at its slipshod, lax, and rambling writing. Granted, it is a classical work that appeared some thousand years ago. Nonetheless, I was born in the same country as its author, and I've spent a fair amount of time studying the old language ever since I was a boy—it's strange that I feel such hatred for this tale, generally thought to be Japan's greatest masterpiece. But the fact is that I have never before encountered a work so difficult to read. I feel more interest in the great classics of the West, the *Iliad*, the *Odyssey*, and so on, so at least I am able to keep reading them; but when it came to *Genji*, a work viewed as a national treasure in the literature of my own country, I found myself yearning, more times than I could count, to hurl it against the wall. Say what you like about the content, the writing is incomparably bad. The very idea of including a work like this in a textbook in this day and age strikes me as absurd. I'm sure even *Genji* would be more engaging when read in an English translation.[61]

When I was in school, I heard Mr. Hatakeyama Takeshi lecture on *Genji* up through the "rainy night ranking."[62] After that, I read a few chapters in Hagiwara Hiromichi's *Genji monogatari hyōshaku*.[63] My purpose in reading it was to study the old language, so I didn't find the book interesting and it made no impression on me. This time, I read the Yūhōdo bunko edition,[64] and I found that if I made adequate use of the notes at the top of the page, I could follow the sense of the writing quite well, and I was able to come into direct contact with the original work in a way that was impossible when I read the clumsy literal translation of *The Dream of the Red Chamber*. Nonetheless, apart from the historical interest I felt in learning about the living conditions, the manners, and the customs of the period, I hardly felt anything at all—there was no sort of artistic gratification. I've read more novels than I can say over the course of my life, but I've never encountered a book as difficult, as unrewarding, and as boring as this one. I read on at the tortuous, plodding pace of a cow until I reached "Suma" and "Akashi"; then arriving at "Eawase" and "Matsukaze," I tossed the work aside and decided it was time to give up. I'm told there is an old phrase that people use when someone reads to this point and then gives up: they refer to this as "Suma *Genji*."[65] I can see why the phrase was invented.

Rather than being filled with extravagant fictions of the sort one encounters in the *kusazōshi* and *yomihon* of the Tokugawa period,[66] the work offers neatly differentiated portraits of the loves and passions men and women felt for each other—descriptions that seem, pallid as they are, to reflect the actualities of the time. The writing, however, is like a line of jellyfish and totally prevents the tale from giving us a true impression of life. In terms of the strength of its descriptions, *The Pillow Book* is vastly superior: its prose is more succinct and makes a deeper impression. People have long observed that *Genji* shows the characters of a variety of women, cultivating throughout a mood of *mono no aware*,[67] but I find it all extremely superficial. True, feelings of jealousy, dejection, and joy do appear in several different forms, but they are like dim shadows of the real thing. An endless parade of scenes featuring underdeveloped characters lacking both spiritual strength and the ability to manage their lives—this was how the tale appeared to me. There's nothing wrong with this, I suppose, since that's how society was at the time, but even in the world of painting, good art doesn't mean just painting a decrepit old man so that he looks decrepit. In the world of sculpture, too, a good work draws out the implicit human strength of the subject in a way that strikes the eye of the viewer, even when the subject is a rundown old man and even though the outward form faithfully represents his weakness. Murasaki Shikibu was a brilliant woman, but a brilliant woman is still a woman. Her grasp of human nature was shallow. In the chapters I read, the only places in which I felt any interest were the sections showing Genji's longing for Fujitsubo and the way he acted toward her, which gave off flashes of human strength, and "Suetsumuhana," which was engaging enough to break the monotony.

It seems that even in the Tokugawa period there were a relatively large number of commentaries on *The Tale of Genji*. If I adopted a scholarly attitude toward old literature, if I did preparatory groundwork and then lost myself in researching the tale, I might discover all kinds of beautiful things in it, and I would be able to reason my way into praising this classic. But I live in contemporary times, in this Taishō period, and the impression I came away with after I sat down without any preconceptions, opened this very long work and read what I could, is that it is extraordinarily uninteresting.

I am not attempting here to write a critical essay on *The Tale of Genji*. As I struggled to read this long piece of writing—one that exerted a huge influence on the literature and arts of later ages and that has been viewed since ancient times as the greatest of Japan's literary works—I thought about Japanese writing. When you read through a work very attentively, the words used, the tone, and the format all give you an idea of the character, the spirit, the cultivation, and the thought of its nation's citizenry. And I have to say that it's a mystery to me how the Japanese of a previous age could have been pleased by writing like this. Writing with a lineage that can be traced back to *Genji* is now considered the purest sort of Japanese. And yet even though my thinking grows more conservative as I age and begin to take pleasure in Japan's traditional aesthetics, it has reached the point that I am unable to invest either my emotions or my thought in writing of this sort. Even classical Chinese literature . . . has more power to move my heart.

Would a contemporary youth with some measure of cultivation in literary matters find, if he opened *Genji* at random and started reading, anything that stimulated his appetite for art, even slightly? Japan has, it seems, a rich store of outstanding artworks in the fields of painting and sculpture, but where literature is concerned, we have had a long line of works so feeble they seem malnourished.

Not long ago, I opened up on my desk a sample copy of a book of literary works from the Edo period that was about to be published on the subscription system, and I spent some time poring over it. I had already read a smattering of works by some of the many writers in the various different genres, and my spotty knowledge allowed me to imagine, more or less, what the rest would be like. Apart from Chikamatsu, Saikaku, and Bashō, where would I find any authors whose works I could reread and still respect?

Only in modern times did Russian literature take off; perhaps it was actually better off that way, since it didn't have to shoulder the heavy burden of a past filled with tedious traditions. There were no outstanding literary geniuses in Japan's past.

Apparently every day before he took up his pen to start writing, [William Makepeace] Thackeray read the Bible. When Rai Sanyō was writing *Nihon gaishi*,[68] he read *The Analects* so that he could use it as the model for his style. And I've heard a story that when the great Ozaki Kōyō[69] was writing "Speechless," he read *The Tale of Genji* every day. I guess the young literati of the early Meiji period, tired of the styles of writers such as Bakin and Shunsui,[70] must have tried to adopt the archaic rhythms of texts like *Genji*, which might be long-winded and weak but still were elegant and had a certain "sketch-like" feel about them.[71] It was only natural that they studied with great pleasure the more succinct style of Saikaku's prose.[72] Recently, I went back for the first time in quite a while and read through *The Life of an Amorous Man* in the Complete Classics[73] edition, and as I was reading it occurred to me that even more than Kōyō and Rohan, Ichiyō[74] had really absorbed a lot from Saikaku's prose. She seems to have studied *Genji* and Saikaku together and used them both to create a style of her own. She looked at the immature, idiosyncratic writing of Saikaku's early works—collections dealing with amorous affairs such as *The Life of an Amorous Man* and *The Life of an Amorous Woman*.[75] The later works, such as *Worldly Mental Calculations*, *A Thousand Scraps*, and *Things Saikaku Left Behind*,[76] no longer exhibit any trace of the astonishing verbal feats he pulled off in his early works; the writing becomes smooth and resonant, so masterly as to be entirely without peer in all of classical Japanese literature.

The shining lights of the early Meiji literary establishment sought models for their writing in the supposedly polished prose of *Genji* and its heirs and in the unlearned mastery of style that is characteristic of Saikaku. Even Mr. Shimazaki Tōson,[77] who had only just made his debut, went to Ishiyama Temple as a young man, during the days when he was aimlessly wandering the countryside, to leave a copy of *Hamlet* as an offering to Murasaki Shikibu. The period when writers took *Genji* and Saikaku as their models didn't, however, last long. A new age saw the rise of a new literature. Writing that had severed its ties with the old Japanese classics began to appear. This was the literature of Kunikida Doppo.[78] (Doppo seemed to feel scorn for both Saikaku and Chikamatsu.) This was the literature of Mushanokōji Saneatsu.

But I, for one, am getting tired of their literature and their style of writing. Humanity's desire for artistry won't be satisfied forever with mere unadorned simplicity. Strong energies, beautiful colors, fragrant perfumes, startling noises . . . all the things that lie waiting in our senses, in our minds and bodies, must emerge in written form.

It's true that the dramatic flourishes that old actors used are so out of date that one can hardly stand to watch them, but then the plays the new troupes put on are so tasteless and grubby that you can hardly stand to watch them, either. And it's just the same with writing. It would be nice to have a literature for this new age whose works would keep getting better and better with each rereading.

The writings of Tanizaki, Satomi, and Akutagawa[79] may be too heavily infused with the scent of the old literatures of China and the Tokugawa period to be enjoyed as trail-blazing writings of a new age, but I still prefer their fictions to most of the other works currently being written, which offer nothing but a string of events.

TRANSLATED BY MICHAEL EMMERICH

ON TRANSLATING *THE TALE OF GENJI* INTO MODERN JAPANESE, 1938

(*Genji monogatari* no gendaigoyaku ni tsuite)

TANIZAKI JUN'ICHIRŌ

Tanizaki Jun'ichirō (1886–1965) is best known as the author of some of the most highly regarded novels and essays of twentieth-century Japan. What is less well known is that his most massive work is a complete translation of *The Tale of Genji* and that this project was directly inspired by Arthur Waley's English translation of *Genji*.[80] There are three versions of the "Tanizaki *Genji*." The earliest, *Jun'ichirō yaku Genji monogatari* (*Jun'ichirō's Translation of The Tale of Genji*, twenty-six volumes), was published between January 1939 and July 1941 while Japan was at war with China. The second, *Jun'ichirō shin'yaku Genji monogatari* (*Jun'ichirō's New Translation of The Tale of Genji*, twelve volumes), was published between May 1951 and December 1954. And the third, *Jun'ichirō shin-shin'yaku Genji monogatari* (*Jun'ichirō's New New Translation of The Tale of Genji*, ten volumes), appeared between November 1964 and October 1965 during the last year of the writer's life. All three translations were commissioned and published by the major Tokyo publishing house Chūōkōronsha. Sales of the various editions of the Tanizaki *Genji* generated enormous income for both the publishing company and the translator, and the successful marketing of the translations to a mass readership has recently become the subject of intense interest.

That Tanizaki published three translations of *Genji* in the space of less than thirty years has led some scholars to make great claims for "the fundamental importance of *The Tale of Genji* to the man and his art."[81] The evidence does not support such a view, however, and Tanizaki himself—despite his admiration for *Genji*—was at pains to distance himself from such a reductive account of his work. Unlike Yosano Akiko, who worked alone on her two translations, Tanizaki benefited from the assistance of a number of collaborators: his first two translations were minutely supervised by Yamada Yoshio (1875–1958), the ultranationalist scholar of Japanese language and literature;[82] revisions to his second translation were overseen by Tamagami Takuya (1915–1996) of the Department of Japanese Language and Literature at Kyoto University; and revisions to his third translation were made by Tokyo University professor Akiyama Ken (b. 1924) and his graduate students.[83]

Tanizaki wrote several essays about *The Tale of Genji* and the process of translating it. His principal essay on the subject, "On Translating *The Tale of Genji* into Modern Japanese," is translated here.[84] Tanizaki admits that the idea of translating *Genji* did not originate with him but with Shimanaka Yūsaku (1887–1949), the president of Chūōkōronsha. Correspondence between the two enables us to date Shimanaka's proposal to late 1933, when he first learned of Arthur Waley's English translation.[85] Shimanaka immediately had a copy of Waley's *Genji* sent to Tanizaki, but not until September 1935 did Tanizaki begin working in earnest. He had hesitated, he claims, because he was "such an exceptionally slow writer" and *Genji* was "such an enormous work." Otherwise, as he states, with characteristic immodesty, "I might well have had the idea and finished the job long before Chūōkōron suggested it." In fact, Tanizaki had been delayed by divorce and remarriage, and severe financial pressure was one of several factors that drove him finally to accept Shimanaka's proposal.

G. G. ROWLEY

I think it must have been young Shimanaka, president of Chūōkōronsha, who had the idea of getting me to translate *The Tale of Genji*. I'm not at all the sort of person to accept at the drop of a hat a plan dreamed up and set before me by a magazine publisher. But this proposal interested me enormously right from the start. Whether a disinterested observer would consider me qualified for the task I cannot say; but even supposing I should decide on my own to translate a work of classical literature, there could be no other choice but *Genji*. I am fully aware, of course, that transforming the original text into modern Japanese is no easy task. But because it has long been considered such a difficult work, commentaries, digests, and other such aids abound. From as early as the Kamakura period, and on into the Muromachi and Tokugawa eras, a truly vast variety of academic studies and reference works has been produced; so many, one might say, that the meaning of virtually every word, every phrase, has been explicated. And from the Meiji period through to the present day, the trend has been toward ever greater attention to fine points of detail. We now have several different editions equipped with modern language glosses; and just since I have undertaken this project, our younger scholars of National Learning have published a wealth of new work. With the possible exception of the *Man'yōshū*, no other work possesses such an abundance of exegetical commentary as does *Genji*. With the aid of the work of these scholars, both ancient and modern, one should experience little difficulty in ascertaining the meaning of the text. This is not to say that there are no doubtful or unclear passages whatever; but these are passages that no scholar in the past has been able to decipher, so I'm not worried that anyone will take me to task for coming up with an interpretation of my own. This being the case, one might say that *Genji* is, in a certain sense, the easiest of all the classics to translate—far easier, at least, than Saikaku or Chikamatsu; just as in English literature Shakespeare is easier to translate than Hardy or Meredith.[86] Assuming, then, that there is no difficulty in ascertaining the meaning of the text, how is one to render it in the most literary manner possible? That is the task to which one must devote the whole of one's energy; and the sort of work that I myself find immensely satisfying. If *Genji* were not such an enormous work, I might well have had the idea and finished the job long before Chūōkōron suggested it. Indeed, the one and only reason for my initial hesitation when they put the proposal to me is that I am such an exceptionally slow writer, four or five pages a day being my maximum rate of progress. How many years would it take me to finish translating such an enormous work? Once begun, I would have no choice but to abandon everything else and give myself up entirely to the task. Yet it was not as if I had no commitments to other magazine publishers; would I be able to spend that many years in such a manner? That was my one and only cause for concern.

It was three years ago, in September 1935, that I first began work in earnest. Since then I have published nothing except "Neko to Shōzō to futari no onna" [A Cat, a Man, and Two Women] in the magazine *Kaizō*, and I have written no new fiction or essays. The way I work is this. First I send the manuscript of my draft translation to Chūōkōronsha. There they make two sets of galleys, one of which I have sent to my collaborator Professor Yamada Yoshio, and one to me. Then, as Yamada's pages, corrected in red ink, come in, I have them sent to me as well. These, which sometimes seem dyed bright red with the professor's corrections, I refer to from time to time; but revision I leave until later and forge ahead without worrying about it. At first I left the headnotes for someone else to do; but then I realized I could never be content not doing them myself, so since then I have appended them one by one as I go along. Proceeding in this manner until a draft translation is complete, I shall then review the entire text from the very beginning with reference to Yamada's advice, and with the intention of incorporating 80 to 90 percent of his suggestions. At present, I have reached a point midway through the Uji chapters in my work on the draft translation. This has taken two years and four months spread over three calendar years, at which rate the draft, albeit a rough one, should be complete by about April. If it is not to be published all at once but at the rate of two or three hundred pages per month over a the span of a year or so, then I should be able to make my corrections while it is being produced. Thus once I have completed at least a draft, I shall finally feel secure.

For me to have studied on my own the multitude of commentaries that have come down to us from of old would have been all but impossible. It was essential, therefore, to find a collaborator who is an authority on this subject. It was I who insisted that they importune some major figure, but it was on the initiative of Chūōkōronsha that we approached Professor Yamada. Thus it was that in the spring of 1935, accompanied by Mr. Amemiya[87] of Chūōkōron, I called at the professor's home in Sendai and first met him. I asked his opinion on several matters; and I can say with total sincerity how extraordinarily grateful I am to have found such a fine collaborator. I have no desire merely to borrow the professor's good name; I really do want him to point out, unsparingly, all of my errors. Which indeed the professor does: wielding his vermilion brush with the most painstaking precision, he has made many valuable suggestions and corrections, not only concerning academic matters but points of style and expression as well. The professor likewise has told me in person how very important he considers this task and has been unstinting in his encouragement. That I should be the beneficiary of someone who would scrutinize my work so obligingly and with such extraordinary attentiveness was something I never expected. I feel quite as if an ally a million strong has come to my aid. Over these past three years, it has been a source of no small sustenance to me that the professor has participated in this project with such unwavering interest and zeal, start to finish.

Professor Yamada suggested that I use the *Kogetsushō* as my text.[88] And since my own knowledge of the *Genji* was acquired through the *Kogetsushō* I decided to base my translation upon it entirely. Of the old commentaries, I found *Mingō nisso* the most helpful. But for a modern person translating into the modern language, the most helpful of all are the vernacular translations published since the Meiji period—such as Yosano Akiko's; Miyata Waichirō's, as revised by Professor Yoshizawa; the seven-volume edition in Zen'yaku ōchō bungaku sōsho; Kubota Utsuho's translation; the *Genji monogatari sōshaku* published by Rakurō

Shoin; and Shimazu Hisamoto's *Genji monogatari kōwa*.[89] Those that are already complete, I have, of course; and those currently in process of publication, I place on my shelves as soon as they appear. Waley's work is so riddled with errors that it is not of much help; but its considerable virtues as a literary translation are a stimulus to effort, so I peruse it from time to time as a source of inspiration. As I said before, my principal aim is to produce a literary translation, a translation that can itself be read as literature without reference to the original text—a translation from which one derives the same fascination that an ancient reader would derive from reading the original. It is not to be a free translation, unfettered by the original, but, in keeping with my aim, one that adheres to the original as closely as possible. At the very least, I intend there should be no phrase in the original text for which there is no corresponding passage in the translation. It may be impossible to achieve perfection in this, but I shall try my best to do so. In short, I mean to work in such a manner that my translation may also be of use as a reference in reading the original text.

There shall, I am sure, be other opportunities to discuss the style [*bun*] of *The Tale of Genji*, so I'll not discuss the matter in any detail here. Were I to venture just one observation, however, I should say that the charm of the original lies, more than in anything else, in its "eroticism" [*iroke*]. The text of *Genji* is truly, to an uncanny degree, erotic. Of all the classics, it is first of all *Genji* and, much later, Saikaku's works that stand out for their eroticism. Is not this one of the reasons *Genji* so utterly outshines the many other fictions of the Heian period? Thus in rendering it in the modern language, I try as hard as I can not to lose that eroticism. To what extent I have succeeded only an expert can judge; but to that end it has been essential to emulate the vagueness of the original—that indirect manner of speaking, fraught with implications, yet so understated that it can be taken in several different senses. I've been unable to write with the daring economy of the original text; but if we posit that the original expresses ten units of meaning using five units of expression, then I have expressed them with seven. So a passage in the original that cannot be understood without reading it ten times over, in my translation should be understandable after two or three readings. This much of the "difficulty" and "impenetrability," I should like it to be understood, has been preserved. And one further point: I have endeavored to keep my vocabulary small. This is something that strikes everyone when they read the *Genji*; but for such a long work and such a sweeping narrative, the variety of words used in it is not great. The adjectives used in describing scenery, describing persons, describing feelings are for the most part unvarying, with *omoshiroshi, okashi, namamekashi,* and the like repeated over and over again. (Though in the process, extremely fine shades of nuance do emerge.) This may well be due to the importance attached to what I have previously described as words fraught with implication; but I think, too, that the number of words in general use at that time must have been small. These characteristics of the original text I have of course done my best to preserve.

If modern persons reading works of modern literature were to delve into the meaning of every word and every phrase the way one does in deciphering a classical text, I am sure they would encounter a great many passages that are quite incomprehensible. But since the text is written in the modern language, they feel they have understood and read on. This sort of reading presents no obstacles to literary appreciation. The relentless pursuit of every word and every phrase is academically indispensable, but it may actually be a hindrance to literary response. By reading on past what is incomprehensible, making no concerted attempt to understand it completely on the first go, we come in the course of repeated readings to a natural understanding of it. I've meant the text of my translation to be more readily understandable than the works of Izumi Kyōka, and hope that my readers will not be deterred by the idea that it is a classic but will read it in the same frame of mind as they would an ordinary novel.

TRANSLATED BY T. HARPER

Notes

1. For Suematsu's activities in England, see Margaret Mehl, "Suematsu Kenchō in Britain, 1878–1886," *Japan Forum* 5, no. 2 (1993): 173–93.

2. On this subject and the impact of Suematsu's English translation in Europe, see Rebekah Clements, "Suematsu Kenchō and the First English Translation of *Genji monogatari*: Translation, Tactics, and the 'Women's Question,'" *Japan Forum* 23, no. 1 (2011): 25–47; and Michael Emmerich, *The Tale of Genji: Translation, Canonization, and World Literature* (New York: Columbia University Press, 2013).

3. [Murasaki Shikibu,] *Genji Monogatari: The Most Celebrated of the Classical Japanese Romances*, trans. Suyematz Kenchio (London: Trübner, 1882), xiv.

4. Mikami Sanji and Takatsu Kuwasaburō, *Nihon bungakushi I* (Tokyo: Kinkōdō, 1890), 5–6, 23, 29. See also Ueda Kazutoshi, "Kokubungaku shogen," and Haga Yaichi and Tachibana Senzaburō, "Kokubungaku tokuhon shoron," both in *Ochiai Nao-*

bumi, Ueda Kazutoshi, Haga Yaichi, Fujioka Sakutarō shū, Meiji bungaku zenshū 44 (Tokyo: Chikuma Shobō, 1968), 107, 198–99.

5. Mikami and Takatsu, *Nihon bungakushi I*, 26–27.

6. Watsuji Tetsurō, "*Genji monogatari* ni tsuite," *Shisō* 15 (1922): 61–76.

7. Tanizaki Jun'ichirō, "Gendai kōgobun no ketten ni tsuite," in *Tanizaki Jun'ichirō zenshū* (Tokyo: Chuōkōronsha, 1982), 20:183.

8. Tanizaki Jun'ichirō, *Bunshō tokuhon*, in *Tanizaki Jun'ichirō zenshū* (Tokyo: Chuōkōronsha, 1983), 21:148–49.

9. Ikeda Kikan, "Murasaki Shikibu," in *Chūgaku kokugo* (Tokyo: Gakkō Tosho, 1951), quoted in Tsushima Tomoaki, "Kyōkasho no naka no *Genji monogatari*," *Genji kenkyū* 8 (2003): 149–50.

10. The translation was republished as [Murasaki Shikibu,] *Genji Monogatari: The Most Celebrated of the Classical Japanese Romances*, trans. Suyematz Kenchio (Yokohama: Maruzen, 1894); in Epiphanius Wilson, ed., *Japanese Literature* (London: Colonial Press, 1900); and as *Genji Monogatari (I): Kiri-Tsubo, Hahaki-Gi, Woots-Semi*, trans. Kenchio Suyematz (Tokyo: San Kaku Sha, 1934).

11. Henry N. Shore, "Remarks on the Character and Social Industries of the Inhabitants of China and Japan," *Journal of the Society of Arts*, May 5, 1882, 631.

12. *Genji Monogatari*, trans. Suyematz, xiv, xvi.

13. Anna Buckland, *The Story of English Literature* (London: Cassell, Petter, Galpin, 1882), 20.

14. Surveys of modern Japanese literature consistently refer to the appearance of Shōyō's treatise *The Essence of the Novel* as the catalytic document of Meiji fiction. Some scholars have questioned its immediate impact, but even his detractors admit that Shōyō was a greatly respected and influential figure in the literary world of his time.

15. Translated from Tsubouchi Shōyō, *Shōsetsu shinzui*, in *Tsubouchi Shōyō shū*, Meiji bungaku zenshū 16 (Tokyo: Chikuma Shobō, 1977), 3–4, 19–20, 48, 53–56.

16. *Jōruri jūnidan*, as this work was known to Shōyō, is a Muromachi-period *otogizōshi* of unknown authorship about Minamoto no Yoshitsune (1159–1189) and his romance with Jōruri Gozen, the daughter of the governor of Mikawa.

17. T. J. Harper, "Norinaga on the Translation of *Waka*: His Preface to *A Kokinshū Telescope*," in *The Distant Isle: Studies and Translations of Japanese Literature in Honor of Robert H. Brower*, ed. Thomas Hare, Robert Borgen, and Sharalyn Orbaugh (Ann Arbor: Center for Japanese Studies, University of Michigan, 1996), 210.

18. Fujita Tokutarō, "Yakubun hon'an," in *Genji monogatari kenkyū shomoku yōran* (Tokyo: Rokubunkan, 1932), 88–95; Rebekah Clements, "Rewriting Murasaki: Vernacular Translation and the Reception of *Genji monogatari* During the Tokugawa Period," *Monumenta Nipponica* 68, no. 1 (2013): 1–36.

19. Translated from Sassa Seisetsu, "Jo," in *Shinshaku Genji monogatari* (Tokyo: Shinchōsha, 1911), 1:1–11.

20. Both of these texts are digest versions of *Genji*. *Osana Genji* by Nonoguchi Ryūho (1595–1669) was first published in 1661, and *Genji monogatari shinobugusa* by Kitamura Koshun (1648–1697), son of Kitamura Kigin, was composed around 1688 and circulated in manuscript form for more than a century before it was published in 1834.

21. The name given to interlinear notes on *Genji* compiled by the early Kamakura-period courtier-scholars Minamoto no Mitsuyuki and his son, Chikayuki. The text survives only as quotations in later commentaries.

22. There is no such title listed in *Kokusho sōmokuroku*, the bibliography of pre-1868 Japanese books and manuscripts. Sassa probably means the *Shimeishō* (ca. 1293–1294), compiled by the monk Sojaku (ca. 1207–1211 to after 1294), younger brother of Minamoto no Chikayuki.

23. All are commentaries on *Genji*: *Sengenshō* (1381) by the Chōkei Emperor (1343–1394; r. 1368?–1383?); *Kakaishō* (ca. 1362–1367) by Yotsutsuji Yoshinari (1326–1402); *Kachō yosei* (1472) by Ichijō Kanera (1402–1481); *Rōkashō* (1510) and *Sairyūshō* (1510–1513), both by Sanjōnishi Sanetaka (1455–1537); *Rin'itsushō* (ca. 1559) by Rin Sōji (1498–1581); *Myōjōshō* (ca. 1552) by Sanjōnishi Kin'eda (1487–1563); and *Mōshinshō* (1575) by Kujō Tanemichi (1507–1594).

24. *Mingō nisso* (1598) by Nakanoin Michikatsu (1556–1610) is the most extensive medieval commentary on *Genji*. For a discussion of *Mingō nisso* and a translation from Kitamura Kigin's *Kogetsushō*, see chapter 6 of this volume.

25. Here Sassa lists what Hagiwara Hiromichi termed the "new commentaries" (*shinchū*) on *Genji*: *Genchū shūi* (completed 1696, first published 1834) by Keichū (1640–1701); *Shijo shichiron* (*Shika shichiron*, 1703) by Andō Tameakira (1659–1716); *Genji monogatari Tama no ogoto* (*The Tale of Genji: A Little Jeweled Koto*) is the title that Motoori Norinaga gave to the results of revisions, made probably between 1768 and 1779, to his earlier commentary on *Genji*, *Shibun yōryō* (1763); and Hiromichi's own *Genji monogatari hyōshaku* (1854–1861).

26. The text reads Hinaya Yaho, a misprint for Ryūho. This is the *haikai* poet now usually known as Nonoguchi Ryūho, author of the digests *Osana Genji* and *Jūjō Genji* (both 1661).

27. *Wakakusa Genji monogatari* (1707) is a vernacular translation of *Genji*, from the end of the "Hahakigi" chapter through "Yūgao," by Baiō (Okumura Masanobu, 1686–1764). *Hinazuru Genji monogatari* (1708), also by Baiō, comprises translations of the "Wakamurasaki" and "Suetsumuhana" chapters. See Rebekah Clements, "Cross-Dressing as Lady Murasaki: Concepts of Vernacular Translation in Early Modern Japan," in "Tradurre il *Genji monogatari*," ed. Andrea Maurizi, special issue, *Testo a fronte* 51 (2014): 29–51.

28. The full title of this *jōruri* play by Chikamatsu Monzaemon (1653–1724) is *Kokiden u no ha no ubuya* (*The Kokiden Cormorant-Feather Birthing Room*, ca. 1714). The cover title (*gedai*) of the work, *U no ha no ubuya*, may also be read *Uwa nari uchi*, meaning "Kokiden kills the later wife." This seems to be the title by which the play was known to Sassa.

29. Ryūtei Tanehiko (1783–1842), *Nise Murasaki inaka Genji* (woodblock ed., 1829–1842). For a detailed discussion of Tanehiko's parody, see Emmerich, *The Tale of Genji*.

30. Yosano Akiko, "Dokusho, mushiboshi, zōsho" (1926), in *Tekkan Akiko zenshū* (Tokyo: Bensei Shuppan, 2007), 23:200.

31. Writers and scholars from Tsubouchi Shōyō through Fujioka Sakutarō (1870–1910) to Akutagawa Ryūnosuke (1892–1927) did not distinguish between *monogatari* (tales) and *shōsetsu* (novels), so view is not peculiar to Akiko, according to Tamura Takashi, "Shōhitsu no yakushutsu: Akiko *Genji* no saikentō," *Bunken tankyū* 43 (2005): 31–34.

32. The extent of Akiko's cuts is tabulated in Seki Reiko, *Ichiyō igo no josei hyōgen: Sutairu, media, jendaa* (Tokyo: Kanrin Shobō, 2003), 306–7.

33. Henri de Régnier (1864–1936) was a poet and novelist associated with the symbolist movement. Hiroshi's account of the Yosanos' meeting with him is in a short piece originally written for the *Tokyo Asahi shinbun* and published on July 20, 1912. See Yosano Hiroshi, "Renie sensei," in *Tekkan Akiko zenshū* (Tokyo: Bensei Shuppan, 2003), 10:122–24. Akiko was deeply moved by her encounter with sculptor Auguste Rodin (1840–1917) and recalled the experience in a rapturous account written in 1916: "Rodan-ō ni atta hi," in *Tekkan Akiko zenshū* (Tokyo: Bensei Shuppan, 2005), 17:222–26.

34. Translated from Yosano Akiko, "Shin'yaku *Genji monogatari* no nochi ni," in *Shin'yaku Genji monogatari*, trans. Yosano Akiko (Tokyo: Kanao Bun'endō, 1913), 4:1–7.

35. *Shin-shin'yaku Genji monogatari*, trans. Yosano Akiko, Nihon no bunko 20–25 (Tokyo: Nihonsha, 1948–1949).

36. Translated from Yosano Akiko, "Atogaki," in *Shin-shin'yaku Genji monogatari*, trans. Yosano Akiko (Tokyo: Kanao Bun'endō, 1939), 6:1–10.

37. For details, see G. G. Rowley, *Yosano Akiko and The Tale of Genji* (Ann Arbor: Center for Japanese Studies, University of Michigan, 2000), 148–50, 181–82. The scholars were Ikeda Kikan (1896–1956), Oka Kazuo (1900–1981), Teramoto Naohiko (1912–1990), and Mitani Kuniaki (1941–2007).

38. Daini no Sanmi Fujiwara Kataiko (Kenshi, 999?–1082?), daughter of Murasaki Shikibu and Fujiwara no Nobutaka (947?–1001).

39. Kume Kunitake (1839–1931), historian and compiler of the official report of the Iwakura mission. In 1892, he was dismissed from his post at (Tokyo) Imperial University for publishing an article describing Shinto as "an outdated custom of heaven worship." He was teaching at Tokyo Senmon Gakkō, later Waseda University, at the time of the publication of the article to which Akiko refers: Kume Kunitake, "*Genji monogatari* no sakusha oyobi sono setsu," *Nōgaku* 7, no. 5 (1909): 1–7.

40. In fact there is only one occurrence of the term *shodayū* in *Genji*, in "Wakana, jō," 15:86. See Murasaki Shikibu, *The Tale of Genji*, trans. Royall Tyler (New York: Viking, 2001), 603.

41. Murasaki to Genji in "Wakana, jō," 15:58; *The Tale of Genji*, trans. Tyler, 593.

42. Kaoru in "Niou Miya," 16:18; *The Tale of Genji*, trans. Tyler, 787.

43. The poem Akiko quotes is actually from the *Senzaiwakashū*, no. 302, KT 1:191c.

44. More recent scholars take the opposite view and understand *murasaki no yukari* to mean "[tales told by] gentlewomen in the service of [the character] Murasaki" ("Takekawa," 16:53; *The Tale of Genji*, trans. Tyler, 805).

45. The figure of twenty-six years appears in Yosano Akiko, "Murasaki Shikibu: Nihon josei retsuden," *Fuji kōron* 20, no. 9 (1935): 214–17. Earlier, in her essay "Murasaki Shikibu shinkō" (1928), Akiko argued that Murasaki Shikibu had written the "first section" (*zenpen*) of *Genji*—that is, the thirty-three chapters from "Kiritsubo" through "Fuji no uraba"—during the years between the death of her husband, Nobutaka, in 1001 and her entering Shōshi's service in 1006 and that Daini no Sanmi had begun writing the "latter section" (*kōhen*)—the chapters from "Wakana" to "Yume no ukihashi"—about 1029.

46. That is, Ukifune's stepfather.

47. Fujiwara no Yorimichi (992–1074), eldest son of Michinaga, was regent for fifty-two years during the reigns of Emperor GoIchijō (1006–1036; r. 1016–1036), GoSuzaku (1009–1045; r. 1036–1045), and GoReizei (1023–1068; r. 1045–1068). Daini no Sanmi was appointed as wet nurse to the future GoReizei Emperor in 1025.

48. The *Daini no Sanmi shū* (also known as *Tō Sanmi shū*, ca. 1068) is extant. See KT 3:94; also appended to *Murasaki Shikibu shū*, ed. Nanba Hiroshi (Tokyo: Iwanami Shoten, 1973).

49. The Sarashina diarist, the Daughter of Sugawara no Takasue (b. 1008), returned to the capital from her father's provincial posting in 1020. It was in the following year, she recalled, that she received copies of "the fifty-some chapters of *Genji*." As Akiko recognized, if the Sarashina diarist's recollection is reliable, *The Tale of Genji* must have existed in something like its present form by this time, that is, by 1021.

50. Jorge Luis Borges, "Lady Murasaki, *The Tale of Genji*," in *Selected Non-Fictions*, ed. Eliot Weinberger, trans. Esther Allen and Suzanne Jill Levine (New York: Viking Penguin, 1999), 187.

51. Arthur Waley, "Notes on Translation" (1958), in *Madly Singing in the Mountains: An Appreciation and Anthology of Arthur Waley*, ed. Ivan Morris (London: Allen & Unwin, 1970), 156.

52. *The Tale of Genji: A Novel in Six Parts, by Lady Murasaki*, trans. Arthur Waley (Boston: Houghton Mifflin, 1935), 1:viii–ix.

53. Virginia Woolf, "The Tale of Genji: The First Volume of Mr. Arthur Waley's Translation of a Great Japanese Novel by the Lady Murasaki," *Vogue* (London), July 1925, in *The Essays of Virginia Woolf*, vol. 4, *1925 to 1928*, ed. Andrew McNeillie (London: Hogarth Press, 1994), 264–69.

54. After Woolf's greatest commercial success, *Orlando* (1928), *Vogue* increased her pay from £20 to £50 an essay. See Hermione Lee, "Virginia Woolf's Essays," in *The Cambridge Companion to Virginia Woolf*, ed. Sue Roe and Susan Sellers (Cambridge: Cambridge University Press, 2000), 91–108; and Jane Garrity, "Virginia Woolf, Intellectual Harlotry, and 1920s *British Vogue*," in *Virginia Woolf in the Age of Mechanical Reproduction*, ed. Pamela L. Caughie (New York: Garland, 2000), 185–218.

55. Tanizaki Jun'ichirō, "Masamune Hakuchō no hihyō o yonde," in *Tanizaki Jun'ichirō zenshū* (Tokyo: Chūōkōronsha, 1982), 20:401–2.

56. Masamune Hakuchō, "Eiyaku *Genji monogatari*," *Kaizō* 15, no. 9 (1933): 196.

57. Chiba Shunji, "*Genji monogatari* to kindai bungaku," in *Genji monogatari kōza 9: Kindai no kyōju to kaigai to no kōryū* (Tokyo: Benseisha, 1992), 9–11.

58. "Bundan futari anku: Dentōryō nesage ron," *Yomiuri shinbun*, September 2, 1933, 4.

59. Translated from Masamune Hakuchō, "Koten o yonde," in *Bungei hyōron* (Tokyo: Kaizōsha, 1927). The other three essays are "Eiyaku *Genji monogatari*" (An English Translation of *Genji monogatari*, 1933), "Futatabi eiyaku *Genji monogatari* ni tsukite" (Further Thoughts on the English Translation of *Genji monogatari*), and "*Genji monogatari*: Hon'yaku to gensaku" (*Genji monogatari*: Translation and Original, 1951). For a translation of the last essay, see Michael Emmerich, "Masamune Hakuchō Reads *Genji*: A Translation of *Genji monogatari*: Hon'yaku to gensaku," *Monumenta Nipponica* 68, no. 1 (2013): 37–68.

60. *Hongloumeng*, which is also known in English as *The Story of the Stone*, is a long work written in the eighteenth century by Cao Xueqin (1715?–1763?).

61. Although *The Sacred Tree: Being the Second Part of "The Tale of Genji," by Lady Murasaki*, was published in February 1926, it is clear that Hakuchō had not set eyes on either of the two volumes; indeed, he wasn't even aware of their existence.

62. The "rainy night ranking" occurs in the second chapter, "Hahakigi." Hatakeyama Takeshi was a scholar of Japanese literature who wrote on various works, most notably the *Man'yōshū* (ca. 785). Hakuchō studied with him at Tōkyō Senmon Gakkō, the predecessor of Waseda University.

63. Hagiwara Hiromichi is known as a "national learning" (*kokugaku*) scholar, but he was also a translator of Chinese literature and a writer of fiction. *Genji monogatari hyōshaku* (1861), his commentary on *The Tale of Genji*, is considered his most important work. For a translation, see chapter 7 of this volume.

64. The Yūhōdō bunko edition of *Genji monogatari* was published in 1926 in four volumes. It provides relatively few notes and is clearly intended for reading; it is not a scholarly edition.

65. The implication of this phrase is that most readers of *Genji* give up at the "Suma" chapter.

66. *Kusazōshi* are sometimes called "picture books"; *yomihon* are "reading books." As a young man, Hakuchō was a great fan of Takizawa Bakin, one of the most popular *yomihon* authors.

67. For clarification of the meaning and history of this important term, see the translation of Motoori Norinaga's *Genji monogatari Tama no ogushi* in chapter 7 of this volume.

68. Rai Sanyō (1780–1832) was a historian and poet known for his writing in Chinese. His *Nihon gaishi* (*An Unofficial History of Japan*, completed 1827, first published 1839–1870), a twenty-two-volume history of Japan that begins with the end of the Heian period and ends with the establishment of the Tokugawa shogunate in 1603, became a best seller in Japan.

69. Ozaki Kōyō (1867–1903), one of the founders of the group Ken'yūsha (Friends of the Inkstone), was a best-selling author whose works tended toward the melodramatic. The Japanese title of the story mentioned is "Fugen fugo."

70. Takizawa Bakin (Kyokutei Bakin, 1767–1848) was a scholar, poet, and best-selling author of numerous *kusazōshi* and *yomihon*, the most famous of which is *Nansō satomi hakkenden* (*Satomi and the Eight Dogs*, 1814–1842). Tamenaga Shunsui (b. 1789) considered himself, rightly or wrongly, the creator of the genre known as *ninjōbon*. His *Shunshoku umegoyomi* (*Spring Love: A Plum Almanac*, 1832–1833) was a best seller.

71. The ideal of the literary "sketch" was popularized by the essayist and haiku poet Masaoka Shiki (1867–1902) beginning in the late 1890s.

72. Ihara Saikaku (1642–1693), a prolific *haikai* poet and writer of prose fiction, inadvertently created the genre that later came to be known as *ukiyozōshi* (tales of the floating world) when in 1682 he published his first work of prose fiction, *The Life of an Amorous Man* (*Kōshoku ichidai otoko*). His writings fell out of fashion after his death until he was rediscovered in the 1880s.

73. The 260-volume series Nihon koten zenshū was published between 1926 and 1944 by Nihon Koten Zenshū Kankōkai. It was edited by the poets Yosano Akiko and Yosano Tekkan and Hakuchō's brother Masamune Atsuo (1881–1958).

74. Higuchi Ichiyō (1872–1896) is one of the few women writers of the Meiji period to have been given a central place in the canon of modern Japanese literature.

75. Ihara Saikaku's *The Life of an Amorous Woman* (*Kōshoku ichidai onna*) was published in 1686.

76. The three works mentioned are *Seken mune san'yō* (1692), *Yorozu no fumihōgu* (1696), and *Saikaku okimiyage* (1693).

77. Shimazaki Tōson (1872–1943) came to be regarded as one of the preeminent naturalist writers.

78. Kunikida Doppo (1871–1908) came to be viewed as a precursor to the naturalist movement.

79. Tanizaki Jun'ichirō, Satomi Ton (1888–1983), and Akutagawa Ryūnosuke (1892–1927) all, in their own ways, represented alternatives to the naturalist writing that had been so prevalent in the preceding decades.

80. As Chiba Shunji, who first documented the connection between the Waley and Tanizaki translations, put it: "Had there been no Waley translation, there would have been no Tanizaki translation" ("Kindai bungaku no naka no *Genji monogatari*," in *Kindai bungaku ni okeru Genji monogatari*, vol. 6 of *Kōza Genji monogatari kenkyū*, ed. Chiba Shunji (Tokyo: Ōfū, 2007), 22.

81. Hata Kōhei, *Tanizaki Jun'ichirō: Genji monogatari taiken* (Tokyo: Chikuma Shobō, 1976), 37.

82. Yamada Yoshio was a professor of Japanese language and literature at Tōhoku Imperial University from 1925 until 1933. In 1940, when the Jingū Kōgakukan in Ise, a government institute devoted to promoting National Shinto, was granted university status, Yamada was appointed president. The university was closed by a GHQ order during the Allied Occupation of Japan, and Yamada was fired. Known more for his studies of Japanese grammar than of literature, Yamada's most notable work on *Genji* is *Genji monogatari no ongaku* (*Music in The Tale of Genji*, 1934).

83. For further details of the collaborative process, see Ibuki Kazuko and G. G. Rowley, "'The Tanizaki Genji': Inception, Process, and Afterthoughts," in *The Grand Old Man and the Great Tradition: Essays on Tanizaki Jun'ichirō in Honor of Adriana Boscaro*, ed. Luisa Bienati and Bonaventura Ruperti (Ann Arbor: Center for Japanese Studies, University of Michigan, 2009), 25–52.

84. Translated from Tanizaki Jun'ichirō, "*Genji monogatari* no gendaigoyaku ni tsuite," in *Tanizaki Jun'ichirō zenshū* (Tokyo: Chūōkōronsha, 1983), 21:321–28.

85. Tanizaki Jun'ichirō to Shimanaka Yūsaku, January 16, January 24, February 4, February 12, February 16, and February 27, 1934, in Minakami Tsutomu and Chiba Shunji, (*Zōho kaiteiban*) *Tanizaki sensei no shokan: Aru shuppansha shachō e no tegami o yomu* (Tokyo: Chūōkōronsha, 2008), 105–9, 345–46, 351–52.

86. The English novelists Thomas Hardy (1840–1928) and George Meredith (1828–1909).

87. Amemiya Yōzō (1903–99), head of the publishing department (*shuppan buchō*) at Chūōkōronsha between 1932 and 1937.

88. The *Kogetsushō* (1673) is a complete text of *Genji* with selected commentary, compiled by Kitamura Kigin (1624–1705). For an excerpt, see chapter 6 of this volume.

89. *Shin'yaku Genji monogatari*, trans. Yosano Akiko, 4 vols. (Tokyo: Kanao Bun'endō, 1912–1913); *Taiyaku Genji monogatari*, trans. Miyata Waichirō, 3 vols. (Tokyo: Yūkōsha, 1938); *Genji monogatari*, trans. Yoshizawa Yoshinari et al., Zen'yaku ōchō bungaku sōsho 4–9 (Kyoto: Ōchō Bungaku Sōsho Kankōkai, 1924–1927); *Genji monogatari*, trans. Kubota Utsuho and Yosano Akiko, Gendaigoyaku kokubungaku zenshū 4–6 (Tokyo: Hibonkaku, 1936–1938); *Genji monogatari sōshaku*, trans. Shimazu Hisamoto, 5 vols. (Tokyo: Rakurō Shoin, 1937–1939); and *Taiyaku Genji monogatari kōwa*, trans. Shimazu Hisamoto, 5 vols. (Tokyo: Chūkōkan, 1930–1942).

Permissions

The editors and publisher acknowledge with thanks permission granted to reproduce in this volume the following material.

From "After *Shin'yaku Genji monogatari*" and "'Afterword,' *Shin-Shin'yaku Genji monogatari*," pp. 186–92 of G. G. Rowley, *Yosano Akiko and The Tale of Genji*, Michigan Monograph Series in Japanese Studies, Number 28 (Ann Arbor: Center for Japanese Studies, The University of Michigan, 2000). Copyright © 2000 the Regents of The University of Michigan. All rights reserved. Used with the permission of the publisher.

"*Genji* Gossip," by T. J. Harper, from pp. 29–44 of *New Leaves: Studies and Translations of Japanese Literature in Honor of Edward Seidensticker*, edited by Aileen Gatten and Anthony Hood Chambers, Michigan Monograph Series in Japanese Studies, Number 11 (Ann Arbor: Center for Japanese Studies, The University of Michigan, 1993). Copyright © 1993 the Regents of The University of Michigan. All rights reserved. Used with the permission of the publisher.

"On Translating *The Tale of Genji* into Modern Japanese," by Tanizaki Jun'ichirō, translated by Thomas Harper, from pp. 25–29 of *The Grand Old Man and the Great Tradition: Essays on Tanizaki Jun'ichirō in Honor of Adriana Boscaro*, edited by Luisa Bienati and Bonaventura Ruperti (Ann Arbor: Center for Japanese Studies, The University of Michigan, 2009). Copyright © 2009 the Regents of The University of Michigan. All rights reserved. Used with the permission of the publisher.

T. J. Harper, "More *Genji* Gossip," *Journal of the Association of Teachers of Japanese* 28, no. 2 (1994): 175–81. Copyright © 1994 American Association of Teachers of Japanese. All rights reserved. Used with the permission of the publisher.

Index

GPSR Authorized Representative: Easy Access System Europe, Mustamäe tee 50, 10621 Tallinn, Estonia, gpsr.requests@easproject.com

www.ingramcontent.com/pod-product-compliance
Lightning Source LLC
Chambersburg PA
CBHW020919310726
48980CB00011B/957/J

* 9 7 8 0 2 3 1 1 6 6 5 8 4 *